SCOTLAND AND EUROPE:
THE MEDIEVAL KINGDOM AND ITS CONTACTS
WITH CHRISTENDOM, c.1215-1545

VOLUME 1: RELIGION, CULTURE AND COMMERCE

Scotland and Europe: The Medieval Kingdom and its Contacts with Christendom, c.1215-1545

Volume 1: Religion, Culture and Commerce

David Ditchburn
University of Aberdeen

TUCKWELL PRESS

First published in paperback in Great Britain in 2001 by

Tuckwell Press
The Mill House
Phantassie
East Linton
East Lothian
Scotland

ISBN 1 86232 172 8

Britsh Library Cataloguing-in-Publication Data

A catalogue record for this book is available
on request from the British Library

Printed and bound in Great Britain by Bookcraft Ltd

Contents

Table of Figures

Acknowledgements

In the era of the Research Assessment Exercise, this book has taken rather too long to write. Its genesis lies in a junior honours course developed by Grant Simpson, which we then jointly taught and which, following Grant's retirement, I adopted as my own. I have learnt much from Grant and from a decade of students, though I am especially grateful to my first class of 1990 – Simon Appleyard, Anna Edgar, Gavin Farquhar, Keith Fellows, Stuart King, Flora Macarthur, Maureen Macnaughtan, Robin Macpherson, John Milne, Margaret O'Hagan, Jacqueline Peter and Stephanie Watson. Their enthusiasm was infectious. Their glazed eyes, whenever I mentioned wool and hides, persuaded me that a more rounded consideration of medieval Scotland's relations with Europe might prove more appealing to students and the general reader. That bigger task, compared with the one I had originally envisaged, is one reason why this study has outlived three indulgent heads of department (Paul Dukes, Roy Bridges and Bob Tyson), though it was never likely to see off the sterner gaze of my current line manager. To all four I am grateful for carrots and sticks, the former including grants from the Mackie bequest. That funding was spent travelling between archives. It would be invidious to single out any particular repository – the staff of all have been more than helpful – but the regular supplies of coffee in Bergen-op-Zoom cannot go unapplauded.

Between archival visits I have benefited greatly from listening to many acquaintances. I would particularly like to record my debt to Steve Boardman and Ian Blanchard, two historians never short of ideas and always ready to challenge my casual assumptions. Alison Rosie provided assistance at the National Archives of Scotland and also alerted me to the material available in Turin. In Aberdeen James Vance goaded me into beginning to write; and, once the writing was underway, Janet Hendry provided emergency supplies of fruit and nicotine, as well as more conventional secretarial assistance. Philip Lyndon helped with the graphs and Alison Sandison with the maps. I am especially grateful to my colleagues Alastair Macdonald, Leslie Macfarlane, Allan Macinnes and Grant Simpson, who, despite their own busy schedules, read drafts and suggested many valuable improvements.

Writing a book requires an element of seclusion. My mother, Janine and Robert Pennel and the extended Família Ferreira kindly lent me quiet corners of Fife, Obwalden, Minho and Ticino to undertake the task – and Kathryn, Johnny, Fabio and Marco provided welcome puerile interruptions. Finally, in latterly fraught and gloomy times, Kirsteen Hay and Andrew Mulholland (the best of flatmates), Michael Boyd, Terry Brotherstone, Gilian Dawson, Mark Evans and Morag Patterson, Catriona and Greig Fraser, and Darren Raphael provided sanity, escape and perspective. More recently so too have Alison Cathcart, Jan Kerr and Micheál Ó Siochrú – despite his attempt to kill me with a B52 and his vow never to read the pages which follow. I am, however, above all grateful to Rosie Mackay and Jane Ohlmeyer – who all too often have been there to pick me up, calm me down and set me back on course. To them, and all, thank you.

Abbreviations

Aberdeen Reg.	*Registrum Episcopatus Aberdonensis* (Spalding and Maitland Clubs, 1845)
ADA	*Acts of the Lords Auditors of Causes and Complaints*, ed. T. Thomson (Edinburgh, 1839)
ADCP	*Acts of the Lords of Council in Public Affairs, 1501-1554*, ed. R.K. Hannay (Edinburgh, 1932)
AND	Archives Départementales du Nord
AH	Archiv der Hansestadt
AN	Archives Nationales
APS	*Acts of the Parliaments of Scotland*, ed. T. Thomson and C. Innes (Edinburgh, 1814-75)
AS	Archivio di Stato
CA	City Archive
CAEB	*Cartulaire de L'ancienne Estaple de Bruges*, ed. L. Gilliodts van Severen (Bruges, 1904-6)
Cal. Carew MSS	*Calendar of the Carew Manuscripts preserved in the archepiscopal library at Lambeth, 1515-74* (London, 1867-73)
CCR	*Calendar of Close Rolls* (London, 1900-)
CDI	*Calendar of Documents relating to Ireland* (London, 1875-86)
CDS	*Calendar of Documents relating to Scotland*, ed. J. Bain *et al.* (Edinburgh, 1881-1986)
'Chron. Auchinleck'	'The 'Auchinleck Chronicle'', ed. C. McGladdery in idem, *James II* (Edinburgh, 1990)
Chron. Bower (Watt)	*Scotichronicon by Walter Bower, in Latin and English*, ed. D.E.R. Watt *et al.* (Aberdeen and Edinburgh, 1987-98)
Chron. Chastellain (Lettenhove)	*Oeuvres des Georges Chastellain*, ed. K de Lettenhove (Brussels, 1863-86)
Chron. d'Escouchy	M. d'Escouchy, *Chronique*, ed. G. du Fresne de Beaucourt (Paris, 1863-4)
Chron. Fordun	John of Fordun, *Chronicle of the Scottish Nation*, ed. W.F. Skene (Llanerch, repr., 1993)
Chron. Froissart (Brereton)	Jean Froissart, *Chronicles*, ed. G. Brereton (Harmondsworth, 1968)
Chron. Froissart (Lettenhove)	*Oeuvres de Jean Froissart*, ed. K. de Lettenhove (Brussels, 1867-77)
Chron. Higden	Ranulph Higden, *Polychronicon*, ed. C. Babington and J.R. Lumby (Roll Series, 1865-66)
Chron. Knighton (Martin)	*Knighton's Chronicle, 1337-1396*, ed. G.H. Martin (Oxford, 1995)

Chron. Lanercost	*Chronicon de Lanercost* (Maitland Club, 1839)
Chron. Le Baker	*Chronicon Galfridi le Baker de Swynebroke*, ed. E.M. Thompson (Oxford, 1889)
Chron. Melrose	*Chronicle of Melrose*, ed. A.O. Anderson and M.O. Anderson (facsimile edn., London, 1936)
Chron. Pluscarden	*Liber Pluscardensis*, ed. F.J.H. Skene (Edinburgh, 1877-80)
Chron. Reading	*Chronica Johannis de Reading et Anonymi Cantuariensis, 1346-1367*, ed. J. Tait (Manchester, 1914)
Chron. Waurin	Jehan de Waurin, *Chroniques et Anchiennes Istoires de la Grant Bretagne* (Roll Series, 1864-91)
Chron. Westminster	*The Westminster Chronicle*, ed. L.C. Hector and B.F. Harvey (Oxford, 1982)
Chron. Wyntoun (Laing)	Androw of Wyntoun, *The Orygynale Cronykil of Scotland*, ed. D. Laing (Edinburgh, 1872-9)
CJRI	*Calendar of the Justiciary Rolls, or the proceedings in the court of the justiciar of Ireland*, ed. J. Mills (Dublin, 1905-14)
Clement VII Letters	*Calendar of Papal Letters to Scotland of Clement VII of Avignon, 1378-1394*, ed. C. Burns (SHS, 1976)
Coupar Angus Chrs.	*Charters of the Abbey of Coupar Angus*, ed. D.E.R. Easson (SHS, 1947)
CPL	*Calendar of the Entries in the Papal Registers relating to Great Britain and Ireland: Letters to the Pope*, ed. W.H. Bliss *et al.* (London, 1893-)
CPP	*Calendar of the Entries in the Papal Registers relating to Great Britain and Ireland: Petitions to the Pope*, ed. W.H. Bliss (London, 1896)
CSP (Milan)	*Calendar of State Papers and Manuscripts, existing in the archives and collections of Milan*, ed. A.B. Hinds (London, 1912)
CSSR	*Calendar of the Scottish Supplications to Rome*, ed. E.R. Lindsay *et al.* (SHS, etc., 1934-)
CPR	*Calendar of the Patent Rolls* (London, 1906-)
Dunbar, *Poems*	*The Poems of William Dunbar*, ed. J.L. Kinsley (Oxford, 1979)
Edin. Recs.	*Extracts from the Records of the Burgh of Edinburgh*, ed. J.D. Marwick (Scottish Burgh Records Soc., 1869-92)
ER	*The Exchequer Rolls of Scotland*, ed. J. Stuart *et al.* (Edinburgh, 1878-1908)
Foedera (O)	*Foedera, Conventiones, Litterae et Cuiuscunque Generis Acta Publica*, original ed., ed. T. Rymer (London, 1704-35)
Foedera (R)	*Foedera, Conventiones, Litterae et Cuiuscunque Generis Acta Publica*, Record Commission ed., ed. T. Rymer (London, 1816-69)

GA	Gemeentearchief
Glasgow Reg.	*Registrum Episcopatus Glasguensis* (Bannatyne and Maitland Clubs, 1843)
GSA	Geheimes Staatsarchiv, Preussischer Kulturbesitz
HA	Historisches Archiv
Halyburton's Ledger	*Ledger of Andrew Halyburton, 1492-1503*, ed. C. Innes (Edinburgh, 1867)
Holm Cultram Reg.	*The Register and Records of Holm Cultram*, ed. F. Grainger and W.G. Collingwood (Cumberland and Westmorland Antiquarian and Archaeological Soc., Record Ser., 1929)
Handelsrechnungen	*Handelsrechnungen des Deutschen Ordens*, ed. C. Sattler (Leipzig, 1887)
Hanseakten	*Hanseakten aus England, 1275-1412*, ed. K. Kunze (Halle, 1891)
HGb	*Hansische Geschichtsblätter*
HR, 1256-1430	*Die Recesse und andere Akten der Hansetage von 1256-1430*, ed. W. Junghans and K. Koppmann (Leipzig, 1879-97)
HR, 1477-1530	*Hanserecesse, 1477-1530*, ed. D. Schäfer (Leipzig, 1881-1913)
HUB	*Hansisches Urkundenbuch*, ed. K. Höhlbaum *et al.* (Halle, etc., 1879-1939)
IAB	*Inventaire des Archives de la Ville de Bruges*, ed. L. Gilliodts van Severen (Bruges, 1883-85)
IR	*Innes Review*
James IV Letters	*The Letters of James the Fourth, 1505-13*, ed. R.K. Hannay and R.L. Mackie (SHS, 1953)
James V Letters	*The Letters of James V*, ed. R.K. Hannay and D. Hay (Edinburgh, 1954)
KRO	Kent Record Office
LA	Linna Archiwi
LAT	Landesarchiv Tirol
L. & P. Henry VIII	*Letters and Papers, Foreign and Domestic, Henry VIII* (London, 1862-1932)
LUB	*Urkundenbuch der Stadt Lübeck* (Lübeck, 1843-1905)
Lindsay, *Satyre*	David Lindsay, *Ane Satyre of the Thrie Estaitis*, ed. R. Lyall (Edinburgh, 1989)
Melrose Liber.	*Liber Sancte Marie de Melros*, ed. C. Innes (Bannatyne Club, 1839)
MM	*Mariner's Mirror*
Moray Reg.	*Registrum Episcopatus Moraviensis*, ed. C. Innes (Bannatyne Club, 1839)
NAS	National Archives Scotland
NfRO	Norfolk Record Office

NH	*Northern History*
NLS	National Library of Scotland
NRO	Northumberland Record Office
NS	*Northern Scotland*
Paisley Reg.	*Registrum Monasterii de Passelet* (Maitland Club, 1832)
Pitscottie, *Historie*	Robert Lindesay of Pitscottie, *The Historie and Cronicles of Scotland* (STS, 1899-1911)
PP	*Past and Present*
PRO	Public Record Office, England and Wales
PRONI	Public Record Office, Northern Ireland
PUB	*Pommerisches Urkundenbuch*, ed. O. Heineman *et al.* (Stettin, 1868-)
PSAS	*Proceedings of the Society of Antiquaries of Scotland*
RA	Rijksarchief/Rigsarkivet
RMS	*Registrum Magni Sigilli Regum Scotorum*, ed. J.M. Thomson *et al.* (Edinburgh, 1882-1914)
Rot. Scot.	*Rotuli Scotiae in Turri Londinensi et in Domo Capitulari Westmonasteriensi asservati*, ed. D. Macpherson *et al.* (Record Commission, 1814-19)
RRS	*Regesta Regum Scottorum*, ed. G.W.S. Barrow *et al.* (Edinburgh, 1960-)
RSCHS	*Records of the Scottish Church History Society*
RSS	*Registrum Secreti Sigilli Regum Scotorum*, ed. M. Livingstone *et al.* (Edinburgh, 1908-)
SA	Staatsarchiv
Scalacronica	*Scalacronica, by Sir Thomas Gray of Heton Knight* (Maitland Club, 1836)
SRO	Suffolk Record Office
StA	Stadtarchiv/Stadsarchief
St Andrews Copiale	*Copiale Prioratus Sanctiandree*, ed. J.H. Baxter (Oxford, 1930)
SHS	Scottish History Society
SHR	*Scottish Historical Review*
Smit, *Bronnen, 1150-1485*	*Bronnen tot de Geschiedenis van den Handel met Engeland, Schotland en Ierland, 1150-1485*, ed. H.J. Smit (The Hague, 1928)
Smit, *Bronnen, 1485-1558*	*Bronnen tot de Geschiedenis van den Handel met Engeland, Schotland en Ierland, 1485-1558*, ed. H.J. Smit (The Hague, 1942)
SRS	Scottish Records Society
Stevenson, *Documents*	*Documents Illustrative of the History of Scotland, 1286-1306*, ed. J. Stevenson (Edinburgh, 1870)
Stevenson, Thesis	A.W.K. Stevenson, Trade between Scotland and the Low Countries in the Later Middle Ages (University of Aberdeen, unpublished PhD thesis, 1982)

STS	Scottish Text Society
TA	*Accounts of the Lord High Treasurer of Scotland*, ed. T. Dickson and J.B. Paul (Edinburgh, 1877-1916)
TDGAS	*Transactions of the Dumfriesshire and Galloway Natural History and Antiquarian Society*
The Bruce (Duncan)	John Barbour, *The Bruce*, ed. A.A.M. Duncan (Edinburgh, 1997)
The Brut	*The Brut or the Chronicles of England*, ed. F.W.D. Brie (Early English Text Soc., 1906-8)
TSES	*Transactions of the Scottish Ecclesiological Society*
UL	University Library
WAP	Wojewódzkiego Archiwum Państwowe
Watt, *Graduates*	D.E.R. Watt, *A Biographical Dictionary of Scottish University Graduates to A.D. 1410* (Oxford, 1977)
Wigtownshire Chrs.	*Wigtownshire Charters*, ed. R.C. Reid (SHS, 1960)
ZA	Zeeuws Archief

Preface

This is the first of a two-volume study. Its aim is to offer a survey of later medieval Scotland's relations with Christendom – a perhaps ambitious task. It is, however, one which can now be contemplated, for recent decades have witnessed a proliferation of publications on various aspects of the topic. Yet, while this particular study is built upon the labours of others, its execution has still presented problems. The topic is vast, synthesis cannot offer comprehension, and so I present my apologies in advance for the many details omitted. I have also struggled with whether to approach the subject chronologically, geographically or thematically. The consequence of opting for a thematic approach is perhaps an undue emphasis on the fifteenth and early sixteenth centuries, for when the source material is fuller, at the expense of the thirteenth century in particular. There is, moreover, in this volume neither sustained analysis of the importance, or otherwise, of contacts with particular areas, nor an overall conclusion. The latter, I feel, would be premature. Instead, my summative remarks (and an attempt to rectify some of the problems inherent in the structure) will appear at the end of the second volume.

The focus of that volume will be political – broadly defined to include ecclesiastical issues such as the Schism, economic issues such as the location of the Staple, as well as 'high politics'. This volume, meanwhile, is concerned with social and economic interaction between Scotland and Christendom from the Fourth Lateran Council of 1215 to the Council of Trent, which was convened in 1545. These dates perhaps require some justification – even although history is only manageable in discrete slices, and the artificial chronological parameters that I have chosen seem as good as any. The choice of 'religious dates' for a study which encompasses culture, commerce and (in the second volume) politics may seem odd. Religion was, however, of fundamental importance not only to Scotland's ecclesiastical contacts with the continent, but also to other aspects of its engagement with Europe. Culture, trade and politics did not, and given the mentality of the times could not, escape from the bounds of thought broadly established by the church. Religious dates, therefore, seemed suitable, and since Innocent III's pontificate arguably marked the high point of the papacy's prestige, while the deliberations at Trent indicated that even what remained of Catholic Europe would not remain unchanged, the period between 1215 and 1545 possesses a certain coherence. By a happy coincidence, for those who remain unconvinced, 1215 and 1545 roughly accord with the traditional regnal approach to delineating time, since Alexander II became king of Scots in 1214 and James V died in 1542.

Of course, the unity of Christendom was already evident in the period before 1215 (or 1214), and it was already beginning to crumble before 1545 (and before 1542). Indeed, the decay of Christendom has perhaps been one reason why many historians have found it more stimulating to approach the later medieval period from the national, rather than international, perspective. This, they might legitimately argue, is more in keeping with the spirit of the times which they seek to interpret. Yet we should be careful not to pre-date the demise of Christendom, and this volume seeks to explore one continuing dynamic behind developments in Scotland which national histories have little time to examine. I leave you, the reader, to decide whether it succeeds.

1
Transport and Travel

MCCCCLXVII quidem Scoti hic fuerunt.[1]

In 1467 some unknown visitors left a message for posterity in the catacomb of San Callisto in Rome. 'Scots, too, were here,' they scrawled, though like most graffiti artists they did not elaborate upon what precisely they were doing there. Rome was, however, the spiritual centre of Latin Christendom, and our anonymous Scots may well have been among the thousands of pilgrims and churchmen who flocked to the city from all over Christendom, some to marvel at the fine collection of relics, others to plead for favours from the pope. If not pilgrims or clerics, our underground visitors may have been students studying at the local university, diplomats or, less probably, merchants, pedlars or even soldiers of fortune. All sorts of Scottish travellers were to be found throughout medieval Christendom and we shall encounter many of them in the pages which follow.

Although the reasons for their travel varied, these Scots shared one similar experience. All contacts between Scotland and Europe depended on the evolution of communication. Yet the precise means by which medieval Scots travelled abroad (and by which foreigners reached Scotland) remains more mysterious, and perhaps more difficult for modern minds to comprehend, than the actual purpose of travel. Very few of the technological and bureaucratic certainties which have made modern travel so routine were available in any recognisable form to the medieval traveller. As I write this paragraph, I am sitting in Engelberg, high in the Swiss Alps. From London, where I purchased an aeroplane ticket by telephone with a credit card, I travelled after breakfast and by car to Heathrow Airport. After arrival at Zürich Airport, I proceeded by train to Engelberg, purchasing my ticket with Swiss francs bought in Scotland. After arrival in Engelberg, I collected my luggage, which I had last seen in London, and then, served by a dark-haired girl with the most sensuous of arms, I lunched in the shadow of the great Benedictine monastery which has dominated the valley since the twelfth century. Had anything gone amiss on the journey, telephones, travel insurance, the consular service, and perhaps the girl with the sensuous arms, were at hand.

A similar journey in the middle ages would have taken at least three weeks longer. It would have necessitated carting heavy luggage along often ill-defined routes and worrying about safety. It would also have involved haggling about the means and cost of transport, searching for often scarce accommodation, changing money several times over and, all along the route, struggling with

---

[1] L.J. Macfarlane and J. McIntyre, eds., *Scotland and the Holy See: The story of Scotland's links with the papacy down the centuries* (Edinburgh, 1982), 6.

not just foreign languages but with regional dialects which changed from valley to valley. Moreover, weariness and tedium might well have set in once the initial novelty of travel had waned.

Even those who have experienced the spartan rigour of modern travel in the company of a Eurorail pass and a tent seem fortunate compared to the tyranny of distance suffered by the medieval traveller. Yet such comparisons between medieval and modern travel are only possible with the benefit of very recent hindsight. Since they could not have occurred to medieval travellers, their seemingly momentous undertakings ought not to be exaggerated. Indeed, it is not surprising that we do not know the identity of the graffiti artists who visited Rome in 1467. So mundane had travel become by then that most travellers came and went completely unnoticed by scribes and chroniclers.

Harbours

We can try to reconstruct the journey of the anonymous Scots who left their mark in fifteenth-century Rome. Their voyage abroad probably began on the Scottish coast. Harbours were the kingdom's gateways to Christendom. Whenever, and for whatever purpose, Scots travelled abroad in the later middle ages, they were liable to undertake at least a part of their journey by sea. There was clearly no other way of reaching either Ireland or continental Europe; and even some of those heading no further than England preferred to take to the water.

All sea journeys began at a port. Ports were not synonymous with towns. Indeed, one of the most striking features of settlement patterns in medieval Scotland is that, although the country is surrounded on three sides by sea, few of its communities were established with an eye to the sea. Of about fifty burghs established by *c.*1250, almost two-thirds were located on inland sites.[2] Although several of these were situated on rivers which were navigable to sea-going vessels – Perth on the River Tay and Stirling on the River Forth are the obvious examples – most riverside towns probably owed their origins less to maritime access than to the convergence of land routes at fording points. Meanwhile, many of the coastal burghs – such as Cullen – were of such minimal significance that they can rarely have featured in the itinerary of those who ventured abroad. Moreover, we cannot be certain that several of the remaining coastal towns were established *because* of their access to the sea. Port facilities often developed as an adjunct to the emergence of other urban functions. Inverkeithing is perhaps a case in point. Although the town may have developed around the natural harbour at the mouth of the Keithing Burn, it is equally conceivable that the original nucleus of Inverkeithing lay on considerably higher ground to the north, around the present Square, near where the land routes to Dunfermline, Perth and eastern Fife converged. At

[2] The statistic is based on information from G.S. Pryde, *The Burghs of Scotland: A critical list* (Oxford, 1965).

Montrose too we may question whether the town developed because of the superb natural harbour afforded by the tidal basin adjacent to the town. The port of medieval Montrose had a distinctive name of its own (Strumnay) which suggests that the port and the town had separate and distinct origins.[3]

There were few exceptions to this predominantly landward vista of the early Scottish burghs. Aberdeen was probably one, particularly if Pat Dennison's plausible identification of the area adjacent to the Denburn harbour as the early nucleus of the town is accepted.[4] Ayr and Dundee were others. Coastal locations such as these were well positioned to exploit the growth in maritime traffic from the twelfth century, an expansion spawned by the growing demand for foreign wheat and wine and the more or less simultaneous emergence of large quantities of wool available for export. It was this trade which necessitated ports and, perhaps fortuitously, fluvial towns such as Perth, Stirling and Rutherglen, discovered that the rivers on which they were located often afforded access to burgeoning commercial activity.

For landward towns, and their inhabitants, muscling in on this increasing maritime traffic was more problematic. Many made use of the nearest convenient haven: in Lothian traffic from Dunbar passed through Belhaven while that from Haddington was directed to Aberlady. Further north Cupar and Elgin were less exclusive in their choice of harbour, both maintaining overseas contacts through a variety of nearby havens.[5] But it was not until the fourteenth century that several of even the more important towns acquired legal rights over their satellite ports. Edinburgh gained (South) Leith in 1329; Dunfermline acquired Gellet (now Limekilns) in 1362; and Linlithgow secured Blackness as late as 1389.[6] Even then, access to satellite ports, and jurisdiction over them, often remained contentious. As late as the early sixteenth century merchants from Cupar found the highway to their port facilities obstructed by a local laird; and it was only in 1389 that Edinburgh acquired land beside the harbour at Leith – though jurisdictional disputes between the Edinburgh authorities and the lords of Restalrig concerning their respective rights in Leith continued to fester into the sixteenth century.[7]

Across Scotland port facilities were normally simple. Even at the larger ports we have no evidence of great waterside cranes of the sort which were erected in Antwerp, Bristol, or Elbing to load and unload vessels.[8] In Scotland

---

[3] *RRS*, i, no. 19; J. Wordsworth *et al*, 'Excavations at Inverkeithing, 1981', *PSAS*, 113 (1982), 520.

[4] E.P.D. Torrie, 'The early urban site of new Aberdeen: a reappraisal of the evidence', *NS*, 12 (1992), 1-18.

[5] For Dunbar and Haddington, see *ER*, iii, passim; for Cupar's use of 'port of Eden', 'port of Motray' and Tayport, see *ER*, v, 189, 226, 260, 299, 337, 375, 427, 494, 554, 624; and for Elgin's use of Findhorn, Aberdeen and Spynie, see *ER*, iv, 625; viii, 632; *Moray Reg.*, no. 163.

[6] *RRS*, v, no. 381; *Registrum de Dunfermelyn* (Bannatyne Club, 1842), no. 391; *RMS*, i, no. 776.

[7] *ADC*, ii, 38-9, 177, 187; iii, 312; J. Colston, *The Town and Port of Leith* (Edinburgh, 1892), 3-7.

[8] H. van der Wee, *The Growth of the Antwerp Market and the European Economy, Fourteenth to Sixteenth Centuries* (The Hague, 1963), ii, 133; J.W. Sherborne, *The Port of Bristol in the Middle Ages* (Bristol, 1965), 16-17; E. Carsten, *Geschichte der Hansestadt Elbing* (Elbing, 1937), 106-7. See too *Danzig: Bild einer Hansestadt* (Berlin, 1980), 46-9; and the frontispiece of E.S. Hunt and J.M.

a harbour often amounted to no more than a beach-head bereft of man-made constructions – hence, perhaps, the equation of 'shore' and 'harbour' in Scots usage.[9] This simplicity seems to have been the case at, for instance, many of the east Fife ports, such as Pittenweem, whose 1541 charter of erection into a royal burgh included specific provision for building a harbour. Presumably no such facility previously existed, even though the town was apparently used as a port in the thirteenth century.[10] Elsewhere too, we hear of harbour constructions only rather belatedly. Those at Perth remain obscure until the early sixteenth century, when work began on a new harbour; and although Blackness was used frequently as a port in the fourteenth and fifteenth centuries, it was not until 1465 that Linlithgow was permitted to construct a harbour there.[11]

The lack of such facilities bespeaks a limited volume of trade at such ports. Quays facilitated the loading and unloading of heavy barrels and containers, since a raised quay obviated the need for steep gangways between vessels and the shoreside. From the later fifteenth century there is, however, considerable evidence of investment in the construction of harbour facilities, even at smaller ports such as Ayr, Kirkcaldy and Montrose – a sign, perhaps, of expanding trade and economic prosperity.[12] And more followed in the sixteenth century. By 1533 it was planned to construct bulwarks, probably breakwaters to protect vessels at anchor, at a number of ports on both the east and west coasts.[13]

Once harbours had been built it was necessary to maintain their structures. The consequences of not doing so were serious. By 1337 the burgesses of Berwick were complaining that their harbour dues had been misappropriated and that 'the said haven is on the point of being lost'.[14] At Dundee, although a levy for the maintenance of the stone-built harbour was imposed from 1447, by 1560 the town's harbour was in a state of decay.[15] Damage was often the result of natural phenomena. Part of the facilities at Ayr 'past away with the storme' in 1546-47.[16] Silting was another problem which required periodic

---

Murray, *A History of Business in Medieval Europe, 1200-1500* (Cambridge, 1999), for an early sixteenth-century depiction of the crane at Bruges by Simon Benning, an artist of possibly Scottish extraction.

[9] I owe this linguistic suggestion to Grant Simpson.

[10] A. Graham, 'Archaeological notes on some harbours in eastern Scotland', *PSAS*, 101 (1968-69), 202; *RMS*, iii, no. 2292.

[11] D. Bowler and R. Cachart, 'Tay Street, Perth: the excavation of an early harbour site', *PSAS*, 124 (1994), 485-7; *CDS*, iv, no. 461; v, nos. 440, 464, 472, 492; *RMS*, ii, no. 257.

[12] D. Adams, 'The harbour: its early history' in G. Jackson and S.G.E. Lythe, eds., *The Port of Montrose* (Tayport, 1993), 27; *Ayr Burgh Accounts, 1534-1624*, ed. G.S. Pryde (SHS, 1937), 80, 88-9; E.P.D. Torrie and R. Coleman, *Historic Kirkcaldy: The archaeological implications of development* (Scottish Burgh Survey, 1995), 13-15.

[13] *TA*, vi, 129-30.

[14] *Northern Petitions Illustrative of Life in Berwick, Cumbria and Durham in the Fourteenth Century*, ed. C.M. Fraser (Surtees Soc., 1981), no. 11.

[15] E.P.D. Torrie, *Medieval Dundee: A town and its people* (Dundee, 1990), 37.

[16] Pryde, *Ayr Burgh Accounts*, 101.

attention at several ports – the navigational channel at Spynie, in Moray, was, for instance, improved in the mid-fourteenth century – while ships wrecked as they attempted to navigate harbour entrances provided a further, if occasional, impediment to maritime access.[17] At Leith wrecks were reportedly the cause of 'heavy and inestimable damages' in 1445. And at Aberdeen it was perhaps an obstruction caused by wrecks which necessitated the redirection of the town's trade through Footdee between 1430 and 1434 and again between 1447 and 1451. During the intervening years a Danzig vessel was certainly wrecked at Aberdeen's harbour – which was difficult to negotiate because of a sandbank at its entrance.[18]

Harbour dues had been imposed since at least the reign of David I (1124-1153) and part of their proceeds were used to keep harbours and their entrances in good repair. There is evidence of such work at Arbroath, Crail and Leith, and possibly also at Aberdeen, in the fourteenth century, and such work continued at various locations in the fifteenth and early sixteenth centuries.[19] In 1428, for instance, a levy was imposed on ships and goods using Leith 'in augmentation of the fabric and reparation of the port'; and it is probably no coincidence that also in the same year the Edinburgh customs collectors ('custumars') had reported the presence of a shipwreck at Leith. The levy was confirmed in 1445, as it was in 1454, 1471 and 1482 – suggesting that repair and building work was an almost perennial task at the harbour, whose entrance-channel was cleared of large stones in 1504 and 1508.[20] At Aberdeen, meanwhile, new developments in the later fifteenth century included the installation of beacons (to guide ships) and fortifications to defend the harbour against attack from the sea.[21] Leith too appears to have possessed beacons by at least the mid-sixteenth century – though these were far from common in medieval Scotland.[22]

Shipbuilding

At least some of the ships which the traveller might have found in a Scottish port had been built in Scotland. Shipbuilding at Inverness is attested in 1249 by the English chronicler Matthew Paris, but the industry remains obscure until the fifteenth century.[23] By then Leith had developed into not only an important port, but also a major centre of shipbuilding. A barge was

---

[17] *Moray Reg.*, no. 163.
[18] *Edin. Recs.*, i, 7; *ER*, iv, 535, 566; v, 306, 341, 389, 431; CA Aberdeen, CR/5/2, 684; Alexander Lindsay, *A Rutter of the Scottish Seas*, ed. A.B. Taylor, I.H. Adams and G. Fortune (National Maritime Museum, 1980), 48. The wreck of a Spanish barge is also noted at Aberdeen in 1484 (CA Aberdeen, CR/6, 598).
[19] E. Ewan, *Townlife in Fourteenth-century Scotland* (Edinburgh, 1990), 6-7.
[20] *Edin. Recs.*, i, 3, 7, 25, 99, 113; *ER*, iv, 439.
[21] J. Murray, ed., *Excavations in the Medieval Burgh of Aberdeen, 1973-81* (Edinburgh, 1982), 37-45; E.P.D. Dennison and J. Stones, *Historic Aberdeen: The archaeological implications of development* (Scottish Burgh Survey, 1997), 83-4. For the installation of beacons, see CA Aberdeen, CR/6, 598.
[22] *Edin. Recs.*, ii, 275-76.
[23] Matthew Paris, *Chronica Majora*, ed. H.R. Luard (Rolls Series, 1872-83), v, 93.

constructed there for James I, along with ship for his queen in 1435. Repair
work on a carvel was carried out in 1450 and again in 1455.[24] There was, then,
already a basis of skill and experience before James IV commenced his
ambitious programme of shipbuilding in the later fifteenth century. Yet, even
allowing for the possibly false impression created by the fuller late fifteenth-
century evidence, James IV's reign does seem to mark a new epoch in the
shipbuilding industry. In 1492 parliament instructed 'idle men' to build fishing
vessels and, although we may wonder how many were actually constructed as
a result of this edict, the king himself set an example.[25] In 1493-94 alone he
spent £512-9s-11d on the construction of a barge and two boats and on the
repair of a warship, the *Christopher*, at Dumbarton.[26] These, however, were
small projects by comparison with what followed. New yards were
established at Airth in Stirlingshire and at Newhaven near Edinburgh, and
before long their products – the *Margaret*, the *Treasure*, the *James* and the most
magnificent vessel of all, the *Great Michael* (launched in 1512) – were to
provide Scotland with a navy.[27]

   Despite James IV's endeavours, the construction of ships in Scotland was
neither cheap nor easy. Many of the raw materials and skilled craftsmen
required for such work had to be imported. On the east coast timber was
scarce. Froissart noted the complaints of the peasantry at the wasteful misuse
of timber by visiting Frenchmen in 1385 and even in the thirteenth century
the monks of Lindores in Fife sought timber for domestic fuel from as far
away as Glen Errocht in Perthshire.[28] For shipbuilding purposes too timber
was often transported considerable distances before reaching the ports where
the ships were built. In 1435 it was sent by sea from the north of the kingdom
to Leith's yards; and for the work carried out at Dumbarton in 1494, it was
floated down the River Leven from the Loch Lomond area.[29] Yet, while
timber supplies were available in the north and west of the country, the most
commonly available species were not always appropriate for shipbuilding
purposes. In 1512 James IV informed the Danish king that a sailor whom he
had commissioned to search out ship masts in the north of Scotland had failed
to find any suitable timber.[30]

   To compensate for the shortage or inaccessibility of Scottish timber
supplies, some wood was imported for shipbuilding purposes. Baltic timber
was used for the construction of ships near Berwick in 1465, while James IV
used Norwegian, French and Netherlandish imports for the construction of

---

[24] *ER*, iv, 626, v, 384, 387; vi, 3.
[25] *APS*, ii, 235.
[26] *TA*, i, 245-54.
[27] W.S. Reid, 'Seapower in the foreign policy of James IV', *Medievalia et Humanistica*, 15 (1963),
97-107; N. Macdougall, "The greattest scheip that ewer saillit in England or France': James IV's
'Great Michael" in idem, ed., *Scotland and War, AD 79-1918* (Edinburgh, 1991), 36-60.
[28] *Chron. Froissart* (Lettenhove), x, 399; J. Dowden, ed., *Chartulary of the Abbey of Lindores, 1195-
1479* (SHS, 1903), 79.
[29] *ER*, iv, 625; *TA*, i, 247-48.
[30] *James IV Letters*, no. 435.

the *Great Michael*.[31] As for masts, one was imported from Zeeland in 1435, although it was probably not felled there, and James IV obtained those he required for his shipbuilding programme from England, Danzig, Holstein and Norway.[32] Timber was not, however, the only commodity which was imported for shipbuilding purposes: coal, hemp, iron and tar were also required, as were skilled workmen. James IV employed Frenchmen and Spaniards in this capacity, as well as Scots, and also a Portuguese man who grumbled about his low remuneration.[33]

That Scottish shipbuilding flourished despite such shortages was in part due to the restrictions imposed upon the sale of ships elsewhere. To limit foreign commercial competition, the Hansa periodically proscribed the sale of ships to aliens from 1426. The Catholic monarchs issued similar restrictions on the sale of Spanish-built ships.[34] Nevertheless, on occasions Scots were able to circumvent these restrictions. In 1445, for instance, a group of Scots acquired a ship called *Rose* as partial compensation for a series of piratical attacks undertaken by sailors from Bremen, and in 1508 at least one Scottish merchant managed to have his vessel refitted at St Sebastian in Spain.[35] But there were other sources of ships old and new too. James IV paid £35 for a 'brokin' Portuguese vessel in 1498, while Breton yards were building ships for the king in 1504 and 1508.[36] More dubiously, a market also existed for pirated vessels. In 1459, for instance, proceeds from two captured English vessels were delivered to the customs officials at Kirkcudbright.[37]

Scottish travellers did not, however, only make use of Scottish-owned ships. Walter Bower, writing in the fifteenth century, tells a somewhat unlikely tale that Alexander III (1249-1286) had prohibited Scottish ships from venturing overseas.[38] If this was so, official policy had changed by the fifteenth century. A parliamentary statute of 1428 ordained that 'qhare scottis schippis may nocht be gottyn that [merchants] may fure thar gudes and thare merchandice in schippis of vther cuntreis'.[39] In reality, however, whatever was decreed during the reigns of Alexander III and James I, Scots demonstrated no discernible prejudice towards chartering either domestic or foreign shipping. In 1229, for instance, we hear of the Berwick merchant Bernard of Alvertone transporting seven sacks of wool on a Dover ship; and at much the same time we hear too of ships owned by the monasteries of Melrose and Coupar Angus.[40] And by the fifteenth century, if not earlier, Scots were making use

[31] *ER*, vii, 370; *James IV Letters*, nos. 41-2, 84, 402; Reid, 'Seapower in the foreign policy of James IV', 101.
[32] *ER*, iv, 626; *James IV Letters*, nos. 213, 230-32, 435-36; *TA*, iv, 296, 331.
[33] *TA*, iv, 75, 335, 341, 482, 502, 511, 527.
[34] P. Dollinger, *Die Hanse* (3rd ed., Stuttgart, 1981), 191; *James IV Letters*, no. 163.
[35] SA Bremen, 1/Bc 1445 Oktober 16; *James IV Letters*, no. 163.
[36] *TA*, i, 388; ii, 445, 461; iii, 135, 182; iv, 460.
[37] *ER*, vi, 495.
[38] *Chron. Bower* (Watt), v, 424-25.
[39] *APS*, ii, 16.
[40] *CDS*, i, nos. 902, 1042, 1086.

not just of Scottish shipping, but also of Danish, English, French, German, Netherlandish, Norwegian and Spanish vessels. Such diversity was, indeed, by no means unusual in medieval Europe: shipping deployed on Anglo-Castilian routes, for instance, was of a similarly cosmopolitan nature.[41]

If common sense dictated the use of whatever shipping was available for a voyage, it also fostered co-operation between those of different social standing and from different locations. In 1444, for instance, three ships bound for Danzig (two of them Scottish, the third from Dunkirk) included cargoes belonging not just to Danzig merchants but also to those from fourteen Scottish towns.[42] Similarly, by at least the fifteenth century, the crews of vessels were sometimes of mixed nationality. In 1478 Richard Mill of Dundee was engaged as a steersman on a Stralsund vessel, while in 1498 John Grant, a Scot, was reported as having had 'the principal rule of the best schippes bilonging to Bristowe'.[43] Foreigners were also employed on Scottish ships. The master of a 150-ton Scottish barge moored at Sluis in 1464 was the seemingly foreign Barthelmieu Breton.[44] The crew of the *Great Michael* included Spaniards, Frenchmen and possibly a German or Netherlandish mariner by the name of Wolf Duchman. James IV also employed a French pilot on the *James*, while the *Gabriel* had a French skipper.[45] The maritime workforce of later medieval Europe was truly cosmopolitan.

Shipping

What, then, did the ship which our traveller may have boarded look like? In 1464, while investigating the possibility of launching a crusade, Burgundian officials compiled an inventory of vessels then docked at Sluis. They found seventy-two ships, in addition to almost forty fishing boats which they deemed useless for their purposes. Among the largest was a 500-ton ship belonging to the bishop of St Andrews which, the Burgundian observers noted, was 'a very fine vessel'. Several of the others moored at Sluis were Scottish too – including a 350-ton barge, whose master was Robert Barton of Leith, and a 140-ton carvel belonging to the bishop of Aberdeen.[46] This list has led some historians to argue that one reason for the infrequency of sailings from Scottish ports was that Scottish vessels were unusually large when compared with those used in other countries. Since their cargo capacity was

[41] W.R. Childs, *Anglo-Castilian Trade in the Later Middle Ages* (Manchester, 1978), 149-57. See too James IV's comments to the French queen in *James IV Letters*, no. 13.
[42] SA Bremen, 1/Bc 1445 Juli 15; 1/Bc 1445 August 4; 1/Bc 1445 August 10; 1/Bc 1445 August 12; 1/Bc 1445 August 13/I; 1/Bc 1445 August 13/II; 1/Z 1444 Juli 4.
[43] CA Aberdeen, CR/6, 557-58; *CDS*, iv, no. 1645.
[44] R. Degryse, 'De schepen in de haven van Sluis in het voorjaar 1464', *Mededelingen van de Marineakademie van Belgie*, 20 (1968), 101.
[45] *TA*, iv, 502-7.
[46] J. Finot, ed., *Inventaire Sommaires des Archives Départmentales du Nord. Tome VIII: Archives Civiles, Série B* (Lille, 1895), i, 291; Degryse, 'De schepen in de haven van Sluis', 95-106.

greater, the number of voyages which they made could be reduced.[47] Scots were certainly capable of constructing vessels which, by European standards, were large – as James IV's grand fleet demonstrates. But we should be careful before assuming that large vessels were the norm. The average tonnage of Scottish vessels included in English safe-conducts of the fifteenth century was only seventy-five tons.[48] Even at Leith, the busiest Scottish port, harbour facilities appear to have been either inadequate, or too congested with smaller vessels, to allow the bigger vessels to enter;[49] and when Nicholas West, an envoy of Henry VIII of England, visited Leith in 1513, he was less than impressed with 'only nine or ten small topmen with other small ballingers and crayers' which he found docked in the harbour.[50] There is, then, much evidence to suggest that many of the vessels which visited Scottish harbours were of a much smaller scale than that belonging to the bishop of St Andrews in the fifteenth century.

By the thirteenth century the most common type of vessel used in northern Europe was the cog, a normally single-masted ship, with a keel and a stern rudder. It was ideally designed for the transport of the bulky commodities which constituted the mainstay of north European trade, and it was typically about 30m long and 9.5m wide with a draught of between three and four metres – though larger and smaller variants were not uncommon. By 1400 the average cog was capable of loading one hundred tons, though some reached a 300-ton capacity.[51] Meanwhile, other ship designs, such as the originally crescent-shaped, flat-bottomed hulk, were modified to compete with the cog (for instance by the incorporation of a keel), to the point that the words 'cog' and 'hulk' were sometimes applied indiscriminately to the same vessel. Linguistically, at least, the latter was to emerge triumphant: hulks, but not cogs, are routinely referred to in the shipping tolls levied at Leith in the fifteenth century.[52] Yet, as these lists indicate, the toll collectors at Leith were familiar with other types of vessel too. Crayers, busses, barges, ballingers and caumfers were all noted and subjected to an identical levy of 5s. The difference between these ship types is not altogether clear. Barges and ballingers, unlike the others, probably included provision for oars, as well as sail power; and caumfers may have been nothing more than vessels which

---

[47] A. Stevenson, 'Trade with the south, 1070-1513' in M. Lynch *et al.*, eds., *The Scottish Medieval Town* (Edinburgh, 1988), 190.

[48] Stevenson, Thesis, 170-72.

[49] A.D.M. Forte, 'The identification of fifteenth-century ship types in Scottish legal records', *MM*, 84 (1998), 8.

[50] *James IV Letters*, p. 321.

[51] R.W. Unger, *The Ship in the Medieval Economy, 600-1600* (London, 1980), 138-40, 163.

[52] Unger, *The Ship in the Medieval Economy*, 168-71; Forte, 'The identification of fifteenth-century ship types', 4. See too Childs, *Anglo-Castilian Trade*, 158, on the 'disappearance' of the cog further south.

routinely sailed to the Netherlandish port of Veere.[53] The identical levy imposed on all five classes of vessel might suggest a broad parity in tonnage and also that these smaller ships were about half the size of hulks which were liable for a 10s levy at Leith. The distinction is not, however, as clear-cut as the toll lists imply. 'Small' ships varied greatly in size and though a typical ballinger bore a capacity of between twenty and fifty tons (compared to an average hulk of by then about 300 tons), some ballingers were as large as 500 tons. Designs varied too, even within the same class of vessel. Some busses were modified with a stern rudder and these were little different from cogs and hulks. Ballingers were originally unsophisticated, oared fishing vessels, though by the fifteenth century some were large, two-masted ships. Meanwhile, it is even more difficult to identify the characteristics of the Aberdeen carvel recorded at Sluis. Although in the Mediterranean a carvel was a highly manoeuvrable, two-masted vessel with lateen sails, sometimes exceeding 400 tons in capacity, in northern Europe the word was often applied to any ship of vaguely Mediterranean design.[54] The bishop of Aberdeen's vessel – at 140 tons – was evidently much smaller than the greatest of true carvels, though it too may be reckoned to figure among the myriad of medium-capacity ships which frequented Scottish ports.

By the later middle ages ships might be owned either by a single individual or by a group of shareholders. Kings, bishops and nobles were often sole proprietors of vessels, though they frequently hired out their ships to others. Thus, in 1409 the *Tay*, owned by the duke of Albany, was hired by a group of Compostella-bound pilgrims, including the abbot of Melrose, Sir James Douglas of Strathbrock and several Edinburgh burgesses; and in 1460 the bishop of Aberdeen sought payment of £7 6s in Flemish money from the merchant Andrew Alaneson, whose goods had been transported on the bishop's ship, the *Christopher* – probably the same vessel noted at Sluis a few years later.[55] Some townsmen, too, were single owners of vessels, but at least by the fifteenth century it was common for several to share ownership of a vessel. Half, quarter and eighth shares are all well attested in Scottish sources, though smaller portions are known too. In 1512, for instance, the Aberdonian widow Elizabeth Sinclair sold the twenty-fourth share in *The Bark* owned by her late husband, a ship's master.[56] Although joint owners usually hailed from the same town, in 1525 another vessel called the *Christopher* belonged to men from both Cupar and St Andrews, while Arthur Bruce, a Scot, and Peter

---

[53] J.W. Sherborne, 'English barges and ballingers of the late fourteenth century', *MM*, 63 (1977), 109-14; Unger, *The Ship in the Medieval Economy*, 171-72, 204; Forte, 'The identification of fifteenth-century ship types', 9-10.

[54] Unger, *The Ship in the Medieval Economy*, 167, 204, 212.

[55] *Calendar of Signet Letters of Henry IV and Henry V, 1399-1422*, ed. J.L. Kirby (London, 1978), no. 741; CA Aberdeen, CR/5/1, 394.

[56] CA Aberdeen, CR/9, 86.

Stralk, from Hamburg, appear to have co-purchased a vessel in 1513.[57] This, however, was unusual.

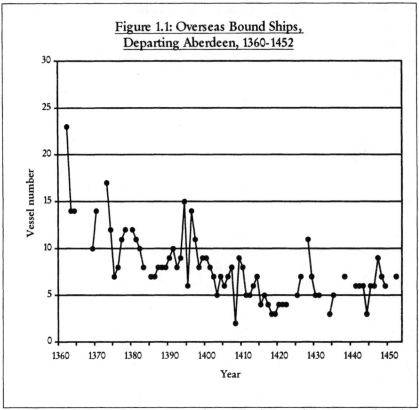

Figure 1.1: Overseas Bound Ships, Departing Aberdeen, 1360-1452

Source: ER, passim. Note: where accounts are for periods of two or three years, vessel numbers have been averaged per year. An additional but unspecified number of boats are also recorded in 1416 and 1431.

Preparations

The immediate factor which governed the length of a journey was the duration of the wait for a suitable vessel. This probably explains why several Scots travelled overland to south-eastern England before sailing abroad, since the frequency of departures from the Channel ports was greater than that from Scotland.[58] The unfortunate traveller from Banff would have had a long wait for a ship in the 1380s – the town's custumars reported in 1389 that none had visited their port for some time.[59] Even at the more important Scottish

[57] *ADCP*, 220; *James IV Letters*, no. 512.
[58] E.g., *CDS*, iv, nos. 142, 194-95, 198, 868, 890.
[59] *ER*, iii, 213.

ports maritime traffic was hardly frequent. As indicated in Figure 1.1, there were rarely more than about ten vessels laden with customable goods leaving the comparatively important port of Aberdeen each year – and in 1409 only two did. Aberdonians and others could, however, overcome their own sometimes meagre contacts with the continent by taking a coaster as far as Leith. Leith became Scotland's main commercial entrepot in the later middle ages and goods (and presumably people) were shipped there from as far away as Dingwall and Tain before onward travel.[60] Yet even at Leith an average of only seventeen ships left port in the 1380s *per annum*, though that would rise to over thirty in the 1510s and forty-nine in 1527-28.[61] Nevertheless, even this was limited by comparison with south-eastern England. Two hundred and fifteen ships left the port of London and its satellite havens in 1480-81 alone.[62]

From London, albeit occasionally, it was possible to sail directly to the Mediterranean. No Scottish ships, so far as we know, sailed through the Straits of Gibraltar, leaving travellers for the Holy Land to face an Alpine crossing, before embarking on another sea voyage, usually from Venice. Direct sailings to the Baltic were also rare before the later fourteenth century, travellers in that direction normally alighting at Hamburg (or further south) before re-boarding at Lübeck. Even once the sea route through the Sound became more frequently used, the number of Scottish vessels heading for the Baltic remained limited. All ships were liable to pay a toll at Elsinore, when entering or leaving the Baltic, and in 1497 Scottish skippers made payments on twenty-one occasions (about 2.6% of the total), though their number had doubled by 1503 and 1528.[63] For most Scottish travellers, however, a sea voyage took them no further than an Irish or North Sea port. Trading records and customs data provide some indication of where exactly they headed, though these are sadly sparse for the west coast. Still, there is no doubt that ships from the west sailed regularly to Ireland: when an arrest order was placed on Scottish vessels in Irish ports in 1306 twelve were apprehended in Dublin, Drogheda and Dundalk alone. There is also some evidence of direct contact with France and Spain, though this was probably not frequent.[64] Meanwhile, by the fourteenth century east-coast vessels headed primarily for the Low Countries. The major Scottish exports – wool, woolfells and hides – were by then legally directed to a staple. Since this was usually located at Bruges, most vessels probably made for Damme or Sluis, the satellite ports of the great Flemish emporium. This was to change in the second half of the fifteenth century. Veere was designated as the staple port in 1508, though it

[60] NAS Edinburgh, E71/29/2; E71/29/3.
[61] *ER*, iii, 52, 65, 86, 116-17, 132, 150, 168, 186, 204; NAS Edinburgh, E71/29/2; E71/29/3; E71/29/3.
[62] *The Overseas Trade of London: Exchequer customs accounts, 1480-1*, ed. H. Cobb (London Record Soc., 1990).
[63] RA København, Øresundtolsregnskaber, 1497; 1503; 1528; *Tabeller over Skibsfart og Varetransport gennem Øresund, 1497-1660*, ed. N.E. Bang (Copenhagen and Leipzig, 1906), i, 2-4.
[64] *CJRI*, ii, 226-227; Stevenson, 'Trade with the south', 186, 196.

had long since supplanted Sluis in the Netherlandish trade, the Zeeland port offering better access to the growing commercial centres of Antwerp and Bergen-op-Zoom than its Flemish rival. More significantly, as indicated in Figure 1.2, the Netherlands lost its dominant position in Scottish trade. Sailings to the ports of Normandy rose markedly from the later fifteenth century and by 1527-28 forty-three per cent of foreign-bound vessels leaving Leith made for Dieppe.[65] Meanwhile, as political tensions between the two kingdoms subsided, the number of sailings to English ports grew markedly too from the later fifteenth century, most of them undertaken by vessels from the Fife ports.

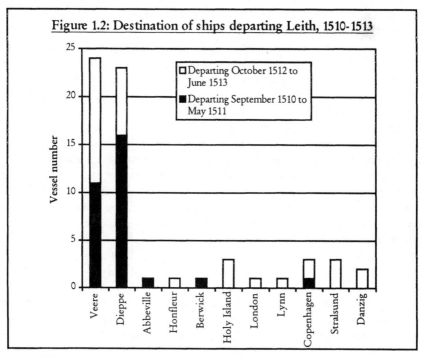

Figure 1.2: Destination of ships departing Leith, 1510-1513

Source: NAS, E71/29/2; E71/29/3.

Sailings to all of these destinations were governed by commercial considerations. In the Netherlands by the later fifteenth century the commercial calendar was focused principally on the great fairs of Bruges, Bergen-op-Zoom and Antwerp. Each town boasted two fairs, providing for virtually year-long business opportunities, though there was a lull in July, August and September between the end of the Pixteren (Whit) markt at Antwerp and the start of the Bamisse markt in Antwerp on 1 October. Shipping from Scotland was geared to coincide with the fairs and accordingly

[65] NAS Edinburgh, E71/29/4.

comparatively few vessels made for the Netherlands in the summer months.[66]
English-bound shipping was also seasonally concentrated, though here it is
much more difficult to detect a rationale to sailing patterns. In the early 1540s,
for instance, the vast majority of Scottish ships arriving at Hull did so in
February and March, though in the early 1520s arrivals had been concentrated
in April and May. June and August had been the favoured months in 1453 and
October in 1511-12.[67] For other areas we are less well informed, though the
presumption must be that most ships sailed for commercial purposes and that
those who travelled for other reasons simply had to plan their journeys
accordingly.

   Once a suitable vessel had been found, travellers had to negotiate the terms
and conditions of their carriage. Aside from any passengers, ships often carried
goods belonging to a large number of merchants, most of whom probably did
not accompany their cargo. Both passengers and cargo were the responsibility
of the skipper, though their interests did not always coincide. In certain
circumstances (for example to escape pirates or to avoid shipwreck) the
skipper might deem it necessary to jettison the cargo. On other occasions
ships did not sail to the agreed destination. It was to safeguard against disputes
arising in such circumstances that in 1438 the Edinburgh town council
stipulated that written contracts be made between skippers and merchants. It
was no doubt at the instigation of the mercantile community that parliament
passed a similar statute in 1467.[68] There was other paperwork to be completed
too before a vessel departed. If it carried custumable goods, duty had to be
paid. This entailed counting or weighing the merchandise at the public tron
and only once merchants had been issued with a sealed letter of cocket,
certifying that duty had been paid on the goods, could the voyage
commence.[69]

Voyages

Once a ship had departed, crew and passengers alike faced a probably
uncomfortable, possibly lengthy and potentially dangerous voyage. Since no
detailed descriptions of Scottish ships survive, it is difficult to recapture the
discomfort of life aboard these probably rickety and rat-infested
constructions. The foul odour was probably especially off-putting. Writing of
a vessel upon which he spent a brief but unpleasant journey, the poet William
Dunbar noted that twenty years of excrement was caked on its side.[70] In

---

[66] Stevenson, Thesis, 301-5, 318-23.
[67] PRO London, E122/60/3; E122/61/71; E122/64/5; E122/64/15; E122/64/15.
[68] *Edin. Recs.*, i, 5; *APS*, ii, 87. Elsewhere in the North Sea world charter-parties long pre-dated this
legislation. See, for instance, R. Ward, 'A surviving charter-party of 1323', *MM*, 81 (1995), 387-401.
[69] The fullest modern accounts of the customs administration are A. Murray, 'The customs
accounts of Kirkcudbright, Wigtown and Dumfries, 1434-1560', *TDGAS*, 40 (1961-62), 136-62;
Stevenson, Thesis, 150-57. See too Stevenson, Thesis, 174-84, for the administration of the Flemish
customs.
[70] Dunbar, *Poems*, no. 23, p. 92.

addition, we may presume that space was often cramped. The hierarchical notions of medieval society were briefly suspended as the wealthy traveller abandoned comparative comfort and mingled with others in the restricted areas available. With limited sleeping accommodation merchants aboard one vessel sailing from the Netherlandish port of Bergen-op-Zoom to Aberdeen took to reposing upon a bale of woad. While this no doubt afforded a measure of comfort in the absence of bunks, their sweat allegedly ruined the cargo.[71] Some ships, such as a Norwegian-bound vessel from Dundee in 1554, carried cooks, but supplies of fresh drinking-water and food were probably limited.[72] And if the necessities of life were in limited supply, the experience of life at sea was all the more miserable in inclement weather conditions. Dunbar 'was not sekir of [his] tayle' and graphically described the excretal consequences. He was probably not alone in also suffering from chronic sea sickness. Even in the Forth this could be severe, Dunbar recounting how, safely ashore on the Bass rock, he 'spewit and kest out many a lathly [horrible] lomp'.[73] More experienced mariners perhaps fared better in the Forth, but elsewhere even they might take fright. The Pentland Firth was described by an English observer in 1542 as 'the most dangerous place in Christendom' and even Scots were wary of passing through its treacherous waters in the winter months.[74] On the open seas, with no possibility of seeking shelter in a port, storms often blew ships well off course. In 1448 Robert Wormot's ship, bound from Aberdeen to London, was driven by storms to Holland.[75] On occasions worse followed as vessels sank or ran aground and travellers drowned. With few ships carrying priests – even those which Christopher Columbus took to the New World in 1492 were priestless – those caught in such circumstances faced the horror of death before final confession and absolution for their sins.[76] This, we should not forget, was an alarming prospect in such an intensely religious society. Less severe storm damage, though frightening, might be repaired *in situ* by carpenters ('timbermen') and caulkers ('caulfetours') who were carried aboard at least some vessels.[77] Skilled craftsmen were, however, espensive. Thomas Wynne, the carpenter aboard the English vessel *Mary Walsyngam*, was paid 28s for a voyage from Bordeaux in 1537, double that of ordinary sailors.[78] It was clearly cheaper to risk doing without the on-board services that such craftsmen provided and instead to rectify storm damage in a port. Accordingly, vessels sailing to and from Scotland frequently sought shelter in havens along the English coastline, even if, while saving body and

[71] CA Aberdeen, CR/8, 84-85.
[72] CA Dundee, BHCB/2, fo. 338.
[73] Dunbar, *Poems*, no. 23, p.92.
[74] *L. & P. Henry VIII*, xvii, no. 514; Taylor, Adams and Fortune, *Alexander Lindsay*, 50.
[75] CA Aberdeen, CR/5/1, 29.
[76] For an exception, see, however, *TA*, iv, 504.
[77] *TA*, iv, 503, 505; *Protocol Book of Gavin Ros, 1512-32*, ed. J. Anderson and F.J. Grant (SRS, 1908), no. 885.
[78] SRO Ipswich, C13/15/1, fo. 134r.

soul from stormy seas, political tensions meant that ships and their cargoes were liable to sequestration and travellers to imprisonment. Thus, in 1365 a Scottish vessel driven into Newcastle by stress of weather was arrested, while in 1368 a Flemish ship sailing from Sluis to Aberdeen put in at Grimsby due to stormy conditions, only for its cargo to be detained on the grounds that the skipper had no safe-conduct.[79]

Storms were but one of the potential natural hazards to be endured by the sea traveller. Disease and illness were others. In 1500 'sekness' was discovered aboard a ship arriving in Aberdeen from Danzig and the passengers were duly quarantined until the nature of the disease had been identified. Shortly afterwards further precautions dictated that part of their cargo be burned.[80] In the confined circumstances of a ship, disease could spread rapidly and often with fatal consequences. Of thirty-six pilgrims bound from Venice to Jaffa in 1508, twenty-seven (including Robert Blacader, bishop of Glasgow) succumbed to plague.[81] But there were also man-made hazards. Flames, for instance, engulfed one ship carrying Scotsmen on the open seas in 1405.[82]

It was partly for these reasons that whenever possible medieval skippers preferred to sail close to the coastline: calling at ports *en route* afforded opportunities to re-provision and repair vessels and for passengers to recover their composure and perhaps health. Thus, when the cleric Robert de Moffet made for the Holy Land in 1414, his ship called at Pola (on the Istrian peninsula), Rhodes and Beirut, before arriving at Jaffa, with another stop at Rhodes on the return leg to Venice.[83] But comfort and safety were not the only reasons for such navigational caution. Navigational techniques in northern Europe were rudimentary compared to those in the Mediterranean and this made progress on the open seas difficult. Most ships probably possessed a sounding line which enabled mariners to calculate the depth of the waters into which they ventured. Compasses (used by the Chinese in the tenth century) are recorded on some North Sea ships from the fourteenth century, though it is not until James IV's reign that we can be certain of their use on Scottish vessels. Dunbar, for instance, noted a compass and an hourglass on the ship which he boarded in the Forth, and James IV purchased several compasses for his ships in 1507.[84] Sea charts, meanwhile, were rare. In their absence reliance was probably placed on celestial observation during voyages on the open sea, though the inaccuracies to which this navigational

[79] *CDS*, iv, nos. 116, 146.

[80] CA Aberdeen, CR/7, 1067-68.

[81] D. Laing, ed., 'Notice of the death of Robert Blackader, archbishop of Glasgow, during a pilgrimage to the Holy Land, in the year 1508', *PSAS*, ii (1859), 224.

[82] *CDS*, v, no. 936.

[83] AS Venezia, Busca 134, fo. 35r. I owe this reference to Anthony Goodman, who in turn obtained it from Stefano Piasentini. On Moffet, see Watt, *Graduates*, 398-99.

[84] Dunbar, *Poems*, no. 23, p. 92; *TA*, iii, 91, 386; iv, 302, vi, 164; viii, 159. For sandglasses see too *TA*, iii, 180, 337; vii, 491.

technique was prone are well documented in the case of Christopher Columbus.

In the absence of such basic maritime tools, the land offered a measure of reassurance. One late medieval Icelandic source offered a vague itinerary for reaching Greenland, recommending sailors leaving the Norwegian port of Bergen to 'turn right' and sail as 'far north as possible from Shetland, so that it can only be seen from the sea on a clear day'.[85] The importance of visual landmarks in calculating direction is self-evident in this advice. Indeed, distance was measured not by standard units of length but rather by 'kennings' – the number of prominent landmarks between two locations. A sea journey between Aberdeen and Leith was thus five kennings, divided by Red Head, Fife Ness, the Isle of May and Inchkeith.[86] Prominent topographical features, such as these, were probably committed to memory by experienced sailors, though by the later middle ages mariners were sometimes also equipped with rutters which included descriptions of this kind, as well as information about tides, bearings and hazards. Few of these now survive – the earliest Scottish example dates from *c*.1540 – but some indication of their content is also afforded by artistic works, such as Jan de Hervy's *View of the Zwin*, which appears to have been based on such a source.[87] In addition to depicting nautical hazards, such as mudflats and sandbars, Hervy's work shows landmarks such as church spires which were visible from the sea. These features were often based upon the depiction of buildings carried on a town's seal. We may perhaps assume that through the transmission of documents symbolic representations were readily associated with their actual location and that they were well known to mariners as they plotted their course. In good visibility the actual landmarks themselves could be recognised from afar by seamen with experience of local waters. If these were not qualities possessed by a crew member, captains could break their journey at a suitable point to engage the services of a pilot who was aware of the local topography. The thirteenth-century laws of Oléron, the basis for maritime law throughout the North and Baltic Seas, advised Scottish-bound ships to recruit a pilot at Yarmouth in Norfolk.[88] By the early sixteenth century pilotage services were beginning to become institutionalised. At Hull, for instance, the guild of the Holy Trinity was asked by the town's shipmasters to provide a pilot service in 1512. It was the difficulties encountered by a Scottish vessel attempting to enter Hull without a pilot, as witnessed personally by Henry VIII in 1541,

[85] N. Ohler, *Reisen im Mittelalter* (Munich and Zürich, 1986), 66-7.
[86] A.D.M. Forte, "Kenning be kenning and course be course': maritime jurimetrics in Scotland and northern Europe, 1400-1600', *The Edinburgh Law Review*, 2 (1998), 56-98; idem, 'Kenning be kenning and course be course': Alexander Lindsay's rutter and the problematics of navigation in fifteenth and sixteenth-century Scotland', *Review of Scottish Culture*, 11 (1998-99), 32-45.
[87] Taylor, Adams and Fortune, *Alexander Lindsay*; A. Roberts, 'The landscape as legal document: Jan de Hervy's 'View of the Zwin', *Burlington Magazine* (February, 1991), 82-6.
[88] *The Black Book of the Admiralty*, T. Twiss (Roll Series, 1873), ii, 226.

which prompted legislation that all alien vessels should be conducted into the Humber port by a brother of the Trinity House guild.[89]

Coastal navigation was not, however, without its own dangers, for ships which ventured cautiously along familiar routes were more vulnerable to the hazards of war and piracy than those which challenged the anonymity of the open seas.[90] Of course, there were several methods by which skippers and shipowners might safeguard themselves against such loss. Safe-conducts were the most obvious. These could be obtained, at a price, from the prince whose territory was being traversed, and they provided for a measure of redress in the event of attack or arrest: the grantee could sue the grantor for compensation in the event of loss. Safe-conducts were, in other words, a primitive form of state travel insurance.[91] In addition, or alternatively, some ships were armed for self-defence. Indeed, many larger vessels were built with small decks or castles fore and aft which were specifically intended for defensive purposes.[92] Well above the water level, these constructions provided the defending crew with the advantage of height over would-be assailants and a launching pad from which to project arrows, lime or, latterly, gunfire on their attackers. Sometimes ships were well-prepared for assailants. In 1416 the crews of Scottish ships visiting Holland were granted the right to arm themselves in times of war, and in 1514 the *Bergenfahrer* of Lübeck, Rostock and Wismar carried weapons in anticipation of an onslaught by Scottish pirates.[93] Meanwhile, calculating upon safety in numbers, convoys were another safeguard against attack. Some were of an impressive size. Those which plied the waters from the Baltic to the Bay of Bourgneuf were often composed of over one hundred vessels. On occasion ships bound for Scotland joined the Bay fleets, leaving the main convoy at an appropriate juncture.[94] Given the limited volume of Scottish trade, convoys to and from Scotland were correspondingly smaller. In 1528, for instance, five Scottish vessels were entered consecutively in the register of ships passing Elsinore, suggesting a convoy; and further east groups of between two and nine Scottish ships apparently arrived in Danzig together in the fifteenth century.[95] Such clusters were less frequent among the Scottish ships which visited English ports,

[89] A. Storey, *Trinity House of Kingston-upon-Hull* (Grimsby, 1967), 37.

[90] D. Ditchburn, 'Piracy and war at sea in late medieval Scotland' in T.C. Smout, ed., *Scotland and the Sea* (Edinburgh, 1992), 37-58.

[91] For those granted by the English crown to Scots, see *Rot. Scot.*, passim. For the handling of safe-conducts by the Scottish government, see *The Register of Brieves*, ed. T.M. Cooper (Stair Soc., 1946), nos. 61-3; *Formulary E: Scottish letters and brieves, 1286-1424*, ed. A.A.M. Duncan (Glasgow, 1976), nos. 61-2; and *TA*, i, 3, for the £10 paid by the Englishman Thomas Black for a Scottish safe-conduct in 1473-74.

[92] Unger, *The Ship in the Medieval Economy*, 139-40.

[93] Smit, *Bronnen, 1150-1485*, i, no. 940; *HR, 1477-1530*, vi, nos. 576, 578, 647.

[94] *HUB*, viii, no. 366.

[95] RA København, Øresundtolsregnskaber 1528, 3; WAP Gdansk, 300/19/1-10, passim.

though the ten Scottish vessels which left Hull within a four-day period in March 1541 perhaps imply a convoy assembling outside the port.[96]

The Speed of Sea Travel

The dangers of sea travel were exacerbated by the length of time which ships spent at sea. Much, of course, depended upon the route which vessels took to reach their destination and the number of stop-overs which their masters chose to make. Much too depended on the chance circumstances of favourable winds. In good conditions a ship might manage an average rate of fifteen kilometres per hour, but in less propitious conditions only four or five kilometres per hour could be maintained.[97] These variables made for considerable differences in the length of journeys. The Lübeck skipper Claus van der Stege left Aberdeen on 20 September 1499 and arrived at Veere on 23 October – a journey time of just over a month – and at least some of the correspondence dispatched to James IV through the Netherlandish ports took about the same length of time to be delivered.[98] We do not know, however, whether either van der Stege or James IV's messengers made a detour on the way to their respective destinations, or whether the winds were particularly unfavourable as they made their voyages from and to Scotland. Certainly, detours were not uncommon. In 1439 a probably Baltic-bound Greifswald ship departed the Low Countries but called at Aberdeen, a diversion which must have added considerably to the duration of the voyage.[99] Indeed, it is this which probably explains why some voyages took even longer than that undertaken by van der Stege, one vessel sailing from Aberdeen to Veere apparently taking forty-seven days to complete the voyage.[100] Moreover, the first departing ship was not necessarily bound even ultimately for the traveller's ideal destination. In 1447 Aberdeen merchants anticipated that their cargo from Danzig might arrive at Rattray or Leith or 'quhar it suld happin the said schip to arrive' rather than at their home port; and in 1515 another Aberdeen merchant, Andrew Cullan, discovered that his cargo of tar and timber had been sent from Danzig, via Copenhagen, to Leith.[101] Clearly travellers had to balance such inconvenience against the prospect of an even longer wait for a vessel sailing exactly where they wanted. Nevertheless, it was certainly possible to cover the route from the Low Countries to Scotland – a distance of some 385 miles – in a much shorter time than the examples cited above would suggest. Mary of Guelders, the bride-to-be of James II, left the Netherlandish port of Sluis at four o'clock on the morning of Thursday 12

---

[96] PRO London, E122/64/15, fos. 9v-10r.

[97] Dollinger, *Hanse*, 192.

[98] NAS Edinburgh, E71/1/1, fo. 5r; *De Tol van Iersekeroord: Documenten en rekeningen, 1321-1572*, ed. W.S. Unger (The Hague, 1939), 511; *James IV Letters*, nos. 130, 164-65. See too Stevenson, Thesis, 168-69.

[99] *LUB*, vii, no. 808.

[100] Stevenson, Thesis, 168.

[101] CA Aberdeen, CR/4, 498; CR/9, 441-442.

June 1449 and arrived in Scotland a week later.[102] Even this seems a lengthy journey compared with that undertaken by Alexander III's daughter Margaret, whose party took a mere two or four days to cover the 400 miles or so from Scotland to Norway in August 1281.[103] Although this was probably a particularly speedy voyage, it suggests a minimum duration for journeys from Leith to Bergen, the Netherlandish ports and London, all of which lay within a radius of approximately 400 miles from Leith. Nevertheless, those who opted to minimise the queasiness of sea travel by travelling south by land could cross to the continent much more quickly: the Welshman Adam of Usk took just a day to sail from Billingsgate in London to Bergen-op-Zoom.[104]

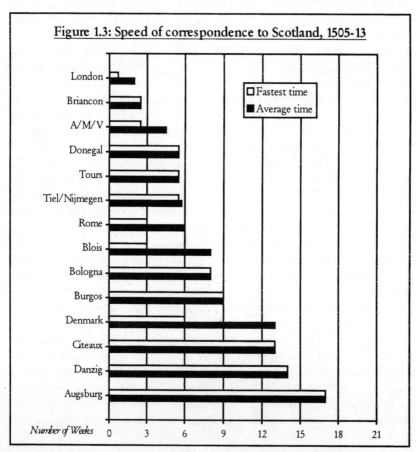

Figure 1.3: Speed of correspondence to Scotland, 1505-13

Source: *James IV Letters*, passim. *Key:* A/M/V = Antwerp, Middelburg and Veere

---

[102] *Chron. d'Escouchy*, i, 176-77.
[103] *Chron. Lanercost*, 104-5; *Chron. Bower* (Watt), v, 411.
[104] *The Chronicle of Adam of Usk, 1377-1421*, ed. C. Given-Wilson (Oxford, 1997), 152-53; *The Chronicle of Adam of Usk A.D. 1377-1421*, ed. E.M. Thompson (repr., Llanerch, 1990), 112.

Sailings elsewhere obviously took longer: Danzig is about 850 miles from Leith and Bordeaux about 1050 miles. One letter, written to James IV and dated at Danzig on 8 October 1508, did not arrive with the king until 13 January 1509. As indicated in Figure 1.3, it took over two months for some messages from the Danish court to reach Scotland too.[105] Still, James 'wondered at the [Danzig] messenger's delay' and his surprise suggests that speedier voyages were possible. In this instance it seems credible that the delay was occasioned by poor weather, for the Baltic was normally closed to shipping during the winter months on account of the hazards of ice.[106]

On routes such as that between Scotland and the Baltic, direct traffic was also less frequent than it was between Scotland and the Low Countries. Delay, in other words, might often have been occasioned by the wait for a ship. Certainly, although it was not unknown for skippers to undertake two Baltic voyages in one season – Hans Dertholt, for instance, is twice recorded as arriving in Danzig from Scotland in 1471 – one return voyage seems to have been the norm.[107]

Land Travel

For most mariners and merchants arrival at port marked the end-point of their journey. For other travellers disembarkation was but the prelude to a further journey. Some had perhaps already planned their onward itinerary before disembarkation: we know, for instance, that there was a travel guide for those visiting the Holy Land in the library of Aberdeen cathedral in the fifteenth century, though it has since been lost.[108] Others took advice upon landing from those in the know. In 1465 Eleanor Stewart, duchess of Tirol, sent a servant to guide her half-brother James Stewart of Auchterhouse from Füssen, on the Austro-Bavarian border, to Innsbruck and Trent, from where a priest from Bozen/Bolzano accompanied him to Rome.[109] We can be sure, however, that the speed with which journeys by land were accomplished was as variable as for those by sea. In 1303 it took three weeks for one of Edward I's messengers to reach him in Scotland from Dover, but only five days for some correspondence to reach Edinburgh from Greenwich in 1513.[110] Meanwhile, a journey from the English Channel to Italy could take between three and seven weeks, Thomas Wale and Thomas Delisle, the English

[105] *James IV Letters*, no. 36, 86, 213.
[106] *HR*, *1256-1430*, viii, nos. 17, 24, 59(17), 63, 67. The Baltic was officially 'closed' from 11 November to 22 February. See too *APS*, ii, 87, for legislation of 1467 prohibiting the export of staple goods from Scotland between 28 October and 2 February. The decree was perhaps pertinent to that year alone, since it seems to have little, if any, effect in subsequent years.
[107] WAP Gdansk, 300/19/3, fos. 131v, 165r; S.G.E. Lythe, 'Scottish trade with the Baltic, 1550-1650' in J.K. Eastham, ed., *Economic Essays in Commemoration of the Dundee School of Economics, 1931-1955* (Coupar Angus, 1955), 73.
[108] *Aberdeen Reg.*, ii, 156.
[109] M. Köfler and S. Caramelle, *Die Beiden Frauen des Erzherogs Sigmund von Oesterreich-Tirol* (Innsbruck, 1982), 91.
[110] M.C. Hill, *The King's Messengers, 1199-1377* (London, 1961), 108; *James IV Letters*, no. 557.

emissaries entrusted with delivering Edward I's response to the bull *Scimus fili*, taking six weeks to cover the route from Dover to Anagni.[111] All being well, we may doubt whether land travellers normally made more than at most fifty kilometres per day. Wale and Delisle averaged a creditable forty-five kilometres per day. By contrast, Annabella Stewart and her party managed an average of only about twenty-two kilometres per day as they journeyed from Veere to Chalons-sur-Saône in September 1445.[112]

The continental journeys of Annabella and her sister Eleanor apart, little information now survives regarding the exact itineraries which Scottish travellers chose once on the continent, but we may presume that their choices were not markedly different from those favoured by other travellers. No doubt many of the Scots who were destined for Rome followed the same path as that taken by the Welshman Adam of Usk in 1402. Usk set off from Bergen-op-Zoom and proceeded via Maastricht to Cologne and then along the course of the Rhine as far as Basel. From there he took the route to Bern, Luzern and 'its wonderful lake' and then the St Gotthard pass where he was 'almost frozen to death from the snow, and blindfolded to stop me seeing the perils of the journey'. Safely over the pass, Usk arrived in Bellinzona whence he passed on through Como, Milan, Piacenza, Pisa, Siena and Viterbo before reaching Rome.[113]   Adam was not alone in his terror of Alpine peaks. A century later, when the Italian artist Benvenuto Cellini crossed the Bernina and Albula passes in deep snow, he confessed that he and his party were 'in danger of our lives'.[114]

Adam crossed the Alps on an ox-drawn waggon, Cellini on horse. Horses offered the quickest means of transport. Athough the elite, such as Annabella Stewart, might gain an additional degree of comfort by use of a chariot, the speed of Annabella's journey was constrained by repairs which had to be undertaken on the vehicle which had been borrowed from the duchess of Burgundy.[115] Roads were often ill-defined and Cellini even found it advisable to abandon his horse when he reached the Walensee, on the northern side of the Alps, and to proceed instead by boat. Indeed, it was not unusual for those travelling inland to progress by both land and river. The choice did not solely depend upon the factors of cost and comfort. Some routes were notorious for brigands, or passed through areas of political conflict, and were best avoided. The advantage of the St Gotthard Pass – the most direct route across the Alps, which had been opened to international traffic in the early thirteenth century – was to some extent negated by the notorious reputation for brigandage which was acquired by the Monte Ceneri (between Bellinzona and Lugano, on

[111] E.L.G. Stones, 'The mission of Thomas Wale and Thomas Delisle from Edward I to Pope Boniface VIII in 1301', *Nottingham Medieval Studies*, 26 (1982), 11.
[112] AS Torino, Inventario 16, Registro 93, fos. 376v-383v.
[113] *Chron. Usk* (Given-Wilson), 152-55; *Chron. Usk* (Thompson), 112-13.
[114] G. Bull, ed., *The Autobiography of Benvenuto Cellini* (Harmondsworth, 1956), 178.
[115] AS Torino, Inventario 16, Registro 93, fo. 383v.

the southern side of the pass) in the later fifteenth century.[116] This may be one reason why some travellers, such as the Rome-bound John Atkinson, made for the more distant, but also lower, Brenner Pass to the east.[117] On other occasions travellers obtained advance warnings of possible attacks and altered their itinerary accordingly. When Eleanor Stewart, the sister of James II, travelled to the Tirol for her marriage to the Archduke of Austria, news reached her party in Belfort both of uncertain political conditions near Basel and of a planned ambush in the region of Lake Constance. Eleanor's route was changed to avoid Basel, and instead she took the longer route via Freiburg im Uchtland, Bern, Luzern and Zürich.[118] To guard against attack, cynical Italians advised travellers to spread false information regarding their itineraries. 'If you are going to Siena,' proclaimed one, 'say you are going to Lucca and you will travel free of evil folk.'[119] But, since attacks were frequently speculative, this precaution was of limited value: brigands might strike anywhere and against anyone, irrespective of status. In 1423 a party of Scottish clergymen, bound for the papal court, was ambushed at Brühl, near Cologne, with one cleric losing his life during the fracas.[120]

Safety, then, was one consideration for the land traveller, as it was at sea – and it was advisable to take much the same precautions on land as at sea by, for instance, procuring a safe-conduct. Other forms of identificatory documentation might also be carried. Pilgrims, for instance, often obtained letters of commendation from their local bishop, or certification that they had completed a penitential visit. Diplomats, meanwhile, would carry letters of credence and procuration, and merchants might possess a licence to trade.[121] A more particular problem for the land traveller was, however, accommodation. Life on board ship might be cramped, but at least there *were* sweat-soaked bales of woad upon which to recline. On land even this might have seemed a luxury. True, some land routes were comparatively well provisioned with lodgings, and in the quest for shelter well-to-do travellers were the most fortunate. The aristocratic community of Christendom was small, tight-knit and looked after its own, frequently offering hospitality to those of a similar social status from abroad. Diplomats were often housed and fed by those

[116] G. Vismara, A. Cavanna & P. Vismara, *Ticino medievale: Storia di una terra lombarda* (Locarno, 1990), 185-202; E. Motta, 'Ladronecci ed assassini al Monte Ceneri nel quatrocento', *Bolletino Storico della Svizzera Italiana*, 16 (1894), 120-23

[117] LAT Innsbruck, Sigm. IVa/181.

[118] Köfler and Caramelle, *Die Beiden Frauen*, 27-8.

[119] *Mercanti Scrittori: Ricordi nella Firenze tra medioevo e rinascimento*, ed. V. Branca (Milan, 1986), 17.

[120] HA Köln, Briefbuch 9, fos. 45-6, 49, 84-5; Hanse U2/72; *HUB*, vi, nos. 478, 532; *St Andrews Copiale*, appendix, no. 23.

[121] *St Andrews Copiale*, no. 42; D. McRoberts, 'A St Andrews pilgrimage certificate of 1333' in idem, ed., *The Medieval Church of St Andrews* (Glasgow, 1976), 155-56; D.E. Queller, *The Office of Ambassador in the Middle Ages* (Princeton, 1967), 111-12. For examples of licences to trade and letters of passage granted by the Scottish crown to foreign merchants and musicians, see *James IV Letters*, nos. 79, 100, 183, 226.

whom they visited. The Scottish envoys who brokered the marriage between James II and Mary of Guelders were entertained by the townsmen of Arnhem in 1446, as well as, in all probability, by the dukes of Guelders and Burgundy.[122] By contrast, when Sir James Douglas arrived with Robert I's heart at Sluis in 1330, he invited local dignitaries aboard his vessel and entertained them for twelve days, serving them generous amounts of wines and spices in gold and silver vessels. It was, thought the snobbish Froissart, a proper display for a lord who represented the king of Scots.[123] Care was also taken of aristocrats travelling on private business. Whilst on pilgrimage to Rome in 1450, the eighth earl of Douglas and his entourage were entertained to a sumptuous banquet at Lille, hosted by the duke of Burgundy and consisting of beef, mutton, pork, hare, pheasant, heron, bittern, rabbit, partridge, goose, water bird, lark, chickens and pigeon.[124] Eleanor Stewart's dietary needs were catered for by her future subjects. Once she entered the domain of her intended husband, they were expected to cater for her needs, though the citizens of Freiburg im Uchtland subsequently moaned about the cost of her week-long stay at their expense.[125]

The experiences of Eleanor Stewart and William, earl of Douglas, were not, however, typical of medieval Scottish travellers. Others might seek shelter with fellow countrymen who were resident abroad, much as Buonacorso Pitti, the Italian merchant and adventurer, stayed with fellow Florentines when passing through Budapest on his way to Prussia.[126] Indeed, the Edinburgh pilgrim Lawrence Green, presumably heading for the Baltic coast on his way back from Rome, seems to have found some fellow Scots with whom to stay on his journey through Poland.[127] Such possibilities were, however, probably more limited for Scots, since the majority of Scottish emigrant communities were settled along the coastal fringes of continental Europe, rather than along it principal inland arteries. As an alternative Scots might seek to stay in monastic houses or at inns, which, in the larger centres of population and along the well-trodden pilgrimage routes, were numerous. This certainly appears to have been the plan of several Scottish abbots as they travelled to the chapters general of the Cistercian order at Cîteaux. In 1222, for instance, the abbot of Deer died at 'the abbey of the valley of the Blessed Mary' (probably Croxden in Staffordshire) while on his way to Cîteaux. The abbot of Dundrennan perished in the same year at the monastery of Auberive, west of Langres, while returning from the chapter general. Others too experienced Cistercian hospitality: in 1256 the abbot of Benedictine

---

[122] GA Arnhem, inv. no. 1245, fo. 7r.

[123] *Chron. Froissart* (Lettenhove), iii, 204-5.

[124] Finot, *Inventaire Sommaire VIII*, i, 23-4. See page 138, below, for the full menu.

[125] Köfler and Caramelle, *Die Beiden Frauen*, 28.

[126] *Two Memoirs of Renaissance Florence: The diaries of Buonaccorso Pitti and Gregorio Dati*, ed. G. Brucker (New York, 1976), 25-6.

[127] T.A. Fischer, *The Scots in Germany* (Edinburgh, 1902), 241.

Dunfermline died at the abbey of Pontigny while making a journey to Rome.[128]

Alternatively, in some places at least, the traveller could make use of inns and taverns. In Scotland it seems unlikely that inns were a commonplace even in towns, since legislation of the 1420s called for their establishment in every burgh.[129] Abroad, however, inns were relatively common in the larger urban centres at least. Alexander Stewart, earl of Mar, found accommodation at the Tin Plate Inn in Paris, during a visit in 1408. Scots visiting Oxford perhaps stayed at the town's Star Inn, a successful business venture owned, as many inns were, by a nearby abbey. To cater for the needs of visitors to the papal court there were about sixty inns in Avignon by 1370.[130] There were several in Bruges and its satellite ports too and in 1456 James II appointed one Sluis innkeeper, Lawrence Pomstraat, as 'host and receiver' of all Scots visiting the town. As a *quid pro quo* for this lucrative monopoly on Scottish business Pomstraat was expected to safeguard Scottish interests in the town.[131] In this instance the function of the medieval 'host' was wider than it is perhaps understood nowadays, and in Scotland too we find James I entrusting innkeepers with official responsibility for witnessing the financial transactions of the foreigners who stayed with them.[132]

Our knowledge of what these buildings looked like and the facilities which they afforded travellers is limited. By the fifteenth century, in Venice at least, some establishments sought to cater for a wealthier clientele by providing more comfortable, and presumably expensive, amenities than those found in most inns, where facilities remained basic. Sleeping accommodation was frequently limited. One inn at Arrezzo recorded 180 overnight guests in a period of nineteen days (an average of fourteen or fifteen guests per night), even though the bedroom furniture of this particular establishment amounted to only four beds and one mattress. In sparsely populated, rural areas even this might have seemed luxurious. In Alpine regions there were a few hospices to provide shelter for the traveller – that on the Great St Bernard dated from Carolingian times, though others, such as that on the St Gotthard (first mentioned in 1237) and that on the Arlberg (built only in 1386), were of more recent foundation.[133]

[128] *Chron. Melrose*, 75; *Chron. Bower* (Watt), v, 319. See also *Chron. Melrose*, 91, for the deaths of the abbots of Coupar Angus (at the abbey of Vaucelles, near Cambrai) and Glenluce (at the unidentified abbey of 'St Remy') in 1243.
[129] *APS*, ii, 6. See too ibid, 346, for similar legislation of 1535, which extended the provision to burghs of barony.
[130] *Chron. Wyntoun* (Laing), iii, 104; E.M. Jope, ed., *Studies in Building History* (London, 1961), 168-69; Ohler, *Reisen im Mittelalter*, 131.
[131] A. Stevenson, 'Medieval Scottish associations with Bruges' in T. Brotherstone and D. Ditchburn, eds., *Freedom and Authority: Scotland, c.1050-c.1650* (East Linton, 2000), 96.
[132] *APS*, ii, 5. See also ibid, ii, 10, 14, 24.
[133] M.W. Labarge, *Medieval Travellers: The rich and the restless* (London, 1982), 27; E. Egli, 'Der Gotthard: Bedeutung und Auswirkung', *Geographica Helvetica* (1991), 63; Ohler, *Reisen im Mittelalter*, 132, 162-64.

For the more humble traveller even a remote hospice would have seemed luxurious. In *c.*1470 a number of Scots were arraigned before the magistrates of Breslau (now Wrocław) on charges of vagabondage: their number included several who were ill and some who confessed to having begged their way along the highways of the continent.[134] Even more affluent travellers were sometimes forced to make the best of poor offerings. Those caught between towns at night made do as best they could. In Flanders Scots who arrived at towns after dusk had to wait until the morning for admission, though in 1387 their new privileges stipulated that they be allowed to enter immediately.[135] When Aeneas Silvius Piccolomini, the Italian humanist, journeyed from Scotland to Newcastle in 1435 he spent an uncomfortable night in the company of the peasant women of Northumbria. The food which he received was, for an Italian aristocrat, spartan, but the future pontiff was particularly perplexed when two young women offered to sleep with him 'as was the custom of the country'. Escaping from the amorous embraces of the loose Northumbrian women, the worthy cleric opted instead to spend an uncomfortable night with their cattle and goats, which disrupted his sleep by stealthily pulling all the straw from his mattress during the night.[136]

Money

While safety and shelter were perhaps the most crucial considerations, they were not the only problems encountered by the medieval traveller. Money eased some of the discomforts to be endured on a long journey, but its use required some appreciation of fluctuating exchange rates. There is an air of informed authority to Andrew Wood's flat refusal to accept payment in English money for goods which he delivered to Grimsby in 1504 on the grounds that it was, he claimed, but 'oaff'.[137] The English currency was, in fact, less susceptible to devaluation than most in the middle ages and Wood's chauvinistic, but firm, refusal to accept English money in England is surprising. Still, a table of exchange rates compiled by an early sixteenth-century Aberdeen council official reveals a familiarity not just with the coinage of neighbouring countries such as England, Flanders and France, but also with more exotic specie from Italy, Spain and Hungary.[138] Foreign coinage was well known in Scotland and by at least the fifteenth century much from Flanders (and increasingly from France too by the early sixteenth century) circulated alongside the produce of the Scottish mint, in towns at least.[139]

---

[134] Fischer, *Germany*, 241-42.
[135] M.P. Rooseboom, *The Scottish Staple in the Netherlands* (The Hague, 1910), appendix no. 11.
[136] Pii II, *Commentarii Rervm Memorabilivm Que Temporibvs Svis Contigervnt*, ed. A. van Heck (Vatican City, 1984), i, 47-8.
[137] E. Gillett, *A History of Grimsby* (London, 1970), 22.
[138] CA Aberdeen, SR/3, 23.
[139] Stevenson, Thesis, 330, Table ix, which charts the number of references to foreign coinage in the Aberdeen council registers between 1434 and 1509.

If an appreciation of the value of foreign coins was probably more widespread than might be supposed, it remained dangerous for travellers to carry large amounts of coin on lengthy journeys. John Chalmers was probably not alone in secreting a linen purse containing seven gold French crowns in a feather bed when he boarded a ship in 1496.[140] Up to a point primitive precautions of this nature could be avoided by making use of loans, credit facilities and banking services. The development of loans and credit arrangements had been one of the key elements of the thirteenth-century commercial revolution and eventually a broad section of both aristocratic and urban society was able to negotiate financial deals of this variety. Evidence of credit and loans is rarely explicit but can be inferred from the more plentiful references to debt. An early fifteenth-century list of the Teutonic Order's debtors included not just the earls of Angus and Douglas but also the humble wife of an Aberdeen litster.[141] It would seem as if credit had been extended to these, and almost forty other, Scottish customers upon delivery of grain supplies by the Order's merchants. Similar facilities were available to Scots abroad. In November 1390 four Scottish knights bound for the northern crusade in Prussia borrowed £26 13s 4d from two Edinburgh burgesses in Bruges. The debt was repayable in Bruges the following Easter, together with half a gold noble 'for the labour' of the two lenders, which clearly implies that an interest payment was being levied on the loan.[142] Deals of this sort, between private individuals, were perhaps common, though more sophisticated transactions could also be arranged through merchant-bankers, pawnbrokers and moneylenders.

There are two types of financial arrangement which we should note. The first is the letter of credit – similar to a modern travellers' cheque – which were sold to all sorts of travellers. The second is the bill of exchange which might be repaid by a representative of the borrower to an agent of the lender in a quite different location to that where the bill had been originally issued. Letters of credit were almost certainly obtained by Scots on a frequent basis. That seems to be the nature of the purchase made by the archdeacon of Dunblane, who in 1269 obtained a £5 letter, redeemable at Bologna. It was probably also a letter of credit, to the value of £10, which the Glasgow canon Thomas Tod acquired before venturing to the continent in 1368, though he seems also to have carried 20s in coin, presumably to cover his immediate travel expenses. And it was perhaps by means of a letter of credit that Albano (?Alan) de Wyntoun deposited 800 ducats with a Venetian banker before setting off on pilgrimage to the Holy Land – though in 1363 Wynton's executors dispatched the knight Walter Leslie to Venice in an attempt to redeem half this sum following Wynton's death.[143] Less certain is the

[140] *ADC*, ii, 39.
[141] *Handelsrechnungen*, 75-7.
[142] NAS Edinburgh, AD1/27.
[143] D.E.R. Watt, 'Scottish student life abroad in the fourteenth century', *SHR*, 59 (1980), 19-20; *CDS*, iv, no. 142; *I Libri Commemoriali della Republica di Venezia: Regesti* (Venice, 1883), iii, nos.

mechanism by which the monks of Coupar Angus arranged for the annual delivery of £20, payable at Troyes in France to Cistercian headquarters at Cîteaux.[144] The sum may have been dispatched by coin or by letter of credit but it is equally conceivable – indeed, perhaps more likely – that the abbey obtained a bill of exchange from merchant-bankers, repaying the loan from the proceeds of its wool sales in the Low Countries. Inexplicit though the evidence is, the example is important, since Troyes was the location of one of the famous cycle of Champagne fairs where merchants from across Christendom transacted their financial business. Thirteenth-century Scots clearly had obtained access to the most important financial centre of their day, though how they did so remains obscure.

Most of the great merchant-bankers were Italian, and much of their business involved delivering the proceeds of papal taxation to the *curia*. The collectors of the later thirteenth-century papal taxes in Scotland were expected to deliver their funds to merchant-bankers from Florence, Lucca and Siena. These men, or their agents, may have ventured to Scotland to take possession of papal dues, offering other financial services as they did so. This would explain how the archdeacon of Dunblane procured his letter of credit in Berwick. But it is also possible that most payments of papal taxation were delivered to merchant-bankers who ventured no closer than London or the Low Countries; and that the receivers collected their dues not in coin dispatched from Scotland, but rather from the proceeds of Scottish wool sold abroad.[145] Although the nature of papal taxation was subsequently transformed, Italian merchant-bankers remained instrumental in its delivery to the *curia*. By at least the fifteenth century leading Scottish clerics (even from the Highlands) were in direct communication with the new generation of merchant-bankers. Popes normally appointed the head of the Rome branch of the Medici bank as their Depository General and Scottish clerics often dealt with Medici employees, such as Bartolomeo de Bardi and Roberto Martelli, when making payments of their annates and common services – the merchant-bankers retaining possession of the clerics' bulls of appointment until such times as they had paid their dues.[146] Much of this business may have been transacted through banking agents in London or Bruges. Since Thomas Tod travelled to the continent via Dover, he perhaps purchased his bill of exchange from bankers in London. For most, the Low Countries was probably the more usual location for financial business. It was through bankers in Bruges

95-6, 145. On Wyntoun's pilgrimage, see *Chron. Bower* (Watt), vii, 159; and on Leslie's visit to Italy, see A. Macquarrie, *Scotland and the Crusades, 1095-1560* (Edinburgh, 1985), 80.
[144] *Coupar Angus Chrs.*, i, no. 51.
[145] A.A.M. Duncan, *Scotland: The making of the kingdom* (Edinburgh, 1975), 428-29, 516; *CPL*, i, 465, 469, 478, 481; 'Bagimond's roll: Statement of the tenths of the kingdom of Scotland', ed. A.I. Dunlop, *SHS Miscellany*, 6 (1939), 25-32; *The Register of John de Halton, Bishop of Carlisle, 1292-1324*, ed. W.N. Thomson and T.F. Tout (Canterbury and York Soc., 1913), i, 16-17, 73-5, 153-54.
[146] A.I. Cameron, *The Apostolic Camera and Scottish Benefices, 1418-1488* (Oxford, 1934), 7, 10, 25, 28-9, 35, 234-35, 261; R. de Roover, *The Rise and Decline of the Medici Bank, 1397-1494* (Cambridge, Mass., 1968), 377.

that Bishop James Kennedy of St Andrews delivered payment of the proceeds of an indulgence in 1463, and it was in Flanders that the bulls appointing the archbishop of St Andrews were collected after payments had been delivered to Giovanni Frescobaldi in the 1500s.[147] The Frescobaldi sometimes also sent agents to Scotland to attend to company business.[148] Normally, however, Scots entrusted conduct of their financial affairs to factors such as Andrew Halyburton who resided in the Netherlands. In the later fifteenth century Halyburton was transacting business on behalf of his Scottish clients with several of the Italian banking agents who also resided in the Low Countries.[149] Indeed, it is striking that the business which Halyburton conducted for clients such as Bishop William Elphinstone of Aberdeen and Archbishop William Schevez of St Andrews more frequently involved financial than commercial transactions. They and others simply evaded the frequent restrictions on the export of coin from Scotland by depositing money with Halyburton in the Low Countries.[150]

Language and Law

Halyburton's dealings in the Low Countries obviated the need for personal communication between his Scottish clients and their Italian bankers, though he himself presumably required linguistic skills as well as business acumen to perform his tasks satisfactorily. We do not know how Halyburton, or indeed other merchants, acquired proficiency in foreign languages though they were perhaps equipped with rudimentary Latin in one of the urban grammar schools established in later medieval Scotland. For much of the period Latin was the west's *lingua franca*. Many merchants possessed a smattering of Latin which was adequate for maintaining their financial records;[151] and the fluency of some Scots in that particular tongue may be gleaned from the invitations which they received to speak publicly in the language. Thomas Livingstone, abbot of Dundrennan, preached on several occasions to the clergymen assembled at the council of Basel and elsewhere in the 1440s, and William Elphinstone deputised for the indisposed bishop of Tournai at church services celebrated in Bruges at Easter 1495.[152] It seems unlikely that the experience of either was unusual for senior clergymen. Latin, meanwhile, remained the language of diplomacy too, and the preferred medium through which the Scottish government transacted business with foreign powers. Nevertheless, it was in Scots rather than Latin that Halyburton kept his business ledger, and it

---

[147] Cameron, *The Apostolic Camera*, 280; *TA*, ii, 240-42.

[148] NAS Edinburgh, CS5/26, fo. 55r.

[149] Stevenson, Thesis, 313-14.

[150] Stevenson, Thesis, 214-18. For the restrictions on Scottish coin exports, see *APS*, ii, 5-6, 86, 105-6, 166.

[151] J. Donnelly, 'Thomas of Coldingham, merchant and burgess of Berwick-upon-Tweed (d.1316)', *SHR*, 59 (1980), 121-25.

[152] J.H. Baxter, 'Four new medieval Scottish authors', *SHR*, 25 (1928), 96-7; D. Shaw, 'Thomas Livingston: a conciliarist', *RSCHS*, 12 (1955), 132; L.J. Macfarlane, *William Elphinstone and the Kingdom of Scotland, 1431-1514* (Aberdeen 1985), 232.

was in German rather than Latin that many fifteenth-century Hanseatic merchants kept their account books.[153] And when in 1528 the Edinburgh council wrote in Latin to officials at Veere, the recipients deemed it necessary for the correspondence to be translated into Low German.[154] By the later fifteenth century Latin was beginning to lose some of its status as an international language of record.

By then we can no longer suppose that French remained the aristocratic *lingua franca* which it too had been, following the Norman diaspora of the eleventh and twelfth centuries. True, a visiting Spanish diplomat still believed at the end of the fifteenth century that 'many [Scots] speak the French language'.[155] But although some fifteenth-century Scots still wrote to English kings in French, even in the thirteenth century the Scottish government, unlike its English counterpart, preferred to transact diplomatic business with France in Latin rather than in French. The gradual demise of French among Scottish aristocrats was accompanied by their growing use of the vernacular. While Christina, countess of March, wrote to Henry IV of England in French, her husband, George Dunbar, fourth earl of March, advised the same king in 1400 to 'marvaile yhe nocht that I write my lettres in englis for that ys mare clere to myne vnderstandyng than latyne or Fraunche'.[156] Of course, the increased popularity of English aided Anglo-Scottish communication, especially once the English aristocracy began to abandon its predilection for French in the later fourteenth century, though the ease of such communication was not always with friendly intent. In fifteenth-century France English-speaking Scottish soldiers were deployed to deceive their English enemies, much to the surprise of the anonymous author of the *Journal d'un Bourgeois de Paris*. He seemed not to appreciate that English was the common tongue of many Scots.[157]

The rise of the vernacular made communication with other foreigners more difficult. In the 1380s the French government had deemed it advisable for an interpreter to accompany a diplomatic mission dispatched to Scotland and by the fifteenth century it often entrusted such business to Franco-Scots such as William Monypenny, lord of Concressault, and Bernard Stuart, lord of Aubigny, who, we may suppose, were fluent in both Scots and French.[158] Much the same development is evident in urban affairs too, with presumably bilingual Netherlandish émigrés such as Thomas Richardson and John Moffet

[153] A. Hanham, 'A medieval Scots merchant's handbook', *SHR*, 50 (1971), 107-20; *Halyburton's Ledger*; LA Tallinn, I/Af/2 – I/Af/25.
[154] ZA Middelburg, inv. no. 243/19.
[155] P. Hume Brown, ed., *Early Travellers in Scotland* (repr. Edinburgh, 1978), 48.
[156] *Facsimiles of the National Manuscripts of Scotland* (London, 1867-71), ii, nos. 52-3. See too ibid, nos. 51 and 54, for other letters written to the same king in French and English.
[157] *A Parisian Journal, 1405-1409*, ed. J. Shirley (Oxford, 1968), 196.
[158] *Chron. Froissart* (Lettenhove), x, 287.

often selected to advance the interests of Netherlandish towns with Scots or in Scotland.[159]

While sensible arrangements of this sort facilitated formal diplomatic contacts, it was altogether less feasible for private individuals to travel abroad in the company of an interpreter. Some relied upon *ad hoc* translation services. In 1548 a Scots notary and a Scottish priest, both of whom could speak French, were required to elucidate the circumstances of a fracas in an Edinburgh house, which erupted between several visiting Frenchmen and during which one of the Frenchmen had died.[160] A Russian whose goods were shipwrecked off the Buchan coast was less fortunate, and in order to instruct an Edinburgh notary in 1556 he required the services of a translator brought all the way from England.[161] More commonly, the predominantly vernacular record of fifteenth- and sixteenth-century court proceedings was often suspended for cases involving foreigners as scribes resorted temporarily to Latin, presumably for the benefit of the foreigners involved. Still, there is remarkably little evidence to suggest that linguistic barriers posed major obstacles for merchants at least. Although Edinburgh's James Lawder informed the Grand Master of the Teutonic Order in 1452 that he was a Scotsman and could not make his points to the Grand Master in verbal German, he did write to the Grand Master in German.[162] It is not clear whether Lawder engaged the facilities of a translator to pen his letters. Despite his modesty, he may have picked up some rusty Low German through interaction with Hanseatic merchants in Danzig. Business abroad, especially as a factor stationed in a foreign country, provided an opportunity for some to acquire language skills and by the mid-sixteenth century Edinburgh merchants were sending their male offspring to Bordeaux specifically so that they might gain proficiency in language and business.[163]

Language and commercial skills aside, one thirteenth-century Norwegian writer recommended that travellers should also possess at least a rudimentary knowledge of the law.[164] There was good sense to his advice that 'if you are acquainted with the law, you will not be annoyed by quibbles', for decrees, statutes and treaties imposed restrictions and penalties on medieval travellers, as well as sometimes offering them a measure of protection. It was pilgrims and crusaders who enjoyed the greatest legal safeguards. The church extended its full protection not only upon the crusader and the pilgrim (who did not therefore require a safe conduct to travel) but also upon the absent traveller's property and family. There were other perquisites too, often of a financial

---

[159] See below, chapter 5.
[160] *Edin. Recs.*, ii, 137-40.
[161] *Illustrations of the Topography and Antiquities of the Shires of Aberdeen and Banff* (Spalding Club, 1847-69), iv, 108-9.
[162] GSA Berlin, OBA 11391/2; *HUB*, viii, no. 172.
[163] *France Ecosse* (Archives Nationales, 1956), nos. 635-36.
[164] Forte, "Kenning be Kenning and course be course", 57.

nature, such as freedom from interest on debt.[165] Those who flouted such laws were subject to spiritual penalties, culminating in excommunication, though it was not just the assailants of pilgrims who faced this severest of penalties. On occasions pirates too were condemned to the religious, and thereby social, exclusion intended by excommunication.[166]

By contrast with pilgrims, traders were subject to an array of regulation. Scottish legislation periodically sought to determine where ships might sail, which goods they might carry and who might board them. The export of bullion, for instance, was regularly prohibited in the fifteenth century, as was that of horses and tallow in 1425 and salt in 1535, while the import of poisons was banned in 1450 and that of 'corrupt and mixed' wine in 1482.[167] In 1458 it was decreed that only those 'of gud fame' might venture abroad for trading purposes – a clear attempt, presumably at the behest of established merchants, to exclude competition from the less affluent.[168] And in the aftermath of the battle of Flodden (1513) Scots were told not to visit England and Englishmen were made unwelcome in Scotland, unless they had procured a special licence.[169] National legislation of this sort was supplemented, in Scotland and elsewhere, by local by-laws which regulated the places and occasions on which both natives and visiting foreign merchants might sell their wares.

There is perhaps something of a paradox between, on the one hand, the international aspirations of canon law and maritime law (which throughout the North and Baltic Seas derived from the laws of Oléron); and, on the other hand, parochial regulation which, while ostensibly designed to safeguard the wellbeing of the wider community, actually protected vested local interests and discriminated against 'strangers'. Yet this paradox encapsulates the nature of medieval Christendom. It was both a highly localised society, in which suspicion of outsiders was intense, and a highly cosmopolitan society which shared many common values. It was the traveller who bridged the chasm. Highways and seaways constituted the arteries of medieval Christendom, travellers its blood. And the flow of people, and the goods, ideas and disease which accompanied them, provided medieval Christendom with its identity.

---

[165] G. Constable, 'The place of the crusader in medieval society', *Viator*, 29 (1988), 391.
[166] *CSSR*, v, no. 740.
[167] *APS*, ii, 5-7, 39, 86, 105, 144, 166, 436.
[168] *APS*, ii, 49. Similar legislation was enacted in 1467 and 1487 (ibid, ii, 86, 178).
[169] NAS Edinburgh, CS5/26, fo. 92v.

2
The Religious Bonds

'Latin Christendom,' in Robert Bartlett's incisive words, 'was not merely a rite or an obedience but a society.'[1] The principal bonding agent of that society was religion. Across the Latin West, whether in Scotland or in Sicily, religion was not a matter of personal choice, nor a matter for ambivalence, nor a concept which could be pigeon-holed as distinct and separate from other aspects of human existence. Religion influenced the very mundanities of life. It shaped the parameters of both personal behaviour (including diet, work and thought) and interaction with other human beings (including familial and sexual relations, as well as broader cultural, social, economic and political experiences).

Of course, religion was not the only factor which influenced the norms of human behaviour. More fundamental, pre-Christian instincts and motivations were also important determinants of human behaviour, and these were tempered by the physical and climatic environment in which women and men lived. But even these factors were cloaked in a veneer of Christian understanding. By categorising pride, envy, wrath, sloth, lust, greed and gluttony as the Seven Deadly Sins, and meekness, charity, patience, chastity, generosity and abstinence, along with spiritual activity, as the chief Christian virtues, the Church offered judgement on human instincts. By attributing natural disaster such as floods, fires and famine to God's will it offered explanation.[2] Religion, in short, provided the society of the medieval West with its teleology.

The basis for the Christian *mentalité* was to be found in a fundamentally common set of religious beliefs, in a fundamentally uniform series of devotional practices to express those beliefs and, at least until the sixteenth century, in a fundamentally unchallenged acceptance of the right of the ecclesiastical authorities, and especially the papacy, to determine the veracity of belief and the validity of practices. While, as we shall see, the religious life of the medieval west was not monolithic, there were developments which made for a standardisation of the religious experience across Christendom. Most notable among these, perhaps, was the extension of papal power between the eleventh and fourteenth centuries, which was exemplified by the papacy's increasing readiness to interfere in local ecclesiastical affairs across Christendom. But the ecclesiastical authorities not only led from the front.

---

[1] R. Bartlett, *The Making of Europe: Conquest, colonization and cultural change, 950-1350* (London, 1993), 23.
[2] A typical example of this may be found in *Chron. Bower* (Watt), iv, 173: 'Whenever terrible thunder or lightning... occurs, I advise those who witness it to assemble piously at the nearest churches and oratories to invoke the majestic power of God.'

They also responded to, and they engaged with, local spiritual impulses. Some of these, such as the cult of Corpus Christi, an originally Netherlandish devotion, subsequently acquired papal authorisation and continental-wide adherence.[3] Many others, such as the cults of Brendan and Brioc on Bute (and Ireland), remained of largely local significance, undisturbed by papal influence and never achieving any great standing elsewhere in Scotland. The religion of the medieval west was an amalgam of the universal and the parochial. It is the former, and how that was exemplified in Scotland and by Scots, which is of particular relevance here.

Religious Education

Later medieval Scotland was an overwhelmingly Christian country. It had no pagan, Islamic or Jewish communities, as some other countries did, although, if the views of chroniclers were at all typical, it shared some of the Latin West's anti-Semitic and anti-Islamic prejudices.[4] Likewise, in matters of Christian doctrine, devotion and discipline, later medieval Scotland followed much the same pattern as other parts of the Latin West. The tenets of the Christian faith, as enunciated over centuries by popes, general councils of the church, learned commentators and academics, were essentially the same in later medieval Scotland as elsewhere. Heaven, hell, purgatory and sin were as real to Scots as they were to others.

Given the training of those charged with disseminating the faith (the clergy), this could hardly have been otherwise. Across the continent clergymen were informed and educated in similar circumstances and with similar ideas, and even the most humble parish priest, wherever he ministered, was expected to be conversant with the Creed, the Ten Commandments, various commonly recited prayers and the procedures for confession. Responsibility for instructing priests lay with their ecclesiastical superiors – archdeacons and bishops – and, although evidence for the means by which they taught priests is sparse for Scotland, we may assume that throughout the later medieval period Scottish practice conformed with that elsewhere in Europe. Training was probably conducted with little innovation across the centuries. Bishop William Elphinstone of Aberdeen (1431-1514) possessed a manual for the instruction of priests which, although published in 1492, had originally been written in 1255. Elphinstone's manual, moreover, was published in Cologne, a reminder that a text presumably intended for a Rhenish market was just as relevant to Scottish circumstances.[5]

[3] M. Rubin, *Corpus Christi: The eucharist in late medieval culture* (Cambridge, 1991), 164-85; *Chron. Bower* (Watt), v, 325-29.

[4] D.E.R. Watt, 'Abbot Walter Bower of Inchcolm and his Scotichronicon', *RSCHS*, 24 (1992), 295-96.

[5] UL Aberdeen, Inc 34; L.J. Macfarlane, *William Elphinstone and the Kingdom of Scotland, 1431-1514* (Aberdeen, 1985), 246-50.

By the later middle ages the senior clergymen commonly received their own initial training in universities: most were graduates.[6] No matter where they matriculated, their studies revolved around a broad but fairly standard collection of mainly Latin texts. Theology *per se* was a subject of postgraduate study, but all students met theological issues in their initial studies, as part of the arts curriculum. The curricular and linguistic internationalism of the educational experience was strengthened, albeit unintentionally, by the limited number of universities. It is worth remembering that before the foundation of St Andrews university in 1412, every Scottish clergyman with a university degree acquired his qualification while mingling with men (and they were all men) who would soon be attending to the spiritual needs of flocks elsewhere in the Latin West. Moreover, on returning to appointments in Scotland after the completion of their studies, clerical graduates could pursue their academic interests in cathedral or monastic libraries whose collections were remarkably similar wherever located. The stocks of Aberdeen cathedral library in 1436, resplendent in biblical texts, theological tomes by Augustus, Aquinas, Isidore and others, commentaries on canon and civil law and service books, would not have seemed out of place in Aachen, Amiens or Armagh;[7] and that Abbot Bower of Inchcolm should devote four lengthy chapters of his chronicle to the transcription of a work on purgatory by the French Dominican John Gobi merely serves as one very specific reminder of the bonds of religious and academic concern which linked a windswept Scottish island with the arid south of France.[8]

While academic study provided one common basis for the clergy's doctrinal knowledge, the pronouncements of the papacy and of councils general of the church on matters of the faith provided another. Such pronouncements were actually quite rare because most matters of belief were accepted as uncontroversial, and it was not therefore thought necessary to define them. On occasions, however, popes issued *ad hoc* declaratory statements concerning belief, usually to adjudge the acceptability or otherwise of novel or dubious propositions advanced by others. These would be communicated to those concerned by means of a papal bull, though it is indicative of how little papal business was devoted to matters of belief, as opposed to matters of organisation and discipline, that of 180 known papal letters sent to Scotland before 1198, only three were even very broadly

---

[6] D.E.R. Watt, 'University graduates in Scottish benefices before 1410', *RSCHS*, 15 (1966), 77-88. The proportion seems, however, to have declined in the later fifteenth and early sixteenth centuries: Macfarlane, *Elphinstone*, 276.

[7] *Aberdeen Reg.*, ii, 127-38.

[8] *Chron. Bower* (Watt), vii, 17-33.

concerned with belief.[9] Of those dispatched to Scotland by Clement VII (1378-94), not one was.[10]

More formal statements of faith were the responsibility of councils general, which bishops from all over Christendom might attend. These met relatively infrequently during the period with which we are concerned: in 1215 (Lateran IV), 1245 (Lyon I), 1274 (Lyon II), 1311-12 (Vienne), 1409 (Pisa), 1414-18 (Constance), 1423-24 (Pavia/Siena), 1431-49 (Basel), 1438-39 (Ferrara/Florence) and 1512-17 (Lateran V). For authoritative effect decisions enacted by these councils required papal ratification. It was for this reason that the wide-ranging decisions of the council of Basel ultimately lacked legitimacy: the pope of the time – Eugenius IV – withdrew his recognition of Basel and refused to accept its pronouncements. Moreover, the decree *Sacrosancta*, issued at Constance in 1415 – which stated that the authority of a general council was superior to that of the pope – was revoked in 1460, amid little opposition, by Pope Pius II.

Circulation of the decrees issued by councils general, no doubt by the hand of the envoys dispatched to Scotland and elsewhere at least by the fifteenth-century councils, was one means by which up-to-date statements of faith were communicated to the corners of Christendom.[11] Attendance at such councils was perhaps a more effective mechanism for disseminating information about conciliar decisions. At least four Scottish bishops attended both the Fourth Lateran and Second Lyon Councils, while David de Bernham, bishop of St Andrews, was present at the first council of Lyon.[12] There was a Scottish delegation at Vienne too. Although its composition remains uncertain, it is likely to have included Robert Wishart, bishop of Glasgow, no stranger to such gatherings. Wishart probably attended the second council of Lyon, and he was certainly at the papal court in Avignon a few months before the Vienne council was convened in October 1311.[13]

Scottish attendance at the fifteenth-century councils was more mixed. There were no Scots, as far as is known, at the council of Pisa which attempted and failed to end the schism between Popes Gregory XII and Benedict XIII. Obdurate Scottish allegiance to Benedict XIII had prevented a Scottish presence, and this too delayed official Scottish attendance at

[9] *Scotia Pontificia: Papal letters to Scotland before the pontificate of Innocent III*, ed. R. Somerville (Oxford, 1982), nos. 2, 3, 140; '*Scotia Pontificia*: additions and corrections', ed. P. Ferguson and R. Somerville, *SHR*, 66 (1987), 176-84.

[10] *Clement VII Letters*, passim.

[11] E.g. *Chron. Bower* (Watt), v, 329.

[12] C. Burns, 'Scottish bishops at the general councils of the middle ages', *IR*, 16 (1965), 135-38; M. Ash, 'David Bernham, bishop of St Andrews, 1239-1253' in D. McRoberts, ed., *The Medieval Church of St Andrews* (Glasgow, 1976), 36-7.

[13] Watt, *Graduates*, 585, 589. William Lamberton, bishop of St Andrews, and Thomas Dalton, bishop of Galloway, were also summoned to attend the council at Vienne, though neither probably attended (ibid, 309, 323). Unlike other monarchs, the then excommunicated Scottish king, Robert I, was not personally summoned to the council (J. Lecler, *Vienne* (Paris, 1964), 25).

Constance until 1418.[14] By then Constance had almost completed its work. Pavia/Siena did little but nominate the venue of the next council, though the abbot of Paisley (a member of the French delegation) did his best to enliven the proceedings by verbally antagonising the English representatives.[15] From 1432 there was, however, a striking Scottish attendance at Basel: over sixty Scottish clerics have been identified as participating in its proceedings, foremost among them Thomas Livingston, abbot of Dundrennan.[16] Although certainly summoned in good time to Ferrara/Florence, it is possible that the Scottish delegation to that council, led by Bishop Kennedy of St Andrews, arrived too late to witness the principal outcome of the deliberations, the union of the Latin and Greek churches.[17] According to James IV, however, no summons was received in Scotland to attend the Fifth Lateran Council.[18]

International gatherings of clerics and their common training ensured that Scottish clergymen were as conversant with the doctrines of the faith as their counterparts elsewhere in Christendom. Lay society, we may assume, was as ignorant of such matters as it was everywhere else. One of the great mysteries of the religion which bound Christendom together is how people came to have faith in that faith. Books were of limited value in disseminating Christian ideas, since this was an essentially illiterate society. Meanwhile, church services were conducted largely in Latin and were of little use in communicating religious instruction to the vast majority of congregations whose members did not understand Latin. Communication through the spoken vernacular was potentially more rewarding, especially when spiritual inducements were offered to those who listened devoutly: in 1345 those Scots who attended the preachings of Roger of Lancaster, a Cistercian monk of Furness abbey, were granted a remission of forty days in purgatory.[19] Yet, although the mendicant orders probably undertook further preaching (and the Observant Franciscans were specifically introduced to Scotland for that purpose in *c*.1463), the number of preachers was probably small and their impact partial beyond the towns where most friaries were located.[20] It is, indeed, revealing that in a survey of religion and society in fifteenth-century Scotland a well-known authority on the subject does not mention the word preaching once.[21]

---

[14] E.W.M. Balfour-Melville, *James I, King of Scots, 1406-1437* (London, 1936), 69-75. Consideration of the schism which afflicted Christendom between 1378 and 1418 will appear in the second volume of this study.

[15] W. Brandmüller, *Das Konzil von Pavia-Siena, 1423-1424* (Münster, 1968), i, 180-88.

[16] J.H. Burns, *Scottish Churchmen and the Council of Basle* (Glasgow, 1962); D. Shaw, 'Thomas Livingston: a conciliarist', *RSCHS*, 12 (1958), 120-35.

[17] Burns, *Churchmen*, 61-2; A.I. Dunlop, *The Life and Times of James Kennedy, Bishop of St Andrews* (Edinburgh, 1950), 27.

[18] *James IV Letters*, nos. 477-78.

[19] *The Coucher Book of Furness Abbey. Volume II*, ed. J. Brownhill (Chetham Soc., 1915-19), iii, 804.

[20] I.B. Cowan and D.E. Easson, *Medieval Religious Houses: Scotland* (2nd ed., London, 1976), 114-42; W.M. Bryce, *The Scottish Greyfriars* (Edinburgh, 1909), i, 58; A. Grant, *Independence and Nationhood: Scotland, 1306-1469* (London, 1984), 106-7.

[21] I.B. Cowan, 'Church and society' in J.M. Brown, ed., *Scottish Society in the Fifteenth Century* (London, 1977), 112-35.

· In the absence of more subtle and sophisticated mechanisms of instruction, oral communication of the faith probably amounted to little more than priests teaching their parishioners certain prayers by heart and training their congregations for confirmation and confession, which, following the decrees of the Fourth Lateran Council, the laity were expected to perform annually. Oral mechanisms of instruction by rote were supplemented by symbolism and visual imagery. Again, neither was quite the equivalent of a 'bible for the illiterate', since both required intellectual sophistication for full appreciation. We may wonder, for instance, what the laity made of the elevation of the Host at communion, and the incensing of the Host, two liturgical practices which first emerged on the continent in the early thirteenth century and which were both adopted in Scotland remarkably quickly.[22] We may doubt that either practice generally inspired detailed reflections among lay society on the nature of the Host and transubstantiation; but, thanks to these crude theatricals, most people probably appreciated that something sacred and significant was happening during the ceremony of the Eucharist.

The effect of artistic imagery was probably similar. Little of this now survives: it is unfortunate, from the vantage point of medieval historians, that sixteenth-century Protestants were both so committed to their denunciation of imagery and so thorough in its destruction. Yet, ironically, records of iconoclasm do provide some indication of the extent of imagery which adorned medieval churches, not just in the towns, but also in rural areas.[23] The Cross, images of the saints, carvings and banners and stained-glass representations, at least in the wealthier churches, provided a rudimentary outline of the key personalities in the Christian message. Nevertheless, detailed instruction of the laity remained limited. That mattered little to the medieval mind, since the purpose of priests was as much to administer the sacraments as it was to instruct. So, although for the performance of confession people had to know what sin was, they did not have to *understand* it. The Ten Commandments were not a discussion document, they were law. Nevertheless, by one means or another most people appear to have acquired a basic, if sometimes muddled, knowledge of the faith. That much is clear from popular expressions of the faith and, as we shall now see, from the limited criticisms which were voiced of the church's message.

Orthodoxy and Heterodoxy
While the fundamental tenets of Christian belief were officially determined by the papacy and councils general, the views of these institutions were increasingly fortified and influenced by opinions emanating from a third institution: the later medieval university. Academics were on the whole arrogant in their defence of orthodox Christian beliefs, and many claimed the

[22] D. McRoberts, 'The medieval Scottish liturgy illustrated by surviving documents', *TSES*, 15 (1957), 29-30.
[23] J. Kirk, 'Iconoclasm and reform', *RSCHS*, 24 (1992), 371-81.

right to determine what constituted deviation from orthodoxy. Indeed, the ability of university teachers to judge such matters was tacitly recognised in the award of inquisitorial powers to several leading scholars, such as Thomas Lyall, subsequently the Scottish rector of Cologne University, whose responsibility it became in 1489 to stamp out heresy in the Rhenish town.[24]

There were, however, exceptions to this general academic defence of orthodoxy. While the potency of doctrinal criticisms emanating from the universities was often minimised by the esoteric nature of academic debate, two of the most significant later medieval heresies (Lollardy in England and Hussitism in Bohemia) did owe their origins to academics (John Wyclif at Oxford University and Jan Hus at the Caroline University of Prague). Their views succeeded, where those of others failed, in percolating beyond the universities to attract a wider audience; and the movements associated with these men, together with Catharism – which, while not strictly Christian at all, did acquire a mass following in Provençal society – were the most serious challenges to orthodox belief faced by the pre-Lutheran church. The impact of all three heresies on Scotland was, however, minimal. Catharism, which became a serious threat to orthodoxy in the later twelfth and early thirteenth centuries, attracted spleen from the contemporary Melrose chronicler but does not appear to have won any Scottish adherents.[25] Hussitism was hardly any more successful. It too received a lambast from a contemporary Scottish chronicler, rather lengthier and better informed than that which the Cathars had won from the Melrose chronicler. Bower's source about Hussitism was, however, probably a participant in the council of Basel, where Jan Hus was tried and burned, rather any Scottish converts to his cause.[26] The efforts of one Scot to embark upon communication with the Hussites seem to have been idiosyncratic; and a Bohemian missionary who had subsequently attempted to proselytise in Scotland was apprehended and burned as a heretic in 1433 before being able to pose a serious challenge to orthodox belief.[27] Nothing more is then heard of his creed in Scotland.

Lollardy and Lutheranism, given their altogether closer origin, might have been expected to have had a much greater impact in Scotland. It was an English Lollard, James Resby, who won the grim distinction of being the first recorded heretic to be burned in Scotland, along with his books.[28] That was in 1408. Thereafter there is little sign of Lollardy in Scotland, save for an unsubstantiated remark by Bower that Resby's writings and opinions were 'still [presumably in the 1440s when Bower was writing] retained by some Lollards in Scotland' and the much later report by John Knox (hardly an

[24] *Mitteilungen aus dem Stadtarchiv von Köln*, ed. J. Hansen, 36-7 (1918), no.1901.
[25] *Chron. Melrose*, 36.
[26] *Chron. Bower* (Watt), viii, 276-87.
[27] T.M.A. McNab, 'Bohemia and the Scottish Lollards', *RSCHS*, 5 (1935), 10-22; L. Moonan, 'Pavel Kravar and some writings once attributed to him', *IR*, 27 (1976), 5-23.
[28] L. Moonan, 'The Inquisitor's arguments against Resby, in 1408', *IR*, 47 (1996), 127-35.

unbiased witness) that in 1494 thirty Lollards were revealed in Kyle by the
bishop of Glasgow.[29]

Protestantism too was slow to gain appeal in Scotland: over forty years
elapsed between Luther's first public challenge of the Church in 1517 and the
advent of the Scottish Reformation in 1560. Modern historians remain divided
as to the strength of Protestant support before 1560. Some adhere to the view
this was limited before the mid-1550s at the earliest.[30] But even those who
consider that it had 'secured a firm foundation in the politically assertive and
progressive areas of Scotland over a generation before the Reformation
parliament in 1560' presumably do not date that appeal before the 1530s at the
earliest.[31] By then Lutheran ideas had made impressive headway not only in
the Empire and Switzerland, but also in the Scandinavian kingdoms, and to
some extent in the Netherlands too. In the international context, Scots were
slow to embrace the reformed religion.

Specific evidence for the appeal of heretical beliefs in Scotland before the
1540s is, then, slight. There is rather more evidence to indicate that church
and state were fully alert to the challenge which heresy could pose to
orthodox belief. At the height of the Lollard threat in the later fourteenth and
early fifteenth centuries, the duke of Rothesay was required to swear on his
appointment as lieutenant of the kingdom in 1399 that he would restrain
heretics.[32] This may be an indication that others felt Rothesay was himself
tainted with heretical sympathies, and his great rival and successor, the duke
of Albany was certainly noted as a hater of all Lollards and heretics.[33]
Orthodoxy was also the stamp of James I's reign. In 1425 parliament ordered
bishops to 'inquyr be the inquisicione of heresy quhar ony sik beis fundyne'
and, in the event of its detection, secular assistance was promised in the
punishment of 'heretikis and lollardis'.[34] Secular assistance meant fanning the

---

[29] *Chron. Bower* (Watt), viii, 68-9 (Bower's account of Lollardy, as that of Hussitism, is hostile but
well-informed: ibid, 66-73); John Knox, *History of the Reformation in Scotland*, ed. W.C.
Dickinson (Edinburgh, 1949), i, 7-11; D.E. Easson, 'The Lollards of Kyle', *Jurdical Review*, 48
(1936), 123-28; M.H.B. Sanderson, *Ayrshire and the Reformation: People and change, 1490-1600*
(East Linton, 1997), 36-47.
[30] M. Lynch, *Edinburgh and the Reformation* (Edinburgh, 1981), 82 and appendix iv; A. White,
'The impact of the Reformation on a burgh community: the case of Aberdeen' in M. Lynch, ed.,
The Early Modern Town in Scotland (London, 1987), 87.
[31] J. Kirk, *Patterns of Reformation: Continuity and change in the Reformation kirk* (Edinburgh,
1989), p.xi. See also J. Durkan, 'Heresy in Scotland: the second phase, 1546-58', *RSCHS*, 24 (1992),
320-65.
[32] *APS*, i, 210-11 (black); 572-3 (red).
[33] *Chron. Wyntoun* (Laing), 100. I owe the comments about Rothesay to Steve Boardman, who has
pointed out to me that Wyntoun's description of Rothesay as 'cunnand in to literature' (*Chron.
Wyntoun* (Laing), iii, 82) and Bower's remark that, after his arrest in 1402, Rothesay was
conducted on a mule and dressed in a russet tunic from St Andrews to Falkland (*Chron. Bower*
(Watt), viii, 39) may be indicative of either the duke's heretical sympathies or an attempt to
besmirch him as a heretic. Lollards placed great emphasis on reading and, as a sign of their
rejection of worldly goods, those in England often adorned themselves in russet (A. Hudson, *The
Premature Reformation: Wycliffite texts and Lollard heresy* (Oxford, 1988), 144-47, 166-68, 174-227.
[34] *APS*, ii, 7.

flames of the guilty as they met their deaths. Scotland's first university, meanwhile, was also on its guard against academic troublemakers. Laurence of Lindores, the first rector and dean of the Faculty of Arts at St Andrews, was appointed as Inquisitor, gaining praise, at least among sympathetic clerics, for giving 'heretics or Lollards no peace anywhere in the kingdom'.[35]

Once the immediacy of the Lollard threat had passed, state and university alike busied themselves with other matters until the Lutheran controversy reared its head in the early sixteenth century. Then, once more, parliament sprang into action. The importation of Lutheran literature was banned in 1525 and again in 1535.[36] Parliamentary edicts were backed up by campaigns against heretics in the localities. Town councils in Aberdeen and Edinburgh, for instance, pursued the small numbers of heretics whom they could identify with such vigour that many suspects fled. It was still with confidence that James V could inform the pope in 1536 that action had been taken against the 'Lutheran plague'.[37]

But James V was too complacent. That in 1541 parliament had found it necessary not only to denounce heresy, but also to uphold the virtues of the sacraments and papal supremacy suggests that the king's confidence of but a few years before had been sadly misplaced.[38] By 1541 there were real signs of governmental panic, presumably inspired by what the authorities feared was the growing appeal of Protestantism. Yet it remains unclear whether earlier measures against heresy, like those of 1541, were taken in response to an actual emergency or whether they were more of a decorative smokescreen behind which no fire flickered. Given the paucity of Scottish ecclesiastical records, it is certainly possible that heresy was more prevalent in the century and a half before 1540 than it now seems. On the other hand, there are cogent hypotheses, in addition to the sturdy defences erected by the authorities, for assuming that foreign heresy failed to take root in medieval Scotland before the advent of the alleged Lutheran plague.

The geographical distance between Scotland and the epicentres of Catharism, Hussitism and for that matter other, lesser heresies such as Waldensianism and Spiritual Franciscanism, might be viewed as explanation enough for the failure of these beliefs to make significant headway in Scotland. Certainly all these heresies developed in milieux into which few Scots stumbled: southern France, Italy and central Europe. Yet the same argument cannot hold for the apparently limited impact of Lollardy or for the belated appeal of Protestantism, both of which emanated from areas which were in regular contact with Scotland. While James Resby disseminated his Lollard creed by 'preaching to simple people', linguistic differences were more of an impediment to the transmission of other heresies, except perhaps in the towns

---

[35] Watt, *Graduates*, 343-45; *Chron. Bower* (Watt), viii, 276-77.
[36] *APS*, ii, 295, 342.
[37] Lynch, *Edinburgh*, appendix iv; A. White, 'The Reformation in Aberdeen' in J. Smith, ed., *New Lights on Medieval Aberdeen* (Aberdeen, 1985), 59; *James V Letters*, 307.
[38] *APS*, ii, 370-71.

where merchants and mariners probably had a working knowledge of French and the Germanic languages.[39]

Low levels of literacy in Scotland, as Alexander Grant has argued, were probably another obstacle to the transmission of heretical notions, especially in the case of Waldensianism, Lollardy and Protestantism which placed particular emphasis on Biblical study in the vernacular.[40] Certainly it is noticeable that many of those whom the authorities of Edinburgh suspected of heresy in the 1530s pursued professions in which a certain degree of literacy might be expected.[41]

More important still was the fact that Catharism, Hussitism, Lutheranism, and arguably (as the Plantagenets gave way to the Lancastrians) Lollardy too, flourished in societies where royal authority was severely constrained and where particular shortcomings were evident in the established church. The coincidence of such circumstances struck little resonance with the Scottish environment until the Marian minority beginning in 1542. Indeed, the comparative simplicity and stability of later medieval Scottish social, religious and political structures was perhaps conducive to a religious conservatism which manifested itself not only in the rejection of foreign heresies, but also in the failure to embrace more orthodox expressions of religious enthusiasm. Neither the Humilitati, nor the Flagellants, nor the beguines and beghards, nor (other in the most rudimentary respect of possession of Books of Hours) the *devotia moderna* were emulated in Scotland. Medieval Scotland, it would seem, was an overwhelmingly orthodox, but also piously conservative, country. And Scottish religious enthusiasm was accordingly channelled in more conventional modes.

Monks, Nuns and Mendicants

The most obvious means by which men and women could express their devotion to God was by joining the clergy. There were two distinct branches of clergy, the seculars and the regulars. The former were mainly priests, but also lesser holy orders whose members were free to marry and whose status was as much a passport for study at university or for professional notarial activity as it was an indication of a religious vocation. The regulars were monks, friars and nuns, who lived in distinct communities and whose lifestyles were conducted in accordance with a set of established rules. The origins of these rules are a complex matter, and need not detain us here, save to note that it was the rule ascribed to St Benedict of Nursia (c.480-c.547) which, though broad enough to allow for marked regional variation in its implementation, formed the basis for mainstream western monasticism.

Everywhere monks and nuns usually took vows of chastity and obedience to their superiors and divided their daily lives between prayer, study and

---

[39] *Chron. Bower* (Watt), viii, 67; on the linguitic abilties of merchants see pages 29-31, above.
[40] Grant, *Independence and Nationhood*, 115.
[41] Lynch, *Edinburgh*, appendix iv.

manual work in accordance with St Benedict's prescriptions of stability and obedience to their abbot or superior. It was not, however, only monks and nuns who lived in religious communities. Enthused by the ideals of Gregorian reform and their emphasis on the separation of lay and clerical society, some priests sought to emulate monastic ideals by developing similar communities whose inhabitants ('canons-regular') conformed to a rule loosely ascribed to St Augustine of Hippo. Monks and canons-regular both, then, followed rules – hence their common designation nowadays as regular clergy – and not surprisingly historians have traditionally seen little difference between them. More recently it has been argued that in England at least there was a genuine emphasis among the Augustinian canons on pastoral concerns which made for a significant contrast with encloistered monks.[42] The Scottish evidence on this is jejune, but similar circumstances may have prevailed at least initially in Scotland too, despite the assumptions of some Scottish historians to the contrary.[43]

Nevertheless, both Benedictinism and Augustinianism made a belated impact on Scotland. The first Benedictines arrived in Scotland as late as *c*.1070, when a small number of monks from Canterbury were invited by Queen (and subsequently Saint) Margaret to settle at Dunfermline. By 1200 another three Benedictine priories (at Coldingham, the Isle of May and Urquhart) and one nunnery (at Lincluden) had been founded; and at about the same time Benedictine rule was introduced to the long-since established monastery of Iona.[44] This, indeed, was just as significant a development as that at Dunfermline. In Iona's reception of mainstream monasticism, and its rejection of Irish models, lies an indication that Scotland was truly emerging from the Celtic twilight. By then the Augustinians too were well-established in Scotland, though it had not been until *c*.1120 that their first Scottish house was established at Scone. Ten other Augustinian houses had been established by 1200 and more followed in the thirteenth century, including two houses of canonesses at Perth and Iona. Similar to the Benedictine takeover of Iona, Augustinians also displaced extant Celtic monastic communities, for instance at Abernethy and Monymusk.[45] Indeed, the popularity of the Augustinians ultimately outstripped that of the Benedictines, perhaps because the more flexible Augustinian rule was more easily adaptable by the existing religious communities of Culdees whom they replaced.[46]

The failure of the Augustinians, but more particularly still the Benedictines, to make even greater headway in Scotland was in the main a reflection of their less than rigorous standards. The quest for the most

---

[42] C.W. Bynum, 'The sprituality of regular canons in the twelfth century' in idem, *Jesus as Mother: Studies in spirituality of the high middle ages* (London, 1982), 22-58.
[43] M. Dilworth, *Scottish Monasteries in the Late Middle Ages* (Edinburgh, 1995), 3-4.
[44] Cowan and Easson, *Religious Houses*, 55-62, 143.
[45] Cowan and Easson, *Religious Houses*, 88-99, 151.
[46] K. Veitch, 'The conversion of native religious communities to the Augustinian rule in twefth- and thirteenth-century *Alba*', *RSCHS*, 29 (1999), 21.

rigorous interpretation of monastic rules was one of the principal features of medieval monasticism, and both traditional Benedictinism and Augustinianism were already lax by European standards when belatedly introduced to Scotland – despite the reform movement among Benedictines in tenth-century England. Had St Margaret's innovations been genuinely revolutionary she would have patronised one of the newer monastic orders which, invigorated by the vision of apostolic poverty, sought to reject the frills and luxuries of contemporary monasticism in favour of an idealised, primitive austerity. As it was, the first wave of monastic reform, most closely identified with the abbey of Cluny in Burgundy, virtually passed Scotland by. Only two Cluniac houses (Paisley and Crossraguel) were successfully established in Scotland, by comparison with about thirty in England and six in the diocese of Liège.[47] By the time that commitment to monastic reform had gained ground in Scotland the mantle of austere ascetiscim had passed on from the Cluniac model.[48]

Among the canons-regular it had been bestowed upon the Premonstratensians, whose revitalised interpretation of St Augustine's rule was centred around the enthusiasms of their preacher-founder St Norbert of Xanten and the customs followed at the monastery of Premontré in France. Among monks it had passed to the variants of Benedictinism observed at the French monasteries of Tiron, Savigny, La Grande Chartreuse, Cîteaux and Val des Choux. The Savigniacs and Carthusians apart, the other fashionable monastic orders of the twelfth century were to have a significant impact on the Scottish landscape. Six Premonstratensian houses, seven Tironensian houses, three Valliscaulian houses and eleven Cistercian monasteries had been established in Scotland by 1300. To these must be added at least eight Cistercian nunneries.[49]

The internationalism of the new monasticism was matched by another type of religious order which found widespread popularity throughout Christendom, at least among men, at much the same time. The military orders of knights fused the ideals of monasticism and crusading into organisations which in their community-based lifestyles and observance of vows were similar to monasticism and yet which in their glorification of the ideals of Christian knighthood appealed to a quite different temperament. Although the introduction of both the order of the Temple and the Hospital of St John of Jerusalem to Scotland remains somewhat obscure, both had established houses in Scotland by the twelfth century, the former at Balantrodoch and the latter at Torphichen. The Temple acquired a second house, at Maryculter, in the thirteenth century.[50]

[47] N. Hunt, *Cluny under Saint Hugh, 1049-1109* (London, 1967), 124-85; D. Knowles and R.N. Hadcock, *Medevial Religious Houses: England and Wales* (3rd ed., London, 1971), 96-103.
[48] Cowan and Easson, *Religious Houses*, 63-5.
[49] Cowan and Easson, *Religious Houses*, 66-85, 100-4.
[50] Cowan and Easson, *Religious Houses*, 157-61.

The new monastic and military foundations contributed towards the Europeanisation of Scotland. Benedictinism and Augustinianism paved the way, by introducing forms of monastic life which were recognisably similar to those followed elsewhere in Christendom. But they did little more than this, for both orders lacked a supra-national organisation which encouraged standardisation and international contact between their members. This was the important advance contributed by the new monasticism and the military orders of the twelfth and thirteenth centuries, though it was more pronounced in some orders than in others. The Scottish Tironensians, for instance, had already lost substantive contact with their French mother-house before the period with which we are concerned.

By contrast the Cistercians made efforts to insist upon a uniform design of buildings, library provision and liturgical observance in all of their houses, wherever located. This was backed up, as we shall see in the next section, by mechanisms of inspection devised to enforce standardisation but also to promote frequent communication between Cistercian monasteries. This internationalism of attitude is illustrated by the content of the thirteenth-century Cistercian chronicle of Melrose. The interests and concerns of the Melrose chronicler were firmly cosmopolitan. His extended prose relates primarily to crusading and to political developments which occurred not only (or even mainly) in Scotland, but rather to the great issues of the day in England, France and the Empire. We may presume that the sources for much of this information were to be found in other Cistercian houses across Christendom. Sometimes an external Cistercian source is specifically acknowledged by the chronicler; elsewhere he provides ample examples of monks from one Cistercian house moving to another, not just within Scotland but also across the Tweed frontier as if, indeed, there were no frontier at all. In this the Cistercians were like the military orders. Very few of the Templars and Hospitallers lodged at the orders' Scottish establishments were actually Scottish, whereas Scottish brethren routinely served in foreign houses.[51]

Vestiges of this internationalism continued until the sixteenth century. Scottish oblates could still be found in continental Carthiusian houses in the fifteenth century and at Cîteaux in the sixteenth century; and, although the Templars had been disbanded by the council of Vienne in 1311, Scottish Hospitallers were still serving at the order's headquarters in Rhodes in the fifteenth and sixteenth centuries.[52] Nevertheless, the high point of cosmopolitan monasticism had been reached in the thirteenth century. Thereafter, it failed to retain its vibrancy. The loss of the Holy Land undermined the position of the military orders and the suppression of the

---

[51] *The Knights of St John of Jerusalem in Scotland*, ed. I.B. Cowan, P.H.R. Mackay and A. Macquarrie (SHS, 1983), p.xx.

[52] W.N.M. Beckett, 'The Perth Charterhouse before 1500', *Analecta Cartusiana*, 128 (1988), 36; M. Dilworth, 'Franco-Scottish efforts at monastic reform, 1500-1560', *RSCHS*, 25 (1994), 217; Dilworth, *Scottish Monasteries*, 35; Cowan *et al.*, *Knights*, pp.xlvi-xlvii.

Templars unleashed a torrent of perhaps long-standing local resentment against the foreigners who represented the order in Scotland.[53] In addition, international political rivalries, both during the Anglo-Scottish wars and the schism, made life difficult for those orders founded on a concept of international uniformity. When, for instance, faced with the choice of adhering to the pope favoured by their Cistercian, Cluniac or Hospitaller superiors, or conforming with often divergent local views, most chose the latter and thereby imperilled their contacts with those who professed obedience to the rival pope. Moral and demographic dilemmas compounded the nationalist challenge which confronted monasticism. All across Christendom, even in the thirteenth century, the popularity of the new orders had begun to stagnate as prosperity softened the austere lifestyle which had been their initial hallmark. While greater comfort was no doubt attractive to many potential recruits, it perhaps alienated the most devout sections of society for whom the attraction of a religious life was its very ardour. Problems of alienation can only have been compounded by the demographic crisis following the Black Death. With a much reduced population, in addition to the steady erosion of initial ideals, it would hardly have been surprising if the extant monasteries, old and new alike, had faced a recruitment crisis.

There is some evidence to support such a notion, particularly in the Highlands, an area which in any case had been far less infiltrated by continental monastic ideals than other parts of Scotland. By *c*.1507 there was reported to have been no monastic life in living memory at Cistercian Saddell, while the Valliscaulian priory of Pluscarden housed only six monks when it was united in 1454 with Benedictine Urquhart.[54] But it was not just the new orders which suffered: by that stage Urquhart itself was home to just two monks. South of the Highland line three nunneries (Benedictine Lincluden in 1389, Cistercian Berwick in *c*.1390 and Augustinian Perth in *c*.1434) were suppressed, along with the Augustinian house at Abernethy in the early fourteenth century. Among those houses which remained, there is evidence in at least some of a decline in monastic numbers: Kelso, for instance, housed only seventeen or eighteen monks, just over half of its full complement, in 1462. Signs of abandoned or depleted cloisters suggest a retrenchment in monasticism which was barely compensated for by new expansion. Only one monastery (the Perth Charterhouse) was established after the Black Death.[55]

Yet the signs were not all gloomy. Some houses, such as Lindores, did apparently maintain their cohort of monks. There, there were twenty-six monks in 1219, only one fewer in 1538, and still nineteen or twenty in the 1540s and 1550s. Even at Kelso there were more monks in 1540 than there had

[53] Cowan *et al.*, *Knights*, pp. xxv-xxvi.
[54] Cowan and Easson, *Religious Houses*, 61, 77-78, 85; A.L. Brown, 'The Cistercian abbey of Saddell, Kintyre', *IR*, 20 (1969), 135-36; *James IV Letters*, 93-4.
[55] Beckett, 'The Perth Charterhouse', 1-74; Cowan and Easson, *Religious Houses*, 86-7.

been in 1462. Of course, steady recruitment is not an indication of spiritual endeavour. But there were efforts at some houses, notably Iona in 1426, to rid the monastery of those whose lax morals caused scandal.[56] There are also signs that the studious element of monastic life was promoted not just, as historians have long since recognised, in the sixteenth century, but in the fourteenth and fifteenth centuries too. Bower's *Scotichronicon* and Wyntoun's laboured verses were both the products of monastic study, and several monks obtained papal permission to attend university. Against this background, the introduction of the Carthusians to Perth in 1429 seems less startling. But it was not without significance. The Carthusians were the one order which did retain its reputation for strict asceticism (along with an undiluted cosmopolitan outlook) and their arrival suggests that the appeal of the *vita apostolica* remained potent.

Traditional monasticism was not, however, the only way by which the *vita apostolica*, as enunciated in the Bible (Acts, ii, 44-45), could be pursued. The relevant passage from the Acts of the Apostles makes reference to religious communities owning everything in common, and monks and nuns had always been expected to renounce personal property. The renunciation of property was taken a step further, however, by the mendicant friars. The friars, foremost among them the Franciscans, the Dominicans and the Carmelites, adopted a voluntary code of poverty and abandoned the encloistered world of traditional monasticism in favour of interaction with secular society. Most, though not all, of their houses were located in towns. In the urban milieu, living initially on charity bequeathed by those whose conscience their humility had disturbed, the impecunious friars established an empathy with the underclass which had emerged in the wake of the thirteenth-century urban expansion, a group whose spiritual needs were not specifically catered for by traditional mechanisms.[57] All of the principal mendicant orders established houses in Scotland: there were friaries in twenty-four Scottish towns, an impressive number when compared with England, where there were friaries in 116 towns, and more especially with much more populous France, where there were friaries in just 155 towns.[58] Most of the Scottish houses had been established in the thirteenth century (in other words before the demographic crisis), and although the mendicants acquired few new foundations thereafter, enthusiasm for mendicant ideals was subsequently evident in support of the Observant Franciscans, a more rigorous offshoot of the original Franciscans. Nine Observantine friaries were established in Scotland from the later fifteenth century, again a striking number when

---

[56] *CSSR*, ii, 139.

[57] See in general C.H. Lawrence, *The Friars: The impact of the early mendicant movement on western society* (Harlow, 1994).

[58] Cowan and Easson, *Religious Houses*, 114-42; Knowles and Hadcock, *Religious Houses*, 212-50; J. Le Goff, 'Ordres mendiants et urbanisation dans la France médiévale', *Annales E.S.C.*, 25 (1970), 924-46.

compared with just six established in England.[59] Although opportunities for women were much more restricted (only one Dominican and two Franciscan nunneries were established after the mid-fifteenth century in Scotland), this too is a striking divergence from England where not one nunnery associated with the male mendicants was founded in the same period.[60]

The popularity of the Observantines is an indication that early mendicancy, no less than monasticism, had succumbed to the seduction of wealth. Yet, at the same time, the progress made by the Observantines is also an indication that medieval monasticism, though apt to lose its way, was also adept at rediscovering its own high-minded ideals. By the end of the middle ages a curious dichotomy prevailed in the monastic world between relaxed and rigorous interpretations of religious rules. Both had their appeal and both continued to acquire new members. It was, and is, easy to mock the former, and the motif of the worldly monk had certainly become a common whipping horse for satirists by the end of the middle ages. 'My monks and I,' proclaimed Sir David Lindsay's abbot, 'we leif richt easilie. Thair is na monks from Carrick to Carraill,' he continued, 'That fairs better, and drinks mair helsum aill...My paramours is baith als fat and fair/ As ony wench into the toun of Air.'[61] Yet, even in ultimately unfulfilled ambitions and enthusiasms, in its reception of monastic and mendicant ideals the experience of southern and eastern Scotland was similar to that of most other parts of Christendom – and the failures were as much an experience shared by Scotland and Europe as the successes.

Religious and Secular: Patrons and Patronage

Sir David Lindsay had a less than original nose for scandal. Had, however, his instincts been commonly shared throughout the later medieval centuries, monasticism would probably never have developed at all. Religious houses existed thanks, in the main, to secular patronage. Their construction cost substantial amounts of money and they had to be built on someone's lands. Provision of the resources necessary to support a religious house was, however, a conspicuous display of piety and one for which benefactors might expect spiritual returns, not least in the form of prayers for their soul, but also sometimes in the form of retirement homes or burial plots.[62] In the exercise of monastic patronage it is not surprising that St Margaret, her sons and their royal successors had led the way: the royal dynasty was probably always the most affluent family in medieval Scotland. Others, however, sought to emulate royal munificence as best they could. Among aristocrats, for instance, Dervorguilla Balliol founded the Cistercian abbey of Sweetheart in 1273 and Reginald Cheyne founded the Tironensian priory of Fyvie in 1285, while on a

---

[59] Cowan and Easson, Religious Houses, 129-33; Knowles and Hadcock, Religious Houses, 230-31.
[60] Cowan and Easson, Religious Houses, 152-55; Knowles and Hadcock, Religious Houses, 285-87.
[61] Lindsay, Satyre, 122.
[62] J. Burton, Monastic and Religious Orders in Britain, 1000-1300 (Cambridge, 1994), chapter 10.

smaller scale burgesses too were frequent donors of property to the religious orders.

At first sight this secular patronage of the monastic orders seems to have declined from the fourteenth century. The great majority of religious houses were built in the thirteenth century, or earlier, and very few were founded in later centuries. But this is not necessarily an indication of secular disillusionment with the regular clergy. After the Black Death aristocrats became strapped for cash and they increasingly redirected their religious patronage towards the cheaper expedient of establishing collegiate churches, that is institutions staffed by secular clergy. Moreover, though few new monastic houses were constructed, traditional donative support of monks and mendicants did not cease completely, as is evident from the progress made by the Observantines from the later fifteenth century. In Aberdeen, for instance, the Observantine friary was founded thanks to grants made by both individual burgesses and the town council, and thereafter the friary continued to enjoy a steady flow of donations in cash, kind and property from aristocrats, clergymen and burgesses, as well as the crown.[63]

Grants of land and alms aside, there were other ways too in which secular support of the religious orders might be expressed. Several orders, such as the Cistercians and the Franciscans, made provision for the membership of lay associates, such as Robert Arbuthnott of that ilk and his wife Mariota Scrymgeour, who in 1487 were received into the privileges of the Observantines by its vicar-general.[64] That Mariota's attachment was to the male Observantines is an indication that female spirituality was not merely channelled towards female orders and this may partly explain why opportunities for religious women were considerably more restricted than those for men. For present purposes, however, the important fact to note is that the spread of the international orders of monks, nuns and mendicants was not a phenomenon which merely led to the Europeanisation of one distinct section of society, the clergy. The religious required, and received, secular support in Scotland as they did elsewhere in Christendom. In giving this support, the royalty, aristocracy and wealthier sections of the urban population in Scotland were demonstrating a full-hearted espousal of international fashions in religious patronage. Analysis of other devotional practices, such as the popularity of certain cults, the collection of relics, the undertaking of pilgrimages and crusades, suggests a similar conformity with Christendom. These expressions of piety are, however, important for another reason too: they encouraged the transmission of ideas, along with the movement of the pious and the penitent, across political and geographical frontiers of Christendom.

[63] Bryce, *Grey Friars*, i, 307-17, 332-42.
[64] NAS Edinburgh, RH1/2/292. See too C. Bing, *The Lairds of Arbuthnott* (Edzell and London, 1993), 36-41.

Sin and Sanctity

The cult of saints and of their relics played a vitally significant role in medieval devotional practice. Women and men prayed to God, to Christ and to the Holy Spirit, but they also prayed to the saints. For most it was probably easier to relate to saints, who had all originally been ordinary people, than to the awe-inspiring Trinity. Though not worshipped, saints were revered and accredited with a special ability to intercede with God. Through the saints God might choose to work miracles or ward off evil. While the spiritual powers of saints might be invoked through prayer, association with saintly relics was thought to place ordinary mortals in more direct contact with the saints themselves. Relics were accordingly collected, bought and even stolen during the medieval centuries.

There were, however, numerous saints and the cults of some were more avidly pursued than those of others. By choosing which feast days were observed in each church, the ecclesiastical authorities played an important role in the propagation of cults, for on these days the deeds of the festal saints were related to the laity during church services. To further popularise a cult, the church might grant indulgences to those who visited a shrine associated with a particular saint, though for a cult to gain a widespread following much depended on the ability of the laity to fully empathise with the deeds and legends associated with the saint in question. Despite, for instance, the support of at least four Scottish bishops, the cult of the thirteenth-century academic St Edmund of Abingdon apparently failed to generate a substantial amount of interest in Scotland.[65] The ecclesiastical authorities did not, then, hold a monopoly on the popularisation of cults and some, such as that which developed in thirteenth-century France surrounding the greyhound Guinefort, were popularised despite the condemnation of the ecclesiastical authorities.[66]

In thirteenth- and fourteenth-century Scotland religious cults were of a curiously cosmopolitan character. To a large measure this was a reflection of the rites for religious services followed in Scottish churches, which, even during the protracted Anglo-Scottish conflict of the fourteenth century, were normally based on English practice. While Scottish clerics adapted the standard Sarum Use of the church in England for the ordering of church services, adaptation was undertaken in a piecemeal fashion. In different localities, while saints with local associations were incorporated in breviaries, insertion proved more popular than deletion. Breviaries accordingly continued to accord a place to many relatively obscure English saints along with those who were internationally revered.[67] The festal days of the Anglo-Saxon king-saints Edmund, Edward and Oswald, for instance, were routinely

[65] D. McRoberts, 'St Edmund in Scotland', *IR*, 13 (1962), 219.
[66] J.C. Schmitt, *The Holy Greyhound* (Cambridge, 1983).
[67] Macfarlane, *Elphinstone*, 232-33; L.J. Macfarlane, 'The Divine Office and the Mass' in J. Geddes, ed., *King's College Chapel, Aberdeen, 1500-2000* (Leeds, 2000), 11-14.

accorded a place in Scottish calendars.[68] Church breviaries are, however, only one indication of the popularity of different saints; ecclesiastical dedications provide a rather different insight. Most parish churches were founded before the mid-thirteenth century and their dedications are, therefore, a guide to saintly veneration of an earlier era. The later medieval period did, however, witness the foundation of many hospitals, and of those first recorded between the mid-thirteenth century and the end of the fourteenth century, the most frequent known dedications were to Mary Magdalene, John the Baptist and Leonard.[69]

Of course, this is not to say that Scots ignored their own saints, or at least all of their own saints, in the thirteenth and fourteenth centuries. True, the cults of St William of Perth (a baker martyred at Rochester) and San Pellegrino (allegedly the son of a Scottish king who renounced his claims to the throne to travel to the Holy Land) seem not to have been known in Scotland.[70] Nevertheless, the royal house in particular displayed an affection for saints with Scottish connections and much has been made of Robert I's veneration of Columba, Ninian and Fillan, whose relics were allegedly paraded before the Scottish army on the eve of Bannockburn.[71] Less well known is Robert II's preference for spending May on his Bute estates, almost certainly to participate in the feast days of the locally revered saints Brendan and Brioc.[72] With the canonisation of St Margaret in 1250, the royal family had also acquired its own distinctive saint – though this particular quest was paralleled by the canonisation of other monarchs, such as Knut (Denmark), Edward the Confessor (England), Olaf Haraldson (Norway), Erik (Sweden) and Louis IX for the Capetian dynasty in France.[73] Beyond the devotions of the monarchy, although decidedly fewer hospitals were dedicated to saints with Scottish connections than to cosmopolitan saints, those in Caithness, Ballencrieff, Kingcase and Turriff were dedicated respectively to SS Magnus, Cuthbert, Ninian and Congan. Nevertheless, that amalgam of reverence commonly found across Christendom of international, national and local saints was perhaps less evident in Scotland. The lack of a distinctive and

---

[68] A.I. Doyle, 'A Scottish Augustinian psalter', *IR*, 8 (1957), 80, 83-4; 'The Holyrood Ordinale', ed. F.C. Eeles, *Book of the Old Edinburgh Club*, 7 (1914), 8, 13, 16.

[69] This and subsequent references to hospital dedications are based on Cowan and Eason, *Religious Houses*, 162-200.

[70] J.S. Richardson, 'St William of Perth and his memorials in England', *TSES*, 2 (1906-9), 122-26; N. Yates, *Faith and Fabric: A history of Rochester Cathedral, 604-1994* (Woodbridge, 1994), 37-8; A. Vauchez, *La Sainteté en Occident aux Derniers Siècles du Moyen Ages* (Rome, 1981), 233.

[71] G.W.S. Barrow, *Robert Bruce and the Community of the Realm of Scotland* (3rd ed., Edinburgh, 1988), 225, 318-19.

[72] S. Boardman, *The Early Stewart Kings: Robert II and Robert III, 1371-1406* (East Linton, 1996), 94.

[73] B. Guenée, *States and Rulers in Later Medieval Europe* (Oxford, 1985), 56-8; B. & P. Sawyer, *Medieval Scandinavia: From conversion to Reformation, c.800-1500* (Mineapolis, 1993), 214-15; Vauchez, *Sainteté*, 187-97, 310-14.

standard Scottish Use in church services meant that the official mechanism simply did not exist to propagate the cult of a group of 'national' saints.

This allegedly began to change in the fifteenth century. In recent years much as been made of a new, 'nationalistic' trend in Scottish religious observation. Greater emphasis, we are told, began to be placed on the cult of distinctively Scottish saints. Church calendars were revised to give greater prominence to the feast days of 'national' saints. The papacy was petitioned for the canonisation of Duthac, a Scot who was buried at Armagh in 1165. A search was mounted for the relics of the almost forgotten apostle of the Irish, Paladius, who had died at Fordoun in the Mearns. His relics, together with those of other saintly Scots which had not been misplaced, were re-housed in ornate and ostentatious surroundings which attracted pilgrims. This patriotic trend allegedly culminated during the career of William Elphinstone, bishop of Aberdeen. Under his guidance a martyrology, illustrating a particular interest in Scottish saints, was compiled and, though the saints included in martyrologies were not necessarily included in liturgical ceremonies, when Elphinstone and his colleagues subsequently produced a new breviary, one quarter of the major feast days in it were given over to the celebration of Scottish saints.[74]

It is right and proper that this 'nationalistic' trend has been acknowledged, but unfortunate that it has been allowed to overshadow the simultaneous, but cosmopolitan, trend in devotional practice which is every bit as evident in Scotland as elsewhere in the Latin west. Foremost among these devotional practices were the cults associated with Christ and the Virgin Mary. Much Christocentric devotion was focused on the suffering of Christ on the cross. The cults of the Five Wounds, the Crown of Thorns and the Holy Blood were celebrated in Scottish churches long before their incorporation in the Aberdeen Breviary gave them official standing. Altars dedicated to the Holy Blood, for instance, were established by gild merchants and others in the churches at Aberdeen, Dundee, Edinburgh, Perth and St Andrews.[75] This possibly reflected the trading connections of these towns with the Low Countries: Bruges was one of the principal centres of that cult on the continent. The popularity of Christocentric themes was not, however, the exclusive preserve of merchants. It is further reflected in contemporary art, drama and literature: the Fetternear banner, dating from the first half of the sixteenth century, displays a powerful image of a bloodied Christ on the cross; King's College in Aberdeen possessed a statue of a flagellated Christ; and at Haddington a stone carving depicted a naked Christ, his arms bound to a pillar, being lashed by two soldiers.[76] Dramatic productions developed the

[74] Macfarlane, *Elphinstone*, 234-43; D.McRoberts, 'The Scottish church and nationalism in the fifteenth century', *IR*, 19 (1968), 7-12; J.Durkan, 'The sanctuary and college of Tain', *IR*, 13 (1962), 147-56.
[75] *Aberdeen Registrum*, i, 333-34; D. McRoberts, 'The Fetternear banner [I]', *IR*, 7 (1956), 76-7.
[76] McRoberts, 'The Fetternear banner [I]', 69-86; D. McRoberts, 'The Fetternear banner [II]', *IR*, 8 (1957); 69-70; F.C. Eeles, *King's College Chapel, Aberdeen* (Edinburgh, 1956), 38; *Angels, Nobles and*

general theme further. The play *ly Haliblude* was performed in Aberdeen at Corpus Christi from 1440, and other Corpus Christi processions or plays were performed in Edinburgh and Perth by the fifteenth century and at Dundee, Haddington and Lanark by the sixteenth century.[77] Meanwhile, William Dunbar's *The Passioun of Christ* and *Surrexit Dominus de sepulchro* are but two of the most obvious poetical considerations of Christ and his death.[78] The morbid focus on divine mortality struck a chord in an era of plague and echoes wider literary and artistic trends evident both in Scotland and elsewhere in Christendom.[79]

Marian cults were, if anything, even more popular than those focussed on Christ. Mary, of course, was the greatest of the saints and her cult continued to attract significant adulation until the very eve of the Reformation in 1560.[80] New Marian feasts, such as the Visitation (2 July) and the Presentation (21 November), began to be celebrated at altars in Scottish churches. New Marian shrines, such as Whitekirk and Loretto, attracted substantial numbers of pilgrims. Marian devotion was accorded a prominent place in prayers, such as the *Ave Maria*, which all Christians were expected to recite frequently. The *Ave* also formed an integral part of the rosary which consisted of fifteen *Ave* couplets, each preceded by the Lord's prayer and followed by the *Gloria Patri*. This prayer compilation was first popularised by the fifteenth-century French Dominican preacher Alan de la Roche, and it was as a memory aid to its recitation that rosary beads became fashionable. All Scottish kings from James III, together with at least some clergymen and burgesses, are known to have possessed a rosary, and rosaries began to be engraved, embroidered and illuminated in a variety of artistic settings.[81] Imagery, as we have seen, was an important means by which the faith was communicated and Marian imagery was prolific.

Marian carvings, of the sort still evident at the church of St Giles in Edinburgh, were perhaps not uncommon, though unfortunately little else of this genre now survives.[82] Some possessed statues of the Virgin: James IV purchased one for himself in 1507 and presented another made of gold to his wife, Queen Margaret, in 1503.[83] Others were decapitated by Protestants at Ayr in 1533 and at Edinburgh in 1556, and there were at least four in King's

Unicorns: Art and Patronage in Medieval Scotland (National Museum of Antiquities, 1982), no. E16.
[77] A.J. Mill, *Medieval Plays in Scotland* (Edinburgh, 1927), 61-73.
[78] Dunbar, *Poems*, 7-15.
[79] J.A.W. Bennett, *Poetry of the Passion: Studies in twelve centuries of English verse* (Oxford, 1982), especially chapter 5; J.M. Clark, *The Dance of Death in the Middle Ages and the Renaissance* (Glasgow, 1950), especially chapter 1.
[80] M. Lynch, *Edinburgh and the Reformation* (Edinburgh, 1981), 29-30.
[81] D. McRoberts, 'The rosary in Scotland', *IR*, 23 (1972), 81-6.
[82] G. Hay, 'The late medieval development of the High Kirk of St Giles, Edinburgh', *PSAS*, 107 (1975-76), 249-50.
[83] *TA*, ii, 217; iii, 363.

College Chapel, Aberdeen by 1542.[84] We do not know what these statues looked like but depictions on seals perhaps provide a clue not only to this but also to the appearance of paintings which may have adorned churches. Among these, representations of Mary cradling the infant Jesus in her arms, emphasising the maternal role of the Virgin and women more generally, were especially common. The majority of these images appear on ecclesiastical seals, but some were also engraved on secular seals, such as that of Walter Biggar, the royal chamberlain in the mid-fourteenth century – an indication that Marian devotion had been successfully propagated among the laity.[85] A probably even greater indication of this is the clay mould, found at Markle in East Lothian and now on display in the National Museum of Scotland. This was used to mass-produce cheap papier mâché images of the Virgin and Child, which were presumably sold to pilgrims visiting the nearby Marian shrine at Whitekirk. Marian devotion was not, however, just the opium of the illiterate. Further evidence of the Virgin's popularity appears in contemporary literature, such as William Dunbar's *Ane Ballat of our Lady* and an anonymous compilation of saints' lives which bestowed particular attention on the life and miracles of the Virgin.[86]

The popularisation of Christocentric and Marian cults encouraged the veneration of other saints associated with Jesus's family. Foremost among these was not Joseph – whose popularity beyond carpenters did not spread until the sixteenth century, though even then it has left little trace in Scotland.[87] Rather, Anne was the chief beneficiary of these trends. Anne was Mary's mother and her cult grew rapidly in the fifteenth century following the official promulgation of her feast day by the Roman pope Urban VI (whom Scots did not recognise) in 1396. Nonetheless, Anne's image was depicted in fifteenth-century books of hours, such as that of Rossdhu, and by 1542 a tapestry depicting scenes from her life adorned the chapel of King's College, Aberdeen.[88] Long before then altars dedicated to Anne had been established in, for instance, the parish churches of Aberdeen and Edinburgh, and they continued to be dedicated in her name until the eve of the Reformation: the secular college established at Cullen in 1543, for instance, included prebendaries of St Mary and St Anne.[89] In Anne's footsteps came the grandchildren of her alleged second and third marriages: James the Lesser,

[84] Kirk, 'Iconoclasm', 371, 381; Eeles, *King's College*, 37-8.
[85] H. Laing, *Descriptive Catalogue of Impressions from Ancient Scottish Seals* (Edinburgh, 1850), passim. See also M. Warner, *Alone of All Her Sex: The myth and the cult of the Virgin Mary* (2nd ed., London, 1990), passim.
[86] Dunbar, *Poems*, 4-7; R.J. Lyall, 'The lost literature of medieval Scotland' in J.D. McClure and M.R.G. Spiller, eds., *Bryght Lanternis: Essays on the language and literature of medieval Scotland* (Aberdeen, 1989), 38.
[87] Joseph was, however, represented on the seal of Bishop Kinnimonth of Aberdeen (1357-1382): Laing, *Seals*, no. 896.
[88] G. Hay and D. McRoberts, 'Rossdhu Church and its book of hours', *IR*, xvi (1965), 7; F.C. Eeles, *King's College Chapel, Aberdeen* (Edinburgh, 1956), 23.
[89] Cowan and Easson, *Religious Houses*, 218.

Simon, Jude; and the other James and John. All of these too, and especially James the Greater, won a treasured place in medieval devotion. James IV, for instance, made offerings to all bar James the Lesser during his reign while the saint whom the king overlooked won a depiction on the seal of James Beaton, archbishop of St Andrews, in the early sixteenth century.[90]

The increasing veneration accorded to Christ's saintly family to some extent took place at the expense of other more traditional saintly figures. It has been calculated that only about eight of the 344 individuals from the fourteenth and fifteenth centuries who were sanctified or beatified acquired international cults, and of these only those associated with St Bridget of Sweden, St Catherine of Siena, St Roche of Montpellier and San Bernadino of Siena had anything of an impact on Scotland.[91] Bower was well-informed of Bridget's at times rather eccentric exploits, while a printed copy of San Bernadino's *De duodecim periculis* was possessed by Archbishop Schevez of St Andrews (1478-1497), though it is difficult to find evidence of other Scots sharing these interests.[92] Bridget's rather less threatening contemporary, Catherine, was certainly celebrated in Scottish churches;[93] but in an era of epidemic disease it is perhaps not surprising that it was the cult of St Roche, along with the older cult of St Sebastian, which acquired particular popularity in Scotland.

Roche had tended plague sufferers in fourteenth-century Italy before eventually succumbing to the disease himself. Sebastian's connections with plague sufferers is less obvious – he was a Roman martyred by Diocletian and, thanks to a Derek Jarman film, is now a gay icon. But in the later middle ages Sebastian was widely invoked on behalf of the sick, initially perhaps because the arrow marks on depictions of his body resembled the buboes which appeared on those of plague victims.[94] In early sixteenth-century Scotland chapels were dedicated to Roche at Dundee, Edinburgh, Glasgow, Paisley and Stirling, while Sebastian's cult was honoured in Aberdeen, Dundee and Edinburgh.[95] The sudden popularity of Sebastian is a reminder that if the circumstances were appropriate an interest in older saints might be rejuvenated. So it was with St George. St George's Day had long since been accorded a place in the calendars of Scottish churches, though there is little indication of a strong Scottish devotion to the saint before the fourteenth

[90] *TA*, i, 101, 126, 308, 374; ii, 77; iii, 62, 69, 76; iv, 43, 177, 180, 190; Laing, *Seals*, no. 879.

[91] D. Hay, *Europe in the Fourteenth and Fifteenth Centuries* (2nd ed., London, 1989), 338.

[92] *Chron. Bower* (Watt), vii, 374-79; J. Durkan and A. Ross, 'Early Scottish libraries', *IR*, 9 (1958), 48.

[93] *TA*, iii, 59, 290. Catherine of Siena (feast day: 30 April) should not be confused with Catherine of Alexandria (feast day: 25 November), whose cult was also popular: see for instance *TA*, i, 125, 170, 369; ii, 256; Laing, *Seals*, no. 892.

[94] M.M. Antony-Schmitt, *La Culte de Saint-Sebastien en Alsace* (Strasbourg, 1977); A. Fliche, 'Le problème de Saint Roch', *Analecta Bollandia*, 68 (1950), 343-61.

[95] W.M. Bryce, 'St Roque's chapel and the lands of Canaan', *Book of the Old Edinburgh Club*, 10 (1918), 167-83; *TA*, i, 324; iv, 182; A. Maxwell, *Old Dundee* (Dundee, 1891), 36.

century.[96] The crusading impulses of a number of David II's knights seem, however, to have revived a veneration for George in the south and east of Scotland, for George was popular with crusaders. His popularity in Scotland was marked by the adoption of the previously unusual Christian name George and the dedication in 1390 of an altar dedicated to the saint in Dundee.[97]

Clearly, then, though Scots were rediscovering their own saints, they were not losing interest in universal cults. Assessing the relative importance of these twin developments is not easy, but to set the 'nationalistic' trend in context it is important not to exaggerate its significance. Rather than, for example, stressing that a quarter of the feast days in the Aberdeen Breviary were now given over to the celebration of Scottish saints, the corollary – that 75% were not – deserves equal emphasis. Indeed, while some writers have detected a bias for Scots among those saints to whom church altars were dedicated in the later medieval period, this is difficult to substantiate across the kingdom.[98] At the parish church of Dundee, for instance, while altars were dedicated to the Scottish saints such as Serf, Duthac, Monan, Columba and Triduana, these amounted to just a fifth of the total number of altars recorded in the church.[99] Similarily, among dedications of hospitals which first appear in the records from the beginning of the fifteenth century, the international saints, led by Leonard, Mary Magdalene and the Virgin, outnumber the Scots by almost fourteen to one.[100] Outwith the churches, it is similarly difficult to find evidence that the popularity of Scottish saints was beginning to outstrip that of international cults. Scottish religious poems and ballads overwhelmingly addressed the subject of the Virgin or the Passion of the Cross rather than the deeds of St Duthac or St Fillan. Seals overwhelmingly depicted the Holy Trinity, the Virgin and saints such as Andrew, Giles, James, Peter and Paul rather than Serf or Ninian. And perhaps even more reflective of ordinary everyday speech and thought, the characters of Sir David Lindsay's *Ane Satire of the Three Estates* rarely invoked Scottish saints in their dialogue, but frequently appealed to a cosmopolitan group of saints led by the Virgin, Paul, Michael and Blaise, a Cappadocian bishop martyred by Diocletian.[101]

This evidence – and much more to the same effect could probably be gathered – suggests that the 'nationalistic' trend in veneration was limited. Moreover, the attempts of the ecclesiastical hierarchy to promote use of Elphinstone's new and distinctively Scottish breviary were essentially a failure. The printer of the breviary complained that Edinburgh merchants were infringing his copyright by importing Sarum brevaries. Breviaries of the Roman Use were also imported, and after its appearance in 1535 the revised Quinones breviary of the Roman Use was also quickly popularised in

[96] Doyle, 'Psalter', 81; Eeles, 'Holyrood Ordinale', 9.
[97] I owe this suggestion to Steve Boardman; Maxwell, *Old Dundee*, 18.
[98] McRoberts, 'Nationalism', 10.
[99] Maxwell, *Old Dundee*, 18-36.
[100] Cowan and Easson, *Religious Houses*, 162-68.
[101] Lindsay, *Satyre*, passim.

Scotland.[102] Interestingly, by contrast with the Sarum breviaries, importation of Roman-style breviaries had never been prohibited, which leads to the suspicion that the whole hierarchically inspired reform was in any case essentially anglophobic rather than genuinely nationalistic in intent. And all this is a further reminder, if one were needed, that trends in medieval religion were as much dictated by popular feelings as by episcopal or governmental fads.

Contacting the Saints: Relics and Pilgrimages

The appeal of popular cults among Scots was reflected in the closely related devotional practice of collecting relics and sculpted or painted images of saints. Relics associated with Scottish saints were obviously the easiest to obtain but several were also acquired from abroad. The assemblage of spiritual wares at Glasgow cathedral included not only part of the Virgin's girdle, but also fragments of her hair and droplets of her milk, along with remnants of St Catherine's tomb, St Mathew's cloak, St Thomas Becket's scourge and the bones of SS Thomas, Bartholomew, Blaise and Eugene.[103] By 1436 Aberdeen cathedral's collection included a hair of St Edmund of Abingdon and the bones of various saints associated with the middle east – Catherine (probably of Alexandria), Helen, Isaac the Patriarch and Margaret (possibly of Antioch) – as well as Marian, Petrine and Pauline artefacts.[104] St Catherine excepted, the cult of none of the eastern saints was especially marked in Scotland and these particular relics were probably acquired by someone who had ventured either on crusade or pilgrimage to the Holy Land. More appropriate acquisitions, given Scottish circumstances, were the wooden fragments of the Cross and the bones of St Augustine, possessed by the Augustinian abbey of Holyrood, and an arm-bone of St Giles, which William Preston gifted to the same saint's parish church of Edinburgh in 1455.[105] This, together with an image of St Giles, was thereafter publicly displayed on Relic Sunday and St Giles Day.[106] Elsewhere the devotion to the great foreign saints was reflected at Holyrood Abbey which, by 1493, also possessed bones of St Catherine, while in 1502, James IV – the king who allegedly lavished his attention on national saints – paid fifteen French crowns for a bone of St Roche.[107] The king's honesty may be contrasted with the alleged dishonesty of William Claxton, the English prior of Coldingham. His devotion to St Ebba and St Margaret supposedly led him to secretly remove their relics to Durham in 1379: though the theft of relics has left little trace in Scotland, it was a

[102] McRoberts, 'Liturgy', 36-8.
[103] *Glasgow Reg.*, ii, no. 339.
[104] *Aberdeen Reg.*, ii, 143.
[105] Eeles, 'Holyrood Ordinale', 214; *Registrum Cartarum Ecclesiae Sancti Egidii de Edinburgh* (Bannatyne Club, 1859).
[106] *Edin. Recs.*, ii, 336, 344, 353, 363.
[107] Eeles, 'Holyrood Ordinale', 214; *TA*, ii, 346.

significant scandal in the Latin West as a whole.[108] Despite the lengths to which some would go to obtain their relics, another well-known scandal – the trade in bogus relics – seems also to have had little impact in Scotland. There is little documentary evidence to suggest that Sir David Lindsay's pardoner – who attempted to pass off the bones of a cow as those of the Irish saint Bride – was at all typical.[109]

While relics were believed to place the devout in closer communion with the saints, pilgrimage was the means by which men and women might come into contact with a saint's relics and the holy places most closely associated with that saint. Pilgrimage was not, however, an essential element of Christian devotional practice. It was a matter of individual choice. Thanks to the influence of Chaucer's *Canterbury Tales* it has become common to regard the medieval pilgrim as a proto-tourist whose ambitions were to seek adventure and to marvel at strange places rather than to pursue any serious spiritual goal. There perhaps were some pilgrims who come into this category and many did at least return home with the souvenir trinkets and badges which were commonly sold at pilgrimage centres. The skeleton with a conch placed in its mouth which was recently excavated on the Isle of May had almost certainly undertaken a pilgrimage to Compostella: the conch was an internationally recognised symbol of that shrine and figured prominently on its associated trinkets.[110] While conches have been excavated elsewhere – for instance at Perth – to date only one lead emblem depicting the conch (dating from *c*.1300) has been found in Scotland, at St Monans in 1996.[111]

For others a pilgrimage was an opportunity to escape some ghastly family row: Bower, for example, implies that Alan de Wynton set off for the Holy Land 'because of the intrigues of the friends of [the relations of] his wife' following a contentious marriage.[112] Yet to tar all pilgrims with an essentially secular motivation would be a mistake. Many pilgrimages originated in a vow and some pilgrims, indeed, took a vow on behalf of a friend or relation: in 1529, for example, George Preston intended to visit two foreign shrines 'for the quhilk he is under a vow for umquhile Symoun Prestoun'.[113] These vows were normally a serious business and those who, for whatever reason, found

---

[108] A. Brown, 'The priory of Coldingham in the late fourteenth century', *IR*, 23 (1972), 93. The standard account of the theft of relics is P.J. Geary, *Furta Sacra: Thefts of relics in the central middle ages* (Princeton, 1978).

[109] Lindsay, *Satyre*, 75. For a rare example of a pardoner at work in Aberdeen in 1496, see I.B. Cowan, 'Church and society' in J.M. Brown, ed., *Scottish Society in the Fifteenth Century* (London, 1977), 114.

[110] P. Yeoman, *Secrets of Fife's Holy Island: The archaeology of the Isle of May* (Glenrothes, 1996), 20-1; B.W. Spencer, 'Medieval pilgrimage badges', *Rotterdam Papers: A contribution to medieval archaeology*, 1 (1968), 143.

[111] For examples of trinkets brought to Scotland from Compostella, see *Santiago de Compostella: 1000 ans de Pèlerinage Européen* (Ghent, 1985), nos. 175, 212, 213. The St Monans find is on permanent display in St Andrews Museum.

[112] *Chron. Bower* (Watt), vii, 158-59. On Wynton's pilgrimage, see also above, p. 27, and below p. 61.

[113] *RSS*, i, no. 4064.

themselves unable to fulfil a vow of pilgrimage often sought official sanction for release from their undertaking: in 1359, for instance, Sir Robert Erskine sought release from a vow on the grounds that the king would not release him from royal service, while in 1437 William de Keith was granted papal permission to commute a pilgrimage to other pious works on the grounds of his 'great infirmities and feebleness of his body'.[114]

The vow to undertake a pilgrimage might be taken in times of crisis or difficulty, when the intercessions of a saint were sought to alleviate a particular problem, or in gratitude for an act of divine assistance. Both motives are neatly encapsulated in the figure of the Aberdonian Alexander Stephenson, who, suffering from worms and sores on his feet, made a pilgrimage to Canterbury in 1445. There he was miraculously cured, and, having celebrated by dancing incessantly for three days, he then decided to offer his thanks by travelling to the shrine at Wilsnack.[115] Other Scottish evidence of motivation is slight, but in one fifteenth-century incident the spur to a vow of pilgrimage was illness, and in another distress at sea – a not uncommon impetus elsewhere too, as is vividly described in the biography of Christopher Columbus by his son, Hernando.[116] Others willingly embarked on a pilgrimage as an act of penance for their sins and yet others were judicially enjoined so to do. In the twelfth century several foreigners fettered in chains, some of them Scots, had arrived at the shrines of St Cuthbert in Durham and Kirkcudbright to atone for their sins.[117] Although such pitiful sightings of Scotsmen were not recorded in the later middle ages, it remained the case that murderers were sometimes sent to the far corners of Christendom to expiate their crimes. In 1471 Peter Black, a Scot who was accused in Danzig of manslaughter, was directed to undertake a penitential visit to Aachen, Einsiedeln, St Adrian and Compostella. Four years later Alexander Gustis was also ordered to undertake a pilgrimage to the Holy Blood (Wilsnack?), after he had wounded a Scottish compatriot in Danzig.[118] Pilgrims such as these were expected to return with certificates to prove that they had undertaken their penance; not surprisingly, perhaps, there is no evidence that Peter Black found his way back to Danzig.

Pilgrimage shrines were widely scattered across Europe. Most were of purely local significance, attracting an essentially local clientele, though the number of visitors which such sites attracted could be substantial. Whitekirk, a Marian shrine in East Lothian which achieved fleeting popularity from the

[114] CPP, i, 346; CSSR, iv, no. 352. For an example of a vow taken 'thoughtlessly in the days of... youth', see ibid, i, 2.
[115] J. Stuart, 'Notice of an original instrument recently discovered among the records of the dean and chapter of Canterbury...', PSAS, 10 (1875), 528-35; S.C. Wilson, 'Scottish Canterbury pilgrims', SHR, 24 (1926-27), 263.
[116] Fischer, *Germany*, 241-42; J.M. Cohen, ed., *Christopher Columbus: The four voyages* (London, 1969), 101-2, 109.
[117] Reginaldi Monaci Dunelmensis, *Libellus de Admirandis Beati Cuthberti Virtutibus* (Surtees Soc., 1835), 164-65, 177-78.
[118] Fischer, *Prussia*, 10-11.

later fourteenth century, allegedly attracted no fewer than 15,653 pilgrims in 1413.[119] Scotland itself could boast few pilgrimage sites of international renown, even though Whitekirk could claim the future Pope Pius II among its visitors in 1435.[120] Elsewhere in Scotland, veneration of St Margaret brought some English visitors to Dunfermline, including part of an English army besieging Loch Leven in 1334, but there is little evidence that the throngs of pilgrims now depicted on street murals in the town – if throngs of any sort there ever were – included many foreigners.[121] Evidence for foreign visitors to St Andrews is only marginally more impressive. Two fifteenth-century pilgrim badges from St Andrews have been found in Zeeland, and at least seventeen others have been excavated in England.[122] The popularity of St Andrew in the Burgundian domains may account for the visits from Zeeland, and, with over six hundred parish churches dedicated to him in England, Andrew was well known there too. Given its location on the fringe of Christendom, St Andrews was also deemed appropriate for the itinerary of some foreign miscreants. In 1319, for instance, Watier Maisière of Kortrijk was directed to Fife after assaulting his wife; and in 1333 William Bondolf from Dunkirk was ordered to visit St Andrews to atone for killing André d'Esquerdes. At Ypres, where expiatory pilgrimages were commonly imposed, St Andrews was the third most common destination for such miscreants.[123] Nevertheless, by 1512 the pilgrimage hospice at St Andrews had apparently fallen into desuetude: St Andrew, it would seem, was no longer working the miracles required to entice pilgrims, while expiatory pilgrimages were no longer so commonly imposed.[124]

Whithorn retained its vibrancy much longer, and it alone among Scottish pilgrimage sites seems to have maintained a regular, if modest, foreign traffic.

---

[119] *Clement VII Letters*, 112; E.B. Rankin, *Saint Mary's Whitekirk, 1356-1914* (Edinburgh, 1914), 6. The supposed number of visitors to Whitekirk in 1413 is modest compared to some other estimates: 60,000 in a week at Munich in 1392 and 142,000 in a day at Aachen in 1496. (Spencer, 'Pilgrimage Badges', 137.) See also J.B. Paul, 'Whitekirk church and its history', *TSES*, 6 (1920-21), 119-24; and, for a survey of other Scottish pilgrimage centres, J.B. Paul, 'Royal pilgrimages in Scotland', *TSES*, 1 (1903-6), 147-55; P. Yeoman, *Pilgrimage in Medieval Scotland* (London, 1999).

[120] Pii II, *Commentarii Rerum Memorabilium Que Temporibvs Svis Contigervnt* (Vatican, 1984), ed. A. van Heck, i, 45; C-E. Naville, *Enea Silvio Piccolomini: L'uomo l'umanista il Pontefice, 1405-1464* (Locarno, 1984), 167.

[121] *Chron. Bower* (Watt), vii, 99.

[122] R.M. Van Heeringen, A.M. Koldeweij and A.A.G. Gaalman, *Heiligen uit de Modder: In Zeeland gevonden pelgrimstekens* (Utrecht, 1988), 101. For a thirteenth-century English pilgrimage to St Andrews, see *CDS*, ii, no. 8. The English finds (eleven from London and one each from Holkwold (Norfolk), Westbury-by-Shenley (Buckinghamshire), Beauchamp Grange (Leicestershire), Canterbury (Kent), Gravesend (Kent) and Saffron Waldon (Essex)) were included in an exhibition staged at St Andrews Museum in 1999.

[123] F. Ganshof, 'Pèlerinages flamands à Saint-Gilles pendant le XIV siècle', *Annales du Midi*, 78 (1966), 401, 404-5; D. McRoberts, 'A St Andrews pilgrimage certificate of 1333 at Saint-Omer' in idem, ed., *The Medieval Church of St Andrews* (Glasgow, 1976), 155-6. See too J.H. Hennes, ed., *Codex Diplomaticus Ordinis Sanctae Mariae Theutonicorum: Urkundenbuch zur Geschichte des Deutschen Ordens* (Mainz, 1845-61), ii, no. 318.

[124] R.G. Cant, *The University of St Andrews: A short history* (3rd ed., St Andrews, 1992), 35.

The future Edward II of England visited St Ninian's shrine there in 1301 and its fame in England was perhaps increased with reports that the Scots had hidden the saint's image from the prince, only to discover that it had miraculously returned to its proper place the following morning. By the fifteenth century Ninian's cult flourished in northern England and both James I and James V extended protection towards foreign pilgrims visiting Whithorn, James V specifically alluding to those who came from England, Ireland and Man.[125]

Some pilgrimage centres were, however, of international repute, and foremost among these were the sites located in the Holy Land, Rome and Compostella. The Holy Land had attracted a substantial pilgrim traffic from the west before the advent of the crusades in the later eleventh century. John of Würzburg noted Scots among the 'people of every race and tongue' who thronged Jerusalem in c.1170 and the city remained a popular destination with Scots and others long after Jerusalem again fell under Saracen control in 1187.[126] There were many sights to be seen and prayed at, and not all of them, such as the Church of the Holy Sepulchre, were in Jerusalem itself. The itinerary of many pilgrims to the Holy Land included a visit to the Church of the Nativity in Bethlehem and to the spot where John reputedly baptised Jesus in the River Jordan. The hardiest travellers, such as Alan de Wyntoun in 1347, also embarked upon the arduous journey across the Sinai desert to the shrine of St Catherine.

In the west Rome was the principal centre of pilgrim traffic.[127] A warehouse of relics, Rome's attractions included the bodies of SS Peter, Paul and Lawrence, along with the heads of SS Peter and Paul, housed at the Lateran, and the Veil of Veronica at St Peter's. These and numerous other revered limbs and artefacts had long since attracted a regular flow of pilgrims from Scotland and elsewhere and continued to do so between the mid-thirteenth and mid-sixteenth centuries. In an effort to further stimulate the Roman pilgrim traffic (and the profits to be made from it) later medieval popes periodically offered pilgrim visitors 'a general amnesty for sin'.[128] Jubilee years were designated in 1300, 1350 and 1390, and again in the fifteenth century, perhaps in 1423 and certainly in 1450, 1475-6 and 1500. In these *anni santi* all pilgrims who trekked to the Eternal city were granted a plenary indulgence – that is, all who undertook a pilgrimage to Rome were to be released from other penances to be undertaken for previously committed sins and, latterly, from the pontificate of Sixtus IV (1471-1484) from those penances which would have to be undertaken in Purgatory. The first two jubilees were scheduled at times which were less than propitious for Scots. The first fell during the wars of independence and the second shortly after the

[125] *CDS*, ii, no. 1225; *James V Letters*, 66, 363; *RSS*, i, no. 2844; D. Palliser, 'Richard III and York' in R. Horrox, ed., *Richard III and the North* (Hull, 1986), 60-1.
[126] J. Wilkinson, J. Hill and W.F. Ryan, eds., *Jerusalem Pilgrimage* (Hakluyt Society, 1988), 273.
[127] See in general D.J. Birch, *Pilgrimage to Rome in the Middle Ages* (Woodbridge, 1998).
[128] The phrase is John Bossy's: *Christianity in the West, 1400-1700* (Oxford, 1985), 3.

advent of the Black Death, though even the dislocations caused by plague did not prevent the abbot of Dunfermline from visiting Rome 'to obtain the general indulgence' in 1350.[129] The third jubilee, during the schism, also presented problems for Scots, since Scotland recognised the Avignonese, rather than Roman, pope. It is, however, instructive of the significance of Rome to the Latin psyche – and of the irrelevance of papal squabbles – that some Scots still sought to venture to Rome for what should have been the jubilee of 1400, had not papal financial expediency dictated its declaration ten years early.[130] The schism concluded, the possible jubilee of 1423 perhaps attracted a few Scots and that of 1450 rather more. There were certainly some Scots in Rome in 1423, though whether they had undertaken a pilgrimage, in addition to other business which they were attending to, is not clear.[131] James Kennedy, bishop of St Andrews, James lord Hamilton and William, earl of Douglas, were among the most prominent Scots to visit Rome in 1450, but others did too and it has been suggested that it was to cater for the large number of Scots who were there in 1450 that a Scottish church and hospice were founded at Sant' Andrea delle Frate.[132]

Compostella, the other great centre of pilgrimage in the west, could offer fewer relics than the Holy Land or Rome, and some even doubted the authenticity of the city's claims to possess the body and head of St James. An early sixteenth-century sceptic who studied at Glasgow informed his readers that 'there is not one heare nor one bone of the saint Iames in Spayne in Compostell, but only, as they say, his stafe, and all the chayne the whyche he was bounde wyth all in prison and the syckle or hooke, the whyche doth lye vpon the mydell of the hyghe aulter, the whych (they sayd) dyd saw and cutte of the head of saint Iames the more'.[133] Nevertheless, astute international promotion by the Galicians ensured that a cult which had barely been heard of beyond the Pyrenees in the tenth century had become, by the later middle ages, a major focus of international attention, attracting not just pilgrims but financial donations from afar too.[134] Some Scots were apparently travelling there by the thirteenth century and they continued to do so at least occasionally until the sixteenth century.[135] This, moreover, was a journey to boast about and those, such as Sir Thomas Maule of Panmure and Marion Pringle, whose seals depicted scallop shells, probably had either visited

[129] *Chron. Bower* (Watt), vii, 277. See too G. Dickson, 'The crowd at the feet of Pope Boniface VIII: pilgrimage, crusade and the first Roman Jubilee, 1300', *Journal of Medieval History*, 25 (1999), 279-307.

[130] *Rot. Scot.*, ii, 154.

[131] *CSSR*, ii, 32, 35, 44.

[132] *CDS*, iv, nos. 1217, 1229; *CPL*, x, 468-70; D. McRoberts, 'The Scottish national churches in Rome', *IR*, 1 (1950), 112-3.

[133] Andrew Borde, *The Fyrst Boke of the Introduction of Knowledge*, ed. F.J. Furnivall (Early English Text Society, 1870), 204.

[134] NAS Edinburgh, GD103/2/1/2.

[135] *Paisley Reg.*, 90-1.

Compostella themselves or had forebears who had done so.[136] Presumably these visitors were oblivious to some of the promotional literature for the Compostellan shrine which alleged that the sexual preference exemplified by the Navarese for mules (graphically described) derived from their supposed Scottish descent.[137]

In addition to the three principal shrines, others visited by Scots in the later middle ages included those of St Magnus at Kirkwall, St Nicholas at Calais, St Andrew at Amalfi (where the Apostle's grave was located) and the church of Wilsnack in Saxony (which rose to fame after 1383 following the discovery of three Hosts which were allegedly oozing blood).[138] In this second division of pilgrimage destinations, those which seem to have attracted the greatest Scottish attention were Canterbury (where the tomb of St Thomas Becket was located) and from the fourteenth century Amiens (where one of medieval Europe's three supposed heads of St John the Baptist might be venerated). Indeed, of those Scots who between 1488 and 1529 sought licences under the privy seal to undertake a pilgrimage abroad, more intended to travel to Amiens than to all the other shrines combined.

Explanations for the choice of destination are rarely made explicit in the surviving evidence, but it is reasonable to assume that different factors may have influenced different pilgrims. Of course, those judicially instructed to undertake a pilgrimage had little choice in determining their destination, and it was probably no accident that the locations chosen for such individuals were often not the closest to hand. Neither, for Scots, were the three greatest centres of Latin pilgrimage. Nevertheless, the very arduousness of journeys to the Holy Land, Rome or Compostella was perhaps for some a part of their attraction, along with the overriding significance which Jerusalem and Rome in particular held in the Christian psyche. Such feelings were no doubt intensified by the promotional literature which was available in Aberdeen and Glasgow, and perhaps elsewhere too, for pilgrimages to these two locations.[139]

For other pilgrims, shrines dedicated to a saint associated with one's name or occupation were among the possible attractions of one site as opposed to another. In 1506, for example, the earl of Crawford decided to visit the shrine of St John at Amiens: the earl's Christian name was John and his family was patron of an altar dedicated to the same saint in the parish church of Dundee.[140] For Crawford, at least, there seems to have been good reason to choose Amiens, though for many of the other Scots who flocked there, it may

---

[136] Laing, *Seals*, nos. 571, 676. See too ibid, no. 879: Archbishop James Beaton's seal, depicting St James the Lesser holding a pilgrim's staff.

[137] *The Pilgrim's Guide to Santiago de Compostela*, ed. W. Melczer (New York, 1993), 95.

[138] E.g. *CDS*, iv, no. 1254; v, no. 840; *Rot. Scot.*, ii, 347; *RRS*, vi, no. 203; *RSS*, i, no. 1606; M. Dilworth, 'Two Scottish pilgrims in Germany', *IR*, 18 (1967), 21. On Calais and Wilsnack as pilgrimage centres, see J. Sumption, *Pilgrimage: An image of medieval religion* (London, 1975), 282-4, 293.

[139] *Aberdeen Reg.*, ii, 156; *Glasgow Reg.*, ii, 604-8.

[140] *RSS*, i, no. 1251; E. Torrie, *Medieval Dundee: A town and its people* (Dundee, 1990), 89.

have been simple word of mouth and fashion which encouraged them in that direction. Amiens, moreover, was not far away from Scotland, and for some convenience was probably an important factor in determining location. In 1508 Master John Watson, parson of Ellem, wished to visit Amalfi, while in 1531 the prior of Blantyre opted for Rome.[141] For both men, however, pilgrimage was essentially an adjunct to other business in Italy: Watson intended to study there, while the prior sought to purchase ecclesiastical benefices in Rome. For yet others, the spiritual perquisites on offer at particular pilgrimage centres were perhaps a deciding factor.

Reports of recent miracles frequently drew pilgrims to particular locations, even if, as at Wilsnack in the fifteenth century, the reports were considered fraudulent by the ecclesiastical authorities. Other frauds were also perpetrated to entice the gullible pilgrim. The church of St Nicholas in Calais, for example, offered what were reputed to be plenary indulgences associated with travel to major shrines, even though in 1402 Boniface IX had revoked the right of lesser churches to advertise these. One further calculation which was perhaps taken into account was political. In the high middle ages many Scots had ventured on pilgrimages to Durham and Canterbury. Despite the more hostile nature of Anglo-Scottish relations in the later middle ages, English pilgrimage sites did not lose their appeal: Canterbury remained popular, perhaps partly because of its association with another victim of the English monarchy, and Walsingham became popular. But Scottish veneration of St Cuthbert, patron of the shrine at Durham, declined markedly after the outbreak of war and few Scots seem to have visited Durham for pilgrimage purposes in the later middle ages. St Cuthbert, whose banner was paraded by English armies invading Scotland, perhaps did not seem the most sympathetic of saints.[142]

Since pilgrimage was an optional component of Christian devotion, and there were in any case many accessible Scottish shrines, economic logic might suggest that foreign pilgrimages were a luxury. If they were a luxury, they were not one which greatly appealed to Scottish royalty. Both Alexander II and his queen ventured as far as Canterbury; David II planned visits to Walsingham and Canterbury; and Margaret Logie (his queen) allegedly died whilst on pilgrimage to Rome. No other king or queen (in our period) ventured beyond the realm on pilgrimage, though James III seems to have seriously considered a pilgrimage to Amiens, while James IV arranged for payments to be made on his behalf at Compostella.[143] Magnates and knights were more frequent foreign pilgrims, as were members of the clergy

---

[141] *RSS*, i, no. 1606; ii, no. 1042.

[142] For the general points made in this paragraph, see J. Sumption, *Pilgrimage*, 282-84; A. Goodman, 'The Anglo-Scottish marches in the fifteenth century' in R.A. Mason, ed., *Scotland and England, 1286-1815* (Edinburgh, 1987), 28-9.

[143] *CDS*, i, nos. 855-56; ii, no. 67; *Rot. Scot.*, i, 881, 887, 899, 900, 901 ii, 453, 455, 457; *Chron. Bower* (Watt), vii, 359; I.H. Stewart, 'Some Scottish ceremonial coins', *PSAS*, 98 (1964-66), 256-61; *TA*, iv, 41.

(especially the regular clergy if the impressionistic nature of the evidence is at all reliable), and to their number at least a few burgesses should be added. On occasions members of the lay elite would also take their wives: in 1362 Margaret Hogg from Edinburgh intended to accompany her burgess husband Roger to Compostella; more unusually, in 1426 Sir Patrick Dunbar and Sir Gilbert Hay sought safe-conducts for their wives to visit Canterbury, apparently without their husbands.[144] Travellers of this social standing were frequently accompanied by large entourages – the earl of Atholl planned to take one hundred horsemen to Canterbury in 1404, and even the abbot of Dunfermline, at about the same time, expected to visit Rome with sixteen horsemen.[145]

Inclusion in such a group perhaps provided an opportunity for some more humble members of Scottish society also to view the major continental shrines. The extant evidence, however, rarely names these more ordinary Scots. Moreover, its very nature (in the form of safe-conducts, licences to travel abroad, papal supplications and chronicle references) not surprisingly conveys an elitist image of foreign pilgrimage which is perhaps not valid. It may be doubted whether the humbler pilgrim, travelling either alone or with those of similar social standing, bothered with safe-conducts. Honoré de Bonet, for one, considered it unnecessary for pilgrims to obtain safe-conducts.[146] Moreover, simple pilgrims were not the sort of people with whom chroniclers were greatly concerned. A chance snippet of evidence from Breslau would, however, suggest that poor pilgrims were by no means unknown. There, in *c*.1470, a number of Scots were arraigned before the local magistrates on charges of vagrancy, presumably while heading for the Baltic in order to sail home. Their number included at least five pilgrims who had been overtaken by illness and penury while allegedly undertaking visits to Rome or Compostella, and in one instance to both.[147]

Fighting for God: The Crusade

Crusades, like pilgrimages, were a voluntary rather than an obligatory element in Christian life. While in the modern popular imagination crusading is inextricably linked with mugging Saracens in the Holy Land, in the middle ages it offered spiritual benefits. Foremost among these was the grant of a plenary remission of sin of the sort which was also bestowed on jubilee pilgrims. Indeed, there is more than a germ of truth in the old adage that a crusade was an armed pilgrimage, since the vows which pilgrims and crusaders took were similar and the rationale behind the first crusade (1096-99) had been to defend Christendom's holiest shrines in the middle east. The success of this venture stimulated further crusading activity which was designed to recover

[144] *Rot. Scot.*, i, 859-60; *CDS*, v, no.999.
[145] *CDS*, iv, nos. 656, 715.
[146] *The Tree of Battles by Honoré Bonnet*, ed. G.W. Copland (Liverpool, 1979), 187-88.
[147] Fischer, *Germany*, 241-42.

formerly Christian lands thought to have been unjustly seized by Islamic powers. It is important to emphasise that these crusades were conceived as defensive undertakings, rather than as intrinsically anti-Islamic adventures, for it was not only in the middle east that Christians perceived a threat to Christendom. In the Iberian peninsula the early medieval advance of Islam had also occupied once Christian territories, while in the lands of the eastern Baltic Christians confronted a pagan population which, although not in possession of previously Christian territory, was still viewed as hostile to Christian missionaries and neighbouring Christian kingdoms. Within the bounds of Christendom, heretics, such as the Cathars in thirteenth-century France and the Hussites in fifteenth-century Bohemia, were perceived as posing a similar threat in that they challenged the true path to salvation.

Traditionally historians regarded only those attempts to recover the Holy Land as valid crusades but a growing school of 'pluralist' historians has argued that crusades in other theatres were viewed by contemporaries as equally just and valid undertakings. This view was shared not least by the medieval papacy which, on behalf of Christ, authorised the Spanish and Baltic crusades, and subsequently others against heretics and schismatics too, bestowing the same spiritual benefits on all crusaders, irrespective of where they fought for the Cross. This redefinition of fundamental crusading terminology has served to focus attention not just on the earlier crusades beyond the Holy Land but also on later medieval crusades in general. Acre, the last Latin outpost in the middle east, fell to the Mameluks in 1291. Thereafter there were few direct attempts to recover possession of the Holy Land itself. But military challenges continued to be mounted in defence of Christendom against what were perceived to be the hostile and threatening forces of Islam, paganism, heresy and schism.[148]

In most western European kingdoms monarchs had traditionally set an example to their fellow countrymen when it came to crusading. To Castilian, Aragonese and Portuguese kings *reconquista* was a way of life and those, such as Henry IV of Castile, who barely even paid lip service to the ideal, faced critical demands to rectify their ways. Some Scandinavian monarchs had participated in the early crusades to the Holy Land and their successors were periodically active in the northern crusades. Most of the twelfth- and thirteenth-century Plantagenet and Capetian kings took the Cross and several actually fulfilled their vows. Scottish monarchs, by contrast, were lacklustre in their enthusiasm for crusade. Of the original royal family, not even the quasi-saintly David I had taken the Cross and Alexander III ignored personal appeals from Popes Innocent V in 1276 and Martin IV in 1282 to do so.[149] The main line of the Stewart dynasty, with the exception of James IV, also displayed

---

[148] The most recent powerful expositions of the pluralist school are J. Riley-Smith, *What Were the Crusades?* (2nd ed., Basingstoke, 1992) and N. Housley, *The Later Crusades: From Lyons to Alcazar, 1274-1580* (Oxford, 1992).

[149] P.C. Ferguson, *Medieval Papal Representatives in Scotland: Legates, nuncios and judges-delegate, 1125-1286* (Stair Soc., 1997), 115.

little passion for crusading either before or after its elevation to the royal dignity.

In the short-lived Bruce dynasty alone was there greater enthusiasm for crusading. Both Robert I's father and grandfather, along with his mother's first husband, had travelled abroad on crusade, and the crusading vow which Robert himself took in later life is well attested. David II, like his father, did not personally undertake a crusade. Nevertheless, his enthusiasm for crusading is recorded by Bower and Wyntoun and exemplified by the trouble which David took to meet the Cypriot King Peter, during the latter's visit to the English court in 1363 in order to raise money and stimulate crusading awareness.[150] But if, the Bruces apart, most Scottish kings displayed little interest in the crusading movement, others were more attracted to the notion. In the later thirteenth century a large number of Scottish and Anglo-Scottish aristocrats, including the earls of March, Carrick and Atholl, numerous lesser barons, knights and their retinues, set off to join the crusades led both by Louis IX of France (to Damietta in 1249 and Tunis in 1270) and by the future Edward I of England (to the Holy Land in 1270).[151] Crusading was the mark of a good knight and even a political foe might be admired for such endeavour. The Englishman Sir Giles d'Argentan, for instance, was lauded by John Barbour as 'the third best knight who lived in his time'. Why? Because 'he fought three campaigns against Saracens, and in each of those campaigns he defeated two Saracens'.[152]

Scottish crusading fervour was, however, seriously dampened by the outbreak of the wars of independence. Appeals from Philip IV of France to participate in a crusade were evaded in 1309, and in 1320 the Declaration of Arbroath was blunt in its assurance to Pope John XXII that '...he from whom nothing is hidden well knows how cheerfully we and our lord the king would go there [i.e. to the Holy Land] if the king of the English would leave us in peace'.[153] Left unsaid, but no doubt fully appreciated by author and recipient of the Declaration alike, was the further obstacle that the pope, who was responsible for authorising crusades, had excommunicated most of the potential stock of Scottish crusaders between 1319 and 1320.[154] Moreover, although this too was wisely omitted from diplomatic correspondence sent to the pope, leading Scottish clerics had insidiously undermined the crusading ideal ever since 1296 by seeking to 'sanctify' the war against England. Robert Wishart, the bishop of Glasgow, for instance, allegedly exclaimed in 1306 that it was 'just as meritorious [to join Robert I's forces] as to go in the service of

---

[150] *Chron. Bower* (Watt), vii, 361; *Chron. Froissart* (Lettenhove), vi, 385.

[151] Macquarrie, *Crusades*, 47-63.

[152] *The Bruce* (Duncan), 496.

[153] *APS*, i, 459; A.A.M. Duncan. *The Nation of Scots and the Declaration of Arbroath* (London, 1970), 36.

[154] G.G. Simpson, 'The Declaration of Arbroath revitalised', *SHR*, 56 (1977), 17-18.

God to the Holy Land'.[155] Fighting the English, it would seem, was more important than fighting for God.

It is hardly surprising, then, that virtually no Scottish crusading activity is recorded in the first half of the fourteenth century, with the single exception of Sir James Douglas's entourage which, with Robert I's heart in tow, lent support to Alfonso XI of Castile's attack on the Moorish citadel of Teba de Hardales in 1330.[156] Yet this episode is instructive. Behind the dark shadow which the Anglo-Scottish conflict has cast over later medieval Scottish history, it is all too easy to lose sight of broader horizons and forget the enormous impact which the fall of Acre, the last Christian outpost in the Holy Land, had had on contemporaries. Early fourteenth-century Christendom was awash with crusading fervour intent on recuperating the losses of 1291. Philip IV's ambitions to lead a crusade appear to have been genuine and had fuelled the imagination of thousands of peasants from England, France, the Low Countries and Germany who in 1309 and again in 1320 left home with the intention of heading for the Holy Land.[157] In the diplomatic correspondence of 1309 and 1320 the Scots were responding to an issue which was of genuine international concern. And given the king's own last wishes and his background – he came, as we have seen, from good crusading stock – it is tempting to accept that the Scots were not just making cynical, anglophobic propaganda points in excusing their participation in crusades. They were also expressing the king's piety.

The mission led by Douglas did not, however, mark an end to the hiatus in Scottish crusading activity any more than the 1328 treaty of Edinburgh-Northampton marked a conclusion of the Anglo-Scottish wars. Only from the 1350s, as Anglo-Scottish conflict became less pronounced, was there a resumption in Scottish crusading fervour. Yet few followed Douglas's example by heading for the Iberian arena. The *reconquista* was pursued only fitfully between the 1330s and the 1480s, so crusading opportunities there were limited. Even once the Catholic monarchs Ferdinand of Aragon and Isabella of Castile had revived the *reconquista* ethos they appear to have won little Scottish support. To date only one Scot (Johannes Villesetun) has been noted in Aragonese service during the campaign which led to the final collapse of the Moorish kingdom of Granada in 1492, to whom the Franco-Scottish lord of Aubigny, Bernard Stewart, can perhaps be added. Years later, ridden with gout, Aubigny was reported spending time with a nostalgic Ferdinand 'en parlant de leurs vielles guerres de Grenade'.[158]

[155] Macquarrie, *Crusades*, 71.
[156] S. Cameron, 'Sir James Douglas, Spain and the Holy Land' in T. Brotherstone and D. Ditchburn, eds., *Freedom and Authority: Scotland c.1050-c.1650* (East Linton, 2000), 108-17; *The Bruce* (Duncan), 750-52.
[157] Housley, *Later Crusades*, 26-9, 32.
[158] Macquarrie, *Crusades*, 106; Jean d'Auton, *Chronique de Louis XI* (Paris, 1889-95), ed. R. de Maulde la Clavière, iv, 357-58.

Only a handful of Scots seem to have been involved in Middle Eastern enterprises too. Robert Erskine had taken a vow to fight Saracens before 1359, but then sought release from his vow.[159] William Ramsay and David Barclay (in 1363) and Walter Moigne and Laurence de Gelybrand (in 1366) received English safe-conducts for themselves and their retinues to travel to the Holy Land, presumably for a crusade, and, if they indeed went, they were perhaps joined by Norman and Walter Leslie, two Scottish esquires who are recorded at Alexandria in 1365. At least one Scottish 'knight' (possibly Norman Leslie) met his death during the Cypriot king's stunning capture of the Egyptian port in 1365.[160] Sir Alexander Stewart (perhaps of Darnley, though possibly of Ralston) joined the Barbary Crusade of 1390 while in c.1395 Alexander and David Lindsay enrolled in Philip de Mezieres's new chivalric order of the Knighthood of the Passion of Jesus Christ, which aimed to reconquer and garrison the Holy Land.[161] In the fifteenth century the Mediterranean continued to offer an outlet for crusading enthusiasm, but even fewer Scots than in the previous century responded. Some, such as Robert Arbuthnott and his wife, made financial contributions to the war against the Turks.[162] Others, such as Sir Colin Campbell of Glenorchy, served with the Knights of St John at their base on Rhodes, but only three Scots (Alexander Preston, Richard Murray and Peter Hunter) are known to have actually taken up arms against Islam in the Mediterranean arena.[163]

If Scots were generally unattracted by Iberian and Middle Eastern adventures, they displayed a greater appetite for the offerings of the Baltic. English safe-conducts for travel to the northern crusade were issued to Moigne, the Leslies and Thomas Bisset and their company in 1357 and to David Barclay of Brechin and his companions in 1362.[164] A fourteen-year Anglo-Scottish truce was confirmed in 1369 and the ensuing years witnessed a spurt of further Scottish crusading activity in the Baltic. In February 1370 Simon Preston, John Abernethy, John Edmonstone, John Tours and Sir John of Monymusk were all in Königsberg, almost certainly to participate in one of the almost annual winter expeditions (*Reisen*) in Prussia.[165] The Austrian poet Peter Suchenwirt noted the involvement of three Scottish knights ('Ekhart, Wilhelm und Ritschart') in a campaign led in 1377 by Albrecht, duke of

[159] *CPP*, i, 346.
[160] *Rot. Scot.*, i, 877, 901;
[161] 'List of Additions to the Department of Manuscripts, 1845' in *Catalogue of Additions to the Manuscripts in the British Museum in the Years MDCCCXLI-MDCCCXLV* (London, 1850), 41. (The identification of Stewart of Ralston is suggested by W. Fraser, *The Douglas Book* (Edinburgh, 1885), i, 18; that of Stewart of Darnley by the *Armorial de Geldre*, on which see below, page 70-1.) N. Jorga, *Philippe de Mezieres, 1327-1405, et La Croisade au XIVe Siècle* (Paris, 1896; repr.,1976), 491.
[162] NAS Edinburgh, RH1/2/284.
[163] Macquarrie, *Crusades*, 93-5.
[164] *Rot. Scot.*, i, 797, 869.
[165] NAS Edinburgh, GD143/1/2; RH1/2/130.

Austria, and the following year Adam Hepburn received an English safe-conduct to join the Prussian crusade.[166]

Following another Anglo-Scottish truce, agreed in 1389, an unnamed Scottish knight was a beneficiary of the largesse distributed by the crucesignatus earl of Derby in 1391.[167] It was probably also in the summer of that year, during the papal schism, that Sir William Douglas of Nithsdale led a contingent of Scots to Prussia which included Sir James and Sir William Douglas of Strathbrock and Sir Robert Stewart of Durisdeer. This expedition began with an infamous brawl between English and Scottish crusaders outside the church of St Mary in Königsberg, which quickly escalated as the adherents of the Roman pope intervened on behalf of the English, while the Scots were supported by those who recognised the Avignon pope.[168] Still, William Douglas's unhappy fate – he was murdered in the *fracas* before the planned crusade – did not dissuade others from venturing to Prussia. In 1400 Abernethy was granted another English safe-conduct for travel there and the French chronicler Enguerran de Monstrelet reported the presence of 'le bastard d'Escoce qui se appeloit conte de Hembe' at the battle of Tannenberg in 1410.[169] Tannenberg, however, marked a horrendous defeat for the Teutonic Order at the hands of the Poles, and though it marked neither the end of the Teutonic Order nor of the northern crusade, it did lead to a sharp decline in the recruitment of foreign crusaders.[170]

In addition to identifiable Scottish participants in the northern crusade, there were no doubt others of whom no specific trace now survives. It seems possible, for instance, that many of the Scottish knights whose arms are displayed in the *Armorial de Gelre* were Prussian crusaders. The arms of Walter Leslie, John Edmonstone and John Abernethy (all known Prussian crusaders) are included among these late fourteenth-century depictions, along

[166] *Scriptores Rerum Prussicarum*, ed. T. Hirsch, M. Toeppen and E. Strehlke (Leipzig, 1861-74), ii, 168; *Rot.Scot.*, ii, 13.

[167] *Expeditions to Prussia and the Holy Land Made by Henry, Earl of Derby*, ed. L.T. Smith (Camden Soc., 1894), 111.

[168] The relevant passages from Scottish, French and Prussian chronicles are published in Fischer, *Germany*, 275-78 and partly in *Documents on the Later Crusades, 1274-1580*, ed. N. Housley (Basingstoke, 1996), 56, 103-4. For a particularly illuminating English account, unnoticed by most modern commentators, see *Chron. Westminster*, 474-77. The incident is discussed by Fischer, *Germany*, 70-2; E. Keyser, 'Die Ermorderung des schottischen Grafen William Douglas in Danzig im Jahre 1391', *Mitteilungen des westpreussichen Geschichtsverein*, 27 (1924); Macquarrie, *Crusades*, 85-7; P. Simson, *Geschichte der Stadt Danzig bis 1926* (Danzig, 1913), i, 104. The pedantic matter of the date and place of William Douglas's death is discussed in Ditchburn, Thesis, 447-9, 453-6. The identity of William Douglas's companions is suggested by financial agreements made at Bruges on 10 November 1390 and subsequently at Danzig (NAS Edinburgh, AD/1/27; *Reports of the Royal Commission on Historical Manuscripts, 11th Report* (London, 1887), 210-11).

[169] *CDS*, iv, no. 593; *La Chronique d'Enguerran de Monstrelet*, ed. L. Douet d'Arcq (Paris, 1857-62), ii, 76. For different suggestions regarding the identity of this character, see Macquarrie, *Crusades*, 88; D. Ditchburn, 'The pirate, the policeman and the pantomime star: Aberdeen's alternative economy in the early fifteenth century', *NS*, 12 (1992), 24-5, 33 n.51.

[170] E. Christiansen, *The Northern Crusades: The Baltic and the Catholic frontier, 1100-1525* (London, 1980), 221-22, 233.

with those of Robert Erskine, David Lindsay, Alexander Stewart of Darnley (who are known to have had other crusading interests) and Thomas Erskine, Patrick Hepburn, James Lindsay, Henry Preston, Alexander Ramsey, John Stewart and 'the lord of Seton', all of whom had at least namesakes if not relations with crusading interests.[171] Scottish knights heading for Prussia might well have passed through Guelders, and been spotted by the compiler of the Armorial as they did so, and it was among some of the families whom he recorded (the Leslies, Prestons and Setons) that the Christian name George found popularity. It was under the banner of St George that the foreign adventurers who assisted the Teutonic Order frequently fought.[172]

Yet, even including this Gueldrian element of conjecture, it remains difficult to accept that the level of Scottish commitment to the northern crusade was striking.[173] The Baltic was the most popular destination for later fourteenth-century Scottish crusaders, but even if the numbers of those who *might* have gone there are tallied, only 78 Scots can be enumerated, or less than two per year.[174] The earls who had graced earlier Scottish crusading expeditions were now also missing, save for the mysterious 'conte de Hembe'. There remained, by and large, lesser knights, many of them, such as the Leslies and David Barclay, clearly crusade junkies. Crusading, in practice, had become the pastime of a committed, but small, knightly minority. It is impossible to know for sure what motivated this minority. Familiarity with the crusade-enthusiast David II was probably one factor: it is this which links Sir Thomas Bisset, Sir David Barclay, Sir Walter Moigne, the Erskines, the Lindsays and the Leslies, and perhaps too the 'sir R [?] Comyn' of the Armorial, if Sir R may be equated with Sir Richard Comyn, a close adherent of Walter Leslie in Ross.[175] There was also a Douglas crusading affinity, exemplified not just by the Douglases already noted, but by their adherents Sir John Edmonstone and, from the *Armorial*, (Sir James?) Sandilands (of Calder?) and Sir Robert Colville. Other families displayed an even more enduring tradition of foreign crusade or pilgrimage. A papal letter of 1455 to Alexander Preston, canon of Glasgow, notes that Preston and his father and many other kinsmen before him had fought the Turks and, as we have seen, Simon Preston and possibly Henry Preston joined the northern crusade, while in 1529 George Preston made plans to visit two foreign pilgrimage shrines following a vow he had made to Simon Preston.[176]

---

[171] A.H. Dunbar, 'Facsimiles of the Scottish coats of arms emblazoned in the *Armorial de Gelre*', *PSAS*, 25 (1890-91), 9-19. I owe this line of enquiry to Steve Boardman.

[172] Housely, *Documents*, 5, 14, 55-8.

[173] Macquarrie, *Crusades*, 84-8.

[174] The figure of seventy-eight includes all those enumerated on safe-conducts; those from other sources likely to have have gone to Prussia; and the twenty-two non-comital figures whose arms appear on the *Armorial*.

[175] Boardman, *Early Stewart Kings*, 14-15, 76-7.

[176] *CPL*, xi, 158-59; *RSS*, i, no. 4064.

For others personal motivations were probably more significant. These were probably fed by word of mouth. In the thirteenth century the papal legate John of Salerno (in 1201) and the bishops of Glasgow and St Andrews (in 1213) had informed their clerical colleagues of imminent crusading plans, and they no doubt told others.[177] Seasoned crusading veterans, such as the French sire de Beaugeau, who visited Scotland in 1352, and the Tyrolean knight Oswald von Wolkenstein, who had served in Prussia between 1377 and 1385 and who was in Scotland in 1388, probably also regaled those whom they met with crusading tales.[178] In addition to informal publicity for its ventures, the Teutonic Order also sent out appeals and agents specifically designed to recruit crusaders. Its grand-masters Conrad and Ulrich von Jungingen (1394-1407; 1407-1410) possessed an address list of European rulers which included the names of Robert III and David, duke of Rothesay.[179] We are, however, ignorant of the precise message which men such as Beaugeau, Wolkenstein and others may have spread. But we can guess. Crusading, like pilgrimage, presented an opportunity to visit remote, foreign lands, with the additional attraction, in the Baltic, of the sumptuous feasting and ceremony which the Teutonic Order laid on for its foreign recruits. During Anglo-Scottish truces crusading also offered knights a chance to continue the pursuit of their martial interests. It proffered the chance to display honour, prowess and other chivalric virtues. The style of warfare employed in the northern crusade – seasonal raids or *Reisen* – was familiar to Scots with their experience of border warfare. But the essential difference which crusading offered from other types of military service was that, at least theoretically, it was performed in the service of God. It bestowed spiritual benefits. Crusaders were subject to ecclesiastical, not secular, courts; they received ecclesiastical assurances that their lands and possessions would not be seized in their absence; they were granted personal confessors who could grant pardon for sins which were normally reserved to the papacy; and they were offered an indulgence.[180] It evidently mattered little that the victims of crusading endeavour in the later medieval Baltic were the Catholic Poles and after 1386 the recently converted Lithuanians or that, in retrospect, the Teutonic Order's wars may be viewed as nothing more than a sordid campaign of secular expansion.

Yet the fact remains that few Scots sought service in God's armies. Some explanations for this meagre contribution to the later medieval crusade have already been offered. For lengthy periods many Scottish knights were preoccupied with the English war, and it is precisely those who displayed a crusading enthusiasm (largely those from the south of the country) who faced these preoccupations most pressingly. The domestic war, moreover, was a war with a *reconquista* spirit of its own as, in the later fourteenth century, the

---

[177] Ferguson, *Medieval Papal Representatives*, 66, 72-3; Macquarrie, *Crusades*, 32, 34.
[178] *Scriptores Rerum Prussicarum*, ii, 173-74; iii, 453.
[179] GSA Berlin, OF3, 5.
[180] For a concise summary of the spiritual benefits bestowed on crusaders, see Riley-Smith, *Crusades?*, 54-63.

Scots nibbled away at the areas of their country still under English occupation. Prominent clergymen, such as that old hypocrite Robert Wishart, and latterly too the bishop of Galloway, had sought to bless the war as a holy one. The general drift of Scottish attitudes was mirrored elsewhere. Secular governments throughout the later medieval West were increasingly reluctant to commit themselves fully to the type of international crusade which had been the hallmark of earlier centuries. Domestic considerations, for them too, were more pressing, while the increasing sophistication of military technology made crusading more and more financially prohibitive for Scots and others alike. In addition to such practical considerations, some historians have argued that changing devotional habits, and in particular the growing importance of private acts of piety as opposed to public expressions of devotion, also made the actual fate of the traditional crusading arenas less significant to the Christian psyche.[181] Not all would agree, but inaction, along with stunning setbacks such as Tannenberg, certainly contributed to a closing down of crusading opportunities. Yet, as Norman Housley has recently demonstrated, governmental inaction did not spell the end of the crusading ideal. No one, in a Scottish context, exemplified this more than James IV whose diplomacy, from 1509 to 1513, was peppered with crusading allusions and proposals. It matters little at one level whether one regards the king's outpourings as insincere diplomatic posturing or as the sincere naiveté of long, bibulous evenings. In either case the assumptions and aspirations revealed in the king's choice of language are instructive. While not many Christians actually went on crusade during the fifteenth century and later, the crusading ideal was still perceived to have resonance.

The Structural Bonds

In the preceding sections we have examined a variety of religious enthusiasms, from monasticism to the crusade. All of these may be defined as devotional expressions within that common framework of religious belief which, as we saw at the beginning of this chapter, bound Christendom together. The third element in the religious bonding of the Latin West was, in modern parlance, its line management structure. At the apex of this structure stood the papacy, boastful of its 'plenitude of power' since the fifth century.[182] Although the underlying theme of ecclesiastical organisation in the period from the thirteenth to the sixteenth centuries was the rise, and many would argue subsequent fall, of ecclesiastical centralisation and papal supremacy, neither centralisation nor supremacy were of the ancient lineage which papal boasts implied. Until the eleventh century bishops had largely been left to their own devices in tending their flocks; monasticism was international only in the sense that most monks adhered to a similar rule; and the laity rarely came into

---

[181] Housley, *Crusades*, 418-19.
[182] R.W. Southern, *Western Society and the Church in the Middle Ages* (Harmondsworth, 1970), 157-58.

contact with clergymen outwith their own diocese. The organisation of Christianity was diffuse, for although in the earlier eleventh century the bishop of Rome was accorded some vague pre-eminence in ecclesiastical affairs, in reality the horizons of the papacy strayed little beyond the narrow world of Roman politics. The obvious focus for centralisation lay semi-dormant, and it is a reasonable assumption that practically no one in tenth-century Scotland, save perhaps monks and a few other clergy, would have even known the pope's name. In the absence of active papal authority there was little in Latin Christendom to ensure uniformity in belief, practice and, ultimately, in coherence. This began to change in the wake of the monastic and papal reform movements which emerged from the eleventh century. The reform movements were in essence moral – concerned with issues such as the rigorous adherence to monastic ideals, the abandonment of clerical marriages and the proscription of simony (the sale of ecclesiastical office) – but to achieve their ambitions the reformers required the application of centralised direction and discipline. In the monasteries this meant that reformed orders such as the Cluniacs and Cistercians insisted on accountability. Unlike the traditional Benedictine monasteries, the Cluniacs, and more especially still the Cistercians, Premonstratensians, Tironensians, Valliscaulians and Carthusians, sought to regulate practice in each house of their respective orders. Inspections were held to ensure that standards were maintained and chapters-general, which the head of each house was expected to attend, were convened to impose standards. At the papacy too centralisation meant informing the local agents of Christianity about their shortcomings and interfering in the running of the localities in order to rectify perceived flaws.[183] In Pope Gregory VII (1073-1085) the reformers found a pope who was fully committed to their ideals and more ready than most of his predecessors had been to take the initiative. What is surprising is that with their newly acquired moral authority Gregory and his successors succeeded. Bishops began to do what they were told; if they did not, they accepted that they might be summonsed by the pope to answer for their actions; they meekly accepted the usurpation of their own powers under what became a welter of organisational and disciplinary instruction from Rome.

Scotland was not immune to the effects of these developments. Among the secular clergy a chain of command was developed which made parish priests, through various promoted ecclesiastical posts, accountable to a bishop. Bishops were in turn normally accountable to an archbishop and archbishops to the pope. Scotland, however, had no archbishop of its own until the elevation of the bishops of St Andrews and Glasgow to that dignity in 1472 and 1492 respectively. Before then the attempts of the archbishop of York to extend his authority to Scottish bishoprics had been at times thwarted and,

---

[183] For the immediate impact of the Gregorian reform movement on Scotland (and Ireland), see B.T. Hudson, 'Gaelic princes and Gregorian Reform' in idem and V. Ziegler, eds., *Crossed Paths: Methodological approaches to the Celtic aspect of the European middle ages* (Lanham, 1991), 61-82.

instead, in 1189 'the Scottish church', including most Scottish dioceses, was declared a 'special daughter' of the papacy and placed in direct obedience to the Holy See.[184] This was an unusual but not a unique arrangement. Bishops in the Basqueland, central Italy and at Kammin on the Baltic coast were granted a similar status.[185] Nor was it unusual that two Scottish bishops (Galloway and, from 1266, the Isles) remained under the jurisdiction of foreign archbishops (York and Trondheim). Ecclesiastical borders did not, in Latin Christendom, always coincide with political boundaries and similar anomalies can be seen in, for instance, the jurisdiction of both the archbishops of Reims and Lyon which extended beyond the bounds of French territory and onto imperial lands.[186] Still, when compared with Ireland, which had four archbishops, the Scottish situation does seem somewhat anomalous. Although explanations for the arrangement which the papacy made with the Scottish church are difficult to find, papal reasoning was probably governed by political considerations. The pope probably did not wish to reward an English king held responsible for the murder of the archbishop of Canterbury by delivering the Scottish church to another English archbishop; but neither did he wish to antagonise one of the most powerful monarchs in the Latin West by granting the Scottish church its own archbishop.

The Scottish bishops, then, were directly dependent on the pope and became 'in an everyday sense the harassed agents of popes, busy in the exercise of the papal plentitude of power.'[187] Yet, for all their direct obedience to the pope, the pope decided that in certain matters bishops could not be trusted. During the thirteenth century, for instance, the right of bishops across Christendom to offer indulgences was curtailed. Their role in the canonisation process was undermined and the nomination of saints, along with the authentification of relics, was instead reserved for the papacy to determine. And in *c*.1233 episcopal determination of heresy was superseded by the Inquisition, whose members were appointed by, and accountable to, the pope personally.[188] Bishops' rights were further undermined by papal grants of exemption from episcopal authority. Certain monasteries, such as the Benedictine house of Iona, were removed from episcopal oversight and local

---

[184] I adopt the date suggested by A.D.M. Barrell, 'The background to *Cum Universi*: Scoto-papal relations, 1159-1192', *IR*, 46 (1995), 116-38, rather then the more traditional date of 1192. The bishopric of Argyll was omitted from the original grant: see ibid, 133-135 and, for a different view, A.A.M. Duncan, *Scotland: The making of the kingdom* (Edinburgh, 1975), 275-76.

[185] L.J. Macfarlane, 'The primacy of the Scottish church, 1472-1521', *IR*, 20 (1969); L.J. Macfarlane, 'The elevation of the diocese of Glasgow into an archbishopric in 1492', *IR*, 43 (1992); R.K. Rose, 'Latin episcopal sees at the end of the thirteenth Century' in A. Mackay and D. Ditchburn, eds., *Atlas of Medieval Europe* (London, 1997), 110-13.

[186] ibid, 111; R.D. Oram. 'In obedience and reverence: Whithorn and York, *c*.1128-*c*.1250', *IR*, 42 (1991), 83-100.

[187] Duncan, *Scotland*, 285.

[188] A.I. Dunlop, 'Remissions and indulgences in fifteenth-century Scotland', *RSCHS*, 15 (1966), 154; E.W. Kemp, *Canonization and Authority in the Western Church* (London, 1948), 106-13; B. Hamilton, *The Medieval Inquisition* (London, 1981), 38, 73.

bishops were then not normally permitted to undertake visitations of these houses.[189] Certain other ecclesiastical foundations were granted similar privileges. In 1470 the collegiate church of St Giles in Edinburgh, for instance, was removed from the oversight of the bishop of St Andrews.[190]

The chain of episcopal command was not, then, as simple as it might at first sight appear.   The chain of command among the regular clergy does not even seem simple. The Benedictines, Augustinians and Valliscaulians were all subject to local episcopal oversight; the Cluniacs, Tironensians, Cistercians, Premonstratensians and Carthusians were not. The Benedictines, Augustinians and, from 1165, the Tironensians were not subject to the authority of external mother-houses; the Cluniacs, Cistercians, Premonstratensians, Valliscaulians and Carthusians were.

The extent of external supervision was, however, variable. That the Scottish Cluniac monasteries of Paisley and Crossraguel were accorded abbatial, as opposed to priory, status bespeaks a degree of autonomy not normally bestowed on other Cluniac foundations. When petitioning for Paisley's elevation in 1219, Alexander II had quite candidly argued that regular visits to Cluny had caused the monks of Paisley 'much danger and injury'.[191]Although thereafter the monks maintained some contacts with Cluny – and in 1517 the abbot of Cluny still claimed the right to adjudicate in disputes between Paisley and Crossraguel – visitations from the continent were apparently rare. By the mid-fifteenth century there is no evidence that the abbots of the two Scottish Cluniac houses attended the chapters-general of their order in Cluny.[192] Meanwhile, in practice the Valliscaulians too appear to have evaded both episcopal and monastic supervision for lengthy periods, while Premonstratensian abbots were being censured by the early sixteenth century for their failure to attend chapters-general at Premontré.[193] By the later middle ages the internationalism of these orders was moribund.

At the other extreme stood the Dominicans and Perth Charterhouse. Even in the early sixteenth century the former were frequently represented at chapters-general of the order, normally held in Italy. Meanwhile, the Charterhouse's links with La Grande Chartreuse remained intimate and, although the Perth prior was excused attendance at chapters-general except in leap years, strict adherence to monastic ideals appears to have been maintained by the Carthusians almost everywhere.[194]

[189] Cowan and Easson, *Religious Houses*, 59.
[190] A.D.M. Barrell, *The Papacy, Scotland and Northern England, 1342-1378* (Cambridge, 1995), 19.
[191] *Pailsey Reg.*, 8.
[192] PRONI Belfast, D623/B/7/1/12; Dilworth, 'Franco-Scottish efforts', 206-8. See too idem, 'Cluniac Paisley: its constitutional status and prestige' and idem, 'Letters from Paisley' in J. Malden, ed., *The Monastery and Abbey of Paisley* (Glasgow, 2000), 23-26, 169-72.
[193] ibid, 208-10; Dilworth, *Scottish Monasteries*, 33-4.
[194] A. Ross, 'Libraries of the Scottish Blackfriars, 1480-1560', *IR*, 20 (1969), 12; W.N.M. Beckett, 'The Perth Charterhouse before 1500', *Analecta Cartusiana*, 128 (1988), 1-74; *James V Letters*, 300.

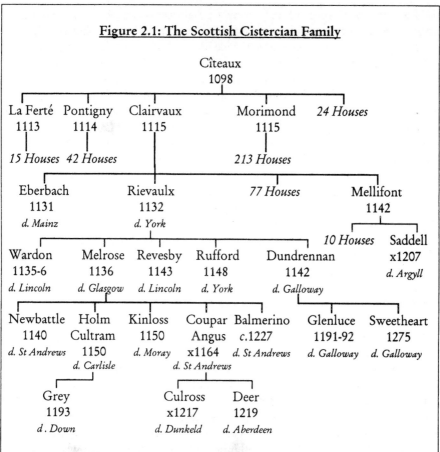

Figure 2.1: The Scottish Cistercian Family

Key: dates = date of foundation; *d.* = located in diocese of.
Source: R.H.C Davis, *History of Medieval Europe* (Harlow, 1970), 273 with additional information
from I.B. Cowan and D.E. Easson, *Medieval Religious Houses Scotland* (2nd ed., Harlow, 1976) and
A. Gwynn and R.N. Hadcock, *Medieval Religious Houses: Ireland* (London, 1970).

While much less successful in maintaining their ideals, the Cistercians too retained at least the vestiges of internationalism. Like the prior of the Charterhouse, Cistercian abbots were granted leave of absence from three out of four of the annual chapters-general of the order. Still, at least in the thirteenth century, the affairs of the order's Scottish houses were frequently debated and we can probably assume that Scottish representatives were present on such occasions.[195] Moreover, Cîteaux appointed visitors to inspect its Scottish offspring. Some were Scottish abbots (and not necessarily any the less rigorous for that), but others were foreign. In 1409, for instance, the abbot

[195] *Statuta Capitolorum Generalium Ordinis Cisterciensis ab anno 1116 ad annum 1786*, ed. J.-M. Canivez (Louvain, 1933-39), i, 67, 360, 427; ii, 63, 15, 226, 267, 295, 345, 359, 382-83, 456; iii, 45, 63, 88, 123-24, 138, 145, 149, 213-14.

of Pontigny undertook an inspection of Scottish houses; in 1488 and 1506 monks from Cîteaux itself visited Scotland; and in 1531 the abbot of Chaalis was appointed to a comparatively well documented inspection which met with local resistance on the grounds of the severity of its proposed reforms.[196] Centralised inspections were supplemented by filial inspections. As indicated in Figure 2.1, each Cistercian monastery had originally been founded by monks from another house. These ties established a mother-daughter relationship among all Cistercian houses. Melrose and Dundrennan were 'mothers' to a number of Scottish houses, and Melrose at least undertook visitations not only of its Scottish daughters but also, at least until the 1470s, of its Cumbrian offshoot at Holm Cultram.[197] Saddell in Argyll had been born of a different lineage to the other Scottish Cistercians, but before its suppression in *c*.1507, it still maintained some contact with its Irish mother, Mellifont. In 1393 – despite the Schism – mother Mellifont had been approached to confirm 'according to the usual custom' the election of a new abbot at Saddell. Such contact did not, however, prevent the disappearance of monastic life by the time of the monastery's suppression.[198] As this demonstrates, it is not structures themselves, but rather their effective implementation that is of actual significance.

Financial Obligations

Interest in the localities was at its most intrusive in matters of finance and provision to clerical office. Financial demands on the clergy of Christendom came from two distinct quarters. Certain monastic orders, such as the Cluniacs and Cistercians, imposed taxation on all the monasteries of their order with the intention, ostensibly at least, of providing funds for the crusades. Quotas were imposed on each house according to its resources, and wealthy Cistercian abbeys, such as Dundrennan, Melrose and Coupar Angus, were bound to pay over substantial sums which ranked alongside those paid by the richest Cistercian abbeys in France.[199] Whether by the fifteenth century these were still being paid with regularity is more doubtful: Cîteaux and Cluny certainly complained that they were not.[200]

The sums to be raised from monastic taxation were, however, paltry when compared to the financial ambitions of the papacy. Some papal dues were of ancient origin, though levies such as Peter's Pence and census (paid by ecclesiastical foundations which were exempt from normal episcopal oversight) appear to have been raised only rarely in Scotland.[201] Scotland, too,

---

[196] Dilworth, 'Franco-Scottish efforts', 215-20; Dilworth, *Scottish Monasteries*, 35, 37-8.
[197] Dilworth, 'Franco-Scottish efforts', 215; *Holm Cultram Reg.* (Kendal, 1929), 149-50.
[198] Cowan and Easson, *Religious Houses*, 77.
[199] P. King, 'Scottish Abbeys and the Cistercian financial system in the fourteenth century', *IR*, 42 (1991), 68-71; *The Tax Book of the Cistercian Order*, ed. A.O. Johnsen and P. King (Oslo, 1979).
[200] Dilworth, 'Franco-Scottish efforts', 215; idem, 'Cluniac Paisley', 31.
[201] B.E. Crawford, 'Peter's pence in Scotland' in G.W.S. Barrow, ed., *The Scottish Tradition* (Edinburgh, 1970); Barrell, *Papacy*, 18-21.

was exempt from tribute, payable by those countries, such as England and Naples, which were at least in theory feudally dependent upon the papacy. There was no escape, however, from procurations and income tax. Procurations were paid on all benefices to visiting papal legates and by certain monasteries exempted from episcopal oversight.[202] Income tax was introduced in 1166 to pay for the cost of the crusades, although at first contributions were voluntary.[203] A greater degree of compulsion was introduced following the deliberations of the Fourth Lateran Council in 1215, and thereafter the tax was imposed on the clergy at a rate of usually either a twentieth or a tenth of their incomes. Although income tax was not apparently extended to the Scottish clergy until c.1220, from then the papacy issued demands for its payment with some regularity: in 1228, possibly in 1239, in 1245 (for three years), in 1275 (for six years) and in 1290 (also for six years).[204]

The fate of the last general crusading tenth, levied in most countries between 1313 and 1319, is, however, instructive. Its imposition coincided with the reign of an excommunicated king (Robert I), whose authority was not recognised by the pope and who therefore denied the admittance of papal agents into his kingdom. Not surprisingly the tax remained uncollected in Scotland. The collection of clerical income tax depended on the co-operation of monarchs. Where, as in most countries, kings were able to pilfer some of the proceeds of clerical income tax for their own ends, they acquiesced in its levy. On three previous occasions, however, the Scottish crown had obstructed papal exactions: in 1229 (when, for reasons unknown, Alexander II refused to admit the collector, Stephen of Anagni, to the kingdom);[205] in the mid-1260s (when Alexander III refused the imposition of a tenth);[206] and thirdly in the 1280s (when Alexander III refused to permit the export of already collected monies).[207] Alexander III's objection to the crusading levies lay in their intended destination: the coffers of King Henry III of England in the 1260s and King Edward I of England in the 1280s. Where royal pilfering was not possible, because the collection machinery was based on geographical rather than political boundaries and generally operated from south of the English border, Scottish kings imposed obstacles.

From the fourteenth century the imposition of Christendom-wide clerical income tax was abandoned. It remained on a kingdom-by-kingdom basis, the king of Scots now got his cut (it helped, for instance, to pay for David II's ransom), but the universality of the system collapsed. Certainly the

[202] Procurations were imposed by visiting papal legates on all benefices in 1239 and 1266: *Chron. Bower* (Watt), v, 357, 472; Ferguson, *Medieval Papal Representatives*, 109-10. For an example of a monastic procuration owed to Cîteaux, see *Coupar Angus Chrs.*, i, nos. 27, 49, 51.
[203] F.A. Cazel, 'Financing the crusades' in K.M. Setton, ed., *History of the Crusades* (Madison, 1969-89), vi, 125-29; 136-39. For a voluntary Scottish levy in 1213, see Ferguson, *Medieval Papal Representatives*, 72-3; Macquarrie, *Crusades*, 35.
[204] Ferguson, *Medieval Papal Representatives*, 84-117, passim.
[205] Ferguson, *Medieval Papal Representatives*, 93; *Chron. Bower* (Watt), v, 142-43.
[206] Ferguson, *Medieval Papal Representatives*, 109-11; *Chron. Bower* (Watt), v, 360-61.
[207] Ferguson, *Medieval Papal Representatives*, 115-16.

significance of the contribution which income tax made to papal revenues declined sharply. Nevertheless, thwarted in one technique, the papacy developed others to shore up its income from Christendom at large. First and foremost among these was the imposition of service taxes and annates. These were one-off payments levied on clergy appointed to office by the papacy. Common services were imposed on bishops and some abbots (usually at about a third of the estimated income of the benefice) and annates were collected from other clergymen (at up to half the income of the benefice).[208] To maximise income from these sources required the papacy to make as many appointments as possible. This, as we shall see, is exactly what happened, and so the proceeds accruing to the papacy from the associated taxes grew correspondingly.

Although lucrative to the papacy, local clergymen remained understandably reluctant to fork out large proportions of their income to the *curia*. Surliness was displayed in prevarication of payment, which from Scotland was sometimes lengthy and, in some instances, amounted to several years.[209] Moreover, clerical resentment at these impositions now found support from the general councils of the church which assembled in the fifteenth century. In pursuit of their conflict over authority with the papacy, the councils often sought to limit papal rights of taxation, and in 1435 the council of Basel went so far as to abolish annates. The general circumstances of the early fifteenth century, where popes were desperate for princely support against, first of all, their rivals during the schism and then against the general councils, were not generally helpful to the maintenance of papal financial interests. Yet, while in several countries (notably France in 1438 and Germany in 1439) secular princes gleefully adopted the conciliar stance and declared annates abolished, the financial exactions imposed upon the Scottish clergy met with little opposition from the Scottish government. The only specific indication of Scottish governmental concern about financial dealings in Rome related not to service taxes or annates, but rather to the practice of 'barratry', that is clergymen travelling to the papal court to 'purches ony pension out of ony benefice secular or religious'.[210] The Scots, then, continued to pay their service taxes and annates to Rome until the Reformation; and for all the bluster from France, Germany and elsewhere, so too, albeit more sporadically and in more limited measures, did clergymen from those countries. Though challenged, the universality and profitabilty of papal exactions remained intact.[211] So too did the system of papal appointment to ecclesiastical office.

---

[208] Barrell, *Papacy*, 27-31, 33-55. Bishops consecrated at the *curia* were liable to payment of two dues termed *sacra* and subdeacon. The former amounted to a twentieth of common services and the latter to a third of *sacra*.

[209] ibid, 29-31, 51-5.

[210] *APS*, ii, 5. This legislation of 1424 was repeated in 1482 and again in 1484 (ibid, 144, 166).

[211] J.A.F. Thomson, *Popes and Princes, 1417-1517: Politics and polity in the late medieval church* (London, 1980), chapter 8.

Appointments

The circumstances in which the papacy claimed the right to make appointments had been gradually extended since 1179. These circumstances reached their pinnacle during the fourteenth century when the popes were normally resident at Avignon. By then they included vacancies arising when the previous incumbent had died within two days of travel from the papal court, along with those which arose following resignations or promotions made at the papal court, those stemming from papal deprivation on the grounds of pluralism, those resulting from the death of members of the papal household and even those caused by the death of jubilee-year pilgrims, such as Abbot Alexander of Dunfermline who had died near Cremona in 1350.[212]

These reservations all related broadly to circumstances in which clerics had visited Rome. But additional chronological reservations were also devised. If an incumbent cleric died in the months of March, June, September and December, then patrons or electors could still exercise their traditional rights of appointment; but in all other months appointments were referred to the papacy.[213] In this broad range of circumstances, the pope could provide a petitioner directly to the benefice in question. But the pope could also issue an 'expectative grace' which allowed the recipient to lay claim to the next vacant benefice in a specified location. Given, too, that papal provision was deemed the most effective method of securing possession of a benefice, many other clergymen sought to secure their title by obtaining papal provision, even though they had been appointed quite legitimately by other means and even though this papal confirmation necessitated the payment of taxes to Rome for which they otherwise would not have been liable.

Taken together, these papal reservations amounted to a vast number of contingencies. It has been calculated that between 1342 and 1370 the papacy provided 364 clerics (an average of thirteen per annum) to Scottish benefices, most of whose appointments proved effective. Although systematic analysis of the situation in later periods has yet to be undertaken, it would seem as if the number of papal provisions grew further, at least in the early fifteenth century.[214]

It is important to examine the subject of papal provisions in the context of ecclesiastical appointments as a whole. In this light the number of papal provisions was not excessive. It amounted in the mid-fourteenth century to little more than one provision per diocese per year – and in the diocese of Aberdeen alone there were almost a hundred benefices. Given life expectancy rates, we may assume that, on average, several benefices became vacant in the diocese of Aberdeen in any single year and that papal provision therefore only accounted for a minority of appointments. Moreover, although there was

---

[212] G. Mollat, *The Popes at Avignon, 1305-1378* (London, 1963), 335-42. On the abbot of Dunfermline, see Barrell, *Papacy*, 221; *Chron. Bower* (Watt), vii, 277.

[213] *St Andrews Copiale* no. 45; *St Andrews Formulare, 1514-1546* , ed. G. Donaldson and C. Macrae (Stair Soc., 1942-4), i, no. 193.

[214] Barrell, *Papacy*, 161.

nothing to prevent the pope from appointing whomsoever he wished to vacant benefices over which his patronage extended, he rarely chose to appoint foreigners to Scottish positions. There were, of course, exceptions. In *c.*1237 Master John of Civitate Antina was appointed to the church of Aberlemno in Angus; Bertrand Cariti, a papal nuncio, had acquired the parsonage of Fettercairn by 1354; the cardinals of St Eusebius and Cortona obtained the commendatorships of Glenluce and Whithorn abbeys in the early sixteenth century; and, true to the notorious nepotistic reputation of the Renaissance papacy, Leo X intruded his nephew, Innocenzo Cibo, as administrator of St Andrews diocese in 1513.[215] But such appointments were rare, perhaps, as most historians assume, because the value of Scottish benefices was not great enough to attract foreign interest.

The few foreigners who did acquire Scottish positions did not arouse the ire evident in many countries where such appointments (including those of several Scottish clerics) were more common; or, indeed, the hostility which Englishmen legitimately in possession of Scottish benefices faced in the later thirteenth century.[216] It was, then, predominantly Scots who benefited from the system of papal provision in Scotland and very often they were Scots whose opportunities for finding a benefice were otherwise limited. Most of those appointed to office by the papacy were university graduates: some 77% of papal provisions were in their favour, the number rising to about 90% during the pontificate of Urban V (1362-70). Given that graduates spent several years abroad, and that during their studies they were out of routine contact with those who might bestow patronage locally, the system clearly, from their point of view, had its advantages. While, no doubt, individual university graduates could (and can) be as grasping, manipulative and temperamentally unsuited to the ministry as anyone else, it was at least difficult to complain about the educational suitability of these appointments.

From the vantage point of others papal provision might have more substantial drawbacks. Papal provision superseded the rights of appointment which belonged traditionally to either local patrons or episcopal electors. Moreover, papal interference in appointments could also curtail the manipulative impulses of secular princes because it limited their opportunities to influence elections. The crown had a vital interest in who was appointed to high office in the church, since clerics often moonlighted as royal bureaucrats. It might, therefore, be thought that papal interference in the matter of appointments would excite heated opposition both from local patrons and from the crown. There was certainly some resentment. In 1363, for instance, the bishop of Glasgow complained about the 'multitude' of people obtaining papal provision which undermined his own exercise of patronage;[217] and in

---

[215] Ferguson, *Medieval Papal Representatives*, 246 (no. 93); *CPL*, iv, 64; *James V Letters*, 13, 31, 41, 48-9, 71-2.

[216] Barrell, *Papacy*, chapter 3. For examples of Scots seeking foreign benefices, see *CSSR*, ii, 10, 34-5.

[217] *CPP*, i, 400.

1428 parliament not only fulminated against 'barratry' but banned clerics from leaving the realm without permission, presumably, as Ian Cowan and Alexander Grant suggest, to obtain benefices at the *curia*.[218] In fact, even if so intended, the statute of 1428 would not have prevented papal provision, since many of those who were provided to benefices by the pope were university graduates not resident in Scotland before their appointment.

Far more effective, in this respect, was the approach taken by parliament in 1485. This suggested that provision to the higher ecclesiastical offices (in effect the bishoprics and wealthier abbatial appointments) should be postponed for six months until the king had time to supplicate the pope for the provision of his favoured nominee. It was this concession (extended to eight months) which Innocent VIII granted in an indult of 1487.[219] Even then it is remarkable that it was not, as in other countries, the system of provision *per se* which was being attacked. Nor, therefore, was it the financial benefits which the papacy derived from the system in the form of common services which came under attack. Nor was the right of the pope to appoint to lesser offices questioned. Rather, the furore of the 1480s was solely concerned with the mechanisms by which the crown might seek to influence the appointment of the most senior clerics of the kingdom. Moreover, the compromise which was reached in 1487 was in practice hardly a major innovation. Since at least David II's reign, kings had submitted lists of clergymen whose provision they recommended to the papacy.[220] Although there were exceptions, popes had generally acquiesced in royal wishes or offered suitable alternative appointments when they did not. By the fifteenth century, although there were still minor squabbles, notably over the appointment of bishops of Glasgow and Dunkeld immediately before the grant of the indult, royal wishes regarding episcopal appointment were ultimately nearly always heeded by the papacy. All that the indult of 1487, therefore, achieved was a formalisation of what had long since been common practice. Moreover, since the indult was not binding on Innocent's successors, the crown still faced occasional disregard of its wishes, most notably during the early years of the pontificate of Leo X (1513-21). Leo took six years to reissue the indult. In the meantime he attempted to make provisions unwelcome to the crown – but failed.[221]

Royal outbursts against papal provision, then, were rare. Unlike other monarchs (notably again in France), Scottish kings generally worked with, rather than against, the system and in the process generally managed to safeguard their own interests. Popes were disposed to accept royal advice about appointments to the higher ecclesiastical offices, and in return they kept

---

[218] *APS*, ii, 16; I.B. Cowan, 'Patronage, provision and reservation: pre-Reformation appointments to benefices' in idem, *The Medieval Church in Scotland*, ed. J. Kirk (Edinburgh, 1995), 200; Grant, *Independence*, 91.

[219] *APS*, ii, 171; J.A.F. Thomson, 'Innocent VIII and the Scottish church', *IR*, 19 (1968), 23-31.

[220] *RRS*, vi, 44-8.

[221] Cowan, 'Patronage', 196-98; Dilworth, *Scottish Monasteries*, 18-19.

their profits from common services and annates. As for other interested parties, non-royal secular patrons had become very much of a rarity in some parts of the country by the fourteenth century. Only half a dozen churches in the diocese of Aberdeen, for instance, remained in secular patronage.[222] Papal provision to ecclesiastical office was not, therefore, much of an encroachment on the exercise of secular lordship. Monastic patronage of churches was much more common than secular patronage, but there were very few papal provisions to such churches, or, indeed, to religious houses themselves in the fourteenth century, though the unfortunate Abbot Alexander of Dunfermline was replaced by a papal nominee in 1351. It would seem, however, as if papal provision to monasteries and their appropriated churches increased in the fifteenth and sixteenth centuries.[223] Yet in so far as the papacy rode roughshod over local patronage rights, these belonged in the main to the episcopate. The resentment of the bishop of Glasgow is therefore perhaps understandable, but this encroachment on his authority was, as we have seen, only part of a much wider undermining of episcopal authority in which bishops had acquiesed for the best part of three centuries.

Justice

If there was little opposition in Scotland to either papal taxation (after the thirteenth century) or to papal appointments (even in the fifteenth century), in common with the rest of Christendom there was even less criticism in Scotland of papal justice.[224] Ever since the tenth century it was generally accepted that the church had jurisdictional rights over all clergymen, whatever the nature of their alleged crime or dispute. It was also accepted that the legal capacity of the church courts extended, in certain circumstances, to lay women and men too. Hence matters of a broadly social nature (including matrimonial and sexual issues, as well as defamation) and matters of a broadly religious nature (including issues of belief and devotion, such as blasphemy and heresy) came within their competence. So did certain matters concerned with death, such as probate and burial issues. And so too did financial and commercial issues when they impinged upon ethical values or religious obligations. The payment of teinds by laymen to their parish church, the imposition of interest on loans, profiteering, broken contracts and certain aspects of the terms and conditions of labour all came within this category. Yet, important though the arbitration of disputes arising from such matters was, papal justice possessed another facet. In certain circumstances the pope was empowered to award dispensations, or exemptions, from the standard norms of the canon law. He could, for instance, dispense priests from the normal canonical rules regarding their age at ordination; he could dispense

---

[222] I.B. Cowan, 'The church in the diocese of Aberdeen' in idem, *Medieval Church*, 106, 122.
[223] Cowan, 'Patronage', 202-4.
[224] See, in general, Barrell, *Papacy*, chapter 7; Brundage, *Canon Law*, chapter 4; and Thomson, *Princes*, chapter 9.

men from bastardy in order that they be admitted to the priesthood; and he could dispense men and women from regulations which would prevent them from marrying. The award of such concessions formed a substantial proportion of the business handled by the ecclesiastical courts.

Many cases within this broad range of jurisdictional competence were handled locally by diocesan courts. These were presided over by the bishop's official or his commissary, who were usually trained lawyers.[225] After the erection of archbishoprics in Scotland, appeals could be directed from a bishop's to an archbishop's court. Both before and after 1472, however, the ultimate source of appeal was the vicar of Christ or, more usually in practice, the vicar's vicars. While the pope together with his cardinals in consistory still heard judicial cases, the pressures of business were such that the pope himself frequently delegated his judicial responsibilities to others. By the fourteenth century this delegated business was dealt with in several forums. Foremost among them was the *Rota*, which took its name ('the wheel') from the room in which it met at Avignon, and latterly the *signatura iustitiae*, which developed into the highest court of appeal. Other more specialised agencies were also established, including the *audientia litterarum contradictarum* (which scrutinised technical aspects of the judicial system), the penitentiary (which dealt with dispensations from canon law) and the chamberlain's court (which dealt with financial matters).

No records of Scottish church courts survive before the sixteenth century and they are extremely patchy for the sixty years before the Reformation too. The opposite problem – an expanding number of courts producing, certainly from the fifteenth century, a profusion of records – has to date prevented comprehensive historical analysis of the papal evidence, though selective examination of these records has begun. Nevertheless, the mismatch of papal and Scottish sources means that it is impossible to determine the proportion of people who did exercise their right of appeal to the papal courts. In the thirteenth century many, it seems, did head to Rome.[226] Indeed, it is probably safe to assume that Scots were as litigiously thirsty as their counterparts elsewhere in Christendom: no less than 38% of the business handled by the official of St Andrews in the early sixteenth century consisted of appeals from lesser ecclesiastical courts.[227] It would also appear, from much of the papal evidence, that the vast majority of Scottish litigants at the *curia* were clergymen. During the pontificate of Clement VII (1378-94) for instance, although laymen sometimes petitioned the papacy on behalf of clergymen, less than 4% of the ultimate beneficiaries of the surviving papal fiats were laymen or women.[228] And during the pontificate of Paul II (1464-71), almost 93% of papal supplications from Scotland were for the benefit of clerics.[229]

[225] G. Donaldson, 'The church courts' in idem, *Scottish Church History* (Edinburgh, 1985), 40-5.
[226] Ferguson, *Medieval Papal Representatives*, 131.
[227] S. Ollivant, *The Court of the Official in Pre-Reformation Scotland* (Stair Soc., 1982), 177.
[228] *Clement VII Letters*, passim.
[229] CSSR, v, 296-463.

This may, however, be something of a misleading picture for not all supplications were registered. Moreover, a study of sample penitentiary records between 1432 and 1560 reveals a much more balanced ratio of clerical and lay petitions.[230] Still, whatever the exact proportion of lay petitioners as opposed to clerical supplicants, it is undeniable that a lot of clergymen were active in the papal courts.

The main reasons for this are simple. As we have already seen, the pope's powers of patronage encouraged benefice hunters to deluge him with appeals for provision to ecclesiastical office. This, together with his powers to grant dispensation from the normal rules regarding age, legitimacy and pluralism for the holding of church office, accounted for the overwhelming amount of Scottish business at the *curia*. If, again, we take the pontificate of Clement VII as an example, 71% of the letters directed to Scotland in one way or another concerned ecclesiastical appointments, most of them in Scotland, though one was of a Scotsman to a Castilian benefice, ten were of appointments as papal chaplains and a further two were about the creation of fourteen notaries. Notaries, like students, were normally tonsured and, though free to marry, technically of clerical status.[231]

The remainder of Scottish business at the *curia* was of small, but diverse, fare. In the twelfth century papal confirmations of endowments made to ecclesiastical foundations, and especially monasteries, had formed a significant proportion (almost 30%) of the papacy's Scottish correspondence.[232] Such grants were far less common in the later middle ages, but on occasions monasteries and others still sought confirmation or authorisation of a change in the status of their possessions. In 1423, for instance, the earl of Douglas petitioned Martin V for the erection of Douglas parish church, of which he was patron, to collegiate status; in 1435 Holm Cultram abbey sought Eugenius IV's approval for the transfer of its patronage of Kirkgunzeon church to the archdeacon of Teviotdale; and other confirmations, especially in the sixteenth century, were sought for church lands which had been feued.[233]

A second category of business concerned the visitations which the higher clergymen were expected to undertake of certain monasteries and parishes within their jurisdiction. We may include in this category correspondence relating to the occasional visits made to Scotland by papal legates and nuncios, such as Guy, cardinal priest of Jerusalem, the legate who visited the kingdom in 1379-80. In addition there were mandates to enable clergymen to study at university; and awards of pensions, some to students and others to aged clerics such as Patrick Locrys, bishop of Brechin, who resigned his see because of

---

[230] J.P. Foggie, 'Archivium Sacrae Paenitentiariae Apostolicae in the Vatican Archives as a source for Scottish historians', *IR*, 47 (1996), 110-26.

[231] J. Durkan, 'The early Scottish notary' in I.B. Cowan and D. Shaw, eds., *The Renaissance and Reformation in Scotland* (Edinburgh, 1983), 22-40.

[232] Somerville, *Scotia Pontificia*, passim.

[233] *CSSR*, ii, 15-16; iv, no. 188; Foggie, 'Archivium', 121-23. See also A.D.M. Barrell, 'The papacy and the regular clergy in Scotland in the fourteenth century', *RSCHS*, 24 (1992), 106-7.

infirmity in 1383. There were permissions for monks to transfer from one religious house or order to another; honorific privileges, often for abbots to wear the mitre, ring and other pontifical insignia; and yet other miscellaneous matters all concerned with the trappings, financing and responsibilities of ecclesiastical office.

Devotional favours were granted to both the laity and the clergy, with a striking proportion intended for women. A few privileges of this sort were exemptions from routine dietary observation: in 1379, for instance, the countess of Douglas and her household were permitted to eat meat, presumably on Fridays and Saturdays when it was normally prohibited, and in 1381 the bishop of St Andrews, on account of his age, was dispensed from fasting in Lent, other feast days and from his own vow of fasting on Wednesdays.[234] Rather more exemptions were granted to hear mass before dawn, to choose a confessor of personal choice, or to possess a portable altar – different privileges which together point towards greater individual religious introspection as opposed to the traditional norm of community worship.

Grants for the plenary remission of sins at the point of death were also popular, no doubt because of the immediacy with which the spectre of the afterlife hung over a society ridden from 1348 with pestilence. Death, of course, was expected to be followed by the experience of purgatory. It was popularly thought that the accumulation of days of indulgence, which were granted in return for devotional acts, would offset the length of stay in purgatory. In fact this was theologically unsound. Days of indulgence gained for devotional acts were actually a substitute for days of penance imposed on sin; besides, purgatory was timeless and not therefore amenable to arithmetic calculations of the sort so often made. Nevertheless, whether fully understood or not, there was certainly a demand for days of indulgence. While plenary (or full) indulgences were granted on great devotional undertakings, such as the jubilee pilgrimages or crusades, partial indulgences were granted for quests which could be taken closer to home. These included visiting and contributing to the upkeep or repair of particular constructions. The financial beneficiaries of such grants were usually ecclesiastical foundations, such as parish churches, hospitals or cathedrals. In 1380, for instance, the cathedral of Aberdeen was given this privilege, along with the chapel of the hospital of Uthrogle in Fife; and the devout who visited these sites received an indulgence of at least one year and forty days in return for alms.[235] On occasions, however, non-ecclesiastical constructions also benefited. In 1384 an indulgence was granted to all those who contributed to the rebuilding of a bridge which had been swept away by floods in Cowal.[236] In other words, indulgences were granted in return for donations. That was not far from the concept which

---

[234] *Clement VII Letters*, 39, 60-1. On religious dietary observation in general, see B.A. Henisch, *Fast and Feast: Food in medieval society* (London, 1976); C. Bynum, *Holy Feast and Holy Fast: The religious significance of food to medieval women* (Berkeley, 1987).
[235] *Clement VII Letters*, 44-5.
[236] *Clement VII Letters*, 103.

Martin Luther so vigorously attacked in the sixteenth century. The medieval church saw it differently. Confession was required before an indulgence was gained and, whatever the purpose of the indulgence, confession restored men and women to grace. Indulgences, therefore, were a legitimate and successful means of pastoral care.

While devotional privileges could be granted to both the laity and the clergy, some spheres of ecclesiastical jurisdiction pertained solely to the laity. Cases pertaining to marital affairs accounted for the overwhelming proportion of this category of appeals and in 1462 alone the Penitentiary considered twenty-nine Scottish cases – a numerically greater number than came from England and, given their respective sizes, a proportionately larger number than came from France.[237] While it is possible that this reflects abnormally high incidents of marital difficulty in Scotland, it seems more likely that appeals to Rome are an indication of the faith which Scots had in papal justice.

The intention behind the majority of marital cases was to rectify an anomaly and to legitimise the relationship (perhaps following a handfasting, a secretive marriage which posed difficulties for the canon lawyers), rather than to end the marriage. Divorce, as such, was rare in the middle ages but there were a few instances in which annulment of marriage or a legal separation short of divorce were sought. The most famous Scottish case probably concerns the marriage between Alexander Stewart, lord of Badenoch, and Euphemia, countess of Ross in her own right. A dispensation on consanguineous grounds had been required in 1382 to secure what initially seemed like an astute political marriage. Ten years later Euphemia had petitioned the pope for a separation 'from bed and board' on the grounds of her husband's persistent adultery and his detention of her goods.[238] By separation from 'bed and board' she presumably meant a release from both co-habitation and the marital debt of sex which husband and wife owed each other. Had the couple remained informally apart the ecclesiastical courts would have been within their rights to order the resumption of both these aspects of the marital relationship. Separation on the grounds of adultery was, however, rare everywhere in Christendom, as were the circumstances which led Alexander's son, Alexander earl of Mar, to seek an annulment of his second marriage. He had married a Brabantine heiress who, unbeknown to him, was already married but had separated from her husband without the knowledge of the church courts, a not uncommon occurrence. On these grounds an annulment was granted in 1415.[239] Yet the annulment was not apparently effective, for after the conclusion of the schism, Mar was petitioning anew, this time for divorce rather than annulment, on the grounds

[237] L. Schmugge, 'Cleansing on consciences: some observations regarding the fifteenth-century registers of the papal penitentiary', *Viator*, 29 (1998), 355.
[238] *Clement VII Letters*, 79, 174, 181.
[239] *Papal Letters to Scotland of Benedict XIII of Avignon, 1394-1419*, ed. F. McGurk (SHS, 1976), 313.

of his wife's long-continued absence from Scotland, a reason which some canonists at least accepted as valid grounds for divorce.[240]

Such instances were, however, the exceptions. Most couples whose cases reached the papal courts sought dispensation from the laws of consanguinity or (but sometimes and) spiritual affinity to allow them to marry. Many Scots added in their supplications that they wished to undertake such marriages in order to end feuds between their families, and this certainly accorded with the basic precept of marriage which was to extend Christian love and affection between families. It was partly for this reason, coupled with the horror of incest, that the church was led to determine the bounds between one family and another.

At the Fourth Lateran Council the laws of affinity for marital partners had been relaxed somewhat, but marriage between those related within four degrees of blood or spiritual affinity (that is related through common great grandparents or through godparents) remained illegal. Some sought backdated dispensations on the grounds of ignorance of the impediments when they had married; a few sought release from the sin of having married in the full knowledge of the legal impediments. Hector Macgileeom and Mor Campbell were guilty of the latter, though wisely they had not consummated their marriage by 1393, or so they claimed. Consummation was necessary for the validity of a marriage, so arguably Hector and Mor had not actually sinned before acquiring their dispensation. The penalties for those who had knowingly contravened the marital legislation, however, could be harsh and included excommunication. It was this fate which by 1386 had befallen James de Valence and Christine Erskine. They had married and consummated their marriage, despite Valence's earlier carnal dalliance with a serving wench who was related to Christine. It was not James's fornication *per se* which had created the problem, though fornication was a sin, denial of which was condemned as heresy. Rather it was his choice of partner: a sexual affinity had been established by their liaison which precluded marriage between James and any close relation of the serving girl.[241]

Such matters were obviously of fundamental importance in people's lives. Had they not been, men and women like James and Christine would not have gone to the time, trouble and expense which was routinely encountered in pursuing litigation at the papal court. But there was the rub: how could most ordinary people afford the expense of protracted judicial proceedings in a far-away place? The temptation is perhaps to assume that this was justice for the wealthy, and a superficial glance through the papal records would appear to support this. Among lay petitions, for instance, the aristocracy features in supplications far beyond its proportion in society as a whole, while, among the regular clergy, abbots and would-be abbots far outnumber the references

---

[240] *CSSR*, ii, 59-60.
[241] *Clement VII Letters*, 112, 188; on the laws of affinity in general, see J.A. Brundage, *Law, Sex and Christian Society in Medieval Europe* (Chicago, 1987), passim.

to the unambitious monk content to reside for life in the same monastery. The papacy itself was aware of the practical problems associated with visiting its courts. In 1386 Clement VII noted that 'the number of appeals made to the pope... are then attended by such delay of justice that the appellants take their cases to the civil court to the prejudice and loss of ecclesiastical liberty'.[242] The message here is slightly contradictory. There is clearly a hint that people were not using the system because it was defective. Yet, there is also an implication that it was the very surfeit of litigation which was clogging up the system, despite the fact that, as one supplicant informed the pope in 1435, he had 'by the greatest of difficulties of roads and perils of the sea' made his way to the papal court.[243]

Awareness of such problems was matched by a willingness to offer remedies. It was not necessary for every litigant to compear personally before the papal courts and there is little in most supplications and petitions to suggest that anything but a minority actually did. In the absence of the litigants themselves business before the courts could be conducted by resident procurators whose qualifications were checked by the *audientia litterarum contradictarum*. Moreover, supplications could be sent to procurators in bulk. This would appear to have been the case with six requests to possess portable altars which came from the Western Isles in October 1433, the same month that the bishop of the Isles requested permission to transfer the location of his cathedral church. It was perhaps the bishop or his agent who delivered all of these petitions to Florence.[244] Here, then, was one means by which supplicants could limit their costs. Another was by taking advantage of delegated papal authority. It had been common in the twelfth century for bishops to be consecrated by three of their peers in Scotland in order to avoid a journey to the *curia*. Although this was less common in the fourteenth and fifteenth centuries, it remained possible. In 1379 the bishop of Dunkeld was given permission for his consecration to be enacted in Scotland, and in a not dissimilar circumstance in 1389 the abbot of Holyrood had been allowed to take his oath of fidelity locally 'in order to save the abbot the fatigue and expense of coming personally to the papal court'.[245]

There were other specific powers too which could be delegated. In 1384 Cardinal Wardlaw was given a blank mandate to dispense fifty men and women of his choosing from the impediment to marriage arising from the fourth degrees of consanguinity and spiritual affinity. This was followed by powers to dispense ten men and women who had already married in ignorance of the same impediments, power to dispense one hundred men from defects of birth thereby enabling them to enter the priesthood, and power to create twenty notaries.[246] Since many of the elite did take their cases to the

---

[242] *Clement VII Letters*, 116.
[243] *CSSR*, iv, no. 205.
[244] *CSSR*, iv, nos. 105-6
[245] *Clement VII Letters*, 23, 146.
[246] *Clement VII Letters*, 105-6.

papal court, we may perhaps assume that at least occasionally the cardinal exercised his powers on behalf of the great mass of ordinary townspeople and country dwellers who rarely figure in the papal records and who have become anonymous to modern historians.

It was not only specific powers that were delegated. Since the thirteenth century it had not been unusual for the pope to refer cases back to judges-delegate in Scotland for determination.[247] From the fourteenth century it became more common still to appoint conservators. The appointees had wider powers than judges-delegate and were empowered to hear appeals immediately from specified individuals or institutions. In 1344, for instance, the abbots of Dunfermline, Coupar Angus and Newbattle were made conservators for the Cluniac monasteries in Scotland.[248] The scope of delegation was expanded still further in 1386 when the bishop of St Andrews was granted power to hear cases which would otherwise have gone on appeal from episcopal courts all over Scotland to the Holy See.[249] In effect this gave him the powers which were normally held by an archbishop. It remains a matter of conjecture whether ordinary people found these delegated mechanisms any less daunting than a journey to the *curia*. Yet, even if the system remained exclusive and defective, remedies were being sought to a problem which had been recognised.

The quest to improve the system was a reflection of the commonly held notion that it was the duty of every monarch to offer his subjects justice. But the *demand* for justice came from below. The pope did not initiate the supplications which came to his court from six Islesmen and their wives in 1433. Indeed, I would even wager my Dunfermline Athletic scarf, that he did not personally care, one way or the other, whether these twelve Gaels had their own altars or not. He was, however, expected to respond to their pleas as he was to the multitude of others which came his way. If, as the Italian humanist Petrarch thought, popes had strangely forgotten their origins as the poor fishermen of Galilee, this was partly because of the burgeoning expectations and demands imposed upon the papacy by the faithful across Christendom. These common demands gave Christendom coherence. So too did the great bureaucratic jungle established by the papacy to cope with the demands. So too did the claims of the papacy to its supremacy over Christendom. So too did the beliefs and the devotional practices which were examined earlier in this chapter. These were all pieces in what many readers may have found to be a rather complicated jigsaw. What moulded them together was canon law.

From the twelfth century canon law provided Christendom with regulations for the conduct of its religious experience. Canonical rules were 'all-pervasive' and 'reached into virtually every nook and cranny of human

[247] Ferguson, *Medieval Papal Representatives*, chapter 4.
[248] Barrell, *Papacy*, 165-70.
[249] *Clement VII Letters*, 116.

conduct'.[250] Walter Bower, for instance, readily resorted to the citation of canonical rules in offering his judgements on matters such as adultery, astrology, leisure pursuits, oaths, politics and the weather, as well as more obviously ecclesiastical business.[251] Canon law was, furthermore, international in its relevance and application, enabling Scottish bishops in their administration of justice to liase not only with the papacy but also with their colleagues across political frontiers, be it in Durham or Roskilde.[252]

Herein lies the significance of the books shelved by the fifteenth century in St Machar's Cathedral, Aberdeen. These were not just dry tomes of academic interest. They were of direct relevance to people's lives and, we may presume, were routinely consulted. John Barbour, for instance, never returned a copy of the church laws (or decretals) which he borrowed from the library. The Aberdeen collection fortunately included several other copies of the decretals, which had been most recently up-dated in the *Liber sextus*, *Constitutiones Clementinae* and *Extravagantes*, the first produced during the pontificate of Boniface VIII (1294-1303) and the other two issued by John XXII (1316-34). In addition to the decretals there were commenteraries on them written by some of the foremost legal minds of the twelfth, thirteenth and fourteenth centuries: Giovanni d'Andrea, William Durand 'The Speculator', William of Monlezun, St Ramón of Penyafort, Henry of Segusio, Tancred, Geoffrey of Trani, and others.[253] These are not names that normally figure prominently in Scottish history. Nevertheless, by providing a common and acceptable legal framework for Christendom and Christians, it was these men and their laws who provided religiously conservative and orthodox Scotland with a point of reference shared by other countries.

[250] Brundage, *Canon Law*, 175.
[251] *Chron. Bower* (Watt), iii, 381, 387, 427; iv, 173, 309, 357-59, 373; v, 45, 291, 329, 401; vi, 61-3, 165, 187, 278, 287; vii, 155, 263, 267, 321.
[252] G. Donaldson, 'Justice across frontiers' in idem, *Scottish Church History*, 54-5.
[253] *Aberdeen Reg.*, ii, 129-34. Brundage, *Canon Law*, 202-30 provides a brief synopsis of the life and works of these and other prominent canon lawyers.

3
The Cultural Bonds

The Christian faith provided the Latin west with one powerfully cohesive bond. There was, however, at least one other factors which also welded these disparate lands together. The Latin west was a 'society organised for war'.[1] Although that phrase was coined with particular reference to Castile, it is an apt description of the entire continent. Despite some regional variations, from the Baltic to the Balearics society was organised for war along broadly similar lines. While, on occasions, peasants and townsmen, and sometimes even clerics and women, engaged in battle, social convention decreed that it was *par excellence* the role of the knight to fight. Knights constituted the secular aristocracy of the medieval west and throughout Christendom they were imbued with a common, militaristic culture. The origins of this knightly culture lay in what is now northern France and were characterised by the mounted warrior, equipped with lance, broadsword and shield, and clad in a coat of iron mail. Near invincible, or so it seemed by the eleventh century, the Frankish military culture spread rapidly from its heartland – to some places, such as England, parts of Ireland, southern Italy and the Baltic lands, by conquest; and to others, such as Scotland, much of Germany and Iberia, by adoption. Throughout these lands the knight, his horse and their armour came to form the backbone of military power. And they continued to do so even although the triumph of the common infantry at the battles of Kortrijk (1302), Bannockburn (1314) and Morgarten (1315) demonstrated that the mounted warrior was not, after all, invincible.

Notwithstanding the growing significance of the common footsoldier (and also of the longbowman and of artillery) in fourteenth-century conflict, the aristocracy clung trenchantly to its horses and traditional weapons. The horse was a mark of status. It continued to distinguish aristocrats and their purpose in society from others, not just militarily, but also socially; and it continued to do so across political frontiers. As a consequence, long after their shared Frankish origin had been diluted by intermarriage with natives and long after their familiarity with the French language had become a little rusty, aristocrats from different countries continued to have much in common.[2] This

[1] E. Lourie, 'A society organised for war: medieval Spain', *Past and Present*, 35 (1966), 54-76.
[2] For the gradual demise of French as the aristocratic *lingua franca* in the British isles, see D. Murison, 'Linguistic relationships in medieval Scotland' in G.W.S. Barrow, ed., *The Scottish Tradition: Essays in honour of Ronald Gordon Cant* (Edinburgh, 1974), 71-83; G.W.S. Barrow, 'French after the style of Petithachengon' in B.E. Crawford, ed., *Church, Chronicle and Learning in Medieval and Early Renaissance Scotland* (Edinburgh, 1999), 187-93; A. Bliss and J. Long, 'Literature in Norman French and English to 1534' in A. Cosgrove, ed., *A New History of Ireland*, vol. 2: *Medieval Ireland, 1169-1534* (Oxford, 1987), 708-36; S. Hussey, 'Nationalism and language in England, c.1300-1500' in C. Bjørn, A. Grant and K.J. Stringer, eds., *Nations, Nationalism and Patriotism in the European Past* (Copenhagen, 1994), 96-108.

shared military inheritance proved an enduring one, even although aristocrats periodically – and from the fourteenth century increasingly – fought each other in 'national' wars. It was an inheritance underpinned by the ethos of chivalry. The somewhat nebulous concept of chivalry is important in this context, for it provided aristocrats throughout the Latin west with a common code of conduct. Courage, honour, largesse, loyalty and prowess were qualities to be admired in a knight and those who upheld these virtues were worthy of praise and renown, even if they were political and military opponents. Warfare had spawned a culture, expressed not just on the battlefield, but also in art, literature, music and sport. Nowhere is this better exemplified than in the chronicles of Jean Froissart and his tales of military exploits gathered (often from personal experience) in Scotland and throughout the lands of the Latin west.

At first sight this bellicose aspect of medieval culture may seem to have been sharply at odds with the powerful message of Christian love and peace propagated by the Church. There were, indeed, tensions and in the central middle ages churchmen had expounded much intellectual energy in seeking to fetter the conflictual edge of aristocratic society. Rules were devised to regulate upon whom and what aristocrats might legitimately vent their bellicosity, and when they might do so. The 'pious warrior' did not attack Christian institutions or defenceless non-combatants. He did not lead his troops into battle between Saturday evening and Monday morning, or during the great religious festivals.[3] Hence, it was with a degree of grudging respect that the northern English chronicler Richard of Hexham noted that David I of Scotland did not commence his attack on Northumberland in 1138 until 'the celebration of Easter was over'.[4] And these broad conventions concerning military engagement (known as the 'peace and truce of God') continued to influence the outlook of even the most ardent admirers of the military ethos. Froissart, for instance, was implicitly critical of his great hero the Black Prince (the son of Edward III of England) for the 'fearful slaughter' which the prince's armies meted out on the non-combatant townspeople of Limoges in 1370.[5] Nonetheless, it is significant that the Church sought to curtail, rather than prohibit, warfare; and in the concept of 'holy war' the interests of clerics and knights neatly coincided. Fighting was just, admirable and worthy of spiritual perquisites if it was undertaken in the name of God. In the cause of crusade the two most powerful sections of medieval society – the clergy and the secular aristocracy – were able to reach a *modus vivendi*.

We have already examined the spiritual purposes of crusade.[6] From a cultural perspective crusades were also important because they provided

---

[3] H.E.J. Cowdry, 'The peace and truce of God in the eleventh century', *Past and Present*, 46 (1970), 42-67.
[4] *Scottish Annals from English Chroniclers A.D.500 to 1286*, ed. A.O. Anderson (London, 1908), 185-86.
[5] *Chron. Froissart* (Lettenhove), viii, 38-9.
[6] See above, pages 65-6.

aristocrats with an opportunity for doing what they did best – fighting. Since warfare was intermittent within Christendom – even during the more intensely conflictual fourteenth century – crusades on the frontiers of the non-Christian world provided the aristocracy with an alternative opportunity for practising and displaying their martial skills. It is surely significant that many who availed themselves of this opportunity were already experienced warriors; and that they chose to fight for God when there was no one to fight in their own back yards. In a Scottish context no one exemplified this better than Sir James Douglas, the veteran general of Robert I's wars. Once an Anglo-Scottish peace had been brokered in 1328, Douglas set off willingly with his late commander's heart to engage the Iberian Muslims – even though political common sense dictated that he remain at home.[7] Douglas was not unique. His distant descendant Sir William Douglas of Nithsdale was a similarly seasoned campaigner, inured to the world of war along the Anglo-Scottish marches, in Ireland and on the Isle of Man, which he had raided in 1388.[8] But in 1391, following the international truces agreed at Leulingham in June 1389, Douglas set forth on crusade, in his case to join the Baltic campaigns of the Teutonic Order.[9] There were others of a similar temperament too: Sir Walter Moigne (captured at Neville's Cross in 1346), Sir Norman Leslie (captured at the battle of Flavigny in 1360), and Sir Robert Stewart of Durisdeer were all war veterans before taking the cross, as were many of those whom they met on crusade.[10] Crusading constituted something akin to an international confraternity for the knightly classes and it provided camaraderie as well as conflict. Froissart provided a perfect – though not Scottish – example of this mindset which saw nothing contradictory in knights fighting together on crusade and then fighting against each other in the battles of the Hundred Years War. In the midst of the battle of Crécy (1346), the beleaguered counts of Eu and Tancerville spotted Sir Thomas Holland, whom they recognised from crusading ventures in Granada and Prussia. The Frenchmen surrendered to the one-eyed English knight and the latter was delighted 'not only because he could spare their lives but also because their capture meant an excellent day's work and a fine haul of valuable prisoners.'[11] The warrior elite fought both with and against its cultural comrades.

---

[7] S. Cameron, 'Sir James Douglas, Spain and the Holy Land', in T. Brotherstone and D. Ditchburn, *Freedom and Authority: Scotland, c.1050-c.1650* (East Linton, 2000), 110.

[8] *Chron. Bower* (Watt), vii, 412-15.

[9] D. Ditchburn, 'Merchants, Pedlars and Pirates: A history of Scotland's relations with northern Germany and the Baltic in the later middle ages' (University of Edinburgh, unpublished PhD thesis, 1988), 450-56.

[10] *Rot. Scot.*, ii, 678; *Scalacronica*, 190; *Chron. Bower* (Watt), vii, 414-15. On the crusading ventures of these men, see above, chapter 2.

[11] The translation is from *Chron. Froissart* (Brereton), 75.

Tournaments

Crusading opportunities were dwindling in the later medieval period. As Christendom's flexible frontiers became more brittally delineated aristocrats were forced to find other methods of expressing their valour in times of peace. Military tournaments, in which knights pitted their military skills against each other, provided one such opportunity. These events had first developed around the time of the first crusade, or perhaps a little earlier in the eleventh century. They were originally devised as an occasion on which the warrior class could practice its skills of horsemanship and combat with the lance. But, although conceived as mock rather than genuine battles, tournaments were dangerous affairs. While participants attempted to capture rather than kill their opponents, the risks of accidental death remained significant. Indeed, mock conflict aside, aristocratic pride wounded on the tournament field was also a potentially murderous animal. It was this, if the English chronicler Matthew Paris is to be believed, which prompted Walter Bisset to murder Patrick, earl of Atholl, following a tournament in which both had fought at Haddington in 1242, for the earl had unhorsed his assassin during the proceedings.[12] Given these dangers, it is not surprising that the Church remained wary of the tournament, its qualms focused especially on the potential for needless spilling of Christian blood. Indeed, the ecclesiastical authorities routinely voiced their objections to the tournament in the twelfth century. Nevertheless, tournament culture flourished throughout the Latin west and in 1316 the papacy quietly abandoned its earlier condemnations of these aristocratic games of death.[13]

That the tournament remained popular throughout the later medieval period, and beyond, was indicative of its adaptable nature. Initially tournaments had often taken the form of mounted encounters which entailed combat between two teams of warriors fighting in a mêlée. By the thirteenth century many tournaments also featured jousting contests. These involved just two participants, the combatants normally running three courses against each other with lances. Both the tournament proper and the joust were fought *à outrance* – that is, under war conditions and using the weapons of war. The mêlée clearly resembled a battlefield and, while the resemblance of jousting to battle conditions might seem more limited, real battles – such as Bannockburn in 1314 and Halidon Hill in 1333 – were often prefigured by single combat of exactly the sort re-enacted in jousts.[14] Both the tournament proper and the joust therefore constituted a highly authentic setting in which the participants

---

[12] Matthew Paris, *Chronica Majora*, ed. H.R. Luard (Roll Series, 1872-83), 200-2; *Chron. Melrose*, 90; Chron. *Bower* (Watt), 178-79; *Chron. Wyntoun* (Laing), ii, 246-47;*Chron. Lanercost*, 49-50.
[13] General histories of the tournament, upon which much of this section is based, include R. Barber and J. Barker, *Tournaments, Chivalry and Pageant in the Middle Ages* (Woodbridge, 1989); J.R.V. Barker, *The Tournament in England, 1100-1400* (Woodbridge, 1986); and J. Vale, *Edward III and Chivalry: Chivalric society and its context, 1270-1350* (Woodbridge, 1982). The English studies, it should be noted, are a good deal wider in scope than their titles suggest.
[14] *The Bruce* (Duncan), 448-51; *Chron. Le Baker*, 51.

might practice the skills required on the battlefield. Meanwhile, one-to-one combat was also a useful preparation for the many duels which were fought, mainly by aristocrats, though in 1216 Pope Innocent III fulminated against those in Scotland who forced the clergy to undergo a duel in person too.[15]

The later middle ages witnessed several developments to these two basic formats of joust and mêlée. Many tournaments, even by the thirteenth century, developed into increasingly ritualised charades as combat *à outrance* became pageant *à plaisance*. Often set to a storyline, enacted upon lavishly constructed sets and frequently fought with blunted weapons, these sanitised tournaments were staged in front of large audiences in which noble women, as well as men, were prominent. On these occasions it was increasingly for a woman's favour, rather than to hone their own military skills, that knights now fought; and, much to the disgust of one English chronicler at least, women reportedly used such occasions to parade themselves and 'wantonly and with disgraceful lubricity' display their bodies.[16] The paradoxically brazen yet passive role of women in such proceedings is one indication of the changing nature of the tournament: an audience had become *de rigeur*. This meant that tournaments were frequently staged in large towns, such as Edinburgh, London and Bruges, which were accessible both to the aristocrats of the surrounding countryside and to a sizeable audience of townspeople. To some extent the later medieval tournament was a cultural phenomenon which melded the martial interests of the rural aristocracy with spectating (and business) opportunities for the urban populace. In London, for instance, Smithfield, on the edge of the built environment, was a favoured location for English tournaments.[17] This was where teams captained by the earls of Kent and Mar jousted in 1406, though London Bridge was the even more spectacular setting for the contest between Sir David Lindsay of Glenesk and Lord Wells in 1390.[18] In Scotland, meanwhile, many of the most famous tournaments were staged at either Stirling or Edinburgh, often below the walls of the towns' castles. The Edinburgh 'barras' – tournament field – was in existence by at least 1337, and this was where Sir Patrick Hamilton challenged the French esquire Jean de Cowpance in 1498-99, even though in 1456 James II had earmarked landed between Canongate and Leith 'for tournaments, sports and proper warlike deeds'.[19]

---

[15] R. Bartlett, *Trial by Fire and Water: The medieval judicial ordeal* (Oxford,1986), 119.

[16] *Chron. Knighton* (Martin), 92-5.

[17] S. Lindenbaum, 'The Smithfield tournament of 1390', *Journal of Medieval and Renaissance Studies*, 20 (1990), 1-20. Lindenbaum, however, refutes the notion that the urban populace figured prominently in this event. On the urban setting of Netherlandish tournaments, see Vale, *Edward III and Chivalry*, chapter 2.

[18] *Chron. Wyntoun* (Laing), iii, 47-50, 102-4; *Chron. Bower* (Watt), viii, 13; *Chron. Westminster*, 434; *CDS*, iv, nos. 404, 410-11; *Rot. Scot.*, ii, 103. G. Neilson, *Trial by Combat* (Glasgow, 1890), 233-38.

[19] *CDS*, iii, p. 359; Pitscottie, *Historie*, i, 234; Neilson, *Trial by Combat*, 284-85; *ER*, xi, 231, 235, 259; *Edin. Chrs.*, 82. See too *ER*, i, 238, for what seems to have been an Anglo-Scottish tournament

If the precise location for such events was significant, so too was the attention given to the stage decor and cast. An audience demanded spectacle. An elaborate set was part of this spectacle and some tournament props – such as the 'botes of Leith' on which men jousted for James IV in 1496 – bore little obvious resemblance to the conditions of an actual battlefield.[20] Still, even on inauthentic sets, participants required armour, weapons and horses. These were expensive commodities and their value is suggested by the occasional inclusion of both horses and armour in the safe-conducts which participants obtained when venturing abroad to display their military skills.[21] Indeed, armour was often procured abroad specifically for prearranged conflictual occasions. In 1367 William Douglas of Dechmont acquired a lance head, daggers and armour in London for a duel to be fought on the border; and James V sought 'cataphract horses' from Denmark for tourneying in 1538.[22]

In addition to magnificent sets and the finest of props, spectacles also required a cast. Sometimes this was assembled following a general challenge by which all-comers were invited to demonstrate their skills. Scots, for instance, were called along with Frenchmen and Englishmen, to the famous tournament staged at St Inglevert, near Boulogne, in 1390; and the lord of Haubourd and sometime Burgundian envoy, Jean de Luxembourg, bastard of St Pol, issued a general invitation to Englishmen, Germans, Scots and Spaniards to participate in a tournament which he hosted near Calais in 1449.[23] Other events featured more carefully selected teams which were of national composition. Arrangements of this sort were devised for the two international tournaments staged at London in May 1390, the first (on 6 May) featuring Lindsay, Wells and their two teams and a second (on 28 May) starring a team of Scots captained by the earl of Moray and an English team led by the earl of Nottingham.[24] Team games, in the middle ages as nowadays, often produced star performers and by the fifteenth century some knights had acquired international renown for their performances. Jacques de Lalaing, councillor and chamberlain of the duke of Burgundy, was one; and Antoine

staged at Edinburgh in 1329. For tournaments at Stirling, see below, n. 25 and also *TA*, iii, 364, 395; v, 381, 411-12; vi, 225.

[20] *TA*, iii, 141. It could perhaps be argued that boats provided an authentic preparation for maritime conflict. The weaponry used for this was similar to that deployed on land: D. Ditchburn, 'Piracy and war at sea in late medieval Scotland' in T.C. Smout, *Scotland and the Sea* (Edinburgh, 1992), 41-2.

[21] *CDS*, iv, nos. 404, 410, 414.

[22] *Rot. Scot.*, i, 916-17; *James V Letters*, 345. See too *CDS*, iv, nos. 283, 462, 584, for the acquisition of swords in Flanders and armour in England.

[23] *Chron. Froissart* (Lettenhove), xiv, 107; Bower and Barber, *Tournaments*, 117. That the St Inglevert tournament received extensive coverage from Wyntoun perhaps suggests Scottish participation: *The Original Chronicle of Andrew of Wyntoun* (STS, 1903-14), vi, 348-354. (This passage is omitted from *Chron. Wyntoun* (Laing), iii.) The event is not, however, mentioned by Bower and no Scots are mentioned in the most recent study of the tournament, E. Gaucher, 'Les joutes de Saint-Inglevert: perception et écriture d'un événement historique pendant la guerre de cent ans', *Le Moyen Age*, 102 (1996), 229-44.

[24] *Chron Westminster*, 436; *The Brut*, 366; *CDS*, iv, 411; *Rot.Scot.*, ii, 103-4. See also above, n. 18.

d'Arces, lord of la Bastie-sur-Melans, was another. Both men brought their travelling show to Scotland. Lalaing's tourneying reputation was forged in the 1440s. He had performed in Ghent in 1445 and Valladolid in 1448, but his career reached its pinnacle in 1449, when he appeared at Stirling in February and Bruges in June. From October Lalaing then prepared to meet all-comers for a year of combat set against the backdrop of a 'Fountain of Tears', constructed at Chalons-sur-Saône – though in the event no one appeared to challenge him until February 1450.[25] At Stirling Lalaing and three Burgundian companions challenged James Douglas, the brother of the eighth earl of Douglas, and three other members of the Douglas affinity. We know of no set upon which their combat was enacted, but the participants arrived in lavish costumes. Lalaing and his uncle Simon, lord of Montigny, were adorned in 'long black robes of velvet, furred with martens', while Hervé de Mériadec appeared in 'a short robe of black satin, furred with fine marten'. They performed their martial skills in front of a large audience which Lalaing's biographer, no doubt with some exaggeration, estimated to be between four and five thousand in size. Significantly, although it had been agreed that the contest should be *à outrance*, which no doubt added to the excitement of the crowd, no one was killed. The opportunities for inflicting mortal blows had arisen, but James II, who presided over the event, intervened to prevent the occurrence of fatalities. In reality, then, this was a tournament *à plaisance* and Lalaing and his compatriots were subsequently feted at a post-tournament feast and regaled with unspecified 'honourable gifts'.[26]

We are better informed of the payment which James IV delivered to d'Arces. The lord of la Bastie, like Lalaing, was a celebrated star of the tournament circuit, having fought in England, France, Portugal and Spain, in addition to two appearances which he made in Scotland, in 1506-7 and again in 1508. On the first occasion he appears to have jousted with the earl of Arran at Stirling in November 1506. Then he performed in a grander tournament, also staged at Stirling, in January 1507, for which he was well rewarded with over £335 in cash and lavish gifts of gold and silver. In 1508 d'Arces returned to Scotland to participate in the second of James IV's pageant-tournaments of 'The Wild Knight and the Black Lady', in which the king himself took the male title role, performing as the champion of a Moorish woman famously celebrated in William Dunbar's (then acceptably) racist phraseology as the 'ladye with the mekle lippis' who 'blinkis als brycht as ane tar barrell'.[27] These events, as the royal expenditure on them reveals, were classic pageant. Elaborate costumes and sets (the latter designed by the clerk of the chapel royal, Sir Thomas Galbraith, and a Dutch painter by the name of Piers) were created for show in front of an international audience

[25] *Chron. Chastellain* (Lettenhove), viii, 82-9, 130-47, 164-79, 189-97, 201-46; *IAB*, v, 498. Lalaing's tourneying exploits are noted in Barber and Barker, *Tournaments*, 118-19, 130; 'Chron. Auchinleck', 164; *Chron. d'Escouchy*, i, 148-53; *Chron. Waurin, 1447-71*, 26.
[26] *Chron. Chastellain* (Lettenhove), 172-73.
[27] Dunbar, *Poems*, no. 33, p. 106.

composed of, if Pitscottie is to be believed, Scots, Danes, English and French. Certainly the king spent 52s on engrossing and illuminating the official announcement of the 1508 tournament which was circulated in France.[28]

Here we are reminded of another vital element in the theatrical transformation of the tournament: spectacle was also propaganda. Tournaments were prestigious occasions and, through their lavish patronage of such events and generous provision of prizes, hosts could use such events to advertise their own chivalric worth in international and domestic circles, and also that of their subjects. The tournament was thus something of a unifying bond between ruler and ruled. There was, perhaps, an element of the artificial to this, for valour in a pageant was not the same as courage on the battlefield. For contemporaries, however, the location was less important than the *display* of prowess. 'A knight,' opined Christian de Pisan, 'is not known but by his deeds of arms.'[29]   And Pitscottie, for one, swallowed the royal propaganda, proclaiming that James IV 'brocht his realme of great manheid and honouris' through his promotion of tournaments. James's tournaments were, he added, attended by 'money forand knychtis ... out of strange contrieis ... because they hard the nobill fame and knychtlie game of the prince of Scotland and of his lordis and barrans and gentillmen'.[30] Indeed, James IV was not alone in using tournaments to propagandistic ends. Perhaps the most famous of all later medieval tournaments was that staged at Bruges in 1430, which concluded with Philip the Good, duke of Burgundy, announcing the creation of his chivalric order of the Golden Fleece.[31] The chivalric glory of the Burgundian ruler was, on this occasion, being loudly proclaimed to a Netherlands recently, but not yet convincingly, united under the dominion of the Valois dukes. The role of the chivalric in unifying the politically fractious and linguistically divergent Burgundian duchy has long been acknowledged by historians, as has the chivalric contribution to re-establishing political harmony in the English kingdom during Edward III's reign. In his promotion of tournaments and creation of a vehicle through which Scottish nobles might demonstrate their chivalric worth, James IV, it might be argued, was following a similar path to the restoration of domestic harmony following the fissure between ruler and ruled which had emerged during his father's reign.

The type of occasion on which Philip the Good chose to stage his magnificent chivalric celebrations of 1430 – that of his marriage to Isabel of Portugal – was not uncommon. Throughout the Latin west moments of

---

[28] D'Arces's career is related in F. Michel, *Les Ecossais en France, Les Français en Ecosse* (London and Edinburgh, 1862), i, 303-5; and in L.O. Fradenburg, *City, Marriage, Tournament: Arts of rule in late medieval Scotland* (Madison, Wis., 1991) 176-77. On his Scottish tournament exploits, see *TA*, iii, pp. xxxviii-lii, 372; iv, 117-18, 124, 127-28.

[29] Christine de Pisan, *The Epistle of Othea translated from the French text by Stephen Scrope*, ed. C.F. Bühler (Early English Text Society, 1970), 88.

[30] Pitscottie, *Historie*, i, 232.

[31] P. Vaughan, *Philip the Good: The Apogee of Burgundy* (London, 1970), 56-7, 160-63. In addition to the sources cited there, see also P. Cockshaw, ed., *L'ordre de la Toison d'Or de Philippe le Bon à Philippe le Beau, 1430-1505: Idéal ou reflet d'une société?* (Brussels, 1996).

dynastic significance and diplomatic importance were frequently marked by a tournament. In 1449, for instance, Philip staged another tournament at Bruges, this time featuring Lalaing, which was designed to celebrate the marriage of Philip's niece, Mary of Guelders, to James II of Scotland.[32] On this occasion the message of Burgundian munificence was probably directed at Mary's father, Duke Arnold of Guelders, who was not only unable to meet the costs of his daughter's dowry, but who, more significantly, was an isolated critic of Burgundian domination of the Low Countries.[33] More provocatively still, James IV organised a tournament in 1496 to celebrate the marriage of Katherine Gordon and Perkin Warbeck, the pretender to the English crown of Henry VII. This attempt to cock a snook at his future father-in-law may have backfired somewhat, for at about the same time, and perhaps as a consequence of over-exuberance in mock battle, James was to complain of a 'sare hand'.[34] He had recovered by the time of his own marriage in 1503, which was similarly marked by jousting in the courtyard of Holyrood Palace.[35] But although marriages were a convenient occasion on which to use tournaments as vehicles of political propaganda, some monarchs needed no such excuse. In 1358 Edward III of England staged a tournament at Windsor with the express intention of celebrating recent English victories in battle against the French and the Scots.[36] Indeed, the Windsor tournament of 1358, in which English champions pitted their skills against Scots, adds weight to those who consider that by the later middle ages 'the palmy days of the tournament as a species of military exercise [were] on the wane'.[37] Here was an event staged not to prepare for war, but to celebrate its outcome. The practice of military skills, the original purpose of the tournament, was on this occasion overshadowed, among the organisers at least, by other motives: a quest for spectacle and naked political triumphalism.

Nevertheless, while many of the most famous later medieval tournaments were marked by a sense of theatre, several still concluded with a tragic twist. John Dunbar, earl of Moray, was perhaps injured following his clash with the earl of Nottingham in London in 1390.[38] Somewhat later, in 1485, Alexander, duke of Albany, James III's exiled brother, met his death at the end of a

---

[32] *IAB*, v, 498.

[33] D. Ditchburn, 'The place of Guelders in Scottish foreign policy, *c.*1449-*c.*1542' in G.G. Simpson, ed., *Scotland and the Low Countries, 1124-1994* (East Linton, 1996), 66-7.

[34] *TA*, i, pp. cxxx-xxxi, 257, 262-63.

[35] J.G. Dunbar, *Scottish Royal Palaces: The architecture of the royal residences during the later medieval and early renaissance periods* (East Linton, 1999), 59, 203.

[36] *Eulogium (Historiarum sive temporis): Chronicon ab orde condition usque...*, ed. F.S. Haydon (Roll Series, 1858-63), iii, 227. Similarly Edward III staged a tournament at Dunstable in 1342 to mark military victory over the Scots: *Chron. Le Baker*, 75.

[37] *TA*, iii, p. xxxviii.

[38] *Rot. Scot.*, ii, 103-4; *CDS*, iv, no. 411; *Chron. Westminster*, 436-37; *The Brut*, ii, 348, where the earl of Mar seems to be mistaken for the earl of Moray. Here the Scot is said to have broken two ribs and, while being carried home in a litter, to have died at York, though rumours of his death were certainly exaggerated. See J.B. Paul, ed., *The Scots Peerage* (Edinburgh, 1904-14), vi, 300-1.

splintered lance while jousting with the French king in Paris.[39] There remained a dangerous element to such activity. Moreover, although many tournaments, such as that staged at Stirling in 1449, remained *à outrance* in name only, even these incorporated the new and significant inclusion of combat with axes and daggers as well as the traditional weapons of lance and broadsword – significant because in real battles mounted warriors were by then increasingly expected to dismount and engage in personal combat with an adversary.[40] This too was common in those tournaments (or 'feats of arms') which, especially during the fourteenth century, were staged in areas far removed from impressionable court circles, in frontier regions which were more familiar with the bloody atrocities which marked real combat. These tournaments remained inextricably linked with the reality of warfare, and not just because they were fought with unblunted weapons and before probably more cynical audiences. Some were judicial duels. Others were staged mid-campaign. The Christmas festivities which briefly interrupted the English invasion of Scotland in 1341 provided a suitable interlude for tourneying activities at Melrose and Roxburgh.[41] Sieges, meanwhile, were the setting for other contests. Thus, as Thomas Randolph, earl of Moray, and Sir James Douglas besieged Henry Percy in the Northumbrian citadel of Alnwick in 1327 'there were great jousts of war by formal agreement'; and in 1338 Alexander Ramsay jousted with an English squire as an Edwardian army besieged Cupar.[42] And yet other feats of arms (some featuring only two individuals and which seem to have been judicial duels, and others involving English and Scottish teams) were arranged along the Anglo-Scottish borders, especially during periods of truce in the 1380s and 1390s.[43] These could be brutal affairs. During that staged at Berwick early in 1342, in which teams of either twelve or twenty Scots and English fought each other, three deaths and several other injuries ensued.[44]

Why, then, did so many (presumably sane) knights expose themselves to such horrendous danger in the name of sport? One explanation perhaps lies in the sharper national animosities which developed in the fourteenth century. The century which witnessed the greatest number of recorded Anglo-Scottish tournaments was also that in which Anglo-Scottish hostilities were at their most intense. As we have seen, some contests were staged mid-campaign and their occurrence may be interpreted as a gamble by the participants to gain psychological advantage immediately prior to the 'real' hostilities. Indeed,

---

[39] *ER*, ix, p. lvi.

[40] *Chron. Chastellain* (Lettenhove), viii, 173. Axes and daggers were also used in the contest between Lindsay and Wells in 1390 (*Chron Westminster*, 434; *Chron. Wyntoun* (Laing), iii, 49).

[41] Adam Murimuth, *Continuatio Chronicarum*, ed. E.M. Thompson (Roll Series, 1889), 123; *Chron. Knighton* (Martin), 38-9; *Chron. Bower* (Watt), 136-37; *Chron. Wyntoun* (Laing), 440-41.

[42] *Scalacronica*, 155; *Chron. Wyntoun* (Laing), ii, 436.

[43] *CDS*, iv, nos. 309, 414, 425, 439, 468, 659, 711. *Rot. Scot.*, ii, 29, 39, 87, 90, 105-6, 111, 117, 119; *Chron. Bower* (Watt), vii, 533.

[44] *Chron. Knighton* (Martin), 38-39; *Chron. Wyntoun* (Laing), ii, 441-46; *Chron. Bower* (Watt), vii, 136-39.

when set against the wider context of Anglo-Scottish conflict, and the seeming impossibility of establishing a lasting peace between the two kingdoms, this factor is likely to have been important during tournaments staged in times of truce too. A morale-boosting victory could be psychologically banked for a future episode of real conflict. Moreover, that several tournaments were staged during periods of truce perhaps lends support to the notion that tournaments provided an outlet for national animosities when the war option itself was in temporary suspension. These are persuasive arguments, but not ones which offer a completely satisfactory explanation for the popularity of the tournament. They do not explain why tournaments were staged during the comparatively peaceful thirteenth century, or why few were seemingly staged during the middle decades of the fourteenth century. We must assume, then, that in explaining the popularity of the tournament other factors also came into play.

One of these factors was the official, governmental attitude. In England, while Edward III and Richard II were enthusiasts for the tournament, Henry IV and Henry V were not;[45] and given that comparatively few tournaments occurred once David II returned from his French exile in 1341 we may wonder whether, for all the other evidence of his chivalric enthusiasms, David too was somewhat sceptical of the benefits of tournaments. Since official permission seems to have been required for staging feats of arms, this perhaps accounts for the comparative frequency of tournaments in the 1330s and early 1340s, their subsequent rarity, and the revival of feats of arms once Robert II had succeeded David II in 1371.[46] But, in determining why tournaments were staged, there are other motives too which we ought to consider, such as the intensity of personal rivalries among the participants. This may be one reason why some war veterans chose to display their martial skills in single combat while others did not. There seems to have been personal rivalry between Percy and Douglas, who organised the jousting at Alnwick in 1327, for both men laid claim to lands in Jedworth Forest. There was clearly also an element of personal acrimony – perhaps regarding lands in Douglasdale – between two other war veterans, William Douglas of Nithsdale and Thomas Clifford, who proposed to undertake feats of arms with each other in 1390.[47] Whether similar personal rivalries influenced other jousting occasions is less clear, though it is noticeable that many tournament participants were either Borderers (such as Ralph, lord Neville) or men with Border experience (such as the earl of Nottingham who had served as keeper of Roxburgh Castle).[48] These were men whose geo-political interests may well have brought them

[45] Barber and Barker, *Tournament*, 37.
[46] Exceptions to the scarcity of evidence between 1341 and 1371 include the Berwick tournament of early 1342 and the judicial duels fought in the Border regions in 1368, for which see *Rot. Scot.*, i, 916-17.
[47] *CDS*, iv, no. 414.
[48] *CDS*, iv, nos. 411, 425.

into adversarial contact with those whom they subsequently opposed on the tournament field.

Yet neither the notion of Border societies inured to war, nor bitter rivalries spawned by territorial disputes or personal enmity, explain why a contingent of at least six Scots or Anglo-Scots fought at the Compiègne tournament of 1278;[49] or why northerners, such as David Lindsay of Glenesk (who fought in London in 1390) or Alexander Stewart, earl of Mar (who fought in London in 1406), also participated in tournaments. To explain this we must resort to what Alastair Macdonald has dubbed the 'non-rational motivations' behind medieval conflict.[50] Fighting, as we have seen, was the *raison d'être* of medieval knights and we should not rule out the possibility that these men, and many Borderers too, simply *enjoyed* fighting. There is some evidence to support this notion. The Compiègne tournament of 1278 featured, among others, both John de Vescy, lord of Sprouston in Roxburghshire, and John Comyn. Vescy was certainly a man of military endeavour. He had accompanied the future Edward I on his crusade in 1271-72 and was later to participate in the same king's Welsh wars of 1277 and 1282. If Comyn may be equated with John Comyn of Badenoch, he was a man of similar temperament who had lent his services voluntarily to the English crown at the battle of Lewes, during the civil wars of the 1260s. And others too conformed to this outlook. A seemingly unexpected offer led Mar to join the duke of Burgundy's campaign against the Liègois in 1408. Neither at Lewes, nor at Liège did either Comyn or Mar have any discernibly rational motives for their participation – other perhaps than using these opportunities to promote solidarity and training in arms among members of their military affinity.[51] Yet even this does not preclude the possibility that they signed up for service because they enjoyed fighting, much as other tournament participants, such as William Douglas of Nithsdale, joined the crusades.

There is another element to the aristocratic mind-set of the middle ages that we must not forget. The chivalric ethos ensured that fighting was not just a function, but a culture. Lalaing was prompted to challenge the Douglases, so his biographer tells us, because he thought constantly of attaining 'la haute vertu de prouesse et bonne renommé'.[52] And although unfettered chivalric notions spawned the tournament *à plaisance*, chivalry was not absent from the grimmer tournament *à outrance*. Even amid the carnage of the tournament

[49] A. de Behault de Doron, 'La noblesse hennuyère au tournoi de Compiègne de 1238 [sic]', *Annales du cercle archéolgique de Mons*, 22 (1890), 61-114. The Scots who particpated in this tournament are listed as: Alexander de Balliol (?lord of Cavers, *fl.* 1246-1309), Richard de Brins (?Robert Bruce), Henry Haliburton (?of Dirleton, *fl.* 1270-96) and William de Soules (?justiciar of Lothian, *c.*1279-*c.*1292). John Vescy (d.1289) and John Comyn were noted among the English contingent. For Lindsay and Mar, see above, n. 18.

[50] A.J. Macdonald, *Border Bloodshed: Scotland and England at war, 1369-1403* (East Linton, 2000), 178.

[51] M. Brown, 'Regional lordship in the north-east. The Badenoch Stewarts, II: Alexander Stewart, earl of Mar', *NS*, 16 (1996), 32.

[52] *Chron. Chastellain* (Lettenhove), viii, 164.

field at Berwick in 1342 there were clearly discernible chivalric elements: courage, largesse and honour. Contemporaries applauded bravery and courage, even in an adversary, and deplored cheating. Those who supervised tournaments awarded prizes for the best performance and at Berwick in 1342, in truly courteous fashion, it was left to the two teams to nominate the best performance among their adversaries. The Scots chose an English knight who had run his lance through William Ramsay's head; and the English, significantly, selected Patrick Graham who killed John Twyford and who would have killed Richard Talbot, had Talbot not worn protective armour beyond that agreed by the two teams prior to their engagement.[53] There was a place for courtesy even in the midst of carnage, and it was with implicit disgust that an English chronicler recorded how 'northerners' (not 'Englishmen') enticed the Scots to Berwick seven years later with false promises of a tournament, only to ambush and slay them in a deceitful fashion.[54]

Visiting the Family

Both crusading and tourneying provided opportunities for pleasure trips abroad, in the case of the crusades to the Baltic and to the Mediterranean and in the case of tournaments mainly to England and France. Pilgrimage, of course, provided similar opportunities and, to those activities which combined leisure and travel, we should also add visits made to friends and relations who resided abroad, though the frequency of these should not be exaggerated. Although, as we shall see in chapter five, many Scots of humble status emigrated in the later medieval period, we know little about the mechanisms by which they maintained contact with relatives, or whether they even did. While one Scot who studied at Oxford in 1255 was visited by a nephew, on balance it seems unlikely, given the cost of transport and the slow pace of travel, that many Scots visited friends and relations abroad, though some emigrants did occasionally make visits to their homeland.[55] By contrast, the aristocratic elite could afford to travel and in the thirteenth and early fourteenth centuries, when international marriages and transnational landholdings were common, they probably did so quite frequently. Before he became king John Balliol visited his familial estates in Picardy in 1289;[56] and in 1305 his successor as king, Robert Bruce, used the opportunity of attending to his late father's English estates (which included a house in London and an estate at Tottenham) to visit his brother Alexander, then a student in

---

[53] *Chron. Knighton* (Martin) 38-9; *Chron. Wyntoun* (Laing), ii, 446; *Chron. Bower* (Watt), vii, 136-39.
[54] *Chron. Knighton* (Martin), 92-3.
[55] Watt, *Graduates*, 45; 'Letters of a Scottish student at Paris and Oxford, *c*.1250', ed. N.R. Ker and W.A. Pantin in *Formularies which Bear on the History of Oxford, c.1204-1420*, ed. H.E. Slater, W.A. Pantin and H.G. Richardson, ii (Oxford Historical Society, 1942), 489, no. 17.
[56] G. Stell, 'The Balliol family and the Great Cause of 1291-2' in K.J. Stringer, ed., *Essays on the Nobility of Medieval Scotland* (Edinburgh, 1985), 154-55.

Cambridge. Robert perhaps also saw his de Clare relations during this visit, and he was to travel abroad again on family business in 1328, when he escorted his nephew William de Burgh to his Ulster earldom.[57] Robert's (and John's) royal predecessors were also internationally peripatetic. Although Alexander III's mother, Marie de Coucy, returned to her native France shortly after her son's tenth birthday in 1250, and married again in 1257, she returned to the British Isles in 1251 for the wedding of her son to Margaret, daughter of Henry III, spending Christmas with her son at York. In 1257, together with her new husband, the son of the king of Jerusalem, she visited Alexander in Scotland.[58] Alexander, meanwhile, also had occasional encounters with his wife's family. The couple was visited by Queen Margaret's brother, the future Edward I, probably in 1266, and Alexander also attended his brother-in-law's coronation in 1274. He met Edward again in 1278 to perform homage for his lands in England.[59]

Such contact was both facilitated by, and helped to promote, the generally cordial nature of Anglo-Scottish relations in the later thirteenth century. The protracted conflict of the fourteenth century changed this. Thereafter few aristocrats (exiles excepted, the first two Stewart kings included) married foreigners and transnational landholding virtually ceased. With neither landed interests nor marital ties abroad, most later medieval Scottish aristocrats no longer possessed one impetus for travel possessed by many of their thirteenth-century counterparts. Indeed, only from the reign of James I did the royal family once again look abroad to contract its marital alliances. The king himself took an English bride, Joan Beaufort, and five of their children took continental partners, a sixth (Annabella) returning to Scotland only after a lengthy betrothal to the count of Geneva failed to materialise into marriage. Nevertheless, the reinvented cosmopolitanism of the fifteenth-century royal family produced a far-flung family network which was bound together by only the loosest of personal contacts. Joan Beaufort never returned to England, either as a wife or as a widow. Although her uncle, Cardinal Beaufort, visited Scotland on diplomatic business in 1429, Joan seems rarely to have seen members of her own family after her arrival in Scotland.[60] Similarly, Joan's daughter-in-law, Mary of Guelders, never returned to the Netherlands following her marriage to James II in 1449. Indeed, she never again saw any of her Netherlandish relatives, though it was presumably at her instigation that her second son, Alexander, duke of Albany, spent four years with his

[57] G.W.S. Barrow, *Robert Bruce and the Community of the Realm of Scotland* (3rd., ed., Edinburgh, 1988), 142-43; Watt, *Graduates*, 66; R. Nicholson, 'A sequel to Robert Bruce's invasion of Ireland', *SHR*, 42 (1963), 35-7. Although the later chronicle assertion that, by sending a symbolic shilling and pair of spurs, Raoul de Morthermer, earl of Gloucester, warned Robert to flee Edward I's wrath in 1305 seems totally fictitious, it seems credible that Robert should have met his Gloucester relations while visiting England that year. (c.f. Barrow, *Bruce*, 139-140; *Chron. Fordun*, ii, 331).
[58] *CDS*, i, nos. 1785, 1804, 1807, 1812, 1815-19, 2083, 2084; *Chron. Melrose*, 109-10; *Chron. Fordun*, ii, 290.
[59] M. Prestwich, *Edward I* (London, 1988), 57-8, 356-57.
[60] *Foedera* (O), x, 408-10.

Gueldrian grandfather between 1460 and 1464.[61] Meanwhile, two of Joan's daughters, Margaret (who married the French Dauphin in 1436) and Isabella (who married the duke of Brittany's son in 1442) remained similarly isolated and their sisters were only marginally less so. Mary (who married the lord of Veere in 1444) entertained her sister Annabella for a fortnight in 1445.[62] Once ensconced at the Savoyard court Annabella was in turn visited by her sister Eleanor as she passed through Savoy on her way to the Tirol, where she married the Archduke Sigismund in 1449. Thereafter Eleanor's only personal contact with her family was probably with her half-brother, James Stewart, earl of Buchan, who visited the Austrian court in 1465.[63]

Although the early fifteenth-century Stewarts devised other means of maintaining family contacts – by dispatch of letters and gifts and through messengers who were no doubt entrusted to relay family news – their direct personal contacts were markedly less close than those evident among members of Alexander III's family. And though too the Stewarts abroad received other Scottish visitors – Annabella, for instance, entertained a bastard of the earl of Douglas for three weeks in January 1455 – for women marriage effectively entailed isolation from both family and friends.[64] Only in the sixteenth century did foreign queens, albeit in widowhood, once again visit their homelands.[65]

We should not assume that the fifteenth-century royal family was somewhat dysfunctional in its emotional attachments. It was reportedly with tears that James I witnessed the departure of his eldest daughter to France in 1436.[66] No doubt he knew that he was unlikely to see her again. James was certainly aware that Margaret's father-in-law, the French king Charles VII, preferred that his daughter-in-law have as few reminders of her homeland around her as possible, so that she might be groomed without prejudice for he role as queen-designate of France.[67] It was not that royal parents lacked affection for their children, but James knew, because conventional wisdom dictated, that it was a ruler's duty to defend his domain. That could not be done if he was visiting family abroad. As a consequence, after the outbreak of war with England in 1296, invasions apart, only three adult Scottish kings willingly ventured abroad: Robert I to Ireland, once peace was temporarily re-established in 1328; David II who probably visited England twice, in 1363 and

[61] Ditchburn, 'The place of Guelders', 68-9; G. Nijsten, *Het Hof van Gelre: Cultuur ten tijde van de hertogen uit het Gulikse en Egmondse huis, 1371-1473* (Kampen, 1992), 320, n.107.
[62] AS Torino, Inventario 16, Registro 93, fos. 376v-377.
[63] AS Torino, Inventario 16, Registro 96, fo. 456r; M. Köfler and S. Caramelle, *Die beiden Frauen des Erzherzogs Sigismund von Österreich-Tirol* (Innsbruck, 1982), 91.
[64] AS Torino, Inventario 16, Registro 104, fo. 264v. For her sister Eleanor's Scottish visitors, see Köfler and S. Caramelle, *Die beiden Frauen des Erzherzogs Sigismund*, 91-2
[65] P.H. Buchanan, *Margaret Tudor, Queen of Scots* (Edinburgh, 1985), chapter 11; R.K. Marshall, *Mary of Guise* (London, 1977), 186. Mary was visited by her brother Claude in 1550 (ibid, 182-83).
[66] L.A. Barbé, *Margaret of Scotland and the Dauphin Louis: An historical study* (London, 1917), 81.
[67] Barbé, *Margaret of Scotland*, 59-60, 65-6.

in 1369;[68] and James V, who travelled to Paris in 1536 for his (first) marriage to Madeleine de Valois. For reasons of state, then, kings were unlikely to visit their offspring who married abroad.

Queens, meanwhile, were shackled to the kingdom as a result of other expectations. It was the fundamental duty of every queen to provide her husband with an heir and preferably, indeed, to guard against the risks of infant mortality by providing him with several reserves too. Obviously this was a role which queens could not perform unless they were frequently at their husband's side. Although, once pregnant, Alexander III's first wife, Margaret of England, visited her mother in 1260-1, this was permitted only once clear agreement had been reached between the two governments, setting out terms and conditions for Margaret's visit, and more importantly (as far as contemporaries were perhaps concerned), for her child's return.[69] The Scottish political community preferred its female figureheads to remain in Scotland, and between the mid-thirteenth century and mid-sixteenth century only two did not – David II's two wives, Joan Plantagenet and Margaret Logie. It is significant, however, that their foreign travels – Joan returned to England in 1357 and died there in 1362, and Margaret died abroad while on her way to the papal court to prevent her husband's attempts to obtain a divorce – occurred only after the irretrievable breakdown of their marriages and after it had become unlikely that either woman would bear the king an heir. Regular trips home were thus taboo and to have undertaken them might have aroused suspicions as to a queen's commitment to her new homeland and her role within that society. As a consequence queens were as unlikely as kings to see their children who married abroad; and, of course, those who did marry abroad were soon lumbered with the similarly restrictive constraints of their new subjects, making a visit home equally difficult.

Sport and Games

Since crusading opportunities were declining, tournaments comparatively infrequent, and family visits to foreign parts rare, it may seem as if continental influences on Scottish leisure activities were limited. Although we are singularly ill-informed about the recreational pursuits of most later medieval Scots, it seems safe to assume that recreation normally revolved around socialising with nearby family and friends and, in the case of men, probably prostitutes too.[70] Much social contact was probably focused on local taverns and churches, where, as we have already seen, important feast days were

---

[68] 'A question about the succession, 1364', ed. A.A.M. Duncan, *SHS Miscellany*, 12 (1994), 1-20.

[69] *CDS*, i, no. 2229.

[70] Little has been written about prostitution in later medieval Scotland, though see E. Ewan, 'Mons Meg and Merchant Meg: women in later medieval Edinburgh' in Brotherstone and Ditchburn, *Freedom and Authority*, 142; D. Ditchburn and A.J. Macdonald, 'Medieval Scotland, 1100-1560' in R.A. Houston and W. Knox, eds., *The Penguin History of Medieval Scotland* (London, 2001, forthcoming); and more generally the excellent synopsis by J.A. Brundage, *Law, Sex and Christian Society in the Medieval Europe* (Chicago, 1987).

accompanied by pageants and processions.[71] For the male population, at least, games and sports (such as wrestling, football and golf) were also popular pursuits which owed little, if anything, to continental contacts. Some of these interests spanned social classes. Despite earlier attempts to ban it in favour of archery, golf was latterly played by kings as well as commoners: James IV paid 6s for two golf clubs and a dozen golf balls in 1506.[72] Other pastimes were more socially exclusive. When not fighting or attending to seigniorial duties, aristocrats often resorted to their estates to indulge in the quintessential aristocratic pursuits of hunting and hawking. These were, of course, private rather than public occasions, and they have left comparatively few traces in the extant documentary record, or material culture, of the period. Still, some measure of their popularity with James IV is suggested by his employment of at least fifty-eight falconers between 1488 and 1513.[73]

James's love of hawking was shared by the aristocracy of the Latin west, and there was certainly an international dimension to its practice. Hawks and falcons were prized possessions and much money was lavished on their acquisition. Despite their availability in Scotland, some were acquired abroad. In 1508, for instance, James IV was presented with hawks sent by the Irish warlord Hugh O'Donnell of Ulster, and in 1540 James V dispatched two servants to the continent to procure hawks.[74] So committed was the latter king to the sport that four years earlier he arranged for coursing horses, falcons and dogs to be sent from Scotland for his use in France, where, prior to his marriage, he was spending time with the French king Francis I.[75] We do not know what became of James's hunting accoutrements, but it would not have been surprising had James bequeathed them to his host, for hunting and hawking paraphernalia were deemed suitable gifts for even the most powerful of princes. In the fifteenth century James lord Hamilton offered to send his step-aunt, Eleanor, duchess of Austria-Tirol, hawks and hounds, and in 1535 James V sent his master falconer to Henry VIII of England 'wyth sex folkounnis unlauborit of this yeir' which he had acquired in the Northern Isles.[76] Others – such as the earl of Kent in 1504 – also sought to procure hawks in Scotland. Even although the most valuable hawks came from Scandinavia, Scotland was clearly well positioned to furnish the European aristocracy with its birds.[77]

Hunting was similarly popular and Scottish greyhounds were sufficiently renowned for Froissart to return to France with a fine white specimen,

---

[71] See above, page 53.

[72] *APS*, ii, 48; *TA*, iii, 187, 206.

[73] J.M. Gilbert, *Hunting and Hunting Reserves in Medieval Scotland* (Edinburgh, 1979), 77-8.

[74] *TA*, iv, 135; *James V Letters*, 397. For hawks acquired in Scotland, see *TA*, passim; for dogs acquired from England in 1503, *TA*, ii, 405; and for a stag acquired from England, *TA*, ii, 415.

[75] *James V Letters*, 326.

[76] LAT Innsbruck, Sigismund IVa/181; *James V Letters*, 300.

[77] *TA*, ii, 465; J. Cummins, *The Hound and the Hawk: The art of medieval hunting* (London, 1988), chapters 14 and 15. See too *TA*, ii, 445, 474, for the dispatch of hawks to France.

following his visit to Scotland in 1365.[78] In Scotland, as in other parts of north-western Europe, hunting generally seems to have conformed to the 'bow and stable' method, whereby stags, boars or foxes were driven by the hunters and their hounds to a predetermined location, where the animal was killed by waiting archers.[79] There were clearly military applications to the skills required for such endeavours. Good horsemanship and skill in the use of weaponry were obvious attributes of both the successful hunter and the successful warrior, though hunting also trained its participants in tactical considerations, tenacity and mental agility.

Hunting and hawking were day-time pursuits. In the evening, though sometimes at other times of the day too, aristocrats resorted to indoor games, several of which had evolved from Christian contacts with non-European peoples. Chess, for instance, passed into the culture of the Latin west from the Islamic world in the eleventh century. The intricately sculpted Lewis chess pieces, now on display in the British Museum and the Museum of Scotland, indicate that by the twelfth century, when the set is thought to have been made, chess had become an entertainment even in that corner of Christendom furthest removed from the Islamic world. Their fine craftsmanship, as well as the hierarchical nature of both individual chess pieces and the moves which they make on a chessboard, leave little doubt that they were the possession of an aristocratic household.[80] The Lewis chessmen were sculpted in the Scandinavian world and other chess pieces were perhaps also purchased abroad.[81] Meanwhile, cards too are based upon notions of a hierarchical society and, like chess, may also have been originally of Islamic invention, though it was not until the 1370s that cards are first recorded in the Latin west. From Italy and Germany their popularity spread quickly. They are recorded in Lille by 1382 and some probably reached Scotland from northern France and Flanders shortly afterwards, though by the early sixteenth century others were certainly imported from England.[82] By then cards were a familiar nocturnal pastime of James IV and Queen Margaret, his playing partners including the bishop of St Andrews and royal familiars, as well as visiting Spaniards in 1497 and the English diplomat Lord Dacre in 1504.[83] James clearly gambled when he played, and this too was probably an important element in other pastimes – such as the 'hasard of dis' [dice] and 'cross and pile' (now, or at least in my schooldays, better known as pitch and toss), the original name probably derived from the marks on French coins.[84] The

[78] *Chron. Froissart* (Lettenhove), xxvii, 216. See too *Rot. Scot.*, ii, 131.
[79] Gilbert, *Hunting*, chapter 4; Cummins, *The Hound and the Hawk*, chapter 3.
[80] Note too that according to the medieval rules of chess, apart from the pawns, the queen was the weakest piece on the board, corresponding with the inferior social status of medieval women.
[81] *Angels, Nobles and Unicorns: Art and patronage in medieval Scotland*, ed. E. Sharrott and D.H. Caldwell (Edinburgh, 1988), nos. B42-43; *TA*, vi, 464.
[82] G. Beal, *Playing-cards and their Story* (Newton Abbot, 1975), 7-8, 29, 45; PRO London, E122/109/9, m. 6v; CA Chester, SB/8, fo. 84v.
[83] *TA*, i, 350; ii, 455; iii, 176, 181.
[84] *TA*, iii, pp.lvii, 376; iv, 89.

cosmopolitan nature of recreational pursuits is further underlined by the same king's interest in both bowls and tennis, the latter of which was apparently played by members of the royal entourage by at least the early fifteenth century and which, unlike most other pastimes, has bequeathed a still visible arena, in the tennis court at Falkland Palace.[85]

Music

Music provided a rather different form of cultural experience, not least because it was a medium appropriate for both inconsequential secular amusement and for more serious religious contemplation. In cathedral churches mass and the Divine Office were sung daily and schools of choristers were established (or expanded) at several, if not all, of these greater churches by the fifteenth century – as they were in other parts of Christendom.[86] Several churches also possessed an organ – that much at any rate is suggested by the two books of organ music shelved in the library of Aberdeen Cathedral in 1436 – and by the early sixteenth century at least some of the non-cathedral churches frequented by royalty (for instance in Edinburgh and Stirling) also did.[87] Organs were used as a musical accompaniment to the mass and other compositions which dealt with predictable themes. Robert Carver, the celebrated sixteenth-century Scottish composer, produced two motets, one in honour of Christ, the other in praise of the Virgin, who was also the centrepiece of the composition *Ave dei patrus*, by the Duns priest Robert Johnston, a contemporary of Carver's.[88]

Unfortunately we know little about the music performed in Scottish churches before this, since – other than the fragments inscribed on slate, recently discovered at Paisley – not a single Scottish score survives from between the mid-thirteenth and early sixteenth centuries. It seems likely, however, that Scottish ecclesiastical music absorbed elements familiar elsewhere in the Latin west. Scores dating from the first half of the thirteenth century contain material of French derivation which has been linked to the Notre-Dame school of music in Paris. Northern French or English influences also have been detected both in the hymn composed to celebrate the wedding of Margaret, daughter of Alexander III, and the Norwegian king in 1282, and in the fifteenth-century Paisley fragments.[89] Meanwhile, the early sixteenth-

[85] Dunbar, *Scottish Royal Palaces*, 205-08.
[86] E.E. Lowinsky, 'Music in the culture of the renaissance', *Journal of the History of Ideas*, 15 (1952), 510-12; I.B. Cowan, 'Church and society' in J.M. Brown, ed., *Scottish Society in the Fifteenth Century* (London, 1977), 122-23; J. Harper, 'Music and ceremonial, c.1500-1560' in J. Geddes, ed., *King's College Chapel, Aberdeen, 1500-2000* (Leeds, 2000), 28-34.
[87] *Aberdeen Reg.*, ii, 136; *TA*, iii, 195, 362; *ER*, vii, 502.
[88] J. Purser, *Scotland's Music* (Edinburgh, 1992), 83, 94.
[89] Purser, *Scotland's Music*, 51-2; J. Beveridge, 'Two Scottish thirteenth-century songs, with the original melodies, recently discovered in Sweden', *PSAS*, 73 (1938-39), 276-88; I. De Geer, 'Music and the twelfth-century Orkney earldom: a cultural crossroads in musicological perspective' in B.E. Crawford, ed., *St Magnus Cathedral and Orkney's Twelfth-century Renaissance* (Aberdeen, 1988), 241-63; K. Elliott, 'The Pailsey abbey fragments', *Musica Scoticana*, 1 (1996), 1-7.

century evidence suggests both Flemish and English influences too. Carver's choir book included compositions similar to those in the Eton choir book, as well as the *Missa l'homme armé*, a mass score by the celebrated Netherlandish composer, Guillaume Dufay, whose mass compositions are first recorded in Italian scores dating from *c.*1470.[90] Carver's own work, it has been noted, was 'florid' and 'very much in the style of English composers in the first years of the sixteenth century'.[91] We can but guess whence this English influence stemmed, but it is perhaps significant that James III acquired the services of the English musician William Rodger, whose skills were held in high regard by Edward IV and who has been credited with establishing a school of musicians in Scotland.[92] Carver's familiarity with Dufay, on the other hand, is likely to have been a product of the Scotsman's continental training, if, as seems likely, he was educated at Leuven in Brabant. Although of an earlier generation than Carver – he died in 1474 – Dufay resided at nearby Cambrai and held a canonry at Bruges. Such was his reputation that his patrons included the duke of Burgundy.[93]

Evidence regarding secular music is similarly scant and even many works which are known to have existed – such as the songs and ballads possessed by James I's daughter Margaret – no longer survive.[94] The leading musicians too are obscure, though some Scots, by at least the later fifteenth century, were travelling abroad to receive musical training.[95] Some musical instruments were also acquired abroad. In the mid-thirteenth century, for instance, the poet Gille-Brígde Albanach was presented with a harp by the king of Thomond in Ireland; in 1504 the crown paid £6 15s for a lute and pair of 'monocordis', bought in Flanders; and in 1507 lute strings were imported from France.[96] Sadly, though, we must take on trust the comment of Gerald of Wales (1146-1223), subsequently copied by Bower, that Scots excelled beyond the Irish in musical science and skill. While even in the sixteenth century 'Irish' (for which, perhaps read 'Gaelic') harpers performed for the Scottish king, none of

[90] Purser, *Scotland's Music*, 51-2, 83; R. Strohm, *Music in Late Medieval Bruges* (rev.ed., Oxford, 1990), 131.
[91] R. Turbet, 'Scotland's greatest composer: an introduction to Robert Carver, 1487-1566', in J.D. McClure and M.R.G. Spillar, eds., *Bryght Lanternis: Essays on the language and literature of renaissance Scotland* (Aberdeen, 1989), 52.
[92] L.J. Macfarlane, *William Elphinstone and the Kingdom of Scotland, 1431-1514* (Aberdeen, 1985), 173; N. Macdougall, *James III: A political study* (Edinburgh, 1982), 164-65. See too G. Donaldson, 'Foundations of Anglo-Scottish union', in idem, *Scottish Church History* (Edinburgh, 1985), 151. It should perhaps be noted that, pace the derogatory comments made here about the peal of English bells, it has recently been established that the bells of King's College, Aberdeen were manufactured in England.
[93] Strohm, *Music in Late Medieval Bruges*, 24.
[94] P. Higgins, 'Parisian nobles, a Scottish princess and the woman's voice in medieval song', *Early Music History*, 10 (1991), 165.
[95] Strohm, *Music in Late Medieval Bruges* 65; *TA*, i, 43, 60, 67; *Edin. Recs.*, ii, 176.
[96] J. Bannerman, 'The *clàrsach* and the *clàrsair*', *Scottish Studies*, 30 (1991), 2; *TA*, ii, 445; iii, 398.

their music survives.[97] By then, however, court preferences were also favourably disposed towards English and Italian harpers and pipers, to Dutch lutars and French organists, and above all to minstrels from England, France and Italy.[98]

We do not know why these musical troops came to Scotland – whether they were invited, or whether they arrived unannounced in search of patronage – or what they performed, though some at least were highly esteemed. In 1530 James V informed the duke of Milan that the musician Thomas de Averencia of Brescia had given him great pleasure and he hoped that the duke would permit Thomas's return before long.[99] Others appear to have been retained on an annual contract. A group of four Italian minstrels, who followed James IV on his travels through the kingdom, performed as far north as Strathbogie and as far south as Dumfries, receiving a 'year's fee' in 1504. The same, or perhaps another, Italian troupe presumably staged similarly regular performances for the king between 1505 and 1507, though on this occasion they were paid at three-monthly intervals.[100] Meanwhile, other performers, such as those (apparently in the employ of the English king) who appeared at Dumbarton in 1328-29 and those employed by the earl of Oxford in 1503, seem only to have staged single concerts.

The traffic in musicians was not, however, one way. A 'Jean d'Ecosse' served as a minstrel to the French king in 1419, while the more limited military uses to which music was put are highlighted by a letter sent from Strasbourg to Frankfurt am Main in 1439, in which the capture was reported of 'Manghomoron', a famous trumpeter of a Scottish captain whose forces had ravaged the Alsace.[101] And the long tradition of Scots busking in London was perhaps commenced by Roger Broun, fiddler, found there in 1483.[102]

Art and Sculpture

The visual arts in later medieval Scotland are shrouded in almost as much obscurity as the performing arts. They were, however, a more exclusive cultural medium. Art was expensive, the artists who frequented the court and their materials costing considerably more *per capita* than the numerically much larger group of musicians who entertained the king. Whereas each of James IV's four Italian minstrels were paid a monthly wage of 29s 4d in 1505, his Dutch painter Piers received a monthly reward of 56s in September

---

[97] Gerald of Wales, *The History and Topography of Ireland*, ed. J.J. O'Meara (Portlaoise, 1982), 103-4; *Chron. Bower* (Watt), viii, 304-5; *TA*, i, 177; iii, 403; C.Ó. Baoill, 'Some Irish harpers in Scotland', *Transactions of the Gaelic Society of Inverness*, 47 (1971-72), 145; Bannerman, 'The clàrsach and the clàrsair', 1-17.

[98] *TA*, i-ix, passim.

[99] *James V Letters*, 169.

[100] *TA*, ii, 431 and passim; iii, 117-26, passim.

[101] *La France Gouvernée par Jean sans peur* (Paris, 1959), ed. B.A. Pocquet du Haut-Jussé, no. 1198; *Frankfurts Reichskorrespondenz, 1376-1519*, ed. J. Janssen (Freiburg in Breisgau, 1863), i, no. 849.

[102] *The Alien Communities of London in the Fifteenth Century: The subsidy rolls of 1440 and 1483-84*, ed. J.L. Bolton (Richard III and Yorkist History Trust, 1998), 96.

1506;[103] and whereas musicians apparently provided their own musical instruments, the king paid £12 on just one occasion in 1506 to supply his artists with 'rede lede, asur, synapur, masticot, orpement and varngreis'.[104] In part, the greater outlay for artists reflected their intricate skills and craftsmanship, though more lavish patronage also reflected the artist's product. Art was intended to be a lasting artefact, unlike the immediacy of the musical or dramatic experience.

Nonetheless, there were also similarities between these media, not least in the dichotomy evident between the religious and secular markets. Much artistic endeavour was devoted to the production of ecclesiastical adornments, in the form of sculpted statues, images (both painted on canvas and illuminated in literary texts) and elaborately decorated tombstones. Little of medieval Scotland's religious art has survived, thanks in no small measure to the iconoclastic efficiency of sixteenth-century Protestants, though a good deal of that which remains betrays evidence of continental influence. The enamelled Christ, from a thirteenth-century crucifix found at Ceres in Fife, was probably manufactured in Limoges and the magnificent fifteenth-century mace of St Salvator's College was commissioned from the Parisian goldsmith Jean Mayelle – possibly an expatriate Scot.[105] Documentary evidence too attests that much was manufactured abroad and then imported. In the early sixteenth century, for instance, George Brown, bishop of Dunkeld, purchased tabernacles and images of SS John and Catherine in Flanders. Other tabernacles and vestments were acquired in England, James IV even buying an image from a visiting English pilgrim.[106] By contrast with altar vestments, the remnants of tombstones are somewhat better preserved. There was clearly a significant traffic in fashionable foreign stones from both England and the continent, especially in Tournai black.[107] Although the stone itself may have been chiselled by masons in Scotland, some were more elaborately finished abroad – that of Robert I in 1329 by Thomas of Chartres in Paris, and that of Bishop George Crichton of Dunkeld, sculpted from black marble and adorned

[103] The comparisons are drawn from *TA*, iii, 118, 325.

[104] *TA*, iii, 193.

[105] J.M.D. Peddie, 'Note of a crucifix of bronze, enamelled, found in the churchyard of Ceres, Fife', *PSAS*, 17 (1882-83), 146-51; D. McRoberts, 'Bishop Kennedy's mace', in idem, ed., *The Medieval Church of St Andrews* (Glasgow, 1976), 167-71; G. Evans, 'The mace of St Salvator's College' in J. Higgitt, ed., *Medieval Art and Architecture in the Diocese of St Andrews* (British Archaeological Association, 1994), 197-212.

[106] *Rentale Dunkaldense*, ed. R.K. Hannay (SHS, 1915), 2-4; PRO London, E122/64/15, fo. 10r; E122/99/26, fo. 4r; *TA*, i, 193.

[107] E.g., from England, *ER*, ii, 300, 348 (for David II and Queen Margaret); 585, 622; iii, 348 (for Robert II and his parents); and from the continent, *Halyburton's Ledger*, 7 (for Archbishop Schevez), 161, 250 (for the archdeacon of St Andrews), 215 (for the duke of Ross). On Tournai stone, see Sharrott and Caldwell, *Angels, Nobles and Unicorns*, nos. C12, C13; A. Stevenson, 'Medieval Scottish associations with Bruges' in Brotherstone and Ditchburn, *Freedom and Authority*, 96; I. Campbell, 'Bishop Elphinstone's tomb' in Geddes, *King's College Chapel*, 115-29. For albaster stones from England, dispatched in the early sixteenth century, see PRO London, E122/60/3, fo. 16r; *TA*, ii, 274; and E122/64/15, fo 10r, for an albaster tabernacle.

with illuminations by the Mechelen painter Jan Mandijn, procured at Antwerp in 1536-37.[108] Frequently the precise specifications elude us, though in a contract of 1529 the Parisian tombmaker Pierre Prisié was commissioned by the priest Robert Elphinstone to engrave two brass strips for a tomb with a coat of arms and an inscription.[109] Even in death aristocrats proclaimed their status.

While religious themes and purposes constituted much of the art trade, by the fifteenth century a market had also developed for profane themes. The heraldic emblems of James I were embroidered on a Flemish-bought tapestry. Those of the 'duke of Flanders' were painted for James IV in 1506, though the most impressive survival of this particular genre is the early sixteenth-century ceiling of St Machar's Cathedral in Old Aberdeen, which qualifies as both a magnificent piece of art and a subtle political statement of the Scottish kingdom's place in Christendom.[110] Landscape scenes have survived less well, though there is a glimpse of a river in the background of William Elphinstone's portrait.[111] Other rural scenes featured on tapestries and in books of hours. Hunting scenes are depicted in the Taymouth Hours (which belonged to Joan, wife of David II) and also on a sixteenth-century tapestry at Mellerstain Castle.[112] 'Arras tapestries' – some of which were made in Bruges rather than Arras, and others of which were perhaps made in Scotland by a seemingly foreign weaver who received regular remuneration from the crown in the mid-fifteenth century – had adorned the royal apartments since at least the fifteenth century.[113] Their content remains largely unknown, though the name given to one which belonged to James IV – 'the cloth of Ercules'– is suggestive of classical images.[114] Similar themes, and others of a biblical nature, figured prominently among over a hundred pieces of tapestry owned by James V, and some idea of their style can perhaps be gleaned from the early sixteenth-century Brussels-made *The Prodigal Son* (now in the Royal Museum of Art and History, Brussels) and *Roumulus on the Throne of Rome* (now in the

---

[108] *ER*, i, 213-14; L. Campbell, 'Scottish patrons and Netherlandish painters in the 15th and 16th centuries' in Simpson, *Scotland and the Low Countries*, 96.

[109] J. Guiffrey, 'Artistes et tombiers parisiens du commencement de XVIe siècle', *Revue de l'art français*, [21-22?] (1896), no. 58, quoted in Campbell, 'Bishop Elphinstone's tomb', 127, n. 13.

[110] *TA*, iii, 355; D. McRoberts, *The Heraldic Ceiling of St Machar's Cathedral Aberdeen* (2nd ed., Aberdeen, 1976); G.G. Simpson and J. Stones, 'New light on the medieval ceiling' in J.H. Alexander *et al*, *The Restoration of St Machar's Cathedral* (Aberdeen, 1991), 21-6.

[111] L. Campbell and J. Dick, 'The portrait of Bishop Elphinstone' in Geddes, *King's College Chapel*, 98-108.

[112] Cummins, *The Hound and the Hawk*, 14, 43.

[113] *ER*, iv, 529, 678, 680; vii, 63, 590-591; viii, 192, 254, 315, 391, 465, 548, 630; ix, 80; *TA*, i, 52-53, 100, 117, 130, 179, 183-184, 195, 240-242, 268, 276, 325, 327, 386, 393 ii, 379, 390, 399, 402, 470; iii, 79, 162, 181, 192, 275, 337-338, 370; iv, 28, 198, 318, 322, 339, 407.

[114] *TA*, iii, 181.

Patrimonio Nacional de España, Madrid), both themes which were included in James's collection too.[115]

Portraiture too became increasingly popular in the fifteenth century and at least four fifteenth-century Scottish kings had their portraits painted. That of James I, included in a sixteenth-century collection by Jacques le Boucq, appears to be a copy of an original painted in a typical Netherlandish style of the 1430s, while James II was sketched by an artist who accompanied the Austrian page Jörg van Ehingen to Scotland in 1458. James III appears on the Trinity altar pieces, though the crudely executed facial features of the king suggest that his likeness was completed by a Scottish artist after the Netherlandish painter Hugo van der Goes had completed the rest of the work.[116] While portraits such as this emphasised the sacral nature of kingship, others struck a more worldly tone. James IV preferred to pose with a hawk on his wrist, in a depiction dated to *c.*1500 which survives only in a seventeenth-century copy.[117] Portraiture was not, however, merely a royal fad. William Elphinstone, bishop of Aberdeen, posed for a portrait of perhaps Netherlandish execution, dating from the later fifteenth or early sixteenth centuries, while a representation of his more-or-less contemporary episcopal colleague, William Schevez of St Andrews, survives in the form of a medal dated to 1491, the depiction attributed to the Brabantine painter Quentin Metsys of Leuven.[118] Perhaps, however, the most famous surviving portrait of a medieval Scot is that of another clergyman, Edward Bonkil, provost of the collegiate church of Holy Trinity in Edinburgh, whose image was 'certainly painted from life', appearing on a triptych of the Trinity altarpiece.[119] Some secular figures were also painted in the fifteenth century. Royalty apart, none of a Scottish figure survives, but depictions of Joan of Arc were circulating in fifteenth-century France, and at least one was acquired in Arras by a passing Scot.[120]

[115] W.G. Thomson, F.P. Thomson and E.S. Thomson, *A History of Tapestry from the Earliest Times until the Present Day* (3rd ed., Wakefield, 1973), 273-74. For the two Brussels tapestries, see the beautifully illustrated G. Delmarcel, *Flemish Tapestry* (London, 1999), 68, 102.
[116] L. Campbell, 'The authorship of the *Recueil d'Arras*', *Journal of the Warburg and Courtauld Institutes*, 40 (1977), 301-13; idem, 'Scottish patrons and Netherlandish artists', 90. The portrait of James I is now in the posession of the Bibliothèque Municipale, Arras. It is reproduced in L. Campbell, *The Early Flemish Pictures in the Collection of her Majesty the Queen* (Cambridge, 1985), Figure 12. That of James II, replete with the famous, firey red mark on the king's cheek is now in the possession of the Württemburgische Landesbibliothek in Stuttgart. It is reproduced on the dustjacket of C. McGladdery, *James II* (Edinburgh, 1990). That of James III is in the National Galleries of Scotland.
[117] D. Macmillan, *Scottish Art, 1460-1990* (Edinburgh, 1990), 29 (Plate 16), 30.
[118] L. Campbell, 'Scottish patrons and Netherlandish artists', 95. The Elphinstone portrait forms the frontispiece of Macfarlane, *Elphinstone*; the Schevez medal is reproduced in Macmillan, *Scottish Art*, 24 (Plate 11).
[119] L. Campbell, 'Edward Bonkil: a Scottish patron of Hugo van der Goes', *Burlington Magazine*, 126 (1984), 272.
[120] *Procès de condemnation de Jeanne d'Arc: Texte, traduction et notes*, ed. P. Champion (Paris, 1921), ii, 66.

Though essentially commemorative, portraiture sometimes also served a quasi-political purpose. At the highest social levels marriages were frequently arranged for diplomatic reasons, between people who had never seen each other prior to their betrothal. Portraits provided prospective partners with an indication of what lay in store for them. Thus, having heard of Egidia Stewart's beauty, the French king Charles VII reportedly sent an artist to secretly 'draw a portrait of her maidenly countenance with a view to taking her to be his own wife' – though in this case no such marriage ensued. [121] More certainly, however, James IV purchased pictures of his wife, her parents and her brother in 1502, painted by Meynart Wewyck, a Netherlandish artist in the employ of the English crown; and James V acquired portraits of his Danish cousins Dorothy, countess-palatine of the Rhine, and Christina, duchess of Milan, whom he was considering marrying. [122]

Here we are reminded of a further purpose served by portraiture. As we have already seen, family visits were rare and in their absence paintings offered an important familial *aide-memoire*. Thus, in *c*.1541 the Scottish queen Mary of Guise was informed by her six-year old French son from a previous marriage, 'My lady, my granny will send me to my lady the Queen, but painted on canvas and as big as I am and I am so very pretty now that I have my hair cut like my uncles.'[123] Mary herself was the subject of a small portrait, now in the Scottish National Portrait Gallery, which has been linked to the French painter Corneille de Lyon, and her marriage to James V may have been the occasion for the famous double portrait of queen and king in the duke of Atholl's collection.[124]

Although some indication of artistic themes may be gleaned from the fragmentary collection of surviving paintings and from documentary sources, much less is known of the means by which art was procured. It is possible that some foreign artists sent samples of their work to Scotland for speculative sales. That, at any rate, seems a credible explanation for the presence of 'a panel decorated with the most beautiful pictures' recorded aboard a vessel coming from Scotland in 1438 for which the owner, Conrad de Eyke of Haarlem, appears to have found no buyer.[125] On the other hand it was relatively easy to acquire paintings directly in the Low Countries. Some, such as the Trinity College altarpiece (attributed on stylistic grounds to Hugo van der Goes) and probably also a book of hours belonging to James IV (which seems to have been a product of the workshop supervised by the Ghent

---

[121] *Chron. Bower* (Watt), vii, 412-13.

[122] *TA*, ii, 304; vi, 250; Pitscottie, *Historie*, i, 354.

[123] L. Campbell, *Renaissance Portraits: European portrait-painting in the 14th, 15th and 16th centuries* (New Haven, 1990), 196.

[124] Macmillan, *Scottish Art*, 32.

[125] Smit, *Bronnen, 1150-1485*, no. 1259(7); Campbell, 'Scottish patrons and Netherlandish artists', 89.

painter Gerard Horenbout), were specifically commissioned.[126] Those with sufficient means added the costs of passage to those of their commission to pose for hand-picked artists, Mark Ker and his wife sitting for the leading Antwerp portrait painter William Key in 1551.[127] But ready-made artefacts were also easily acquired. Carved and painted altar pieces were produced in substantial number in Antwerp from the later fifteenth century, both to commission and ready-made, the latter sold publicly at the church of Onser Liever Vrouwen Pand from 1460.[128] Some Scots were certainly active in the Antwerp art market – it was there that the Edinburgh burgess William Knox acquired a 'gilded panel with images', painted by an artist from Mechelen, in 1439, while in 1495 Andrew Halyburton picked up an image of St Thomas Becket for another Scottish client.[129] Meanwhile, two merchants from Perth and St Andrews commissioned work from the sculptor Gielis van der Sluys in 1506.[130] Bruges, too, hosted a public art market by 1466, from when the town's artists were permitted to sell their wares at St John's Bridge.[131] Artists in both towns, then, appear to have produced and sold substantial amounts of cheap art for the export market – in Bruges on canvas, in Antwerp in the form of figures depicted in the town's distinctive manneristic style, grouped in a graphic narrative.

It was not just paintings which were shipped across the North Sea. By at least the early sixteenth century, painters came too. In 1505 James IV asked Andrew Halyburton, the Scottish Conservator in the Low Countries, to dispatch a Netherlandish artist and this appears to have resulted in the arrival of Piers the painter, who worked in Edinburgh Castle, the chapel royal at Stirling, and perhaps elsewhere too, between 1505 and 1508.[132] Halyburton was particularly well placed to attend to the king's desire. His wife, Cornelia Benning, was the daughter of Sanders (or Alexander) Benning, an accomplished illuminator probably of Scottish extraction, who was the master of the gild of painters in Ghent in 1469. Halyburton's mother-in-law was therefore Catherine van der Goes, daughter of Hugo; and his brother-in-law

---

[126] C. Thompson and L. Campbell, *Hugo van der Goes and the Trinity Panels in Edinburgh* (Edinburgh, 1974); T. Tolley, 'Hugo van der Goes's altarpiece for Trinity College Church in Edinburgh and Mary of Guelders, queen of Scotland' in Higgitt, *Art and Architecture of the Diocese of St Andrews*, 213-31; L.J. Macfarlane, 'The book of hours of James IV and Margaret Tudor', *IR*, 11 (1960), 3-21. Horenbout's career is discussed by L. Campbell and S. Foister, 'Gerard, Lucas and Susanna Horenbout', *Burlington Magazine*, 128 (1986), 719-27.

[127] Macmillan, *Scottish Art*, 39 (Plate 24), 40.

[128] L. Campbell, 'The art market in the southern Netherlands in the fifteenth century', *Burlington Magazine*, 118 (1976), 195-96; K. Woods, 'Some sixteenth-century Antwerp carved-wooden altar-pieces in England', *Burlington Magazine*, 141 (1999), 144.

[129] 'Documenten voor de geschiedenis van de beeldhowkunst te Antwerpen in de XVe eeuw', ed. G. Asaert, *Jaarboek van het Koninklijk Museum voor Schone Kunst, Antwerpen* (1972), no. 6; *Halyburton's Ledger*, 9.

[130] StA Antwerpen, Schebenbrieven 129, fos. 8v, 138r.

[131] M.P.J. Martens, 'Some aspects of the origins of the art market in fifteenth-century Bruges' in M. North and D. Ormrod, eds., *Art Markets in Europe, 1400-1800* (Aldershot, 1998), 21.

[132] *TA*, iii, 158, 162 and passim; iv, 113 and passim.

was Simon Benning, another famous Flemish illuminator. The Bennings and van der Goeses seem to have been related to the Antwerp painter Goswijn van der Weyden – and he, together with Cornelia and her father, appointed guardians for Halyburton's children in 1506. Goswijn's apprentice in 1503 was one Peerken Bovelant – perhaps the same Piers who came to Scotland in 1505.[133]

Piers was not the only foreign painter to find employment in early sixteenth-century Scotland. George Brown, bishop of Dunkeld, employed the Flemish painter William Wallauch, who can perhaps be identified as Willem Wallinc, master of the Bruges gild of painters in 1506.[134] And, though evidence of his work is obscure, the French artist Pierre Quesnel was attached to the household of Queen Mary of Guise in the 1540s; he is perhaps to be equated with an unnamed artist who worked at Falkland Palace in 1542.

The number of foreign artists who practised their craft in Scotland should not, however, be exaggerated. Of sixty painters who can be identified plying their craft in Scotland between 1301 and 1560, only a handful came from overseas.[135] The overwhelming majority were Scots. We know little about how and where these Scottish artists learned their craft, but, just as some Scottish musicians travelled abroad to be trained, some Scottish artists also ventured overseas, some of them perhaps to develop their skills. James Polworth, while in Tours, painted a banner for Joan of Arc;[136] and 'Johan Bron, Escochois' and 'Sanders Escochois' (possibly Sanders Benning) were among the artists hired to decorate the surroundings for the wedding of Charles the Bold, duke of Burgundy, and Margaret of York at Bruges in 1468.

Benning and his father Alexander were artists of international repute. Alexander has been credited with the illumination of several books of hours, including those produced for the Castilian queen, Isabella the Catholic, and for aristocrats such as William, Lord Hastings and Engelbert of Nassau. Alexander was perhaps also responsible for the Glasgow breviary of 1494.[137] Simon's work, meanwhile, features in the Grimani breviary (on which he perhaps collaborated with his father), as well as in a genealogy of the Portuguese royal house and several other religious texts, including a prayer

---

[133] StA Antwerp, Certificatieboeken 3, fo. 170r; D. McRoberts, 'Notes on Scoto-Flemish artistic contacts, *IR*, 10 (1959), 94; Campbell, 'Scottish patrons and Netherlandish artists', 90-1. The suggestion regarding Piers is not neccesarily negated by three descriptions of him as a Frenchman, which may simply allude to the language which he spoke while in Scotland. (*TA*, iv, 134, 136, 138).

[134] Hannay, *Rentale Dunkeldense*, passim; Campbell, 'Scottish patrons and Netherlandish painters', 95-6.

[135] M.R. Apted and S. Hannabuss, *Painters in Scotland, 1301-1700: A biographical dictionary* (Edinburgh, 1978), passim. For Quesnel, see ibid, 77, 114-15.

[136] S. Cursiter, *Scottish Art* (London, 1949), 14.

[137] J.A. Testa, 'An unpublished manuscript by Simon Bening', *Burlington Magazine*, 136 (1994), 418-19. See also *The Master of Mary of Burgundy: A book of hours for Engelbert of Nassau*, ed. J.G. Alexander (London, 1970); *The Hastings Hours*, ed. D.H. Turner (London, 1983); N. Thorp, *The Glory of the Page: Medieval and renaissance illuminated manuscripts from Glasgow University Library* (London, 1987), 189.

book for a German cardinal and a book of hours now in possession of the
duke of Norfolk.[138] The cosmopolitan nature of this patronage speaks for
itself. That, however, is less important for present purposes than the
indication that Scotland and Scots were an integral part of the wider northern
European art market. From at least the later fifteenth century its rulers
patronised men like van der Goes, Horenbout and Metsys, who figured
among the foremost artists of their day.

Books

Similar to the acquisition of art, the study of literature was an exclusive
pastime in the middle ages: in a largely illiterate society it could hardly be
otherwise. Illiteracy limited the demand for books, but their supply was
simultaneously hampered by the slow, intensive and expensive means by
which they were produced. Each volume had to be transcribed manually and
many works were then dispatched to specialist illuminators before being
delivered to a reader. Books were works of art, and it is little wonder that
these valuable commodities were frequently chained to library desks (or, in
the case of the psalter acquired by Aberdeen Cathedral in 1488, to the choir
stalls), and that many were inscribed by an anathema directed against
thieves.[139] Yet even before the invention of the printing press, the remarkable
fall in the price of paper during the fifteenth century led to a sizeable increase
in the number of manuscript books in circulation.[140] Literate clerics were the
chief, but not sole, purchaser. In the fifteenth century Philip the Good, duke
of Burgundy, acquired over six hundred manuscripts and, although we do not
know whether the library of Scottish kings was as extensive, they too seem to
have assembled an impressive collection of books over the centuries.[141] While
imprisoned in Edinburgh Castle between 1355 and 1359 and commencing
work on his *Scalacronica*, the English knight Sir Thomas Gray of Heton was
able to consult an impressive array of verse and prose written in Latin, French
and English.[142] This collection was probably the royal library, for Edinburgh
Castle certainly stored the thirteenth-century royal archive. It was perhaps
there too that the volumes purchased for David II in 1330 (and those for later

---

[138] Testa, 'An unpublished manuscript', 416-26. See also *The Grimani Breviary*, ed. M. Salimi and
G.L. Mellini (London, 1972). It should be noted that five Binning artists from Edinburgh are
known of between 1538 and 1633: Apted and Hannabuss, *Painters in Scotland*, 26-30.
[139] J. Durkan and A. Ross, 'Early Scottish libraries', *IR*, 9 (1958), 8, 11; A. Ross, 'Libraries of the
Scottish Blackfriars 1481-1560', *IR*, 20 (1969), 6; J. Higgitt, 'Manuscripts and libraries in the diocese
of Glasgow before the Reformation' in R. Fawcett, ed., *Medieval Art and Architecture in the
Diocese of Glasgow* (British Archaeological Association, 1998), 103.
[140] On paper prices, see R.J. Lyall, 'Materials: the paper revolution' in J. Griffiths and D. Pearsal,
eds., *Book Production and Publishing in Britain, 1375-1475* (Cambridge, 1989), 11.
[141] W. Blockmans, 'Manuscript acquisition by the Burgundian court and the market for books in
the fifteenth-century Netherlands', in North and Ormrod, *Art Markets*, 7.
[142] A. Gransden, *Historical Writing in England II: c.1307 to the Early Sixteenth Century* (London,
1982), 92-3.

monarchs) were stored.[143] Unfortunately, neither the royal library nor any other medieval Scottish library – with the arguable exception of that belonging to King's College, Aberdeen – has survived even moderately intact.

Secular aristocrats probably followed the royal example in assembling stocks of books. As early as 1390 James Douglas of Dalkeith made provision in his will for an unspecified number of tomes, covering topics as diverse as law, grammar, dialectic and romance.[144] Other testatory evidence is less impressive. In 1499 only two books featured in the disputed estate of the late Lord Lyle; and there are no references to books in the wills of Alexander Sutherland of Dunbeath (1456) or Sir David Sinclair of Swynbrocht (1506).[145] We should not, however, place too much emphasis on such evidence, for the methodological approach to the determination of book ownership which relies upon testatory references is flawed.[146] Lyle was the owner of three English books stolen by the earl of Buchan in 1483, while Sutherland possessed a 'primar buk' (a book of hours) for which he left no provision.[147] In other words, despite the paucity of testimonial evidence, it would not be surprising if by the later fifteenth century most aristocrats possessed books; and by at least the sixteenth century some burgesses did too.[148] We can only guess at the size of their collections; but in England – and there is no reason to suppose that Scotland was any different – a fifteenth-century knight and well known bibliophile such as Sir John Paston possessed only about twenty volumes. More modest aristocratic enthusiasm probably made for very modest collections indeed.

We can, too, but guess what kings, nobles and townsmen did with their books. They may have remained unopened, more important as decorative status symbols than as reading material. Or they may have been read aloud by the literate clerks who were routinely attached to royal and aristocratic households – though by the sixteenth century it seems likely that a growing number of secular book owners were literate and able to read the material for themselves. The largest market for books in medieval Scotland was, however, always a clerical one. Monasteries, in particular, possessed extensive collections and though the abbey of Kinloss was famed for its investment in early sixteenth-century books, and may have spent a disproportionately large sum on them, the collections of other houses, amassed over centuries, cannot have been inconsiderable. We know very little about these collections, but in the early fourteenth century the Franciscans compiled an inventory of books

[143] *APS*, i, 112-13; *ER*, i, 297.
[144] *Registrum Honoris de Morton* (Bannatyne Club, 1853), ii, no. 193
[145] G. Neilson and H. Paton, eds., *Acts of the Lords of Council in Civil Causes, 1496-1501* (Edinburgh, 1918), 296; *The Bannatyne Miscellany* (Bannatyne Club, 1827-55), iii, 89-110.
[146] M. Deansley, 'Vernacular books in England in the fourteenth and fifteenth centuries', *Modern Language Review*, 15 (1920), 349-358; K. Harris, 'Patrons, buyers and owners: the evidence for ownership and the role of book owners in book production and the book trade' in Griffiths and Pearsall, *Book Production*, 163-64.
[147] *ADA*, 112*; *The Bannatyne Miscellany*, iii, 94.
[148] Durkan and Ross, 'Early Scottish libraries', 6.

stored in the libraries of other religious orders, including those possessed by seven Scottish monasteries. Melrose boasted the best collection (102 titles), though this was far smaller not only than that of Canterbury, but also lesser English houses such as Woburn and Guisborough. Still, the survey was selective – its compilers were not interested in legal, medical or scientific texts, concentrating instead on works by the early Fathers and commentators on them.[149] Moreover, with time the Scottish libraries probably expanded. By 1517 Arbroath possessed two hundred volumes and perhaps even more titles, since it was common to bind several books into one volume.[150] Friaries too were major book depositories, the Edinburgh Dominicans owning at least a hundred volumes on the eve of the Reformation. Indeed, this library was of a roughly similar size to that of the Blackfriars in Dijon and Mantua, though it was markedly smaller than that of the Dominican friary in the university town of Bologna.[151]

Students, of course, required books and many members of the secular clergy, who constituted the vast majority of the student population, began (and perhaps finished) their personal book collections as students. Some, however, amassed large collections as their careers progressed, John Lindsay, archdeacon of Aberdeen, bequeathing seventy-five volumes in his will of 1495.[152] That senior members of the clergy (such as Lindsay) and cathedral churches (such as Aberdeen) could boast extensive libraries is hardly surprising, but it is indicative of an increasingly educated parish clergy that at least four early sixteenth-century rectors of Dysart were also book owners.[153] The books owned by the four Fife rectors were of an eclectic nature. They included classical works by Livy, Cassiodorus, Seneca and Ptolemy; the patristic work *Enarrationes in psalmos* by Augustine; studies by the famous Parisian academics Pierre d'Ailly (1350-1420) and Jean Gerson (1363-1429); and two more contemporary works – a collection of the acts of the Scottish parliament (published in Edinburgh in 1541) and *De inventoribus rerum* by the humanist scholar Polydore Vergil. The four men may have had other books too which have not survived, and they almost certainly would have possessed ecclesiastical service books and a bible. Up to a point this collection is reflective of broader clerical reading material, at least towards the end of our period, though as the sixteenth century progressed there was a marked redirection of reading interests as fashionable humanist scholars such as Polydore Vergil and above all Erasmus, whose work is well represented in

[149] R.H. Rouse and M.A. Rouse, *Registrum Anglie de Libris Doctorum et Auctorum Veterum* (London, 1991), 303-8. The other Scottish houses covered were Jedburgh (82 titles), Kelso (96), Newbattle (34), St Andrews (95), Holyrood (28) and Dunfermline (46).
[150] Durkan and Ross, 'Early Scottish libraries', 12.
[151] Ross, 'Libraries of the Scottish Blackfriars', 7-11, 14, 20.
[152] W.M. Bryce, *The Scottish Greyfriars* (Edinburgh, 1909), ii, 334.
[153] Durkan and Ross, 'Early Scottish libraries', 83, 87-8, 120; J. Durkan, 'Further additions to 'Durkan and Ross': some newly discovered Scottish pre-Reformation provenances', *The Bibliotheck*, 10 (1980-81), 95.

other collections, began to eclipse increasingly old-fashioned medieval theological tomes.[154] Nonetheless, esoteric theological works also graced the royal library, James IV's purchases including biblical commentaries by the celebrated thirteenth-century Scottish academic John Duns Scotus and works by other famed theologians such as Gerson, the fourteenth-century English Franciscan Robert Holkot and the fifteenth-century Poitier professor Nicholas de Orbellis.[155]

While the bulk of reading material possessed by both the clerical and the secular audiences was probably of a broadly religious nature, legal and medical texts were also reasonably common. Gratian's Decretals, the first (twelfth-century) compilation of canon law, the subsequent additions to it and commentaries on them reached Scotland in both manuscript and printed format. We have already seen that the library of Aberdeen Cathedral possessed these texts by the first half of the fifteenth century and printed versions were subsequently acquired by, among others, James IV, Bishop Elphinstone of Aberdeen (a noted canon lawyer) and Robert Reid, bishop of Orkney.[156] Meanwhile, Archbishop William Schevez of St Andrews was complimented in the 1490s on his library, which, his Netherlandish admirer informs us, was particularly strong in scientific and medical texts. Indeed, among medical works, Galen's standard work was possessed by some in printed form and by the early sixteenth century other popular medical texts, such as the anonymous *Ortus sanitatus*, which went through several editions from 1471, were also possessed by some clerics and aristocrats.[157]

Theological, legal and medical texts might, with some justification, be regarded as rather heavy reading material. For lighter relief, though still with a clear religious purpose, many clerics possessed the famous compilation of saintly lives by James de Voragine. There seems to have been a copy of it in the cathedral library at either Aberdeen or Elgin before c.1400, and, once printed, it became popular with lesser clerics too, surviving in editions published in Nuremberg in 1476, Cologne in 1485, Lyon in 1493, 1502, 1510 and 1554, along with others with no date or place of imprint.[158] Voragine's sermons were also popular with friars, as were those of the 'witty and pithy' Dominican preacher Pepin, and both served a clear, if entertaining, purpose with those specifically expected to undertake preaching duties.[159] It seems probable that lay readers too, when it came to religious themes, generally preferred something more practical or entertaining than the more taxing texts

---

[154] Durkan and Ross, 'Early Scottish libraries', 20; Ross, 'Libraries of the Scottish Blackfriars', 25.

[155] *TA*, ii, 21, 359, 364.

[156] See above, page 92; *TA*, iii, 364; Durkan and Ross, 'Early Scottish libraries', 31-3, 44.

[157] R.J. Lyall, 'Books and book owners in fifteenth-century Scotland', 246; Durkan and Ross, 'Early Scottish libraries', 41-2, 81, 105; Durkan, 'Further additions to 'Durkan and Ross'', 90; *TA*, ii, 34.

[158] James de Voragine, *The Golden Legend*, ed. G. Ryan and H. Ripperger (Salem, 1987); Lyall, 'Books and book owners in fifteenth-century Scotland', 240; Durkan and Ross, 'Early Scottish libraries', passim.

[159] Durkan and Ross, 'Early Scottish libraries', 19, 74, 122, 152.

favoured by the academics. Duchess Eleanor of Austria, for instance, possessed
a psalter decorated with the arms of Austria and Scotland, and many others
possessed service books.[160] Books of hours – which included a series of short
religious services to be recited at different times of the day – were also a
common aristocratic possession. Some, such as the Playfair Hours, were
manufactured in Rouen and specifically tailored to Scottish audiences by the
inclusion of passages relating to Scottish saints. Others – such as that
commissioned by James IV on the occasion of his marriage to Margaret Tudor
– were Netherlandish products, in this particular instance from the workshop
of Simon Benning and Gerard Horenbout.[161] In addition James owned
another broadly devotional text, *The Art of Dying*.[162]

Fewer books of a more profane nature have survived, but it seems
probable that the English poet Thomas Hoccleve was expressing a widespread
aristocratic prejudice when he advised the Lollard knight John Oldcastle to
put away his bible and, instead, concentrate his reading on the romance
Lancelot of the Lake, accounts of the siege of Troy or Thebes and the treatise
on war by Vegetius.[163] It would not be surprising had the military treatise by
Vegetius circulated in Scotland too for it was the standard work on the
subject. Its popularity throughout Christendom is indicative of the common
martial interests of the aristocracy, and other texts of a broadly military and
chivalric nature were certainly acquired by Scots. In the mid-fifteenth century,
for instance, William Sinclair, earl of Orkney, commissioned translations of
Honoré de Bonet's fourteenth-century *Tree of Battles* and of the anonymous
Buke of the Governaunce of Princis and *Le livre de l'ordre de chevalerie*.
Meanwhile, another 'handbook of good behaviour', Alain Chartier's fifteenth-
century *Le bréviaire des nobles*, was translated by an Aberdeen notary in
c.1490.[164] Other aristocratic interests which we have already examined were
also reflected in literary products. Chess, for instance, was sufficiently popular
to provide the literary motif for the moralising tale *Ludud scaccorum* by the
thirteenth-century Italian James of Cessoli. This was copied and translated
throughout the Latin west, in Scotland as the early sixteenth-century *Buke of
Chess* – though references to the game can be gleaned from thirteenth-century

[160] Köfler and Caramelle, *Die beiden Frauen des Erzherzogs Sigismund*, 98.
[161] *The Playfair Hours: A late fifteenth-century illuminated manuscript from Rouen*, ed. R. Watson
(London, 1984); L.J. Macfarlane, 'The book of hours of James IV and Margaret Tudor', 3-21. See
too D. McRoberts, 'Dean Brown's book of hours', *IR*, 19 (1968), 146-67, and more generally
French Connections: Scotland and the arts of France (Royal Scottish Museum, 1985), 26-8.
[162] *TA*, ii, 359.
[163] *Hoccleve's Works I: The minor poems*, ed. F.J. Furnivall (Early English Text Society, 1892), 14-
15.
[164] *Gilbert of the Haye's Prose Manuscript (AD 1456)*, ed. J.H. Stevenson (STS, 1901-14); I.
Cunnigham, 'The Asloan manuscript' in A.A.MacDonald, M. Lynch and I.B. Cowan, eds., *The
Renaissance in Scotland: Studies in literature, religion, history and culture* (Leiden, 1994), 109-10; C.
van Buuren, 'John Asloan and his manuscript: an Edinburgh notary and scribe in the days of
James III, James IV and James V, c.1470-c.1530' in J.H. Williams, ed., *Stewart Style, 1513-1542:
Essays on the court of James V* (East Linton, 1996), 23-4. See too *The Deidis of Armorie: A heraldic
treatise and bestiary*, ed. L.A.J.R. Houwen (STS, 1994).

romances such as *Fergus* and *La Manekine*, both of which were partly set in Scotland. Tournaments, hawking and hunting too were also a common literary theme, especially in romances.[165]

Unfortunately we do not know the precise content of Lord Lyle's 'buik of storeis' or the romances which were owned by James Douglas of Dalkeith. Still, there is no doubt that later medieval Scottish aristocrats were familiar with both the *roman antiques*, which dealt with classical themes, and those romances which focused on King Arthur and his entourage. John Barbour, the fourteenth-century author of *The Bruce*, compared Robert I with Tydeus, the hero of the *Roman de Thebes*, and the possibly Scottish author of the early thirteenth-century *Fergus* drew on the work of Chrétien de Troyes (*fl. c.*1170-1190), father of the Arthurian romances. Moreover, a mirror case excavated at Perth reveals a familiarity with the story of the other great romance heroes, Tristan and Iseut.[166] In one sense romance was a dying genre from the fourteenth century. Few new works were composed – Froissart's *Méliador* was an exception[167] – but there remained an avid readership for the older works. Robert I allegedly read a romance to his followers as they crossed Loch Lomond in 1306;[168] and Eleanor Stewart, duchess of Austria, possessed a copy of the Lancelot romance – a gift from the duke of Bavaria. She, indeed, seems to have been responsible for translating the French *Pontus and Sidonia*, itself a translation and adaptation of the Anglo-Norman *Horn and Rimenhild*, into German.[169] Here, moreover, is a splendid example of the international nature of medieval culture surviving the rise of the vernacular and in fifteenth-century Scotland too new translations appeared of established favourites. *The Buik of King Alexander the Conquerour* was translated from the *Roman d'Alixandre* while another thirteenth-century French text provided the basis of *Lancelot of the Laik*. English romance translations also circulated, Marion Lyle of Houston possessing Lydgate's *Siege of Thebes* and the disgraced Thomas Boyd, earl of Arran, borrowing a copy of the same book from the Paston collections.[170]

---

[165] *The Buke of the Chess*, ed. C. van Buuren (STS, 1997); D.D.R. Owen, *William the Lion: Kingship and culture, 1143-1214* (East Linton, 1997), 118, 122, 134-35, 144-45, 171.

[166] *The Bruce* (Duncan), 106-8, 232-39; Owen, *William the Lion*, 124, 130-31, 148-49, 188-92. Owen suggests that William Malvoisin, bishop of St Andrews, was the author of *Fergus*, but see the review of his book by W.W. Scott in *SHR*, 78 (1999), 256-57.

[167] Jean Froissart, *Méliador*, ed. A. Longnon (Paris, 1895-99); D.F. Dembowski, *Jean Froissart and his Méliador: Context, craft and sense* (Lexington, 1983).

[168] *The Bruce* (Duncan), 132-33.

[169] A. Stewart, 'The Austrian Connection, *c.*1450-1483: Eleanora and the intertextuality of *Pontus und Sidonia*' in McClure and Spiller, *Bryght Lanternis*, 129-49; Köfler and Caramelle, *Die beiden Frauen des Erzherzogs Sigismund*, 93-5. Eleanor also possessed a translation of Boccacio's *De praeclaris mulieribus*, a copy of Jerome's *Epistae* and perhaps a manuscript of work by Virgil. She presented the duke of Bavaria with another book in 1478 (Köfler and Caramelle, *Die beiden Frauen des Erzherzogs Sigismund*, 94, 98; A. Cherry, *Princes, Poets and Patrons: The Stuarts and Scotland* (Edinburgh, 1987), 18.)

[170] *The Buik of King Alexander the Conquerour*, ed. J. Cartwright (STS, 1986-90); *The Buik of Alexander or The Buik of the Most Noble and Valiant Conquerour Alexander the Grit*, ed. R.L.G.

While the enduring appeal of romance, with its stories of courtly love and military endeavour, is a clear indication of the vibrancy of chivalric culture, there was a market for other works of English, Irish and French provenance too. The French poem *Le débat de l'omme et de la femme* by the fifteenth-century monk Guillaume Alexis was translated in early sixteenth-century Aberdeen. Its circulation (taken together with references in some of Dunbar's poetry and at least a belated knowledge of Christine de Pisan's *Epistle to the God of Love*) suggests a familiarity with the vexed controversy concerning the nature of women which, as we shall see in chapter six, gripped literary circles in Spain and elsewhere.[171] On the other hand, it is perhaps surprising that so little work by Christine de Pisan and for that matter by François Villon – two of the greatest of fifteenth-century French writers – is known to have reached a Scottish audience, even through English translations. Still, the great fifteenth-century Scottish writers were certainly familiar with widely circulated Latin texts, and with English works by Chaucer, Gower, Lydgate and Hoccleve. So were others. Gower's work featured in an inventory of belongings of the Orcadian bishop Robert Maxwell in 1540. That of Lydgate appears in the predominantly Gaelic compilation, *The Book of the Dean of Lismore*, though Irish influences were naturally more profound than English in the Gaelic-speaking regions of the west.[172] Yet literary traffic was by no means one way. Scottish Gaels were to be found in Ireland – Giolla Críost Brúilngeach, for instance, composing poems while on a visit to Roscommon in the mid-fifteenth century.[173] *Fergus* influenced the later French romances *Huon de Bordeaux* and *Aucassin et Nicolette*. And in the later fifteenth and early sixteenth centuries the work of great Scottish writers Robert Henryson, William Dunbar, Gavin Douglas and David Lindsay ought to be regarded as one of the country's most significant exports south of the Border.[174]

There is one other group of works which we must consider: histories and chronicles. It is perhaps surprising that the works of Froissart, whose chronicles covered Scotland and whose romance *Méliador* was largely set in

Ritchie (STS, 1921-29); *Lancelot of the Laik*, ed. M.M. Gray (STS, 1912); Lyall, 'Books and book owners in fifteenth-century Scotland', 240; *The Paston Letters, AD 1422-1509*, ed. J. Gairdner (London, 1904), v, no. 804.

[171] P. Bawcutt, 'An early Scottish debate-poem on women', *Scottish Literary Journal*, 23 (1996), 35-42; idem, 'Images of women in the poems of Dunbar', *Études Écossaises*, 1 (1991), 49-58.

[172] A.A. MacDonald, 'The Latin original of Robert Henryson's Annunciation lyric' in MacDonald, Lynch and Cowan, *The Renaissance in Scotland*, 45-65; Lyall, 'Books and book owners in fifteenth-century Scotland', 240; W. Fraser, *Memoirs of the Maxwells of Pollok* (Edinburgh, 1863), i, 410; D.E. Meek, 'The Scots-Gaelic scribes of late medieval Perthshire: an overview of the orthography and contents of the Book of the Dean of Lismore' in Williams, *Stewart Style*, 265-66; E.M.B. Ó Mainnín, 'The same in origin and in blood: bardic windows on the relationship between Irish and Scottish Gaels, c.1200-1650', *Cambrian Medieval Celtic Studies*, 38 (1999), 1-52.

[173] *Scottish Verse from the Book of the Dean of Lismore*, ed. W.J. Watson (Edinburgh, 1937), 32-59.

[174] Owen, *William the Lion*, 152; G. Kratzmann, *Anglo-Scottish Literary Relations, 1430-1550* (Cambridge, 1980); A.A. MacDonald, 'Anglo-Scottish literary relations: problems and possibilities', *Studies in Scottish Literature*, 26 (1991), 172-84.

Scotland, were not apparently possessed in Scotland until long after his death.[175] Still, other foreign histories (as well as those written by Scots) were certainly in circulation. Fordun (and Bower) were familiar with many English works, such as Bede's *Ecclesiastical History of the English People*, the Anglo-Saxon Chronicle, Geoffrey of Monmouth's *History of Britain*, as well as the works of the twelfth-century writers William of Malmesbury and Henry of Huntingdon and, later still, the thirteenth-century *Polychronicon* of Ranulph Higden. In addition, the two Scottish writers had access to a number of continental sources, including Martin of Troppau's thirteenth-century chronicle and, above all, to a late copy of Vincent of Beauvais's *Speculum Historiale*, probably compiled shortly after 1254.[176] Where exactly Bower and Fordun consulted these works remains unknown. In the case of Bower, it was perhaps in Dunfermline Abbey, which was not far distant from the abbot's island priory of Inchcolm; or perhaps in Edinburgh Castle, if the library which Thomas Gray consulted in the 1350s still existed. Yet it is significant that none of Bower's foreign historical sources date from the fourteenth or fifteenth centuries, and it is tempting to assume that the long conflict with England caused something of an intellectual breach not just with England, but with continental Europe too, at least in so far as the transmission of foreign chronicles to Scotland was concerned. This too is suggested by the seemingly limited circulation in Scotland of works by Pisan, Villon and Chartier. Nevertheless, some of the earlier works used by both Fordun and Bower remained popular once they had been printed. Geoffrey of Monmouth's somewhat fabulous history, for instance, was possessed by at least two sixteenth-century clerics. Meanwhile, a late fifteenth-century manuscript of Suetonius's *Lives of the Caesars* circulated among a number of north-eastern owners and Henry Sinclair, bishop of Ross, possessed a 1521 edition of Einhard's ninth-century *Life* of Charlemagne, which drew on the text by Suetonius. There was also a market for (sometimes pseudo-factual) travellers' tales. In 1467 James III commissioned a copy of Sir John Mandeville's hugely popular travels and the new spirit of exploration which captured the post-Columban world was reflected in William Hay's acquisition of an early sixteenth-century account of Amerigo Vespucci's voyages of discovery.[177]

All this begs the question of how and where later medieval Scots came to acquire foreign texts, for there were probably no bookshops in Scotland until the sixteenth century. Before the invention of the printing press our evidence is patchy, but it seems likely that many texts, such as those which the Perth Carthusians obtained from Ghent and Valbonne, were borrowed from foreign

---

[175] Mary, Queen of Scots, may have acquired an English edition of the *Chronicles*: M.A. Bald, 'Vernacular books imported into Scotland, 1500-1625', *SHR*, 23 (1925-6), 262.

[176] *Chron. Bower* (Watt), ix, 234-51; 260-80.

[177] Durkan and Ross, 'Early Scottish libraries', 51, 66, 108, 113; J. Durkan and J. Russel, 'Further additions (including manuscripts) to John Durkan and Anthony Ross, *Early Scottish Libraries* at the National Library of Scotland', *The Bibliotheck*, 12 (1984-85), 86-7, 89-90; *ER*, vii, 500.

sources and perhaps then copied, most of them in monastic scriptoria.[178] Indeed, the early fourteenth-century catalogue compiled by the Franciscans was perhaps intended as a primitive database for inter-library loans.[179] Alternatively, Scots who ventured abroad copied texts elsewhere (or had them copied) and then brought them home – sometimes perhaps as war booty.[180] Many of the extant twelfth and thirteenth-century manuscripts have been ascribed to English or Irish sources – and this may explain the close similarity between Scottish and English handwriting in the twelfth and thirteenth centuries.[181] Still, even in this early period some texts came from the continent. A gloss of St Matthew belonging the priory of the Isle of May seems to be of French origin and by the later thirteenth century other texts probably originated in both France and the Low Countries.[182] Somewhat later William Elphinstone (senior) copied at least three books of lecture notes while studying at Leuven in the 1430s and later still his son, while studying in Paris, hired the scribe 'R de S' to copy several other books.[183] It was, however, also possible to acquire manuscripts from the specialised booksellers who had emerged in the greater Flemish towns by the fourteenth century, and earlier still in France, and in whose workshops multiples of popular texts were speculatively copied.[184]

Book circulation was greatly facilitated once the laborious task of manual copying had been superseded by the invention of the printing press by Johannes Gensfleisch zum Gutenberg in the 1450s. Books then became much like any other commodity of trade, with one notable exception. They have survived better than most of the other articles handled by medieval merchants, and most of them provide an explicit indication of when and where they were produced. The thousand or so fifteenth and sixteenth-century Scottish-owned books examined by Anthony Ross and John Durkan were published in almost forty different locations across western Europe, with the notable exception of the Iberian peninsula. Few of them, however, were manufactured in Scotland itself – where the first printing press was established

---

[178] W.N.M. Beckett, 'The Perth Charterhouse before 1500', *Analecta Cartusiana*, 128 (1988), 53, 57.

[179] Rouse and Rouse, *Registrum Anglie*, p. cxlvi.

[180] F. Henry and G.L. Marsh-Michell, 'A century of Irish illumination, 1070-1170', *Proceedings of the Royal Irish Academy*, C62 (1961-63), 155.

[181] G.G. Simpson, *Scottish Handwriting, 1150-1650* (Aberdeen, 1973), 5-6. For the divergence of Scottish and English handwriting styles from the fourteenth century, and the introduction of French and Italian handwriting styles in the early sixteenth century, see ibid, 6, 15-24.

[182] *Pagine scelte in due codici appartenuti alla badia di S. Maria di Coupar-Angus in Scozia*, ed. H.M. Bannister (Rome, 1910); Sharrott and Caldwell, *Angels, Nobles and Unicorns*, nos. B17-18, B20, B22, C19, C21-2, C24-9; V. Glenn, 'Court patronage in Scotland, 1240-1340' in Fawcett, *Art and Architecture in the Diocese of Glasgow*, 111-14.

[183] L.J. Macfarlane, 'William Elphinstone's Library', *Aberdeen University Review*, 37 (1957-58), 253-71.

[184] Blockmans, 'Manuscript acquisition by the Burgundian court', 9; D. Pearsal, 'Introduction' in Griffiths and Pearsall, *Book Production*, 3-6; L. Febvre and H-J. Martin, *The Coming of the Book: The impact of printing, 1450-1800* (2nd ed., London, 1990), 25-8.

(in Edinburgh) in 1507 – or in England, where, as in Spain, the volume of book production remained limited.[185] Instead, the vast majority were published in Paris or Basel, which together accounted for 60% of the total, the proportion of French volumes rising notably from the reign of James V.[186]

No doubt some books were acquired by their owners in the places where they were published. It seems likely, for instance, that Bishop Elphinstone acquired his *Manuale parochialium sacerdotum*, published at Cologne in *c*.1492, while visiting the Rhenish city on diplomatic business the same year; and it is probably no coincidence that Italian books featured prominently in the collection of John Adamson, provincial prior of the Dominican order in Scotland, who visited Genoa (in 1513) and Rome (in 1518) to attend the general chapter of his order.[187] But there were other means too by which books could be acquired from the continent. Merchants and scholars can be found acting as middlemen between foreign sellers and Scottish readers.[188] The nineteen volumes which James IV acquired in 1503 were delivered by two Scottish merchants (including presumably the same Andrew Millar who jointly established Scotland's first printing press), and the king obtained further reading material through the endeavours of Master John Harvey, directly from Paris.[189] More came from England. On 22 April 1541 the *Trinity* of Dysart left Hull laden with forty 'old books'; and yet others came from the Netherlands: in 1493 Andrew Halyburton sent a 'kyst of bukis' from the Low Countries to Master James Cumming in Scotland.[190]

Neither of these consignments necessarily contained books published in the country whence they were delivered, for by no means all books were acquired fresh from the printing press or in bulk from foreign centres of commerce. The Dominicans recommended that theirs should be received as alms, both from the secular population and from novices. Others too were the recipients of donations. We have already seen that in 1488 Aberdeen Cathedral received a gloss on a psalter, published three years earlier in Strasbourg. And those which remained in private hands often had a succession of owners: one book of logic owned by a St Andrews student was at various other times the possession of friars from Bristol, Cork and Worcester too.[191] Whether this particular volume was sold, bequeathed or thieved we know not, but the value of books was such that they constituted an emergency honey pot for the impecunious student. William de Clapham, a Scottish

---

[185] Febvre and Martin, *The Coming of the Book*, 190-91.
[186] Durkan and Ross, 'Early Scottish libraries', 15-16.
[187] UL Aberdeen, Inc. 34; Ross, 'Libraries of Scottish Blackfriars', 15.
[188] 'The wills of Thomas Bassandyne and other printers [1577-1687]' in *The Bannatyne Miscellany* (Bannatyne Club, 1827-55), ii, 186-296. See too *CDS*, iv, no. 967.
[189] *TA*, ii, 206, 359, 364.
[190] *Halyburton's Ledger*, 100. See also ibid, 273, for a consignment of eight legal volumes dispatched in January 1505 to Master Richard Lawson.
[191] Ross, 'Libraries of Scottish Blackfriars', 15.

student studying in Paris, left a book of decretals as a pledge for his fees. He subsequently redeemed the text by selling another book.[192]

Architecture

Architecture, like other forms of culture which we have examined, was an interest of the elite – though unlike most of those forms architecture was a medium visible to all. Most buildings which were constructed in late medieval Scotland were of a simple timber design which, as Froissart noted, could be erected and destroyed in a matter of three days.[193] Stone by contrast was a symbol of power. The craftsmen who constructed such edifices were highly skilled and expensive and in most localities only the church and secular aristocrats could afford their services. Remarkably little is known of the men who undertook these great building projects, some of which took decades to complete. Some masons were certainly of foreign extraction. Irish influence is evident in the west – Donald Ó Brolchán worked at Iona in the mid-fifteenth century and Mael-Sechlainn Ó Cuinn at Oronsay slightly later[194] – and English masons were engaged periodically in the Borders. John Lewyn, an experienced builder of castles and religious houses, was recruited to fortify the English-held castle of Roxburgh in 1378 and he may also have assisted in the redevelopment of Melrose Abbey in the later 1380s, where the window tracery perhaps suggests English influence.[195] In this instance the English king Richard II contributed indirectly to the cost of the abbey's refurbishment, and he perhaps therefore influenced the design, but elsewhere too English skills were occasionally recruited.[196] In 1506 the English plumber John Burwel secured the contract for installing the lead roof of King's College Chapel, Aberdeen, three of whose bells were also of English manufacture.[197] There was, indeed, a long tradition of looking to England for architectural exemplars, as is evident from the similarities between the Romanesque elements of Dunfermline Abbey and Durham Priory and the early Gothic styles of St Andrews Cathedral and York Minster.[198] Yet it was not routinely

---

[192] Watt, *Graduates*, 99.

[193] *Chron. Froissart* (Lettenhove), x, 336.

[194] K.A. Steer and J.W.M. Bannerman, *Late Medieval Monumental Sculpture in the West Highlands* (Edinburgh, 1977), 106-9, 119-20.

[195] H. Colvin, ed., *The History of the King's Works* (London, 1963-75), ii, 820; R. Fawcett, *Scottish Architecture from the Accession of the Stewarts to the Reformation, 1371-1560* (Edinburgh, 1994), 11, 29, 31-4.

[196] *CDS*, iv, nos. 397, 398.

[197] *Fasti Aberdonenses: Selections from the records of the university and King's College of Aberdeen, 1494-1854*, ed. C. Innes (Spalding Club, 1854), p. lvii; J. Geddes, 'The Bells' in idem, ed., *King's College Chapel, Aberdeen, 1500-2000* (Leeds, 2000), 111-12.

[198] E. Fernie, 'The Romanesque churches of Dunfermline Abbey' in Higgitt, *Medieval Art and Architecture of the Diocese of St Andrews*, 47-60; N. Cameron, 'The Romanesque sculpture of Dunfermline: Durham versus the vicinal' in ibid, 118-23; M. Thurlby, 'St Andrews Cathedral-Priory and the beginnings of Gothic architecture in northern Britain' in ibid, 47-60. See too idem, 'Jedburgh Abbey church: the Romanesque fabric', *PSAS*, 125 (1995), 793-812; idem, 'Aspects of the architectural history of Kirkwall Cathedral', *PSAS*, 127 (1997), 855-88.

to England that the patrons of great building works looked for inspiration in the later middle ages.

Following the deposition of Richard II, English models were abandoned at Melrose and instead the abbey turned to the continent. At least some of its later stonework was supervised by the French mason John Morow, whose inscription was twice inserted into the west wall of the south transept. Moreover, to furnish the renovations the abbey turned to the Bruges carpenter Cornelius van Aeltre. His new choir stalls, delivered in the 1440s, were modelled according to the monks' specifications on those at the Cistercian houses of Ter Duinen and Ter Doest in the Netherlands.[199] The cosmopolitan patronage of Melrose was by no mean unique. Morow was well known in late fourteenth and early fifteenth-century Scotland, having secured contracts for his services at the cathedrals of St Andrews and Glasgow, Paisley Abbey and the collegiate church of Lincluden.[200] Other French and Netherlandish craftsmen were to find royal patronage in early sixteenth-century Scotland. The French mason Moyse Martin worked at Dunbar Castle and Holyrood Palace before his appointment as master mason for the crown in December 1536. The following year Martin was engaged in the major remodelling of Falkland Palace, where he was succeeded, after his death in 1538, by another French mason, Nicholas Roy, who worked on the palace until 1541. Roy collaborated with three French assistants but other Frenchmen also worked on the Fife palace, including the pargeoner Hector Beato and the painter Pierre Quesnel. Netherlanders were also recruited, the carver Peter Flemishman sculpting statues for the chapel buttresses.[201]

It is reasonable to assume that building designs resulted from, amongst other things, an amalgam of the stylistic desires of patrons who paid for the work and the skills of the masons who carried it out. By the sixteenth century we can sense this process in the making. Moyse Martin had accompanied James V on his visit to France in 1536-37 and it seems highly plausible that the courtyard facades at Falkland were modelled on those at Fontainebleau (which featured on the itinerary of the king and his mason) and Villers-Cotterêts (which lay close to their route). Falkland did not, however, conform to a single model. Construction was prolonged and conducted under the direction of several masons – many of them Scots – who are likely to have brought their own experiences to bear on the different parts of the palace for which

---

[199] 'L'abbaye de Melrose et les ouvrier Flamandes', ed. O. Delepierre, *Miscellanies of the Philobiblon Society*, 5 (1858-59); 'Documents from the records of west Flanders relative to the carved stalls at Melrose Abbey', ed. M.O. Delepierre, *Archaeologia*, 31 (1846), 346-49.
[200] J.A. Smith, 'Notes on Melrose abbey, especially in reference to the inscriptions on the wall of the south transept', *PSAS*, 2 (1854-7), 166-75; R. Fawcett, 'Scottish medieval window tracery' in D.J. Breeze, ed., *Studies in Scottish Antiquity presented to Stewart Cruden* (Edinburgh, 1984), 155-57. The inscription indicates several other locations at which Morow worked.
[201] Dunbar, *Scottish Royal Palaces*, 31-6, 228

they were responsible.[202] Little is known of how or where most of these masons were trained or the nature of the royal wishes which influenced their work. Falkland, moreover, is comparatively well documented. Elsewhere we may speculate that patrons acquired architectural ideas during their travels abroad. Thus, the work which James I financed at Linlithgow may have been modelled on the palace of Sheen, with which the king had become familiar during his captivity in England. Yet few kings were as well travelled as James I and on balance their generally better travelled wives may have been a more significant influence on the architectural design of royal buildings. The castles of Dirleton and Bothwell, for instance, betray similarities to Coucy-le-Château, built by Enguerrand de Coucy, father of the thirteenth-century Scottish queen Marie de Coucy.[203]   Large galleries were common in the fifteenth-century Netherlands and it is tempting to see the hand of Mary of Guelders, a queen whose building interests elsewhere are well attested, behind the gallery built at Falkland in the mid-fifteenth century. Parallels have also been drawn between some of the sixteenth-century features at Stirling Castle and those at the French châteaux of Châteaudun, Nancy and Joinville. Again, a queen provides the link, for Châteaudun was the home of Mary of Guise's first husband, Nancy belonged to her uncle and Joinville to her father. Moreover, Nicholas Roy and five other French masons working in Scotland were recommended to James V by the Guise family.[204]

While similarities between Scottish and continental constructions can sometimes be linked by the itinerary of particular patrons, only rarely can they be attributed directly to a particular mason – though the strikingly Italianate features of roof corbels in the great hall of Edinburgh Castle may well be the work of the Italian mason Cressent, employed by the crown in 1511-12.[205] All too often, however, such links cannot be established – especially for building work carried out before the sixteenth century. Neither is it possible to detect a link between printed architectural studies and buildings which were actually constructed, even though the mid-sixteenth-century lawyer John Marjoribanks acquired two of the earliest such studies ever published – Alberti's *De re aedificatoria* (Florence, 1485) and Vitruvius's *De architectura* (Rome, c.1486).[206] In the absence of such vital information, architectural historians have been left to ponder the implications of the similarities between Scottish styles and those evident in other countries.

[202] D. Bentley-Cranch, 'An early sixteenth-century architectural source for the palace of Falkland', *Review of Scottish Culture*, 2 (1986), 85-95; J.G. Dunbar, 'Some sixteenth-century parallels for the palace of Falkland', *Review of Scottish Culture*, 7 (1991), 3-8; Dunbar, *Scottish Royal Palaces*, 36.
[203] F. Watson, 'The expression of power in a medieval kingdom: thirteenth-century Scottish castles' in S. Foster, A. Macinnes and R. MacInnes, eds., *Scottish Power Centres from the Early Middle Ages to the Twentieth Century* (Glasgow, 1998), 61.
[204] Dunbar, *Scottish Royal Palaces*, 8, 23, 52, 55; *Foreign Correspondence with Marie de Lorraine, Queen of Scotland, 1537-1548*, ed. M. Wood (SHS, 1923-25), i, nos. 11. 17.
[205] *TA*, iv, 271, 439; Dunbar, *Scottish Royal Palaces*, 79.
[206] Durkan and Ross, 'Early Scottish libraries', 128.

These are numerous. We have already noted the influence of English and French styles on Scottish architecture and historians have traditionally assumed that after the wars of independence the former were gradually abandoned in favour of the latter. More recently, however, this neat transformation has been undermined by the observation of other parallels. Richard Fawcett has argued that Netherlandish styles influenced all types of late Scottish Gothic construction, from baronial tower houses to churches built or modified in towns such as Aberdeen, Dundee, Haddington and Perth.[207] Ian Campbell, on the other hand, has detected a quite different trend, claiming a Romanesque revival in Scotland from the later fourteenth century which was influenced less by continental models and more by anglophobia. This, he argues, was a politically conscious development which, by returning to Scottish styles of the pre-wars of independence era and rejecting newer developments in England, sought to emphasise political differences with England in a cultural context. The return to the Romanesque (the predominant architectural style of the twelfth century) made for similarities with Italian architecture (which had never fully embraced the later north European Gothic style). Moreover, this paved the way for the direct adoption of Italian renaissance styles in the later fifteenth century. The best example of this, Campbell argues, is in the remodelling by James III and James IV of Linlithgow Palace, whose quadrangular form and square corner towers resemble the designs of the Italian architect Filarete.[208] So, while both agree that later medieval architecture owed little to English models, Fawcett has argued that Scottish architecture was primarily the second-hand recipient of Netherlandish styles, while Campbell sees Scottish buildings as pioneering exemplars of Italian architectural design north of the Alps.

There are merits in both of these arguments. Both, however, require intellectual leaps of faith which may not be wholly justified. For a start, it is not self-evident that Scottish architects would have consciously turned their backs on English models. We have already seen similar devotional patterns in the two countries and also how they shared a common chivalric tradition. There were musical, linguistic and literary connections too. Given these cultural exchanges, it would be strange if architecture was somehow different. Indeed, both Fawcett and Campbell have somewhat grudgingly recognised limited English influences in Scottish architecture, especially in the construction of the crown steeples on church towers at Dundee, Edinburgh,

---

[207] R. Fawcett, 'Late Gothic architecture in Scotland: considerations on the influence of the Low Countries', *PSAS*, 112 (1982), 477-96; Fawcett, *Scottish Architecture*, 19-20, 187, 190, 196, 210. See too D. Howard, *Scottish Architecture: Reformation to Restoration, 1560-1660* (Edinburgh, 1995), 2, 16-17, 83, 86.

[208] I. Campbell, 'A Romanesque revival and the early renaissance in Scotland, *c*.1380-1513', *Journal of the Society of Architectural Historians*, 54 (1995), 302-25; idem, 'Linlithgow's 'princely palace' and its influence in Europe', *Architectural Heritage*, 5 (1994), 1-20. See too R. Stalley, 'Ireland and Scotland in the middle ages' in Higgitt, *Art and Architecture of the Diocese of St Andrews*, 108-17, in which the author compares the Scottish and Irish rejection of the English Perpendicular style.

Linlithgow, Haddington and King's College, Aberdeen. If we follow their methodology, this is readily explicable. By the fifteenth century traders from these towns were regularly to be found in towns such as London and Newcastle, where some churches bore similar attributes.[209] Following the same approach, it seems eminently sensible for John Dunbar to have sought an English parallel for James I's rebuilding of Linlithgow Palace – since, albeit unwillingly, that Scottish king was more familiar with England than most. He, moreover, had an English wife and we have already noted the potentially important contribution of queens to the design of royal buildings.

    This is not to argue that English architecture was the main, or even one of the main, inspirations behind Scottish architectural design in the later medieval period. Yet, at least in the examples cited relating to both English and French influences, it is possible to detect a connection between patron and possible models. This is much less clear in the other models which have been proffered. Let us firstly examine the north European link. In its favour are two circumstantial factors. The Scots who commissioned building work were (kings apart) frequent visitors to both the Netherlands and France. We can therefore assume that they were familiar with architectural designs *in parts* of those regions. Secondly, we know that the furnishings for Scottish buildings were sometimes acquired in the same places. In addition to the Melrose choir stalls, those at King's College, Aberdeen are reckoned to conform to Flemish designs. More certainly three of the chapel's bells – as well others at St John's church in Perth and St Giles's church in Edinburgh – were manufactured at Mechelen.[210] Floor tiles too were occasionally imported from the Netherlands, as were some beds and chairs for the royal chambers.[211] Still, modern Ikea shoppers do not construct Scandinavian homes for their chic Scandinavian fittings, and we may wonder whether just because Bishop Elphinstone acquired Netherlandish decorations for King's College, he necessarily looked to the Low Countries for architectural inspiration. True, Fawcett has shown that the windows of the college chapel bear a striking resemblance to those at the cathedrals of s'Hertogenbosch and Utrecht, but we have not a shred of evidence that Elphinstone or his associates visited either of these Dutch towns. Few, if any, Scots did. Similarly, James I's Linlithgow may well resemble La Ferté-Milon, but there is no evidence that he or any other Scot visited the French palace.[212]

---

[209] Fawcett, *Scottish Architecture*, 163; R. Fawcett, 'The medieval building' in Geddes, *King's College Chapel*, 55-8.

[210] S. Simpson, 'The choir stalls and rood screen' in Geddes, *King's College Chapel*, 74-97; Geddes, 'The bells', 111; R.W.M. Clouston, 'The bells of Perthshire: St John's kirk, Perth', *PSAS*, 124 (1994), 527-41; G.H.M. Thoms, 'The bells of St Giles, Edinburgh', *PSAS*, 18 (1883-84), 95.

[211] *Halyburton's Ledger*, 162, 251; *ER*, iv, 434, 626; C. Norton, 'Medieval floor tiles in Scotland' in Higgitt, *Art and Architecture in the Diocese of St Andrews*, 149-53. Some French tilers recruited to work for the duke of Hamilton in 1553 were captured on their voyage to Scotland and ransomed (*TA*, x, 206, 208).

[212] Fawcett, 'The medieval building', 47-8; Campbell, 'Linlithgow's 'princely palace'', 2.

The Italian connection meanwhile hinges on just one, albeit slightly more solid, link. This is afforded by Anselm Adornes, a Bruges citizen with close Scottish links, who had become keeper of Linlithgow Palace by 1477. Adornes visited Italy and was, moreover, a man whose family was fond of architectural experiment, as is evident from the Jeruzalemkapel in Bruges, founded by Anselm's father and uncle and modelled on the Holy Sepulchre.[213] Yet it is strange that allegedly Italianate kings such as James III and James IV – who engaged the services of Italian dancers, minstrels and trumpeters and whose predecessors patronised Italian moneyers and glaziers – seem not, with the brief exception of Cressent, to have patronised Italian masons.[214]

There is, then, as yet little consensus on the predominant continental influences on medieval Scottish architecture. None is likely to emerge until such times as architectural historians reconcile their at times disconcerting disagreements over identification of the most fitting foreign parallels for Scottish buildings. Meanwhile, in the absence of more concrete evidence regarding the provenance and training of masons and the itinerary of their patrons, a degree of caution would be wise before attributing architectural styles to the influence of particular countries. Other factors, such as the availability of building materials and the costs of construction, also require closer consideration. At best we may conjecture that Scots picked and chose between various haphazardly remembered or reported foreign designs and then melded these with native traditions – which probably remained the predominant architectural influence – before producing a construction which, for them, was cost-effective, functional and aesthetically, rather than necessarily politically, pleasing.

The Other Side of the Coin?

Culture is an amorphous subject. Yet there were two common threads to the cultural experience of later medieval Christendom. The military interests of the aristocracy were reflected not only in the war-like games of the tournament field and the hunting reserve, but also in the literature of chronicle and romance, the music of the trumpet, the art of the tapestry and the architecture of the castle. This violent streak to the medieval mentality was tempered by religious convictions which were unashamedly displayed in the art and literature of devotion, the music of the mass and the architecture of the church.

[213] A. Macquarrie, 'Anselm Adornes of Bruges: traveller in the east and friend of James III', *IR*, 33 (1982), 15-21; A. Stevenson, 'Medieval Scottish associations with Bruges' in Brotherstone and Ditchburn, *Freedom and Authority*, 101-2.
[214] *APS*, i, 569; C.P. Graves, 'Medieval stained and painted window glass in the diocese of St Andrews' in Higgitt, *Art and Architecture in the Diocese of St Andrews*, 125. The glazier was Francesco Domenico Livi da Gambassi who returned from Scotland to Florence in 1434 to work on the city's cathedral. For an Italian architect who worked on the fortifications of Edinburgh Castle in 1547-48, see *TA*, ix, 163.

A culture whose chief media of expression were stone, script and iron was, of course, exclusive. Few could afford extensive outlay on stone or iron, and few understood script. This supposes that there is another side to the coin of medieval culture. The peasant experience is, however, one of which only occasional glimpses can be discerned.[215] We may suppose that it was markedly less cosmopolitan than that of the aristocracy, though that is difficult to verify. Still, even peasants did not inhabit an environment with no horizon beyond their own locality. Bower displayed his customary snobbishness in dismissing 'the foolish common folk' who 'with gawping enthusiasm' celebrated the deeds of the legendary English outlaws Robin Hood and Little John.[216] The means by which these tales had passed into fifteenth-century popular culture are not clear, and we cannot rule out the possibility that, like the ballad, the Robin Hood legend had percolated to a wider audience from an originally aristocratic milieu. Nevertheless, by at least the early sixteenth century it was the pious but violent English hero who had been adopted as the central figure of the May Day and other celebrations in many Scottish towns. Turning the world upside down was part of the May Day ethos and Robin's nationality, as well as the social origins of those who played him, perhaps made him a particularly suitable figure to preside over the celebrations. Yet, whatever the case, here again is an example of a borrowing from English culture (itself based on a melding of the English tale and the thirteenth-century French play *Robin et Marion*), grafted on to a perhaps older Scottish tradition which featured the 'abbot of unreason'.[217] Even at a popular level some aspects of culture transcended national boundaries.

By contrast, the cosmopolitan dimension of the aristocratic cultural ambience is quite clearly discernible. It is perhaps surprising that this survived despite the sharpening of national animosities and the rise of the vernacular languages in the later middle ages. It survived too despite what most historians consider to have been the increasingly difficult economic circumstances encountered by aristocrats in the aftermath of the Black Death. Investment in culture seems not to have been the first casualty of declining revenue from land. Indeed, although the hypothesis requires closer examination, anecdotal evidence would suggest that fifteenth and sixteenth century aristocrats invested just as much in lavish cultural pursuits as their twelfth and thirteenth-century predecessors had done – if not more so. Why this was so, and how aristocrats were able to afford their cultural inclinations, are big questions.

The first is probably easier to answer. Culture was a mark of status or, as Robert Lopez suggested, 'the password which admitted a man or a nation to

---

[215] See, however, J.J. McGavin, 'Robert III's 'Rough Music': charivari and diplomacy in a medieval Scottish court', *SHR*, 74 (1995).

[216] *Chron. Bower* (Watt), v, 355.

[217] A.J. Mill, *Medieval Plays in Scotland* (Edinburgh, 1927), 19-35; E.P.D. Torrie, *Medieval Dundee: A town and its people* (Dundee, 1990), 95; Macfarlane, *Elphinstone*, 271-72; J. Holt, *Robin Hood* (London, 1982), 159-60.

the elite'.[218] The importance of cultural largesse was perhaps all the more important in a country like Scotland which during the course of the fourteenth century witnessed the elevation of new royal and comital dynasties. Of the thirteenth-century comital families only two – the earls of March and Sutherland – survived into the fifteenth century. New men (and women) are apt to flaunt their new wealth to underline their social arrival, not least, perhaps, when the economic gulf between them and their social inferiors was less pronounced than it had been in the thirteenth century. There are other signs too that the new aristocracy lacked confidence in its position. In the fifteenth century sumptuary legislation sought to regulate what men and women might wear: silk, the luxury cloth *par excellence*, was largely reserved for the knightly class.[219] And in the same century noble houses, such as the Drummonds, invented fictitious lineages for themselves designed to display their supposedly illustrious origins – much as perhaps the greatest patrons of the medieval arts, the Medici, did in Florence.[220] The social transformation of the aristocracy, in other words, perhaps encouraged cultural largesse. Yet this was not the central correlation identified by Lopez. For him it was the 'hard times' of the post-plague years, rather than social transformations of the era, which were accompanied by 'investment in culture'.[221] To determine the relevance of his hypothesis to the Scottish milieu, we must now turn to a consideration of economic matters.

[218] R.S. Lopez, 'Hard times and investment in culture' in W.K. Ferguson *et al.*, *The Renaissance: Six essays* (New York, 1962), 48.

[219] *APS*, ii, 49, 100.

[220] W. Drummond, *The Genealogy of the Most Noble and Ancient House of Drummond* (Edinburgh, 1831), 96; G.A. Brucker, *Renaissance Florence* (New York, 1969), 91.

[221] Lopez, 'Hard times and investment in culture', 29-52. See too J.H. Munro, 'Economic depression and the arts in the fifteenth-century Low Countries', *Renaissance and Reformation*, 19 (1983), 235-50; W. Blockmans, 'The social and economic context of investment in art in Flanders around 1400' in M. Smeyers and B. Cardon, eds., *Flanders in a European Perspective: Manuscript illumination around 1400 in Flanders and abroad* (Leuven, 1997).

4
The Economic Bonds

'Der Mensch ist was er ißt' (Ludwig Feuerbach)

In 1450 William, earl of Douglas, decided to participate in the jubilee pilgrimage. The earl journeyed to Rome via the Low Countries and, finding himself at Lille on Monday, 12 October 1450, he and his companions were entertained to a meal by the duke of Burgundy. The menu included beef, veal, mutton, pork, two hares, ten pheasant, one heron, four bittern, 156 rabbits, seventy-two partridge, ten geese, twelve water birds, thirty-four dozen lark, twenty-two capons, 231 chickens and fifty-six brace of pigeon. The selection of vegetables was more limited: cabbage, though cheese and patisserie were also served. There were a further eighteen loaves and 120 rolls (both brown and white) to accompany the meal, which was garnished with mustard, onion, parsley, milk, cream, butter, salt, pepper, verjuice, vinegar and aspic jelly. Presumably too there was much drink: the ingredients of the aspic jelly alone included a liberal dose of white wine.[1]

Earl William's reaction to the sumptuous feast is not recorded. If, however, he raised an eyebrow at what he was served, it was probably more in surprise at the quantity, rather than the quality, of the fare. Although he might have been disappointed by the limited offering of spices and by the absence of game – the aristocratic meat *par excellence* – the earl would have been well acquainted with everything else. The aristocratic palate was essentially an international one. It had been formulated in the eleventh century, moulded by essentially French agricultural circumstances and popularised across Christendom in the wake of the Norman diaspora of the eleventh and twelfth centuries. Admittedly ale was rarely served south of the Alps and the Pyrenees, while olive oil figured infrequently on dining tables in the north, but otherwise there was remarkably little variation in aristocratic tastes across the territorial frontiers of the Latin west.[2] Neither was there much change in aristocratic tastes over the centuries with which we are concerned, save for a growing preference for sweet wines and beer which can be discerned from the fifteenth century. These, however, were mere adornments to the staples of meat or fish, wheat and wine. Of course, not everyone could afford the lavish banquet served up by the duke of Burgundy

---

[1] *Inventaire Sommaires des Archives Départmental du Nord. Tome VIII: Archives Civiles, Série B*, ed. J. Finot (Lille, 1895), i, 23-4.

[2] J.L. Flandrin, 'Internationalisme, nationalisme et régionalisme dans la cuisine des XIVe et XVe siècle: le témoinage des livres de cuisines' in D. Menjot, ed., *Manger et Boire au Moyen Age* (2 vols, Nice, 1984), ii, 75-91; C.B. Hieatt, 'Sorting through the titles of medieval dishes: what is, or is not, *blanc manger?*' in M.W. Adamson, ed., *Food in the Middle Ages: A book of essays* (New York, 1995).

in 1450. But what was fitting fare for the aristocracy became a fashionable diet to which other social groups might also aspire.

It was not, however, just aristocratic tastes which fashioned the food market. Food was imbued with powerful religious, as well as social, significance. It was the coin of both charity and asceticism. The extremely devout abstained from eating for lengthy periods, while the aristocracy demonstrated not just its largesse and status, but also its piety, in the distribution of alms to the less fortunate members of society. For our purposes, however, it is the way in which religion fashioned diet which is of significance. Had the earl of Douglas visited the duke of Burgundy on another day, or in a different week, their banquet would (or should) have been stripped of meat and fowl. Birds and animals were associated with man's sinfulness, for, when Adam's sins were revealed, God had retorted 'cursed is the ground for thy sake.' It followed that when the religious calendar dictated that special attention be accorded to human sin, all but the most vulnerable members of society (the poor, the sick, the young and the aged) were expected to abstain from the consumption of tainted beasts and their products. This meant that in theory meat was removed from menus on Fridays (in memory of the crucifixion on Good Friday), on Saturdays (in memory of the Virgin Mary) and on Wednesdays too (since it had been on a Wednesday that Judas had accepted his forty pieces of silver to betray Christ). Moreover, these weekly days of abstinence were augmented by Ember Days, the eves of great feast days, lengthier periods in Advent and after Whitsun and by the forty days of Lent, the latter calculated in imitation of Christ's spell in the wilderness. On these days too meat and dairy produce was supposedly anathema, though Annabella Stewart was probably not alone in forsaking meat, but neither cheese nor eggs, on Friday, 10 September 1445.[3] On such a day, however, convention dictated that 'fish was king' – and Princess Annabella, then travelling between Valenciennes and Guise, was duly served with fruits and fish.[4] By living in water fish had both escaped God's wrath and succeeded in associating themselves with Christianity's most potent symbol of purification, water. Religious beliefs thus ensured that for approximately half the year fish substituted meat as the principal dish on medieval menus.

Culture and religion fashioned drinking habits too. The church's sacramental requirements dictated a regular demand for wine. There was no acceptable alternative to this 'blood of Christ', as was clarified by the pope's refusal to allow the Norwegian archbishop of Trondheim to use beer, instead of wine, for communion services in 1186.[5] Clerical dogma was complemented by aristocratic fad. The Anglo-French elite which had settled in Scotland from the twelfth century brought its continental palate for wine to the north and

[3] AS Torino, Inventario 16, Registro 93, fo. 379r.
[4] B.A. Henisch, *Fast and Feast: Food in medieval sociey* (London, 1976), 33.
[5] K. Friedland, 'Kaufmannsgruppen in frühen hansisch-norwegischen Handel' in idem, ed., *Bergen als Handelszentrum des beginnenden Spätmittelalters*(Cologne and Vienna, 1971), 42.

Norman tastes were quickly adopted by the indigenous aristocracy. The urban populace too became a significant consumer of wine. Gifts of wine were often required from those who sought admission to gilds, reflecting the importance of conviviality in gild activities. On other occasions the urban population might purchase wine in the taverns which dotted the town landscape. Taverns, however, were also a feature of rural life – and rural taverns suggest a rural market for wine, since it is unlikely that these establishments catered solely for the needs of the local lord.[6]

If cultural and religious attitudes fashioned demand for food and drink, its supply was governed by climatic considerations. Analysis of the medieval climate has progressed considerably since H.H. Lamb postulated the theory of a 'medieval warm period', lasting from *c.*1100 to *c.*1300. This, Lamb argued, was followed by a period of cooler and wetter weather which continued until the end of the middle ages and beyond.[7] More recent studies have refuted the notion of climatic regression south of the Alps, and qualified Lamb's theory for northern Europe – suggesting, instead, a more complicated pattern of generally wetter and cooler weather, especially between the mid-thirteenth and mid-fourteenth centuries, tempered, however, by some comparatively dry and warm decades.[8]

The Scottish evidence, jejune though it is, would appear to confirm the notion of a climatically stable early thirteenth century. Bower, admittedly a later witness, records crop failures only in 1205 and 1209.[9] The subsequent temperature decline was not dramatic: average summer temperatures dropped by perhaps only 1°C in cooler decades, and annual rainfall in the growing season increased by perhaps 70mm. Nevertheless, in marginal areas such as much of Scotland, this resulted in a crucial shortening of the growing season and a growth in the chances of crop failure.[10] Again, the patchy and not necessarily reliable Scottish evidence tends to support the notion of less propitious climatic conditions from the mid-thirteenth century. Bower records crop failures in the early 1260s which broadly conforms with similar conditions then prevalent in Ireland. Further problems arose in 1272 (perhaps a mistake for 1271 when dearth is recorded in both England and Ireland), 1293 (again in accordance with the fuller Irish evidence), 1337 and 1358 (in

---

[6] A.A.M. Duncan, *Scotland: The making of the kingdom* (Edinburgh, 1975), 491-92.

[7] H.H. Lamb, *Climate: Present, past and future* (London, 1972-77), ii, chapter 17; idem, *Climate, History and the Modern World* (London, 1982), chapters 10-11.

[8] P. Alexandre, *Le Climat en Europe au Moyen Âge: Contribution à l'histoire des variations climatiques de 1000 à 1425* (Paris, 1987); M.K. Hughes & H.F. Diaz, 'Was there a 'medieval warm period', and if so where and when?', *Climatic Change*, 26 (1994), 109-42; F. Serre-Bachet, 'Middle ages temperature reconstructions in Europe', *Climatic Change*, 26 (1994), 213-24; A. Ogilvie and G. Farmer, 'Documenting the medieval climate' in M. Hulme and E. Barrow, eds., *Climates of the British Isles: Present, past and future* (London, 1997), 112-33.

[9] *Chron. Bower* (Watt), iv, 437, 457.

[10] M.L. Parry, *Climatic Change, Agriculture and Settlement* (Folkestone, 1978), 96-102.

Lothian).[11] These individual years of harvest mishap were probably augmented by two cumulative harvest failures in the early fourteenth century. The first of these was between 1308 and 1310. John of Fordun noted that in 1310 'so great was the famine and dearth of provisions in the kingdom of Scotland, that, in most places many were driven, by the pinch of hunger, to feed on the flesh of horses and other unclean animals.'[12] Bower ascribed this to the effects of war, which is possible, but the fuller evidence for Ireland suggests that there, at least, there was a climatically induced famine in 1310 which came on the back of poor harvests in 1308 and 1309. In Ireland this was the first cumulative disaster since the 1220s, but it was soon followed by another, between 1315 and 1318. This affected not only Ireland, but also the whole of north-western Europe from England to Scandinavia. The famine of 1315-18 was, moreover, was one of the most extreme ever known in western Europe, before or since.[13] Although there is little explicit evidence that Scotland suffered what its neighbours endured, it is perhaps telling that when the Scots invaded Ireland in 1315 one of the first things they did was to dispatch four shiploads of 'goods of the land of Ireland' (very probably grain) back to Scotland.[14] Similar raids for 'goods and chattels' were mounted on Anglesey and we know too that the English officials at Berwick reported 'many dying from hunger' in 1315, and again in 1316. In the latter year the garrison mounted a foray in search of food: perhaps significantly it foraged as far as Melrose, some forty kilometres away.[15]

The activities of the Berwick garrison remind us that there was another factor too which influenced the supply of food. The climatic regression of the fourteenth century was accompanied by more unstable political conditions, especially during the recurrent bouts of both Anglo-Scottish conflict and civil war between 1296 and 1357. Those who cultivated fruits and crops were particularly vulnerable amid this strife. Fruit-bearing trees took years to replace if cut down, and the English army which destroyed the orchard of Coldstream nunnery in 1296 was presumably well aware of the long-term impact of its actions.[16] Meanwhile, if they did not witness their crops devoured by invading armies, arable farmers were likely to see the harvest burned to chaff as the Scots deployed scorched earth tactics on their northwards retreats. True, prior warning of hostilities enabled shepherds to

---

[11] *Chron. Bower* (Watt), v, 325, 335, 385; vi, 41; vii, 127; *Chron. Fordun*, ii, 367. A bad harvest was apparently also expected in 1297, but does not appear to have materialised (*Chron. Bower* (Watt), vi, 87). For Ireland, see M.C. Lyons, 'Weather, famine, pestilence and plague in Ireland, 900-1500' in E. Crawford, ed., *Famine: The Irish Experience, 900-1900: Subsistence crises and famines in Ireland* (Edinburgh, 1989), 39-40, 58-61.

[12] *Chron. Fordun*, ii, 338. Compare with *Chron. Bower* (Watt), vi, 347.

[13] Lyons, 'Weather', 41-3, 62-3; W.C. Jordan, *The Great Famine: Northern Europe in the early fourteenth century* (Princeton, 1996).

[14] *Chartularies of St Mary's Abbey, Dublin*, ed. J.T. Gilbert (Roll Series, 1884), ii, 346.

[15] CDS, iii, nos. 451-52, 470, 477.

[16] Stevenson, *Documents*, ii, 32.

herd their flocks in the direction of safer pastures;[17] but this was not always feasible, and in 1296 the sheep flocks of Coldstream nunnery – amounting to about a thousand beasts – were attacked by marauding English soldiers. The nuns were probably unusual only in that they pleaded successfully for compensation.[18]

The impact of political calamities on the food chain was compounded by the effects of disease. The Black Death was arguably the single most traumatic event in the medieval Scottish experience, and the impact of the death of perhaps a third of the European population on the level of supply and demand for all goods, was profound. But plague affected trade in other ways too. Lack of understanding as to how the disease was transmitted prompted precautionary measures of uncertain medical validity which caused damage to commercial activity throughout the later middle ages. A Danzig ship, among whose crew the infection lurked, was placed in quarantine at Aberdeen in August 1500 and its cargo burnt. Similarly, two years earlier the Edinburgh authorities instructed the incineration of suspect English cloth which had arrived at Leith.[19] Disease was not, however, only a human problem. Bower noted the (to him) inexplicable death of cattle, deer and sheep in 1268 and among animals more generally in 1272. Scab was a recurring problem among later medieval sheep flocks – it was noted, for instance, in Lothian in 1268 and on Deeside in 1328. Although government attempted to regulate the movement of infected beasts suggests, the success of such action is less certain.[20] If any quarantine measures were imposed in 1344, they did nothing to prevent a virulent outbreak of fowl pest which reputedly culled the entire poultry population of Scotland.[21] Even if, as Aeneas Silvius Piccolomini reported, it was normal for 'the common people eat flesh and fish to repletion', adverse weather conditions, political instability and disease combined to create a food chain which was rusted with uncertainty.[22]

Flesh and Fish
The Scottish environment was better suited to supply some of the culturally and religiously determined requirements than others. On 'meat-eating days' preferences were broad-ranging, and, while beef, veal, lamb and mutton were the principal fare of the carnivore's calendar, pork, rabbit, chicken, goose, pigeon were also widely consumed. Swan, and above all game, provided the aristocratic elite with other options, though both were no doubt poached by

---

[17] *CDS*, iii, no. 14.
[18] Stevenson, *Documents*, ii, 32-5.
[19] CA Aberdeen, CR/7, 1067-68; *Edin. Recs.*, i, 74.
[20] *Chron. Lanercost*, 85; *ER*, i, 148; *Formulary E Scottish Letters and Brieves, 1286-1424*, ed. A.A.M. Duncan, (Glasgow, 1976), no. 16. On the dating of this, see too G.W.S. Barrow, *Robert Bruce and the Community of the Realm of Scotland* (3rd ed., Edinburgh, 1988), 298.
[21] *Chron. Fordun*, ii, 358.
[22] Pii II, *Commentarii Rervm Memorabilivm Que Temporibus Svis Contigervnt*, ed. A. van Heck (Vatican City, 1984), i, 46.

the poor too.[23] By comparison with fish exports, however, comparatively little meat was sent abroad. There were exceptions: two barrels of meat are recorded aboard a St Andrews ship which was arrested in England in 1388; three swine carcasses were aboard a Bremen vessel which was either about to visit Scotland, or just had, when it was attacked in 1404; a Scottish merchant arrived with meat at Sluis in 1428; and bacon and six barrels of meat were sent to Dieppe in October 1510.[24] But on the whole it seems likely that at least until the mid-sixteenth century most Scottish meat was consumed in Scotland and that only the skin and leather remnants of beasts were frequently dispatched overseas.

If Scotland was well provided with meat, fish too was readily available, if the vessels were there to catch them. Parliamentary legislation of 1471 and 1493 – instructing landlords and towns to build ships and to make fishing nets – may suggest that they were not.[25] It is perhaps more credible, however, to interpret this legislation as official encouragement to exploit more intensely an important resource for which there was abundant foreign, as well as domestic, demand. Herring appears to have been the most commonly caught species of sea fish in Scottish waters: it, at least, predominates in the documentary evidence of fish consumption. Tastes were, however, liberal and on occasions herring was supplemented or substituted on Scottish plates by cod, hake, haddock, lamprey, ling, gurnard, oysters, plaice, ray, turbot, wrasse and even shark.[26] Porpoise, sturgeon and whale were also consumed, though on the Isle of Man (and no doubt in Scotland too) they were supposedly reserved for royal consumption – providing seafood of a status to match that of game.[27] The consumption of sea fish was not, however, confined to coastal regions. Herring were salted or smoked, and cod dried or salted, both for out-of-season consumption and for distribution inland. There they provided an alternative to fresh water species, such as eel, pike, and, above all, salmon, though these too were preserved with salt for distribution elsewhere.

---

[23] E. Gemill and N. Mayhew, *Changing Values in Medieval Scotland: A study of prices, money and weights and measures* (Cambridge, 1995), 230-77; G.W.I. Hodgson and A. Jones, 'The animal bone' in J.C. Murray, ed., *Excavations in the Medieval Burgh of Aberdeen* (Edinburgh, 1982), 229-38; C. Smith, 'Perth: the animal remains' in J.A. Stones, ed., *Three Scottish Carmelite Friaries: Excavations at Aberdeen, Linlithgow and Perth, 1980-86* (Edinburgh, 1989), 166; R. Grove, 'The animal bone', in G. Ewart, ed., 'Inchaffray Abbey, Perth & Kinross: excavations and research, 1987', *PSAS*, 126 (1996), 509-11; C. Smith, 'The animal bone' in A. Cox, ed., 'Backland activities in medieval Perth', *PSAS*, 126 (1996), 792-94 ; Hill, *Whithorn and St Ninian*, 605-13.
[24] *CCR, 1385-88*, 401; *Hanseakten*, nos. 334-36; *IAB*, iv, 437; NAS Edinburgh, E71/29/2. See too *ER*, v, 25.
[25] *APS*, ii, 100, 235.
[26] E.g. Gemill and Mayhew, *Changing Values*, 303-23; *ER*, ii, 369, 451; iii, 42, 108-9; P. Holdsworth, ed., *Excavations in the Medieval Burgh of Perth, 1979-1981* (Edinburgh, 1987), 153, 199; P. Hill et al, *Whithorn and St Ninian: The excavation of a monastic town, 1984-91* (Stroud, 1997), 602-3.
[27] *Legislation by Three of the Thirteen Stanleys, Kings of Man*, ed. W. Mackenzie (Manx Soc., 1860), 83.

Fish was, then, in abundant supply. Much was probably exported. In the thirteenth century *aberdaan* was a Flemish by-word for cod, though salmon and herring were also dispatched overseas: certainly to St Omer, probably to Lynn, and no doubt elsewhere too. Indeed, fishermen from Nieuwpoort in Flanders were already catching herring off the Scottish coast by 1274.[28] Salmon was still exported in the fourteenth century – we hear of it at Bruges, for instance, in 1302 and 1382 and of its frequent dispatch to England.[29] By then there is, however, remarkably little evidence of cod exports, or even of cod consumption in Scotland. References to herring exports are also scarce in the fourteenth century, though the crown continued to acquire substantial supplies, mainly from Crail.[30] Some herring was, however, also imported from England in the fourteenth century, and as early as 1329 Scanian herring too was acquired by the royal household.[31] The fairs of the Scanian peninsula were the main centre of the European herring trade and by at least the later fourteenth century they were visited by Scottish merchants too. Some of the fish in which Scottish merchants dealt was exported to the Low Countries, but a little also reached Scotland, sometimes from pirated vessels – a source of Dutch herring too in the sixteenth century.[32]

Foreign competition at the Scanian fairs was viewed with alarm by the Hanseatic League, which used its military victory over Denmark (confirmed by the Peace of Stralsund in 1370) to restrict the presence of foreigners in Danish Scania. Already anticipating success, the Hanseatic diet outlawed Scots and other foreigners from salting herring at the fairs in October 1369: herring could not be transported for any great distance unless it was salted. This edict was repeated in 1377, and the following year the diet decreed that Netherlanders, English and Scots were to be excluded from *Vitte*, the strips of land possessed by the Haneatic towns at the fairs and upon which the herring were landed.[33] Yet the Hanseatic victory was comparatively shortlived, for by the early fifteenth century the Scanian fairs were in decline following several poor catches. Scanian competition is perhaps one reason why we hear so little of Scottish herring exports in the fourteenth century. That Scottish merchants had muscled in on the Scanian trade suggests that it was more profitable to

[28] A. Stevenson, 'Trade with the south, 1070-1513' in M. Lynch, M. Spearman and G. Stell, eds., *The Scottish Medieval Town* (Edinburgh, 1988), 186; *CDS*, ii, no. 9; *The Making of King's Lynn: A documentary survey*, ed. D.M. Owen (London, 1984), no. 77; R. Degryse, 'De laatmiddeleeuwse herringvisserij', *Bijdragen voor de Geschiedenis der Nederlanden*, 21 (1966-67), 86-7.

[29] *CAEB*, i, no. 136; *IAB*, iv, 435; *ER*, iii, 90, 96, 662. For fourteenth-century salmon shipments to Newcastle, see PRO London, E122/106/5, m. 9v; E122/106/16; E122/106/21, m. 1r, 3r; E122/106/24, m.2r; E122/138/21, m. 6r; to Ipswich, see *CDS*, iii, no. 853; and for London, see *Rot. Scot.*, ii, 106-7.

[30] PRO London, E122/106/21, m. 1r; *CDS*, v, no. 864; *ER*, i-iii, passim.

[31] PRO London, E122/138/21, m. 6r; *ER*, i, 134-35.

[32] Smit, *Bronnen, 1150-1485*, i, nos. 584, 718; *CDS*, iv, nos. 283, 300; *CCR, 1377-81*, 276-277, 500; *CCR, 1389-92*, 426; *Rot. Scot.*, ii, 22; *Hanseakten*, nos. 329(1), 337(1). For Scottish attacks on Dutch fishermen in the 1540s, see GA Rotterdam, Oud Stads Archief 15, pp. 132, 194, 239.

[33] *HR, 1256-1413*, i, nos. 510(11), 522; ii, nos. 150, 158(10-11).

procure herring from northern Europe's most famous fishing grounds than from around the Scottish coast. In the longer term, however, Hanseatic protectionism and the unpredictable migratory habits of Baltic herring spawned a revival in the Scottish herring industry.

In addition to herring, salmon and grilse (a small salmon) were the mainstay of later medieval Scotland's fish trade. Cod, by contrast, remained a comparatively insignificant export until the sixteenth century, though 'mudfish', a word used to describe cod and ling, do appear regularly among exports to England from the fifteenth century.[34] Other types of fish and fish products were not subject to an export duty in Scotland, though some were shipped abroad nonetheless. At Newcastle, alone in England, there was a considerable market for Scottish oysters.[35] Fish oil featured more commonly among exports elsewhere and there are more occasional references to the overseas dispatch of porpoise, dried skate and stockfish (dried cod) – though Norway was western Europe's principal supplier of stockfish.[36] Some of Scotland's exported fish was clearly dried too, though considerably more was salted and some was perhaps fresh.

By the mid-fifteenth century, in contrast to the earlier period, little Scottish fish seems to have found its way to the Low Countries, save that which the Dutch fished themselves. Andrew Halyburton sold small quantities of salmon and trout to his Netherlandish customers, but no Scottish sea fish.[37] A similar pattern is revealed by the early Scottish customs particulars. Although 464 barrels of salmon were dispatched from Aberdeen in 1499-1500, not one was sent to the Netherlands; and only 24 barrels of salmon, out of a total of 510 exported barrels, were sent from Leith to Veere in 1510-1511.[38] In neither period of account was any sea fish sent to the Netherlands. Given that the Low Countries remained the most densely urbanised region of northern Europe, and therefore an area likely to require greater supplies of all types of food than other places, this may seem strange. The virtual exclusion of Scots from this market is probably to be explained by the precocious development of the Netherlandish fishing fleet. Indeed, advances in the design of fishing vessels and in the art of fish curing meant that Netherlandish fishermen were working ever more frequently off the Scottish coast as well as their own.[39]

---

[34] For the volume of fish exports, see M. Lynch and A. Stevenson, 'Overseas trade: the middle ages to the sixteenth century' in P.G.B. McNeill and H.L. MacQueen, eds., *Atlas of Scottish History to 1707* (Edinburgh, 1996), 256-58; Guy, 'The Scottish export trade', 77-9.

[35] PRO London, E122/106/21, m. 1r; E122/106/22, m. 1r; E122/106/24, m. 2r; E122/138/21, m. 1r, 6r; E122/106/41, fo. 1r; E122/107/48, m. 1r, 1d; E122/107/57, m. 4r, 4d, 5d, 6r; E122/108/2, m. 1r.

[36] PRO London, E122/64/16, fos. 3v, 4v, 5v; E122/61/71, m. 3r; E122/62/7, m. 3d; E122/62/9, m. 1d; E122/60/3, m. 9d, 14r.

[37] *Halyburton's Ledger*, 46-7, 87-8, 134, 139, 159, 177, 180, 182, 186, 188, 195, 218-19, 234, 242, 248, 255, 263. See too CA Aberdeen, CR/6, 312, 314.

[38] NAS Edinburgh, E71/1/1; E71/29/2.

[39] Degryse, 'De laatmiddeleeuwse harringvisserij', 82-121; idem, 'De Vlaamse haringvisserij in de XVe eeuw', *Annales de la Société d'Emulations de Bruges*, 88 (1951), 116-33; R.W. Unger, 'The

Here perhaps was one impetus behind the Scottish legislation of 1471 and 1493: envy of Dutch enterprise.

If the Netherlands ultimately provided only a limited outlet for Scottish fish, France and England remained rather more significant markets. Scottish trade with France focused on two distinct regions: Normandy and Gascony. It seems unlikely that either was important in the fish trade until the conclusion of the Hundred Years War in 1453, and even thereafter there is little evidence to suggest that Scottish fish were regularly dispatched to Gascony.[40] Normandy, however, was to become an important destination of Scottish fish. Although in 1499-1500 only twenty-eight of the 464 barrels of salmon exported from Aberdeen were destined for Dieppe, the Norman ports received 68% of the salmon and 99% of the herring exported from Leith in 1510-11 and 1512-13 – some 2,448 barrels of fish in total. Most of the rest was dispatched to England.[41] Yet these figures perhaps give an unduly modest impression of Scotland's fish trade with England.

During periods of truce in the later fourteenth century London fishmongers had regularly sought the permission of the English crown to purchase fish in Scotland;[42] and by at least the later fifteenth century Scottish vessels routinely appeared in the ports of eastern England with cargoes of fish. Berwick, Blakeney, Boston, Bridlington, Grimsby, Hull, Lynn, Newcastle, Scarborough, Whitby and Yarmouth were among their ports of call, though the significance of the trade varied enormously from port to port and from year to year. At Boston, for instance, only three barrels of trayne (whale blubber) were off-loaded by one Scottish ship in 1528-29. Eight years later, however, seven Scottish ships delivered nineteen barrels of salmon, one last and six barrels of grill, twenty-six lasts of herring, six lasts and 1,850 salted fish, six and a half lasts of barrelled fish and two barrels of trayne oil.[43] Boston, however, was a comparative latecomer to the trade and never its most important centre. Newcastle, Lynn and especially Hull were far more important, though even here the delivery of Scottish fish was not an annual occurrence. Still, as the trade peaked in the early sixteenth century, ten or eleven Scottish ships arrived with fish at Lynn in 1538-39, while seventeen Scottish vessels unloaded fish in the Hull customs precinct in 1541-42.[44]

Scottish fish were also to be found as far south as Dover, Faversham, London and Sandwich.[45] Salmon, in particular, continued to find a ready

Netherlands herring industry in the later middle ages: the false legend of Willem Beukels of Biervlet', *Viator*, 9 (1978), 335-56.

[40] See, however, *ER*, i, 456, 465, 479, 506, for salmon sent to David II during his exile in France; and *ER*, viii, 542-44, for herring sent to La Rochelle in 1486-87.

[41] NAS Edinburgh, E71/1/1; E71/29/2; E71/29/3.

[42] *CCR, 1377-81*, 87; *Rot. Scot.*, ii, 106-7, 120, 124, 129, 135-36, 158; PRO London, E122/161/11, m. 9v.

[43] PRO London, E122/12/8, fo. 4a; E122/12/12, m. 1r, 2v.

[44] PRO London, E122/99/24, fos. 7r-10v, 13v, 14; E122/64/16, fos. 1r, 3v-6v, 12r, 13v.

[45] PRO London, E122/76/38, m. 5v; E122/130/12, fo. 3v; E122/208/3, fos. 15r, 20r, 20v; E122/208/4, fo. 6v. Accounts for these ports rarely indicate the home port of shipping.

market in fifteenth-century London, as it had in the later fourteenth century.[46] Rarely, however, did Scottish fish appear in southern or western England. There is no hint of them at, for instance, Bridgewater, Bristol, or at the Welsh ports. Even at Chester, the largest port of north-western England, their appearance was extremely rare.[47] Most of Chester's fish supplies came from the Isle of Man, Wales and Ireland, and, since these areas were major exporters of fish, it seems unlikely that Scottish fish found a major outlet anywhere around the Irish Sea littoral.[48] That said, in 1306 government officials arrested nine Scottish boats in Drogheda, three in Dublin and at least one in Dundalk, most if not all of which were laden with herring of uncertain provenance. Several of the merchants who owned these fish came from Rutherglen and they, at least, seem to have been selling, rather than buying, fish.[49] Thereafter, however, the Irish market, if it remained, is obscure.

Yet we cannot doubt that from at least the later fifteenth century supplies of cod and herring were as copious in the west as in the east – large enough, indeed, to attract the attention of some east-coast vessels. On 9 November 1559 Matthew Jamieson, merchant of Ayr 'laid in ane boat to pass to ane schip of Leith yan beand at yer gar loche four lastis of herring'.[50] We do not know the destination of this particular vessel, or whether it sailed through the Irish Sea or the Pentland Firth. If, however, it chose the southern route, its destination was probably France. Indeed, by the early sixteenth century French fishermen were themselves operating as far north as the Western Isles.[51] Meanwhile, supplies of fish in western regions were matched by those around the Northern Isles. For most of the period with which we are concerned Orkney and Shetland were not, of course, part of the Scottish kingdom. Moreover, their fish trade was of a quite different nature to that of the mainland. Both island groups were legally locked into the trade routes which emanated from Bergen in Norway, and in theory their fish (mainly cod) was delivered there, largely for purchase by Hansard merchants. By the later fifteenth century, however, merchants from Bremen and Hamburg in particular were visiting the isles directly, thereby circumventing the Bergen

---

[46] E.g., *CDS*, iv, nos. 992, 1061, 1064, 1078, 1102, 1107, 1124, 1130, 1148; v, no. 1025; CA Aberdeen, CR/6, 167-68; PRO London, E122/76/38, m. 5v. See too CA Aberdeen, CR/6, 230, 376, 422.

[47] PRO London, E122/16-22 and various other classifications (Bristol accounts); E122/25-27 (Bridgewater accounts); E.A. Lewis, ed., 'A contribution to the commercial history of medieval Wales', *Y Cymmrodor*, 24 (1913), 86-188. For the rare examples of Scottish ships appearing at Chester, see CA Chester SB/4, fo. 128 (for the *Antony* of Ayr in 1499); SB/8, fo. 84v (for a Leith ship in 1543).

[48] J. Kermode, 'The trade of late medieval Chester, 1500-1550' in R. Britnell and J. Hatcher, eds., *Progress and Problems in Medieval England: Essays in honour of Edward Miller* (Cambridge, 1996), 290-92.

[49] *CJRI, 1305-1307*, 226-27.

[50] NAS Edinburgh, E71/3/1, fo. 2v. For cod and herring exports from west coast ports, see Lynch and Stevenson, 'Overseas trade: the middle ages to the sixteenth century', 257.

[51] *Wigtownshire Chrs.*, no. 119.

staple and undermining the dominance which merchants from Lübeck, Wismar and Rostock traditionally exercised over later medieval Norwegian trade.[52]

Figure 4.1: Scottish Trade Links (selected)

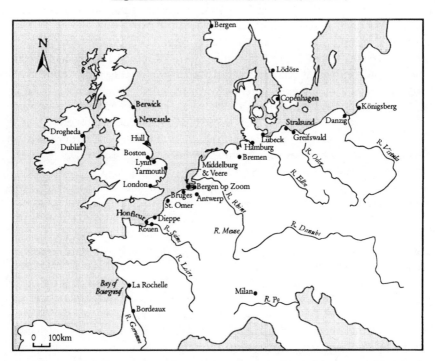

Unfortunately, there is no statistical evidence regarding the volume of the fish trade of the Northern Isles. It is also difficult, in the absence of a complete run of Scottish, English or French customs accounts, to assess the comparative importance of the eastern English and western French markets for fishermen from the Scottish mainland. The Leith accounts of 1510-11 and 1512-13 (see Figure 1.2) clearly suggest that France was the bigger market. Yet, if we add the amounts of fish delivered to Hull and Lynn, the sums were not insignificant and were growing. In 1466-67 202½ barrels of salmon and 52 barrels of herring arrived on Scottish ships at the two ports; by 1540-41 Hull and Lynn together received at least 137 barrels of salmon and 2,033 barrels of

---

[52] *HR,1256-1430*, vi, nos. 262, 275-76; *HR, 1477-1530*, i, nos. 350, 510; ii, nos. 160, 270(28); iii, nos. 353, 356; iv, nos. 68, 79); K. Friedland, 'Der hansische Shetlandhandel' in *Stadt und Land in der Geschichte der Ostseeraums* (Lübeck, 1973), reprinted in idem, *Mensch und Seefahrt zur Hansezeit* (Cologne, 1995), 190-205; idem, 'Hanseatic merchants and their trade with Shetland' in D.J. Withrington, ed., *Shetland and the Outside World, 1469-1969* (Oxford, 1983), 90-3.

herring.[53] This, indeed, is a minimum figure for Scottish imports, since several incoming English vessels may also have been carrying Scottish fish – unfortunately the English customs officials recorded only the home port of each vessel (if indeed even that), rather that its port of departure. Nevertheless, it is clear that eastern England a significant market. It was, however, a vulnerable market, liable to closure not just because of political tension between England and Scotland, but also for environmental reasons. On 6 March 1514 the Scottish lords of council decreed that 'na scottis man tak apon hand to pass in Ingland with na manner of of [sic] victualis, fische or vthir stuff.'[54] The impact was dramatic. Not a single Scottish vessel appeared in Lynn or Sandwich that year.[55] It may seem as if there was a measure of political vindictiveness in such a decree and, since the French market was not similarly targeted, perhaps there was. But similar legislation of 1535 – the impact of which is less easy to determine – was prompted by domestic dearth.[56] Fish, it would seem, were the first substitute for grain in the event of a poor harvest.

The Grain and the Grape

Wheat and wine were rather less naturally abundant in Scotland than meat and fish. In part the scarcity of wheat was a consequence of the decision to graze sheep on viable arable land – a human decision, made for reasons of economic advantage and one to which we shall return presently. In the main, however, the paucity of wheat and wine was a reflection of climatic conditions. The limits of viticulture lay well to the south of Scotland and, although sown in medieval Scottish fields, the sensitivity of wheat to precipitation and temperature makes the Scottish environment less than ideal for its cultivation. Scotland as a whole possesses a more marginal climate for cereal cultivation than southern Scandinavia, and even within Scotland there is a marked variation between the wet, windy and less fertile west, where cool summers are a more significant determinant of wheat production than mild winters, and the drier and more fertile east, even though the latter is apt to suffer harsher winters.[57] In those areas of the country where wheat was grown, yields were good by medieval standards. A ratio of as much as 4:1 was apparently expected, low compared to English norms, but favourable when compared with a ratio of 2:1 in parts of northern Europe and perhaps only 4:1

---

[53] PRO London, E122/62/9; E122/96/8; E122/64/15; E122/99/26. Calculations are based upon the equation of 12 barrels with 1 last.

[54] NAS Edinburgh, CS5/26, fos. 92v-93r.

[55] PRO London, E122/99/3; E122/130/2. Accounts for other east-coast ports have not survived for this year.

[56] *APS*, ii, 346-47.

[57] Parry, *Climatic Change, Agriculture and Settlement*, 82-5; I. Morrison, 'Climatic changes in human geography: Scotland in a North Atlantic context', *Northern Studies*, 27 (1990), 4-5; I Morrison, 'Evidence of climatic change in Scotland before the age of agricultural improvement', *Scottish Archives*, 1 (1995), 6-8.

in parts of France.[58] Very occasionally the harvest was large enough to permit the export of grain to the comparatively densely populated Netherlands.[59] The problem was that relatively little Scottish land could sustain such good growth and in years of adverse weather conditions the crops could fail even on these more fertile lands. As a consequence, and despite legislation of 1457 to force peasants to grow wheat, it and other types of grain were frequently imported to make good the domestic shortfall.[60]

During the thirteenth century Ireland was the traditional source of western Scotland's foreign grain imports. The abbeys of Glenluce, Dundrennan, Kilwinning and Whithorn all periodically sought supplies of Irish grain, as did a number of secular lords, including the future king, John Balliol, then lord of Galloway.[61] Many of these purchases were probably made in the market towns of eastern Ireland, though some Scottish consumers are likely to have acquired supplies from Irish land which they held *in absentia* – Dundrennan, for instance, possessed an estate at Burtonstown in Co. Meath.[62] Yet, in the longer term, Irish grain supplies failed to meet Scottish demand. Political hostilities between the English crown and Scotland disrupted Scottish-Irish trade. Trade embargoes were periodically imposed and Scottish-owned estates were confiscated, often for good. Trade resumed during times of peace – and even in the fifteenth century Dundrennan was clamouring to regain its Burtonstown estate.[63] But longer-term cultural, climatic and demographic trends meditated against the revival of thirteenth-century trade patterns. In the wake of Gaelic resurgence, climatic regression and the Black Death, much of Ireland's arable land was gradually converted to pasture. Ireland was transformed from a net exporter of grain into a net importer.[64]

In eastern Scotland, meanwhile, the shortfall in grain production had traditionally been made good by deliveries from England, especially from the

---

[58] Gemill and Mayhew, *Changing Values*, 145; J. Thirsk, ed., *The Agrarian History of England and Wales* (Cambridge, 1967-), ii, 289-93, 381-82, 394, 407-8, 449-50; G. Bois, *The Crisis of Feudalism: Economy and Society in Eastern Normandy c.1300-1550* (Cambridge, 1984), 204-7; W.C. Jordan, *The Great Famine: Northern Europe in the early fourteenth century* (Princeton, 1996), 25-6.
[59] *HUB*, x, no. 472.
[60] *APS*, ii, 51.
[61] *CDI*, i, nos. 545, 943, 982, 1093, 1370, 1532, 2424, 2830, 2931; ii, nos. 100, 627, 1736, 2166, 1928; iii, nos. 32, 902, 932, 945, 1136-38; *CDS*, i, nos. 617, 765, 795, 850, 933, 974, 982, 1148, 1372, 1891, 1899, 2163; ii, nos. 182, 211, 535, 635.
[62] *CDS*, iii, nos. 967, 969, 1157.
[63] *Rotulorum Patentium et Clausorum Cancellariae Hiberniae Calendarium*, ed. E. Tresham (Dublin, 1828), i, 9, 34, 94, 96-7, 139, 143, 151, 171, 201; 'Accounts on the great rolls of the pipe of the Irish exchequer in the reign of Edward II', *Reports of the Deputy Keeper of the Public Records in Ireland* (Dublin, 1869-), 42 (1911), 17, 25; 'Catalogue of accounts on the great pipe rolls of the pipe of the Irish exchequer for the reign of Edward III', *Reports of the Deputy Keeper of the Public Records in Ireland* (Dublin, 1869-), 43 (1912), 20; 44 (1912), 57; 47 (1915), 47, 73; 53 (1926), 49; *CDS*, iv, no. 668; *Rot. Scot.*, i, 135, 293, 392, 437, 491, 519, 525, 526, 754, 815, 822, 933; ii, 47, 172.
[64] W. Childs and T. O'Neill, 'Overseas trade' in A. Cosgrove, ed., *A New History of Ireland. Volume II: Medieval Ireland, 1169-1534* (Oxford, 1987), 503.

East Anglian port of Lynn.[65] Here too political conflict disrupted trade after
1296, though to some extent this interruption in traditional trading patterns
was perhaps mitigated by ransom payments made in grain on behalf of
captured Englishmen.[66] The remaining shortfall in supplies was partially
compensated by the acquisition of grain from Normandy and Picardy, and
small amounts of Norman grain continued to be dispatched to Scotland in the
fifteenth and sixteenth centuries.[67] By the early fifteenth century grain was
also reaching Scotland from the Baltic. Sometimes it arrived in the form of
flour or malt, but more usually as unprocessed wheat, rye, or occasionally also
as barley or oatmeal.[68] In terms of value, indeed, grain constituted 18% of all
exports from Danzig to Scotland between 1460 and 1530. Other Baltic ports
also participated in this trade, and it was probably with an eye to the poor
harvests of the early 1450s that in February 1454 James II granted merchants
from Bremen his special protection if they visited Scotland. Similar thoughts
may have provoked an analogous grant to Wismar in 1440.[69] Yet, while the
Hanseatic towns perhaps constituted an emergency source of grain supplies,
more corn arrived aboard just one Dordrecht ship than aboard ten Hanseatic
vessels which docked at Dundee in 1551 – unless, that is, the substantial
quantities of 'beir' which the Hansards imported was barley, rather than beer.
It could be either, or both.[70]

Neither northern France nor the Baltic offered a completely satisfactory
replacement for English grain supplies. Both were more distant than England
and, although Baltic grain was comparatively cheap, transportation costs were
correspondingly greater than those from south of the Border. It is not,
therefore, surprising that in times of truce Scottish merchants were soon to be
found visiting English ports in search of their traditional supplies of grain.
Their prime targets were the ports of the Hull customs precinct and Lynn.
Lesser amounts were procured in Newcastle, Yarmouth and occasionally also
in Barton-on-Humber, Boston, Grimsby and Ipswich, though even some of
the smaller English creeks saw potential in the Scottish grain trade. In 1376
Lincolnshire merchants illegally loaded a hundred quarts of wheat for

[65] *CDS*, i, nos. 877, 907, 934, 1044, 2257.
[66] E.g. *Rot. Scot.*, ii, 31, 35, 72, 83, 85, 91-2.
[67] *CDS*, iii, no, 960; iv, no. 151; *CCR, 1369-74*, 27; *James IV Letters*, nos. 328, 402; *Compatabilité du Port de Dieppe au XVe Siècle*, ed. M. Mollat (Paris, 1951), 38. For the international traffic in Norman grain, see Z.W. Sneller, 'Le commerce du blé des Hollandais dans la région de la Somme au XV siècle', *Bulletin de la Societé des Antiquaires de Picardie*, 42 (1947), 140-60.
[68] *Handelsrechnungen*, 20-1, 23, 76-7, 82, 269. For other examples of wheat and malt, see CA Aberdeen, CR/4, 498; CR/5/1, 592; CR/8, 1017; for rye, see CA Aberdeen, CR/5/2, 687; CR/7, 135; for barley, see *TA*, v, 99.
[69] StA Wismar, II Hanseatica C/25; *HUB*, vii (1), no. 556; viii, no. 223. The grant of 1454 is now missing from SA Bremen. For the poor harvests of the early 1450s, see *APS*, ii, 36, 41.
[70] H. Samsonowicz, 'Engländer und Schotten in Danzig im Spätmittelalter' in K. Friedland and F. Irsigler, eds., *Seehandel und Wirtschaftswege Nordeuropas im 17. und 18. Jahrhundert* (Ostfildern, 1981), 50; CA Dundee, BHCB/2, fos. 48r, 52v, 53r, 54r, 54v, 55v, 57r, 67v, 68r, 88v.

Scotland at Saltfleet, and another hundred quarts at Mablethorpe.[71] Malt, however, was the main item of the English grain trade, though wheat and barley featured regularly too, much of it, in the later fourteenth and early fifteenth centuries at least, destined for aristocratic households.[72]

The English grain trade was, however, subject to considerable fluctuation. This is not only explicable by reference to adverse political developments and the imposition of trade embargoes. In 1383, for instance, the English crown granted twenty licences for the export of, in total, 840 quarts of wheat and over 6,280 quarts of malt (and a little barley) to Scotland; but it granted only one such licence in 1382.[73] And somewhat later all seven Scottish ships which left Lynn in 1526-27 were laden with grain, though only one of the eleven Scottish vessels which departed Lynn in 1538-39 was so laden.[74] Sometimes fluctuations of this sort were an indication of poor harvests in England: domestic dearth led to the cessation of grain exports in, for instance, 1389. More often, however, the fluctuating level of exports probably provides a glimpse of years in which the Scottish harvest was poor. And in such years England continued to provide Scotland with an emergency granary.

The grain-based element of the Scottish diet – consumed as gruel, oatcake or bread – was accompanied by liquid refreshment. While water, ale and, perhaps among the lower orders, whisky were the most commonly consumed beverages in Scotland, variation on these basic staples came from abroad. They included occasional imports of foreign ale and mead, and also cider, trade in the latter chiefly associated with Normandy. There the increasing cultivation of apple trees following the Hundred Years War allowed cider to displace wine as the staple drink, though it failed to achieve such widespread popularity in Scotland.[75] Beer too, though more widely consumed than cider, remained a predominantly elitist, and perhaps largely east-coast, tipple. In 1503 the gildsmen of Dunfermline spent 64% of their Christmas drinks budget on beer; but in Ayr ale and wine remained the council's favoured options for entertaining those who visited the town in the early sixteenth century.[76] This seeming divergence in consumption patterns between east and west coasts is perhaps to be explained by the origin of beer. Made, unlike ale, with hops, it was brewed predominantly in the German-speaking world and imported (though not necessarily directly) from the towns along the southern coast of

---

[71] *Records of Some of the Sessions of the Peace in Lincolnshire, 1360-1375*, ed. R. Sillem (Lincoln Record Soc., 1936), nos. 444-45; *CCR, 1377-81*, 140. For Barton, Grimsby and Ipswich, see *CDS*, iii, no. 853; *Rot. Scot.*, ii, 47, 148, 150, 159; and for the other named English ports, *Rot. Scot.*, ii, passim and PRO London E122, passim.

[72] *CDS*, iv, nos. 372, 569, 570, 763; v, no. 864, 2020; *Rot. Scot.*, ii, 32, 41, 47, 49, 50, 91, 132, 156, 186, 193.

[73] *Rot. Scot.*, ii, 41, 47-51, 54.

[74] PRO London, E122/205/3; E122/99/24, fo. 1v.

[75] For examples of ale, mead and cider, see *Hanseakten*, nos. 334-36; *TA*, i, 343. On cider production in Normandy, see Bois, *The Crisis of Feudalism*, 197-98.

[76] *The Gild Court Book of Dunfermline, 1433-1597*, ed. E.P.D. Torrie (SRS, 1986), 46; *Ayr Burgh Accounts, 1534-1624*, ed. G.S. Pryde (SHS, 1937), passim.

the Baltic and above all from Hamburg.[77] The volume of these imports in the fourteenth and fifteenth centuries remains obscure, but, if the brewers of Stralsund are to be believed, Scotland was one of their most lucrative markets. Warfare in the Baltic region, they claimed in 1428, had severely damaged their livelihood by disrupting exports to Scotland and Scandinavia.[78]

All of these liquid imports probably paled into insignificance compared with those of wine. A wide variety of vintages from western and southern Europe were consumed in medieval Scotland. By the fifteenth century osay and malmsey (the sweet wines of Portugal, Greece and the Mediterranean) had begun to make inroads into the Scottish market, though neither challenged the dominance of traditional reds and whites.[79] A number of regions specialised in the production of these mainstays of the wine trade. Some Spanish wines were consumed in Scotland by the fourteenth century, and it was perhaps from Spain too that both 'garnache' and 'bastard' were derived: that, at least, was the designation of the latter in the anonymous fifteenth-century poem *The Libelle of Englysche Polycye*.[80] On balance, however, it was primarily French and German products which were consumed in Scotland, wine described as 'Rhenish' probably including the produce of the Mosel and Alsace as well as that of the Rhineland proper.[81] In France, meanwhile, production was focused on a number of provinces. Gascony was perhaps the most notable source of production, but in addition to the wines of Bordeaux and La Rochelle, those from Orléans and Burgundy also reached Scotland.[82]

In the thirteenth century Bordeaux merchants had been responsible for the import of at least some Gascon wine. One of their number, John Mazun, was involved in lengthy court proceedings in an attempt to recoup debts left unpaid by King Alexander III.[83] Archaeological evidence – such as the French wine jugs found at Glenluce – also points to contact with the La Rochelle

---

[77] E.g. *ER*, v, 36; vi, 114, 117-18, 131; vii, 60; xi, 235; *TA*, ii, 256; *LUB*, x, no. 532; CA Aberdeen, CR/4, 413; CR/5/1, 509; CR/5/2, 700; CR/9, 728. On the brewing industry in the Hanseatic world, see K. Fritze, *Am Wendepunkt der Hanse: Untersuchungen zur Wirtschafts- und Sozialgeschichte wendischer Hansestädte in der ersten Hälfte des 15. Jahrhunderts* (Berlin, 1967), 25-7.
[78] Fritze, *Am Wendepunkt der Hanse*, 226.
[79] For the sweet wines see, for example, *ER*, iii, 3; iv, 406; v, 36, 300, 340, 381; vi, 295; vii, 289; x, 38; xii, 369; xiii, 486; *TA*, ii, 454; iv, 470, 474; CA Aberdeen, CR/6, 482; PRO London, E122/29/4, fo. 14r. For the price of sweet and other wines, see Gemmill and Mayhew, *Changing Values*, 215-30. See too *TA*, iv, 81, for the rare import of muscat from Ferrara in 1507.
[80] *The Libelle of Englysche Polycye: A poem on the use of sea power, 1436*, ed. G. Warner (Oxford, 1926), 4. For its consumption in Scotland, see, for example, *ER*, i, 609; iii, 81; iv, 499, 681; vi, 295; xi, 72; CA Aberdeen, CR/4, 172; CA Dundee, BHCB/1, fo. 40v.
[81] E.g. *ER*, i, 609, 617; ii, 6, 78, 133, 222, 454, 475, 531, 620; iii, 40, 655; iv, 436, 450, 564; vi, 308, 499, 502; vii, 95, 163; viii, 256; x, 488, 611; xi, 265; xii, 114, 375, 470, 600; xiii, 235; *TA*, ii, 44, 127, 475.
[82] E.g. *ER*, ii, 222; iv, 568, 620-23, 626, 628; v, 100, 150, 552, 616; vi, 4, 384, 658; vii, 7-8; viii, 149; ix, 344, 358, 448; xiv, 118-19, 200-1; xvi, 299; PRO London, E122/107/57, m. 6r; E122/99/27, fo. 3r. On French wine production generally, see M. Lachiver, *Vins, Vignes et Vignerons: Histoire du vignoble français* (Paris, 1988).
[83] *CDS*, i, nos. 935, 1694; ii, nos. 252, 264, 297, 353, 359, 402, 434, 686-88.

region, though we cannot be certain that either the ceramics, or the wine which they contained, arrived in Galloway directly from France. Similar pottery has been discovered in both England and Ireland and it is possible, indeed perhaps likely, that much French wine was re-exported to Scotland from English and Irish ports.[84] Several of the safe-conducts granted in the thirteenth century to Scots seeking grain in Ireland stipulated that they might also purchase wine there.[85]

Evidence of direct commercial contact between Scotland and Gascony in the fourteenth and early fifteenth centuries is meagre, although in 1385 a Waterford ship carried wine from La Rochelle to Scotland.[86] In the early fifteenth century a few Scottish merchants also procured safe-conducts to visit Bordeaux and La Rochelle, but whether they reached their intended destination is less certain.[87] Not one Scottish ship can be traced in the extant Bordeaux customs accounts of the fourteenth and early fifteenth centuries.[88] Moreover, that King Robert II normally sought wine supplies for his Bute estates in Linlithgow and Edinburgh suggests that wine supplies arrived infrequently on the west coast – though they did occasionally.[89] It would seem, then, that wine was more regularly imported at this juncture on the east coast. Indeed, it was primarily to the Netherlands that Scottish merchants looked for their wine supplies in the fourteenth and early fifteenth centuries – and even in the later fifteenth century the Scottish merchant Andrew Halyburton acquired substantial quantities and different qualities there. His supplies of Rhenish wines were usually acquired in Bergen-op-Zoom – though previously Dordrecht had been the recognised entrepot for Rhenish wines.[90] For malmsey and other wines (from unspecified locations) Halyburton looked to Middelburg, but for French wines it was to Damme, the satellite port of Bruges and the French wine staple, that he turned.[91] His purchases there included the produce of Orléans and Gascon claret, and it was perhaps from

[84] S. Cruden, 'Glenluce abbey: finds discovered during excavations, part I', *TDGAS*, 29 (1952), 179-80; P. Wallace, 'North European pottery imported into Dublin, 1200-1500' in P. Davey and R. Hodges, eds., *Ceramics and Trade* (Sheffield, 1983), 227.

[85] *CDI*, i, nos. 2931, 2937; ii, no. 1928; iii, nos. 902, 932; *CDS*, ii, nos. 211, 535.

[86] *CPR, 1391-96*, 634.

[87] *CDS*, iv, nos. 794, 962; *Rot. Scot.*, ii, 191. See too *HUB*, vii, no. 469, for a ship of La Rochelle sailing from Scotland to Danzig in 1439.

[88] PRO London, E101/156/5; E101/158/2; E101/160/3; E101/160/8; E101/161/3; E101162/1; E101/162/5; E101/163/2; E101/163/4; E101/173/4; E101/181/10; E101/182/11; E101/183/11; E101/184/19; E101/185/3; E101/185/7; E101/185/9; E101/188/12; E101/188/14; E101/190/6; E101/191/3; E101/192/1; E101/194/3; E101/195/19; EXT6/151; EXT6/158. Berwick ships are, however, occasionally recorded: see, for example, E101/160/3, fo. 80v; E101/161/3, fo. 44v.

[89] *ER*, ii, 520, 553, 605; iii, 2, 8, 50, 53, 65, 82, 173, 654. See too *ER*, ii, 551; iii, 59, 122, 173 for wine sent from Blackness to Renfrew and Glasgow. For wine arrivals at the west coast: *ER*, i, 495; *CCR, 1381-85*, 35, 355.

[90] *Halyburton's Ledger*, 22, 25, 90, 109, 110, 123. For earlier shipments of wine from the Low Countries to Scotland see, for example, *CDS*, iv, nos. 10, 146 and probably no. 462.

[91] *Halyburton's Ledger*, 15-17, 21, 23-6, 91, 111, 123, 181; J. Craeybeckx, *Un Grand Commerce d'Importation: Les vins de France aux ancien Pays-Bas, XIIIe-XVIe siècle* (Paris, 1958), 21-2, 93-4.

Damme too that other French wines, including the expensive vintages of Beaune in Burgundy, were dispatched to Scotland. The Netherlands was not, however, the only transit location in which wine could be obtained. Several shipments also reached Scotland from England – some of them of poor quality.[92] In 1366 wine which was unsaleable in London 'on account of its thinness' was dispatched north, as perhaps were twenty tons of Gascon wine 'of poor colour', sent from Yarmouth in 1374.[93]

The later fifteenth century was to witness a geographical expansion of Scotland's wine trade. Some Beaune and Orléans clarets, along with whites from Blois and Bagneaux (near Paris) were by then reaching Scotland not just from England and the Netherlands, but also from the Norman ports of Dieppe and Honfleur.[94] This area (and Brittany too) was also becoming an increasingly important source of Gascon wines. Rouen merchants were selling these more southerly French wines at Leith in 1517; and 291 tons of wine, at least some of it from Gascony, arrived at Dundee, mainly on Dieppe vessels, in 1551.[95] Neverthless, by the later fifteenth century Gascon wines were also being shipped regularly and directly from Bordeaux and La Rochelle, both to the east coast ports and to western ports such as Kircudbright, Wigtown, Irvine and Dumbarton.[96] By the mid-sixteenth century those wines arriving at east coast ports were generally higher priced than those arriving in the west – though whether this was a reflection of the volume of supply or the level of demand remains uncertain.[97] Meanwhile, how much Spanish and Portuguese wine was imported directly from the Iberian peninsula is less certain. Specific

---

[92] E.g. PRO London, E122/64/15, fo. 16r; E122/29/24, fo. 14r, E122/99/27, fo. 3r; E122/106/22, m. 3v; E122/138/21, m. 6; E122/108/8, m. 4r; E122/109/19, m. 6v; NfRO Norwich, Y/C4/104, m. 15v; *CDS*, v, nos. 967, 1102; *Rot. Scot.*, ii, 32, 41, 120, 124, 129, 132, 134, 158, 159. For the customs levy imposed on wine imported into England, see *ER*, viii-xviii, passim. See too E122/107/57, m. 6v, for wine re-exported from Scotland to Newcastle in 1465-66; SA Bremen, 1/Bc 1445 Juli 15; *HUB*, x, no. 715; CA Aberdeen, CR/7, 653, 769, for wine re-exported from Scotland to the Baltic in 1444, 1479, 1495 and 1496; and *ER*, xiv, 268 for wine re-exported from Edinburgh to Bergen in 1517.

[93] *CDS*, v, nos. 122, 214.

[94] *James IV Letters*, nos. 493, 497; Mollat, *Compatabilité du Port de Dieppe*, 43. For the wine trade of fourteenth-century Normandy, which seems not to have extended to Scotland, see A. Sadourny, 'Le commerce du vin à Rouen dans la seconde moité du XIVe siècle', *Annales de Normandie*, 2 (1968), 117-34.

[95] A. Derville, 'Le marché du vin à Saint-Omer: ses fluctuations au XVe siècle', *Revue Belge de Philologie et d'Histoire*, 40 (1962), 348-70; NAS Edinburgh, CS5/30, fos. 123, 154v, 168r; CA Dundee, BHCB/2, fos. 40r, 42v, 51r, 57r, 62r, 88r, 104r.

[96] E.g. *ER*, v, 224, 269; vi, 295; vi, 7, 8; viii, 343, 345; ix, 442; *TA*, i, 392-93; ii, 279; iv, 318, 398, 408, 487, 490, 491, 497-98; *Wigtownshire Chrs.*, no. 112; *CDS*, v, no. 1080; *Navires et Gens de Mer à Bordeaux, vers 1400 - vers 1550*, ed. J. Bernard (Paris, 1968), iii, 16-17, 70-1, 74-5, 82-3, 86-7, 100-1, 118-19, 146-47, 162-63, 376-77, 380-81, 392-93, 402-3, 406-7, 466-67, 488-89; H. Touchard, *Le Commerce Maritime Breton à la Fin du Moyen Age* (Paris, 1967), 183 n. 16. See too *Livres des Priviléges* (Bordeaux, 1878), ii, 18, in which King Charles VIII of France, in confirming Bordeaux's privileges in 1483, appeared to anticipate the presence of Scottish merchants in the town.

[97] *RPS*, i, 52-3, 128-29; *Edin. Recs.*, ii, 120, 124-26, 144, 185. Bordeaux wines tended to fetch a higher price than those from La Rochelle, on both sides of the country.

evidence of Iberian trading contacts with Scotland is rare, and the deliveries of bastard and osay to Dumbarton in the mid-1450s may have come from elsewhere.[98] Still, some Iberians did make the long trek north. A Portuguese merchant was selling wine at Dumbarton in 1498, as was a Spanish merchant at Wigtown in 1513.[99]

Timber, Spice and Other Things Nice

Besides the essentials of the fish, meat, grain and grape based products, most other items of food were regarded with comparatively little esteem by medieval society. Dairy products were an exception, but were rarely traded with foreign countries.[100] By contrast, as we have already seen, fruit and vegetables barely featured on the menu served to the earl of Douglas at Lille in 1450. Nevertheless, according to one foreign observer there was so much fruit in Scotland that the population did not know what to do with it. The excremental remains of fruits seeds suggest otherwise.[101] Still, while berries of various sorts were common, and the orchards of the elite were stocked with apples, cherries, pears, and plums, fruit was also imported to supplement domestic production. Andrew Halyburton, for instance, bought two barrels of apples in Middelburg for the abbot of Holyrood in 1496; and in 1503 Halyburton sent twelve pounds of plums, purchased in Bruges, to Master Richard Lawson.[102] Some fruit came from England too. James I acquired apples, pears and prunes there in 1424, and half a barrel of prunes and a thousand oranges were laden on the *Trinity* of Dysart at Hull in 1541-42.[103] Mediterranean fruits were more usually purchased in the Low Countries, Halyburton's acquisitions including a substantial number of dates, raisins and figs. These more exotic fruits (and nuts) were consumed at the royal court; but archaeological evidence also points to the consumption of figs, at least, in the east-coast towns.[104] More rarely, we hear too of olives – delivered to the abbot of Holyrood in 1500 – and grapes are recorded at Ayr in 1501.[105] Still, the fruit trade was essentially limited, as was that in vegetables. Although the Berwick customs tariffs of the thirteenth century suggest that peas and beans were shipped through the port, subsequent evidence points to only the occasional arrival of beans, leeks, peas and onions from England in the thirteenth century and latterly from the continent too. Some onions were

---

[98] *ER*, vi, 295.

[99] *TA*, i, 391-392; *Wigtownshire Chrs.*, no. 110.

[100] See Gemmill and Mayhew, *Changing Values*, 290-96, for the consumption of butter and cheese.

[101] P. Hume Brown, ed., *Early Travellers in Scotland* (repr., Edinburgh, 1978), 44; Murray, *Excavations in the Medieval Burgh of Aberdeen*, 240-41.

[102] *Halyburton's Ledger*, 15, 271.

[103] *CDS*, iv, no. 967; PRO London, E122/64/16, fo. 17r. See too E122/64/15, fos. 9v, 10r for prunes sent from Hull; and *TA*, i, 330-31; iii, 400; vii, 184, 465; ix, 393, for oranges.

[104] *Halyburton's Ledger*, 10, 15-16, 32, 34, 43, 47, 54, 58, 67, 70, 97, 104-5, 116, 118, 198, 202, 271, 272; *ER*, ii, 213-16, 371, 441, 443, 467, 508, 548; Murray, *Excavations in Aberdeen*, 240-42.

[105] *Halyburton's Ledger*, 253; *TA*, ii, 103.

meanwhile also exported, though vegetable imports were markedly more numerous than those of fruit in mid-sixteenth-century Dundee.[106]

Considerably more important for the elite, at least, was the import of foreign spices. These were used not to preserve, but rather to flavour other foods, both fresh and salted. Their importance may be gleaned from the variety of spices which Robert I acquired in Flanders for the celebrations which marked the marriage of his son, the future David II, to Joan of England. Robert's purchases included cinnamon, cumin, galingale, ginger, grain of Paris, mace, nutmeg, pepper, saffron, and spikenard.[107] Spices, we may assume, were a prerequisite for a good medieval party. Yet their purchase by the royal court was no extraordinary matter. The wardrobe accounts for the period 1372-75 and 1376-78 reveal the crown's regular expenditure on cinnamon, galingale, ginger, pepper, saffron and other spices – and also almonds, rice and sugar.[108] We are less well informed about aristocratic spice consumption, but should not doubt that nobles too acquired spices, albeit in perhaps smaller quantities than the crown. Spices circulated in the towns too. Their frequent use as the price of admission to merchant gilds and burgess-ships symbolised their expense and exclusivity – they were evidently available even in smaller towns such as Dunfermline.[109]

By the end of the fifteenth century spice preferences had changed little from Robert I's day. In terms of weight, pepper and ginger (in that order) were the most common acquisitions made by Halyburton. In terms of the number of consignments which Halyburton sent to Scotland, these were marginally more frequent not only than the other 'cheap' spices (cinnamon, cloves, grain of Paris, nutmeg and 'sandry' (?sandlewood oil), but also than the more expensive mace and galingale and the most expensive spice of all, saffron. Almonds, rice and sugar also featured prominently among what both Robert I and Halyburton considered spice acquisitions; and both also purchased vinegar.[110]

There is, however, one important development which we must note. Although it was the Netherlands which provided Scotland with its spices for most of the medieval period, suddenly from 1538-39 another source emerged: England. There is no indication in the English customs accounts that Scots had sought to purchase spices there before this. But in that year four of the ten or eleven Scottish ships leaving Lynn carried saffron and/or other unspecified spices; and two years later six of the seventeen Scottish ships

---

[106] Duncan, *Scotland*, 324, 498, 506; *CDS*, i, no. 907; iii, no. 1502; iv, no. 146; v, no. 219; *Hanseakten*, nos. 334-36; CA Dundee, BHCB/1, fo. 20r; BHCB/2, fos. 57r, 89v, 154r, 187v, 194r; *Edin. Recs.*, ii, 132; PRO London E122/98/8, m. 1v; E122/205/3, fo. 18r.

[107] *ER*, i, 119.

[108] *ER*, ii, 370, 440-41, 446-47, 507-8, 547-48.

[109] Torrie, *Gild Court Book of Medieval Dunfermline*, 9, 11, 13-14 [all for the 1440s]; *The Perth Guildry Book, 1452-1601*, ed. M.L. Stavert (SRS, 1993), nos. 2-6, 8, 12-13 [all for 1453]; *Edin. Recs.*, i, 13-14, 20, 26.

[110] *Halyburton's Ledger*, 22, 53, 65, 179, 198, 223, 232, 272.

leaving Hull carried spices, the cargo of the *Mawdelyn* of Kirkcaldy, for instance, including four pounds of mace, four pounds of saffron, two pounds of pepper and one pound of nutmeg, as well as some mustard.[111]

The importance of plants to dietary needs was matched by their use for industrial and medicinal purposes. Madder, woad and weld were all occasionally imported from the Netherlands and England for use as mordants in the cloth industry – probably, indeed, as early as the thirteenth century.[112] Other dyes were sometimes exported: a barrel of litmus was sent from Leith to Newcastle in 1454-55 and a hundred pounds of madder was carried along the same route in 1494-95.[113] Hemp, meanwhile, was imported from the Baltic, the Netherlands and, from the sixteenth century, England. Used for the production of rope and canvas (the latter of which was also imported from Brittany by the early sixteenth century), hemp also possessed medicinal qualities.[114] The archaeological excavation of Paisley Abbey's drain and the hospital at Soutra have shed further light upon the cultivation and use of plants for medical purposes. The finds include great celandine (used as an eye ointment) and white opium poppy (used as an anaesthetic or painkiller) and at least some of these plants were of foreign origin.[115] Andrew Halyburton made his own distinctive contribution to this trade, providing one of his clients with aniseed laxative.[116]

Among plant imports, more important still was timber. We have already seen that timber was scarce in Scotland for shipbuilding purposes, and the signs are that its limited availability prompted conservation measures even in the thirteenth century. When Alexander II granted Alloway to the burgesses of Ayr, it was on condition that the trees were felled for building, rather than burning.[117] The timber shortage was to remain acute throughout the middle ages, not least because wood remained the most essential material in the construction industry. Apart from the great stone-built castles and cathedrals, most buildings were made from wood. While, normally perhaps, there was sufficient local wood for such purposes, the greater building projects

---

[111] PRO London, E122/99/24, fos. 8v, 9r, 15r, 15v; E122/64/15, fo. 10r. Sugar and nuts featured very rarely in shipments from England, but see E122/64/15, fo. 16r for sugar; and E122/99/16, fo. 3r for walnuts.

[112] Duncan, *Scotland*, 490, 508; *CDS*, iv, no. 146; *ER*, viii, 545; *Halyburton's Ledger*, 179, 208, 220, 221-24, 263.

[113] PRO London, E122/107/48, m. 1r; E122/108/8, m. 1r.

[114] Gemmill and Mayhew, *Changing Values*, 331-37; GSA Berlin, OBA 7433; OF/13, 413-415; *HUB*, vii (1), no. 343; *Halyburton's Ledger*, 136, 180; PRO London, E122/12/10, fo. 3r; E122/64/15, fos. 9v, 10r, 17r; E122/64/16, fos. 7v, 9v, 10v, 17r.

[115] P. Yeoman, *Medieval Scotland* (London, 1995), 31-3; C. Dickson, 'Food, medicinal and other plants from the drain' in J. Malden, ed., *The Monastery and Abbey of Paisley* (Glasgow, 2000), 215-16, 218.

[116] *Halyburton's Ledger*, 41. For Halyburton's other dealings in drugs, mainly acquired in Bruges, see ibid, 15-16, 21, 103, 213.

[117] See above, chapter 1; *Charters of the Royal Burgh of Ayr* (Ayr and Wigtown Archaeological Assoc., 1883), no. 5.

consumed so much timber, and in such a short space of time, that recourse was routinely made to additional supplies from abroad.

The first indications that foreign timber was being used in Scotland date from the early fourteenth century: in 1329 'Eastland boards' were used to build a chapel above Robert I's tomb at Dunfermline.[118] Thereafter their import is frequently recorded in royal accounts, since they were often used on the great royal construction projects. In the 1460s, for instance, their arrival is recorded at Dundee, Edinburgh, Linlithgow, North Berwick and Perth; and they were used in building work at the castles of Dunbar, Edinburgh and Stirling and the palaces of Falkland and Linlithgow, as well as for shipbuilding purposes near Berwick and for the repair of the tron (the public weighbeam) at Perth.[119] Eastland boards were presumably planks of timber, but latterly we hear of other types of timber too which came from abroad: clapholt, wainscot, barrel staves, masts, oars, as well as seemingly unprocessed trees. Important too were the sylvan by-products, chief among them pitch, tar and ash.

The origin of these imports is less certain. 'Eastland' suggests that the boards came from the Baltic. Tar and pitch were certainly sent from Danzig to Scotland: together they were worth 14% of Danzig's exports to Scotland in the fifteenth century. But wood was a more unusual cargo from the Prussian port, and was worth only 1% of the goods sent to Scotland between the mid-fifteenth and early sixteenth centuries. At least one early fourteenth-century supply was delivered by a Hamburg merchant, but there is little evidence to suggest that this city engaged frequently in Scottish trade.[120] It is more likely that Baltic timber came to Scotland from Stralsund, a Hanseatic port with which Scotland did have regular contacts. Since that town's customs records have not survived, we cannot be certain, though six vessels from Stralsund, Hamburg and neighbouring Rostock delivered over a thousand wainscot and over a thousand clapholt to Dundee in 1551.[121] From the end of the fifteenth century we can, however, be sure that a good deal of timber reached Scotland not from the southern Baltic, but rather from Scandinavia. Norwegian merchants were dealing in timber at Aberdeen by the 1490s; and Swedish boards are recorded in Scotland from 1512.[122] Indeed, wherever earlier imports may have come from, by the mid-sixteenth century Scandinavia had come to dominate this particular trade. All sixteen Scottish ships which left the Swedish port of Lödöse in 1546 carried timber, in the main spruce and oak, though some also brought lime. Almost all of Lödöse's exported oak in that year seems to have been bound for Scotland.[123] And between 1550 and 1555 at

---

[118] *ER*, i, 215.
[119] *ER*, vii, 288, 370, 401, 404, 425, 585, 587, 660.
[120] *CDS*, v, no. 492(iv).
[121] CA Dundee, BHCB/2, fos. 53r, 54r, 54v, 55v, 67v, 88v.
[122] CA Aberdeen, SR/1, 650-651, 750; *TA*, iv, 290, 292, 295, 481. See too *DN*, ii(2), no. 978; CA Dundee, BHCB/1, fo. 146.
[123] J. Dow, 'Scottish trade with Sweden, 1512-1580', *SHR*, 48 (1969), 69-70.

least one Swedish, ten Danish and a dozen Norwegian ships docked at Dundee alone, laden mainly with fir and oak.[124]

Since by the later fifteenth century Scotland received much of its imported timber from Scandinavia, it may seem likely that this was also the source of earlier timber imports. This is possible, but doubtful. Although both the extant Scottish and Scandinavian sources are far from complete, there is remarkably little indication of commercial contact between Scotland and the Scandinavian countries (Scania excepted) before the later fifteenth century. Indeed, we should be wary about pre-dating the development of the Scandinavian timber trade, which owed much to the technological innovation of saw-milling. This was introduced into Sweden from Germany in the 1460s and only became common in Norway from the sixteenth century.[125] We are left, then, with the conundrum of the origin of earlier Eastland boards. England is one possible source. Some fir, wainscot and clapholt, possibly of Baltic extraction, and also pitch, tar, lime and bark, was dispatched from there on Scottish ships in the early sixteenth century.[126] But pre-sixteenth century English customs accounts provide little evidence that Scots acquired timber there, though they did occasionally acquire tar and pitch.[127] Apart from that which came directly from the Baltic towns, the most likely source for Scotland's Eastland boards was, then, the Netherlands, where Scots presumably picked up re-exported Baltic wares. That, certainly, was where James I acquired a mast for one of his ships. Yet very little timber was sent from the Low Countries to Scotland in the later fifteenth and sixteenth centuries – it was a commodity in which Andrew Halyburton, trading there in the 1490s and 1500s, rarely dealt. The development of Scandinavian trade at the close of the middle ages was perhaps one nail in the coffin of Scotland's Netherlandish trade.

Beasts and their Bodies
The extensive use made of plant products was matched by the use to which animals were put. There was, of course, a domestic trade in live animals, but the size and mobility of live beasts made their overseas dispatch difficult. There was, as we have already seen, an international trade in falcons and hunting dogs and some other animals were also traded across the land border with England. In 1276, for instance, the English king dispatched a servant to

---

[124] For the Norwegian and Swedish vessels, CA Dundee, BHCB/2, fos. 49v, 54r, 68r, 76v, 79v, 152v, 155r, 170v, 246v, 294r, 303r, 328v, 329r. For the Danish vessels, T. Riis, *Should Auld Acquaintance Be Forgot: Scottish-Danish relations, c.1450-1707* (Odense, 1988), i, 69.

[125] D. Ditchburn, 'A note on Scandinavian trade with Scotland in the later middle ages' in G.G. Simpson, ed., *Scotland and Scandinavia, 800-1800* (Edinburgh, 1990), 73-89; A. Lillehammer, 'The Scottish-Norwegian timber trade in the Stavanger area in the sixteenth and seventeenth centuries' in T.C. Smout, ed., *Scotland and Europe, c.1200-1850* (Edinburgh, 1986), 99-100.

[126] PRO London, E122/64/2, fo. 26v; E122/64/10, fo. 20v; E122/64/15, fos. 9v, 16v; E122/64/16, fos. 9v-10v, 17r-18v.

[127] PRO London, E122/62/7, m. 3d; E122/62/9, m. 5a.

procure horses at the Stirling fair. Such trade was not one-way. James IV bought English horses at Dumfries in 1504, and on other occasions he either bought or was given Danish, French, Irish and Portuguese horses too. Despite legislation of 1426 which prohibited the export of young horses, some Scottish horses were also dispatched abroad, to Flanders, for instance, in 1368 and to Dieppe in 1511.[128] This was, however, unusual. Apart from small quantities of honey, and rather more of wax (crucial for lighting), most animal-based exports were the products of already slaughtered beasts.[129]

The most valuable among these exports were the furs of marten and polecat which were highly esteemed by aristocrats and converted into clothing.[130] There are few insights into this trade, for these skins were rarely taxed, the levy imposed on them by James I soon falling into abeyance.[131] Still, for the later 1420s and early 1430s, the Scottish customs accounts provide a glimpse of this exclusive trade. Dominated by Inverness, it was not large. Only six marten skins were exported from the town in 1427-28 and from then until 1434 an average of less than a dozen was exported annually.[132] Halyburton too rarely handled marten skins, and when he did they were in small number.[133] There apart some deer, fox, goat, otter and squirrel skins were exported, mainly from east-coast ports, along with rather more substantial amounts of cheaper rabbit skins – over two thousand from Edinburgh, for instance, in 1424-25.[134] Perhaps, however, the most significant dimension of this trade is that it provided even the far north with a rare opportunity to trade with the continent, even though the rabbit skins exported from Wick in 1430-31 were customed at Inverness and shipped from Aberdeen.[135] We do not know the ultimate destination of these particular skins, but the market for skins was diverse, and they may have ended up anywhere around the North Sea littoral. Goatskins and deer skins (the latter of bucks, doe and roe) were exported to England throughout the period, both by sea and by land – in 1389-90, for instance, a Lincoln merchant carried otter skins across the frontier. The trade was not, however, one way and Scottish merchants periodically purchased calf skins in England.[136] Across the North

---

[128] *CDS*, ii, no. 79; *TA*, i, 96, 129, 204, 289, 340; ii, 21, 197, 465; iii, 36, 148, 379, 390, 398; iv, 87, 311, 398; *CCR, 1364-68*, 451; *APS*, ii, 7; NAS Edinburgh, E71/19/2.

[129] For wax, see Gemmill and Mayhew, *Changing Values*, 298-303. For its import, and that of honey, see, for example, WAP Gdansk, 300/19/2a, passim.

[130] E.g. *ER*, v, 149, 156, 186, 296, 311, 465, 501; *TA*, ii, 20, 198.

[131] *APS*, ii, 6; *Edin. Recs.*, i, 13.

[132] *CDS*, iii, no. 853; *ER*, iv, 452, 497, 538, 577. For further evidence of Inverness's role in this trade, see *ER*, vi, 392, 483.

[133] *Halyburton's Ledger*, 268.

[134] *ER*, iv, 380, 386, 442, 451, 452, 497, 509, 525, 534, 535, 538, 559, 577, 608.

[135] *ER*, iv, 537.

[136] PRO London, E122/12/10, fo. 4v; E122/62/7, m. 2r; 2d; 3d; E122/62/9, m. 2r; E122/64/2, fo. 22r; E122/64/5, fos. 15v, 21v; E122/64/16, fo. 13v; E122/99/24, fo. 10r; E122/138/21, m. 6; E122/106/24, m. 1d; E122/106/22, m. 1r, 1d; E122/106/21, m. 1r, 1d, 3r; *CDS*, v, no. 864. For calfskins purchased in England, see E122/60/3, fo. 18r; E122/64/2, fo. 26r; E122/99/16, fo. 2v; E122/99/18, fo. 1v; E122/99/27, fo. 3r.

Sea, meanwhile, we find Scottish goatskins and hogskins sent to the Low Countries; calf, deer and ox skins dispatched to France; and rabbit skins taken to Zeeland and the Baltic.[137]

Far more common in international trade than the skins of these animals were, however, those of cows, converted into 'hides' or leather. Given the abundance of Scottish cattle, hides were comparatively cheap. They provided all sections of society with an important material, used for making bags, belts, jerkins, leggings, shoes, stirrups and many other things too.[138] Moreover, these uses were not merely of Scottish application. In areas of comparatively dense urban population (such as the Low Countries), and in places where the prevailing agricultural activity was arable, the demand for hides was likely to be high. It is little surprise, then, that hide exports were second only to those of wool in their importance to the medieval Scottish economy – though (as with wool) fifteenth-century hide exports fell short of their fourteenth century levels, recovering (unlike wool) episodically in the earlier sixteenth century.[139]

In geographical terms, though not in volume, the market for hides was more limited than that for other animal skins. Few Scottish hides are recorded in English sources, and in 1426 a Berwick merchant was to complain that Scots would not sell him any.[140] Indeed, some 'well tanned' hides were even purchased in England by Scots, notably at Boston in the early sixteenth century.[141] The Baltic, by contrast, provided a steady, but small market. Hides were worth 3% of Scottish imports at Danzig between the mid-fifteenth and early sixteenth centuries.[142] For most of the period, however, Scottish hides presumably accompanied wool exports in dispatch to the Netherlands.[143] There is, at least, little evidence that they found a large market elsewhere – though Irish hides found a major outlet in fifteenth-century Italy.[144] Yet from the later fifteenth century the pattern of wool and hide exports began to diverge. Halyburton dealt with very few Scottish hides in the Netherlands, and that he sold some of his rare supply to merchants from Rouen in 1508 suggests where the principal market now lay. This is confirmed by the

---

[137] NAS Edinburgh, E71/29/2; E71/29/3; *Halyburton's Ledger*, 240; *CDS*, ii, no. 9; *HUB*, viii, no. 1255.
[138] Gemmill and Mayhew, *Changing Values*, 277-83; Spearman, 'Workshops, materials, debris', 138-41.
[139] Lynch and Stevenson, 'Overseas trade: the middle ages to the sixteenth century', 241, 253; Guy, 'Scottish export trade', 74.
[140] *Northern Petitions: Illustrative of life in Berwick, Cumbria and Durham in the fourteenth century*, ed. C.M. Fraser, (Surtees Soc., 1981), no. 29.
[141] PRO London, E122/12/12, m. 1r, 2v; E122/12/10, fo. 2r, 3r, 4v; E122/12/8, fo. 4r.
[142] Samsonowicz, 'Engländer und Schotten', 50.
[143] *CDS*, iii, no. 1097; iv, nos. 107, 1014; v, nos. 632-33, 636; *ER*, vi, 298, 384, 530; viii, 547; *Bronnen voor de Economische Geschiedenis van het Beneden-Maasgebied*, J.F. Niermeijer (The Hague, 1968), no. 447(4); Smit, *Bronnen, 1150-1485*, i, nos. 267, 482, 720.
[144] M.E. Mallett, 'Anglo-Florentine commercial relations, 1465-1491', *Economic History Review*, second series, 15 (1962), 265.

Scottish customs accounts. Although only two ships left Aberdeen for Dieppe in 1499-1500, almost half of the town's hide exports were sent there, rather than to the Zeeland port of Veere. Similarly, France (mainly Dieppe) was the recipient of 86% of hide exports from Leith in 1510-11; 89% in 1512-13; and 97% in 1527-28.[145] And it was this major new market for hides – which wool producers never found to the same extent – which ensured that, although the value of hide exports never outstripped that of wool, they remained comparatively rather more buoyant.[146]

'Man does not live by bread alone'

Wool, as Alexander Grant has remarked, was the equivalent of North Sea oil to the medieval Scottish economy.[147] The later medieval countryside was awash with sheep and, while their dung provided useful fertiliser, their fleeces earned hard currency.[148] Wool was traded in several different guises. White wool dominated the export trade, though by at least the later fifteenth century some cheaper brown wool was also sent abroad.[149] In addition to this mainstay of the trade, woolfells, futfells (the skins of lambs which died soon after birth), lentrinware (other, less valuable, lambskins), schorlings (the skin of and/or wool of dead sheep) and scaldings (sheepskins) were all carefully distinguished by producers and consumers alike – though for woolfells alone was there a substantial demand abroad. Together, however, these sheep-derived products constituted Scotland's most valuable exports, wool itself still accounting for the largest single proportion of customs receipts in the 1530s, even although shipments abroad were by then running at only about a quarter of the level seen in the 1370s. With an average of 881 tonnes exported annually, together with an additional 114,000 woolfells, that decade had marked the zenith of the wool trade, though only marginally smaller quantities had been dispatched abroad earlier in the fourteenth century, and perhaps in the thirteenth century too.[150] We have no figures for exports in that century, but historians are in little doubt that the burgeoning wool trade partly explains a healthy balance of payments surplus, and the monetisation of the Scottish economy.[151]

The origins of the wool trade lie in the period before that with which we are concerned. The commercial development of wool farming probably owed much to the new monastic orders (and especially the Cistercians) which

---

[145] *Halyburton's Ledger*, 14, 158, 169, 211, 246; NAS Edinburgh, E71/1/1; E71/29/2; E71/29/3; E71/29/4.

[146] Lynch and Stevenson, 'Overseas trade: the middle ages to the sixteenth century', 241.

[147] A. Grant, *Independence and Nationhood: Scotland, 1306-1469* (London, 1984), 72.

[148] Stevenson, 'Trade with the south', 183.

[149] G. de Poerck, *La Draperie Médiévale en Flandre et en Artois: Technique et terminologie* (Bruges, 1951), i, 27; *Halyburton's Ledger*, 24, 42, 56, 64, 66, 68, 71, 76, 89, 107, 113, 119-20.

[150] Lynch and Stevenson, 'Overseas trade: the middle ages to the sixteenth century', 241, 244.

[151] Grant, *Independence and Nationhood*, 69-72; N. Mayhew, 'Alexander III – a silver age? An essay in Scottish medieval economic history' in N. Reid, ed., *Scotland in the Reign of Alexander III, 1249-1286* (Edinburgh, 1990), 61-2.

arrived in Scotland from the twelfth century. Certainly monks were among the first to produce substantial surpluses of wool from their estates. These they sought to sell overseas – in the case of the monks of Melrose probably as early as the 1180s, by when they had been granted freedom from tolls imposed on goods (perhaps wool) sent to Flanders.[152] How much wool, or how many sheep, the abbey then possessed remains unknown, though, on the basis of its export of about ten tonnes of wool per year, it has been estimated that Melrose possessed approximately 17,000 sheep by the 1390s.[153] This was an abnormally large number of beasts. In 1296 the Border nunnery of Coldstream owned 497 ewes 'with as many lambs' and a further one hundred sheep; and in 1391-92 another south-eastern lord, the earl of March, exported 4.13 tonnes of wool, suggesting a flock of perhaps 7,000 sheep.[154] Even these were probably unusually large herds. The earl's exports amounted to no more than a paltry 0.53% of known Scottish wool exports in 1391-92, and even Melrose (with 11.6 tonnes) could claim a share of only 1.48% of the exported Scottish wool clip in the same year.[155] Since the biggest owners commanded only a minute proportion of the export market, we may suppose that much of the wool dispatched overseas was sheared from peasant-owned sheep.

Where perhaps the owners of larger flocks stood at an advantage over small producers was in their ability to deliver bulk supplies. Less certainly, they were perhaps also able to deliver a better quality of product. At least in the thirteenth century the wools marketed by the greatest monastic producers were graded into three different qualities which fetched different prices. Most other producers, including abbeys such as Jedburgh, seem often to have mixed their wools and commanded only aggregated prices.[156] In the Borders Jedburgh's wool fetched a lower price than that for the best Melrose produce and elsewhere too price differentials between the wool of neighbouring localities suggests qualitative differences. In early fifteenth-century Aberdeen, for instance, the great lords of Buchan (who presumably owned the largest flocks of the region) received a better price for their wool than the free tenants of the same region.[157] Quality was not, however, a constant.

The wools of Melrose were well enough renowned by the thirteenth century to be included in a list of 'British' wool prices compiled at Douai in c.1270. The list was probably intended for merchants of the same town, then one of the leading Flemish textile producers, and in the price schedule Melrose

---

[152] *Melrose Liber*, i, nos. 14-15.
[153] Lynch and Stevenson, 'Overseas trade: the middle ages to the sixteenth century', 251.
[154] *Chartulary of the Cistercian Priory of Coldstream*, ed. C. Rodgers (Grampian Club, 1879), 77-80; *ER*, iii, 291. The metric tonne calculation is based upon the assumption of one sack equating with 24 stones, 1 stone equating with 15lbs and 1lb equating with 15oz.
[155] *ER*, iii, 283-304. The percentage calculations are based solely on wool exports, and include neither English wool exported from Scotland, nor Scottish wool exported from Berwick.
[156] Francesco Balducci Pegolotti, *La Pratica della Mercatura*, ed. A. Evans (Cambridge, Mass., 1936), 259.
[157] Gemmill and Mayhew, *Changing Values*, 285.

wool was valued at £35 *livre parisis* (= £10.938 sterling) per sack-weight of 364
lb.[158] Yet, by the early fourteenth century Melrose wool was quoted in
another price guide, compiled by the Italian merchant Francesco Pegolotti, at
an equivalent rate of only £10.677 sterling.[159] By contrast the value of clips
from the four other Scottish monasteries mentioned in the Douai schedule
had all increased, that of Coupar Angus now ranking foremost among
Scottish wools, at £12.333 sterling, with those of Dundrennan and Glenluce
not far behind. The Pegolotti schedule includes prices for the clips of a further
ten Scottish houses not mentioned in the Douai list, though none matched the
wools of Coupar Angus, the Galloway houses or even Melrose – those of
Dunfermline, for instance, selling at only three-quarters of the price of those
of Dundrennan.

Unfortunately, the dating of the Pegolotti tract remains contentious –
suggestions span the period from the mid-1270s to 1318-21 – and consequently
the causes for the diminution in the value of the Melrose clip remain
uncertain. Biological phenomena (such as a localised outbreak of sheep scab)
provide one possible explanation, though the effects of Anglo-Scottish war
may be another, if, that is, the schedule can be dated to the period after 1296
and before 1308. Melrose lay close to the routes favoured by invading English
armies from 1296, while the effects of political conflict on Gallovidian wools
from Dundrennan and Glenluce (which held up better in the Pegolotti
schedule than those of Melrose) are unlikely to have set in before the savage
devastation mounted by Bruce forces in Galloway in 1308.

Whatever the cause for the slump in the value of the Melrose clip, it is
clear from both the Douai and the Pegolotti schedules not only that different
Scottish wools were differently priced, but also that in general Scottish wools
were less expensive (and probably therefore of lesser quality) than many
(though by no means all) English and Welsh wools. In the Douai schedule
Melrose wool was valued lower, and in some instances considerably lower,
than the prices recorded for twenty-five other brands of 'British' monastic
wool. That of Margam in Glamorgan was, at £50 per sack, the most expensive;
that of Culross (rated at £28) ranked (along with the produce of Waltham
Abbey in Essex) as the cheapest of all fifty-four entries. The difference in
quality between Scottish wools, and their English and Welsh counterparts
remained in later centuries, for, although there is less specific information for
the later fourteenth, fifteenth and early sixteenth centuries, Scottish wools (in
general) were differentiated detrimentally from most English clips by
consumers in the Low Countries. The difference is important because it
meant that English and Scottish producers were not, by and large, rivals. They

[158] J.H. Monro, 'Wool-price schedules and the qualities of English wools in the later middle ages,
c.1270-1499', *Textile History*, 9 (1978), 121-22.
[159] Pegolotti, *La Practica della Mercatura*, 259. The sterling equivalent is derived from the
calculation in J.H. Monro, 'Wool-price schedules', 121-22.

generally catered for different markets and it was only with the poorer quality wools of northern England that Scottish produce stood in direct competition.

Before, however, we examine the market for wool, let us pause to consider how producers delivered their wool to continental markets. In the thirteenth century the Cistercians probably traded abroad directly, without recourse to merchants in Scottish towns. Indeed, there is much to commend A.A.M. Duncan's hypothesis that the entire Cistercian wool clip was delivered to either Berwick or Perth, where the monasteries of Melrose and Coupar Angus respectively assumed responsibility for its onward dispatch.[160] While at least one other Cistercian house (Newbattle) had apparently traded abroad in the twelfth century – by 1189 it had been granted toll freedom within the domains of the Angevin king Henry II – there is no explicit evidence that it, or most other Cistercian houses, did so by the thirteenth century.[161] By contrast, both Melrose and Coupar Angus are known to have shipped their own wool abroad in this period. In 1225, amid tense Anglo-French relations, both monasteries deemed it prudent to acquire an English safe conduct for their trading activities.[162] We know too that by 1230 Melrose possessed its own ship, and that it owned property in the port town of Berwick. Coupar Angus, meanwhile, though it had rented out its own Berwick property, held a tenement in another port town, Perth.[163]   These urban properties were presumably used for the storage of wool, as well as for organising and transacting commercial business prior to the dispatch of wool cargoes overseas.

Yet Duncan's hypothesis perhaps requires a modicum of refinement. It seems conceivable that wool from the northern Cistercian houses (Balmerino, Deer, Kinloss and the nunnery of Elcho) was shipped or carted to Perth prior to continental dispatch. Likewise, it seems conceivable that wool from the south-eastern houses (Newbattle, Culross and the nunneries of Eccles, North Berwick, Haddington, Manuel and St Bothan's) was brought to Berwick. On the other hand, it seems most unlikely that wool was routinely carted overland to either Berwick or Perth from western regions. The merchants of Ayr complained when Edward I instructed them to do this in 1297.[164] Moreover, that the Gallovidian Cistercian houses maintained their own direct contacts with the continent is suggested not only by the distinctiveness with which their clips were recognised on the continent (after all that was true of other Cistercian houses, such as Balmerino and Kinloss, too) but also by the fact that both Gallovidian houses maintained direct commercial contacts with

---

[160] Duncan, *Scotland*, 513.
[161] *CDS*, ii, no. 624.
[162] *CDS*, i, no. 904.
[163] *CPR, 1225-32*, 332; W.B. Stevenson, 'The monastic presence in Scottish burghs in the twelfth and thirteenth centuries', *SHR*, 60 (1981), 117; W.B. Stevenson, 'The monastic presence: Berwick in the twelfth and thirteenth centuries' in Lynch *et al.*, *Medieval Town*, 111.
[164] *Rot. Scot.*, i, 40.

Ireland.[165] With ample wool of its own for sale, Ireland was an improbable market for Gallovidian wool. Nevertheless, both Dundrennan and Glenluce might well have gained access to their Netherlandish markets via Irish ports, for Irish wool was certainly reaching Bruges by the later thirteenth century. Alternatively, the Galloway houses may have co-operated with another nearby Cistercian house. Holm Cultram in Cumbria, a daughter house of Melrose, not only maintained close Scottish (and Irish) contacts, but also undertook east-coast commercial ventures via the land route through Hexham to Newcastle and at the fairs of Boston.[166] Tapping into this trading nexus may explain why Dundrennan sought permission to export its wool to England in 1266.[167]

It remains unclear if or when the Cistercians abandoned their own overseas trading ventures and turned instead to the facilities provided by secular merchants – though there is little evidence that monks continued to trade abroad from the fourteenth century. Neither do we have explicit evidence from this period, as we do for the thirteenth century, of the greater wool producers selling their wool directly to foreign merchants, as Coldingham, for instance, had done in 1290.[168] Still, that the earl of March seemingly dispatched his own wool abroad in 1391-92 suggests either that the earl had made direct arrangements with an overseas buyer, or that he had secured the services of a factor on the continent who would make a deal on his behalf. The latter was certainly the option favoured by a number of producers in the later fifteenth century, who looked to Andrew Halyburton to sell their wares in Netherlandish markets.

While this was perhaps the arrangement favoured by larger landowners, it seems highly likely that the small peasant producers sold their wares to merchants based in Scotland. A few Scottish merchants traded in large quantities of wool – in 1249, for instance, the Berwick burgess Philip of Ryedale sold forty sacks (6.12 tonnes) to Jakemes di Cauderliers of Ypres.[169] Ryedale may have acquired his stocks *en masse* from one of the larger suppliers, rather than accumulating small quantities from several sources; but many other merchants dealt in only a few sacks, suggesting that they had acquired their supplies from smaller producers. In 1229, for instance, another Berwick merchant, Robert Stater, was arrested in Kent in possession of just three sacks (0.46 tonnes) of wool, and in 1503-04 ten Haddington merchants shared in the export of just 4.79 tonnes of wool.[170]

---

[165] *CDS*, i, nos. 765, 933, 974, 1891; ii, no. 182; *CDI*, i, nos. 943, 1370, 1532; ii, nos. 100, 1736; iii, no. 32. See too *CDI*, i, no. 1093; iii, no. 1138, which may also relate to trade.

[166] *Holm Cultram Reg.*, nos. 257, 258, 267a.

[167] *CDS*, i, no. 2414.

[168] UL Durham, Dean and Chapter Muniments, Miscellaneous Charters, no. 3418. I am grateful to Grant Simpson for drawing this document to my attention.

[169] *CDS*, i, no. 1050; *Analyses de Reconnaissances de Dettes Passées devant L'échevin d'Ypres, 1249-1291*, ed. C. Wyffels (Brussels, 1991), no. 459.

[170] *CDS*, i, no. 1051; NAS Edinburgh, E71/16/1, fos. 4-5; *ER*, xii, 259.

Most of the secular merchants who dealt in wool came from the east-coast towns. While we have little thirteenth-century evidence, wool constituted the bulk of fourteenth-century exports from Ayr alone among the west-coast towns, but even Ayr's wool trade had all but disappeared by the fifteenth century. In the east Berwick was clearly a major centre of the thirteenth-century wool trade. Aberdeen, Montrose and Perth probably also handled a sizeable amount of trade, since it was by these towns (and Berwick) that the authorities of St Omer sought to differentiate between the different brands of Scottish wool in the later thirteenth century.[171] If this was indeed the case, the following centuries were to witness a radical transformation in the pattern of the wool trade. While Berwick remained an important centre of exports, still exporting on average 316 sacks of Scottish and English wool between 1404 and 1432, the volume of exports passing through the town had fallen sharply from the 3,753 sacks recorded in 1333.[172] Aberdeen, and more particularly Perth and Montrose, also witnessed a substantial fall in their wool exports in the fifteenth century. Since total wool exports were in decline, this was to be expected, but this trend masks another. Edinburgh had come to dominate the trade in the fifteenth and sixteenth centuries, its port of Leith handling 90% of all Scottish wool exports by the 1530s.

Foreign demand for Scottish wool was geographically restricted. Textile production in Scandinavia, the Baltic lands and much of France was largely geared towards the supply of local markets and producers in these regions seem in the main to have made use of local wool clips and, in southern France, of Spanish wools.[173] Only from the later fifteenth century were large consignments of Scottish wool shipped to Dieppe, presumably for onward dispatch to the newly important cloth manufacturers of Normandy.[174] Further south, although Spain too was a major producer of wool (and therefore an unlikely market for the Scottish produce), Italy could boast an important textile industry which required supplies of foreign wools. In the thirteenth century Scottish wool was on the shopping list of at least some Italians, such as Guido Hugonis of Florence who purchased Coldingham's wool in 1290, though how much, if any, of this actually found its way to

[171] *Recueil de Documents Relatifs à l'Histoire de l'Industrie Drapière en Flandre. Première partie: des origines à l'époque bourguignonne*, ed. G. Espinas and H. Pirenne (Brussels, 1906-24), iii, no. 651(6).
[172] A. Tuck, 'A medieval tax-haven: Berwick-upon-Tweed and the English crown, 1333-1461' in Britnell and Hatcher, *Progress and Problems*, 148-67.
[173] P. Wolff, *Commerce et Marchands de Toulouse* (Paris, 1954), 244.
[174] While no Scottish wool imports are discernible in the Dieppe customs accounts of the 1470s, wool was dispatched from Leith on thirteen out of sixteen Dieppe bound vessels in 1510-11, and on five out of seven in 1512-13. (Mollat, *Compatabilité du Port de Dieppe*, 31, 38-111 passim; NAS Edinburgh, E71/29/2; E71/29/3). See too *Les Affaires de Jacques Coeur: Journal du Procureur Dauvet*, ed. M. Mollat (Paris, 1952-53), ii, 510, 549-51, 610-15. On the development of French production, see M. Mollat, *Le Commerce Maritime Normand à la Fin du Moyen Age* (Paris, 1952), 273-77; J-F Belhoste, 'La maison, la fabrique et la ville: l'industrie du drap fin en France, XVe-XVIIIe siècles', *Histoire, Economie et Société*, 13 (1994), 458-59, 462-64.

Italy, rather than to the Netherlandish markets, remains uncertain.[175] In later centuries, however, there is little evidence to suggest that Scottish wool found its way to Italy on a regular basis: by then transaction costs were probably prohibitive.[176]

Meanwhile, penetration of Anglo-Irish markets was also problematic, though for quite different reasons. Both England and Ireland developed flourishing cloth industries and both were therefore in need of wool. Some Scottish wool was certainly reaching eastern England in the thirteenth century. In 1229 the prominent London merchant Gervaise le Cordwainer received a safe-conduct for the dispatch of wool from Berwick to London; and in 1242 several East Anglian merchants from Dunwich, Yarmouth and Ipswich were in possession of seventy-five sacks of Scottish wool.[177] It remains uncertain whether English or Netherlandish looms were the ultimate destination of these purchases. By the later fourteenth century, however, considerable quantities of wool from both Teviotdale and elsewhere in Scotland were dispatched to Berwick (by then in English hands) and these consignments, lured by the town's advantageous customs rates, were certainly destined for export overseas.[178] Indeed, it seems likely that on the other rare occasions upon which Scottish wool was dispatched to England, it too was intended for re-export, as indeed were the considerable quantities of English wool which were sent to Scotland, especially in the later fourteenth century.[179]

Most, if not all, of this wool was shipped to the Netherlands. Sold in the markets of Bruges and Ypres in the thirteenth century, and also in the fairs of Antwerp and Bergen-op-Zoom and at Middelburg by the fifteenth century, Scottish wool was purchased to feed a Netherlandish textile industry hungry for its most essential raw material. It was foreign wool which had enabled the industry to develop into a major exporting concern by the twelfth century.[180]

---

[175] UL Durham, Dean and Chapter Muniments, Miscellaneous Charters, no. 3418.

[176] Several recent studies of the wool used in Italy make no mention of Scottish clips. See, for instance, H. Hoshino, *L'arte della Lana in Firenze in Basso Medieovo* (Florence, 1980); G. Pampaloni, 'Un nuovo studio sulla produzione e il commercio della lana a Firenze fra trecento e cinquecento', *Archivo Storico Italiano*, 140 (1982), 197-213. Neither does Scottish, unlike English, wool appear in the Savoyard customs tariffs for transalpine commerce: J.F. Bergier, 'Peages du XVe siècle au pays de Vaud', *Beiträge zur Witschafts- und Stadtgeschichte* (Wiesbaden, 1965), 286-95. On the other hand, see R. Davidsohn, *Storia di Firenze* (Florence, 1956-68), vi, 117, 120-21, 123, 726.

[177] *CPR, 1225-1232*, 261; *CDS*, i, no. 1594.

[178] See, for instance, PRO London, E122/3/4, E122/3/11; E122/3/13, wherein English and Scottish wool exports from late fourteenth-century Berwick are clearly distinguished from each other.

[179] For a rare example of Scottish wool being sent to England, see, NfRO Norwich, Y/C4/169, m.16a (for a sack sent to Yarmouth in 1464-65). For English wool exported through Scotland, see 'The wool customs accounts for Newcastle-upon-Tyne for the reign of Edward I', ed. J.C. Davies *Archaeolgia Aeliana*, 32 (1954), 295-96; *ER*, iii, 111-445, passim.

[180] D. Nicholas, *Medieval Flanders* (Harlow, 1992), 112-15; H. van der Wee, 'Industrial dynamics and the process of urbanization and deurbanization in the Low Countries from the later middle

Figure 4.2: Centres of Netherlandish cloth production (selected)

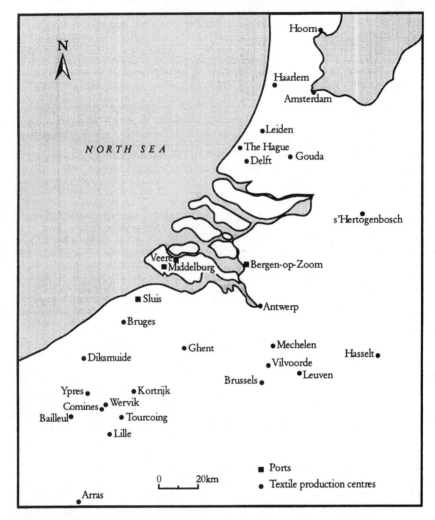

Yet the Netherlandish market was neither an open nor a homogenous one. By the thirteenth century the cloth-making pre-eminence of Artesian towns such as St Omer and Arras had passed to the Brabantine towns of Mechelen, Leuven and Brussels. By the later fourteenth century these towns in turn faced increasing competition from the developing Dutch textile towns, such as Leiden and Amsterdam. This northerly drift of Netherlandish manufacturing

ages to the eighteenth century: a synthesis' in idem, ed., *The Rise and Decline of Urban Industries in Italy and the Low Countries* (Leuven, 1988), 321. For the sale of Scottish wools in the towns noted, see *Halyburton's Ledger*, passim; *De Tol van Iersekrood: Documenten en rekeningen, 1321-1572*, ed. W.S. Unger (The Hague, 1939), part C, passim.

was simultaneously accompanied by a shift of production within existing regions of manufacture, from the larger towns to the plethora of *nouvelle draperie* located in the small towns and villages of the rural Low Countries. This was especially the case in Flanders, where by the fourteenth century the *grande draperies* of the the *drie steden* encountered growing competition from the *nouvelle draperie* of small towns such as Kortrijk, Poperinghe and Wervik. This geographical expansion in the location of the textile industry was matched by a diversity of manufacture. Three types of textile, broadly speaking were produced in the Low Countries. 'Small cloths' of an inferior quality were manufactured across the Netherlands and were intended chiefly for purchase by the poor, both in the Low Countries and elsewhere. It was, however, for the production of light says (often a hybrid made from wool and either cotton or linen) and of heavy, expensive woollen cloths that Artesian, Flemish and Brabantine manufacturers were renowned. Both of these cloth types found a market as far away as the Mediterranean.[181]

At different times Scottish wools were probably used for the production of all three types of cloth. While little thirteenth-century evidence survives regarding the manufacture of small cloths, by the fifteenth century Scottish wool was certainly used for such purposes at Bruges, Brussels, Comines, s'Hertogenbosch and Wervik.[182] It was probably used at Ghent too. There it was ordained in c.1456 that small cloths (*halvekins*) should be made from 'pyewulle, van lamwulle ende schuerlinge', the second and third of which certainly figured among fifteenth-century Scottish exports. Indeed, elsewhere the Ghent authorities indicated that *halvekins* were to be manufactured from Newcastle, Scottish and Rhenish wools; and in 1467-68 at least sixteen sacks and three pokes of Scottish wool were brought into the city, presumably to facilitate such production.[183]

There is no reason to suppose that Scottish wools were not used for the manufacture of similar cloths in the thirteenth century, though then, at least,

---

[181] H.C. Krueger, 'The Genoese exportation of northern cloths to the Mediterranean ports, twelfth century' *Revue Belge de Philologie et d'Histoire*, 65 (1987), 722-50; P. Chorley, 'The cloth exports of Flanders and northern France during the thirteenth century: a luxury trade', *Economic History Review*, 40 (1987), 349-87.

[182] J. Vermaut, 'Structural transformation in a textile centre: Bruges from the sixteenth to the nineteenth Century' in H. van der Wee, ed., *The Rise and Decline of Urban Industries in Italy and the Low Countries* (Leuven, 1988), 189-90 (though the author does not note the significance of the difference between small and luxury cloths); 'Note et documents sur l'aparration de la 'nouvelle draperie' à Bruxelles, 1441-1443', ed. F. Favresse, *Handelingen van de Koninklijke Commissie voor Geschiedenis*, 112 (1947), no. 3(1); *Receuil de Documents Relatifs à l'Histoire de l'Industrie Drapière en Flandre. Deuxième Partie: Le sud-oeust de la Flandre depuis l'époque bourguignonne*, ed. H.E. Sagher (Brussels, 1951-66), ii, no. 220; iii, nos. 582-84; GA s'Hertogenbosch, Inv. Chartres en privilegiën, no. 293.

[183] 'Nieuw teksten over de Gentse draperie: wolaanvoier, productiewijze en controlepraktijken, c.1456-1468', ed. M. Boone, *Handelingen van de Koninklijke Commissie voor Geschiedenis*, 154 (1988), 1-61. For the export of lambswool and schorlings from Scotland, see Lynch and Stevenson, 'Overseas trade: the middle ages to the sixteenth century', 254; Guy, 'The Scottish export trade', 75-76, though neither differentiates between the different types of skin.

they were perhaps also used in the manufacture of better quality products. In the old established centre of Bruges an ordinance of 1282 apparently ranked cloth by quality, and that manufactured from Scottish wool ranked second only behind English-based woollens.[184] Although this hardly proves that Scottish wools were deemed adequate for the production of the better quality heavy woollens of the thirteenth century, subsequent attempts to prohibit the use of Scottish wools for such purposes imply that they previously had been. It is also possible that the Scottish wools used in thirteenth-century Bruges, and for that matter in Ypres too, were intended for the production of says, and it seems highly probable that the famous thirteenth-century *sayetterie* of St Omer made use of Scottish wools in its manufactures.[185]

Thereafter important structural changes in the nature of Netherlandish textile production began to influence the demand for Scottish wools. As competition between the textile manufacturing centres increased, the older centres of production sought to protect their commercial interests by military, legal and economic means.[186] It is the third of these strategies which is of greatest concern to us here, for in the fourteenth century the more renowned centres of textile production abandoned the use of all but the best quality English wools in an attempt to increase the distinctive quality of their heavy woollens. In this drive for exclusivity the lead was taken by the *drie steden* of Bruges, Ghent and Ypres. Ypres, for instance, prohibited the use of Scottish wool in the production of its quality cloths in 1390.[187] Its regulations were soon imitated by many of its Brabantine and Dutch neighbours and by many of the *nouvelle draperie* in Flanders too. Maastricht introduced prohibitions on its use from 1399. Leiden regularly issued ordinances forbidding the use of Scottish, Irish and northern English wools from 1406. Brussels did likewise from 1444; and in *c.*1447 the magistrates of Wervik in Flanders informed producers that they must 'annually take an oath upon the cross to use none but English wools'.[188] Those who contravened the rules faced draconian penalties. When, in 1476, Griele Kerstant, a carpenter's wife,

---

[184] Espinas and Pirenne, *Receuil de Documents*, i, no. 140(67). See too G. Espinas, *La Draperie dans la Flandre Française au Moyen Age* (Paris, 1923), ii, 43, for a similar ranking at St Omer and Arras. At Oudenbourg, however, Scottish wools were placed third behind those of English and Flemish origin in the fourteenth century (Espinas and Pirenne, *Receuil de Documents*, iii, no. 622 (86).)

[185] Espinas and Pirenne, *Receuil de Documents*, iii, no. 651(6); A. Derville, 'Les draperies flamandes et artésiennes vers 1250-1350: quelches considerations critiques et problematiques', *Revue du Nord*, 54 (1972), 365.

[186] H. Van der Wee, 'Structural changes and specialization in the industry of the southern Netherlands, 1100-1600', *Economic History Review*, 2nd ser., 28 (1975), 207-11.

[187] Espinas and Pirenne, *Receuil de Documents*, iii, 637. For similar edicts at Ardenburg and Bruges, see Espinas and Pirenne, *Receuil de Documents*, i, no. 20(21) and O. Delepierre and M.F. Willems, eds., *Collections des Keuren ou Status de tous les Métiers de Bruges* (Ghent, 1842), 42.

[188] *Raadsverdragen van Maastricht, 1367-1428*, ed. M.A. van der Eerden-Vonk, W.J. Alberts and T.J. van Rensch (The Hague, 1992), nos. 914, 1123; *Bronnen tot de Geshiedenis van de Leidsche Textielnijverheid, 1333-1795*, ed. N.W. Posthumus (The Hague, 1910-22), i, nos. 58, 69, 74, 115-16, 132, 166; Sagher, *Recueil de Documents*, iii, 577, 586(195); J. Munro, *Wool, Cloth and Gold: The struggle for bullion in Anglo-Burgundian trade, 1340-1478* (Brussels, 1972), 3.

surreptitiously brought Scottish wool into Leiden, she was threatened with banishment.[189]

Not all of the *nouvelle draperie* followed suit. At Audenarde the use of Scottish wool was still permitted in cloth manufacture by a statute of *c.*1387. The author of the fifteenth-century *Libelle of Englysche Polycye* indicated that Scottish wool also supplied the looms of Poperinghe and Bailleul, and later in the century merchants from another of the new draperies, Tourcoing, were among Andrew Halyburton's most prolific customers. Diksmuide, meanwhile, was using Scottish wools for its production of woollens in the sixteenth century.[190] These draperies were all located in west Flanders, but in Holland too Scottish wool still found a market. By the early fifteenth century it appears to have been used by cloth manufacturers in towns such as Gouda and Haarlem;[191] and by 1418 Dutch imports of Scottish wool were sufficiently large to be taxed by the local count.[192] At a rate of 96 *groten* a sack, half the rate imposed on sacks of English wool, the 1418 *pontgeld* was perhaps a temporary inducement for Dutch manufacturers to utilise more Scottish wool – had it not been for the fact that many Dutch towns (notably Amsterdam and Leiden) opted, like their Flemish and Brabantine competitors, to produce quality woollens. Nevertheless, several Dutch producers were still using Scottish wool in the later fifteenth and sixteenth centuries. Manufacturers in Gouda and Haarlem apparently continued to do so and much of Andrew Halyburton's wool was sold to merchants from Delft, Hoorn and The Hague. Those from The Hague, in particular, also purchased large numbers of woolfells.[193] Scottish wool was purchased elsewhere too, by, for instance, merchants from s'Hertogenbosch in Brabant and from Hasselt in Limburg.[194] Excluded from the *grande draperie* there remained, then, a market for Scottish wools in many of the lesser *nouvelle draperie*.

This important development in the *draperie ointe* (which produced the heavy woollens) was accompanied from the early fourteenth century by the eclipse of the *draperies légères* and their production of says. Although the production and export of says continued to a limited extent thereafter,

[189] Posthumus, *Bronnen*, i, no. 474.

[190] Espinas and Pirenne, *Receuil de Documents*, i, no. 121; Warner, *The Libelle of Englysche Polycye*, 13; *Halyburton's Ledger*, passim; Sagher, *Receuil de Documents*, ii, nos. 245(1), 247(1), 248(1), 248(1), 251(1).

[191] *Rechtsbronnen der Stad Gouda*, ed. L.M. Rollin Conquerque and A. Meerkamp van Embden (The Hague, 1917), no. 24; *Rechtsbronnen de Stad Haarlem*, ed. J. Huizinga (The Hague, 1911), 103, 108-9.

[192] J.A.M.Y. Bos-Rops, *Graven op Zoek naar Geld: De inkomsten van de graven van Holland en Zeeland, 1389-1433* (Hilversum, 1993), 180. For tariff rates at Antwerp, which also placed required smaller payments on Scottish wool, see HA Köln, Hanse IVK/22B, fos. 7v, 28v.

[193] Conquerque and Meerkamps, *Rechtsbronnen Gouda*, 638, 648-49; Huizinga, *Rechtsbronnen Haarlem*, 185, 216-17; *Halyburton's Ledger*, 21-2, 40, 62, 64, 71, 76, 107, 120. See too H. Kaptein, *De Hollandse Textielnijverheid, 1350-1600: Conjunctuur & continuïteit* (Hilversum, 1998), 79-80.

[194] StA Antwerpen, Certificatieboeken 3, fo. 111r; GA Bergen-op-Zoom, inv. no. 5268, fo. 59v. See too N.H.L. van de Heuvel, *De Ambachtsgelden van s'Hertogenbosch voor 1629* (Utrecht, 1946), ii, 362-63.

notably in and from Arras and Hondschoote, other say-producing towns, such as St Omer, found that they could no longer find a market for their fabrics. Many, such as Douai, abandoned their manufacture of says entirely in the early fourteenth century.[195] Only from the mid-fifteenth century (at Hondscoote and Bergue-Saint-Winoc) or later still (at Lille, Amiens, Arras and St Omer) can signs of a revival in the production and export of says be detected. It was, however, limited. At St Omer, for instance, manufactures had fallen from about 40,000 cloths in 1290 to only about four or five hundred per year by 1467.[196] The reasons for this decline of say production, and its subsequent revival, remain contentious.[197] But although the reinvigorated cloth industry at Hondschoote, Lille, St Omer and no doubt elsewhere too, appears to have made use of Scottish wools, from the vantage point of Scottish wool producers, the fourteenth-century hiatus in production made for another closed door.[198]

These developments present something of a conundrum. We might expect that Netherlandish demand for Scottish wools would have contracted from the later fourteenth century as stricter regulations on the use of wools were introduced in the *grand draperie* and as the production of the *sayetteries* declined. It did. But one might then have expected wool exports to have expanded in the fifteenth and early sixteenth centuries with the revival of the *sayetteries* and the expansion of the *draperie nouvelle* which used Scottish wools. Yet, wool exports declined markedly from the first decade of the fifteenth century and, despite some short-lived but minor upturns, they never regained their fourteenth-century peaks.[199] Of course, some dwindling of demand can be attributed to the general population decline after the Black Death, especially once population levels reached their nadir in the early fifteenth century. But other factors are also important in explaining the sluggishness of Scottish wool exports. It has, for instance, been suggested that Netherlandish restrictions on the use of Scottish wool were a response to a decline the quality of that wool, caused by the climatic regression of the later middle ages.[200] This is possible, but economic rather than environmental explanations are perhaps still more important. The quest for exclusivity in the manufacture of Netherlandish cloth was a response to growing competition,

[195] Espinas and Pirenne, *Receuil de Document*, ii, no. 389.

[196] A. Derville, ed., *Histoire de Saint-Omer* (Lille, 1981), 43, 85.

[197] J.H. Munro, 'The origin of the English 'new draperies': the resurrection of an old Flemish industry, 1270-1570' in N.B. Harte, ed., *The New Draperies in the Low Countries and England, 1300-1800* (Oxford, 1997), 54, 65-87.

[198] Sagher, *Receuil de Documents*, ii, no. 290; E. Coornaert, *Un Centre Industriel d'Autrefois: La draperies-sayetteries d'Hondschoote, XIVe-XVIIIe siècles* (Paris, 1930), 189-90; M. Vanhaek, *Histoire de la Sayetteries à Lille* (Lille, 1910), ii, no. 10; Derville, *Histoire de Saint-Omer*, 85; *Halyburton's Ledger*, 49, 107.

[199] Various attempts have been made to chart the volume of Scottish wool exports. See Lynch and Stevenson, 'Overseas trade: the middle ages to the sixteenth century', 241; Grant, *Independence and Nationhood*, 236-37; Guy, 'The Scottish export trade', 69-70.

[200] Stevenson, Thesis, 22-5.

increasing costs and shrinking markets in the cloth trade. At the same time it
was not just cloth manufacturers who faced competition. Scottish wool
producers did too.

This competition came not only from the British Isles, but also from the
often over-looked Netherlandish wools and also from the produce of the
Iberian peninsula, the Rhineland and the Baltic.[201] At Vilvoorde, for instance,
the looms used to manufacture cheaper woollens were supplied with Irish,
rather than Scottish, wool; and at Naarden, one of the principal
manufacturing centres of cheap cloths bound for Baltic markets, the draperies
used Rhenish wool.[202] Small quantities of Spanish wools had long since been
used in Netherlandish cloth production too. In the thirteenth century their
quality had been abysmal – and even in the early fifteenth century the author
of the *Libelle* thought them 'of lytell valeue'.[203] Initially, then, Iberian wool
had posed little competition at least to the better quality Scottish wools,
though by the 1420s Spanish wool was routinely used in *nouvelle draperie*
such as Poperinghe, Bailleuil, Tournai and Tourcoing. Here it stood in direct
competition with Scottish wool, by now excluded from the *grand draperie*.
Meanwhile, the quality of some Iberian wool was transformed following the
cross-breeding of indigenous Spanish stocks with merinid sheep introduced
from North Africa from the mid-fourteenth century. Even as the author of
the *Libelle* penned his dismissive remarks on Spanish wool, the more highly
prized clip of the merino sheep was being imported into the Netherlands.
This wool did not begin to challenge its English counterpart until the later
fifteenth century. The old *draperie ointe* clung trenchantly to their traditional
supplier until the rise in English wool prices at the end of the fifteenth
century encouraged them to seek regular supplies elsewhere. But then it was
to Spain, rather than Scotland, that they looked. Between 1497 and 1523
several thousand sacks of Spanish wool penetrated the Netherlands market
annually.[204]

This alternative source of supply had important implications for
Scotland.[205] Scottish wools were still, of course, largely excluded from the

[201] A. Verhulst, 'La laine indigène dans les anciens Pays-Bas entre le XIIe et le XVIIe siècle', *Revue Historique*, 248 (1972), 281-322; H. Pohl, 'Zur Geschichte von Wollhandel im Rheinland, in Westfalen und Hessen vom 12. Bis 17. Jahrhundert' and A. Maczak, 'Wool production and the wool trade in east-central Europe from the fourteenth to the seventeenth centuries' in M. Spallanzani, ed., *La Lana come Materia Prima: I fenomeni della sua produzione e circolazione nei secoli XIII-XVII* (Florence, 1974), 89-96, 353-67.
[202] 'Bouwstoffen voor de geschiedenis der laatmiddeleeuwse stadsdraperie in een klein Brabants produktiecentrum: Vilvoorde, 1357-1578', ed. J.P. Peeters *Handelingen van de Koninklijke Commissie voor Geschiedenis*, 151 (1985), no. 11(5); A.C.J. Vrankrijker, 'De textielindustrie van Naarden, I: De laken industrie in de 15e en 16e eeuw', *Tijdschrift voor Geschiedenis*, 51 (1936), 155, 157-58.
[203] Warner, *Libelle*, 6.
[204] C.R. Philips, 'The Spanish wool trade, 1500-1780', *Journal of Economic History*, 42 (1982), 777-79.
[205] The subtleties of these developments are discussed in the excellent article by I. Blanchard, 'Northern wools and Netherlandish markets at the close of the middle ages' in G.G. Simpson, ed.,

manufacture of quality cloths. Moreover, the growing price stability of quality cloths (which recourse to an alternative supply of quality wool from the later fifteenth century afforded) meant that the manufacturers of cheaper cloths were henceforth denied the brief but recurrent opportunity of expanding their sales (and therefore production) when the cost of the quality woollens rose. However, the cheaper woollens generally sold more consistently in the Baltic, where currency debasement in the later fifteenth and early sixteenth centuries depressed the market for quality cloths, and consumers turned to cheaper alternatives. This thriving northern market for cheaper Netherlandish cloths might have boded well for Scottish wool, but for the fact that the Baltic debasement, especially after 1515, made Baltic exports cheaper in the markets of western Europe. These exports included low grade wools from Pomerania, Poland and Silesia, which, together with Rhenish and Netherlandish wools, were used in, for instance, the say production of Hondschoote.[206] Indeed, the price advantage which these wools began to enjoy was heightened by the lower customs tariffs to which they were subjected by comparison with Scottish wool. In 1519, for instance, Rhenish and Baltic wools were liable to only two thirds of the payment required for Scottish wools in Zeeland.[207] And it is this new Baltic competition in the *draperie nouvelle*, together with that from Ireland, Newcastle, the Rhineland and the Netherlands, which probably explains why Scottish wool exports fell to their medieval nadir in the 1520s.

Cloth and Clothing

The importance of wool in the medieval economy derived from its role in cloth manufacture. It was with woollen-based garments that, north of the Alps and the Pyrenees, most people clothed themselves. Given that Scotland produced copious amounts of wool, one might have expected that it would also have been a major producer of cloth. A good deal was indeed manufactured, probably as much in the countryside as in the towns. Indeed, it seems likely that, as wool exports declined from the later fourteenth century, wool was redirected from Netherlandish looms to Scottish weavers. This, of course, is what happened in England, partly because there the customs duty on cloth was much lower than that on wool – providing English cloth producers, who did not pay a custom on wool, with a considerable economic advantage over their foreign competitors in the Low Countries, who did. This element of the equation was paralleled in Scotland, where the export duty on cloth amounted to about 10% of its value, compared with a levy of about 25% of the value of wool.[208] Yet, although wool exports fell from the later

Scotland and the Low Countries, 1124-1994 (East Linton, 1996), 76-88, upon which this whole paragraph is largely based.
[206] Coornaert, *Un Centre Industriel d'Autrefois*, 189-90.
[207] HA Köln, Hanse III/K35, fo. 83.
[208] Stevenson, 'Trade with the south', 194.

fourteenth century and cloth was certainly exported, Scotland never emerged as the major exporter of cloth that England and Ireland did.

The flight from wool to cloth, such as it was, is most obvious in the south-west. By the fifteenth century very little wool was customed at the Solway and Clyde ports, and Kirkcudbright in particular emerged as a major exporter of cloth once export duties were levied on cloth from 1425. In 1434-35 the Solway town accounted for 28.4% of all Scottish cloth exports, and, although its volume and share of total cloth exports subsequently declined, the Galloway towns still accounted for 13% of total cloth exports in the 1470s.[209] The destination of these exports remains obscure. Little, if any, reached western England, as is revealed by the almost total absence of Scottish shipping from the extant customs accounts for the ports of western England.[210] Instead, it seems likely that Solway-Clyde cloths were dispatched to south-western France and to Spain, providing a return cargo for shipment of French and Spanish wine and iron.[211] Unfortunately, there is little evidence with which to substantiate this hypothesis. We do know, however, that cheap Irish cloths reached Spain and Italy in some quantity throughout the middle ages;[212] and it is possible that, as awareness of their actual origin declined with the distance they were transported, the 'Irish serge' of Spanish and Italian records had become a generic term which encompassed the perhaps similar cloths of Scotland and Ireland. That said, Scottish and Irish cloths *were* differentiated in a Milanese price schedule dating from about the mid-fourteenth century – Irish says were valued at only 70% of their Scottish equivalents – though whether these Scottish cloths arrived in Lombardy from western Scotland, eastern Scotland, or indeed from Netherlandish manufacturers who used Scottish and Irish wools in their manufactures, remains unclear.[213]

Despite the special importance of cloth to the commerce of the south-west, most Scottish cloth was exported from east-coast ports. At Aberdeen wool remained an important export, and woollen cloth exports were correspondingly less significant, but elsewhere (most notably at Dundee) decline in the wool trade was accompanied by a rise in the comparative importance of woollen cloth exports. Thus, whereas only 164 dozen ells of cloth were exported from Aberdeen in 1527-28 and 1528-29, 1,547 dozen ells

[209] Stevenson, 'Trade with the south', 195-96; Lynch and Stevenson, 'Overseas trade: the middle ages to the sixteenth century', 255.
[210] PRO London, E122, passim; Lewis, 'A contribution to the commercial history of medieval Wales', 86-188; CA Chester, MB/1-4, passim; SB/1-9, passim.
[211] Stevenson, 'Trade with the south', 195.
[212] For Irish cloths in Spain and Italy, see, for example, *Statuti dell'arte dei Rigattieri e Linaioli di Firenze, 1296-1340*, ed. F. Sartini (Florence, 1940), 40; A. Esch, 'Importe in das Rom der Renaissance: Die Zollregister der Jahre 1470 bis 1480', *Quellen und Forschungen aus Italienischen Archiven und Bibliotheken*, 74 (1994), 377; P. Chorley, 'English cloth exports during the thirteenth and fourteenth centuries: the continental evidence', *Historical Research*, 61 (1988), 8.
[213] Chorley, 'English cloth exports during the thirteenth and fourteenth centuries', 7.

were exported from Dundee in the same period.[214] It was, however, Edinburgh and its port of Leith which dominated this branch of the cloth trade, accounting for 75% of all Scottish woollen cloth exports in the 1430s, and for over 80% by the 1530s.[215]

Some of the east-coast cloth trade was directed towards the Baltic – and it is surely significant in this respect that whereas Dundonian vessels passed the Sound on at least ten occasions in 1528, not one Aberdonian ship apparently did so.[216] Some of the cloth which these and other Scottish vessels carried was delivered to Denmark and to southern Sweden, though 760 of the 1159 ells which reached Lödöse aboard Scottish ships in 1546 were actually of English manufacture.[217] The adjacent Wendish towns of Anklam, Hamburg, Lübeck and Stralsund also received Scottish cloth, some of which was re-exported eastwards to Pomerania, Mecklenburg and even, in 1444, as far as Reval (now the Latvian town of Tallinn).[218] The origins of this Baltic trade probably date back to the later fourteenth century. At much the same time as the Wendish towns were attempting to exclude Scots and other foreigners from the Scanian herring fairs, the sale of Scottish cloth was prohibited in Stralsund.[219] A date of c.1370 also seems far more likely than 1330 for the imposition of a similar ban imposed at Anklam, for it seems reasonable to assume that Scottish merchants would have brought cloth to the Baltic and returned to western Europe with fish.[220] As, however, with other items of Scottish-Baltic trade, the main Baltic market for Scottish cloth was to be found not in the western Baltic, but rather in Danzig. There, measured by value, cloth accounted for at least 17% of all Scottish imports, and perhaps an even greater amount if, as seems reasonable, we assume that cloth constituted a substantial element

[214] *ER*, xv, 440, 443, 511, 514. I have assumed a 'long hundred' of 120 in the calculation of ells.
[215] M. Lynch and A Stevenson, 'Restructing urban economies in the later middle ages' in P.G.B. McNeill and H.L. MacQueen, eds., *Atlas of Scottish History to 1707* (Edinburgh, 1996), 244-46; Lynch and Stevenson, 'Overseas trade: the middle ages to the sixteenth century', 255.
[216] RA Københaven, Øresundtolregnskaber 1528, 4, 6, 11, 19, 24.
[217] NAS Edinburgh, E71/29/3, fos. 2v, 12r; Dow, 'Scottish trade with Sweden', 71; CA Dundee, BHCB/1, fo. 147r.
[218] *ADCP*, 489; NAS Edinburgh, E71/29/3, fos. 12r; E71/29/4, fo. 6r; *Hamburger Burspraken, 1346 bis 1594*, ed. J. Bolland (Hamburg, 1960), ii, 190-91; *LUB*, x, no. 532; 'Die lübeckischen Pfundzollbücher von 1492-96', ed. F. Bruns *HGb*, 13 (1907), 460; *Kämmereibuch der Stadt Reval, 1432-63*, R. Vogelsang (Cologne and Vienna, 1976), i, 356. For a sixteenth-century shipment of Scottish cloth, see TLA Tallinn, I/Af/21, 147.
[219] *HUB*, iv, no. 335, n. 4.
[220] T.A. Fischer, *The Scots in Eastern and Western Prussia* (Edinburgh, 1903), 4. On the doubtful dating of this no longer extant document, see I. von Wechmar and R. Biederstedt, 'Die Schottische Einwanderung in Vorpommerm im 16. und 17. Jahrhundert', *Greifswald-Stralunder Jahrbuch*, v (1965), 19, n. 4. On the other hand, Berwick merchants were trading at nearby Stralsund by 1312: *CDS*, iii, no. 258; *HUB*, ii, no. 206; *PUB*, v, no. 2713. See too *PUB*, ix, no. 5324; C.A. Christensen, ed., *Diplomatarium Danicum, 2. Raekke*, xi (Copenhagen, 1950), no. 241, dated 1335 and which refers to an attempt to exclude Scots, Danes and Wends [?Slavs] from the trading community at Anklam.

among the undifferentiated packs of Scottish goods unloaded at the Prussian port.[221]

In western Europe some cloth was shipped to France.[222] Perhaps surprisingly, given its own vibrant cloth industry, England too provided an important market. This was, however, in the main of a quite different nature to that shipped to the Baltic. Woollens dominated the Baltic trade and, although some woollen cloth was also exported to England, most exports to England were of linen. The Baltic and English trades were, however, interdependent, for from the early fifteenth century flax (the raw material from which linen was made) constituted one of the most important shipments from Danzig to Scotland. It was freighted aboard every one of the fourteen Scottish-bound ships leaving the port in 1477 and constituted 60% of all Danzig exports to Scotland in the later fifteenth and early sixteenth centuries.[223] Much was presumably used to feed a Scottish linen industry which has left remarkably little evidence of its importance to the Scottish economy. Neither imports of flax, nor exports of linen were taxed, so neither appears in the Scottish customs data. Archaeology too provides little evidence of the linen industry, since linen survives less well than woollen cloth. Still, a flax-breaking mallet has been discovered at Perth, and flax seeds have been found in a number of locations on the east coast.[224] Nevertheless, the English customs data provides an unusually specific insight into this now otherwise almost invisible industry. Linen figured among Scottish exports to both Newcastle and Hull by the mid-fifteenth century – and over 600 yards, worth £8 19s, was sent to Hull alone in 1540-41, compared with other cloths only to the value of £1 3s 4d.[225] By then, if not earlier, Boston, Lynn and no doubt ports elsewhere in eastern England too were also receiving shipments of linen.[226]

Yet, whether for linen or for woollens, the overseas market for these cloths was limited. Demand for linen was comparatively small and Scottish

[221] Samsonowicz, 'Engländer und Schotten', 50.

[222] NAS Edinburgh, E71/29/2; E71/29/3; E71/29/4; Mollat, *Compatabilité du Port de Dieppe*, 45, 89, 91, 93; Mollat, *Les Affaires de Jacques Coeur*, i, 69, 91..

[223] WAP Gdansk, 300/19/2a, 187-203; Samsonowicz, 'Engländer und Schotten', 50. See too WAP Gdansk, 300/27/3, 52; GSA Berlin, OBA 7433; OF/13, 413-415; CA Aberdeen, CR/6, 502; *HUB*, vi, no. 844; vii(1), no. 343.

[224] R.M. Spearman, 'Workshops, materials and debris - evidence of early industries' in Lynch *et al*, *Medieval Town* (Edinburgh, 1988), 137, 141; J.C. Murray, ed., *Excavations in Medieval Aberdeen, 1973-81* (Edinburgh, 1982), 241. For the cultivation of flax in medieval Scotland, see K.J. Edwards and G. Whittington, 'Palynological evidence for the growing of *cannabis sativa* L. (hemp) in medieval and historical Scotland', *Transactions of the Institute of British Geographers*, new series, 15 (1990), 60-9.

[225] PRO London, E122/107/48, m. 1d; E122/108/2, m. 1r; E122/108/8, m. 2d; E122/61/91, m. 2r-3r; E122/62/7, m. 2r-4r; E122/62/9, m. 2r-4r; E122/62/19, m. 3r (to Scarborough); E122/63/2, m. 2d; E122/60/3, fos. 1r, 10r; E122/64/2, fos. 10v, 21v, 22r; E122/64/5, fo. 15v; E122/64/6, fo. 1r; E122/64/15, fos. 4r, 5v, 7r, 15r; E122/64/16, fos. 1r, 3v, 4r, 5v, 6v, 13v.

[226] PRO London, E122/12/8, fo. 4r; E122/12/9, m. 1d; E122/12/12, m. 2d; E122/99/24, fo. 10r; E122/99/26, fos. 3r, 5r, 6v.

producers had to compete with those from Holland and Brittany. In the Baltic, meanwhile, Scottish woollens faced competition from both English and Netherlandish products. Many of the latter were ironically made from Scottish wool, though the Baltic debasements of the early sixteenth century (which stimulated the export of the cheaper Netherlandish cloths to the Baltic) probably also encouraged Scottish exports, as the better quality cloths of the Netherlands and England became too expensive for Baltic customers. Scottish merchants were also able to exploit moments of Anglo-Hanseatic tension to expand their cloth trade in the Baltic. In 1474 twelve ships arrived in Danzig from Scotland, compared with only two from England. This, however, was at the tail end of a serious rupture in Anglo-Hanseatic relations, and in the following years, as the number of arrivals from England rose to seven in 1475 and at least fourteen in 1476, Scottish arrivals fell to eight in 1475 and seven in 1476.[227]

If the cloth trade to the Baltic was of a 'stop-go' character, that to the Netherlandish markets faced even greater hurdles. Despite the welcome extended to virtually every other commodity which was sent there from Scotland, cloth manufacturers encountered difficulty in accessing Netherlandish markets. As major cloth manufacturers themselves, the leading Flemish towns in particular had no desire to engage in competition with foreign producers, though in 1400 the duke of Burgundy conceded that cheap foreign textiles from Scotland and elsewhere might be brought to Sluis for dyeing. This, however, was on condition that they were not sold, but instead re-exported. The privilege was confirmed by the commercial treaty agreed between the Scottish and Burgundian authorities at Leiden in 1427, and subsequent concessions relaxed the anti-competitive ethos still further.[228] By the mid-fifteenth century small, narrow Scottish-produced cloths ('scotbrede') were being sold in Flanders, finding a niche market for the clothing of the poor. Indeed, so important had this source of supply become for the urban poor of the Netherlands that a public outcry forced the duke of Burgundy to exempt these inferior imports from a general embargo which he sought to introduce on imported cloths in 1497.[229] This partial opening-up of the Netherlandish market towards the end of the fifteenth century is further reflected in the business activities of Andrew Halyburton, who sold small quantities of Scottish cloth in Antwerp, Bergen-op-Zoom and Bruges. We

---

[227] WAP Gdansk, 300/19/15, passim; H. Samsonowicz, 'Handel zagraniczny Gdanska w drugiej polowie XV wieku', *Przeglad Historyczny*, 47 (1956), 302-3; V. Lauffer, 'Danzigs Schiffs- und Waarenverkehr am Ende des XV. Jahrhunderts', *Zeitschrift des Westpreussischen Geschichtsverein*, 33 (1894), 22-3. The English figures quoted are derived from the revision of Lauffer's figures presented in J.D. Fudge, *Cargoes, Embargoes and Emissaries: The commercial and political interaction of England and the German Hanse, 1450-1510* (Toronto, 1995), 215-16.

[228] *IAB*, iii, 427-34; v, 301; vi, 12, 39; Rooseboom, *The Scottish Staple*, nos. 21, 26; J.H. Munro, 'Industrial protectionism in medieval Flanders: urban or national?' in H.A. Miskimin, D. Herlihy and A.L. Udovitch, *The Medieval City* (London, 1977), 234-36, 240-42.

[229] Munro, 'Industrial protectionism', 242.

cannot doubt that cloth which was 'ettin with mottis' was destined for a less affluent member of society.[230]

Although Scotland was an exporter of fabrics, cloth also featured prominently among the country's imports. Much was of a type and quality not manufactured in Scotland. Prime among these were the silk-based materials, including velvet, satin, damask and taffeta, most of which were Italian in origin. All of these found a ready market at the court, long before the *Treasurer's Accounts* provide extensive, and barely as yet analysed, information about royal cloth purchases from the end of the fifteenth century.[231] The accounts of the clerk of the royal wardrobe, extant for five years between 1372 and 1378, reveal regular expenditure on gold, satin and taffeta silks. Meanwhile gold silks, at least some of which were produced in Venice and Cyprus, featured annually on the royal shopping list between 1444 and 1454.[232] Most of these were purchased in the Low Countries, where Andrew Halyburton also regularly bought damask, satin and taffeta in the later fifteenth century.[233] From the later 1530s similar cloths were, however, also acquired in English ports such as Hull and Lynn.[234]

These silk-based fabrics were among the most expensive cloths. Although sumptuary legislation of the fifteenth century suggests that non-aristocratic sections of society could also afford to purchase them, they were in the main an exclusive item of trade destined for the elite.[235] Most of these materials came by the yard or as sowing silk. Both were presumably destined for Scottish tailors, who turned them into capes, coats, collars, doublets, gowns, hose and pantaloons – and it was presumably the finished products, rather than the materials from which they were made, which provoked the curiosity of some foreign observers. When Mary of Guelders married James II in 1449, the new queen was dressed in violet robes, lined with ermine, which were deemed 'of a most unusual and peculiar style judged by French standards.'[236] Yet Scottish tailors were forced to learn foreign ways. Parliamentary legislation of 1458 decreed that the wives of townsmen should wear head dress which accorded with English and Flemish styles.[237]

Those Scots who were dressed foreign cloths were far more likely to wear linen and especially woollen-based garments than silk, and both linens and woollens – generally of a better quality than that produced in Scotland – were frequently purchased abroad. In the fourteenth century most came from the

---

[230] *Halyburton's Ledger*, 29, 64, 81-4, 89, 132-33. See too HA Köln, Hanse III/K35, fo. 77, for the toll rates imposed on 'Scottish cloth' and 'Scottish carsays' imposed in Zeeland in 1519.
[231] Gemmill and Mayhew, *Changing Values*, 353, 355.
[232] *ER*, ii, 371, 439, 465, 506, 546; v, 148, 222, 273, 309, 345, 346, 384, 436, 498, 615.
[233] *Halyburton's Ledger*, 19, 22, 37, 50, 55, 88, 108, 117, 123, 178, 200, 206.
[234] PRO London, E122/99/24, fo. 15v; E122/99/26, fos. 5r, 6v, 7r; E122/99/27, fos. 1v, 2v, 3r; E122/64/16, fos. 7v, 9v, 17r.
[235] *APS*, ii, 49. See too *Edin. Recs.*, ii, 4.
[236] *Chron. d'Escouchy*, i, 181-82.
[237] *APS*, ii, 49.

Low Countries. Between 1373 and 1378 the crown spent over £700 on cloth. Although some of this went on silks, most was in return for the quality woollens of Ypres and Kortrijk.[238] On other occasions, especially from the fifteenth century, acquisitions were made of scarlet – the most expensive of all the woollen-based cloths, which, despite its name, came in a variety of different colours.[239] Not all of those fabrics which Scottish merchants purchased in the Low Countries were, however, Netherlandish in origin. Halyburton purchased five ells of Rouen cloth in 1500; John Moffet bought English cloth from a Brussels merchant, as well as black velvet from a Florentine merchant in 1508; and it was perhaps from the Netherlands too that James IV acquired his supplies of Milanese fustian.[240] Yet it seems unlikely that it was just for the elite that cloth merchants catered. Though some scarlets came from England too, most of those cloths which came from south of the border were medium-grade, relatively cheap kerseys, russets and worsteds, manufactured the length of England from Kendal to London, along with some friezes from Bristol and London and some fustians.[241] Halyburton too made occasional purchases of cheaper cloths manufactured in Holland and, among these, the cloths of Naarden were both bought and re-sold by Scottish merchants, sometimes in England.[242] More common still were Halyburton's purchases of says and cloths from Lille – and Lille, as we have seen, was not one of the draperies most renowned for the quality and expense of its products.[243] More rarely, cheaper linens were also imported – some from the Netherlands and others from Brittany. Cloth from both areas, at least some of it of linen, was frequently used by the monarchy to make sheets and shirts.[244]

Since imports, other than those from England and Ireland, were not subject to a customs duty, it is difficult to determine whether Scotland's cloth exports were balanced by its cloth imports. Yet there can be no doubt that Scotland never emerged as the major exporter of cloth which England did, or that the Scottish market for imported cloths remained strong. We can but speculate as to why this was. One possibility is that, despite the local availability of wool, there were insufficient numbers and concentrations of craftsmen to develop a flourishing cloth industry in Scotland. There is some evidence to substantiate this theory, not least from the indications that urban

---

[238] *ER*, ii, 439, 465, 506, 546.
[239] E.g. *ER*, v, 261, 265, 296, 306, 342. On scarlets generally, see J.H. Munro, 'The medieval scarlets and the economics of sartorial splendour' in N.B. Harte and K.G. Ponting, eds., *Cloth and Clothing in Medieval Europe* (London, 1983), 13-70.
[240] *Halyburton's Ledger*, 260; StA Antwerpen, Certificatieboeken 3, fo. 181r; *TA*, i-iv, passim.
[241] E.g. PRO London, E122/161/11, m. 9d; *CDS*, iv, no. 802.
[242] *Halburton's Ledger*, 12, 30, 63. For Naarden cloths bought in England, see PRO London, E122/99/26, fo. 3r; and for Naarden cloth sold in England PRO London, E122/64/2, fo. 22r; E122/64/15, fo. 6r; E122/64/16, fo. 3v, 4r, 5v, 12r, 13v.
[243] For says, see *Halyburton's Ledger*, 87, 90, 103, 165, 235, 254; for cloth from Lille, ibid., 19, 30, 50, 114, 169, 208, 240, 254, 260. See too Gemmill and Mayhew, *Changing Values*, 354, 357.
[244] *Halyburton's Ledger*, 87, 159; *TA*, i-x, passim.

cloth production was squeezed even in the thirteenth century by both small scale rural production (which cornered the market for the cheapest cloths) and Netherlandish manufactures (which dominated the market for the more exclusive woollens). Important too was the quality of Scottish wool. As we have seen, on the whole this was of an inferior calibre to that of England and latterly Spain. Consequently, even the most skilled craftsmen would not have been able to compete qualitatively with the producers of the cloths made from these wools. However, this in itself cannot have inhibited the production of Scottish woollens, for the largest, albeit not the most lucrative, market for cloth was among the lower social orders who sought cheap fabrics with which to clothe themselves. This is the market which one might have expected Scottish manufacturers to have tapped more extensively than they did.

There are perhaps three reasons why they did not. Firstly, in the thirteenth century and early fourteenth century there had been little incentive for them to do so, for the demand for wool in the Low Countries had been buoyant. Secondly, once that demand fell in the later fourteenth century, the manufacturers of cheap cloths were faced by rising transportation costs and greater risks, resulting from more unstable political conditions in the North Sea and Baltic worlds. Quality cloths could by and large be priced at a level to absorb these additional burdens; but the profits on cheaper cloths were savagely cut. This, it has been suggested, was one reason why the Netherlandish producers abandoned their production of the cheaper says in favour of the quality woollens; and it may partly explain why the reorientation from wool to cloth was limited in Scotland. No fat profits could be expected from the Scottish cloth trade – which is very probably why very few foreign, as opposed to Scottish, merchants exported cloth from Scotland. At Edinburgh, for instance, 1,113 separate consignments of cloth were exported by merchants (including over thirty by women) in 1539. Their number included only nine clearly identified foreigners – seven 'Dutchman' (either Netherlanders or Germans) and two Frenchmen.[245] Foreign merchants did, of course, trade in other cheaper cloths, and this brings us to the final point. Scottish cloth, like Scottish wool, faced stiff competition. Irish woollens seem to have dominated much of the remaining Mediterranean market for cheap northern woollens, while in the North Sea region northern English cloths and the cheaper Netherlandish products from Holland vied with Scottish manufactures for much the same market. Ironically, then, it was partly the success of Scottish wool producers in finding an outlet in the Dutch textile centres which limited the opportunity for Scottish cloth producers to expand their production.

Minerals
While food and (in the cool climes of Scotland) effective clothing are essential to human welfare, the preparation of both was greatly facilitated by minerals

---

[245] NAS Edinburgh, E71/30/4.

and mineral-based artefacts. Metal tools aided peasants and craftsmen in their agricultural and industrial work, while armour, weaponry and horseshoes were the hallmarks of the fighting class and its favoured mode of transport. Castles and the greater ecclesiastical buildings, moreover, were adorned with lead roofing and piping, and with iron, lead or copper fixtures and fittings of doors, gates, locks and windows. These functional uses of metal products were supplemented by highly-regarded, luxury manufactures made from gold and silver, which, of course, together with copper, were also used in the minting of coins. Metalworks and metalworkers, however, required fuel to extract and mould their metals. Timber and peat were one source of energy, though, as we have already seen, timber supplies became increasingly scarce in the south and east of the country. In some areas coal provided an alternative, which was used for domestic heating purposes even by the poor, as well as for industrial purposes. Yet, of all the mineral products used by medieval society, salt was perhaps the most important, since it provided the most common means of preserving food for out-of-season consumption.

On the whole we are inadequately informed about the mineral resources of medieval Scotland. Both iron and lead were mined in Scotland, though neither industry is extensively recorded in either documentary or archaeological sources. These metalworks were often located in rural areas remote from the main centres of population. Iron, for instance, was extracted at Duchray in Stirlingshire, at Rannoch, at Strathgartney on the shores of Loch Katrine and in Sutherland, while lead was obtained from Crawford in Lanarkshire and, by the sixteenth century, in Islay and Leadhills.[246] Gold and silver were much scarcer, though the significance of David I's occupation of Cumberland in the twelfth century largely lay in that region's silver mines, which provided part of the wherewithal for furnishing the new royal mints.[247] Coal and salt works are somewhat better recorded. Coal had been mined in the region of the Forth since at least the thirteenth century, and this area also produced a good deal of salt.[248] Both, however, were extracted elsewhere too. The monks of Holm Cultram, for instance, possessed a coastal salt pan on the Solway estuary and the monks of Coupar Angus possessed a saltpan near Aberdeen.[249]

The greatest salt and coal production was, however, focused on the Forth estuary and small quantities of both were exported by the fifteenth century. Inferior to the produce of the great continental salt mines, such as that at

---

[246] W.G. Aitken, 'Excavations of bloomeries in Rannoch', *PSAS*, 102 (1969-70), 188-204; *ER*, i, 30; vi, 278; ix, 38, 113, 189, 239, 330, 410-11, 493, 563, 596; xi, 34, 85, 158, 288; xii, 12, 23, 59, 142, 213, 320, 411, 495, 677; xiii, 58, 264, 321, 447, 529, 531; *TA*, iv, 273-74, 386, 396, 408.
[247] I. Blanchard, 'Lothian and beyond: the economy of the 'English empire' of David I' in Britnell and Hatcher, *Progress and Problems*, 23-45. See too *TA*, v, 19, for sixteenth-century gold extraction at Crawford.
[248] Gemmill and Mayhew, *Changing Values*, 345-50.
[249] *Holm Cultram Reg.*, nos. 120, 135; *Coupar Angus Chrs.*, i, no. 48. See too Duncan, *Scotland*, 361-62.

Lüneburg where salt was extracted from brine, Scottish salt struggled to compete with the lower-grade produce of the Bay of Bourgneuf. Indeed, the impact of Biscayan competition in the later middle ages is revealed by the sudden surge of Scottish salt exports in the last quarter of the sixteenth century, when the price of French salt rose.[250] This French salt, like that of Scotland and the Netherlands, was derived from sea water, though while that from France was sun-dried, the Scottish produce was boiled. Hence the close connection in Scotland between the salt and coal industries. The different methods of extraction produced different qualities of salt. That from France tended to be coarser than that from Scotland (and better for preserving fish), though both contained impurities. Since those in Scottish salt were fewer, in western Europe Scottish salt was often described as white and that of France as grey.

Scottish salt was regularly dispatched to England, almost all of it on ships from the Forth ports and most of it on vessels from Dysart and Kirkcaldy. Newcastle – with both local supplies and Bay imports – took little.[251] Hull took rather more. In 1453 Scottish ships delivered 126 chalders to the Humber port. Despite a temporary ban on salt exports, imposed by the Scottish parliament in 1535, even political conflict did not disrupt the trade.[252] In the same year that Scottish troops were being slaughtered at Solway Moss, Scottish ships were delivering salt to Hull. Indeed, salt constituted a major of item of Scottish trade not only with Hull, but also with the nearby ports of Bridlington, Grimsby and Scarborough.[253] Further south it is more difficult to assess the delivery of Scottish commodities since English customs officials often failed to note the home port of visiting vessels. Still, it is clear that by at least the later fifteenth century Scottish salt was regularly sent to Lynn, though normally in smaller quantities than were sent to Hull.[254] Boston too received regular shipments by the 1530s, though Yarmouth (perhaps surprisingly since it was a more important fishing port than either Lynn or Boston) was a rather more occasional recipient of Scottish salt.[255] Small amounts percolated further south too. At Faversham one Dysart vessel

[250] Lynch and Stevenson, 'Overseas trade: the middle ages to the sixteenth century', 259.

[251] PRO London, E122/107/57, m. 2d, 3r.

[252] PRO London, E122/202/6; *APS*, ii, 346.

[253] PRO London, E122/61/71, m. 2-4; E122/62/5, m.2d; E122/62/7, m. 2-4; E122/62/9, m. 1d-4r; E122/62/14, m. 1d; E122/62/19, m. 3r; E122/63/8, m. 2d; E122/60/3, fos. 1, 10v, 11v, 14r; E122/64/2, fos. 9v, 10v, 21v, 22r; E122/64/5, fos. 15v, 21; E122/64/6, fos. 1r, 5v; E122/202/5, fo. 19v; E122/64/15, fos. 5v-7v; E122/64/16, fos. 1r, 5v, 7r, 12r, 13v; E. Gillett, *A History of Grimsby* (London, 1970), 29.

[254] PRO London, E122/97/6, m. 2d; E122/97/10, fo. 3v; E122/98/5; E122/98/8, m. 1d; E122/98/10, m. 1r; E122/205/2, fo. 11r; E122/205/3, fos. 14-17; E122/99/12, fos. 12v, 15v; E122/99/23, fos. 7, 10v; E122/99/24, fos. 8-10, 13v-14v; E122/99/26, fos. 5-6; E122/99/27, fos. 4-5. See too N.J. Williams, *The Maritime Trade of the East Anglian Ports, 1550-1590* (Oxford, 1988), 81-5.

[255] For Boston, PRO London, E122/12/8, m. 4r; E122/12/9, m. 1d; E122/12/10, fo. 4v; E122/12/12, m. 2d, 3r; for Yarmouth, PRO London, E122/152/5; NfRO Norwich, Y/C4/169, m. 15d; Y/C4/171, m. 14r; Y/C4/172, m. 3r.

delivered twenty ways of Scottish salt in 1540, returning a month later with one way of Bay salt.[256]

There was also a market for Scottish salt in the Baltic, despite the availability of supplies from Lüneburg. Indeed, towards the end of the fifteenth century Lüneburg was becoming increasingly nervous about foreign competition. In 1471 it had sought to restrict the sale of French and other foreign salt in Denmark; and in 1495 it complained that merchants from Stralsund were regrating the produce of the Lüneburg mine with Scottish salt.[257] The incentive behind this deception was, of course, economic. In 1485 Lüneburg salt was priced at 38 marks per last in Danzig, compared to only 22 marks per last for Scottish salt.[258] Still, the Wendish towns were probably not regular recipients of Scottish salt. No ships left Leith for these towns in 1510-11, and not one of the three vessels bound for Stralsund in 1512-13 was laden with salt. Neither was any salt aboard the two vessels which left Leith for Hamburg in 1527-28, though it did constitute the sole cargo aboard another Stralsund bound ship which departed Leith on 22 February 1528.[259] Scottish salt was, however, delivered regularly to Prussia. It was recorded on the cargo list of most Scottish ships arriving at Danzig in the fifteenth century, and some was then transported as far inland as Torun.[260] Indeed, at Danzig its value constituted 27% of that of all Scottish imports between 1460 and 1530.[261] The western Baltic too was a regular recipient of Scottish salt. In 1510-11 thirty chalders were sent from Leith to Copenhagen, and another seven chalders were laden on one of two Copenhagen bound vessels in 1512-13. Even more was dispatched in 1527-28: twenty-eight chalders for Holstein and twelve lasts and thirty-four chalders to three unidentified Danish ports.[262] By the mid-sixteenth century Sweden too had become a recipient of Scottish salt. In 1546 it was the most common cargo aboard the eleven Scottish ships arriving at Lödöse.[263] Still, the volume of these exports should not be exaggerated. While at Lödöse Scottish salt amounted to 18.7% of the town's salt imports, at Danzig, despite the regularity of its supplies, Scottish salt accounted for 2.8% of the town's total salt imports in 1476 and for only 1.9% in 1506.[264]

Salt exports were, however, balanced by imports, especially north of Tay, where local supplies were limited and demand (especially for the preservation

[256] PRO London, E122/130/12, fos. 3v, 4r.
[257] StA Lüneburg, AH IV, no. 1(a)5, a.3043; AB6(1), 96; *HUB*, xi, nos. 866, 872.
[258] P. Dollinger, *Die Hanse* (3rd ed., Stuttgart, 1981), 512.
[259] NAS Edinburgh, E71/29/2; E71/29/3, fo. 12r; E71/29/4, fos. 5v, 6r.
[260] E.g. WAP Gdansk, 300/19/1, fos. 3v, 25v; 300/19/3, fos. 60v, 65v, 85r, 86r, 91v, 92v, 131v, 132r, 165r, 175v-177r, 180v, 188r; 300/19/5, pp. 9, 13, 31, 119, 135, 146, 173, 221, 245, 251, 257, 363; 300/19/8, 55, 126; 300D/68/270. See too *HUB*, viii, no. 1019; ix, no. 46.
[261] Samsonowicz, 'Engländer und Schotten in Danzig im Spätmittelalter', 50.
[262] NAS Edinburgh, E71/29/2; E71/29/3; E71/29/4, fos. 5r, 10r, 10v, 11r.
[263] Dow, 'Scottish trade with Sweden', 71.
[264] H. Samsonowicz, 'Handel zagraniczny Gdańska w drugiej połowiej, XV wieku', *Przegald Historyczny*, 47 (1956), 303, 325.

of fish) was high. The singular importance of salt as a preservative is, indeed, inferred by the somewhat alarmed tones in which the Aberdeen council dispatched David Menzies to Flanders in 1449 to procure a cargo of salt. He was to depart 'in al haste'.[265] The Netherlands was not, however, the only source of salt imports. A little came from England – in 1437 a London fishmonger wisely planned to take salt with him before heading to Aberdeen to procure salmon. More came from the Bay of Bourgneuf, some of it via England.[266] And by the early sixteenth century still more came from the Baltic. It was presumably Lüneburg salt that merchants from Stralsund and Greifswald delivered to Edinburgh in 1508 and 1514.[267]

Coal exports too faced competition, especially from north-eastern England. Indeed, in the later fourteenth century towns north of Tay often looked to Newcastle, rather than to the Forth, to supply their carbon needs. In some years almost one hundred chalders were laden on Scottish vessels visiting the Tyne, most of them from Aberdeen, Dundee and Perth.[268] Although some coal continued to be sent to Scotland from Newcastle, the trade became much less regular in the later fifteenth and sixteenth centuries – a sign, perhaps, that Scottish coal production was expanding, as is indeed suggested by the growing customs payments paid on coal in Scotland.[269] Nevertheless, most continental markets were still served predominantly from the Tyne rather than the Forth. The French, for example, were among the major customers for English coal: 7,398 of the 10,402 chalders exported from Newcastle between 1499 and 1509 went on French ships.[270] By contrast, none was sent from Leith to France in 1510-11 or 1512-13, though small shipments are recorded on other occasions – for instance to Dieppe in 1478-79 and again in 1527-28.[271] Occasional shipments to English ports are also recorded.[272] But the steadiest market for Scottish coal was probably to be found in the Baltic

---

[265] CA Aberdeen, CR/5/2, 741. For examples of other Netherlandish salt imports, mainly to Aberdeen, see *CDS*, iv, nos. 146, 462; v, no. 1036; *Halyburton's Ledger*, 178-79, 181, 194-95, 223, 227-28, 230, 232; CA Aberdeen, CR/5/1, 304; CR/9, 536.

[266] E.g. *ER*, iv, 474; vii, 578; viii, 389, 455, 539, 545, 620; ix, 63, 145; xiii, 391; *Rot. Scot.*, ii, 124, 150; *CDS*, iv, no. 1102; v, no. 1080; Bernard, *Navires et Gens de Mer à Bordeaux*, iii, 70-1; PRO London, E122/12/10, fo. 4v; E122/60/3, fo. 18r; E122/64/16, fo. 9r; E122/99/24 fo. 15r; E122/99/26, fo. 5a; E122/138/21, m. 6.

[267] *Edin. Recs.*, i, 114-16, 148-49.

[268] PRO London, E122/106/5, m. 1-3r, 9d; E122/106/16; E122/106/18, m. 1r, 2r; E122/106/19, m. 1r, 3r; E122/106/21, m. 1r, 2r, 2d, 3d; E122/106/22, m. 3d, 4r, 4d; E122/138/21, m. 6; E122/106/41, fo. 1v; E122/106/42, fo. 1v. See too J.B. Blake, 'The medieval coal trade of north-east England: some fourteenth-century evidence', *NH*, 2 (1967), 1-16.

[269] PRO London, E122/107/57, m. 4d; E122/108/2, m. 1r; E122/108/4, m. 6r; E122/108/7, m. 5d; *The Accounts of the Chamberlains of Newcastle-upon-Tyne, 1508-1511*, ed. C.M. Fraser (Newcastle, 1987), 200; *ER*, ix, 63; xii, 368. For Scottish coal exports, see Lynch and Stevenson, 'Overseas trade: the middle ages to the sixteenth century', 260; Guy, 'The Scottish export trade', 80.

[270] J.F. Wade, 'The overseas trade of Newcastle-upon-Tyne in the late middle ages', *NH*, 30 (1994), 40.

[271] NAS Edinburgh, E71/29/2; E71/29/3; E71/29/4, fo. 9r; Mollat, *Compatabilité du Port de Dieppe*, 93.

[272] E.g. PRO London, E122/62/5, m.2d; NfRO Norwich, Y/C4/169, m. 16r; Y/C4/193, m. 1r.

and the Netherlands. Although none was sent from Leith in 1510-11, six chalders were dispatched to Copenhagen, and six more to Stralsund, in 1512-13. Another eighteen chalders were bound for Hamburg, five for Holstein and three for Danzig in 1527-28. In the same year forty-one chalders were sent from Leith to Veere, Middelburg and Amsterdam.[273] Danzig, however, probably obtained most of its coal supplies from Polish mines and none was sent from Scotland to Lödöse in 1546.[274]

Other minerals featured much more prominently among Scottish imports than exports. The prohibition imposed by the English crown in *c.*1282 on Scottish, Norwegian and Manx trade with Wales included a specific embargo on iron, but this was probably a precautionary measure, rather than an indication of Scottish supplies reaching the rebellious Welsh.[275] Still, the Isle of Man was one source of minerals, and some of its ore was sought by Scots. In 1292 John Comyn, earl of Buchan, requested permission from the English crown to extract lead from the Calf of Man, for construction work which he was undertaking at Cruggleton Castle in Galloway.[276] On the east coast lead featured prominently among Newcastle's exports, and by at least the later fourteenth century some was dispatched to Scotland – almost seventy hundredweight, for instance, aboard two Dundee vessels in 1391-92.[277] By the early sixteenth century, however, lead was acquired more frequently from Hull than Newcastle and, to a lesser extent, from Scarborough, Boston and Lynn too.[278] Halyburton, meanwhile, rarely purchased lead in the Netherlands for his Scottish customers.[279]

Iron imports came from a variety of sources. Prussian iron is recorded from the earlier fifteenth century. It subsequently accounted for about 3% of the total value of exports to Scotland from Danzig in the later fifteenth and early sixteenth centuries. By 1546 iron was also one of the key elements in Swedish trade: it was freighted on fourteen of the sixteen Scottish ships leaving Lödöse in 1546.[280] Meanwhile, Spanish and French iron is commonly recorded in Scotland from the fifteenth century, though among the crown's

---

[273] NAS Edinburgh, E71/29/3, fos. 2v, 12r; E71/29/4, fos. 2r-3v, 6r, 7v, 10r, 11r.
[274] See, however, Dow, 'Scottish trade with Sweden', 72, for small amounts of coal sent to Nylöse in the 1560s.
[275] *CDS*, v, no. 46.
[276] *CDS*, ii, no, 616.
[277] PRO London, E122/106/21, m. 2v; E122/138/21/21, m. 6; E122/108/8, m. 1r, 4r.
[278] For Hull, PRO London, E122/60/3, fo. 17v, 18r, 25r, 26r; E122/64/6, fo. 6v; E122/64/15, fo. 9v, 10r; E122/64/16, fo. 10; for Scarborough, PRO London, E122/64/10, fo. 20v; for Boston, E122/12/12, m. 1r; for Lynn, PRO London, E122/99/16, fo. 2v; E122/99/24, fo. 8v, 15; E122/99/26, fo. 3v, 5r. See too *ER*, viii, 199; xii, 84, xiii, 90.
[279] *Halyburton's Ledger*, 117. By the early sixteenth century some lead was also re-exported to Denmark: NAS Edinburgh, E71/29/4, fos. 10v, 11r.
[280] For iron in general, see Gemmill and Mayhew, *Changing Values*, 338-44. For references to Prussian iron, see for example, *ER*, iv, 437; v, 150; *TA*, ix, 105, 114, 260, 283, 348, 408, 415; x, 10, 50, 90; H. Samsonowicz, 'Engländer und Schotten in Danzig im Spätmittelalter', 50. For Swedish iron, see *ER*, iv, 412; Dow, 'Scottish trade with Sweden', 69; CA Dundee, BHCB/2, fos. 57r, 155r.

purchases the latter declined from the 1540s as supplies of Danzig iron grew.[281] Some iron, like lead, was also laden aboard Scottish vessels in the eastern English ports.[282] Not all of these imports arrived in Scotland direct from source. Much of that which came from England is likely to have been of continental origin and re-exported to Scotland; and much of that described as Prussian was probably re-exported Swedish ware. The occasional presence of Spanish merchants in Scottish ports is probably connected with the iron or wine trades; and when in 1432 the Dundee merchant John Lovell was dispossessed of 180 iron bars near Oléron, we may presume that he had acquired his cargo either in France or Spain.[283] Yet, even in the early sixteenth century, much iron was purchased in the Low Countries.[284]

Aside from iron and lead, copper and tin were also imported. The Baltic was a source of copper, though other supplies – including sixty pounds of 'old copper' laden on a Dysart vessel at Hull in 1510-11 – came from England and the Netherlands, two areas from which tin (mined above all in Cornwall) was also procured.[285] Nevertheless, neither of these metals, nor alum, was traded in substantial amounts, not only by comparison with iron and lead, but also when set against the supplies of pewter which were imported by the early sixteenth century.[286] The greatest premium among metal imports was, however, placed on silver, a commodity in scarce circulation in the fifteenth century, yet one which was deemed essential for the production of currency. Parliamentary statutes regularly implored that, whatever else they brought from foreign parts, merchants should also seek to return home with supplies of silver.[287]

A Miscellany of Manufactures

Although raw materials dominated medieval Scotland's international trading links, for the elite at least trade served another important purpose: it provided

---

[281] For additional examples of French iron, not included in the prices lists compiled by Gemmill and Mayhew, see *ER*, vi, 496; *TA*, ii, 276; vii, 211, 228-29, 342, 345, 358, 489; ix, 165; x, 121, 128; Mollat, *Compatabilité du Port de Dieppe*, 92. For additional examples of Spanish iron, see *TA*, i, 249-50; ii, 85, 276- 77; vii, 215, 221, 228, 345, 358, 360, 488, 496, 500, 502; viii, 118, 121, 177, 188, 192, 446, 448; ix, 64, 105, 114, 213, 251.

[282] For Newcastle, PRO London, E122/108/4, m. 6r; for Hull, PRO London, E122/64/15, fos. 9v, 10r. 16v; E122/64/16, fos. 9v, 10, 17r, 18r; for Lynn, PRO London, E122/99/24, fo. 15; E122/99/26, fo. 3v. See too *ER*, viii, 63, 145, 464, for the import of iron from England.

[283] *A Calendar of Early Chancery Proceedings Relating to West Country Shipping, 1388-1493*, ed. D.M. Gardiner, (Devon and Cornwall Record Soc., 1976), nos. 24-5; *CDS*, v, nos 1012, 1014; *CPR 1426-36*, 197-98.

[284] *Halyburton's Ledger*, 11-12, 34, 39, 43, 48, 57-5, 69, 72, 75, 114, 116, 125, 168, 201, 203, 207-8, 232; *CDS*, iv, no. 146.

[285] *TA*, iv, 254, 284, 301, 481, 514; v, 99; PRO London, E122/60/3, fo. 26r. For alum, used in cloth manufacturing, see for example PRO London, E122/109/9; *Halyburton's Ledger*, 201; *TA*, iv, 90, 511.

[286] PRO London, E122/60/3, fo. 25r; E122/64/15, fo. 16v; E122/64/16, fos. 9v-10v, 17r, 18r.

[287] *APS*, ii, 23, 37, 46, 86, 90, 92, 105, 221; *Edin. Recs.*, ii, 203. On the dearth of silver in fifteenth-century Europe, see J. Day, 'The great bullion famine of the fifteenth century', *PP*, 79 (1978), 3-54.

noble households with the means to acquire the finer things of life which were part and parcel of aristocratic culture across the Latin west. We have already witnessed some aspects of this trade: the development of the art market, the acquisition of books and hunting accoutrements and the trade in silks and spices. But there were other non-essentials too with which, with their greater disposable income, the aristocracies of town and country also chose to indulge themselves.

Although much cloth was imported by the yard, some ready-made clothes and soft furnishings also came from abroad. James IV, for instance, purchased a pair of velvet pantouns from the Netherlands in 1503 and some ready-made hose, made from English cloth, at Dumfries in 1504. Meanwhile, the Dysart ship *Trinity* carried three silk girdles from Hull in 1541-42.[288] Hats and bonnets, however, were the most commonly acquired items of clothing. In 1499 the Aberdeen merchant Andrew Cullan stocked up with almost fifty hats of different colours. These were bought in the Low Countries, as were those of Master Richard Lawson, whose new headgear included two items 'of the nyow fasson'. Those made from velvet (acquired in both England and the Netherlands) were particularly popular, though in 1411 the duke of Albany preferred three scarlet caps.[289] By the early sixteenth century boots, shoes and slippers too were being shipped from England – not in great quantities, the four pairs of boots and five pairs of shoes, freighted aboard the Wemyss ship *Petyr* in 1541-42, being fairly typical.[290] James IV, however, acquired a pair of shoes made from Portuguese leather.[291]

Aside from clothing, leading aristocratic households were also bedecked with other fabric-based items. Featherbeds were especially popular towards the end of the period. Halyburton acquired no less than eight in Antwerp for the duke of Ross in 1495 and James IV bought nine, made in Flanders, in 1501.[292] In addition cushions and cushion coverings were imported. Those described at Boston as 'course' were presumably not intended for the wealthiest customer, though aristocrats certainly were among the buyers of mats and carpets, acquired in both England, France and the Netherlands from the later fifteenth century.[293]

Manufactured metal products had traditionally been purchased in Netherlandish markets. In addition to functional pots, locks, keys, mortars and pestles, expensive chalices and goblets of silver and copper and ornamental objects, such as candlesticks and candelabra, came too – as did personal

[288] *TA*, ii, 212, 323; PRO London, E122/64/16, fo. 10r
[289] *Halyburton's Ledger*, 160, 180, 184, 235, 271; PRO London, E122/64/15, fo. 9v; E122/99/26, fos. 5r, 7r; E122/99/27, fo. 3v; *CDS*, iv, nos. 462, 802; *TA*, ii, 212, 222; iv, 198-99, 203-4, 206.
[290] PRO London, E122/64/15, fo. 9v; E122/64/16, fos. 10r, 10v, 17r-18r.
[291] *TA*, ii, 212.
[292] *Halyburton's Ledger*, 12, 87; TA, ii, 35, 216; *CDS*, v, no. 1080; PRO London, E122/64/16, fo. 10v.
[293] *TA*, ii, 43; vi, 314; PRO London, E122/12/9, fo. 2r; E122/64/16, fos. 10r, 17r; *Halyburton's Ledger*, 162, 165, 251.

jewellery.[294] In 1368 three gold rings, worth £10, were freighted aboard an Aberdeen bound ship from Sluis and in the 1490s Andrew Halyburton acquired several rings, some adorned with rubies and sapphires, for his more well-to-do clients, such as the duke of Ross and the archdeacon of St Andrews.[295] James I and James IV both bought gold rings made in Flanders, and the latter probably acquired others in France.[296] Pearls alone among the fashionable stones were available in number from Scotland.[297]

The developing trade with both England and France from the fifteenth century also encompassed the exchange of more mundane metallic objects. The abbot of Glenluce had purchased six shovels and six spades from France by the 1520s, and iron pots figured among the cargo of a Dieppe vessel which docked at Dundee in 1551.[298] Some equally basic accoutrements, though in much greater quantity, came from England. James I returned to Scotland from his captivity in England with cups, tin vessels and pewter pots and also two candelabra. By the early sixteenth century pewter dishes and vessels were relatively common Scottish acquisitions south of the border, but iron and brass pots came too, along with occasional candlesticks.[299] More alarmingly, from a dietician's perspective, that nemesis of the modern Scottish diet, the frying pan, also made its appearance. Five of them, together with three drying pans, ten kettles, 120 shovels and 150 pots, were laden on the *Clement* of Kirkcaldy, which left Hull on 8 March 1542.[300]

Some metal objects were intended to have a more immediate impact on health. Bows and crossbows were made at Edinburgh Castle in the later fourteenth and fifteenth centuries and James IV acquired several daggers and swords from a Scottish cutler – but both arms and armour were also imported. Ten swords, three of them 'old', were brought from Flanders in 1395. It was there too that arrows and armour for James II and a military engine delivered to Stirling Castle were acquired in the 1440s.[301] In moments of peace England too was a source of arms. The duke of Albany sought two sets of armour there in 1401, while James I returned from captivity in 1424 with bows, crossbows and their fittings.[302] Knights also required saddles for

[294] *CDS*, iv, nos. 146, 462; *Halyburton's Ledger*, 87-8, 108, 114, 159-60, 162, 184, 249-51, 254, 273; *TA*, ii, 241.

[295] *CDS*, iv, nos. 146, 462; *Halyburton's Ledger*, 12, 87-8, 108, 114, 154, 156, 159-60, 162, 165, 176, 184, 216-17, 249-51, 254, 273.

[296] *ER*, iv, 681-82; *TA*, ii, 199, 240; iv, 331.

[297] For the export of pearls, see for example SA Bremen, 1/Bc 1445 August 4; *Halyburton's Ledger*, 139; Pii II, *Commentarii*, i, 46; *Quellen zur Geschichte des Kölner Handels und Verkehrs*, ed. B. Kuske (Bonn, 1917-34), ii, 411-12; Mollat, *Les Affaires de Jacques Coeur*, i, 134.

[298] *Wigtownshire Chrs.*, no. 45; CA Dundee, BHCB/2, fo. 104r.

[299] *ER*, iv, 628; *CDS*, iv, no. 967; PRO London, E122/64/15, fos. 9v, 10r, 16r; E122/64/16, fos. 10r, 10v, 17r; E122/99/16, fo. 2v; E122/99/26, fos. 3r, 6r, 7r.

[300] PRO London, E122/64/16, fo. 10r.

[301] *CDS*, ii, nos. 283, 462; *ER*, iii, 82; v, 149, 382; vi, 310, 499, 582; *TA*, ii, 22, 28, 202, 205, 207, 223, 230, 233.

[302] *CDS*, iv, nos. 584, 967.

their horses and Halyburton made occasional purchases of these in the Netherlands in the 1490s, though James I bought at least one in England and James IV looked more frequently to France for his.[303] Halyburton, however, did not deal in arms, his only purchase of gunpowder intended for the peaceful bishop of Aberdeen, probably in connection with the construction work being carried out on King's College.[304]

Altogether less harmful was soap. This, indeed, was a frequent import, both from the Netherlands and England, as, less certainly, was glass and, less frequently, clocks.[305] Occasionally too we find items for industrial or agricultural use. Combs for carding wool were brought from Flanders in 1395, along with shuttles for weavers; and on one of the very rare occasions upon which a Scottish ship put in at Southampton, probably on its return from France in 1435-36, it was carrying quernstones, used for grinding grain.[306]

It is difficult to avoid a list-like approach to discussion of manufactured imports. They were multifarious and Scots, or the wealthier among them, seem to have possessed an insatiable desire for foreign manufactures. Yet, by contrast with this diverse array of imports, very few goods manufactured in Scotland, aside from cloth, were exported. The 1460s appears to have seen a surfeit of glove production – or at least attempts to flog over fifty pairs of them, and over a hundred purses, in Hull and Scarborough. A few daggers were sold in England in this decade too, as were some shoes. On other occasions some leather doublets found their way to England.[307] The list is considerably shorter, and it is this apparent imbalance in the trade of manufactures, combined with the fall in exports of wool and hides, which has prompted many historians to argue that later medieval Scotland was living beyond its means. It had not always been so.

Balancing the Books

The thirteenth-century evidence points to a booming economy in which money supply increased sharply. Of course, this was not a panacea for all. Simultaneous population growth probably made for more intense competition for land, for higher rents, for smaller peasant holdings and for the cultivation of less fertile lands. Nevertheless, peasants who possessed their own sheep are still likely to have prospered, since wool sales seem to have remained buoyant for most of the century.[308] Of course, the demand for wool

---

[303] *Halyburton's Ledger*, 12, 136; PRO London, E122/161/11, m. 9d; *TA*, i, 330; ii, 22, 31, 33-4, 41, 204, 223, 230; iii, 51, 206, 252, 263, 365; iv, 118-19, 122, 308, 412. See too *ER*, v, 382.

[304] *Halyburton's Ledger*, 183.

[305] *ER*, viii, 545; *Halyburton's Ledger*, 41, 43, 53, 59, 63, 65, 67, 76, 83, 91, 168, 179, 191, 203, 223; PRO London, E122/60/3, fo. 26r; E122/64/2, fo. 26r; E122/64/16, fos. 10r, 17v; E122/99/24, fo. 14r

[306] *CDS*, iv, no. 462; *The Local Port Book for Southampton, 1435-36*, ed. D.B. Foster (Southampton, 1963), 2.

[307] PRO London, E122/61/71, m. 3r; E122/62/7, m. 2r-3v; E122/62/9, m. 2r; E122/64/16, fo. 13v; E122/99/26, fo. 4v.

[308] Gemill and Mayhew, *Changing Values*, 362-64; Mayhew, 'Alexander III – a silver age?', 53-73.

worked primarily to the advantage of aristocratic landholders who owned bigger flocks. Moreover, their income was often enhanced by sizeable foreign assets. Kings had long since held territorial interests in England, and, although their attempts to assert political control over the northern counties of England ultimately failed, the resolution of the border issue in 1237 had left Alexander II and his son with extensive estates in Northumberland and Cumberland.[309] King John was in a still more favourable situation, for in addition to his share of the existing royal lands, he was able to add a sizeable familial inheritance, not just in England, but also in Picardy.[310] The foreign possessions of the royal dynasties were unusually vast, but many other secular lords also possessed estates in England and/or Ireland. While some, such as Alan of Galloway and Thomas, earl of Atholl, in the early thirteenth century, saw their hold on Irish lands crumble almost as quickly as they had been acquired, other holdings proved more durable. Indeed, by the end of the thirteenth century virtually every Scottish earl and a good many lesser barons possessed estates in England and/or Ireland – as did at least eight Scottish monasteries, if we include the possessions which Whithorn acquired on the Isle of Man in the early fourteenth century.[311] These lands remain a much neglected topic of study and how precisely, and to what extent, they enriched their owners remains uncertain, though profit from such holdings they surely did.[312]

The income from both wool sales and overseas assets declined dramatically from the fourteenth century, though the catalyst for this turnaround remains a matter of debate. One school of thought postulates war as the great harbinger of economic decline.[313] There is clearly some merit to this thesis, for conflict with England led to the forfeiture of Scottish-owned lands in England and Ireland and to the periodic disruption of thirteenth-century patterns of commercial activity within the British Isles. It also, as the chroniclers were quick to point out, led to intermittent, but nonetheless savagely destructive, attacks upon both towns and the countryside. Indeed, one might take the war thesis further, for conflict in Flanders and tension between France and England disrupted the demand for and the supply of Scottish wool as well. Yet these arguments have not gone unchallenged, and the emphasis of other scholars has been more firmly placed on plague, rather than war, as the great

---

[309] M.F. Moore, *Lands of the Scottish Kings in England* (London, 1915), passim.

[310] G. Stell, 'The Balliol family and the Great Cause of 1291-2' in K.J. Stringer, ed., *The Nobility of Medieval Scotland* (Edinburgh, 1985), 150-65.

[311] B.R.S. Megaw, 'The barony of St Trinian's in the Isle of Man', *TDGAS*, 27 (1950), 173-82.

[312] See, however, K.J. Stringer, *Earl David of Huntingdon, 1152-1219* (Edinburgh, 1985); idem, 'Periphery and core in thirteenth-century Scotland: Alan son of Roland, lord of Galloway and constable of Scotland' in A. Grant and K.J. Stringer, eds., *Medieval Scotland: Crown, lordship and community* (Edinburgh, 1993), 82-113; A. Ross, 'Men for all seasons? The Strathbogie earls of Atholl and the wars of independence, c.1290-c.1335', *NS*, 20 (2000), 27-30.

[313] Stevenson, 'Trade with the south', 187-88; M. Lynch, *Scotland: A new history* (London, 1992), 70-3.

stimulus behind fourteenth-century economic change.[314] Put simply, while war disrupted trade and stimulated the redirection of commercial contacts, plague killed trade by removing, at the swoop of a flea, perhaps a third of the producers and consumers upon whom commercial activity depended. Of course, the correlation between plague deaths and trading levels was neither direct nor simultaneous. The disposable income of survivors increased and to some extent sustained demand at least until the later fourteenth century. Nevertheless, it is difficult not to concur with the assumption that the Black Death had the most profound effect on the economy of not just Scotland, but Europe as a whole. Moreover, and this is surely significant, the first statistical evidence of a decline in Scottish exports comes not from the years of conflict before 1357, but from the later fourteenth-century customs accounts.

The Scottish customs accounts are not, however, an infallible source. Indeed, the great canard of a post-plague (or post-war) trading deficit rests primarily on the partial glimpse of overseas trade which they afford. Admittedly there is seemingly corroborative evidence for the gloomy commercial picture which the customs data provide. The dearth of bullion was repeatedly bewailed in the Scottish parliament and, according to Netherlandish journalese, 'nothing is to be had in the country [and] things come ready made from Flanders'.[315] The scarcity of bullion could have been the consequence, as Froissart implied, of costly imports outstripping exports. Froissart, however, like most journalists, possessed an almost incurable predilection for exaggeration and a limited awareness of wider contexts. It is important to note that the great silver dearth of the fifteenth century was not simply a Scottish phenomenon. Most of Europe suffered a similar ailment, caused by a balance of payments deficit with the Levant and resulting in currency devaluation almost everywhere. Scottish devaluation, though considerably greater than that in England, was no worse than that in the wealthy commercial emporium of Milan and less severe than that in Castile.[316] That is not to minimise the problems which Scotland suffered. Yet, in seeking to attribute blame for the situation, it was often at clerics, rather than merchants, that parliament wagged its collective finger, for the former exported silver not to pay for goods, but rather to obtain preferment at the papal court. There are, then, other possible culprits for the Scottish bullion shortage, and we cannot assume that the predicament was necessarily the fault of spendthrift merchants. The corroborative evidence for a Scottish trade

---

[314] Gemmill and Mayhew, *Changing Values*, 364-71; Grant, *Independence and Nationhood*, 73-6.

[315] *Chron. Froissart* (Lettenhove), x, 336.

[316] J. Day, 'The great bullion famine of the fifteenth century', *PP*, 79 (1978), 3-54; C. Cipolla, 'Currency depreciation in medieval Europe' in S.L. Thrupp, ed., *Change in Medieval Society: Europe north of the Alps, 1050-1500* (New York, 1964), 227-36; R. Nicholson, 'Scottish monetary problems in the fourteenth and fifteenth centuries', and C.E. Challis, 'Debasement: the Scottish experience in the fifteenth and sixteenth centuries' in D.M. Metclaf, ed., *Coinage in Medieval Scotland, 1100-1600* (Oxford, 1977), 103-14, 171-82.

deficit is therefore suspect, and, in order to prove its existence, we are thrown back onto the Scottish customs accounts.

Aside from the unreliability of the transcriptions presented in the printed version of the customs accounts, the essential problem with the customs data is that it offers only partial illumination of medieval Scottish trade. The decline in wool and hide exports which they reveal from the later fourteenth century is, no doubt, broadly accurate, as is the inability of the crown to raise significant sums from the levies imposed on other commodities from the fifteenth century. On the other hand, the customs accounts reveal little about imports, since only those from England and Ireland were taxed, and nothing about a range of exports which were exempt from taxation or upon which customs had lapsed. They do not, for instance, take any account of goods to the value of £4,618-18s-0d (mainly cloth) which were dispatched by almost 150 Scottish merchants to Danzig in 1444 – and upon which one might have expected almost £300 to have accrued to the exchequer in customs payments on cloth alone. Only once in the fifteenth century, it may be noted, did the cloth custom yield more than £300 *per annum* – in 1499.[317] This was clearly a substantial amount of cloth which Scottish merchants had found to export in 1444. We only happen to know about it because it fell into the hands of Bremen pirates. Yet its existence begs the question of how many similarly lucrative cargoes have escaped the historical record.

Meanwhile, we should not underestimate the value of other seemingly unglamorous exports, such as fish and salt, which together with cheap cloth constituted the bulk of exports to England. Anglo-Scottish trade seems to have been generally, and increasingly, profitable. At Hull, for instance, annual sales outstripped purchases by less than £100 in the later fifteenth century, but by between £200 and £400 in the 1530s and 1540s, despite the increasing purchases which Scots made of expensive spices and manufactured articles in the later period.[318] Unfortunately, only for a few English ports is this sort of calculation possible. But since exports to France were of a broadly similar nature and (on the basis of the Leith customs accounts of 1510-11 and 1512-13) of a comparable, if not greater, volume, we may wonder whether Franco-Scottish trade was not similarly profitable. There may even be lessons to learn from the English evidence with regard to Netherlandish trade. Although the Low Countries market for Scottish fish was negligible towards the end of our period, the proceeds from wool sales, however diminishing, may still have been adequate to satisfy the broad range of imports which Scots acquired there. Some, though not all, of Halyburton's customers prospered from their wool dealings. In 1494, for instance, John Patterson bought expensive cloths

[317] D. Ditchburn, 'Bremen piracy and Scottish periphery: the North Sea world in the 1440s' in A. Macinnes, T. Riis and F. Pedersen, eds., *Gun, Ships and Bibles* (East Linton, 2000, forthcoming).
[318] PRO London, E122/62/5; E122/62/7; E122/62/9; E122/64/15; E122/64/16.

to the value of over £88 from the proceeds of five sacks of wool worth over £120.[319]

Despite this relatively optimistic assessment of the Scottish economy – which finds some support in a recent analysis of Scottish price movements in the later medieval period[320] – it is important not to exaggerate. Foreign trade probably accounted for only a small proportion of Scotland's gross domestic product and, in overall European terms, the volume of Scottish trade was small. Scottish ships accounted for only 3% of the total which visited Newcastle in the later fifteenth century; for 6.9% of those anchored at Sluis in 1464; for only 5% of those from Holland and Zeeland which visited Danzig in 1476; and for only 3.8% of those that passed the Sound in the early sixteenth century.[321] In terms of value Scottish trade was also limited, accounting for only about 3% of Danzig's imports and for about 6% of Hull's imports (excluding wine) in the later fifteenth century.[322] Still, by at least the sixteenth century, the proportionate significance of Scottish trade was growing in at least some ports. Scottish vessels accounted for 47% of maritime traffic at Hull in 1541-42 and for 23.5% of vessel movements at Lödöse by 1546.[323] Of course, neither Hull nor Lödöse figured among the great commercial loci of early sixteenth-century trade, and it would perhaps be wise not to read too much into this apparent upsurge in commercial activity. The total volume of goods passing through Hull, at least, was lower in the later fifteenth and early sixteenth century than it been before. There the Scots had cornered a larger share of a diminishing cake. Moreover, even if Scotland's overseas trade was a good deal more lucrative than is often suggested, the vast bulk of the population is less likely to have shared in the commercial prosperity of the fifteenth and sixteenth centuries than it had in the thirteenth century. Many of the 'new' exports, such as fish and salt, were less widely owned than sheep, the main origin of thirteenth-century foreign earnings. And while in the early sixteenth century William Dunbar heaped his wrath upon the growing wealth of Edinburgh merchants, others had decided that emigration offered a more secure future than the Scottish landscape.[324]

---

[319] *Halyburton's Ledger*, 36-7; but see ibid, 130-31, for a loss of £1-9s-2d on the dealings of Edward Spyttall.

[320] Gemill and Mayhew, *Changing Values*.

[321] J.F. Wade, 'The overseas trade of Newcastle-upon-Tyne in the late middle ages', *NH*, 30 (1994), 34; R. Degryse, 'De schepen in de haven van Sluis in het voorjaar 1464', *Mededelingen van de Marineakademie van belgie*, 20 (1968), 97-8; Samsonowicz, 'Handel zagraniczny Gdanska', 303, 336; RA København, Øresundtolregnskaber, 1503; 1527.

[322] Samsonowicz, 'Engländer und Schotten', 53; PRO London, E122/62/5; E122/62/7; E122/62/9.

[323] PRO London, E122/64/16; Dow, 'Scottish trade with Sweden', 68.

[324] Dunbar, *Poems*, 201-3.

5
Immigrants and Emigrants

Rotten, Skotten, Hollender und zegenn
Verderben's allerwegen
Da die seyn
Kann nichts gedien.[1]

In the Dark Ages Latin Christendom was under assault. Between the fourth and tenth centuries a great *Völkerwanderung* had witnessed Germanic tribes cross the Straits of Gibraltar and Vikings venture as far as Vinland. The migration of these and other pagan peoples was to have a profound impact not only on continental Europe but also on the land the Romans had called Caledonia. One tribe of Irish insurgents provided the medieval kingdom with its name. The gradual fusion of these *Scotti* with incoming Anglians and Scandinavians (and also with indigenous Picts and Britons) was to provide Scotland with its unusually complex, but not yet complete, ethnic mix. Anglo-French and Flemish settlers were still required to lace the cocktail and they did not arrive until the twelfth century.[2]

By then the pagan invaders had been Christianised. Indeed, not only had Latin Christendom survived the pagan onslaught. Its inhabitants were themselves on the march from 1096 as children and shepherds, churchmen and cavalry set out to claim new lands for Christ – and for themselves. While many of Christ's more humble soldiers ended up dead or in slavery, better organised crusading armies had successfully pushed the frontiers of Christendom out to more distant horizons. New kingdoms were established in the Holy Land, old kingdoms were expanded in Iberia and heathen territories were Catholicised around the Baltic. At the same time many of those who had remained at home made their own contribution to the expansion of Christendom's frontiers. In the under-populated recesses of the continent trees were felled, marshes were drained and wastelands were introduced to the plough.

The expansion of Europe, both internal and external, had been fuelled by an expanding population: more farmland had been required to feed more mouths. Demographic factors are also important in explaining why the two medieval ages of migration stuttered to a halt in the later middle ages. Demographic contraction was evident across much of Europe by the early

---

[1] 'Rats, Scots and Dutch are everywhere destructive; where they are nothing can thrive.' This late sixteenth-century German poem is noted in H. Marwick, *Merchant Lairds of Long Ago* (Kirkwall, 1939), ii, 46.
[2] G.W.S. Barrow, *The Anglo-Norman Era in Scottish History* (Oxford, 1996); L. Toorians, 'Twelfth-century Flemish settlement in Scotland' in G.G. Simpson, ed., *Scotland and the Low Countries, 1124-1994* (East Linton, 1996), 1-14.

fourteenth century. This was exacerbated by the advent of the Black Death in the mid-fourteenth century and population levels dwindled further as plague became recurrent and other deadly diseases, such as syphilis, took their toll. The pool of surplus manpower which had threatened Latin Christendom in the Dark Ages, and then been responsible for its expansion in the high middle ages, was no more. It followed that such migration as there was in the later middle ages was more in the genre of an *Einzelwanderung* than a *Völkerwanderung*. Even then, the attractions offered by Scotland to later medieval foreign migrants proved limited.

Immigrants: Rural Society

Contemporary estimates of the death rate ascribed to plague and other diseases are notoriously sparse for Scotland. The chronicler John of Fordun suggested that a third of the population succumbed to the first outbreak of plague in the mid-fourteenth century.[3] His estimate was low compared with the wilder sensationalism of many foreign chroniclers, perhaps suggesting that Scotland fared less badly than elsewhere. Yet, even if we allow for a measure of exaggeration in Fordun's seemingly cautious calculations, plague occasioned a haemorrhage in the demographic polity. Warfare with England, especially between 1296 and 1337, took its toll too. Nevertheless, it seems clear that peasant families wiped out by disease, war or natural impotence were not replaced by an influx of farmers and labourers from abroad.[4] Instead, where once cultivated land was not simply abandoned the size of native landholdings increased.

Meanwhile similar scourges had taken their toll on the aristocracy. These afflictions were met with a similar response. In the later middle ages aristocratic replenishment came not from outwith the realm, but rather from within. Heiresses, who in earlier centuries had often married Anglo-Norman incomers, were now routinely betrothed to natives. Such rare attempts as there were to intrude new foreign nobles – for instance the elevation of Wolfert van Borselen to the earldom of Buchan following his marriage to Mary Stewart in 1444 – produced little long term impact on the complexion of the higher aristocracy: their two sons both predeceased their father.[5] Similarly, in the thirteenth century male aristocrats had often looked abroad for wives: James the Stewart, for instance, had married Egidia de Burgh from Ireland in *c.*1290x96 and David de Strathbogie, earl of Atholl wed the Englishwoman Isabella de Dover before 1266.[6] But cross-border marriages

---

[3] *Chron. Fordun*, ii, 359; *Chron. Bower* (Watt), vii, 272-75.

[4] A few foreign miners (often of Germanic origin) are, however, recorded. See, for instance, *ER*, vii, 144.

[5] G.W. Watson, 'Wolfart van Borssele, earl of Buchan', *The Genealogist* (new series), 14 (1898), 10-11; idem, 'Wolfart van Borssele, earl of Buchan', *The Genealogist* (new series), 16 (1900), 136.

[6] G. Barrow and A. Royan, 'James, fifth Stewart of Scotland, 1260(?)-1309' in K.J. Stringer, ed., *Essays on the Nobility of Medieval Scotland* (Edinburgh, 1985), 166, 168; A. Ross, 'Men for all

were more unusual in later centuries. One famous exception was the marriage of Alexander Stewart, earl of Mar, and the Brabantine heiress Marie de Hoorn in 1408. It is suitably symbolic of the later 'Scotticisation' of the aristocracy that the couple cohabited for a mere eight days, parting in acrimony before Marie ever witnessed her husband's Scottish estates.[7]

Alien incomers were equally rare in between the social extremities of peasant and aristocrat. The foreigner most likely to have been encountered by a thirteenth-century Scot would probably have been a priest. Several foreigners had then occupied prominent ecclesiastical office: perhaps ten of the eighty-four men known to have held episcopal office in the thirteenth century were foreigners, most of them English, though their number also included one from Holland (Florence, bishop of Glasgow) and another from France (William Malvoisin, bishop of St Andrews).[8] It is likely that aliens were even more numerous at parish level. The identity of most of these ordinary priests remains obscure for the greater part of the thirteenth century, but when Anglo-Scottish hostilities broke out in 1296 at least twenty-six English priests were ejected from Scottish benefices.[9] Scottish political leaders were evidently wary of their allegiance. Equally convinced of their loyalty, and probably also of their value in explaining the English cause to largely illiterate parishioners, Edward I attempted to install a substantial number of Englishmen in Scottish parish churches once he had gained control of Scotland in 1296.[10] Indeed, he went further. At Jedburgh Scottish canons of suspect loyalty were evicted and replaced wholesale by a spiritual garrison of English regulars. They, in turn, were ejected by the resurgent Scots in 1313, the hapless English abbot, William of Yarm, and eleven canons seeking shelter in Thornton-on-Humber.[11]

As both Scots and English interfered with clerical livelihoods, their actions may well have politicised, or further politicised, ordinary clergymen. In 1296 one chaplain was so aggrieved by the English king's actions that he audaciously excommunicated Edward in Edinburgh's High Street.[12] We do not know what prompted this brave outburst by Thomas the chaplain, but it is perhaps as likely to have been fuelled by economic considerations as nationalistic sentiments, as Scots clergymen witnessed what they perhaps

---

seasons? The Strathbogie earls of Atholl and the wars of independence, *c.*1290-*c.*1335', *NS*, 20 (2000), 2.

[7] D. Ditchburn, 'The pirate, the policeman and the pantomime star: Aberdeen's alternative economy in the early fifteenth century,' *NS*, 12 (1992), 27. For other exceptions, concerning Islesmen seeking wives in Ireland, see, for example, *CDS*, iv, nos. 380, 792.

[8] On Florence, see *RRS*, ii, 30, 60. He was probably an absentee for much of his tenure of episcopal office. On Malvoisin, see Watt, *Graduates*, 374-79.

[9] *Chron. Fordun*, ii, 318; *Chron. Bower* (Watt), vi, 60-1; *The Correspondence, Inventories, Account Rolls and Law Proceedings of the Priory of Coldingham*, ed. J. Raine (Surtees Soc., 1841), 248, 251.

[10] E.g., Stevenson, *Documents*, ii, no. 368; *CDS*, ii, nos. 961, 998, 1000, 1008, 1017, 1023.

[11] Cowan and Easson, *Religious Houses*, 92.

[12] 'A plea roll of Edward I's army in Scotland, 1296', ed. C. Neville in *SHS Miscellany*, 11 (1990), no. 115.

regarded as their own livelihoods being distributed to Englishmen. Certainly Scottish clerics had long since acquired a reputation for frustrating the appointment of foreigners to church livings. Pope Nicholas IV had complained of their surliness in this respect in 1289.[13] It had perhaps been against the odds that, as we have seen, several Englishmen had obtained ecclesiastical preferment in Scotland before 1296. Whatever the case, few foreign clergymen can be traced in Scotland after the long years of warfare with England.

Immigrants: Court Society

Some clerics were probably brought to Scotland in the train of foreign queens. Queens, indeed, were important in making the court into a cosmopolitan institution, for they were often accompanied to their new homeland by a number of retainers. Mary of Guelders, for instance, appointed a number of Netherlandish officials to her own household, including Dutch masters of the stable and keepers of the wardrobe, as well as a tutor, a Gueldrian physician and more menial cooks.[14] Kings too recruited foreign retainers, the court of James IV including several black attendants, messengers and even a Moorish drummer, as well as a Danish cook and a French blacksmith.[15] More expensive services were provided by medical experts. These included many foreign educated Scottish doctors, though foreigners were also to be found – such as the Milanese Maninius Maneris (who attended Robert I), the Englishman John (during David II's reign), the Venetian Serapion (who served James II) and a 'Dutch' (?German) doctor from Sweden (retained by James IV).[16] There were other highly skilled specialists too – including Robert I's notary Rayner, son of James of Podiobonici; and the late fourteenth-century moneyer Bonagio.[17] Perhaps, however, the most visible foreigners were those whose expertise was military.

　　In most countries, and most notably of all in Italy, the development of paid military service provided a conduit for the social and political advancement of outsiders. By contrast, army recruitment in Scotland remained untainted by the professionalism of military endeavour evident elsewhere. When assembling their forces Scottish kings relied largely on the traditional obligation of all able bodied men to furnish unpaid service and only in the more specialist defence occupations did some foreigners find employment in Scotland. There was, however, a long tradition of this. Robert I had recruited the Flemish sea captain John Crabb. He was subsequently to

[13] *Foedera* (R), i, pt. ii, 707.

[14] *ER*, v, 386-87, 500, 535; vii, 49.

[15] M.E. Robbins, 'Black Africans at the court of James IV', *Review of Scottish Culture*, 12 (1999-2000), 34-45; *TA*, iii, 369, 386, 388, 391; iv, 59, 62, 75, 95, 97-8, 100, 118.

[16] *ER*, i, 169, 238, 616; vi, 3, 6, 12, 580, 625, 641; vii, 34, 144, 150; *TA*, iii, 103, 167-68, 176-77, 179, 190. For foreign educated Scottish medics, see, for instance, Watt, *Graduates*, 386, 427-29, 583.

[17] *RRS*, v, nos. 345, 554; *ER*, iii, 82, 655.

defect to the English but later kings too were to man their vessels with foreigners possessed of specialised seafaring skills.[18] The development of artillery from the mid-fourteenth century encouraged the recruitment of other specialists. James II retained a German gunner called Dietrich. His skills were probably required to service the great cannon Mons Meg, sent to the king by Duke Philip of Burgundy in 1457.[19] Other gunners, along with gunsmiths, gunwrights and manufacturers of gunpowder, were to find service with James III and James IV, notably the gunner Hannis, who served the latter consistently from *c*.1494 to 1508. Most of these artillery experts were of Germanic or Netherlandish origin – perhaps a reflection of the importance of the armaments industry in towns such as Cologne, Liège and Mons – though during James IV's reign and that of James V others gunners came from France.[20]

Artillery experts were well paid. Indeed, with a monthly wage of £5-6s-8d in 1513, the master-gunner Jakob received considerably greater remuneration than not only his Scottish counterparts but also many other foreign craftsmen engaged by the crown. The Flemish painter Piers, for example, earned only £2-16s-0d per month.[21] While there was perhaps a financial limit to the number of skilled gunners that the crown could afford, as yet few battles were won or lost on the basis of gunpowder. The overwhelming imperative to invest in these skilled practitioners in warfare and their equipment still, then, lay in the future.

If the science of medieval warfare placed a limited demand on specialist talents, the crown's unambitious military objectives also forestalled expensive military innovations. Following the aggressive acquisition of the Western Isles in the mid-thirteenth century, royal campaigns were generally geared towards the defence or recovery of the realm, rather than towards its expansion. In this official policy stood in marked contrast to that of the English crown, which maintained protracted and predatory interests in France and Scotland and more briefly in the Iberian peninsula too. As a consequence, Scottish kings had less need than their belligerent English counterparts to pay for mercenaries. Moreover, with the comparatively brief exception of the period from 1296 to the mid-1330s (and even then not consistently), the Scottish

---

[18] E.W.M. Balfour-Melville, 'Two John Crabbs', *SHR*, 39 (1960), 31-4; *TA*, iv, 503-7.

[19] *ER*, vi, 385, 496, 498-99, 581; vii, 32, 34, 144, 211, 362, 422, 501, 589-90, 663; viii, 120; C. Gaier, 'The origin of Mons Meg', *Journal of the Arms and Armour Society*, 5 (1967), 425-31. Dietrich was replaced by Hannis, another gunner of Germanic origin, for whom see *ER*, viii, 189, 253; *TA*, i, 71.

[20] For Hannis, see *TA*, i, 232, 236, 284, 295, 300, 302, 306, 310, 320, 323, 345, 347, 387; ii, 25, 94, 275, 293, 333, 431, 443, 452, 473; iii, 118, 121, 125, 139, 141, 200, 203, 327, 332-33, 350, 395; iv, 69, 97-8, 100-1, 110, 113, 115, 122, 126, 131, 135. For artillery experts from France, see, for example, *TA*, i, 232, 236, 299; iv, 126-27, 276-77, 348, 372, 378, 439; v, 439; and for the probably German George of Almane, Jakob and another Hannis, *TA*, iv, 63, 106, 108-9, 127, 277, 293, 372, 480, 482, 492.

[21] *TA*, iii, 325; iv, 277, 480.

polity was rarely subjected to the sustained military pressure endured by several other states in the Latin west. It was precisely such pressure, coupled with the unreliability and depletion of local manpower, which prompted the French crown and many of the Italian states to recruit large mercenary forces. Indeed, Scottish military conservatism was arguably more a reflection of political success, than it was of financial impoverishment.

With little need to recruit soldiers, foreign troops were more likely to witness Scottish terrain either as loyal allies or as hostile opponents in English service. Small contingents of French soldiers were occasionally dispatched to aid the Scots in the wars with England during the fourteenth century and a larger force arrived under the command of Jean de Vienne in 1385. Meanwhile, the Edwardian armies which invaded Scotland between 1296 and 1337 included not only large English and Welsh contingents, but also a sizeable Irish element. Lightly armed, but highly mobile, mounted Irish hobelars were so well suited to Scottish conditions that Edward I attempted to have Englishmen imitate them.[22] Subsequently continental soldiers too were to experience the Scottish wars. In 1314, at the battle of Bannockburn, Edward II's force included not only men from England, Wales and Ireland, but also the count of Hainault 'and with him men that worthi war, Off Gascoyne and off Almany And off the duche of Bretayngny'.[23] The count of Hainault, together with his comital neighbours from Jülich and Namur, also served in Edward III's campaigns of the 1330s. By then there were others too from the imperial lands. Forty German knights accompanied the king's stooge, Edward Balliol, to the battle of Dupplin Moor in 1332.[24] And a few came from even more exotic locations. Four Savoyards served the king in 1335, while John de Ispaynea was to be found in the earl of Oxford's retinue, summoned to serve in Scotland in 1336. And the following year Sir Ralph Neville's company included the exotically nicknamed Sarasyn Henry.[25]

Immigrants: Urban Society
Large English invasions of Scotland were infrequent after 1337 but English-controlled fortifications in the south still had to be manned – especially at Berwick and Roxburgh which remained in English hands for the greater part

---

[22] J.F. Lydon, 'Edward I, Ireland and the war in Scotland, 1303-4 in idem, ed., *England and Ireland in the Later Middle Ages* (Blackrock, 1981), 43-61; idem, 'The hobelar: an Irish contribution to medieval warfare', *The Irish Sword*, 2 (1954-56), 12-16; idem, 'An Irish army in Scotland, 1296' and 'Irish levies in the Scottish wars, 1296-1301', *The Irish Sword*, 5 (1962), 184-190; 207-17; S. Duffy, 'The Anglo Norman era in Scotland' in T.M. Devine and J.F. McMillan, eds., *Celebrating Columba: Irish-Scottish connections, 597-1997* (Edinburgh, 1999), 25-7.
[23] *The Bruce* (Duncan), 409.
[24] R. Nicholson, *Edward III and the Scots* (Oxford, 1965), 13, 20-2, 24, 35-40, 75, 87, 175, 199, 201, 212-14, 218, 249; F. Trautz, *Die Könige von England und das Reich, 1272-1377* (Heildelberg, 1961), 194-216.
[25] Nicholson, *Edward III and the Scots*, 175, 249; A. Ayton, *Knights and Warhorses: Military Service and the English Aristocracy under Edward III* (Woodbridge, 1994), 187.

of the fourteenth and fifteenth centuries. At times these garrisons, most of which were in castles located adjacent to towns, were of a substantial size. They reached a peak in 1299 when there were almost 2,000 men stationed in the major strongholds of Berwick, Edinburgh, Jedburgh, Roxburgh and Stirling alone. Although garrison numbers were to fall substantially thereafter, there were still about 500 men serving in these key castles in 1303; and 116 men at Edinburgh Castle in 1335.[26] While most of those retained for garrison duty were of either English or Scottish extraction, six Germans were among the 160 soldiers who constituted the Edinburgh garrison of 1335-36.[27] Although the Germans had disappeared from the slimmed-down list of ninety garrison members recorded in 1336-37, a few other Germans were retained elsewhere. Sir John de Whitefeld served at Stirling in 1338, and Gerard de Aldenove was remunerated for his service in Scotland before 1341.[28] It was at Berwick, however, that most soldiers were quartered. The contingent there included James van Felle from Brabant (in 1385) and Christian 'Duche Esterling' (in 1386).[29] Still, in the longer term foreign soldiers enclosed in a garrison did little to change the ethnic complexion of urban Scotland.

In other spheres too foreign visitors had only a transient impact on the Scottish landscape. Although the larger ports were routinely visited by foreign vessels, bringing with them an influx of merchants and mariners, and occasionally soldiers and pilgrims too, most of these visitors stayed for only a short time. Their number, moreover, was probably small. Between 1331 and 1333, when alien merchants were usually subject to additional customs levies at all Scottish ports except Berwick, substantial foreign mercantile activity is evident only at Aberdeen, Dundee and Inverkeithing.[30] By the early sixteenth century visits by foreign merchants to these ports had declined substantially. Inverkeithing had dwindled into an international backwater, 'dekeyit and fallin in povertie', with minimal overseas trade.[31] And although Aberdeen and Dundee remained of greater commercial significance, clearly identifiable foreign merchants accounted for less than 5% of consignments dispatched from Aberdeen between 1522 and 1524 and for fewer than twenty out of almost three hundred consignments shipped from Dundee in 1526-27.[32]

If transient aliens were limited in number, resident aliens were even scarcer in the Scottish towns. Berwick, the only truly cosmopolitan Scottish town of the thirteenth century, was an exception brutally snuffed out by the wars of independence. The town's English inhabitants were expelled by the Scottish

[26] F. Watson, *Under the Hammer: Edward I and Scotland, 1286-1307* (East Linton, 1998), 70, 73; Nicholson, *Edward III and the Scots*, 223.
[27] *CDS*, iii, 360-363.
[28] *CCR, 1337-39*, 613; *CCR, 1341-43*, 164.
[29] *CDS*, v, nos. 4207, 4220.
[30] A. Stevenson, 'Foreign traffic and bullion exports, 1331-1333' in P.G.B. McNeill and H.L. MacQueen, eds., *Atlas of Scottish History to 1707* (Edinburgh, 1996), 248-49.
[31] *Edin. Recs.*, ii, 81-2.
[32] NAS Edinburgh, E71/1/2; E71/12/1

authorities on the eve of hostilities breaking out between the two countries in 1296 and thirty Flemish merchants, then residing at the town's Red Hall, were massacred by Edward I's army.[33] Although there are indications that the Red Hall had been rebuilt by 1314, there is little evidence of a Flemish mercantile community resuming residence there.[34] Even if such a community did re-establish itself, the fate of Berwick's Rhenish settlers would suggest that it did not survive the renewal of hostilities in the 1330s. Thereafter a handful of earlier inhabitants, bearing the patronymic 'of Cologne' and residing in or near the town, had disappeared without trace.[35] The fate of one of their associates, the burgess and merchant Christopher of Cologne, was perhaps not untypical. He had been detained in Newcastle for his Scottish sympathies between 1333 and 1335, only to re-emerge at Aberdeen in the 1340s.[36] Subsequently, though a handful of alien residents can be identified elsewhere in Scotland – such as the Genoese merchant Lazerene de Grelis who possessed a house at Kirkcudbright in the mid-fifteenth century – even Edinburgh (the largest later medieval town) failed to attract a large and settled community of resident foreigners.[37] There were some exotic exceptions – notably the Greek bishop of Dromore in Ireland, whose property on the Castlehill was granted, upon his death in 1529, to a Neapolitan banker married to a local woman.[38] Nevertheless, experiments by some Hansards to station resident factors in early fifteenth-century Edinburgh proved short lived, and it is tempting to assume that sheer loneliness contributed to the suicide of one of their agents in 1425.[39]

With few resident aliens it follows that the topography of Scottish towns was largely undisturbed by the needs of such communities. Whereas Scots abroad often possessed their own religious shrines, the Luccese are the only foreigners who perhaps maintained their own altar in Scotland. Even then, the altar dedicated to the San Volto of Lucca (located in the parish church of Edinburgh) is not recorded until the mid-sixteenth century.[40] By then Scots abroad had collectively inhabited particular quarters of several towns, frequently bequeathing their name to a particular street. There were no similar developments in later medieval Scotland.

[33] *CDS*, ii, no. 868; *The Chronicle of Walter of Guisborough*, ed. H. Rothwell (Camden Soc., 1957), 275.

[34] *CDS*, v, no. 596.

[35] *CDS*, iii, nos. 1128-29; *CPR, 1330-34*, 554; *Rot. Scot.*, i, 264, 266, 274, 336; Stevenson, *Documents*, ii, 96, 154.

[36] *Northern Petitions*, ed. C. Fraser (Surtees Soc., 1981), no. 54; *ER*, i, 531.

[37] *ER*, vii, 378. Lazerene served as a custumar of the town between 1455 and 1460 (*ER*, vi, 125, 202, 303, 395-96, 494, 594).

[38] D. McRoberts, 'The Greek bishop of Dromore', *IR*, 28 (1977), 22-37.

[39] *Handelsrechnungen*, 11, 20-1, 23, 28; WAP Gdansk, 300/27/3, fos. 19-20; *HUB*, vi, no. 618; *ER*, iv, 412-13.

[40] NAS Edinburgh, NP/1/12, fos. 119-20. For the veneration of the San Volto by Luccese abroad, see L. Mirot, 'La colonie lucquois à Paris', *Bibliothèque de l'Ecole des Chartres*, 88 (1927), 50-86; R. de Roover, *Money, Banking and Credit in medieval Bruges* (Cambridge, Mass., 1948), 18.

Emigrants: Merchants, Sailors and Fishermen

If later medieval Scotland was no longer a land of immigrants, its long history as a land of emigrants was to begin in the fourteenth century. The most obvious starting point for searching out those Scots who emigrated is in the foreign ports at which their ships first docked. Of course, the sojourn of many of those who disembarked was brief. Envoys and clergymen normally had business to attend to elsewhere and soon moved on. Others, especially merchants and mariners, dallied only until such times as their vessels were once again ready for departure. Not all Scots, however, were temporary visitors. Of those who stayed longer in the port towns, many sought employment in the maritime related occupations of commerce, seafaring and fishing.

For émigré merchants opportunities arose as a result of the increasingly sedentary nature of their counterparts at home. Advances in literacy and greater sophistication in the nature of both business partnerships and capital transactions meant that by the later middle ages merchants were increasingly able to direct their commercial affairs from a single base. The practical matter of selling and buying in foreign markets was instead delegated to an overseas agent. These developments allowed merchants to undertake several simultaneous business ventures. They were still further commercially advantageous since an agent stationed abroad could be expected to possess a more sensitive appreciation of local market conditions than an itinerant alien merchant. Sometimes the services of a foreigner were engaged for the purpose of buying and selling overseas. This perhaps explains the joint business venture involving the Scottish merchant John Raa and the Englishman William Calver of Holkham in Norfolk. In 1375 they jointly proposed to sell a consignment of malt at Newcastle.[41] But the innate medieval suspicion of foreigners, coupled with the comparative ease and linguistic advantage of hiring fellow countrymen, meant that often as not it was an expatriate Scot who performed the task of overseas agent. Sometimes indeed, and perhaps ideally, the factor's duties were entrusted to a familial relation. It seems likely that it was on his father's behalf that the 'son of the *prepositus* of Kirkcudbright' was in Dublin in the later twelfth century or early thirteenth century. The commercial bond of the familial unit is more explicitly evident in the case of David White, recorded in 1490 as 'procurator and factor' in Aberdeen for his brother who was resident in Danzig; and in the case of Andrew Fudes, active in the Netherlands, who was 'son and factor' of the Aberdeen burgess William Fudes in 1500.[42] Nonetheless, far from all business partnerships revolved around the family.

The most celebrated of all Scottish ex-patriate agents, Andrew Halyburton, was active in the Netherlands in the later fifteenth and early

[41] *CCR, 1374-77*, 171-72.
[42] *The Dublin Guild Merchant Roll, c.1190-1265*, ed. P. Connolly and G. Martin (Dublin, 1992), 45; CA Aberdeen, CR/7, 167; *Halyburton's Ledger*, 233.

sixteenth centuries on behalf of a wide range of his most eminent countrymen. They included his brothers-in-law; but they also included two archbishops of St Andrews, a bishop of Aberdeen, an abbot of Holyrood, three knights, eight graduates, and a host of burgesses, mainly from Aberdeen and Edinburgh. Halyburton's quasi-consular role as conservator of Scottish privileges in the Low Countries clearly did not preclude his simultaneous pursuit of extensive business interests in Antwerp, Bergen-op-Zoom, Bruges and Middelburg.[43] Indeed, it probably enhanced his attraction as a factor.

The prominence which Halyburton has been accorded stems form the chance survival of his business ledger. Yet, in his diverse range of partners, he was probably not unusual, as is suggested from the glimpses which we can catch of John Moffet's career. Born in Abbeville, Moffet began his business career as Halyburton's servant and factor.[44] He ended it, like his erstwhile employer, as conservator.[45] Moffet's association with Halyburton was clearly close – he was a trustee for Halyburton's children and appointed Halyburton's father-in-law Sanders as his own agent in Antwerp – and it was probably from the late conservator that he learned many of his diplomatic as well as commercial skills.[46] Even before his own appointment as conservator in 1527 Moffet was much involved in diplomatic activity, playing a prominent role in Middelburg's efforts to acquire the Scottish staple in 1517 and 1518.[47] His diplomatic duties increased substantially after his appointment as conservator. This was presumably why in 1532 James V agreed to exempt Moffet from the obligation to return annually to Scotland to report on his activities. Still, Moffet seems to have made at least one more journey across the North Sea (in 1541), though by then his son, Erasmus, had been officially appointed to assist in the duties of conservator.[48] Meanwhile, Moffet senior also had commercial business to attend to. Like Halyburton, he was frequently to be found in Antwerp, Bergen-op-Zoom, Middelburg and Veere and, in addition to his trade with Scotland, Moffet's business contacts included merchants from England and Italy, as well as Netherlandish merchants from as far apart as Amsterdam and Brussels.[49]

Halyburton and Moffet, then, were both as much merchants as consuls and it was presumably to facilitate their commercial interests that both deemed it advantageous to acquire citizenship of a continental town – in their case Bergen-op-Zoom, where Halyburton became a burgess in 1491 and

[43] *Halyburton's Ledger*, passim.
[44] *Halyburton's Ledger*, 273; GA Bergen-op-Zoom, inv. no. 317, fo. 148; Smit, *Bronnen 1485-1585*, i, no. 194.
[45] RA Brussel, inv. no. 169/I, 405/1, 4-5; *APS*, ii, 331.
[46] StA Antwerpen, Certificatieboeken/3, fos. 170r, 183r.
[47] Smit, *Bronnen, 1485-1585*, i, nos 327, 329, 332, 348.
[48] Smit, *Bronnen, 1485-1585*, i, nos. 544, 629, 684; *RSS*, ii, nos. 1380, 3116.
[49] StA Antwerpen, Certificatieboeken/3, fo. 181r; GA Bergen-op-Zoom, inv. no. 5272, fos. 30r-v; Smit, *Bronnen, 1485-1585*, i, p. 222 n.1 and nos. 443, 575, 691, 770. Moffet was aided in business activities by his own factors, for whom see ibid, i, 337 n.1, 434 n.1 and no. 684.

Moffet in 1509.[50] A handful of other Scottish merchants obtained similar status in Bergen-op-Zoom between 1472 and 1522 and in Antwerp between 1537 and 1545.[51] Other Scots acquired burgess privileges in the neighbouring towns of Bruges, Veere and probably Middelburg, and it seems likely that at least some were merchants.[52] Elsewhere, and presumably for much the same reason, a substantial number of Scottish merchants had acquired membership of the Dublin gild in the thirteenth century.[53] At a later date we also find Scottish merchants obtaining citizenship in the French port of Dieppe;[54] and in the Baltic towns of Greifswald, Stralsund and Danzig.[55] And at least one Scot (John Reid), perhaps from Shetland, was a burgess of Bergen in Norway by 1488.[56] All of these merchant emigrants, we may presume, spent a good deal of their lives in those towns where they acquired citizenship or membership of the local gild. The costs and obligations of such a status, whatever the ensuing commercial advantages, were far from negligible and are unlikely to have enticed the casual, short-term visitor. Nevertheless, many of these men did not abandon their homelands entirely. Thomas Smith was a citizen of Edinburgh as well as Stralsund and died in 1464 whilst

---

[50] GA Bergen-op-Zoom, inv. no. 3092, fos. 39v, 91r. Moffet's burgess-ship was seemingly confirmed in 1522: ibid, fo. 131v.

[51] GA Bergen-op-Zoom, inv. no. 3092, fos. 15r (Jasper de Smit uit Heyentongeren (?Haddington): 1480), 22r (Jan Janssen uit Schotland, koopman: 1483), 55v (Jansz Hillebrant uit Schotland, poorterij: 1498), 72r (Jan Janz uit Schotland, poorterij: 1503); SA Antwerpen, Poortersboeken, 1464-1533, Vierschaar 142, 38 (Jacop Henricxone, Schotland, koopman: 1537), 39 (Jan Forster, Leith, koopman: 1537); Vierschaar 143, 18 (Jan Anderson, Scotland, koopman: 1539); Vierschaar 144, 8 (Robert Blackha, Scotland, koopman: 1544 and Jan Hop, Scotland, koopman: 1544); Vierschaar 145, 11 (Georges Thod, Edinburgh, koopman: 1545).

[52] ZA Middelburg, Archief Veere, inv. no. 920, passim; W.H. Finlayson, 'The Scottish nation of merchants in Bruges' (University of Glasgow, unpublished PhD thesis, 1951), 189-193. The Veere and Bruges lists rarely occupations. The Middelburg records perished in World War II, so comparable records for that town are not available.

[53] Connolly and Martin, *Dublin Guild Merchant Roll*, passim. Of almost 8,500 gildsmen (and three women) recorded in the roll, between 2% and 3% had names which include a possibly Scottish place name element. There was a particularly heavy concentration from Ayr, which furnished Dublin with perhaps forty-nine gild members between 1222 and 1265.

[54] M. Mollat, *Le commerce maritime normand à la fin du moyen age* (Paris, 1952), 171; *Protocol Book of John Foular, 1503-1513*, ed. W. Macleod and M. Woods (SRS, 1940-41), i, no. 345.

[55] I. von Wechmar and R. Biederstedt, 'Die schottische Einwanderung in Vorpommern im 16. und frühen 17. Jahrhundert', *Greifswald-Stralsunder Jahrbuch*, 5 (1965), appendix, 23-7, which includes the names of sixteen Scots entered between 1493 and 1560 in the *Bürgerbuch* of Stralsund; and two Scots from those entered before 1560 in the *Bürgermatrikel* of Greifswald. For further instances of Scottish merchant-burgesses from Stralsund (in 1464) and Greifswald (in 1529), see AH Lübeck, Anglicana 155a; NLS Edinburgh, ch. 57; *James V Letters*, 154. No list of new burgesses survives for fifteenth-century Danzig, but for examples of Scottish merchants described as citizens of Danzig, see WAP Gdansk, 300/27/6, fos. 252-53; *HUB*, ix, no. 46; for the sixteenth century, see Fischer, *Prussia*, 193; H. Penners-Ellwart, *Die Danziger Bürgerschaft nach Herkunft und Beruf, 1536-1709* (Marburg/Lahn, 1964). No Scots are recorded as burgesses of Elbing, though there is an extensive gap in the burgess records from 1457 until 1519 (WAP Gdansk, 369I/131).

[56] *Records of the Earldom of Orkney, 1299-1614*, ed. J.S. Clouston (SHS, 1914), 333. For Bergen, see also H. Marwick, *Merchant Lairds of Long Ago* (Kirkwall, 1939), ii, 46.

accompanying a cargo of beer from the Baltic to Scotland.[57] It remains a moot point whether men such as Smith, who were episodic or seasonal migrants, may be deemed genuine emigrants.

A similar degree of caution must be exercised in applying the word 'emigrant' to those who found employment in other maritime related activities. Sailors, in particular, pursued a peripatetic existence which, by the fifteenth century at least, had facilitated the emergence of an international market for their services. Crews were often of mixed nationality: in 1346, for instance, at least one Scot was in the service of the French corsair Jean Marant;[58] and the larger the port which sailors visited, the greater the opportunity for them to contract their labour to a different employer. During a career which spanned more than thirty years John Grant enjoyed 'the principal rule of the best schippes belonging to Bristol'.[59] He, at least, appears to have maintained an allegiance to English vessels for some considerable time and in 1498 Grant duly sought denizenship in England. In this he was unusual for very few Scottish sailors appear to have acquired the status which Grant did, either in England or elsewhere.[60] In part this was perhaps a reflection of an itinerant lifestyle which militated against the establishment of sustained attachments to any one location; but it was also a reflection of the humble social status of the average sailor. Unlike those of merchants, the names of dead sailors were normally not deemed worthy of inclusion in accounts of shipwreck or attack.

Much the same might be noted of fishermen, though as with sailors there are frequent allusions to Scots plying this trade in foreign parts. It was presumably the popularity of such employment, blended with political hostility, which prompted the merchant gild of Berwick to decree that 'no man or freman of thys town shall hyer ne suffir skottisman to ffysche for hym' on the Tweed in the early sixteenth century.[61] Of course, those Scots who had earned the disapproval of the Berwick gild were perhaps more akin to the modern phenomenon of the *Grenzgänger* – the worker who lives in one country and works in another. Others, including Robert and Andrew Scott, Scottish fishermen recorded in the Yorkshire port of Whitby in 1441-42, were perhaps seasonal migrants.[62] But fishing was not confined to the Tweed and North Sea. Although we do not know for certain what the handful of Scots to be found in the Sussex towns of Rye, Hastings and Winchelsea were actually doing in 1525, their presence was perhaps connected with the bitter complaints advanced in 1538 that aliens were threatening the livelihood of

---

[57] AH Lübeck, Anglicana 155a; NLS Edinburgh, ch. 57.

[58] *Registres du Trésor des Chartres*, ed. J. Viard and A. Vallée (Paris, 1978-84), iii, no. 6217.

[59] *CDS*, iv, nos. 1644-45.

[60] For an exception – the ship's carpenter Hans Gheron (?Heron), burgess of Stralsund in 1515 – see Wechmar and Biederstedt, 'Die schottishe Einwanderung in Vorpommern', appendix, no. 28.

[61] NRO Berwick-upon-Tweed, B1/1, fo. 5v.

[62] PRO London, E179/270/31, fo. 42.

native fishermen by manufacturing cheap fishing nets.[63] Given that there is no indication of even an irregular direct trade between Scotland and Sussex before the later sixteenth century, it is difficult to explain the Scottish presence on the English south coast in terms of conventional commercial activity.

Emigrants: Craftsmen and Labourers

Port towns offered particular employment opportunities in the maritime related occupations of trading, seafaring and fishing. Nevertheless, the occupational structure of only the smallest ports was overwhelmingly maritime related. Most towns hosted a much wider array of both skilled and unskilled labour to service the needs of fishing and trading communities. Hence we find a Scottish smith, a Scottish wool worker (*wolweerker*), a Scottish shoemaker, a Scottish clockmaker (*horenmaker*) and two Scottish labourers in early sixteenth-century Bergen-op-Zoom;[64] a Scottish baker, two Scottish labourers and a Scottish shoemaker at Veere;[65] and a Scottish baker, a Scottish bricklayer, a Scottish saddler and three Scottish tanners in Malmø before 1550.[66] Of course, employment of this variety was to be found in rural areas and in market towns as well as in coastal locations and there too we can often find significant numbers of Scots. Indeed, they were sufficiently numerous in Northumberland by 1398 to be deemed a political threat. The English government sought their removal south of the river Tyne.[67] We do not know exactly what these Scots were doing in Norhumberland. But the most plausible explanation for their presence is that they had found work as labourers or domestic servants, or perhaps as craftsmen, in a region severely depopulated by the combined effects of plague and war. Despite the strictures of the English government, that was certainly what other Scotsmen – and women too – were doing in Northumberland by the mid-fifteenth century. Indeed, by then the careers which these Northumberland Scots pursued were of an eclectic nature: there were labourers, skinners, salters, colliers, chaplains and even a 'kapknytter' called Margaret, all resident in the county in 1439-40.[68] Elsewhere in fifteenth-century England there were also Scottish bakers, brewers, butchers, coopers, fleshers, millers, porters, servants, smiths and tailors – and even in 1441-42 a swineherd at Carnaby, near Bridlington

---

[63] *The Lay Subsidy Rolls for the County of Sussex, 1524-25*, ed. J. Cornwall (Sussex Record Soc., 1956), 164-66; G. Mayhew, *Tudor Rye* (Falmer, 1987), 81. See also *CPR, 1461-67*, 280, for reports that Scottish spies were active in Sussex in 1463.
[64] GA Bergen-op-Zoom, inv. no. 5151, fos. 28r-v; inv. no. 5155, fos. 175v, 176; inv. no. 5167, fo. 37v.
[65] ZA Middelburg, Archief Veere, inv. no. 920: Jonij Bredde, baker, 1537; David Glennij, labourer, 1533; Thomas Jooris from Edinburgh, labourer, 1559; Thoams Claess, shoemaker, 1547.
[66] T. Riis, *Should Auld Acquaintance Be Forgot... Scottish-Danish relations, c.1450-1707* (Odense, 1988), i, 200. See also ibid, i, 224 for a butcher, a mason and two furriers from Scotland in Copenhagen before 1550.
[67] *Foedera* (O), viii, 55.
[68] PRO London, E179/158/41.

(Yorkshire) and a husbandman, who in 1480 was residing in the Hertfordshire village of Ashwell, near Letchworth.[69]

Notwithstanding such occupational diversity, we may broadly distinguish between four different types of employment among secular migrants: the unskilled; the skilled craftsmen; vagrants; and soldiers. The first of these categories comprises those who worked as either servants or labourers. Some from Shetland had found employment of this variety by at least the early sixteenth century in Norway.[70] Jejune source material, rather than limited mobility, may explain the apparent absence of servants and labourers elsewhere on the continent. Nevertheless, large numbers of servants and labourers worked in England. Indeed, in the northern counties of England unskilled migrants seem to have formed the bulk of the Scottish emigrant population. Of forty-three aliens taxed in Cumberland in 1441-42 (most, if not all of whom, were Scots) every one was described as a servant. And two years later, of sixty-four aliens liable for the alien subsidy in Cumberland, all of whom were Scots, all but seventeen were servants.[71] Although the relative preponderance of servants was less marked in the eastern counties of England, servants and labourers were also commonly engaged in Northumberland and Yorkshire, and sometimes further south too. William Roo, for instance, had found work as a labourer in Somersham, between Huntingdon and Ely, by 1480.[72]

The employers of these unskilled migrants included a broad range of English society. Among the clergymen who employed Scots were the chaplain of Broughton (near Cockermouth), the parson of Hayton, the vicar of Irthington, the rector of Kirkoswald, and the priors of Carlisle and Lanercost, both of whom employed two Scots in 1441-42. The chief employers of Scottish servants were, however, secular landowners. Some migrants were probably attached to the greater aristocratic households, in the northern counties at least, though in the Cumbrian evidence already cited only one employer was explicitly described as a knight. Initially, at least, it would seem that those who worked for the elite were exempted from the periodic tax imposed in England on aliens. What is, however, clear from the records of the alien taxation is that many lesser landowners also employed foreign labour. We may perhaps presume that these men, having augmented their lands through acquisition of vacant holdings, had benefited from the redistribution of estates following the Black Death. And, we may further presume, they now needed assistance to run their larger estates, especially perhaps at harvest time.

---

[69] For these specific examples, see PRO London, E179/270/31, fo. 14; *CPR, 1476-85*, 199. References to other occupations are drawn more widely from the alien subsidy accounts (PRO London, E179) and letters of denization and oaths of allegiance recorded in *CPR*.

[70] Marwick, *Merchant Lairds of Long Ago*, ii, 45-6.

[71] PRO London, E179/90/29; E179/90/30.

[72] *CPR, 1476-85*, 220. See too *The Alien Communities of London in the Fifteenth Century: The subsidy rolls of 1440 and 1483-84*, ed. J.L. Bolton (Richard III and Yorkist History Trust, 1998), 70, 75, 77, 82, 93, 95-6, 101, 104.

Indeed, some of the migrant Scots in their employ might well have been seasonal workers who laboured their way north in tandem with the harvest. Yet not all of this assistance was necessarily earmarked for the field. In Cumberland almost half the servants recorded in 1441-42 and 1443-44 were women and, though women were as adept as men at performing agricultural chores, it seems likely that many would have assisted their employers in other household tasks. The important point to note, however, is that northern England provided Scottish women, as well as men, with significant employment opportunities.

That was less obviously the case with the second group of emigrants, the skilled artisans. The crafts which these men had mastered were, as we have seen, diverse. Nevertheless, a substantial proportion of emigrants seems to have been engaged in the various branches of the textile trade. Some were relatively affluent, possessed of sufficient wealth and status to have acquired property or citizenship in their new homes. In 1483, for instance, two Scottish tailors in the Norfolk town of Lynn were registered as householders. Meanwhile, the cripple and tailor Jan Meyerton acquired citizenship in Antwerp in 1502, as did another tailor, William Drummond, in 1537. At least six tailors, one quiltmaker, a mender of old clothes and a kersay maker became burgesses of Bruges between 1429 and 1489; two tailors and two linen weavers became burgesses of Bergen-op-Zoom in the early sixteenth century; and there were two Scottish tailors who became burgesses of Veere in the early sixteenth century.[73] Other craftsmen enjoyed a less settled existence. The two Lynn tailors had a Scottish colleague who was not a householder. Neither was another Scottish tailor residing in the village of Wormegay, some eight kilometres south of Lynn. And there is no indication that the linen weavers who apparently formed the nucleus of the Alt-Schottland community in Danzig were possessed of such status. Weavers, however, were a generally less prestigious group than the elite tailors and perhaps the peripatetic and insecure experience of the linen weaver Simon of Dysart, who had worked in Hamburg and Lübeck before being arraigned for vagrancy in Breslau in c.1470, was not untypical.[74] Why he lost, or left, his job we do not know; but the fluctuating fortunes of the market place made for a fine line between employment and vagrancy.

---

[73] N.J.M. Kerling, 'Aliens in the county of Norfolk, 1436-85', *Norfolk Archaeology*, 33 (1965), 208; StA Antwerpen, Schepenbrieven 121, fo. 140v; Poortersboeken, Vierschaar 142, 37; Finlayson, 'The Scottish nation at Bruges', 254-59; GA Bergen-op-Zoom, inv. no. 3092, fos. 34v (Willem Henricss, linen weaver: 1489), 62v (Thomas Janssen, linen weaver: 1501), 85v (Willem Cavelinge from Linlithgow, tailor: 1507), 105r (Jan Morros, tailor: 1513); ZA Middelburg, Archief Veere, inv. no. 920 (Jan Janss of Leith, tailor: 30 May 1524; Willem Thomassen of Perth, tailor: 18 July, 1546). See also Riis, *Auld Acquaintance*, i, 200, for four tailors, two weavers and a draper in pre-1550 Malmø; and Viard and Vallée, *Registres du Trésor des Chartres*, iii, no. 5400, for a dressmaker (*couturier*) at Noyon, near Amiens, in the 1340s.
[74] T.A. Fischer, *The Scots in Germany* (Edinburgh, 1902), 242.

Emigrants: Hucksters and Vagabonds

Simon of Dysart's travels are a clear indication that the Scottish infiltration of Christendom was not confined to the coastal regions of the continent. Moreover, his disturbing encounter with the authorities of Breslau was not unusual. On 19 May 1473 the magistrates of Cologne ordered the expulsion of Scots from their city. Two months later officials were appointed to track down and imprison those who had not complied with the instruction. That the expulsion was re-enacted in 1486 suggests that it had been of only limited effect.[75] Unfortunately, it is not clear from these magisterial fiats what these individually unidentified Scots had been doing to incite such retribution. It seems unlikely that that it was the city's community of Scottish students which the council had in its sights. Neither does it seem likely that its eyes were fixed on *bone fide* craftsmen, such as Simon the Needlemaker and his wife Gillian, or other propertied Scottish residents, such as Robert Gillespie and his wife Elizabeth Fuller, who had settled in Cologne.[76] Instead, it seems probable the council's attention was focused on rather less well-to-do migrants, such as the 'Scots' who, in return for a measure of beer, were offered temporary employment in 1513 to clean the graves adjacent to St Gereon's church.[77] These men, though not necessarily unskilled, clearly lacked full-time employment when the Cologne authorities set them to work on the town's tombstones.

What, however, did they normally do to eke out a livelihood? One clue is perhaps to be gleaned from the association of Scots with Poles in the first of the edicts issued by the Cologne authorities in 1473. The Poles seem then to have been deemed guilty of similar misdemeanours to the Scots. Poles, it is reasonable to assume, would have arrived in Cologne from the east – and it was perhaps from the same direction that the city's unwanted Scottish visitors also hailed. In the 1470s, in other words, Cologne appears to have witnessed an influx of vagrants from the east.

Now, it is noticeable that in the same decade as some Scots were making a nuisance of themselves in Cologne, similar, but more specific, complaints about the activities of other Scots were also circulating in the towns of Prussia, towns which had been ceded to Poland in 1466. In 1473 Scots (again unidentified) were accused of selling goods in the villages and small towns of the Prussian hinterland 'das vor ny keinen gewonheit ist geweszen'.[78] So, it

---

[75] *Akten zur Geschichte der Verfassung der Stadt Köln im 14. und 15. Jahrhundert*, ed. W. Stein (Bonn, 1895), ii, nos. 331, 455.

[76] HA Köln, Schreinsurkunden Schöffenrein, 2/548/37 [undated, but of the later fifteenth century]; Briefbuch 34/35, fo. 99 [anno 1484].

[77] HA Köln, Ratsprotokoll 1a, fo. 93; Ratsprotokoll 1b, fo. 90v; *Beschlüsse des Rates Köln, 1320-1550*, ed. M. Huiskes and M. Groeten (Düsseldorf, 1988-90), ii, 115 (no. 937). I am extremely grateful to Drs Huiskes and Groeten for guiding me through the difficult palaeography of the *Ratsprotokollbücher* during the first archival visit I ever made.

[78] *Acten der Ständetage Preussens unter der Herrschaft des Deutschen Ordens*, ed. M. Toeppen (Leipzig, 1878-86), v, no. 90.

was a crime of recent manifestation of which the Scots were guilty. It was also a crime which undermined the interests of established merchants in the Prussian towns for the Scots of the Prussian hinterland, and perhaps those of the Rhineland too, were hucksters. By hawking their cut-price merchandise around rural areas, they were threatening the livelihood of established traders. They dealt in 'gefelschten gutte, cromerey, vorkorcztem gewichte und kleynen mose', flouting conventional urban regulations regarding the size and weight of goods which they sold.[79] They acquired a particular toehold in the cloth trade. We may presume that such activity was on a relatively large scale for it to have incited the indignation which it did. Quite how widespread that was is evident from the geographical distribution of complaints about the activities of Scots. In letters to the town council of Danzig, its counterparts in Königsberg (in 1490 and 1510), Lauenburg (in 1488 and 1490), Thorn (in 1478, 1488, 1490 and 1493) all railed against the activities of these itinerant Scottish pedlars.[80] The pedlar problem was further discussed by representatives of the Prussian towns who assembled in 1482, 1483, 1484, 1487, 1489 and 1494.[81] The persistence of such discussion is surely an indication that, despite attempts to prohibit Scottish traders resorting to the countryside, the traders themselves were taking little notice of the injunctions against their activities. By the sixteenth century some, at least, knew that they were not supposed to wander around the countryside selling their wares.[82] Nonetheless, discussions among the Prussian towns regarding the pedlar problem and edicts prohibiting the peripatetic trade remained common.[83] The hucksters may have been a threat to established mercantile interests, not least in towns such as Lauenburg, whose prosperity depended more on rural than sea-borne trade. Yet the Scots were clearly providing a welcome service to the inhabitants of rural Prussia.

It was not just in Prussia that these itinerant Scots were to win notoriety. As we have seen, some were apparently to percolate as far west as the Rhineland but there were others to be found in the intervening regions too. In Scandianvia, the first restrictions placed upon the trading activities of Scottish pedlars date from 1496. At that juncture they had apparently been active in the vicinity of Køge in Zealand. During the course of the next half century they were also to be found in Scania. Malmø and Ystad both complained

---

[79] WAP Gdansk, 300D/68/203.

[80] WAP Gdansk, 300D/67/158; 300D/67/294 [both letters from Königsberg to Danzig]; 300D/36A/88; 300D/67/96 [both letters from Lauenburg to Danzig]; 300D/68/203; 300D/68/302; 300D69/32; 300D/69/34; GSA Berlin, OB89, 47-48; *Acta Stanów Prus Królewskich*, ed. M. Biskup *et al.* (Torun, 1955-75), i, no. 269; ii, nos. 85, 142; iii, 41, 87 [letters from Thorn to Danzig]. Some of these letters are published in *HUB*, xi, nos. 226, 355, 370, 641.

[81] GSA Berlin, OF18A, 83; Toeppen, *Acten*, v, nos. 125(28), 142; Biskup, *Acta*, i, nos. 109, 148, 241, 247.

[82] T.A. Fischer, *The Scots in Eastern and Western Prussia* (Edinburgh, 1903), 20-1.

[83] See, for instance, Biskup, *Acta*, v, no. 131 (dated 1508); Fischer, *Prussia*, 22-3, 33-4, 157 (for complaints dated 1525, 1530, 1531, 1542, 1545, 1556 and 1558).

about the activity of pedlars in their rural hinterlands in the 1530s, and there, as in Prussia, they were accused of travelling around the countryside and retailing 'armfuls of smallwares', including linen and cloth.[84] Further south, more were to be found along the shores of the Baltic. In 1467, for instance, Robert Mitchelson, a pedlar from Brechin, was imprisoned in Lübeck for his 'unspeakable trade'.[85] Such incidents are a rarity in the immediate vicinity of the Hanseatic capital, but a few miles further east merchants from the island of Rügen wrote to their counterparts of Stralsund complaining about a swarm of Scottish pedlars who had infested the island with their servants by 1539. The Scots were trading their goods on holy days as well as on work days, moving from house to house and setting up their stalls in churchyards and villages across the island.[86] Still further south, in c.1470 one pedlar who had been working at Meissen in Saxony was subsequently apprehended at Breslau, along with Simon of Dysart, on charges of vagrancy.[87] Indeed, it would seem as if the Scottish pedlar problem had even reached southern Germany. In 1493 a complaint about their trading activities was published in the Bavarian town of Bamberg and, given its similarly landward location, it seems likely that it was itinerant pedlars, rather than traditional merchants, who were active in neighbouring Regensburg by the same date.[88] So common had the sight of the Scottish huckster become in central Europe that the word 'Scot' was to become a synonym for pedlar.[89]

From where did these pedlars come? The obvious, but overly simplistic, answer would be Scotland. Very few of the pedlars can be identified individually. Although some of those who can, such as Robert Mitchelson in Lübeck and Walter of Dyce in Breslau, were clearly of Scottish origin, once the words 'Scot' and 'pedlar' became almost interchangeable, not all pedlars were necessarily of Scottish extraction. For instance, Johan Steynwerde, known as *Leffelmecher*, a 'Scot' who fell foul of the Cologne authorities in 1513, does not appear to bear a Scottish name.[90] Yet, the ambiguity of the word 'Scot' would surely not have arisen had there not been a genuine and substantial Scottish element among the pedlars who first won such notoriety in the later decades of the fifteenth century.

[84] J. Dow, '*Skotter* in sixteenth-century Scania', *SHR* 44 (1965), 39, 45-9; Riis, *Auld Acquaintance*, i, 74-8.
[85] *HUB*, ix, no. 397.
[86] E.V.K. Brill, 'A sixteenth-century complaint against the Scots', *SHR* 27 (1948), 185-89.
[87] Fischer, *Germany*, 241-42.
[88] Brill, 'A sixteenth-century complaint', 190; L. Hammermeyer, 'Deutsche Schottenklöster, schottische Reformation, katolische Reform und Gegenreformation in West- und Mitteleuropa, 1560-80', *Zeitschrift für bayerische Landesgeschichte*, 26 (1963), 172-75.
[89] Dow, '*Skotter*', 40-3; Wechmar and Biederstedt, 'Die schottische Einwanderung in Vorpommern', 10-11.
[90] HA Köln, Ratsprotokoll 1a, fos. 94v, 95r; Ratsprotokoll 1b, fos. 91v, 92r; Huiskes and Groeten, *Beschlüsse*, ii, 116-17 (nos. 944, 948).

There is more evidence, albeit of the circumstantial variety, to support the notion that the pedlar problem was in origin a specifically Scottish problem. An examination of the fifteenth-century cargoes arriving in Danzig by sea from Scotland reveals that most (some 52%) were composed of *Krämerwaren*. These small packs contained a miscellany of produce in small measures – exactly the diversity and quantity of merchandise for which the hucksters of the Prussian hinterland were renowned.[91] It would seem that, in the eastern Baltic at least, many of the pedlars were supplied with their wares by ships from Scotland. And that towns such as Königsberg, Lauenburg and Thorn all complained to Danzig about the Scottish pedlars suggests that they too perceived a Danzig connection. This is further suggested by the down-on-their luck vagrants detained at Breslau in *c.*1470: many claimed merely to be passing through the town *en route* for the Prussian port. Danzig, it would seem, had become a conduit not just for Scottish migrants, but for their supplies too.

Further west other Baltic port towns probably fulfilled a similar function. Admittedly the explicit correlation evident at Danzig between the import of Scottish *Krämerwaren* and the activities of Scottish pedlars in the town's hinterland can not be made in Denmark. Still, there is evidence to suggest that the pedlars who operated in the Danish countryside obtained their goods in the Baltic ports of Copenhagen, Elsinore, Malmø and Ystad.[92] Moreover, all of these ports were convenient stopping-off locations for Danzig-bound ships, their holds replete with *Krämerwaren*. Ships were bound, indeed, to call at Elsinore to pay the duty levied on all shipping passing the Sound and some of their *Krämerwaren* may well have been off-loaded at the same time.

The circumstantial evidence which suggests a link between Scotland and the Scottish pedlars of the continental countryside is further enhanced by an examination of developments in England. While there were no complaints (so far as I am aware) about Scottish pedlars there, there is substantial evidence that Scottish vagrants were traversing the countryside of northern England. The first indications of their presence date from the mid-fifteenth century: Gilbert Scott and his wife, for instance, then in Kirk Skitby near Hull, were among a handful of Scots designated as vagabonds in the East Riding of Yorkshire in 1441-42.[93] Gilbert and his wife seem not to have bothered the authorities who, despite their designation, considered them liable for payment of the alien tax. Towards the end of the century, however, as elsewhere in northern Europe, the number of these itinerant Scots in England seems to have risen. Christine Newman discerned a clear trend in this direction at Northallerton in the 1490s. It seems unlikely that this small north Yorkshire market town was a lone magnet for travelling Scots and rather more probable

[91] H. Samsonowicz, 'Engländer und Schotten in Danzig im Spätmittelalter: Zwei Formen der Handelstätigkeit' in K. Friedland and F. Irsigler, eds., *Seehandel und Wirtschaftswege Nordeuropas im 17. und 18. Jahrhundert* (Ostfildern, 1981), 50.
[92] Riis, *Auld Acquaintance*, i, 75-7.
[93] PRO London, E179/270/31, fo. 23.

that the Great North Road and Northallerton were mere funnels through which they passed on their way south.[94]

By then the English government was convinced that itinerant Scots were a cause for alarm. In June 1477 it had instigated an inquiry into reports that diverse Scots, women as well as men, were wandering round Yorkshire burning houses and other buildings.[95] More explicitly still, in 1490 Henry VII proclaimed his 'perfect knowledge' that 'great numbers of Scots' had resorted to the northern counties 'applying themselves to idleness and begging'.[96] These objects of the king's wrath were not, he stated explicitly, the servants and householders of Scottish extraction who, as we have seen, had long since laboured in settled occupations throughout northern and eastern England. Instead, the royal edict was directed against vagabonds and they were told to go home.

That they did not do, any more than their counterparts elsewhere in northern Europe did. Nevertheless, the English evidence is problematic and perhaps *sui generis*. It appears to complete the geographical jigsaw depicting a swarm of itinerant Scots from Cumberland to Königsberg. It also coincides chronologically with the impression from elsewhere in northern Europe that the last quarter of the fifteenth century witnessed a substantial increase in their numbers. We cannot be certain, however, that the English and Prussian migrants were of a similar character. In Prussia (and Scandinavia) the talk was of pedlars – of men who provided a service. In England (and the Rhineland) it is of vagabonds – of men and women who sought charity. Yet there are hints – and no more than that – that one government's pedlar was another government's vagrant. In Breslau we have seen how at least one pedlar, Walter of Dyce, was arraigned for vagrancy in *c.*1470. And much later, in 1557, the pedlar Thomas Gibson claimed that he had been reduced to begging once he emerged from prison, where he had been delivered following the sequestration of his goods in Rastenberg. The Polish king Sigismund Augustus was also to link Scots and their mercery wares with vagabonds in an edict of 1556.[97] The equation between pedlar and vagrant in these instances hardly constitutes a solid argument; but the predicament faced by both Walter and Thomas does demonstrate that the pedlar bereft of merchandise, whether through sale, theft or seizure, faced a precarious existence. Physically detached from his kin, he depended on the charity of others for survival.

Meanwhile, the English evidence may not be all it seems. In the royal writ of 1490 the problem of vagabonds was linked directly to the 'likely

---

[94] C.M. Newman, 'Order and community in the north: the liberty of Allertonshire in the later fifteenth century' in A.J. Pollard, ed., *The North of England in the Age of Richard III* (Stroud, 1996), 63-4.

[95] *CPR, 1476-85*, 50.

[96] *Tudor Royal Proclamations*, ed. P.L. Hughes and J.F. Larkin (New Haven, Conn., 1964), i, no. 22; *CPR, 1485-94*, 322.

[97] Fischer, *Prussia*, 20-1, 157.

impoverishment' of the king's 'poor, true and faithful subjects'. The logic of this correlation is not immediately obvious. It does, however, suggest that the vagabonds were doing *something* to undermine the income of loyal Englishmen. The Scottish migrants were explicitly accused of begging – though not, it should be noted, of thieving. There are signs that charitable donations to the poor grew significantly in late fifteenth-century England, perhaps suggesting an increase in the number of beggars. But we can hardly expect a fifteenth-century king to have worried *per se* about his subjects dispensing alms to miserable migrants. Instead, we may suppose that other concerns guided the governmental action of 1490. One possibility is that the king's lieges were parting with their money in order to procure labour or goods from the vagabonds. Perhaps too, in delivering their labour or goods, the vagabonds were undercutting the wages or prices of local craftsmen or merchants. The vagrants, if we follow this line of enquiry, may have been transient labourers, perhaps on short-term contracts, who, on the expiry of their employment roamed around the countryside in search of other, or better, wages and conditions. Alternatively, as in Prussia, the English vagabonds may also have been itinerant hucksters. There was certainly a precedent for both in England. Migrant labour in search of inflated remuneration had been the target of much legislation after the Black Death in the later fourteenth century. Hucksters, meanwhile, had already attracted criticism in the smaller towns of pre-plague England, as they competed for custom with traditional merchants.[98] Both types of migrant, it might be argued, were contributing to the impoverishment of the better off.

On the other hand, we should perhaps seek social and political explanations, rather than economic ones, for the governmental concern with vagrants. The Tudor interest in vagrancy coincided with a period of political instability in England, with a new and fragile royal dynasty nervous of Yorkist pretenders who received succour from the Scottish government. Moreover, the mobility of the English workforce had been significant ever since the Black Death and some have argued that this mobility generated a profound social problem. The traditional medieval suspicion of the outsider mingled with a breakdown of social control, since itinerants were less respectful of employers and immune to the traditional influence exercised by the landlord. The Tudor government's concern with vagrancy was perhaps then 'a fashion in rhetoric' rather than 'a response to real changes in levels of unemployment'. And it was perhaps the transient nature of vagrants and the social and political implications of their mobility, rather than the number of vagrants or their economic activities, which caused such concern.[99]

---

[98] R.H. Hilton, 'Lords, burgesses and huxters', *PP*, 97 (1982), 3-15.
[99] R.H. Britnell, 'The English economy and the government, 1450-1550' in J.L. Watts, ed., *The End of the Middle Ages?* (Stroud, 1998), 105-7; M.K. McIntosh, 'Local change and community control in England, 1465-1500', *Huntingdon Library Quarterly*, 49 (1986), 219-42.

Whatever the case, we should certainly not assume that all vagrants were constantly impoverished. On occasions some, such as the Scots seeking poor relief in Northallerton or those who were ill and destitute in Breslau, certainly were. But when 'vagabonds' such as Gilbert Scott and his wife appear on Yorkshire tax lists, we may assume that officials supposed that they possessed some means with which to pay the taxman, even if many aliens, though assessed, did not pay. Indeed, on the continent some pedlars were of sufficient means to acquire citizenship of the towns in which they plied their trade. David Learmonth, for instance, became a burgess of Frankfurt-am-Main in 1471; and the *Kremer* Adam Ritzmon, Robrecht Gourla, Thomas Thomas, Jan Stavaert, Thomas Wrichter and Jan de Vlaeminck (all Scots) acquired a similar status in Antwerp between 1539 and 1544.[100] Fifty-three other Scots were to obtain citizenship of Regensburg between 1484 and 1559.[101] Although none was identified as a vagrant or pedlar, it is inconceivable that these men had regular trading contacts with their homeland. Located far from the North Sea ports, the most likely explanation for their presence in Bavaria was that they were small-time traders made good. The life of the vagrant was an uncertain one which might encompass radical shifts of fortune. And while the successful might prosper, the unfortunate encountered difficult circumstances often without the cushion of support afforded by traditional social bonds of the landlord, gild, long-standing neighbour and extended family.

Emigrants: Soldiers

Thus far two things are clear. Firstly, many Scots were to be found carving a niche for themselves as merchants, craftsmen or labourers in the urban centres around the North Sea and Baltic coasts. Secondly, many of their compatriots journeyed inland from the coastal regions, eking out a livelihood as hucksters or craftsmen. It would be misleading, however, to assume that overseas employment opportunities only afforded themselves to those of a commercial or manufacturing disposition. The continental magnet was as alluring to those who fought and those who prayed as it was to those who worked. To be sure, for knightly members of society, those who fought, the attraction of continental adventures was more strongly counteracted by the need to protect landed interests at home than it was for the often more rootless members of urban society. On the other hand the gradual emergence of paid armies from the fourteenth century presented the knightly class with the attractive prospect of shoring up the diminishing returns which, especially after the Black Death, it received from its estates. In addition, mercenary service provided many knights with a pursuit which they enjoyed and one which they found honourable. It was also one which, after the long years of warfare with England, they found familiar, though, even before the outbreak of

---

[100] StA Frankfurt-am-Main, Bürgerbuch, iv, fo. 340r; StA Antwerpen, Poorterboeken, Vierschaar 143, 18; Vierschaar 144, 8, 35-7.
[101] Fischer, *Prussia*, 235-36.

Anglo-Scottish hostilities and the advent of handsomely remunerated mercenary service, some had served in Henry III's armies during the Gascon wars of the 1250s. Others, notably John Comyn, lord of Badenoch, had appeared in the same king's entourage as he encountered his baronial foes at Lewes in 1264.[102]

At much the same time the first signs emerge of the numerically much more significant galloglass (*gaillóglaich*) who in the ensuing centuries were to become familiar figures on the Irish landscape. The annals of Connacht note a skirmish at Ballyshannon in 1247 in which a king of Argyll died. This king has been plausibly identified as Duncan, lord of Lorn. His presence in Ireland, in support of O'Donnell attempts to curb the power of Maurice Fitzgerald, lord of Sligo, is the first indication of someone from the Scottish mainland leading Scottish warriors and dying in the service of an Irish warlord, though Hebridean fleets had been employed by Irish leaders since at least the eleventh century.[103] The word 'galloglass' itself, meaning foreign warrior, was not explicitly coined until 1290, though by then galloglass in all but name were well established in Ulster and had been a feature of Connacht politics for at least thirty years too.[104] Before the end of the thirteenth century galloglass had become a nuisance to the unfortunate natives of the north and west of Ireland who were forced by their social superiors to billet these foreign warriors. Clerics condemned their ravenous exactions from the Irish peasantry in 1297, 1310 and 1316, yet Gaelic and Anglo-Irish magnates alike valued these, by Irish standards, loyal and heavily armoured mercenaries. Lethally equipped with a double-edged axe on a long shaft they were of particular use in open battle – even though in 1311 six hundred were reportedly slain in Thomond while in the service of William de Burgh, the earl of Ulster's cousin. Not all of the galloglass were Scots and those who died in Thomond may have been led by a Welshman.[105] Still, if accurate, the reports of those slain in 1311 provides some measure of the numbers who were recruited by just one warlord. Moreover, the apparent ease with which galloglass continued to be recruited between 1296 and 1337 – years of international and civil strife in Scotland – is an indication that the vicissitudes of political fortune were not long drawn out wars of attrition which soaked up the local reservoirs of military manpower. Rather, conflict was sharp and decisive in areas such as Galloway and the west Highlands, from whence the galloglass chiefly came. Many of the galloglass – MacSweens and Macdonalds from the thirteenth century, MacDowells,

---

[102] *CDS*, i, nos. 1985, 2226, 2678; *Chron. Melrose*, 125; *Chron. Bower* (Watt), v, 352-53; A. Young, *Robert Bruce's Rivals: The Comyns, 1212-1314* (East Linton, 1997), 81.

[103] D. Ditchburn and B. Hudson, 'Economy and trade' in S. Duffy, ed., *New History of the Isle of Man. Volume III: The medieval period, 1000-1405* (Liverpool, forthcoming).

[104] J. Lydon, 'The Scottish soldier in medieval Ireland: the Bruce invasion and the galloglass' in G.G. Simpson, ed., *The Scottish Soldier Abroad, 1247-1967* (Edinburgh, 1992), 6-7, 14 n.47.

[105] Lydon, 'The Scottish soldier', 8-9; K. Simms, 'Gaelic warfare in the middle ages' in T. Bartlett and K. Jeffrey, eds., *A Military History of Ireland* (Cambridge, 1996), 108.

MacRories and others from the fourteenth century – were exiles, ousted from their homelands.

In the east and south of Scotland things were different. There civil war between Bruce and Balliol adherents and national war between Scotland and England did preoccupy the fighting classes for most of the early and mid-fourteenth century. During these decades very few Scots from the south and the east fought abroad, whether as crusaders or as mercenaries. There were, of course, exceptions. Sir William Douglas and with him 'a great many Scots', assisted the French at the battle of Poitiers in 1356;[106] Norman Leslie 'who had come from Scotland to help the French', was captured at Flavigny in 1360;[107] and English chroniclers noted the capture of several Scots fighting for the Trastameran cause at the battle of Najera in 1367.[108] It is possible too that Renaud de la Haye, who had been installed as captain of Barfleur on behalf of the mercurial Navarese king Charles the Bad in 1364, was of Scottish extraction.[109] Yet, many of these mid fourteenth-century soldiers found themselves engaged in foreign service almost by accident. Douglas had merely been passing through France, intending to make a pilgrimage, when he stumbled across King John's forces and joined them. France was not yet the magnet for mercenary service which it was to become in the fifteenth and sixteenth centuries.

Instead, it was the English armies which were to provide the main initial recruiting ground for Lowland Scottish soldiers. As in Ireland, exiles who had fallen foul of the Bruce regime were among the first to enter English service. Many, of course, served initially with the armies of Edward II, Edward III and Edward Balliol in what was to be a forlorn attempt to regain their dispossessed lands in Scotland. For them, and for their heirs, enrolment in the English armies which visited France with increasing regularity from the later 1330s, and Ireland, was almost a natural progression of their emigrant careers. In 1359, for instance, Henry Comyn planned to campaign in the service of John, earl of Richmond, while in 1363 John Comyn travelled to Ireland in the service of the duchess of Clarence, having previously already been included in her husband's retinue on the occasion of his visit to Lombardy.[110] The careers of (presumably) the descendants of exiled Comyns were not unique. Following his defection in 1400 George Dunbar, tenth earl of March, was to prove his military ability fighting in support of Henry IV's cause against English rebels at the battle of Shrewsbury in 1403. In this he was perhaps aided by a substantial number of retainers who had crossed the border with

---

[106] *Chron. Bower* (Watt), vii, 299; *Chron. Fordun*, ii, 365; *Chron. Froissart* (Lettenhove), v, 428, wherein the author states that two hundred Scots were present at Poitiers; *Scalacronica*, 175; *Chron. Reading*, 197.

[107] *Scalacronica*, 190.

[108] *Chron. Reading*, 184; *The Brut* , ii, 320. See also the comments of A. Goodman, 'A letter from an earl of Douglas to a king of Castile', *SHR*, 64 (1985), 69.

[109] Galbraith, 'Scottish seals from the continent', no. 40.

[110] *CDS*, iv, nos. 34, 80, 183.

their lord. In 1407 the earl appeared with eighty-two Scots, armed with bows and lances, in the aftermath of a violent brawl instigated by thirty-five of their compatriots in the Lincolnshire village of Navenby.[111] March eventually reverted to the Scottish allegiance in 1409. Others did not. Having failed to fight his way back to favour, following James II's murder of the eighth earl of Douglas in 1452, the exiled ninth earl found service with the English forces bound for France in 1474-75. So too did another exile, Robert, Lord Boyd, on the run following his removal from power by James III, in 1469.[112]

By then the more peaceful direction of Anglo-Scottish relations following the treaty of Berwick (1357) had proven conducive to the appearance of other Scots in English armies. Both the earls of Angus and Mar obtained safe-conducts for travel to France in 1359. That for Angus specifically indicated the earl's intention to participate in the English war effort and he has often been equated with Froissart's 'Hagre l'Escot', a captain among the companies active in Burgundy in 1360.[113] Others were serving closer to home. As early as 1356 Adam Prendergast from Berwickshire was a member of the Berwick garrison and by 1361 others were allegedly serving as grooms in the English garrison of Roxburgh.[114] Recruitment to English armies probably declined once the treaty of Brétigny (1360) ushered in a nine-year lull in the main Anglo-French conflict. Nonetheless, many battle-hardened soldiers chose not to disband. Hagre l'Escot joined the Black Prince's expedition to Castile in 1366, designed to further the cause of Pedro the Cruel in the Castilian king's civil war with his francophile half-brother Henry of Trastamara.[115] Others preferred instead to enlist in the Great Companies which terrorised southern France before turning their attentions to Italy. Walter and Norman Leslie (the latter now released from his captivity after Flavigny) witnessed an agreement made in 1364 by Sir John Hawkwood's White Company and the commune of Florence. Hawkwood and his men were thereby engaged in Florentine service against the Tuscan town's old rival, and Hawkwood's erstwhile employer, Pisa. It has been assumed that this was a purely accidental encounter into which the Leslies had stumbled while en route for a crusade in the Holy Land.[116] That remains assumption, but even if the belligerent Leslie brothers developed a more formal association with Hawkwood, their experience does not seem to have been a common one for Scots.

It was the revived outbreak of Anglo-French war in 1369, coupled with the shortage of manpower after the Black Death, which did most to boost English

---

[111] *Select Cases in the Court of King's Bench under Richard II, Henry IV and Henry V*, ed. G.O. Sayles (Selden Soc., 1971), i, 187-89.

[112] *CDS*, iv, nos. 1423, 1428.

[113] *Rot. Scot.*, i, 840-42; *Chron. Froissart* (Lettenhove), vi, 328, 331; F. Michel, *Les Ecossais en France, Les Français en Ecosse* (London and Edinburgh, 1862), 73.

[114] *CDS*, iii, no. 1619; iv, no. 64. Adam of Prendergast was in English allegiance at the time and his lands were occupied by the Scots.

[115] Michel, *Les Ecossais en France*, i, 73.

[116] A. Macquarrie, *Scotland and the Crusades, 1095-1560* (Edinburgh, 1985), 80.

recruitment of Scottish soldiers. Not only did English garrisons at Calais, Brest and elsewhere have to be defended against a resurgent French monarchy, but the period between 1369 and 1374 witnessed some of the largest and most far-reaching raids ever mounted by the English in France. By 1373 Froissart's mysterious messire d'Angorisses (whom Michel, surely mistakenly, identifies as the earl of Angus) was serving as captain of the garrison at Noirot (Dep. Deux Sèvres).[117] More certainly, at least 144 Scots, including knights, archers, bowmen and valets, served in the Calais garrison in 1369-70, when fears for the town's safety were at their greatest, and others were to serve there periodically throughout the later fourteenth century.[118] In addition, some Scots enlisted with Edward III for the campaign of 1369. Others (both men-at-arms and archers) were sought for service in the retinues of the great magnates who subsequently led the English armies across the Channel.[119] About a hundred Scottish men-at-arms joined Sir Robert Knolles on the great *chevauchée* through the Ille de France, Brittany and Poitou in 1370;[120] and Sir John Swinton, reputedly in the company of three hundred other Scots, joined the equally devastating expedition from Calais to Bordeaux, led by John of Gaunt, duke of Lancaster, in 1373.[121] Swinton then planned to join the esquires William of Monymusk and Robert Cateneys in the company of the earl of Cambridge's Breton expedition of 1375; and others intended to engage for the same campaign with the English earl of March.[122] Two years later, in 1377, Swinton was again in France, this time in Gascony, together with Sir John Sibbald and one hundred men and, though indications of Scots fighting with the English armies tail off in the later 1370s, one Scottish esquire, John Lamb, was still to win renown and reward in 1378 for his murder of Owain Lawgoch, a Welsh rebel in French service.[123] Thereafter Scots did not pass by the remaining, if more limited, opportunities which came their way: some were to join Gaunt in his invasions of Castile in 1386 and of Aquitaine in 1394, and the knight Walter Stewart, apparently with nineteen others, was to

[117] *Chron. Froissart* (Lettenhove), viii, 165, 218, 220, 225, 227, 230, 232, 234; xx, 8-9; Michel, *Les Ecossais en France*, i, 73.
[118] *Issue Roll of Thomas de Brantingham, Lord High Treasurer of England... , 1370*, ed. F. Devon (London, 1835), 83-85; *CDS*, iv, nos. 165, 173, 216, 447; v, no. 843. For the background to the large reinforcements sent to Calais in 1369, see J. Sherborne, 'John of Gaunt, Edward III's retinue and the French campaign of 1369' in R.A. Griffiths and J. Sherborne, eds., *Kings and Nobles in the Later Middle Ages* (Gloucester, 1986), 42; and on Calais in general, see J. Le Patourel, 'L'occupation anglaise de Calais au XIVe siècle', *Revue du Nord*, 33 (1951), 228-41.
[119] *Rot. Scot.*, i, 931; J.W. Sherborne, 'Indentured retinues and English expeditions to France, 1369-1380', *English Historical Review*, 79 (1964), 719.
[120] *Chron. Froissart* (Lettenhove), viii, 46, 48. See P. Contamine, *War in the Middle Ages* (Oxford, 1985), 126, for equation of the term 'lance' (in the source previously cited) with man-at-arms; and see also *CDS*, iv, no. 170 for an English safe-conduct granted to some of them.
[121] *John of Gaunt's Register*, ed. S. Armitage-Smith (Camden Soc., 1911), ii, nos. 1457, 1670; *Chron. Froissart* (Lettenhove), viii, 268, 280.
[122] *CDS*, iv, nos. 217-19, 221.
[123] *CDS*, iv, nos. 254, 273. On Lamb, see also *Chron. Froissart* (Lettenhove), ix, 73-6, 508; Sherborne, 'Indentured retinues', 735, n.2.

engage in royal service for life in 1393, subsequently serving in Richard II's expedition to Ireland in 1399.[124] Richard, however, was to show little enthusiasm for campaigning in France. The earl of Buckingham was to lead the last major English expedition to France in the fourteenth century in 1380.

Thereafter English demand for Scottish recruits was to decline markedly from its apparent peak in the years from 1369 to 1373. Yet, during these years Scots appear to have constituted a significant proportion of the English military endeavour in France. Recent research has estimated that approximately 6,000 men joined the great *chevauchée* of 1373 and some sources, as we have seen, suggest that several hundred Scots joined them.[125] Of course, neither the estimates of chroniclers, nor the numbers stipulated on safe-conducts, provide a completely reliable indication of those who actually participated in these formidable military passages: the former were prone to exaggeration, while the latter are more a statement of intent to serve than a reflection of actual service. If, however, the evidence to hand is taken at face value some 5% of the English force was of Scottish origin. In reality the proportion was probably smaller, but there is still sufficient evidence to suggest that something in the region of at least one hundred Scots entered English service annually during these years.

By comparison with recruitment in England's armies and the probably larger still numbers who were attracted to Ireland, comparatively few Scottish soldiers seem to have sought service elsewhere in the later fourteenth century. Two from Irvine – perhaps laid-off veterans of the Hundred Years War following the agreement of an Anglo-French truce in 1389 – found employment with the city guard of Cologne in 1391.[126] A few others had been engaged by the French crown: the knight Nicholas Erskine, for instance, entered French royal service in 1372 and late in 1390 Charles VI dispatched two recruiting officers to acquire further military support in Scotland.[127] The success of this mission remains uncertain, but that 100 Scottish archers were paid off by the king's son, Louis, duke of Touraine, the following June suggests that Charles's ambition of engaging Scottish mercenaries was more than speculative.[128] Still, there is little evidence that Scots soldiers were to be found in great numbers among the French forces even in the late fourteenth century.

That was soon to change. The fifteenth century witnessed a radical shift in the recruiting patterns of Scottish soldiers. Enlistment in English armies became much less significant than it had been in the later fourteenth century.

[124] *CDS*, iv, nos. 354, 456-58, 461, 518. See also *Chron. Westminster*, 142-43, for Gaunt's confidence is being able to recruit 'the flower of Scotland's chivalry' for his Iberian expedition of 1386.
[125] Sherborne, 'Indentured retinues', 729-30.
[126] HA Köln, Haupturkundenarchiv, K/4308.
[127] AN Paris, J621/77; *St Andrews Copiale*, appendix, no. 2a. See also *Chron. Froissart* (Lettenhove), x, 287 for a Scottish sergeant-at-arms, Janekin Campenois, who was in the service of the French crown in the 1380s.
[128] *St Andrews Copiale*, appendix, no. 2b.

Although it remained an option for some aside from the political exiles, not a single Scottish man-at-arms was apparently serving the English crown in the mid-fifteenth century during the Lancastrian occupation of northern France.[129] On the other hand, Ireland remained an important fighting arena for those recruited in the Highlands and Isles. By the fifteenth century galloglass were to be found in their hundreds not just in the north of Ireland, in the service of Gaelic warlords, but also in the great southern earldoms of Kildare and Ormond, and even in the pay of the English administration in Dublin. In *c*.1515 an anonymous informant of the English crown reported that the army of most Irish lordships included five hundred galloglass; and by the 1530s estimates of galloglass numbers in all of Ireland varied between two thousand and well over three thousand.[130] Indeed, Ireland's significance as a recruiting ground for Scottish soldiers was to increase still further once Gaelic war lords began to employ seasonal fighting men, in addition to those more established galloglass, such as the Sweenys and Macdonalds, who had by now become permanently settled on lands granted by their masters. It is from 1428, at Niall Garbh O'Donnell's siege of Carrickfergus, that the first indications date of seasonal 'redshanks' joining their more established compatriots in Ireland.[131] Two years later it was reported in Dublin that the Gaelic Irish joined by 'a grete multitude of Scottes send unto thayme oute of Scotteland' had overrun most of Munster.[132] By 1433 others were amassing in support of Niall O'Donnell's rival, Eoghan O'Neill, and were to win notoriety for burning Ardglass before joining O'Neill in forcing O'Donnell to peace.[133] Although large numbers of incursive Islesmen are not again reported in the mid-fifteenth century, thereafter the redshanks were to appear periodically and in their thousands. In 1474, for instance, the Irish parliament reported that 10,000 Scots were in Ulster while in 1539 the constable of Carrickfergus Castle reported that the bishop of Derry had sent to Scotland for 6,000 redshanks.[134] Even if one allows for a large degree of exaggeration in the number reported by the embattled Anglo-Irish establishment, Ulster was clearly awash with Scots.

---

[129] *CDS*, iv, nos. 606, 612, 641, 766, 780; *CPR, 1401-5*, 102; A. Curry, 'The nationality of men-at-arms serving in English armies in Normandy and the *pays de conquête*, 1415-1450: a preliminary survey', *Reading Medieval Studies*, 18 (1992), 136-63.

[130] *L. & P. Henry VIII*, ii, no. 1366; G.A. Hayes-McCoy, *Scots Mercenary Forces in Ireland, 1563-1603* (Dublin, 1937), 36-7; Lydon, 'The Scottish soldier', 10-14.

[131] K. Simms, *From Kings to Warlords: The Changing Structure of Gaelic Ireland in the Later Middle Ages* (Woodbridge, 1987), 126-27; idem, 'Gaelic warfare in the middle ages', 112-14.

[132] A.J. Otway-Ruthven, *A History of Medieval Ireland* (London, 1968), 367-68.

[133] A. Cosgrove, 'Ireland beyond the Pale, 1399-1460', idem, ed., *A New History of Ireland. Volume II: Medieval Ireland, 1169-1534* (Oxford, 1986), 575. The activity of Scots in Ireland is also reported in *CDS*, v, no. 1091, *sub anno* 1468.

[134] D. Bryan, *The Great Earl of Kildare* (Dublin & Cork, 1933), 19; *Cal. Carew MSS*, i, no. 132. For further attempts to recruit Scots in the 1530s, see M. Ó Siochrú, 'Foreign involvement in the revolt of Silken Thomas, 1534-35', *Proceedings of the Royal Irish Academy*, C96 (1996), 60. I am grateful to the author for drawing my attention to this article.

Similar numbers of Scots were to be found, at least in the early fifteenth century, in France. As we have already seen, some Scots had been recruited by Louis, duke of Touraine in 1391, and in the early fifteenth century he was to acquire the services of others. Most notable among these was David Lindsay, earl of Crawford, who entered Louis's service on 1 January 1402.[135] By then others had found service with Louis's great rival, John the Fearless, duke of Burgundy – the effective ruler of not only the Low Countries but of much of France too from 1407. Among the first to enter Burgundian service was Alexander Stewart, earl of Mar. Together with a contingent of either eighty men (according to a French chronicler) or one hundred men (according to a Scottish source), he joined the 5,000-strong Burgundian army which soundly defeated the Liègois at the battle of Othée in 1408.[136] Mar's recruitment into Burgundian service – similar to that of Sir William Douglas into French service in 1357 – appears to have been the result of an accidental encounter as the earl returned from a social visit to Paris. But other Scots, notably from the Douglas affinity, were more deliberately recruited into the duke's army. Payments were made to a Douglas retainer for a 'certain number' of Scottish archers who served the Burgundians at the siege of Ham, a town on the Somme, in 1411 and it was perhaps in relation to the same occasion that several men-at-arms also received payment from the Burgundians. In 1413 Archibald, earl of Douglas, promised to deliver 4,000 fighting men to the Burgundians.[137]

The year 1413 was to mark the apogee of Duke John's influence within the French kingdom. He was then effectively ousted from power and only briefly resumed his influence at the heart of French government – by seizing control of Paris and with it of the mad King Charles VI in 1418 – before being assassinated on the bridge of Montereau in 1419. Still, this temporary reassertion of Burgundian power in France had occurred at an important moment. The English king Henry V had resumed English intervention abroad by invading France in August 1415 and, the famous victory of Agincourt behind him, Henry had spent the following three years re-establishing English control over much of Normandy. He had hoped for Burgundian acquiescence; but in May 1418 the duke of Burgundy found himself in control of the French government and responsible for masterminding the response to the Lancastrian invasion. By September John was once again seeking Scottish recruits by dispatching his Scottish *echanson* Patrick Legget across the North Sea to recruit men-at-arms and archers in Scotland. Some certainly responded,

---

[135] AN Paris, K57/9/12. Crawford was just one of several aristocratic foreigners whose personal alliance the duke sought at about this time. Others include the count of Guelders (K57/9/8), the margrave of Baden (K56A/6) and the count of Nassau-Saarbrücken (K56A/12).

[136] *La Chronique d'Enguerran de Monstrelet*, ed. L. Douet d'Arcq (Paris, 1857-62), i, 354; *Chron. Wyntoun* (Laing), iii, 102-16; R. Vaughan, *John the Fearless: The Growth of Burgundian Power* (London, 1966), 55-8.

[137] ADN Lille, B4086, fo. 99v; *St Andrews Copiale*, appendix, nos. 7, 9a, 9b.

for in 1419 Thomas Seton, an esquire, served in the duke's bodyguard, as did Andrew Bannatyne, who received payment for services in 1420. In the same year John Gray, a Scottish esquire and captain of a company of men-at-arms, received payment of 500 *livres tournois* 'for services to the king and to the duke and against the king's enemies'.[138] By then Burgundy's 'enemies' no longer meant the English.

The assassination of John the Fearless in 1419 plunged France into a civil war which pitted the new Burgundian duke, Philip the Good, against the perpetrators of John's death, whose loyalties lay with Charles VI's son, the Dauphin and future king Charles VII. The Dauphin now found himself in beleaguered circumstances. His feeble-minded father remained in Paris under Burgundian control. Meanwhile, the Dauphin's inheritance was threatened by the unlikely but potent alliance forged by Henry V with the Burgundians. Moreover, since much of France's native fighting stock had perished at Agincourt in 1415, a combination of the dead and the disaffected left the hapless Dauphin with little choice but to seek military support from abroad. Much came from Italy; more from Spain; and yet more from Scotland. At times these foreigners together accounted for over half of the Dauphin's forces and the Scots alone may have accounted for no less than a quarter of his armies.[139] Indeed, it has been estimated that between 1419 and 1424 over 15,000 Scots were recruited to aid the cause of the future Charles VII.[140]

Unlike the individuals who entered English service in the fourteenth century, or the kin-based galloglass who fought for disparate Irish warlords, most of the Scots who fought in early fifteenth-century France constituted one single and distinctive Scottish army: hence the appointment of John Stewart, lord of Darnley, as 'constable of the *Scottish* army' in 1424. In contrast too with those who had found service in English and Irish armies of the fourteenth century this was an army led by some of the leading magnates of the kingdom. John Stewart, earl of Buchan, and his brother-in-law, Archibald Douglas, earl of Wigtown, served regularly in the campaigns of 1419-24. They were joined in 1423 by the latter's father, Archibald Douglas, fourth earl of Douglas. These were among the most powerful men of the Scottish realm and it is little wonder that their military endeavours in France, unlike those of lesser men in England or Ireland before them, were officially sanctioned by the Scottish government.[141] Official authorisation did not make this a royal army. Indeed, although the captive King James I was himself waging war in France, he did so in support of Henry V and against his

[138] Galbraith, 'Scottish seals from the continent', nos. 14, 55; *La France Gouvernée par Jean sans Peur: Les dépenses du Receveur Général du royaume*, ed. B-A. Pocquet du Haut-Jussé (Paris, 1959), nos. 366, 443, 1241.
[139] P. Contamine, 'La guerre de cent ans: le XV siècle du 'roi de Bourges' au 'très victorieux roi de France" in idem, ed., *Histoire militaire de la France*, i, (Paris, 1992), 193.
[140] P. Contamine, 'Scottish soldiers in France in the second half of the fifteenth century: mercenaries, immigrants or Frenchmen in the making?' in Simpson, *Scottish Soldier*, 26 n.3
[141] *Chron. Bower* (Watt), viii, 113; *Chron. Pluscarden*, ii, 265.

compatriots. Nonetheless, that the Scottish regime *in situ* officially condoned the expeditions of Buchan, Wigtown, Douglas and their followers can only have facilitated recruitment to what was one of the largest Scottish armies ever assembled in the middle ages. It was in practice, if not in theory, a national army.

Of course, the bulk of this army was not made up of magnates or even of lesser barons. Most of those who fought in France between 1419 and 1424 were probably mounted archers, who appear to have outnumbered the men-at-arms by a ratio of two to one. This was much in keeping with the English forces whom they encountered and with at least some of the Scottish contingents which had fought on behalf of the English crown in the 1370s; but it marked a shift of emphasis from the inverse ratio of bowmen to men-at-arms found in French armies until the battle of Agincourt.[142] England's foes were gradually learning the lesson of the lethal impact which rapidly mobile archers could have when fighting in conjunction with men-at-arms. Indeed, it has been surmised that it was the influence of their Scottish mercenaries that led the French to replace their own slow firing crossbowmen with mounted archers.[143] James I, who felt obliged to instruct his subjects to practice their archery instead of football, may have doubted that his fellow countrymen were in a position to advise the French about such matters. Yet, whatever the instigation, mounted archers normally out numbered men-at-arms by two to one in later fifteenth-century French armies, though this fell far short of the ratios of up to 10:1 found in English armies by the mid- fifteenth century.[144]

The Scottish archer was to remain an important element in the French royal armies long after long after the Scottish army, already depleted by its defeat at Cravant in 1423, met a grisly end at the battle of Verneuil on 17 August 1424.[145] Christin Chambers was serving as captain of the Scots archers in the king's guard by 1438.[146] And from the mid-fifteenth century up to a hundred or so archers were to be found in the immediate entourage of the French king, some forming his personal bodyguard and others serving with a smaller number of men-at-arms as members of the wider royal guard. It was these men who, from the reign of Louis XI (1461-1483), were to become known as the Scots Guard and they were to be led from 1461 by a series of Scottish captains – William Stuyer (1461-64), Thomas Stuyer (1465-72), Robert Cunningham (1473-78) and Bérault (Scotticised as Bernard) Stuart (1493-1508). Meanwhile, other Scots were to find employment in the

[142] B. Chevalier, 'Les Ecossais dans les armées de Charles VII jusqu'à la bataille de Verneuil' in R. Pernoud, ed., *Jeanne d'Arc: Une Epoque, une rayonnement* (Paris, 1982), 87; Contamine, 'La guerre de cent ans', 198; idem, *War in the Middle Ages*, 129.
[143] Contamine, 'La guerre de cent ans', 198.
[144] *APS*, ii, 6; Galbraith, 'Scottish seals from the continent', no. 25; C.T. Allmand, *The Hundred Years War* (Cambridge, 1988), 63.
[145] *The Brut*, ii, 441, 497-98, 564-67; *Chron. Bower* (Watt), viii, 114-15, 124-27, 294-95.
[146] Galbraith, 'Scottish seals from the continent', nos. 16-17. Chambers had served in 1428 as captain of the Scots men-at-arms of the royal bodyguard.

companies of the *grande ordonnance*, or standing army, which the French crown established from *c.*1445. These included both archers and men-at-arms, who were often to be found in the same ratio of 2:1 as found in the 1420s. Similar to the Scots Guard, the companies which most (but not all) of these recruits joined were overwhelmingly of Scottish descent and normally commanded by a senior captain of Scottish origin. In 1446, for instance, Robin Pettillow was placed in command of forty men-at-arms and eighty archers who were based in Gévaudan and Vivrais, while Robert Cunningham led an Auvergne-based company of one hundred and twenty soldiers from 1446 until 1455. He then fell into temporary disgrace, but was restored to the captaincy of four hundred men from 1465 until his transfer to the Scots Guard in 1473. At that point he was succeeded as company commander by his son, Joachim. Bernard Stuart too served in the *grand ordonnance* from 1483 until his transfer to the Scots Guard in 1493. By 1498 his nephew, Robert Stuart, was in command of another company of the *ordonnance*.[147]

Compared with the thousands who had served in France between 1419 and 1424 it is likely that in any one year only between six and seven hundred Scots continued to find employment in the restructured French armies which emerged during the second half of the fifteenth century. Whereas in the earlier period Scots had constituted about 25% of the French armies, that proportion had now fallen to about 10-20% between 1425 and 1440. It was to fall still further as French kings turned increasingly to other foreign mercenaries to fill their swelling armies of the later fifteenth and early sixteenth centuries. Some 5,000 Swiss, Germans and Gueldrians served under Charles VIII in 1495, and no less than 10,000 Swiss were in the pay of Francis I by 1523. But although increasingly outnumbered by Swiss in particular, the several hundred strong Scottish contingent was still a sizeable number of men, especially given the population of Scotland. So, for many Scots, employment in the French army still offered a lifetime career. The average length of service of those who served in the standing army was twelve years, while for those in the Scots Guard it was twenty-three years, and, as we have seen, transfers between the two were not uncommon. Of course, many of the Scots came from families long established in France. Bernard Stuart, for instance, was the grandson of the constable in the 1420s, John Stewart. But although a family tradition of service in the French armies had clearly developed among the émigré Scottish community by the second half of the fifteenth century, many of the other thirty to forty Scottish recruits who enrolled annually in France still arrived fresh from Scotland.[148]

That the number of Scots serving in later fifteenth-century France had declined from its astronomical peak of the 1420s was, in part of course, a

---

[147] Contamine, 'Scottish soldiers', 17-18; idem, 'La guerre de cent ans', 202; idem, 'La première modernité: Louis XI, tensions et innovations' in idem, *Histoire militaire*, i, 220.
[148] Contamine, 'Scottish soldiers', 17, 19-20; idem, 'La première modernité: des guerres d'Italie aux guerre de religion, un novel art militaire' in idem, *Histoire militaire*, i, 240.

reflection of the changed political fortunes of the French monarchy. Its ultimate victory in the Hundred Years War in 1453 laid to rest the original *raison d'être* for the recruitment of foreign soldiers. Although Bernard Stuart was apparently to lead a small Franco-Scottish force which fought in support of Henry Tudor against Richard III at the battle of Bosworth (1485), fighting the English was to become a comparatively rare occurrence for those who engaged in French service from the later fifteenth century.[149] Instead, members of the guard were entrusted with the duty of ensuring the king's personal protection. There was an element of ceremonial to such duty. In 1515 twenty-four of their number, 'armed with halberds, arrayed in white cloth jerkins with gold borders, white hose and helmets with white plumes' accompanied the new French king, Francis I (1515-47) on a procession through Paris following his coronation. It was perhaps too the Scots guard who constituted the twenty-four 'archers de la garde de son [i.e. the king's] corps, auec leurs hallebardes & hocquetons blancs' who marched on either side of Henry II, during his belated ceremonial entry of Paris in 1549.[150] At the other end of the royal life cycle the Scots guards were among the last to take their leave of a dead king's coffin. Twenty-five guards attended the body of Louis XII (1498-1515) as it awaited burial in the crypt of St Denis on the night of 12-13 January 1515; and the Scots, together with their Swiss and French colleagues, were among the last to take their leave of Francis I, following almost two months of ceremonial after the king's death on 31 March 1547.[151]

The role of the guard was not merely ceremonial, important though that was in communicating monarchical propaganda to a still largely illiterate society. During the reign of Louis XII, of the four companies of the royal bodyguard, that of the Scots was given responsibility for protection of the king after dark.[152] On occasions the guard was also assigned to protect other members of the royal family. In 1494, for instance, 100 Scots archers were dispatched to defend the Dauphin at Chateau d'Amboise.[153] Yet active service was a possibility for the guard too. Its members, along with those Scots enlisted in the *compagnies d'ordonnance*, were to travel with the king and his armies to Italy, which from 1494 became the object of a new French autarchy. Bernard Stuart was to lead one contingent of the French army which in 1494 crossed the Alps. From there he and his followers journeyed to the east of the

---

[149] No contemporary English source mentions a Scottish presence at Bosworth (M. Bennett, *The Battle of Bosworth* (Stroud, 1985), 9; A. Conway, *Henry VII's Relations with Scotland and Ireland, 1485-98* (Cambridge, 1932), 5-7), though Scots are recorded in sixteenth-century Scottish accounts of the battle (e.g. Pitscottie, *Historie*, i, 191).
[150] E. Cust, *Some Account of the Stuarts of Aubigny in France, 1422-1672* (London, 1891), 56; *C'est l'ordre qui a este tenv a la nouvelle et ioevse entrée...* (Paris, 1549), fo. 25v, reprinted as appendix to I.D. McFarlane, *The Entry of Henri II into Paris, 16 June 1549* (Binghampton, 1982).
[151] F.J. Baumgartner, *Louis XII* (Woodbridge, 1994), 244; R.E. Giesy, *The Royal Funeral Ceremony in Renaissance France* (Geneva, 1960), 16.
[152] Baumgartner, *Louis XII*, 59.
[153] Y. Labaude-Mailfert, *Charles VIII: Le vouloir et la destinée* (Paris, 1986), 216.

Apennines, sacking Mordano near Imola, before crossing the mountains to Arezzo and Siena and beginning their descent on first Rome and then Naples. The quest to install and maintain Charles VIII as king of Naples led to a prolonged stay for Stuart in the *mezzogiorno*. Aragonese attempts to dislodge the French led to frequent military encounters, including that on 12 June 1495 at Seminara in Calabria, when Stuart won a stunning victory against his Spanish adversaries. For three years Stuart served in Italy – as constable of the army, royal lieutenant in Calabria and a member of Charles's Neapolitan council – before the French were temporarily ousted from the kingdom of Naples.

Stuart was to return with other Scots at the behest of Louis XII in 1499. He fell ill at Asti and progressed little further, though he was named governor of the Valtellina, the rugged valley which stretches from Chiavenna to Tirano, into which several of the central Alpine passes descend. His nephew, Robert, meanwhile, was to command a Franco-Scottish garrison in nearby Como. Bernard was again in Italy from 1500, when he was named governor of Milan, until his defeat and imprisonment following the second battle of Seminara on 21 April 1503. Released under the terms of the treaty of Gaeta (1503) and after a sojourn in France, in 1507 he commanded the troops which stormed Genoa on Louis's behalf. Although Stuart himself was to die – in Scotland – in 1508, his nephew and other Scots were repeatedly to accompany both Louis and his successor Francis I on their further but still ultimately futile expeditions to Italy. They served, for instance, at the battles of Agnadello (1509) and Ravenna (1512), in the defence of Brescia (1512) and at the later battles of Marignano (1515) and Pavia (1525), where the new lord of Aubigny, Robert Stuart, was captured along with Francis I.[154]

It was, then, Ireland and France which provided the most important recruiting ground for Scottish soldiers in the fifteenth and sixteenth centuries. These were not the only areas in which Scottish soldiers saw action – though elsewhere opportunities were more limited. By the sixteenth century some were again enlisting in English service: in the 1540s Elis Gruffudd, a loquacious Welsh veteran of Henry VIII's campaigns, reported that the Henrician armies in the Pas de Calais consisted of 'many depraved brutish foreign soldiers from all nations under the sun, [including] Scots'.[155] More significantly, it was also in the sixteenth century that the first signs emerge of Scots being recruited into the armies of the Baltic world. The marriage of James III and Margaret of Denmark in 1468 had been accompanied by a full

[154] P. Contamine, 'Entre France et Ecosse: Bérault Stuart, seigneur d'Aubigny (vers 1452-1508), chef de guerre, diplomate, écrivain militaire' in J. Laidlaw, ed., *The Auld Alliance: France and Scotland over 700 years* (Edinburgh, 1999), 63-7; Cust, *Stuarts of Aubigny*, chapters 3 and 4, passim; Labaude-Mailfert, *Charles VIII: Le vouloir*, passim; idem, *Charles VIII et son milieu, 1470-98: La jeunesse au pouvoir* (Paris, 1975), passim; J. Jacquart, 'Les Stuarts et les guerre d'Italie' in *Actes du Colloque: Des Chardon et des Lys* (Bourges, 1992), 61-8.

[155] G.J. Miller, *Tudor Mercenaries and Auxiliaries, 1485-1547* (Charlotesville, 1980), 48.

diplomatic alliance between Scotland and Denmark, although the military aspects of the treaty appear to have remained largely inoperative for the remainder of the fifteenth century.[156] By the early sixteenth century the Danish crown was facing growing difficulty in retaining control over Sweden and as a consequence, between 1505 and 1512, King John of Denmark dispatched almost annual requests to Scotland for assistance against the rebellious Swedes.[157] These pleas were repeatedly fobbed off by a Scottish crown severely chastened by the ignominious experience of a two-thousand strong army dispatched to Scandinavia in 1502 which, even James IV subsequently admitted, 'achieved less than it should have done'.[158] This was royal gloss on what had proved to be both a military and financial embarrassment. Although the king's force participated in the successful siege of Elvsborg, other enemy-held fortresses in Norway resisted Scottish attack and at Akershus several Scots were killed and the remainder either fled or deserted. The eventual reestablishment of Danish royal authority in Norway owed little to the Scots.[159] Meanwhile, James IV was still attempting to collect arrears of the taxation levied to pay for the expedition in 1506-7.[160]

In future the Scottish crown was more circumspect about sending official aid to Denmark, though it did nothing to prevent individual Scots from joining Danish service. Some did, lured perhaps by the amnesty which in 1519 was offered to criminals willing to fight with the Danes. Certainly the following year a modest contingent of Scots joined the Danes in the siege of Stockholm. Others Scottish soldiers too were to be found in Denmark, some in the service of the bishop of Roskilde and one by 1524 in the service of Malmø, where he had found employment as the municipal gunner.[161] Meanwhile, as the fissure in the Scandinavian union deepened, the Swedes too sought foreign recruits. Readily identified as staunch adherents of the Danes, it is hardly surprising that few Scots joined them at first. Nevertheless, one unidentified Scottish sea captain had been enlisted in Swedish service by 1534 and in 1556 five Scottish soldiers had joined Gustav Vasa's armies at their own instigation – the early trickle of what in the later sixteenth century was to become a force of several thousand.[162] By then some had progressed further east still, into tsarist service, though even in 1507 four Scots metalworkers

---

[156] For the text of the 1468 Scottish-Danish treaty of Copenhagen, see *ER*, viii, pp. lxxvii-lxxxviii; *Charters and other Records of the City and Royal Burgh of Kirkwall*, ed. J. Mooney (Spalding Club, 1952), 96-118.

[157] *James IV Letters*, nos. 3-4, 46, 151, 210, 259-60, 278, 286, 321, 330, 387, 411.

[158] *James IV Letters*, no. 37.

[159] B. Crawford, 'Foreign relations: Scandinavia' in J.M. Brown, ed., *Scottish Society in the Fifteenth Century* (London, 1977), 91-3.

[160] *TA*, iii, 10, 32, 138, 141, 244.

[161] Riis, *Auld Acquaintance*, i, 83-5, 214.

[162] A. N. L. Grosjean, 'Scots and the Swedish State: Diplomacy, military service and ennoblement, 1611-1660' (University of Aberdeen, unpublished PhD thesis, 1998), 49-53. See also A. Åberg, 'Scottish soldiers in the Swedish armies in the sixteenth and seventeenth centuries' in Simpson, *Scottish Soldier*, 90 (dating the appearance of Scots in Sweden to the Northern War of 1563-70).

with expertise in artillery had found their way to Russia, perhaps on Danish recommendation since the Danes and Russians were allied from 1493.[163] This was as yet an isolated example, but as in Sweden, it proved to be the precursor of a substantial Scottish engagement in tsarist, and for that matter also Polish, service from the later sixteenth century.[164]

Yet even in the later middle ages, as we have seen, vast numbers of Scots had entered foreign military service. If there is one aspect of their careers about which remarkably little is known, it is their training. For the sons of nobles there was a well-established pattern of military tuition within the household. Others no doubt received informal paternal or other familial instruction; and some perhaps learned while on the job. But in France at least the growing professionalism of the fighting classes reflected in the emergence of what was in essence a form of military apprenticeship. Pages and valets were enlisted in the *grand ordonnance* in their mid to later teens, and instructed in the arts of combat by serving men-at-arms and archers.[165] Education, it is worth reminding ourselves, takes many forms and few military men were to be found in the austere and elite environment of the medieval university.

Emigrants: The Clergy

By the end of the middle ages the demarcation between the traditional tripartite divisions of society into those who worked, those fought and those who prayed were becoming frayed. Soldiers had never been of an exclusively aristocratic background and by the later middle ages soldiering had become a full-time, professional activity for many who were not aristocrats. For them, fighting was working. Meanwhile, those who prayed had always constituted a socially diverse amalgam. They encompassed an episcopal elite drawn mainly from baronial or burgess backgrounds and also a frequently impoverished rump which constituted the bulk of unpromoted and often unbeneficed priests. Many of those at both ends of the clerical spectrum were to spend time abroad, though for rather different reasons.

Most members of the elite began their careers at university.[166] It was there that men (and only men) went for instruction in the arts of words and ideas. The distinction between teacher and pupil was more blurred in the middle

[163] J.W. Barnhill and P. Dukes, 'North-east Scots in Muscovy in the seventeenth century', *NS*, 1 (1972), 50; W. Westergaard, 'Denmark, Russia and the Swedish revolution, 1480-1503', *Slavonic Review*, 16 (1937-38), 133.

[164] P. Dukes, 'Scottish soldiers in Muscovy' in *The Caledonian Phalanx: Scots in Russia* (National Library of Scotland, 1987), 9-12; D. Fedosov, *The Caledonian Connection: Scotland-Russia ties... A concise biographical list* (Aberdeen, 1996), 18, 36, 59, 70 (wherein the earliest Scottish troops in Muscovite service, all dating from the later sixteenth century, are cited); Fischer, *Germany*, 72; Fischer, *Prussia*, 125 (both volumes by Fischer dating the first appearance of Scots in the service of Danzig to 1577).

[165] Contamine, 'Louis XI', 222.

[166] See above, chapter 2.

ages than it is nowadays. The age difference between students and masters was less pronounced than today and much of the teaching cohort was formed by men in their thirties who were simultaneously studying for advanced degrees in theology and law. It was, however, with a basic arts course that most students began their academic lives. Besides gender and baptism there were few formal restrictions on university entrance. At Paris it had been decreed that students must be at least twenty-one years of age before receiving their licentiate in arts, but dispensations could be obtained and some began their studies as young as fourteen. This, however, was unusual, though at the English universities new students were normally aged between fifteen and seventeen. In theory almost any male was welcome, though in practice by the fifteenth century prior attendance at school was normal and a certain degree of affluence was advisable for fees had to be paid, as well as day-to-day living expenses.[167] Although Scottish students abroad were often described in university matriculation lists as 'paupers' – and thereby absolved, partially at least, from payment of fees – their poverty was probably relative to other students, not absolute.[168] About a quarter of Scottish students between 1340 and 1410 claimed noble or episcopal family connections, though they might be distant, and it is difficult to believe that the earl of Douglas's son, recorded as a pauper student at Cologne in 1443, was genuinely poor. The social origin of others remains, however, obscure.[169]

Whatever their background, the numbers who went to university were small. Before the foundation of the first Scottish university – at St Andrews in 1412 – some 1,100 Scots are known to have studied at universities abroad, making for an average of only about four new students per year. Actual numbers may have been slightly greater: the lack of matriculation lists for most universities before the fourteenth century makes accurate calculation of the student population impossible.[170] Although no similar analysis has been undertaken of students after 1410, the foundation of three Scottish universities before 1500 did not quell the student exodus. If anything the number of those going abroad actually increased.

Some took second degrees on the continent after a period of study in Scotland, but as in earlier centuries many still began their studies abroad. Many, indeed, attended several foreign institutions before completing their studies. In the fifteenth century those who commenced work at Leuven

[167] R.C. Schwinges, 'Admission' in H. de Ridder-Symoens, ed., *A History of the University in Europe. Volume 1: Universities in the middle ages* (Cambridge, 1992), 171-94.
[168] D.E.R. Watt, 'Scottish student life abroad in the fourteenth century', *SHR*, 59 (1980), 17-19. See too R.J. Lyall, 'Scottish students and masters at the universities of Cologne and Louvain in the fifteenth century', *IR*, 36 (1985), 67, in which the author seems to imply the contrary interpretation.
[169] A.I. Dunlop, 'Scottish student life in the fifteenth century', *SHR*, 27 (1947), 62-3; D.E.R. Watt, 'Scottish university men of the thirteenth and fourteenth centuries' in T.C. Smout, ed., *Scotland and Europe, 1200-1850* (Edinburgh, 1986), 2-3.
[170] Watt, *Graduates*.

frequently progressed to Cologne, while William Cameron began his academic career at Cologne in 1458 before undertaking further studies in Bologna and then Ferrara.[171] Still, the proportion of Scots at any one university was small. At Cambridge, for instance, they accounted for less than 1% of the medieval university's known alumni, while the percentage at Oxford was only slightly higher. At Orléans alone were they deemed a sufficiently large group to constitute their own 'nation' – the administrative units into which universities were commonly divided. Even there, however, there were at times only a handful of Scots in attendance.[172]

In the thirteenth century the choice of where to study was limited by the small number of extant universities. The two earliest centres of higher education – Paris (famed for its theological studies as well as for its basic arts degree) and Bologna (renowned for its law schools) – both attracted a sizeable number of Scots. Oxford also attracted some, and Cambridge rather fewer, though neither of medieval England's universities were ever as cosmopolitan in their student intake as Paris.

In the fourteenth century patterns of Scottish recruitment were to change markedly. Few, if any, Scots seem then to have ventured to Italy, perhaps a consequence of the relocation of the papacy to Avignon. Meanwhile, it has often been assumed that Scottish students increasingly turned their backs on England too. Both political discord and the religious division occasioned by the Schism – which saw Scotland and England recognising different popes – created hurdles of suspicion between Scots and English, though they were not insuperable. The son of the earl of Ross was studying at Cambridge in 1306, while Richard II of England granted large numbers of Scots safe conduct to pursue their studies at Oxford during the Schism, albeit under the mindful eye of the authorities.[173] Indeed, notwithstanding the political and religious differences between the two kingdoms, ninety Scottish students were named on 117 safe conducts granted for study at Oxford or Cambridge between 1357 and 1400. There is perhaps an unwarranted degree of scepticism in assuming that, because their presence in England cannot otherwise be corroborated, few actually headed in that direction.[174] Whether or not they did, it seems likely that the French universities remained the most successful in attracting Scottish students in the fourteenth century – even during the later stages of the Schism when Scotland and France differed in their papal allegiances. Paris, where Scottish students were the most numerous nationality among those assigned to the misleadingly named English-German nation, still predominated: there

[171] Lyall, 'Scottish students and masters', 59; R.J. Mitchell, 'Scottish law students in Italy in the later middle ages', *Juridical Review*, 49 (1937), 21-2.
[172] T.H. Aston, 'Oxford's medieval alumni', *PP*, 74 (1977), 22; T.H. Aston, G.D. Duncan and T.A.R. Evans, 'The medieval alumni of the university of Cambridge', *PP*, 86 (1980), 35; 'The Scottish nation at Orléans, 1336-1538', ed. J. Kirkpatrick, *SHS Miscellany*, 2 (1904), 47-102.
[173] *CDS*, ii, no. 1937; *Rot. Scot.*, ii, 45-6.
[174] Watt, 'Scottish university men of the thirteenth and fourteenth centuries', 4.

were at least twenty-nine Scots there in 1329-30.[175] But Scots were also to be found at Orléans and Montpellier in the fourteenth century. At least one studied at Angers too and, once the papal court had settled there, rather more visited the new university of Avignon, founded in 1303.[176]

Figure 5.1: Universities attended by Scots in the later middle ages

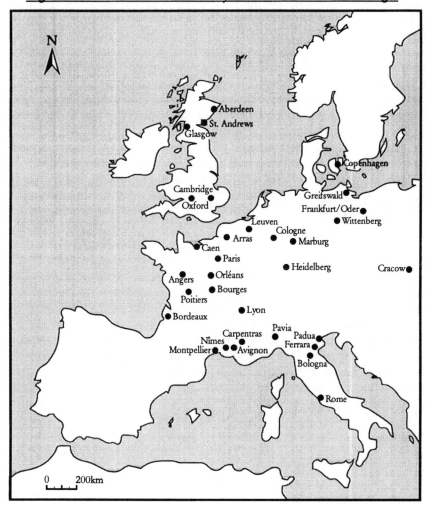

[175] W.J. Courtenay, *Parisian Scholars in the Early Fourteenth Century: A social portrait* (Cambridge, 1999), 118.
[176] R. Swanson, 'The university of St Andrews and the Great Schism, 1410-1419', *Journal of Ecclesaistical History*, 26 (1975), 227-29; D.E.R. Watt, 'Scottish masters and students at Paris in the fourteenth century', *Aberdeen University Review*, 36 (1955-56), 169-80; Kirkpatrick, 'The Scottish nation at Orléans, 1336-1538', 47-102; D.E.R. Watt, 'University graduates in Scottish benefices before 1410', *RSCHS*, 15 (1964), 78.

The diffusion of student recruitment was to become even greater in the following two centuries. The northern Italian universities were once again to attract some Scots in the fifteenth century, as indeed was Rome.[177] By then new universities had also been established within imperial bounds. Although no Scottish connection has been traced with the first of these institutions – the Caroline university at Prague, established in 1348 – by the early fifteenth century comparatively large numbers of Scots were attending the two west German universities of Cologne (founded in 1388 and where Scots can be traced from 1419) and Leuven (founded in 1425, with a Scottish presence from 1426). As indicated in Figure 5.1, penny numbers of Scots were also to be found in Cracow, Greifswald, Heildelberg, Marburg and Wittenberg by 1550, as well as at many of the new provincial universities in France.[178] There were Scottish teachers too in several of these institutions and also at Copenhagen, founded in 1475. The teaching staff of the first Danish university included the Aberdonian Peter Davidson, a graduate of (and then teacher at) Cologne.[179] Yet, despite the growing number of opportunities for scholars as new universities opened their doors across the continent, Paris probably remained the academic magnet for Scots. It was certainly there that many of Scotland's greatest intellectuals – such as the philosopher John Ireland, the theologian John Major and James Liddel, the first living Scot to publish a book – were trained.[180]

It is relatively easy to plot where Scottish students went to university. It is altogether more difficult to account for the comparative popularity of the different locations at which they could be found. Geography, we may suppose, was one determinant. Arguably it was little more difficult for a student from Aberdeenshire to reach Leuven than it was to reach St Andrews. More certainly, in the middle ages as now, some students were attracted by the academic reputation of particular institutions. This alone would explain the enduring appeal of Paris to students from all over Christendom. Subject choice was, however, another consideration. It is this which probably accounts for the popularity of Bologna and Orléans where (unlike Paris) Roman law was taught. It is noticeable too that most of those who went to

---

[177] Mitchell, 'Scottish law students in Italy', 19-24; A.F. Steuart, 'The Scottish 'nation' at the university of Padua', *SHR*, 3 (1905-6), 53-4; *CSSR*, v, nos. 552, 569-70, 573, 586, 616, 674, 817, 836, 1074. See to Watt, *Graduates*, 257, for Andrew de Hawyk, who studied at Siena in the 1420s.
[178] *Papers relating to the Scots in Poland*, ed. A.F. Steuart (SHS, 1915), 347-51; Fischer, *Germany*, 305, 313; J. Durkan, 'The French connection in the sixteenth and early seventeenth centuries' in Smout, *Scotland and Europe*, 36-42.
[179] *Matrikel der Universität Köln*, ed. H. Keussen (Cologne, 1928-31), i, no. 313(97); *Miteilungen aus dem Stadtarchiv Köln*, 36-37 (1918), ed. J. Hansen, no. 1702; Riis, *Auld Acquantaince*, i, 113; ii, 187.
[180] A.I. Cameron, 'Scottish students at Paris, 1466-1492', *Juridical Review*, 48 (1936), 228-53; A. Broadie, *The Shadow of Scotus: Philosophy and faith in pre-Reformation Scotland* (Edinburgh, 1995), 4-6.

Cambridge and Oxford seem to have studied canon law.[181] Montpellier's reputation, meanwhile, rested on the medical training which it offered.

Closely related to both the reputation of particular universities and the subjects which were studied in them was the reputation of individual teachers. This is vividly portrayed in Abelard's account of the competitive intellectual, and bitter personal, disputes associated with the nascent university of Paris in the early twelfth century.[182] The viscious nature of such rivalry subsided in later centuries as the corporate fame of institutions began to outweigh that of the masters who taught in them. Nonetheless, there can be no doubt that some students still sought to study with particular scholars. This seems to explain the initial popularity of Cologne among legal students. In the 1410s the university's teachers included famed lawyers trained in Italy, though from the 1420s other students were attracted to Cologne by the presence of Heimrich van der Vede and Johann Kuyck, notable advocates of the realist philosophical approach originally championed by the Dominican scholar Albert the Great. This, moreover, was an approach to intellectual endeavour which did not find favour at contemporary St Andrews – perhaps another reason for studying abroad.[183] Others, meanwhile, opted for a measure of familiarity while abroad by studying under fellow countrymen. Archibald Whitelaw supervised several Scots during his career at Cologne in the 1440s, though not all Scottish masters welcomed such arrangements. Robert Stoddart, who taught at Cologne between the 1460s and 1480s, seems largely to have shunned fellow Scots, as indeed did perhaps the most accomplished of all Scottish academics, John Duns Scotus, who studied at Cambridge, Oxford and Paris in the thirteenth century.[184]

Whether in the company of a famous scholar or a fellow countryman, we should not suppose that medieval students, any more than their modern counterparts, attended university solely to satisfy their intellectual curiosities. Even more than nowadays, in the middle ages a degree offered employment opportunities. Both secular governments and the church recruited graduates and career prospects may well have influenced the choice of university for some at least. Thomas Muirhead, a student at Bologna in the 1460s, was by no means unusual in petitioning the pope for an ecclesiastical benefice, the income from which would probably have been used to finance his studies. But Muirhead seems to have been hinting at something greater when, in 1461, he remarked that 'students at Rome have greater opportunities of obtaining benefices that those at Bologna'.[185] As papal powers of provision to ecclesiastical office grew from the fourteenth century, proximity to this

---

[181] Aston, 'Oxford's medieval alumni', 22-23; Aston, Duncan and Evans, 'The medieval alumni of the university of Cambridge', 35.
[182] *The Letters of Abelard and Heloise*, ed. B. Radice (Harmondsworth, 1974).
[183] Lyall, 'Scottish students and masters', 55-56, 61, 63. See too Courtenay, *Parisian Scholars*, 87.
[184] Lyall, 'Scottish students and masters', 61, 64; Watt, *Graduates*, 168.
[185] *CSSR*, v, no. 817.

important source of patronage was increasingly attractive to the career-minded student. Hence, very probably, the appearance of Scots at Avignon in the fourteenth century and then at Rome, once the papacy resumed its residence in Italy. Still, even universities far removed from the *curia* sought to look after their own. Many petitioned both the papacy and secular powers, seeking ecclesiastical advancement on behalf of their students – Cologne, for instance, wrote to both James II (in 1446) and Pope Nicholas V (in 1450) on behalf of the Scot John Athilmer.[186]

Yet, wherever they went and for whatever reasons, academic life in medieval universities was remarkably similar, both in terms of the curriculum and in terms of its delivery. The key elements of teaching were the lecture, during which texts were normally read out and explanations of them offered by the lecturer, and the disputation, during which contentious questions regarding the application of knowledge were debated. For some there was perhaps a measure of excitement to a routine which placed a particularly heavy emphasis on the acquisition of grammatical, rhetorical and above all logical skills. There was certainly a measure of quasi-monastic discipline to a lifestyle which theoretically entailed avoidance of women and weapons and, for those who lived in halls, a regulated diet and detachment from the outside world once doors were firmly locked for the night. And there was also poverty – not the self-imposed poverty of the ascetic monk but rather short-term financial problems caused by outlays on fees, books, accommodation and general living expenses.

Not all were temperamentally suited to the rigours of student life. Many aspiring graduates did not complete their degrees. Drop out rates were as high as 50% in the two English universities and even higher in the fifteenth-century German institutions. There only one in ten students who matriculated emerged with a master's degree at the end of their studies.[187] Others clearly fell short of the moral expectations. Together with his mistress, Alexander of Scotland, probably a student in Cologne, was accused of assaulting another man's wife in c.1500 and even Robert Stoddart had an inauspicious start to his academic career there, being fined ten marks for an assault on another Scottish student in 1457.[188]

As for cash-flow problems, many alleviated financial hardship by pawning their books, and one Scot at Cracow even mortgaged his mattress along with his books.[189] There were, however, means of financial support for students beyond that provided by families or patrons or by part-time teaching duties. Bursaries existed – notably that for Scots established at Paris in 1326 on the

---

[186] HA Köln, Universität 26, fos. 19r-20r, 32v. See too D.E.R. Watt, 'University clerks and rolls of petition for benefices, *Speculum*, 34 (1959), 213-29.
[187] A. Cobban, *English University Life in the Middle Ages* (London, 1999), 24; J. Verger, 'Teachers' in Ridder-Symoens, *History of the University*, 146-47.
[188] Hansen, *Mitteilungen*, no. 2317; Lyall, 'Scottish students and masters', 63.
[189] Steuart, *Papers relating to the Scots in Poland*, 348.

basis of an income from a property at Grisy (Dep. Seine-et-Marne) – and some institutions developed loan arrangements for students. Many students also drew an income from ecclesiastical benefices: in 1466, for instance, William Whithill sought papal appointment to a canonry of Dunkeld in order that, after eight years of study, he might meet the expense of obtaining his doctorate from the university of Rome.[190] Yet, however funded, the Scottish student faced problems in having an income from Scotland delivered to his place of study. The mechanisms by which this was undertaken remain largely unclear, though in 1269 a Bolognese student had £5 couriered from Dunblane to Berwick and exchanged for a letter of credit, purchased from Florentine merchants. The letter was then dispatched to Italy and redeemed by the student in Bologna. Such arrangements avoided the danger of robbery associated with sending coin by hand, but they depended upon regular access to Italian bankers. In later centuries Italian financiers were more likely to be found in the Netherlandish towns than in Berwick. By then it had also been written into the Scottish staple treaty of 1469 that Scottish cloth earmarked for the friends and relatives of students studying at Cologne, Leuven and Paris might pass through Bruges unmolested.[191] The precise details of these shipments remain obscure; but that they were guaranteed by treaty suggests that by the later fifteenth century at least supply routes to the more popular universities were already well established.

Most students stayed abroad for only a limited period. A bachelorate in arts might be acquired within three years of commencing study, though, as we have seen, those studying for higher degrees took much longer to obtain their qualifications. But whatever the passing-out point, study opened up career prospects in secular governments and the church and for most preferment occurred at home. Only a few stayed on to teach full-time, among them Thomas Lyall, who having studied at Paris, Leuven and Cologne, went on to serve as rector of his last academic home in 1489, 1502 and 1509. Of these more permanent emigrants some supplemented their academic income by obtaining local benefices. William Lawder, who taught law at Angers, was rector of Pliverut in the diocese of St Malo, in addition to holding canonries at St Malo, Lodève and Rennes, in the later fourteenth century; and Robert Stoddart of Cologne University became a canon of St Mariengraden in the same city.[192] There were also a few like the Orléans student John Kirkmichael who, having finished their studies, embarked upon full-time ecclesiastical posts abroad – in his case, from 1426 to 1438, as bishop of Orléans.[193] Few others

---

[190] *CSSR*, v, no. 1074. More generally on student finances, see Watt, 'Scottish student life abroad', 11-21; Schwinges, 'Student education, student life', 237-41.

[191] Watt, 'Scottish student life abroad', 19-20; M.P. Rooseboom, *The Scottish Staple in the Netherlands* (The Hague, 1910), appendix, no. 26.

[192] *Calendar of Papal Letters to Scotland of Benedict XIII of Avignon, 1394-1419*, ed. F. McGurk (SHS, 1976), 21, 109, 169-171; HA Köln, Haupturkundenarchiv, 2/14124.

[193] Watt, *Graduates*, 311-12

reached the dizzy heights of the episcopate, though by 1496 the graduate monk Laurence Harrison almost acquired the regular equivalent, by becoming prior of the Augustinian house of Newark in Surrey.[194]

Figure 5.2: Loyal Scots in English Lands, 1453-1498

	Number of all Scots	*Number of Clergy*
North		
Co. Durham	2	
Yorkshire	4	
East		
Cambridgeshire	1	1
Essex	14	8
Huntingdonshire	2	1
Lincolnshire	5	
Norfolk	12	4
South		
Bedfordshire	1	1
Berkshire	2	1
Hampshire	1	1
Hertfordshire	4	
Kent	20	9
London	31	3
Middlesex	8	1
Oxfordshire	2	
Surrey	1	
Sussex	3	3
West		
Somerset	1	
Wiltshire	1	
Midlands		
Warwickshire	1	
France		
Calais	1	
Unknown	59	19
TOTAL	176	52

Source: *CPR*, passim.

Historians have dwelt long on the careers forged by prominent graduate clergymen but further down the social scale there was also a substantial exodus of lesser priests too. Most were members of the secular clergy though

---

[194] *CDS*, iv, nos. 1623, 1629.

some regulars went too. In 1425, for instance, a Dominican friar was expelled from Tours in the company of other Scots, while in 1475 John Gaunt, a monk from Perth, was dwelling at the Cistercian house of Warden in Bedfordshire.[195] There were also the Scots who installed themselves in the Irish monastery at Regensburg, some eleven of them, plus an abbot by 1525.[196]

The first Scottish abbot of Regensburg, John Thomson, had originally been a secular priest; and at least a few of his secular colleagues also found employment on the continent. Both the Leuven graduate Stephen Angus (who possibly served as chaplain of St Ninian's aisle in the Carmelite church at Bruges in the 1430s) and Alexander Dume (who by 1545 combined a pastoral role in the reformed church of St James in Greifswald with a professorial appointment in theology at the local university) may perhaps be counted as members of the elite.[197] Both were certainly familiar with university. But we have no indication that either the unnamed Scottish priest resident in Stralsund by 1515 or Robert Lyle, vicar in Danzig by 1543, were so trained;[198] or that the vast majority of their colleagues ministering to English flocks were university educated.

In England some Scots secured valuable benefices: by the 1480s, for instance, both Cuthbert Karre and Adam Ridley were rectors, the former of an Essex parish and the latter of a church in the Romney Marsh district of Kent.[199] Most emigrant priests were, however, mere clerks or chaplains. They generally secured less lucrative appointments than those obtained by Karre and Ridley though, as indicated in Figure 5.2, most were also to be found in the eastern and southern counties of England. This settlement pattern clearly mirrors the distribution of other Scottish migrants in England. Unfortunately, that is not where the similarities between the two groups end: the exact number of both remains uncertain. Still, we do know that in the second half of the fifteenth century about fifty priests sought to formalise and protect their position in England, either by applying for letters of denization or by taking oaths of allegiance to the English crown. This was not the sum total of Scottish clerics then in England: their number does not, for instance,

[195] B.G.H. Ditcham, 'Mutton guzzlers and wine bags: Foreign soldiers and native reactions in fifteenth-century France' in C.T. Allmand, ed., *Power, Culture and Religion in France, c.1350-c.1550* (Woodbridge, 1989), 7; *CPR, 1467-77*, 469.

[196] M. Dilworth, 'The Schottenklöster at the Reformation' in D. McRoberts, ed., *Essays on the Scottish Reformation, 1515-1625* (Glasgow, 1962), 241; idem, 'The first Scottish monks in Ratisbon', *IR*, 16 (1965), 180-98.

[197] A. Stevenson, 'Medieval Scottish associations with Bruges' in T. Brotherstone and D. Ditchburn, eds., *Freedom and Authority: Scotland c.1050-1650* (East Linton, 2000), 101; Wechmar and Biederstedt, 'Die schottische Einwanderung in Vorpommern' 12.

[198] StA Stralsund, St Marien Urkunden, no. 63; NAS Edinburgh, B30/1/4, fo. 71r.

[199] *CPR, 1476-85*, 211, 246; *CPR, 1485-94*, 381. On Ridley, see too J.A.F. Thomson, 'Scots in England in the fifteenth century', *SHR*, 79 (2000), 6.

include the Rochester chaplain Andrew Trail *(fl.1464)*.[200] Indeed, a perhaps more reliable indication of the number of Scottish priests resident in England is afforded by evidence from 1480 and 1481. These were years of Anglo-Scottish warfare during which many Scottish emigrants in England scurried to protect themselves by pledging allegiance to the English crown. And in these two years alone some twenty-seven Scottish clergymen emerged from their chapels and churches to profess their loyalty to the English crown.

The Emigrant Experience: Political Shadows

In England national animosities placed emigrant Scots in an unusually precarious position. Even in times of peace between the two countries, to accuse an Englishmen of being Scottish was deemed abusive and many *bona fide* Englishmen sought redress from such calumny.[201] Women faced similar abuse: one Grimsby women was condemned by another as a 'Scottyshmanhore'.[202] Unfortunately we are left to wonder about the catcalling which genuine Scots were forced to endure in England. In times of war this was exacerbated by state harassment. In 1513, for instance, the English government decreed that all Scots living in England were to be deemed enemies. Their goods were to be seized and their persons banished.[203] It is little wonder that in times of conflict between the two kingdoms, the wary took precautions, either by applying for denizenship or by taking an oath of loyalty to the crown. Both offered a measure of protection against imprisonment and the arrest of property. Ralph Griffiths has noted that between 1447 and 1453 over half of these safeguards were sought in 1449, as hostilities briefly resumed on the border.[204] An even more striking cluster was evident in the 1480s. Of the 188 Scots whose position the English crown formalised between 1450 and 1500, no fewer than 133 of them had sought protection during the war years of 1480 and 1481.[205] Nonetheless, even precautions of this nature were not fail-safe: in 1384 Robert Blackwood was imprisoned in England as an enemy, despite having taken an oath of allegiance to the English crown.[206]

---

[200] KRO Maidstone, DRb/PWr2, fos. 284v-85r. This will made by Trail includes a bequest to his unnamed sister, resident in Bruges, and also provision for the donation of his best breviary to the altar of St Ninian in Bruges.

[201] E.g. *CCR, 1441-47*, 365; *CDS*, v, nos. 1102, 1105; *The York House Books, 1461-1490*, ed. L.C. Attreed, (York, 1991), i, 109-10, 131, 238, 356; ii, 510-11, 520-21, 523-24, 728-29; *Select Cases on Defamation to 1600*, ed. R.H. Helmholz (Selden Soc., 1985), p. xxviii n.7.

[202] E. Gillet, *A History of Grimsby* (London, 1970), 21.

[203] *L. & P. Henry VIII*, i, nos. 2207, 2438, 2467. Those married to Englishwomen were exempt from banishment, but still faced the seizure of half of their property.

[204] R. A. Griffiths, *The Reign of Henry VI* (London, 1981), 553; *CPR, 1447-52*, passim; *CPR, 1452-61*, passim.

[205] The figures are drawn from entries in *CPR, 1446-52, CPR, 1452-61, CPR, 1461-67, CPR, 1467-77, CPR, 1476-85, CPR, 1485-94, CPR, 1494-1509*.

[206] *CDS*, iv, no. 329.

Though a more persistent shadow in England than elsewhere, similar circumstances were not unknown on the continent too. In 1425, for instance, eighteen Scottish inhabitants were expelled from Tours as part of the town's efforts to preclude another Scot succeeding the unwelcome overlordship of the earl of Douglas, who had died at the battle of Verneuil in the previous year.[207] Even more disastrously, in 1513 Maximilian, the Emperor-elect and *de facto* ruler of the Burgundian Netherlands, had told Scots to quit his domains, a decision which, had it been enforced, would have affected not just a sizeable number of emigrants without the protection of local citizenship, but also a significant proportion of Scotland's trade.[208] It is perhaps as well for James IV's reputation that he already lay dead at Flodden and did not have to answer for the bungling ineptitude of his francophile diplomacy. Nevertheless, another arrest order was placed on Netherlandish-based Scots in 1544 and on this occasion the most prominent casualty was the conservator John Moffet, whose French birth and Netherlandish citizenship proved no protection against detention.[209]

Emigrants were, then, often the first victims of political conflict. Indeed, emigrant Scots arguably suffered more than most. They were often difficult to distinguish from Englishmen – hence the credibility of slurs of Scottishness on *bona fide* Englishmen – and since the English government had more enemies than most in the middle ages confusion between English and Scot was potentially dangerous. Given his name, there is an air of inevitability about the troubles encountered in France by the Berwick dressmaker William the Scot called the Englishman. In 1326 – in the aftermath of the Anglo-French war of St Sardos – William had been arrested along with Englishmen in France.[210] On confirmation of his Scottish origins he had been released and furnished with official documentation authenticating his place of birth and nationality, but in 1342 he was once again being harassed as a suspected Englishmen by royal officials in the Vermandois. William, at least, survived the experience. Four of his fellow countrymen were less fortunate. They were murdered in *c.*1349 by three youthful French esquires (one of them only sixteen years old), on the grounds that the assailants thought their victims were English.[211] We may charitably suppose that this was a genuine mistake. Still, that Honoré de Bonet could construct one of the hypothetical paradigms of his *Tree of Battles* around a case which involved the misidentification of Scots as English suggests that such occurrences were rather more common than the surviving evidence indicates.[212]

[207] Ditcham, 'Mutton guzzlers', 7.
[208] *James V Letters*, 7.
[209] RA Brussel, inv. no. 169/I, 405/1, 4-8.
[210] Edward II had declared war on France in July 1326: M. McKissack, *The Fourteenth Century, 1307-1399* (Oxford, 1959), 110.
[211] Viard and Vallée, *Registres du Trésor des Chartres*, iii, nos. 2636, 5400, 7094, 7179.
[212] Honoré Bonet, *The Tree of Battles*, ed. G.W. Coopland (Liverpool, 1949), 186.

Of course, by the fifteenth century many French and others too were well acquainted with Scots. Some seemed to live harmoniously with the new arrivals. Little friction is evident at Orléans, for instance, which seems to have fared well in the early fifteenth century under the protection of John Stewart, lord of Darnley, and John Kirkmichael, the local bishop. Danzig too did little to swell the influx of Scots to, and through, its walls. It rejected appeals at the Hanseatic diet of 1498 to stop granting Scots burgess-ship on the grounds that 'if all foreigners were to be expelled from the town, it would remain half-deserted'.[213] Elsewhere, however, the Scots gained a rather more unwelcome familiarity. In parts of France, and Poland and Ireland too, large immigrant communities faced considerable hostility albeit of a different variety from that evident in the English crown's domains. In some areas natives perceived the Scots as an economic threat and in the Prussian hinterland and latterly in Scandinavia they began to agitate for restrictions on pedlars' activities. By contrast, many French regarded Scots more as a physical or social threat. There was some justification to this. Soldiers who killed enemies were welcome but they had a bad habit of harming the non-combatant too. Even once the English had been ousted from Gascony in 1453 the Scots fought on in France, now against their supposed Spanish allies, their murderous brawls continuing for another four years. Between 1450 and 1464 over 30% of crimes committed in Gascony were perpetrated by soldiers, many of them Scottish.[214] Meanwhile, Scottish military leaders had already usurped the traditional role of the native nobility. The social pretensions of subordinate Scots clearly irked the Dax shoemaker who, mid quarrel, bellowed 'damned Scots villain, I'm as well born a man as you are.'[215] Immigrant aspirations became the subject of wild conspiracy theories. The French chronicler Thomas Basin was probably not alone in the *Schadenfreude* which he expressed when his Scottish allies were trounced at the battle of Verneuil in 1424. Had they defeated the English, he thought, they would have proceeded to murder the nobility of Anjou, Touraine and Berry; and then to have seized aristocratic houses, lands, riches and women: they were savage and barbarian, these Scots who had come to his fellow countrymen's rescue.[216] Basin had been only twelve years old when the Scottish army was crushed at Verneuil, but the legend of their greedy aspirations lived on.

Those who had recruited or welcomed Scottish armies did little to counteract such sentiment. Charles VII's scornful remarks to the townspeople of Lyon are well known. 'Anyway,' he wrote in 1423, making light of the defeat which his forces had suffered at the battle of Cravant, 'at the said siege there were very few nobles of our realm, almost none in fact, but only Scots,

---

[213] Ditcham, 'Mutton guzzlers', 7-8; *HR,1477-1530*, iv, no. 81.
[214] R. Harris, *Valois Guyenne: A study in politics, government and society in late medieval France* (Woodbridge, 1994), 142-43.
[215] Ditcham, 'Mutton guzzlers', 10.
[216] Thomas Basin, *Histoire de Charles VII*, ed., C. Samarins (Paris, 1964-65), i, 98-101.

Spaniards and other foreigners who normally live off the land, so the harm done was not great.'[217] His comments might as easily have been made by an Irish warlord too. Indeed in 1504 the earl of Kildare was only marginally more circumspect in anticipation of the battle of Knocktoe. 'Kall me the Capttayne of the Galegals,' he allegedly proclaimed, 'for he and his shall begine this game for it ys lesse forsse of their lostys then it is of our yonge men.'[218] Foreign soldiers were expected to reap victories on the battlefield. But if not, their lives were cheap and expendable. The master of the mercenary was a fickle beast too.

The Emigrant Experience: Living Together

Native hostility to immigrants perhaps partly explains why emigrant Scots often found it desirable to live in close proximity to one another – though doubtless many found such arrangements congenial, as well as prudent, since they afforded opportunities for social and commercial networking. In Durham the Scottish population, which was probably composed primarily of poorer labourers and journeymen, congregated in the backdwellings of the old borough, while in London they were particularly numerous in Cripplegate and Farringdon.[219] In Bergen-op-Zoom the Scots were located in the area beyond the Steenbergsepoort, which by the early sixteenth century had become known as Schotse vest ('Scottish moat').[220] In other towns too Scots gave their names to the streets which they inhabited. In Bruges the thirteenth-century Schottendijk was supplemented in following centuries by a Scottish bridge, place, street and gate, as well as several Scottish houses. In Stralsund a Schottengang is recorded by the early sixteenth century. In Greifswald a Schottenstrasse had appeared by 1557 and in Danzig the suburb of Alt Schottland had emerged by the sixteenth century.[221] Whether a Scottish presence was also responsible for the naming of Cologne's Schottingasse (a name found repeatedly in the thirteenth century before subsequently falling into desuetude) and the Parisian rue d'Ecosse in the parish of St Hilaire (which before 1313 had been known as the rue due Chaudron), remains uncertain.[222]

Of course, there were exceptions to this apparent emigrant clubbishness. Not all of Bergen-op-Zoom's Scots lived in the same district of the town: the

[217] L. Caillet, *Etudes sur les relations de la commune de Lyon avec Charles VII et Louis XI* (Paris and Lyon, 1909), 106-7; Y. Lequin, *La Mosaïque France: Histoire des etrangers et de l'immigration* (Paris, 1988), 166-67.

[218] Bryan, *Great Earl of Kildare*, 245; *Cal. Carew MSS*, vi, 183.

[219] M. Bonney, *Lordship and Urban Community: Durham and its overlords, 1250-1540* (Cambridge, 1990), 187-88; Bolton, *Alien Communities of London*, 93-6, 99-104.

[220] C.J.F. Slootmans, *Paas- en Koudemarkten te Bergen-op-Zoom, 1365-1565* (Tilberg, 1985), i, 336-42.

[221] Stevenson, 'Medieval Scottish associations with Bruges', 93, 98, 108; Wechmar and Biederstedt, 'Die schottishe Einwanderung in Vorpommern', 13; P. Simson, *Geschichte der Stadt Danzig bis 1926* (Gdansk, 1913), i, 376-77.

[222] H. Keussen, *Topographie der Stadt Köln im Mittelalter* (Bonn, 1910), ii, 276; Michel, *Les Ecossais en France*, i, 10.

conservator John Moffet seems to have preferred the Lieve Vrowestraat to the Schotse vest; and the family of the merchant Thomas Richardson resided in the Wowerstraat.[223] In university towns such as Paris several Scots might seek to lodge together in the same abode, though these lodgings do not appear to have been concentrated in the same neighbourhood as those of other Scots. Nowhere do Scottish students seem to have congregated in particular colleges, not even at Balliol College in Oxford, despite the Scottish connections of its founder.[224] An even greater degree of isolation from fellow countrymen is evident among many of the more humble emigrants who headed for rural areas. The nearest compatriot of the Scottish baker in Burnham (Norfolk) was twenty miles away in Lynn. Yet, concentrations of Scots emerged even in some rural areas. When Margaret the 'kapknytter' from Ponteland put down her knitting needles for the night, she might well have amused herself not only with her husband, but also with the nine other Scots who were living in the Northumberland village in 1439-40.[225] This, indeed, was the norm in many parts of rural Northumberland – and it may explain the apparent ease with which the future Pope Pius II was spirited by his Scottish guide across the Anglo-Scottish frontier, apparently undetected, in 1435.[226]

In areas where Scots resided in close proximity, their Scottish identity was probably more enduring than it was elsewhere, not least because these communities were recognisable to those in whose midst they lived. Even after spending several decades in Bergen-op-Zoom, the cloth merchant Thomas Richardson was still clearly Scottish as far as the town's authorities were concerned. As a very old man of over seventy years, they deemed Richardson the most suitable character to lure Scottish merchants to the town in 1487-88 and 1488-89.[227] Where numerous enough, emigrants also continued to use their own language in everyday conversation. Scots, for instance, remained the language of the Scots Guard in France in the sixteenth century.[228] Sometimes too they married among themselves. Indeed, Margaret Manuel, an early sixteenth-century inhabitant of Middleburg, acquired two successive Scottish husbands.[229] Elsewhere, emigrant Scots often transacted business among themselves: property in Bergen-op-Zoom's Schotse vest, for instance, was regularly conveyed from one Scot to another.[230]

[223] Slootmans, *Paas- en Koudemarkten*, 932, 939.
[224] Watt, 'Scottish student life abroad', 7-11; Aston, 'Oxford's medieval alumini', 23; J. Jones, *Balliol College Oxford: A history, 1263-1939* (Oxford, 1988), 2-10.
[225] Kerling, 'Aliens in Norfolk', 208; PRO London, E179/158/41, fo. 6.
[226] I owe this idea to discussion with Anthony Goodman.
[227] GA Bergen-op-Zoom, inv. no. 759/760, fos. 43, 132; Smit, *Bronnen, 1485-1585*, i, nos. 24, 30. Richardson was described as 68 years old in 1484: GA Bergen-op-Zoom, inv. no. 5269, fo. 125v; Smit, *Bronnen, 1150-1485*, ii, no. 1819.
[228] Ditcham, 'Mutton guzzlers', 7.
[229] *James IV Letters*, no. 10.
[230] Slootmans, *Paas- en Koudemarkten*, 336-43.

In some foreign towns communal religious bonds reinforced a distinct sense of Scottishness. At the university of Orléans, where Scottish students uniquely constituted their own administrative unit or 'nation', St Andrew's Day was a special feast day.[231] Elsewhere, Scottish altars, which provided a focus for national worship, were maintained at churches in Bruges by the fourteenth century and Danzig (in the church of the black monks) by the later fifteenth century. Others had been founded by the early sixteenth century in Bergen-op-Zoom (in the church of St Ontcommeren), Copenhagen (in the church of St Mary), Dieppe (in the church of St James), Elsinore (in the church of St Olai) and Regensburg.[232] Moreover, all of these altars were dedicated to St Ninian and/or to St Andrew. Although veneration of neither saint was uniquely Scottish – Ninian was revered all around the Irish Sea littoral, while Andrew was popular with the Burgundians as well as the Scots – their combination was highly distinctive.

In at least some instances these bonds of identity were further fostered by frequent written communication with relatives at home. Most students were certainly possessed of the skills necessary for such a task and we are fortunate to possess a collection of some eighteen (probably draft) letters which one thirteenth-century Scottish student, who studied in Paris and Oxford, wrote to family and friends. The letters relate much about the author's activities and associates while at university. They also demonstrate a keen interest in the collection of various tithes, principally from Inchture in Perthshire, with which William de Bernham sought to support his studies.[233] Students were not alone in maintaining such contact. We have already seen how some merchants undertook business abroad on behalf of relatives in Scotland. This presupposed that they were literate, or had access to the services of those who were, since satisfactory business relationships depended upon communication between the partners. There is, indeed, some more solid evidence to demonstrate such contact: in 1543, for instance, John Darg, an inhabitant of Danzig, wrote home to his native Haddington.[234] Additionally, or (for those who were not literate) alternatively, some emigrants seem to have made periodic visits home. This presumably explains the reason why one Scotsman was in Newcastle in 1515, while his wife and children were in Dieppe; and

[231] Watt, 'Scottish student life abroad', 7. See too Kirkpatrick, 'The Scottish nation at the university of Orléans', 60, for the nation's emblem, a cross of St Andrews.

[232] M. Dilworth, *The Scots in Franconia* (Edinburgh, 1974), 19; G. Hay, 'A Scottish altarpiece in Copenhagen', *IR*, 7 (1956), 5-10; Mollat, *Le commerce normand*, 171; Riis, *Auld Acquaintance*, i, 196-97, 240-41; A. Stevenson, 'Notice of an early sixteenth-century Scottish colony at Bergen-op-Zoom and an altar once dedicated to St Ninian', *IR*, 26 (1975), 50-2; idem, 'Medieval Scottish associations with Bruges', 98-100; WAP Gdansk, 300/43/2b, fo. 377. That no similar altar existed in Middelburg is suggested by that town's undertaking of 1541 to establish a Scottish chapel or an altar should the Scottish staple be relocated there: Smit, *Bronnen, 1485-1585*, i, nos. 658, 667.

[233] 'Letters of a Scottish student at Paris and Oxford, c.1250', ed. N.P. Kerr and W.A. Pantin, *Formularies which Bear on the History of Oxford, c.1204-1420*, ed. H.E. Slater and W.A. Pantin (Oxford Historical Soc., 1942), 472-91.

[234] NAS Edinburgh, B30/1/4, fos. 69r-72r.

perhaps also the presence of one Colette, pregnant with twins in Dundee, while her husband soldier was in France in 1484.[235]

The longer, however, emigrants remained abroad, the greater the prospects of their assimilation into native society. This occurred even in areas where Scots were numerous. In some instances we find Scots changing their names or having had them changed by locals. Presumably this was to suit local speech patterns, though possibly also it was designed to facilitate acceptance by natives. By 1466 Gilbert Richardson, originally from Edinburgh, was known as Albert Scot in Lübeck; and both are perhaps to be equated with the Albert Schotte alias von dem Berge (?Edinburgh) recorded at Stralsund in 1463.[236] It would seem as if Balthasar Daniel too had adapted his name to suit local circumstances in Stralsund. He himself was sufficiently conscious of his origins to seek James V's assistance in 1542 when denied the commercial privileges of Scottish merchants in Denmark. Yet it is telling that Daniel's difficulties arose when harbour masters in Elsinore assumed (presumably on linguistic grounds) that Daniel must have been German.[237]

Daniel had married locally in Stralsund and this no doubt was an important catalyst in his assimilation process. In this he was not alone. Political exiles, merchants, soldiers and others too often married foreigners; and in Ireland the MacSweens even invented improbable Irish genealogical origins which linked the family with the native O'Neils.[238] Of course marital ties and residence abroad did not immediately override the national allegiance of birth. This is best of all demonstrated by the Scotswoman who, having lived in Cumberland for forty years, still risked her life in 1389 to forewarn her compatriots of an English raiding party by lighting a beacon on a border hill.[239] Yet, one wonders whether her children, if she had any, would have taken similar action.

Property interests further welded the immigrant to his or her new homeland. It was often cumbersome and inconvenient for relatives in Scotland to utilise goods and lands bequeathed to them by emigrants and *vice versa*. Some found it simpler to sever this familial bond by disposing of such interests to locals. Thus, in 1556 the Scottish merchant John Langlands purchased the Polish inheritance of the late David Logan from the latter's brother, John, in Restalrig; and in 1531 Alexander Scott, resident in Middelburg, granted his Edinburgh properties to his son, William.[240] Often,

---

[235] *L. & P. Henry VIII*, ii, no. 378; Contamine, 'Scottish soldiers in France', 20. It is also possible that Colette was impregnated by someone other than her husband.
[236] AH Lübeck, Anglicana 155b; NLS Edinburgh, ch. 58; *Der Stralsunder Liber Memoriales*, ed. H.D. Schroeder (Schwerin etc., 1964-82), v, no. 598.
[237] *James V Letters*, 441.
[238] Simms, *From Warlords to Kings*, 122, 124.
[239] H. Summerson, 'Crime and society in medieval Cumberland', *Transactions of the Cumberland and Westmorland Antiquarian and Archaeological Society*, 82 (1982), 114.
[240] NAS Edinburgh, NP1/12, fos. 123r-23v; *Protocol Book of John Foular, 1528-34*, ed. J. Durkan (SRS, 1985), no. 306.

however, there were legal impediments to emigrants disposing of their estate, unless they had obtained formal rights of citizenship – another assimilatory inducement. This problem was only overcome in France in 1513 when Louis XII granted all Scots in France similar testatory rights to those already enjoyed by French natives.[241] His concession was in part perhaps made in response to the problems encountered by John Cockburn, on whose behalf James IV had intervened with the French government, following the detention of his father's inheritance.[242]

The Emigrant Experience: Accolades and Anonymity

Differences in the demographic concentration, social status and economic wherewithal make it facile to generalise about the experience of emigrant Scots. Some were astoundingly successful in their new environments, most notably perhaps Bernard Stuart, lord of Aubigny.[243] Dubbed one of 'only two top military commanders of first-class quality' produced by medieval Scotland, Stuart was, however, more than a soldier.[244] He was an intimate of kings. In his later, gout-ridden years he and the Aragonese monarch, Ferdinand the Catholic, reminisced at length, as old men do, of their campaigns against the Moors.[245] He was feted by the Scottish monarch, James IV, as 'the father of war'.[246] He played hand-tennis (*paume*) with the French monarch, Charles VIII, and was party to an examination of the physical attributes of a naked Anne of Brittany, prior to her betrothal to the same king.[247] He was also a diplomat, leading French missions to Milan in 1491, to Ferrara, Mantua and Florence in 1494 and to Scotland in 1484 and 1508.[248] Artists made portraits of him and William Dunbar eulogised him in 'The Ballad of Lord Bernard Stewart' and an 'Elegy on the Death of Bernard

---

[241] AN Paris, J687/33; *James IV Letters*, no. 565. These rights were confirmed in 1558 (*Inventaire Sommaires des Registres de la Jurade, 1520 à 1783*, ed. D. le Vacher (Bordeaux, 1896-1947), v, 67). Applications for naturalisation in fifteenth-century France are recorded in AN Paris, series JJ, passim, e.g. JJ197/265, JJ197/411, JJ226/373.)

[242] *James IV Letters*, no. 35; *RSS*, i, no. 1298. For the protracted wrangling concerning the inheritance of Donald Crum, resident of Middelburg, see *James IV Letters*, nos. 9-11, 29, 31, 152, 172; and for that of David Morton, resident of Copenhagen, see *James IV Letters*, no. 288.

[243] The lordship of Aubigny had been granted to Bernard's grandfather, John Stewart of Darnley, in 1423: AN Paris, K168/20; *Inventaire Analytique des Ordonnances Enregistrées au Parliament de Paris, jusqu'à la mort de Louis XII*, ed. H. Stein (Paris, 1908), no. 429.

[244] G.G. Simpson, 'Introduction' in Simpson, *Scottish Soldier*, p.xi. The other top military commander, Simpson claims, was Robert I.

[245] Jean d'Auton, *Chroniques de Louis XII*, R. de Maulde la Clavière (Paris, 1889-95), iv, 357-58.

[246] Pitscottie, *Historie*, i, 241-42.

[247] Labaude-Mailfert, *Charles VIII et son milieu*, 143; idem, *Charles VIII: Le vouloir*, 132.

[248] *Lettres de Charles VIII, Roi de France*, ed. P. Pélicier (Paris, 1898-1905), iii, no. 590; iv, nos. 757, 761, 773- 74 and p. 334; *Negocations Diplomatique de la France avec la Toscane*, ed. A. Desjardin (Paris, 1875-76), i, 410; *ER*, ix, 340; xiii, 123; *James IV Letters*, nos. 175, 177-81, 189; *TA*, iv, 110, 112-13, 117-18, 122, 128.

Stewart'.[249] Stuart's own *Traité sur l'Art de la Guerre*, dictated to his secretary, Etienne le Jeune of Aubigny, was part of a long established *genre* of warfare studies. Although his thought lacked originality, Stuart is the only Scotsman of the middle ages known to have penned such a work.[250] Success and stature brought rewards. In addition to his ancestral title of lord of Aubigny, Stuart was created duke of Terre Nove, marquis of Girace and Squilazzo, and count of Beamont, Acry and Venassac. We may doubt, if his ancestors had stayed in Scotland, whether Stuart would have won such international renown.

Much the same might be said of a sprinkling of Scottish academics. Arguably only John Duns Scotus, who had studied at Cambridge, Oxford and Paris before his death at Cologne in *c.*1308, was of truly international academic stature.[251] Nonetheless, several others acquired important positions in their own universities and some won wider recognition outside academia. John Major attracted a galaxy of budding intellectual stars to his Parisian classroom, while Thomas Lyall was perhaps the most prominent of all later medieval Scots at Cologne, serving as rector of the university in 1489, 1502 and 1509. He was rigorously orthodox – or so we may suspect given his appointment to assist the Inquisitor Jakob Sprengler in 1489. In 1513 Lyall was asked by the emperor-elect Maximilian to examine allegedly heretical passages concerning the Virgin Mary in the Talmud, a corpus of ancient Rabbinic writings which constituted the basis of religious authority for Judaism. This matter arose as a result of the accusations levelled against Johannes Reuchlin, who, in something of a *cause celebre*, had been accused of heresy on account of his alleged 'favour and friendship to the blind and accursed Jews'.[252]

Bernard Stuart, John Duns Scotus and Thomas Lyall were certainly not typical of emigrant Scots. A few won fame in their respective professions, but the vast majority of emigrants remain obscure. Even among the merchant émigrés few acquired the political prominence in urban affairs which their counterparts at home exercised. Others, like the tailor Andrew Henderson of Edinburgh who went to Rome 'for the sake of adventure and his trade', failed even to make a modest income. Having been reduced to begging for his daily bread, the miserable Henderson reportedly stuck to every penny he received. Henderson was one of ten of his compatriots to be apprehended on similar

---

[249] G. Menzies, ed., *The Scottish Nation* (London, 1972), Plate 7; Cust, *Stuarts of Aubigny*, frontispiece; Dunbar, *Poems*, 108-12.

[250] Bérault Stuart, *Traité sur l'art de la guerre*, ed. E. de Comminges (The Hague, 1976); Contamine, *War in the Middle Ages*, 119-20, 210-18; idem, 'The war literature of the late middle ages: the treatises of Robert de Balsac and Béraud, lord of Aubigny' in C.T. Allmand, ed., *War, Literature and Politics* (Liverpool, 1976), 116-21.

[251] Watt, *Graduates*, 168; C. Balić, 'The life and works of John Duns Scotus' in J.K. Ryan and B.M. Bonansea, eds., *John Duns Scotus, 1265-1965* (Washington D.C., 1965); Broadie, *Shadow of Scotus*, 7-51.

[252] Lyall, 'Scottish students and masters', 64; Hansen, *Mitteilungen*, nos. 1091, 2667; HA Köln, Ratsprotokoll 1a, fo. 44v; Huiskes and Groeten, *Beschlüsse des Rates Köln*, ii, 99 (no. 484).

charges at Breslau in *c.*1470; others, down on their luck, were to found in Northallerton in Yorkshire, where the local *maison dieu* housed an increasing number of poor, itinerant Scots from the 1490s.[253] Yet we may wonder whether their lives would have been vastly more enriching had they stayed at home. And even their experiences were preferable to the nameless thousands who died soon after arrival on the battlefields of France, Ireland and Italy.

International acclaim and anonymous death were the extremes of the emigrant experience. For those who survived the battlefield, the experience of life abroad lay somewhere in between these polarities. Certainly the rewards of emigration should not be exaggerated. Although perhaps not an unbiased witness, the English king Henry V was scornful that Scots and Spaniards received only twenty or twenty-four francs per month from the French, 'the which money is feble that it passath not a good English noble a month'.[254] Henry overlooked the point that had they stayed at home these warriors would not have been paid at all for their military service. Moreover, many acquired lands which otherwise they would perhaps not have done in Scotland. Some, it is true, were a mirage: John Stewart of Darnley was made count of Evreux in 1427, though Evreux was itself still in English hands;[255] and although the fourth earl of Douglas did obtain physical possession of part of the duchy of Touraine in 1423, after the new duke's death at Verneuil it was swiftly removed from the clutch of his heirs and reallocated to the young Louis III d'Anjou, the titular king of Sicily, and his mother, Yolande of Anjou.[256] In this phase of the Hundred Years War many of the grants made by the French crown were speculative and had either to be won from the English or defended against Charles VII's casual redistribution of lands belonging to absentee landlords. In this, by effectively emigrating and making their new lands their normal place of residence, the Stuarts of Aubigny (and galloglass such as the MacSweens settled in Tír Conaill) were altogether more successful than their Douglas compatriots.[257] Aubigny-sur-Nère was to remain in Stuart hands from 1423 until 1672. By contrast, the Douglases not only lost Touraine. In 1402 Countess Isabella of Mar found it more convenient to sell an earlier Douglas acquisition at St Saëns in Normandy than to administer it from her distant *caput* in Kildrummy.[258]

---

[253] Fischer, *Germany*, 241-42; C.M. Newman, 'Order and community in the north: the liberty of Allertonshire in the later fifteenth century' in A.J. Pollard, ed., *The North of England in the Age of Richard III* (Stroud, 1996), 63.

[254] *Foedera* (O), x, 163.

[255] D.L. Galbraith, 'Scottish seals from the continent', *SHR*, 27 (1948), no. 61; Michel, *Les Ecossais en France*, i, 154-55; Stein, *Inventaire analytique*, no. 446.

[256] AN Paris, J680/70; B. Chevalier, *Tours, ville royale, 1356-1520: Origine et développement d'une capitale à la fin du moyen age* (Leuven, 1975), 7. Douglas's duchy included the castellanies of Tours, Loches, Châtillon and Langeais, but not Chinon, which seems to have remained in the possession of the French queen, Marie d'Anjou.

[257] On MacSween acquisitions in Ireland, see Simms, *From Kings to Warlords*, 123.

[258] M. L'abbé Cochet, 'Notice historique et archéologique sur l'eglise et l'abbaye de Saint-Saëns (Seine-inférieure)', *Bulletin de la Societé des Antiquaires de Normandie*, 20 (18??), 455.

It terms of landed wealth, then, the balance sheet is mixed, for aristocrats at least. But it would be misleading to suppose that this was the only factor to feature on the aristocratic agenda. As Alastair Macdonald has reminded us, aristocrats fought for other reasons too;[259] and in terms of winning chivalric glory, pursuing nationalist animosity towards the English, acquiring international fame and the pure, simple enjoyment of battle, the Douglases fared rather better. It was a priceless accolade which they acquired when a Piacenzan family sought to invent grand aristocratic associations for itself by obtaining imperial permission to be styled the Douglas Scotti.[260] Whether similar sentiments influenced the non-aristocratic element in society is open to question, though some may well have opted to emigrate because fighting was an enjoyable career option not available in Scotland. Nonetheless, profit perhaps loomed rather more exclusively in non-aristocratic considerations; and it was not just selected aristocrats who acquired reward. Once the English had been ousted from their French possessions in 1453 the land market in France flourished. This enabled an otherwise obscure archer, John Bron of Coulton, to pay 60 *écus d'or* for half of a seigneurie near St-Sever. His commanding officer, Robin Petillow, perhaps scoffed: he paid nothing for the lordship of Sauveterre, which, along with several other presumably well remunerated administrative and military positions, he was granted by the crown.[261] Yet, if we are to judge the emigrant experience, we must do so on individual rather than comparative terms or, at least judge like with like. Unfortunately, we know insufficient about the vast majority of (non-aristocratic) emigrants, or their counterparts at home, to be able to undertake such an exercise in any meaningful way.

The Number of Emigrants

If it is impossible to generalise about the experience of medieval Scotland's migrants, it is equally difficult to establish how many actually emigrated. Medieval demography is more an intuition than a science since few of the tools of which modern demographers make use are extant for the medieval period. Some sources have perished and others were never even compiled. Although estimates of the number who emigrated can be reached for some professions, some places and some periods, we remain largely ignorant of the true number who left their homeland, the proportion of the Scottish population they constituted and the proportion of the population they

---

[259] A.J. Macdonald, 'Profit, politics and personality: war and the later medieval Scottish nobility' in Brotherstone and Ditchburn, *Freedom and Authority*, 118-30.

[260] D.M. Bueno de Mesquita, 'Ludovico Sforza and his vassals' in E.F. Jacob, *Italian Renaissance Studies: A tribute to the late Cecilia M. Ady* (London, 1960), 187; J. Heers, *Family Clans in the Middle Ages: A study of political and social structures in urban areas* (Amsterdam, 1977), 43. I have been available to track down Heer's source: E.N. Rocca, 'Le origine della famiglia Scotti', *Piacenza* (1933). See too M. Brown, *The Black Douglases: War and lordship in later medieval Scotland* (East Linton, 1998), 210-24, for a general survey of Douglas contacts with Europe.

[261] Harris, *Valois Guyenne*, 28.

amounted to in their new abodes. Yet some tentative estimates are called for if we are to attempt to assess the significance of the late medieval diaspora.

The problem begins with attempting to calculate the population of late medieval Scotland. The most convincing arguments suggest that at its peak towards the end of the thirteenth century the population of Scotland was about one million.[262] The demographic crisis of the fourteenth century, introduced by war, continued by famine and culminating in plague, probably reduced that number substantially. Following Fordun's cautious estimate of plague deaths and considering comparative evidence for elsewhere in Europe, we can reckon on the loss of about a third of the population. This would leave a population of about 700,000. Renewed outbreaks of plague and other diseases ensured that in most countries of the Latin west population fell further, reaching its nadir in the late fourteenth and early fifteenth centuries and only showing significant signs of recovery towards the end of the fifteenth century. If Scotland followed this pattern, the population peak of the late thirteenth century would not have been reached again until about 1700.

What, then, of the number of emigrants? Despite the population growth of the thirteenth century, it is difficult to find evidence of substantial emigration in that period. Students who travelled abroad constituted only a minuscule proportion of the population as a whole and the exodus of galloglass was only just beginning. There were clearly some other emigrants who settled in England, Ireland and perhaps in France too. Nevertheless, the best efforts of the English government to seize lands belonging to those living under its jurisdiction in 1296, at the start of the wars of independence, seem to have resulted in the discovery of well under a hundred suspects.[263] Meanwhile, although a Henri d'Ecosse is recorded as a burgess of Valenciennes in 1247-48 and almost sixty inhabitants of Paris in 1292 were identified by tax assessors with names such as 'Escoz' or 'l'Escot', we cannot be certain that they were indeed Scots.[264] Similarly, the significance of the topographical evidence from Bruges and Cologne (where the Schottendijk and Schottingasse were already established) remains obscure. In neither town can large numbers of individual Scots be identified at this juncture. It seems unlikely too that well-known thirteenth-century families such as the Schotte in Soest or the Scotti in Piacenza were themselves of Scottish extraction. Their names were more probably derived from some distant mercantile contacts with Scotland.[265] Our evidence for the thirteenth century is, of course, patchy. But it would be rash to conclude that growing population at home sparked substantial emigration

---

[262] A. Grant, *Independence and Nationhood: Scotland, 1306-1468* (London, 1984), 72-5.

[263] *CDS*, ii, nos. 736, 834, 838, 841; *CJRI, 1295-1303* (London, 1905), 158.

[264] *Archives Departmental du Nord: Repertoire numerique. Serie H, Tome II*, ed., P. & A.M. Piétresson (Avesnes-sur-Helpes, 1943), 148; Michel, *Les Ecossais en France*, i, 11; *Documents Origineaux de L'histoire de France* (Archives Nationales, 1872), no. 302.

[265] F. von Klocke, *Alt Soester Bürgeremeister aus sechs Jahrhunderten, ihre Familien und Ihre Standesverhältnisse* (Soest, 1927), 101; for Scotti merchants trading in thirteenth-century England, see *CDS*, ii, nos. 167, 698.

abroad. Population growth was a factor common to most of the Latin west in the thirteenth century and there were few attractive opportunities anywhere in Christendom for the would-be economic migrant.

This was, of course, to change in the fourteenth century. Warfare began the change and scattered the population of *ante-bellum* Berwick, or at least those who survived the Edwardian onslaught of 1296. Some, such as the dressmaker William the Scot, ventured far from the turbulent town, in his case to Noyon in France by the 1320s. But famine and then plague eased the pressure on resources and probably acted as something of a brake on population dispersal abroad as the living enjoyed the fruits of their inheritance from the dead and limited the number of potential economic migrants. The student population, of course, was still travelling abroad – but still in small numbers – as was the merchant community. Its contacts were chiefly with the staple town of Bruges. Although there was evidently a sizeable Scottish community there by the mid-fourteenth century – large enough to establish a religious confraternity and rich enough to make provision for its own chapel and burial ground – the concentration of Scottish trade on Bruges for most of the fourteenth century makes it unlikely that similar communities existed elsewhere.[266]

Instead, it is to the later fourteenth century that we must turn for the first signs of a major exodus of Scots. The possibility that the novel scale of late fourteenth-century migration is merely a mirage, created by the greater abundance of source material, should not, of course, be discounted. Nevertheless, there is a striking chronological coincidence in this period between signs of emigration and new reasons for it. On the one hand, hundreds of Scots entered English military service and a sufficiently large group of others was resident in northern England to be taken notice of in an Anglo-Scottish truce of 1398.[267] On the other hand, landowners faced pressing financial problems and the cost of labour spiralled as population levels approached their nadir. Elsewhere in Europe economic self-interest had spawned greater demographic mobility, and there is no reason to suppose that Scots were immune to the lure of lucrative incomes – even if they were to be found in England on the territory of a long-standing enemy.

In the fifteenth century the exodus continued. The most credible calculations of its size relate to the soldiering element. As we have seen, it has been argued that between 1419 and 1424 about 15,000 Scots rallied to the beleaguered Dauphin's cause alone. If correct that would suggest that an astonishing 2%, maybe even 2.5%, of the Scottish population saw service in France. That, of course, was an extraordinary episode. But although in the later fifteenth century the number of soldiers in France was to be reckoned in hundreds rather thousands (and a more modest 0.1% of the Scottish

---

[266] Stevenson, 'Medieval Scottish associations with Bruges', 94-5, 100.
[267] *Foedera* (O), viii, 55. For specific examples of Scots resident in England and Calais in the late fourteenth century, see *CDS*, iv, nos. 344, 390, 449, 544, 594.

population), their number was supplemented by those in Ireland. There were, on occasions, between perhaps two and three thousand active galloglass in the later fifteenth and early sixteenth centuries, say between another 0.3% and 0.4% of the Scottish population. All in all, then, approximately 0.5% of the Scottish population was fighting abroad towards the end of the middle ages.

To their number we must add students, manual workers and traders. Students constituted a relatively small, though growing, number. Whereas in the fourteenth century only five or six headed abroad to commence study each year, an average of between five and six Scots matriculated annually at Cologne alone between 1428 and 1500. At Leuven the average number was between three and four each year from 1427 and 1500. The duration of their studies varied: a baccalaureate might be obtained within two years, but a degree in one of the higher faculties might take between six and eight years. If we assume an average of four years study per matriculated student, between about thirty and forty Scots would have been attending these two universities at any one time. Considerably more, of course, might be expected to have been in Paris and smaller numbers elsewhere. Nevertheless, at most we might reckon upon an average of about a hundred Scots studying abroad in any one year of the fifteenth century, a statistically minuscule proportion, of say 0.01%, of the Scottish population.

Rather more significant, but even more difficult to quantify, were the various groups of emigrant labourers and traders. As we have seen, complaints about itinerant Scots began to find expression across much of northern Europe in the last quarter of the fifteenth century, suggesting that by then Scots possessed a marked nuisance value. How many Scots were required to constitute a nuisance remains difficult to establish. The argument already noted, that complaints against vagrancy were more a reflection of political, social or moral values than of the number of vagrants, is an unsettling one for our purposes. It implies that there was not necessarily an increase in the number of Scottish vagrants in later fifteenth-century England or, if similar circumstances prevailed, elsewhere. Yet, in one sense this does not matter. Even if we cannot be certain that there was an increase in Scottish vagrancy, there were clearly large numbers of itinerant Scots in fifteenth-century Europe.

Evidence from England substantiates this. There, records of the tax levied on aliens provide the first extant survey of the immigrant population in any country of the Latin west. The alien subsidy was first introduced in 1440. It was levied again in each of the four following years and then revived in 1449. From 1453 it became an annual tax, normally granted by the English parliament for the duration of a reign. It was not, however, comprehensive. Various groups were, at different times, exempted: children under twelve years of age, regular clergymen and alien women married to Englishmen were routinely overlooked, while servants in aristocratic households escaped (initially at least), as, for most of the period, did foreign merchants. It was, then, the poorer aliens upon whom the tax collectors predominantly set their eyes. In those areas for which figures survive, they identified approximately 13,262 aliens in 1440, of whom perhaps as many as 1,329 (some 10%) were Scots. Most were to be found in the northern counties. Indeed, there the alien population was overwhelmingly Scottish. There were only three clearly identifiable continentals in Northumberland, compared with some 741 aliens who were either certainly or probably Scots. In neighbouring Cumberland there were at least 142 Scots. The assessors failed to record the origin of the remaining 168 aliens in the county, but they may well have been predominantly or entirely Scots too. In Westmorland, where aliens were similarly undesignated, it seems likely that Scots constituted a good proportion of the 105 aliens identified. And in Yorkshire – the only other northern county for which figures survive – the Scots accounted for 137 of the 1,104 aliens, or about 12.4% of the total. Further south thirty-six more Scots were to be found scattered throughout sixteen counties.[268] There were very probably others too. No subsidy records survive for London from 1440, though by 1442 there was a further handful of Scots to be found there. Neither, for 1440, is there any evidence from Co. Durham and Cheshire (both palatine jurisdictions), though one might reasonably assume a large contingent of them in Durham at least. Lancashire too is likely to have been home to at least a small number of Scots. If generous allowance is made for the unknown numbers of Scots in Durham, in aristocratic households throughout England, and for those who evaded detection by the assessors or were too young for assessment; if a more modest allowance is made for other counties and towns for which no figures survive (Bristol, Coventry, Hull, London, Bedfordshire, Derbyshire, parts of Lincolnshire, Lancashire and Oxfordshire); and if most of the undesignated aliens in the north are factored in, we can perhaps reckon upon about 2,000 Scots residing in England in 1440.

Whether or not this pattern of emigration changed over the following decades still awaits a more detailed scrutiny of the voluminous surviving subsidy records. But while there does not seem to have been much of an increase in the number of Scots in Norfolk by the early 1480s, by 1483 London had become the home to a sizeable community of 161 Scots, who constituted approximately 10% of the city's assessed alien population.[269] Meanwhile, as we have seen in the form of applications for denizenship in the 1480s and the royal proclamation of 1490 against itinerant Scots, anecdotal evidence suggests that the number of Scots in late fifteenth-century England had increased. Still, if we err on the side of caution, we may conclude that about 0.3% of the Scottish population emigrated to England in the fifteenth

[268] S.L. Thrupp, 'A survey of the alien population of England in 1440', *Speculum*, 32 (1957), 270-72. I have amended Thrupp's figures to exclude her estimates for some missing areas on the basis of later, and probably less full, returns.
[269] S.L. Thrupp, 'Aliens in and around London in the fifteenth century' in A.E.J. Hollaender and W. Kellaway, eds., *Studies in London History* (London, 1969), 260; Bolton, *Alien Communities of London*, 29.

century. Whether it took similar numbers of Scots to excite the complaints evident in Prussia in the later fifteenth century, and then Scandinavia, perhaps requires a leap of faith too far. The only reliable estimates for this region suggest that about 200 Scots were living in the two Danish towns of Elsinore and Malmø.[270] Although the pace of emigration to Prussia and Poland probably quickened in the last quarter of the sixteenth century, it would not be outrageous to suggest that two or three thousand Scots were already there by the last quarter of the fifteenth century.[271] Scrappy and unsatisfactory though the evidence is, we may reckon on about 2,000 Scots in England in any one year, perhaps 2,000 more in the southern Baltic region, another 2,000 in Ireland, and perhaps 1,000 in France, the Low Countries and elsewhere. Such calculations are perhaps conservative. Aggregated they produce an overall estimate of about 7,000 Scots resident abroad in the final quarter of the fifteenth century. If we assume a Scottish population of, at that date, still around 700,000, that would make for an exodus rate of 1% of the population. While no similar calculations have been attempted for the sixteenth century, such a figure is only slightly higher than one recently advanced for the first half of the seventeenth century.[272]

Reasons for Emigration

If estimating the number of Scots who emigrated in the later middle ages is an inexact exercise, explaining why they went is more problematic still. None has left us a detailed account or diary of the sort which has so personalised the traumatic eighteenth- and nineteenth-century clearances. Recent historiography provides little help either. Those who argue that the later medieval Scottish economy was severely depressed have a tailor-made explanation for emigration; but elsewhere I have argued that this was not the case. Another recent study of pedlars has ventured an essentially geographical explanation. Since the Scottish pedlars of northern Europe had their parallels elsewhere in the continent – the inner Swiss and northern Savoyards engaged in similar activities in lowland areas north of the Alps, while those from southern Savoy and the Dauphiné penetrated southern France – it followed that peddling was *une affaire des montagnards*.[273] Indeed, the proposition might have been extended since the Swiss, like the Scots, were renowned mercenaries too. It is not, however, certain that either the Scottish pedlars or the Scottish mercenaries (save for those in Ireland) were predominantly from the

---

[270] Riis, *Auld Acquaintance*, ii, 9-10, 18-20.

[271] T.C. Smout, N.C. Landsman and T.M. Devine, 'Scottish emigration in the seventeenth and eighteenth centuries' in N. Canny, ed., *Europeans on the Move: Studies on European migration, 1500-1800* (Oxford, 1994), 80-81. See to A. Bieganska, 'A note on the Scots in Poland' in T.C. Smout, ed., *Scotland and Europe, 1200-1850* (Edinburgh, 1986), 157-65.

[272] Smout, Landsman and Devine, 'Scottish emigration in the seventeenth and eighteenth centuries', 85, in which Smout suggests a figure of between 0.7% and 1.2% for the period between 1600 and 1650.

[273] L. Fontaine, *Histoire du Colportage en Europe, XVe-XIXe Siècle* (Paris, 1993), 19.

mountainous Highland regions of Scotland. While the origin of most Scottish pedlars and mercenaries remains unknown, those for whom evidence is available had an overwhelmingly Lowland origin. Whatever else induced Scottish emigration, it seems unlikely that it was the comparative infertility of their native farming lands.

A rather different explanation for the medieval diaspora was provided by the fifteenth-century chronicler Walter Bower. Describing the events of 1337, Bower claimed that years of warfare then induced a famine. As a result, he concluded, 'many people from the kingdom of Scotland left their native soil and settled with people in England or abroad' and their descendants were still to be found there.[274] At first sight, and in the absence of other detailed evidence, this seems a persuasive enough explanation. The correlation between, on the one hand, famine and warfare and, on the other hand, emigration is an equation familiar to students of later periods. Bower had, it would seem, identified two of the plausible 'push factors' so beloved by historians of later migration.

Yet, the abbot's account is not without its problems. For a start, neither warfare nor famine were new to 1337. Warfare had been a persistent scourge of the Scottish landscape for some forty years by then – and a remorselessly consistent factor between 1333 and 1337, as Edward Balliol and Edward III of England sought to remove the fragile grip of the Bruce regime. Meanwhile, though famine had been less of a constant, it too had made its debut on the Scottish stage long before 1337, notably between 1308 and 1310 and again between 1315 and 1318. Bower was seemingly unaware of the latter outbreak, though it was probably the worst in recorded history. He did note the earlier instance, again ascribing its cause to warfare, though on this occasion he did not claim that the catastrophic combination of war and famine led to emigration. For Bower, then, 1337 witnessed a unique coincidence of war, famine and emigration. Unfortunately there is little other evidence to suggest that emigration was particularly significant in this year.

Bower was not, of course, a historian and he was not constrained by the bounds of reliable evidence and rational interpretation. Indeed, the abbot's source of information for his interpretation of the events of 1337 is unknown, though it was not his principal informant on fourteenth-century developments, the chronicler John of Fordun. Fordun mentions the horrendous effects of warfare which left parts of Gowrie and the Mearns like 'a hopeless wilderness' in 1337 but he does not mention emigration.[275] Bower may have had access to another written source, now unknown, or he may have picked up a mid-fifteenth-century oral tradition in his west Fife homeland. We cannot, then, dismiss his claims out of hand. However, it is far from inconceivable that the abbot fabricated his comments on migration in

[274] *Chron. Bower* (Watt), vii, 127.
[275] *Chron. Fordun*, ii, 353.

order to explain a phenomenon which he knew to be current in his own day – and which we know, from the evidence of the English alien subsidy accounts, to have been current when he compiled his *Scotichronicon* in the 1440s.

If the uniqueness of the circumstances in 1337 may be questioned, there can be little doubt that ever since the outbreak of Anglo-Scottish warfare in 1296 many had felt compelled to leave Scotland. Two Balliol kings and two Bruce kings fled, along with a clutch of prominent aristocrats and politically active clergymen, all no doubt accompanied by their more humble retainers. In 1307 many Gallovidian peasants too had scuttled across the border into Inglewood forest, as Edward Bruce's armies attempted to wrest control of the province.[276] Most of these kings, clerics and peasants were more akin to refugees than emigrants. Most probably planned (or at least hoped) to return home once the political circumstances turned to their advantage, though for some departure proved permanent. Aristocratic Comyns and Strathbogies carved out new careers for themselves in England, while some members of the vanquished Gallovidian MacDowell family settled in Ireland.[277] Others preferred France. The demoralised King John, ensconced on his Picard estates from 1302 until his death in 1313, is the most prominent example, though it was near Paris, a notable home to exiles from across Europe, that Bishop William Fraser of St Andrews died in 1297. We have also seen how one dressmaker deserted Berwick for Noyon. The effects of warfare, famine, or both seem a plausible explanation for what seems to have been his permanent relocation to France. Berwick had been sacked in 1296 and was attacked again in 1297, 1316 and 1318. Neither had it escaped the great famine of 1315-18. In 1315 English officials reported many starving to death in the town; and in 1316 the garrison had foraged for food as far as Melrose, some forty kilometres away. This, surely, was a good reason to go for good.

The key problem is not, however, identifying emigrants (or at least exiles and refugees) who left Scotland in times of war or famine. It is instead in determining how significant an inducement to emigration warfare and famine actually were. Emigration, as we have seen, appears to have grown steadily from the later fourteenth century, reaching a peak in the last quarter of the fifteenth century. Anglo-Scottish warfare, by contrast, was at its peak between 1296 and 1337, intermittent in the later fourteenth century and rare in the fifteenth century, only to rekindle periodically in the first half of the sixteenth century. Of course, infrequent Anglo-Scottish conflict did not necessarily make for a peaceful kingdom. Many political historians have argued that the

---

[276] *CDS*, iii, no. 14. It should also be noted that, supposedly in 1330, the small Baltic town of Anklam sought to regulate the activity of Scottish dealers in linen ware and other retail goods. The relevant document has long since disappeared, but it looks suspiciously as if it has been mis-dated, since the circumstances fit better with much later developments in neighbouring towns. (Fischer, *Prussia*, 4 n.2.)

[277] *CDS*, iii, no. 857; Lydon, 'The Scottish soldier in medieval Ireland', 8; Hayes-McCoy, *Scots Mercenary Forces in Ireland*, 23.

later fourteenth and fifteenth centuries were characterised by brutal struggle between magnate factions. Presumably it was local communities who were at the cutting edge of this conflict.[278] Here, perhaps, is more fertile ground for detecting a conflictual spur to emigration. Other historians, however, remain unconvinced of this supposedly grim edge to domestic politics, besides which their opponents have yet to spell out the full impact of the struggle which they perceive on the vast, non-aristocratic majority of the population. For the moment, then, we are left with the possibility that war and emigration moved in opposite trajectories. Meanwhile, it is similarly difficult to relate the spurt of emigration from the later fourteenth century to famine. Like warfare, famine would appear to have been a more regular occurrence in the fourteenth century than it was in the fifteenth and early sixteenth centuries. Still, poor harvests in the Borders in 1435 and more widespread food shortages in the early 1450s, (perhaps) early 1480s and in c.1508 possibly prompted some to migrate in search of food.[279]

If neither famine nor warfare are completely satisfactory explanations for emigration from the later fourteenth century, we must look for other reasons. Some are obvious. Exiles are self explanatory. Criminals offered an amnesty to fight in early sixteenth-century Scandinavia require little further consideration either.[280] Meanwhile, for those who were inured to the violent but glorious life of soldiering, France or Ireland were predictable hunting grounds, once the Anglo-Scottish conflict of the early fourteenth century turned into the largely cold war of attrition of later decades. Similarly, for much of the period those who wished to attend university had no option but to travel abroad; and even after the foundation of three Scottish universities in the fifteenth century many considered that these only offered a preparatory experience before progressing to more advanced study elsewhere. There were others too for whom a foreign education or training was the stimulus to departure. Music and business studies may form part of the modern university curriculum, but medieval musicians and businessmen had to look elsewhere to learn their trades. James III sponsored a lengthy sojourn in Bruges between 1472 and 1474 for his 'litill lutare', John Browne, who went there to 'lere his craft'; and the Edinburgh council granted James Lawder 'prebender of thair queir' licence to spend a year in England and France 'that he may have and get better eruditioun in musik and playing'.[281] Whether artists too were sent

---

[278] This idea (developed by my co-author) is elaborated in D. Ditchburn and A.J. Macdonald, 'Medieval Scotland' in R.A. Houston and W. Knox, eds., *The Penguin History of Scotland* (Harmondsworth, 2001, forthcoming).

[279] *Chron. Bower* (Watt), viii, 293, 299; *APS*, ii, 36, 41, 119; D. Ditchburn, 'Piracy and war at sea in late medieval Scotland' in T.C. Smout, ed., *Scotland and the Sea* (Edinburgh, 1992), 49-50; *James IV Letters*, nos. 167-68, 328. See too ibid, no. 326.

[280] Riis, *Auld Acquaintance*, i, 84; *ADCP*, 144-45.

[281] R. Strohm, *Music in Late Medieval Bruges* (rev. ed., Oxford, 1990), 65; *TA*, i, 43, 60, 67; *Edin. Recs.*, ii, 176.

abroad for training remains unknown;[282] some perhaps did, though most, like the majority of musicians, probably gained their skills in Scotland. The same no doubt applied for most businessmen, although by the sixteenth century at the latest some Edinburgh merchants were dispatching their children to Bordeaux, specifically so that they might learn a foreign language and acquire proficiency in the conduct of commerce.[283]

Pursuit of a foreign education was, in part, often undertaken with a view to longer-term career prospects. Others were attracted abroad by the prospect of more immediate material gain. When asked why he had come to Rastenburg in 1557, the pedlar Thomas Gibson was blunt in his response: 'I should like to make some money,' he said.[284] Pedlars clearly, and correctly, sensed economic opportunities in the north German, Polish and Scandinavian countryside; and that merchants and others gravitated towards Baltic ports such as Stralsund and Danzig and to the Netherlandish towns was no geographical accident. Danzig's economy was booming by the fifteenth century, thanks to the growing demand in the west for Polish grain which was shipped through the town. Meanwhile, in the west the Netherlands remained the commercial hub of northern Europe, where the sheer volume of traffic and exchange far exceeded that in even the largest Scottish towns. And, although there is little concensus on the matter, some historians have also argued that the English economy too expanded rapidly in the later fifteenth century, thereby creating employment opportunities for migrants.[285]

The reverse side of the Dick Whittington syndrome, or the 'pull' factors as historians of later periods prefer to label them, was that, for many, opportunities abroad seemed better than those at home. We need not look to famine or warfare as explanations for this since both were at least as prevalent abroad as they were in Scotland. Besides, warfare attracted as many Scottish emigrants as it drove away. Neither is it necessary to accept that the Scottish economy was severely depressed to advance individual poverty as one reason for emigration. Some emigrants had clearly fallen on hard times. This is vividly illustrated by John Darg of Haddington who had moved to Danzig by the 1540s. Darg was not a man of poor origins. His father was a burgess of Haddington and when he died Darg inherited his father's property in the town. Rather than return home to take possession of the tenement, Darg made arrangements for it to be given to his brother-in-law, John Sharp, who had given Darg 'certane greit sowmes of monye'. More pertinently he had also

[282] M.R. Apted and S. Hannabuss, *Painters in Scotland, 1301-1700: A biographical dictionary* (Edinburgh, 1978), 2.

[283] *France Ecosse* (Archives Nationales, 1956), nos. 635-36.

[284] Fischer, *Prussia*, 20-1.

[285] G.D. Snooks, *Economics without Time: A science blind to the forces of historical change* (Basingstoke, 1993), esp. chapter 7; I. Blanchard, *The Middle Ages: A concept too many ?* (Avonbridge, 1996), 23-6. For a more sceptical interpretation of the English economy, see R.H. Britnell, 'The English economy and the government, 1450-1550' in J.L. Watts, ed., *The End of the Middle Ages?* (Stroud, 1998), 89-116.

paid off Darg's creditors: Darg was clearly a man in debt.[286] Similar circumstances may explain why in 1484 the Cologne emigrant Robert Gillespie alienated property inherited from his late father in Aberdeen. He too was clearly not a man of poor origins and it seems likely that he was related to the family of the same name whose members were both politically and commercially prominent in fifteenth-century Aberdeen.[287] Both of these examples concern young men who seem to have drifted into debt at home before the death of their reasonably affluent fathers. Here, unfortunately, the line of enquiry fizzles out. The circumstances which explain Darg's predicament, and possibly that of Gillespie, remain unknown: they lie perhaps in the field of poor familial business acumen; or perhaps in the field of youthful ambition frustrated by an older generation; or perhaps even in an over-exuberance at the gambling table. Yet, for whatever reason, both men seem to have looked abroad to ease financial problems which could not be solved so readily at home.

Poverty takes many forms. Impecunious merchants had their counterparts among the aristocracy and peasantry. Certainly the later middle ages witnessed a crisis in aristocratic incomes as the returns from land fell and the price of labour escalated in the wake of depopulation. To weather the storm aristocrats sought out new forms of income. Some expanded their landholdings to uphold their income; others sought pensions from the crown to maintain their lifestyle. Similar sources of wealth might be acquired abroad too as Scottish aristocratic vultures circled over the French body politic and the fractious Irish landscape. If indeed there was money to be made from booty, ransom and blackmail on the Anglo-Scottish border, there was more still to be had (or so it may have seemed) abroad.

A more pressing variety of poverty can be discerned among elements of the Scottish peasantry. Although, on further consideration, Bower's seemingly seductive reasoning is of limited assistance, perhaps Sir David Lindsay's blatantly fictitious characters provide us with an ultimately more convincing explanation for the migratory inclinations of these later medieval Scots. In his *Satyre of the Thrie Estaitis*, the character Gude Counsall proclaims, 'Thir pure commouns daylie as ye may see declynis doun till extreme povertie.'[288] The reason for their poverty, in Lindsay's view, was feuing – the process by which landlords granted peasants life-long tenancies at fixed rents, in return for substantial initial payments from each peasant. Those who could afford these payments gained a tenurial security not hitherto enjoyed by most peasants, but John Major, though sympathetic to feuing on the grounds that it solved the problem of short-term tenancies and might thereby encourage investment, was also aware of the drawback. 'The land of the whole realm,' he conceded, might 'be offered to the highest bidder and most of the farmers be forthwith

---

[286] NAS Edinburgh, B30/1/4, fo. 70v.
[287] HA Köln, Briefbuch, 34/35, fo. 99.
[288] Lindsay, *Satyre*, 93-4.

driven from their holdings to their ruin and the disturbance of the kingdom'.[289]   Lindsay was more blunt. Those who could not pay were 'plainlie harlit out be the heid'.

Feuing was not a practice new to the sixteenth century. Indeed, its origins have been traced back to the thirteenth century. Nevertheless, the pace of feuing seems to have quickened in the fifteenth and sixteenth centuries. Although most feued land, perhaps over 60% of it, was taken up by sitting tenants, elsewhere peasants remained liable to eviction if the new feuar brought new tenants with him. Of course this was not always the case. Indeed, surprisingly little litigation arose regarding evictions, which has led the most recent authoritative commentator on the subject to conclude that feuing was not the 'fatal revolution' which Lindsay would have us believe.[290] Still, we may wonder how many of those evicted bothered to take their grievances to court, even though, for those forced off the land, options were then limited. According to Major, writing in 1512, the culture of the apprenticeship was weak among rural inhabitants. Many, he claimed, remained 'untrained and idle'.[291] It is this which perhaps explains the sudden concern of the Scottish parliament with idle men in 1425 and beggars in 1427.[292] That the unemployed and unfortunate were the victims of feuing is suggested by the parliamentary record of 1428, wherein James I won the agreement of landlords to curtail their evictions for a year.[293] This, however, was merely a stay of execution for parliament was to return to the vexed and apparently related problems of feuing and vagrancy in 1458, by when the crown seems to have become a committed advocate of feuing.[294] Feuing continued. So, it would seem, did vagrancy. Vagrants once again featured on the parliamentary agenda of 1478 and 1503; and in 1515 Aberdeen's council ordered that the town be searched for 'strangers, ganglers and beggars'.[295] Those found were to be removed from the burgh. Yet, other than draconian measures to curtail vagrancy – in 1458 beggars were to be branded on the cheek and banished from the country – parliament offered no real solution to what was clearly an on-going problem.[296]

The solution, it seems likely, was found in emigration. Itinerant and unskilled beggars were unlikely to have been constrained by political frontiers. Indeed, it is exactly these sorts of people who, it might be expected, constituted the unskilled labourers and servants to be found in England.

---

[289] John Major, *A History of Greater Britain*, ed. A. Constable (SHS, 1892), 30-31; J.H. Burns, 'The Scotland of John Major', *IR*, 2 (1951), 67.
[290] M. H. B. Sanderson, *Scottish Rural Society in the Sixteenth Century* (Edinburgh, 1982), 166.
[291] Burns, 'The Scotland of John Major', 68.
[292] *APS*, ii, 11, 15.
[293] *APS*, ii, 17.
[294] *APS*, ii, 49-51. See too ibid, ii, 36, 43, 45; and R. Nicholson, *Scotland: The later middle ages* (Edinburgh, 1974), 381-83.
[295] *APS*, ii, 119; 251; CA Aberdeen, CR/9, 444.
[296] *APS*, ii, 50.

Others perhaps became soldiers, for, as Major noted in 1530, 'farmers, accustomed to long labour beneath the sun and open sky, suddenly show themselves the hardiest of soldiers in the day of battle'.[297] Yet others perhaps joined the vagrants and pedlars to be found in England and elsewhere. Migrants from the countryside, it is worth considering, might well have possessed a particular aptitude for recognising the needs of rural inhabitants elsewhere in Europe.

Feuing provides an obvious source of the manpower which fuelled emigration. There is, however, another (and not necessarily contradictory) explanation which must also be considered. That is that emigration was a consequence of an expanding population. Some recovery in population levels would, of course, be expected after the initial outbreak of plague had struck mid-fourteenth-century Scotland. In many other countries, however, natural population recovery was offset by the regular recurrence of pestilence in later decades as plague became endemic. Scotland too witnessed renewed outbreaks of plague – at least one is recorded in almost every decade between the 1370s and 1550s. Nevertheless, there are grounds for supposing that Scotland was not as badly affected by plague as some other countries. Fordun, as we have seen, was more cautious than many of his continental counterparts in estimating the death toll in the mid-fourteenth century. Since bubonic plague generally thrives in warmer climes than those of Scotland, this seems feasible. Moreover, many of the later outbreaks of plague seem to have occurred in the winter months. Although these were probably of the pneumonic strain of plague, which was even more deadly than the bubonic variety, the speed of death suffered by victims of pneumonic plague, coupled with the low demographic density and the small size of towns, probably served to limit Scottish death tolls. Victims were dead before the infectious pneumonic strain of the disease had spread too far. As a consequence the later outbreaks of plague, though frequent, were often localised. If so, the brake which plague applied to natural population growth elsewhere in Europe was less severely applied in Scotland.

If we follow the optimists among the English historical confraternity, then in England population increase from the end of the fifteenth century coincided with vibrant economic growth. The latter, indeed, was perhaps on a par with growth rates witnessed in the period after the Second World War.[298] Such a scenario provides a meaningful context for explaining Scottish migration to England, at least from the later fifteenth century. Economic growth created work which, in turn, attracted migrants. Of course, while some economists and historians have detected a link between the two phenomena, rising population was not a necessary determinant for economic growth. Structural economic changes, such as the level of urbanisation, the

[297] Burns, 'The Scotland of John Major', 66.
[298] See note 285, above.

development of trade and the expansion of agricultural productivity were as, if not more, important in establishing the pre-conditions for growth. In Scotland there are, indeed, some signs of structural change in the economy. Urbanisation was probably increasing, albeit from a lowly base; and feuing, if Major was correct, ought to have encouraged greater agricultural productivity. Yet, even if these conditions encouraged some growth in the Scottish economy, we must conclude that it was at best sluggish. It was certainly inadequate to present a perhaps rising population with sufficient employment opportunities at home.

6
Perceptions

'... we beseech your holiness... to admonish and exhort the king of England... to leave in peace us Scots, who live in this poor little Scotland beyond which there is no dwelling-place at all...'[1]

It was with these emotive words that in 1320 the barons and freeholders of Scotland appealed to the pope's sense of justice in their on-going battle with the tyrannous English. The political purpose of their message was clear enough. Despite the defeat of its army at Bannockburn (1314), an obdurate English crown persistently refused to acknowledge the legitimacy of Robert I's kingship. So too did the papacy. Although two decades earlier a different pope had brazenly rebuked the English crown for its interference in Scotland, now a barrage of hostile papal bulls sought to bring the Scottish king and his bishops to book for their flagrant disregard of a papally sponsored truce between the two warring kingdoms.[2] The Declaration of Arbroath, as the letter of 1320 subsequently became known, was an attempt to assuage this growing papal hostility. Perhaps too it is an indication that King Robert now considered that a friendly papacy might use its diplomatic skills to soften English intransigence on the issue of Scottish independence. Whatever the case, quoting liberally from the Bible and Bede, and from Sallust and John of Salisbury, the unknown author deployed a sophisticated arsenal of rhetoric in his passionate defence of King Robert's position. He was clearly a highly educated man, and, since there were no universities then established in Scotland, his familiarity with esoteric scholarly texts was presumably acquired abroad. Meanwhile, with rather less subtlety, the author of the Declaration of Arbroath also turned three well-known clichés about his homeland to good use. In attempting to invoke the pope's pity, he sought to portray Scotland as remote, as poor and as a hapless victim of its hostile neighbour to the south.

Isolation
Scotland's isolation was a refrain with which the pope was perhaps familiar. Others certainly were. Although the existence of Iceland and Ireland made rational nonsense of its supposedly remote location, medieval cartographers often positioned Scotland at the end of the known world. Numerous *mappae mundi* produced between the twelfth and fourteenth centuries depict a global landmass divided by waters which usually take the shape of the letter 'T'. Land and sea are set inside a circular world and hence the technical designation of such designs as 'T-O maps'. With east normally at the top, and Asia above the bar of the T, Europe was usually located in the lower left segment of these maps and Africa at the lower right. Scotland routinely featured close to the European portion of the world's circumference. On some *mappae mundi*, such as the famous thirteenth-century

---

[1] A.A.M. Duncan, *The Nation of Scots and the Declaration of Arbroath* (London, 1970), 36.
[2] For the diplomatic background to the Declaration of Arbroath, see G.G. Simpson, 'The Declaration of Arbroath revitalised', *SHR*, 56 (1977), 11-33.

version produced in Lincoln and now in Hereford Cathedral, it is depicted as a self-standing island. In this instance the designer had perhaps drawn on an earlier cartographic tradition, associated with the seventh-century encyclopaedic works of Isidore, bishop of Seville, and the eight-century commentaries on the Apocalypse of St John by Beatus of Liebana. In the maps included in both of these Dark Age works Scotland appears in a similarly detached form. Indeed, these earlier designs were frequently copied and latterly printed, the 'island' of Scotland clearly visible among the fish of the sea in, for instance, the British Library's copy of a Beatus map. On the Hereford map, probably produced in the 1280s, the isolation of Scotland is partly tempered by the presence of an island to the north of Ireland and west of Scotland, which is closer than Scotland to the edge of the world. However, the impact of this is in turn superseded by the appearance of a ferocious beast, drawn on the circumference of the world, whose threatening red tongue is licking the western-most fringe of the Scottish landmass.[3]

Not all cartographers were convinced that Scotland was an island. On the map incorporated in the thirteenth-century chronicle by the St Albans monk Matthew Paris it was clearly linked to England. A narrow but distinct causeway also linked the two kingdoms in the map of c.1320 by Pietro Vesconte, a Genoese cartographer, resident in Venice. Neither on the map in Ranulph Higden's chronicle, nor on Vesconte's chart was Scotland placed literally on the edge of the world. Indeed, Vesconte's depiction of the British Isles was very roughly accurate in its alignment of Scotland, England and Ireland, with Ireland markedly closer to the world's circumference than Scotland.[4] This reveals a distinct development in the Genovese's knowledge, for in his atlas dating from 1313 Vesconte plotted neither Scotland, nor Ireland, including only a misshapen England which came to an abrupt end just north of Berwick. No longer *terra incognita* by 1320, and not even *in finibus orbi*, Scotland remained, however, distinctly peripheral on the Vesconte map of c.1320.[5]

Vesconte's work exemplifies a major development in cartography – the emergence of the portolan chart, characterised by distinctive 'rhumb lines' which intersected on large circles. Whereas 'T-O maps' of the Hereford variety were probably of decorative purpose, sometimes appearing as altar backdrops or as wall paintings, portolan charts were probably intended to be of practical value to maritime navigators, although the precise means by which they were used remains uncertain.[6] The new charts also provided detailed information on coastal towns and landmarks, and a generally more realistic topographical outline than those depicted on the 'T-O maps'. They were, however, Mediterranean in origin, and the earliest extant example (the *carte pisane*, dating from the thirteenth century) does not depict

[3] P.D.A. Harvey, *Medieval Maps* (London, 1991), 22-3, 31.

[4] Harvey, *Medieval Maps*, 34-5. The relevant segment of Paris's map is reproduced in *Facsimiles of the National Manuscripts of Scotland* (London, 1867-71), ii, no. 5a; Harvey, *Medieval Maps*, 74.

[5] T. Campbell, 'Portelan charts from the late thirteenth century to 1500' in J.B. Hawley and D. Woodward, eds., *The History of Cartography. Volume I: Cartography in prehistoric, ancient and medieval Europe and the Mediterranean* (Chicago, 1987), 406-9.

[6] Campbell, 'Portelan charts', 439-44.

Scotland at all.[7] Vesconte's portolan of c.1320 was one of the earliest to do so. His map was, however, largely devoid of Scottish coastal details, and, although markedly more was added to the portolans of the sixteenth century, its accuracy was often dubious, especially north of Forth and in the west. Aberdeen, for instance, sometimes appeared south of Dundee, which, in turn, was occasionally plotted far distant from the Tay.[8] Indeed, it was not just with regard to coastal locations that some of the new map makers were found wanting. Vesconte (like Paris before him) had exaggerated the estuarine inroads of the Forth and Clyde, leaving only a narrow causeway at Stirling linking the north and south of the Scottish kingdom. Still, Paris and Vesconte had identified the strategic significance of Stirling. Many later chart makers demonstrated less precision, even with regard to the Anglo-Scottish border. On fifteenth-century maps the Tweed was frequently misidentified as the Tyne, the Humber or the Forth.[9] Indeed, although two rivers which sprang from a common mountain range were by then taken as marking the border, on some maps the rivers featured as great estuaries, reminiscent of the earlier depictions of the Forth-Clyde axis by Paris and Vesconte. The map drawn by Grazioso Benincasa at Venice in c.1469 left little space even for the mountain between the two rivers.[10] Others disposed of it altogether. Thus, on the sixteenth-century charts designed by the Majorcans Jaume Olives and Matheus Prunes, Scotland and England were physically separated, as (more surprisingly given his origin) they also were on the 1542 map by the Dieppe cartographer John Rotz.[11] For all the advances in cartographic skill, many portolans remained less impressive in their depiction of Scotland than the maps composed by the Englishmen Matthew Paris in the thirteenth century and John Harding in the fourteenth century – a sure indication that few Mediterranean mariners (and even some from Dieppe) sailed as far north as Scotland, even in the sixteenth century.

Meanwhile, although the presence of Ireland protected Scotland from the western periphery of the new portolans, it now stood isolated in a different direction, with no discernible dwelling place to the north. Atlantic exploration exacerbated this trend, as is evident on Zuane Pizzigano's portolan of 1424.[12] Here the western perimeter of the inhabited world was extended to allow for inclusion of the Azores, 're-discovered' by the Portuguese by 1427. But Atlantic exploration was not matched by navigational penetration of the Arctic regions, leaving Scotland resolutely isolated to the north of the map. On Benincasa's map the Caithness coast almost clipped the top of the page, the designer deeming it appropriate to note, 'here is the end of Scotland'. His audience might have been forgiven for adding

[7] M. Mollat and M. de la Roncière, *Sea Charts of the Early Explorers, 13th to 17th Centuries* (Fribourg, 1984), Plate 1.
[8] M.C. Andrews, 'Scotland in the portolan charts', *The Scottish Geographical Magazine*, 42 (1926), 195-96.
[9] M.C. Andrews, 'The boundary between Scotland and England in the portolan charts', *PSAS*, 60 (1925-26), 40-3.
[10] Harvey, *Medieval Maps*, 63; Mollat and de la Roncière, *Sea Charts*, Plate 19.
[11] Andrews, 'The boundary between England and Scotland', 48-49; Mollat and de la Roncière, *Sea Charts*, Plate 40.
[12] *Discovering Western Civilization through Maps and Views*, ed. G.A. Danzer and D. Buisseret (New York, 1991), no. S37.

'and the world'. The Latin translations of Ptolemy's geography, dating from the early fifteenth century and first printed in 1475, did nothing to redress this peripheral image. Indeed, on maps of this derivation not only does Scotland appear on the north-western most fringe of the inhabited world, but also in an oddly elongated shape, pointing in the direction of Scandinavia.[13]

Maps, of course, were neither commonly possessed nor used in the middle ages.[14] Nevertheless, the image delivered by the cartographers informed, or reflected, the knowledge of other sections of society too. A fourteenth-century Spanish Franciscan thought Scotland was an island.[15] In 1461 Prospero da Comogli wrote to the duke of Milan suggesting that the western coast of Scotland could only be approached through the Irish Sea in small vessels 'because of a tide that lasts six hours'.[16] In 1474 Christofforo di Bollato, the Milanese ambassador to the French court, was more explicit still. For him Scotland was *in finibus orbi*.[17] Others proffered more profound inaccuracies. In describing *le tre parti del mondo divise*, the celebrated fifteenth-century Italian traveller Benedetto Dei followed cartographic convention in dividing the world into the three continents of Asia, Africa and Europe. But in locating Scotland, he chose to place the country between Denmark and Sweden.[18] More vaguely, but also robustly, Galeazzo Maria Sforza, duke of Milan, declared that 'if we had one daughter ... we should not want to marry her so far off as Scotland.'[19] The duke did not explain his sentiments, and they perhaps arose from nothing more than the unlikely prospect of ever seeing a daughter of whom he was presumably fond, should she reside in (from Italy) such a far-away land.

For others, Scotland's isolation provided a suitable setting for strange and sometimes dangerous phenomena. Scandinavian sources depicted Scots as exceptionally quick of foot, faster, indeed, than animals.[20] Others transplanted the tale about trees from which fruit grew in the form of geese from Ireland to Scotland – though Holy Island too had possessed an unusual species of bird which allegedly nested under the altar and pecked priests as they celebrated mass.[21] There is a hint of something altogether more menacing in the comments of the thirteenth-century French king Louis IX. According to his biographer, Louis advised his son to make himself loved by all his subjects 'for I would rather have a Scot come from Scotland to govern the people of this kingdom well and justly than that you should

[13] Danzer and Buisseret, *Maps and Views*, no. S15; Harvey, *Medieval Maps*, 56-7; *The Mapping of the World: Early printed maps, 1472-1700*, ed. R.W. Shirley (London, 1983), Plate 20.

[14] Harvey, *Medieval Maps*, 7.

[15] *Book of the Knowledge of all the Kingdoms*, ed. C. Markham (Hakluyt Soc., 1912), 11.

[16] *Dispatches with Related Documents of Milanese Ambassadors in France and Burgundy, 1450-1483*, ed. P.M. Kendall and V. Illardi (Athens, Ohio, 1970-81), ii, no. 110.

[17] *CSP (Milan)*, no. 270.

[18] Benedetto Dei, *La Cronica dall'anno 1400 all'anno 1500*, ed. R. Barducci (Florence, 1984), 139.

[19] *CSP (Milan)*, no. 272.

[20] E. Ebel, 'Das Bild der Fremden in den altwestnordlischen Quellen', *HGb*, 100 (1982), 52-3.

[21] For the location of this myth in Ireland, see, for example, Markam, *Book of the Knowledge*, 13; *Chron. Higden*, i, 334-35; *Cal. Carew MSS*, v, 31. For its transplantation to Scotland, see Pii II, *Commentarii Rerum Memorabilium Que Temporibus Svis Contigerunt*, ed. A. van Heck (Vatican City, 1984), i, 46; UL Aberdeen, Inc. 42, fo. 239v; A.M. Stewart, 'Do they mean us? The Nuremberg Chronicle (1493) and Scotland' in W. Ritchie, J.C. Stone and A.S. Mather, eds., *Essays for Professor R.E.H. Mellor* (Aberdeen, 1980), 269-70. For the Holy island ducks, see SA Stralsund, Städtische Urkunden, no. 1786; CA Aberdeen, SR/1, 167.

govern them ill in the sight of all the world.'[22] The thinking behind this inexplicit, but undoubtedly contemptuous, remark was perhaps similar to that which prompted another Frenchman, Jean Juvenal des Ursins, to suggest in the fifteenth century that 'savage Scotland' – the Highlands – was the home of the devil.[23] Scotland's demonic associations were implied by others too. Andrew Borde, an Englishman who studied at Glasgow in 1536, surmised that the 'devilish disposition' of Scots explained their reluctance to love or favour Englishmen.[24] Somewhat more graphically, Guibert, an early twelfth-century abbot of Nogent, recorded a dream in which devilish figures appeared 'carrying pouches slung around their haunches in the Scottish manner'. Their leader too was a Scot whose failure to secure alms led him to viciously assault a monk.[25]

Even this was tame compared with the use to which Scotland was put by the Aragonese writer Juan de Flores. His romance *Grisel y Mirabella*, published in *c.*1495, was set in Scotland and revolved around an illicit love affair between Grisel, a household knight, and Mirabella, the daughter of a fictitious Scottish king. The lovers were caught *in flagrante delicto* and the king organised a trial to determine which of the two partners was more guilty. Mirabella was defended by Braçayda, a character based upon Cressida from the popular romance *Troilus and Cressida*. Grisel's case, meanwhile, was advanced by Pere Torrellas, who ultimately convinced the king's (male) councillors of Mirabella's guilt by exposing the supposed vices of women in general. Sentenced to execution, Mirabella instead jumped from a window to her death in the royal menagerie below. Braçayda and the female members of the court then plotted their revenge on the misogynist Torrellas, who, meanwhile, had fallen in love with Braçayda. Lured to a tryst with Braçayda, the unsuspecting Torrellas was set upon by the ladies of the court. Bound, gagged and stripped, Torrellas was tied to a pillar, the women proceeding to apply different torments to the hapless Spaniard's naked body. He was scratched, bitten and tortured with flaming tongues before his flesh was finally ripped from his bones and his corpse burned. There is here, perhaps, an echo of St. Jerome's assertion that the *Scoti* were cannibals.[26]

The novel by Flores was a serious contribution to the ongoing debate among Spanish intellectuals regarding the nature of women. It constituted an explicit attack on the one factual character in the novel, Pere Torrellas, a noted author and critic of women.[27] We may doubt whether later medieval Spaniards really believed that Scotland was a land inhabited by vengeful and voracious women. It is nonetheless telling that at least one later medieval Spaniard fixed upon Scotland as a fitting location for an incredible story: strange things happened in remote countries.

---

[22] M.R.B. Shaw, ed., *Joinville and Villehardouin: Chronicles of the crusades* (Harmondsworth, 1963), 167.

[23] F. Michel, *Les Ecossais en France, Les Français en Ecosse* (London and Edinburgh, 1862), i, 2.

[24] Andrew Borde, *The Fyrst Boke of the Introduction of Knowledge*, ed. F.J. Furnivall (Early English Text Soc., 1870), 137.

[25] *A Monk's Confession: The memoirs of Guibert of Nogent*, ed. P.J. Archambault (Univ. Park, Penn., 1996), 113-14.

[26] 'Adversus Jovinianum' in *Patrologia Latina*, ed. J.P. Migne, xxiii (Paris, 1845), col. 296.

[27] B. Matulka, *The Novels of Juan de Flores and their European Diffusion: A study in comparative literature* (New York, 1931).

Indeed, other Spaniards too had unusual perceptions of Scotland. One tenth-century Asturian chronicler, in affixing somewhat abusive stereotypes to the different peoples of the world, decided that while the Bretons were famous for their ire, the Saxons for their rudeness, and the Jews for their envy, the Scots were renowned for their libido.[28] And this perhaps explains why a much later commentator accounted for what he considered to be the unnatural nature of Navarese sexual practices ('the Navarese affixes a lock to the behind of his mule or horse so that no one else but he may have access to them. And he kisses lasciviously the vulva of women and mules ... ') by reference to their supposed descent from 'the race of the Scots'.[29]

In accounts such as these voracious and unusual sexual appetites were probably, like the fate of Pere Torrellas, code for a lack of civility and a degree of barbarism. There are also echoes of this among twelfth-century English chroniclers who often juxtaposed comment on male nudity and sexual promiscuity among the Scots with exaggerated descriptions of their cruelty. Ailred of Rievaulx took special note of the 'half-bare buttocks' displayed by the Scots who invaded England in 1138, while Ralph Diceto, writing in 1173, revealed that Scots were unclothed, as well as bald and cruel. The combination of sexual licentiousness and barbarity was particularly explicit in the work of John of Hexham who wrote with disapproval of 'Scottish promiscuity' as the Scots carried off English women during their invasion of 1138. He was even more disgusted by the 'bestial men who regard as nothing adultery, incest and other crimes' and of the 'irreverent' and 'lewd' acts which they committed even in consecrated places.[30] Fordun, it is worth noting, had similar stories to tell of the Irish.[31]

The contempt shown by some English chroniclers for Scottish civilisation was more guarded than that which they (and Fordun) reserved for the Irish. The reason for this was connected with the introduction of Anglo-French settlers from the twelfth century. Ranulph Higden was probably not untypical in considering that, although the Scots were 'cruelle and wylde', they 'amendede thro the admixtion of Englische men'.[32] Nevertheless, the resumption of Anglo-Scottish hostilities in the fourteenth century proved fertile ground for English chroniclers to resurrect their unfavourable images of Scots. By then some commentators used overtly racist images, sometimes still with a sexual undertone, to depict Scottish barbarism. In the Luttrell Psalter, compiled before 1345 for the Lincolnshire knight and war veteran Geoffrey Luttrell, Scots were illustrated with the swarthy complexion of Saracens, the artist perhaps employing the same idea as that which had informed popular thirteenth-century notions of *nigras Scottorum*.[33] Black, we should note, conjured up

[28] *Chroniques Asturiennes*, ed. Y. Bonnaz (Paris, 1982), 11-12. It should be noted, however, given the date of this chronicle, that the reference to Scots was perhaps intended as a description of the Irish.
[29] *The Pilgrim's Guide to Santiago de Compostella*, ed. W. Melczer (New York, 1993), 95.
[30] *Scottish Annals from English Chroniclers, AD 500 to 1286*, ed. A.O. Anderson (London, 1908), 180-81, 187, 197, 247.
[31] S. Duffy, 'The Anglo Norman era in Scotland: convergence and diversity' in T.M. Devine and J.F. McMillan, eds., *Celebrating Columba: Irish-Scottish connections, 597-1997* (Edinburgh, 1999), 15-16.
[32] *Chron. Higden*, i, 387. The quotation derives from Higden's translator, John of Treviso.
[33] *The Political Songs of England from King John to King Edward II*, ed. T. Wright (Camden Soc., 1839), 20.

not only diabolical but also simian images, and apes were commonly understood to signify sin, and especially lust and unnatural vice.[34] For those who missed the symbolism, folio 169r of the psalter offered a less subtle picture of vengeful Scots attacking unarmed men and old widows, and hacking babies to pieces with a sword.[35] Similar atrocities were reported by English and Anglo-Irish chroniclers and even in official records.[36]

Such hyperbole was less common among continental commentators. Yet even for them barbarity lingered beyond the borderland with Gaeldom. In the fourteenth century Froissart wrote of 'le sauvage Escoce' and in the fifteenth century Don Pedro Ayala, a Spanish envoy, wrote of 'the language of the savages who live in some parts of Scotland'. It was there too that Jean Juvenal located his devil.[37] We should not underestimate the extent to which such views informed and reflected European perceptions of Scotland. Froissart's chronicle was widely copied and the work of Juan de Flores was published in several Spanish, Italian and French editions in the early sixteenth century.

Poverty

In his depiction of a remote country 'beyond which there is no dwelling place at all', the author of the Declaration of Arbroath clearly had good grounds for supposing that his words might strike a chord with a receptive audience. But it was not just on his homeland's isolated reputation that the anonymous author played in the letter of 1320. Isolation went hand in hand with poverty. At first sight this is an assertion which found less support among contemporary writers, especially from those further north. According the Icelandic *Laxdaela Saga*, composed in about 1245, there was 'good living' in Scotland.[38] Further south the thirteenth-century Italian Franciscan, Salimbene, displayed perspicacity in announcing 'the land of Normandy give[s] you fish; England wheat; Scotland milk; France wine'.[39] He was presumably alluding to the pastoral nature of much Scottish agriculture. Although it is possible that by 'Scotland' Salimbene understood Ireland, his comments are echoed by others who are likely to have possessed a keener awareness of the difference between Scotland and Ireland. Another thirteenth-century Franciscan, Bartholomew the Englishman, and the sixteenth-century Greek commentator, Nicander Nucius, both noted that the Scots lived off milk, butter, cheese and meat, among other things, and the prodigious quantities of meat which were consumed

---

[34] M. Camille, *Mirror in Parchment: The Luttrell Psalter and the making of medieval England* (London, 1998), 286-87; F. Fernández-Armesto, *Before Columbus: Exploration and colonisation from the Mediterranean to the Atlantic, 1229-1492* (Basingstoke, 1987), 227. For the perpetuation of the association between Scots and Moors in the early sixteenth century, see A.H. Williamson, 'Scots, Indians and empire: the Scottish politics of civilisation, 1519-1609, *Past and Present*, 150 (1996), 49-50.

[35] Camille, *Mirror in Parchment*, 284-85.

[36] E.g., *Chron. Lanercost*, 173-74; *Chron. Knighton*, 527; *Chron. Westminster*, 87; *Cal. Carew MSS*, v, 132.

[37] *Chron. Froissart* (Lettenhove), x, 336, 338; P. Hume Brown, ed., *Early Travellers in Scotland* (repr., Edinburgh, 1978), 39; Unfortunately I have not been able to track down a copy of N. Chareyon, 'La sauvage Ecosse dans la chronique de Jean le Bel', *Nouveaux Mondes et Mondes Nouveaux au Moyen Age* (Greifswald, 1994), 19-27.

[38] *Laxdaela Saga*, ed. M. Magnusson and H. Pálsson (Harmondsworth, 1969), 49.

[39] Salimbene de Adam, *Cronica*, ed. G. Scalia (Bari, 1966), i, 317.

by even the common people were noted by Italian and Spanish visitors too.[40] Supplies of fish, meanwhile, attracted even greater attention. In remarking upon the ready supply of salmon, herring and cod, the Spanish envoy Don Pedro de Ayala, who visited Scotland in 1498, noted an old proverb, *piscinata Scotia*.[41] Ayala's observations also informed the comments of the Venetian diplomat Andrea Trevisano, who dispatched a similar account to his Italian masters in *c.*1500.[42] This was no mere diplomatic flattery, for even in the thirteenth century the word *l'abberdan* ('Aberdeen') was synonymous with cod across much of north-western Europe.[43]

There was, however, another side of the coin. The Moroccan writer Abu Abdallah Muhammad al-Sharif al-Idrisi offered a particularly bleak assessment of Scotland. This was delivered in the twelfth-century *Book of Roger*, compiled for the Sicilian king, Roger II. Scotland, al-Idrisi noted, 'adjoins the island of England and is a long peninsula to the north of the larger island. It is uninhabited and has neither town nor village.'[44] This was perhaps a coded comment, for towns were regarded as agents of civilisation. William of Malmesbury, writing in the twelfth century, made a similar point, though he preferred to contrast the Anglo-French world with Ireland, rather than Scotland. The countryside, he noted, was replete with 'only a ragged mob of rustic Irishmen'; but the English and the French, he continued, 'with their more civilised way of life live in towns and carry on trade and commerce.'[45] By Malmesbury's day Scotland had towns and Anglo-French settlers and perhaps, therefore, escaped hostile comments of the sort many Anglo-French writers reserved for Ireland. By and large, however, later commentators were not impressed with the vitality of Scottish townlife. True, the thirteenth-century Lanercost chronicler preposterously compared Berwick with the great Egyptian town of Alexandria; but the fifteenth-century Burgundian traveller Ghillebert de Lannoy saw little which was worthy of note, save that the five towns which he visited (Dunbar, St Andrews, Perth, Stirling and Dumfries) were unwalled and that Dunbar was 'une ville désolée des guerres'.[46] The normally garrulous Ayala was similarly reticent about townlife. He too was struck by there being 'not more than one fortified town in Scotland' – presumably, despite Lannoy's comments, Perth. Ayala was, however, quite inaccurate in asserting that urban houses were 'all built of hewn stone'.[47] Froissart, meanwhile, damned with faint praise. 'Edinburgh,' he commented, 'is the Paris of Scotland', but with only four hundred houses it was not as big as the bustling, but second-rank, Netherlandish towns of Tournai and

[40] P. Contamine, 'Froissart and Scotland' in G. Simpson, ed., *Scotland and the Low Countries, 1124-1994* (East Linton, 1996), 45; Hume Brown, *Early Travellers*, 27, 43, 61.

[41] Hume Brown, *Early Travellers*, 44.

[42] Hume Brown, *Early Travellers*, 50-4.

[43] A. Stevenson, 'Trade with the south' in M. Lynch, M. Spearman and G. Stell, eds., *The Scottish Medieval Town* (Edinburgh, 1988), 186; B. Kuske, ed., *Quellen zur Geschichte des Kölner Handels und Verkehrs* (Bonn, 1817-34), iv, 480.

[44] B. Lewis, *The Muslim Discovery of Europe* (London, 1982), 147; 'Idrisi's account of the British Isles', ed. A.F.L. Beetson, *Bulletin of the School of Oriental Studies*, 13 (1949-50), 265-80.

[45] William of Malmesbury, *Gesta Regum Anglorum*, ed. R.A.B. Maynors *et al.* (Oxford, 1988-99), i, 739-41.

[46] *Chron. Lanercost*, 185; Ghillebert de Lannoy, *Oeuvre*, ed. C. Potvin (Louvain, 1878), 168.

[47] Hume Bown, *Early Travellers*, 47.

Valenciennes. It is telling too that Edinburgh was insufficiently large to host the influx of French troops in 1385, who were quartered out to Dunfermline, Kelso, Dunbar, Dalkeith *and other villages*.[48] Indeed, Jacques de Lalaing's biographer considered even Edinburgh to be 'a small village'.[49] Urban life barely surpassed the critical hurdle of Anglo-French judgement.

Rural Scotland escaped little better. Piccolomini, his comments repeated by Schedel at the end of the fifteenth century, wrote of the naked poor begging at churches. Ayala thought the Scots poor and lacking industriousness.[50] The poverty of the people was matched by the barren landscape. The knights who accompanied Jean de Vienne to Scotland in 1385, quartered in villages rather than the ornate castles of their homeland, began to wonder 'what can have brought us here?'[51] The Scottish countryside ravaged by warfare, the French herald Gilles le Bouvier reported that it was necessary for travellers to carry all the supplies which they would need on their journey.[52] As if to prove the point Duke John of Brabant, travelling to Jedburgh in 1292-93, hired a hackney to fetch the nightshirt which he had left in Berwick.[53] But it is Froissart to whom we must once again turn for the seemingly most damning (and historiographically influential) impression of Scotland. His comment that 'there was neither iron to shoe horses, nor leather to make horses, saddles or bridles' is still used as a fittingly negative starting point for discussions of the Scottish economy.[54]

It might be expected that closer proximity would have tempered English estimations of Scottish poverty. To some extent, the poverty line was indeed one which retreated northwards in English eyes. The bleak terms applied by others to Scotland were instead reserved by some English observers for the northern isles. In 1542 Orkney was described as 'dangerous and full of rocks' with little in the way of animal inhabitation, save for 'beasts which are so wild that they can only be taken by dogs'.[55] Other English observers were, however, contemptuous of even the more hospitable parts of the kingdom. Distance may explain why the duke of Milan did not wish to marry his daughter to a Scot; but King Henry VII of England expressed similar reservations about sending his daughter to marry the king of what he considered to be such a poor country – though in the event he did.[56] The English king did not elaborate upon his understanding of poverty, but he was perhaps thinking along similar lines to the thirteenth-century monk Ranulph Higden. His seemingly complimentary remarks that the Scots 'fedde more with flesche, fisches, white meat and with fruits' were tempered by the observation that

[48] *Chron. Froissart* (Lettenhove), x, 335.
[49] *Chron. Chastellain* (Lettenhove), viii, 167.
[50] Hume Brown, *Early Travellers*, 26, 43; UL Aberdeen, Inc. 42, fo. 239v.
[51] *Chron. Froissart* (Lettenhove), x, 336-37.
[52] M.W. Labarge, *Medieval Travellers: The rich and the restless* (London, 1982), 9, citing Gilles le Bouvier, dit Berry, *Le Livre de la Description des Pays*, ed. E.T. Hamy (Paris, 1908), 118-20.
[53] 'Account of the expenses of John of Brabant and Thomas and Henry of Lancaster, A.D. 1292-3', ed. J. Burtt, *Camden Miscellany*, 2 (1853), 2.
[54] *Chron. Froissart* (Lettenhove), x, 336; A. Stevenson, 'Trade with the south', 189.
[55] *L. & P. Henry VIII*, xvii, 514.
[56] *CSP (Milan)*, no. 601.

these items were more important in their diet than bread.[57] The 'wheat line', which divided those areas where wheat could be grown in abundance from those where it could not, was psychologically important to the Anglo-French elite. Eleventh and twelfth-century English kings had encountered difficulty in persuading Norman settlers to take land beyond the wheat line in Cumbria and Northumbria.[58] The on-going contempt for pastoral economies was reflected not only by the fifteenth-century French in their dismissal of those Scots who came to their aid as 'mutton guzzlers', but also by the anonymous author of *The Libelle of Englysche Policye*. Despite the importance of wool to the English economy, he wrote disparagingly of the 'moste rude ware' traded by the Scots.[59] Writing in the mid-sixteenth century, Ludovico Guiccardini was a less critical observer, but even he, in describing the trade of Antwerp, found little in Scotland's exports to compliment. Even though its marten skins were 'perhaps the best which one could find', Scottish cloth was 'mal fatta' and Scottish pearls were 'large and pleasant' but lacking in value compared to those to be found in the Orient.[60]

Yet one is reminded of the English adage, 'where there's muck, there's brass'. As we have seen, the economy of Scotland, though it lacked the industrial and commercial sophistication of other parts of the continent, was far from poor. Poverty, of course, was in the eye of the beholder and literate clerics who hobnobbed with aristocrats were perhaps not the best judges of economic matters. Yet even if we judge places by medieval, rather than by our own standards, it is perhaps time to put to rest Froissart's disparaging comments about the lack of horseshoes and suchlike things. Quite apart from the fact that we find horseshoes and 'Scottish iron' *exported* from Scotland to Hull in the 1460s, and that whatever else Scotland might have been short of it cannot have been leather, Froissart's thundering comments have been taken out of context.[61] He was noting what the English found when they invaded the country. Scots had long since taken to scorched earth tactics to frustrate their enemy's advance: of course the English found nothing! And we may take Froissart's comments more as an indication of the success of Scottish military tactics in 1385 than as telling insight into the country's poverty.

Anglophobia

While foreign observers often remarked upon Scotland's isolation and poverty, they rarely demonstrated much awareness of political developments within the kingdom, and even the Icelandic writers began to loose interest in, or contact with, political developments in Scotland after the late thirteenth century.[62] News of James I's

[57] *Chron. Higden*, i, 389.
[58] W.E. Kapelle, *The Norman Conquest of the North: The region and its transformation, 1000-1135* (London, 1979), 213-30.
[59] *Chron. Pluscarden*, i, 357; *The Libelle of Englysche Polycye: A poem on the use of sea-power, 1436*, ed. G. Warner (Oxford, 1926), 14.
[60] Ludovico Guiccardini, *Descrittione di Tutti i Paesi Bassi* (Antwerp, 1567), 122-23.
[61] PRO London, E122/62/6, m.3r; E122/62/9, m. 3d.
[62] R. Power, 'Scotland in the Norse sagas' in G.G. Simpson, ed., *Scotland and Scandinavia, 800-1800* (Edinburgh, 1990), 13-24.

murder – which was reported in England, France, Germany and Italy – was one gory exception, shocking enough to warrant widespread foreign comment.[63] This apart the brief snippets of information which reached continental writers from Scotland were often woefully inaccurate – Benedetto Dei, for instance, placed James III's death in 1475.[64] Even comparatively well-known aspects of Anglo-Scottish conflict were frequently riddled with factual error. The capture of David II by English forces at the battle of Neville's Cross provides a good example. Although one Italian chronicle noted with minimalist accuracy the king's capture in 1346, the Castilian chancellor and poet Pero López de Ayala misdated the event to 1356, as did a Cologne chronicler, while a French commentator explained the king's capture as a consequence of his ill-fated siege of London.[65] Nevertheless, even if their comments were sometimes factually unreliable and unhelpfully terse, many writers who had otherwise nothing to note about Scotland homed in on the conflictual dimension to interaction between the two British kingdoms.

This, of course, was a feeling fuelled by the long years of warfare with England from 1296, and it is not difficult to trace many instances of such sentiment in both later medieval Scottish and English writing. Walter Bower's fifteenth-century chronicle is, for instance, remorselessly anglophobic in tone. 'An Englishman is an angel,' he wrote, 'whom no one can believe; when he greets you, beware of him as an enemy,' the abbot proceeding to compare Englishmen with slippery eels. Indeed, in the abbot's view, the English were worse than eels, for they were treacherous, wicked, deceitful and warlike.[66] Such sentiments were not the preserve of the literate elite. Piccolomini noted that abuse heaped on Englishmen greatly pleased the Scots. Ribald jokes circulated among Scots – and for that matter among the Castilians, French and Germans too – that their English enemies possessed tails, a sign of God's disapproval of their wickedness; and when the Black Death first made its appearance in mid-fourteenth-century England, the Scots were quick to see this too as a sign of God's displeasure with their old enemies.[67] Similar hostility to Scots is evident in many English chronicles, and was accompanied by assertions of superiority over Scotland. The latter was evident not just in the assertions of

---

[63] 'The Dethe of the Kynge of Scotis: a new edition', ed. M. Connolly, *SHR*, 71 (1992), 47-69; *La Chronique d'Enguerran de Monstrelet*, ed. L. Douet-d'Arcq (Paris, 1857-62), v, 275-79; *Chron. Waurin, 1431-47*, 208-16; 'Kölner Jahrbücher des 14. und 15. Jahrhunderts: Recension D' in *Chroniken der deutschen Städten*, xiv, 174; *HR, 1431-76*, ii, no. 68; D. Weiss, 'The earliest account of the murder of James I of Scotland', *English Historical Review*, 52 (1937), 479-91. James II's death received less attention, but see *Chron. Waurin, 1447-71*, 392.

[64] Dei, *La Cronica dall'anno 1400 all'anno 1500*, 100.

[65] *Corpus Chronicorum Bononiensium*, ed. A. Sorbelli (Bologna, 1906-38), ii, 559; Pero Lopez de Ayala, *Crónica del Rey Don Pedro y del Rey Don Enrique*, ed. G. Orduna (Buenos Aires, 1994), i, 248; *Chronique de Guillaume de Nangis de 1113 à 1300 et de ses continuateurs de 1300 à 1368*, ed. H. Geraud (Paris, 1843), ii, 208. For Netherlandish notices of the battle of Neville's Cross see, for example, *De Gelderse Kroniek van Willem van Berchen*, ed. A.J. de Mooy (Arnhem, 1950), 4-5; *Het Haagse Handschrift van Heraut Beyeren*, ed. J. Verbij-Schillings (Hilversum, 1999), 150.

[66] *Chron. Bower* (Watt), vii, 85-7.

[67] *Pii II, Commentarii*, i, 46; G. Neilson, 'Caudatus Anglicus: a medieval slander', *Transactions of the Glasgow Archaeological Soc.*, new series, 2 (1896), 441-47; L. Barbé, 'The story of the 'long-tail' myth' in idem, *In Byways of Scottish History* (London, 1924), 291-360; L.M.C. Randall, 'A medieval slander', *Art Bulletin*, 17 (1960), 32-7; *Chron. Knighton*, 101-3.

historical and political overlordship made by various English kings, but also in the arguments advanced at the general councils of the church held at Constance and Siena. In 1417 English delegates had argued that they should constitute their own nation, rather than be absorbed by the German nation. The English, they argued, represented an extensive block of territories, including Scotland and Orkney, as well as five distinct linguistic groups, including the speakers of English in both England and Scotland. Since the Scots remained aloof from the proceedings at Constance, it was left to the French to refute the English claims, but the matter was raised again in 1423-24 at Siena by the abbot of Paisley, who attended as procurator of the French king Charles VII.[68] Yet perhaps the most bizarre expression of English superiority was penned by the fifteenth-century judge John Fortescue. In his estimation Scots were cowards because they were not hanged for robbery, but rather for larceny: theft in the absence of the owner. Englishmen, by contrast, were courageous, as was proven not only from the large number whom Fortescue and his fellow judges convicted of robbery and manslaughter, but also by the fact English criminals attacked their victims despite being outnumbered.[69]

Not surprisingly, given the long-standing alliance between France and Scotland and their common experience of English aggression, French-speaking writers were particularly well informed about Anglo-Scottish hostility, none more so than the Valenciennes clerk and chronicler of chivalry, Jean Froissart. Anglo-Scottish battles provided the well-travelled Froissart (who visited Scotland in 1365) with many suitable examples of 'honourable enterprises, noble adventures and deeds of arms' which he recorded so that 'brave men should be inspired to follow such examples'.[70] Of course Froissart shamelessly plagiarised the work of the Liège canon Jean le Bel for the early parts of his chronicle; but neither was original in the francophone world in regarding Anglo-Scottish conflict as a fitting topic for discussion. William the Lion's tribulations with the English were briefly recorded in the *Chronique de Saint-Pierre-le-Vif de Sens*, and the early fourteenth-century *Chronique parisienne anonyme* informed its readers at considerable length of 'how and in what way the kingdom of Scotland belongs to the king of England and why, how and when war broke out.'[71] A fourteenth-century Gascon chronicle noted the resumption of Anglo-Scottish hostilities in 1333 and the *Chronique des Quatre Premiere Valois* recorded David II's departure for exile in France in 1334, together with several subsequent military encounters on the Anglo-Scottish frontier. In these accounts the author was keen to stress the role of William, first earl of Douglas, who in his youth had spent several years in France and who had acquired lands at

---

[68] L.R. Loomis, 'Nationality at the council of Constance: an Anglo-French dispute', *American Historical Review*, 44 (1939), 508-27; W. Brandmüller, *Das Konzil von Pavia-Siena, 1423-1424* (Münster, 1968-74), i, 180-88.
[69] John Fortescue, *The Governance of England*, ed. C. Plummer (Oxford, 1885), 141-42.
[70] *Chron. Froissart* (Brereton), 37.
[71] *Chronique de Saint-Pierre-le-Vif de Sens*, ed. R.H. Bautier and M. Gillies (Paris, 1979), 128-29; P. Contamine, 'Froissart and Scotland' in G.G. Simpson, ed., *Scotland and the Low Countries, 1124-1994* (East Linton, 1996), 45-6.

St Säens in Normandy.[72] And for fifteenth-century writers the interest in Scotland continued as a result of the extensive military aid extended by Scots to the beleaguered French in their efforts to resist the English in the early fifteenth century. The fortunes of the Scottish armies which fought against the English at Baugé (1421), Cravant (1423) and Verneuil (1424) are noted in some detail by, for instance, Berry Herald, Jean le Févre, Thomas Basin and Jehan de Waurin.[73] Moreover, despite the contempt which, as we have seen, some sections of French society reserved for the 'mutton guzzlers and wine bags', two of the army's leaders (the earls of Buchan and Douglas) were marked out for celebration, along with twenty-two French nobles, in Chastellain's poem *La mort du roy Charles VII*.[74]

Further afield too there was recognition that Scotland and England were enemies – and the corollary that the king of Scots was, in Francesco Guiccardini's words, 'the ancient ally' of the French.[75] The fourteenth-century Florentine writer Giovanni Villani had heard 'del valente Ruberto di Brus' and of the 'great war and battles which he fought'.[76] In 1346 the archbishop of Armagh informed the pope that the Irish and the Scots were 'always enemies of the English'.[77] The Valencian author of *Tirant lo Blanc* was sufficiently impressed by the exploits of Sir John Stewart of Darnley in fifteenth-century France to nominate him as one of the three most valiant knights of his time.[78] Germans too were aware of the large numbers of Scots who rallied to the aid of the French in the early fifteenth century. They fought manfully at the battle of Verneuil in 1424, noted a Lübeck writer, hitting many Englishmen to the ground, though ultimately suffering complete defeat.[79] Set-piece battles such as this particularly caught the attention of these more distant writers. Other stunning Scottish defeats – such as those suffered at Flodden in 1513 and Solway Moss in 1542 – were noted by, for instance, Francesco and Ludovico Guiccardini, though from their Florentine perspective the Scots played a distinctly marginal role in the dramatic unfolding of early sixteenth-century international politics.[80]

If recognition of Anglo-Scottish hostility was widespread, few foreign accounts demonstrate much awareness as to the cause of the enmity. It was left to Philippe de Commynes to offer a more theoretical explanation of sorts for the animosity of the two 'British' kingdoms. 'All things considered,' he wrote, 'it seems to me that

[72] *Livre des Coutumes*, ed. H. Barkhausen (Bordeaux, 1890), 687; *Chronique des Quatre Premiers Valois, 1327-1393*, ed. S. Luce (Paris, 1862), 4, 31-2, 45, 53, 284; M. Brown, *The Black Douglases* (East Linton, 1998), 210-11.
[73] G. le Bouvier, dit le Hérault Berry, *Les Chroniques du Roi Charles VII*, ed. H. Courteault and L. Celier *et al.* (Paris, 1979), 99-101, 114-18; *Chronique de Jean le Févre*, ed. F. Morand (Paris, 1862), 78, 86; Thomas Basin, *Histoire de Charles VII*, ed. C. Samaran (Paris, 1964-65), i, 76-7, 92-9; *Chron. Waurin, 1422-31*, 68-9, 114-16.
[74] *Chron. Chastellain* (Lettenhove), vi, 447-48.
[75] Francesco Guiccardini, *Storia d'Italia*, ed. L. Felici (Rome, 1967-68), iv, 1064. See too Fernão Lopes, *Crónica de D. João I*, edd. M. Lopes de Almeida and A. de Magalhães Basto (Porto, 1945), ii, 196, 305.
[76] *Cronica di Giovanni Villani* (Florence, 1823), v, 278-79. See too ibid, iv, 151.
[77] J.A. Watt, 'Gaelic polity and cultural identity' in A. Cosgrove, ed., *A New History of Ireland, Volume II: Medieval Ireland, 1169-1534* (Oxford, 1987), 343.
[78] Joanot Martorell and Marti Joan de Galba, *Tirant lo Blanc*, ed. D.H. Rosenthal (London, 1984), 48.
[79] *Die Chroniken der Deutschen Städten vom 14. bis 16. Jahrhundert*, xxviii, 200-1.
[80] Guiccardini, *Storia d'Italia*, iv, 1069-70; Ludovico Guiccardini, *Commentarii* (Venice, 1565), 39.

God has created neither man nor beast in this world without establishing some counterpart to oppose him, in order to keep him in humility and fear.' It was for this reason that the Portuguese existed (to oppose the Spaniards) and that the English existed (to oppose the French). And, of course, Commynes's insight into national matter and anti-matter told him that the divine purpose of the Scots was to oppose the English.[81] Pope Martin V made the point more succinctly. The Scots, he allegedly commented in 1420, were 'truly an antidote to the English'.[82]

Such theories had practical applications. The 'natural' hostility between the two 'British' kingdoms figured in the political calculations of many foreigners. Scottish kings had often invaded northern England at the instigation of their French allies – for instance in 1385 and 1513. Other interventions were touted by those of a francophone disposition. Waldemar III of Denmark had proposed a tripartite alliance between Denmark, France and Scotland, with the object of attacking England and freeing the captured French king John II.[83] Indeed, although Scottish invasions of northern England rarely resulted in territorial gain, the ambition of those who pondered such matters were sometimes awesome. In Jean Juvénal's *Loquar in tribulatione*, written in the 1440s, the hawks in Charles VII's entourage informed the king that with Scottish aid he might not only rid France of its English enemies, but also conquer England itself.[84] In the previous century David II too had fondly imagined that soon after his invasion of England in 1346 he would be celebrating Christmas in London with the French.[85] He did, though not quite in the way that he had presumably envisaged.

For others Scottish anglophobia was less welcome since it potentially constrained England from playing an active role in continental politics. In the early fourteenth century, suddenly in need of English support against a hostile French crown, the papacy abandoned its previous support of the Scots. Much later the Burgundian dukes Philip the Good and Charles the Bold both sought to temper Scottish intervention in England – the former in 1461 and the latter by sponsoring an Anglo-Scottish royal marriage in 1474.[86] We may doubt too whether Scottish emigrants or the merchant class was greatly enamoured by the Scottish government's hostility towards England, even though some merchants and mariners were active in hostilities with England throughout the period. Nevertheless, from the later fifteenth century England was once again becoming an increasingly important market for Scottish traders and Anglo-Scottish hostility not only disrupted, but also threatened to curtail, this lucrative trade. It also damaged commercial contacts with the continent, as anglophone powers expelled Scottish

---

[81] *The Memoirs of Philippe de Commynes*, ed. S. Kinser (Columbia, SC, 1969-73), i, 353. See too J. Blanchard, *Commynes L'Européen: L'invention du politique* (Geneva, 1996), 214-21, for more detailed discussion of the medieval theory of political balance as expressed by Commynes.

[82] *Chron. Bower* (Watt), viii, 121.

[83] R. Cazelles, *Société, Politique, Noblesse et Couronne sous Jean le Bon et Charles V* (Geneva, 1982), 361. For similar tripartite anti-English alliances, see R.G. Nicholson, 'The Franco-Scottish and Franco-Norwegian treaties of 1295', *SHR*, 38 (1959), 114-32; *Chron. Reading*, 181.

[84] *Écrits Politique de Jean Juvénal des Ursins*, ed. P.S. Lewis (Paris, 1978-85), i, 390.

[85] C.J. Rogers, 'The Scottish invasion of 1346', *NH*, 34 (1998), 55.

[86] *Chron. Waurin, 1447-71*, 354-56; Stevenson, Thesis, 107-8.

traders and as English privateers were unleashed on Scottish merchant shipping. This is not to suggest that the merchant class of later medieval Scotland was the hapless victim of an increasingly futile anglophobic foreign policy, determined by over-ambitious kings and bellicose nobles. On occasions merchants and mariners pursued their own animosities at sea, sometimes with even more distant ramifications than their social superiors. No Scottish king succeeded, as fifteenth-century Scottish mariners did, in provoking indignation as far away as Thorn (now) in central Poland and Zürich in Switzerland.[87] These, however, are issues and tensions which shall be explored in the next volume of this study.

[87] WAP Torun, Kat. Inv. 686; SA Zürich, BIV/ I, no. 210.

Select Bibliography

MANUSCRIPT AND EARLY PRINTED SOURCES

Aberdeen, City Archive
CR	Council Register, vols. 1-16, 1398-1541
SR	Sasine Register, vols. 1-3, 1484-1514

Aberdeen, University Library
Inc. 34	*Manuale parrochialium sacerdotum* (Cologne, 1492)
Inc. 42	H. Schedel, *Liber Cronicarum* (Augsburg, 1497)

Antwerp/Antwerpen, Stadsarchief
Certificatieboeken	Certification books, vols. 1-14, 1488-1559
Poortersboeken	Register of burgesses, 1464-1533
Schepenbrieven	Letters of magistrates, 1394-1551

Arnhem, Gemeentearchief
inv. no. 1245	Town accounts, 1446-1452

Belfast, Public Record Office Northern Ireland
D.623/B/7/1-13	Abercorn papers, 1219-1520

Bergen-op-Zoom, Gemeentearchief
inv. no. 780-815	Town accounts, 1413-1550
inv. no. 3092	Register of burgesses, 1472-1522
inv. no. 5119-5170	Protocol van rentbrieven en recognitiën, 1432-1524
inv. no. 5268-5272	Register van procuaties en certificaties, 1466-1547

Berlin, Geheimes Staatsarchiv, Preussischer Kulturbesitz
OBA	Correspondence to the Grand Masters of the Teutonic Order
OF	Registers of the Grand Masters of the Teutonic Order

Berwick-upon-Tweed, Northumberland Record Office
B1/1	Guild minute book, 1509-1568
B2/1	Draft guild minute book, 1505-c.1535

Bremen, Staatsarchiv
1/Bc, 1/Z	Correspondence to Bremen, 1440s

Brussels/Brussel, Rijksarchief
inv. no. 169/I	State papers, 405/1: negotiations with Scotland, 1540-1570

Chester, City Archive
MB	Mayor's books, vols. 1-10, 1392-1509
SB	Sheriffs' books, vols. 1-9, 1422-1550

Cologne/Köln, Historisches Archiv
Briefbuch   Council letter books, vols. 1-50, 1367-1520
Hanse U2   Hanseatic documents
Hanse IIIK   Hanseatic correspondence and acts to 1530
Hanse IVK   Acts of the Hanseatic *Kontors* in Bruges,
                                    Antwerp and London
Haupturkundenarchiv   Main document archive
Universität 26   University collection
Ratsprotokoll   Council protocol books, vols. 1-8, 1513-31
Schreinsurkunden Schöffenrein, 2/548/37
Copenhagen/København, Rigsarkivet
Øresundtolregnskaber   Sound Toll Registers, 1497-1541.
Dundee, City Archive
BHCB/1-2   Burgh Head Court Book, vols. 1-2, 1454-1555
Durham, University Library
Dean and Chapter Muniments   Miscellaneous charters, no. 3418.
Edinburgh, National Archives of Scotland
AD   Crown Office writs
B30/1/4   Protocol book of James Harlaw
CS5   Acts of the Lords of Council
E71   Exchequer, Scottish customs accounts
NP1/12   Protocol book of Alexander Symson
RH1   Transcripts and photocopies
Edinburgh, National Library of Scotland
ch. 57, ch. 58   copies of letters in AH Lübeck
Frankfurt-am-Main, Stadtarchiv
Bürgerbuch/4   Burgess book, vol. 4.
Gdansk/Danzig, Wojewódzkiego Arciwum Państwowe
300/19   Danzig customs accounts, 1460-1521
300/27   Correspondence from Danzig, 1420-1516
300/43   Judicial records, 1426-1513
300/59   Council registers, 1380-1533
300D   Correspondence to Danzig
369I/131   Burgess lists of Elbing, 1413-1664
s'Hertogenbosch, Gemeentearchief
Inv. chartres en privilegiën, 293   Cloth ordinance, 20 September 1403
Innsbruck, Landesarchiv Tirol
Sigismund IVa/181   Letter to Duchess Eleanor of Austria, undated
Ipswich, Suffolk Record Office
C13/15/1   Account book of Henry Tooley, 1521-1550
Lille, Archives Départementales du Nord
B4086   Account book of Godfrey le Lainiage, receiver
                                    general of Flanders and Artois
London, Public Record Office, England and Wales
E101   Exchequer, Bordeaux customs accounts

E122	Exchequer, English customs accounts
E179	Exchequer, Alien subsidy accounts
EXT6	Bordeaux customs accounts
Lübeck, Archiv der Hansestadt	
Anglicana	Correspondence relating to Scotland
Lüneburg, Stadtarchiv	
AB6/1	*Liber memoriales*, 1408-1614
AHIV	Miscellaneous documents
Maidstone, Kent Record Office	
DRb/PWr2, fos. 284-85	Will of Andrew Trail, 19 September 1464
Middelburg, Zeeuws Archief	
inv. no. 243/19	Papers of the admiralty at Veere, 1528-35
Archief Veere, inv. no. 920	Register of burgesses, Veere, 1473-1550
Norwich, Norfolk Record Office	
Y/C4/93-226	Yarmouth burgh court rolls, 1381-1524
Paris, Archives Nationales	
J621/77	Homage of Nicholas Erskine, 1372
J677-680	Treaties and other diplomatic documents relating to Scotland, 1295-1558
JJ197, 226	Registers of royal chancery
K56/K57	Bonds of the duke of Orléans, 1397-1412
Rotterdam, Gemeentearchief	
Oud Stads Archief 15	Resolutions of the town council, 1540s
Stralsund, Stadtarchiv	
Städtische Urkunden	Documents relating to Stralsund
St Marien Urkunden	Documents relating to church of St Mary
Tallinn, Linna Arhiiwi	
I/Af/2 – I/Af/25	Merchant account books
I/Ag/1-4	Ship tax lists, 1426-1492
Torun/Thorn, Wojewódzkiego Arciwum Państwowe	
Kat. Inv. 686	Letter to Aberdeen, 1 December 1410.
Turin/Torino, Archivio di Stato	
Inventario 16, Registro 93	Accounts of the Treasurer General of Savoy, 1445-46
Inventario 16, Registro 96	Accounts of the Treasurer General of Savoy, 1447-49
Inventario 16, Registro 104	Accounts of the Treasurer General of Savoy, 1453-54
Venice/Venezia, Archivio di Stato	
Busca 134	Account book of Francesco Querini, 1414.
Wismar, Stadtarchiv	
II Hanseatica C/25	Letter from James II, 15 April 1440
Zürich, Staatsarchiv	
BIV/1, no. 210	Letter to Louis XI, 24 September 1482

PUBLISHED SOURCES

Record Sources

'Abbaye de Melrose et les ouvrier Flamandes', ed. O. Delepierre, *Miscellanies of the Philobiblon Society*, 5 (1858-59).

Accounts of the Chamberlains of Newcastle-upon-Tyne, 1508-1511, ed. C.M. Fraser (Newcastle, 1987).

'Accounts on the great rolls of the pipe of the Irish exchequer in the reign of Edward II', *Reports of the Deputy Keeper of the Public Records in Ireland*, 42 (1911).

'Account of the expenses of John of Brabant and Thomas and Henry of Lancaster, A.D. 1292-3', ed. J. Burtt, *Camden Miscellany*, 2 (1853).

Accounts of the Lord High Treasurer of Scotland, ed. T. Dickson and J.B. Paul (Edinburgh, 1877-1916).

Acta Stanów Prus Królewskich, ed. M. Biskup *et al.* (Torun, 1955-75).

Acten der Ständetage Preussens unter der Herrschaft des Deutschen Ordens, ed. M. Toeppen (Leipzig, 1878-86).

Acts of the Lords of Council in Civil Causes, 1496-1501, ed. G. Neilson and H. Paton (Edinburgh, 1918).

Acts of the Lords of Council in Public Affairs, 1501-1554: Selections from Acta Dominorum Concilii, ed. R.K. Hannay (Edinburgh, 1932).

Acts of the Lords Auditors of Causes and Complaints, ed. T. Thomson (Edinburgh, 1839).

Acts of the Parliaments of Scotland, ed. T. Thomson and C. Innes (Edinburgh, 1814-75).

Affaires de Jacques Coeur, Les: Journal du procureur Dauvet, ed. M. Mollat (Paris, 1952-53).

Akten zur Geschichte der Verfassung der Stadt Köln im 14. Und 15. Jahrhundert, ed. W. Stein (Bonn, 1895).

Alien Communities of London in the Fifteenth Century: The subsidy rolls of 1440 and 1483-84, ed. J.L. Bolton (Richard III and Yorkist History Trust, 1998).

Analyses de Reconnaissances de Dettes Passées devant L'échevin d'Ypres, 1249-1291, ed. C. Wyffels (Brussels, 1991).

Archives Departmental du Nord: Repertoire numerique, Serie H, Tome II, ed. P. & A.M. Piétresson (Avesnes-sur-Helpes, 1943).

Ayr Burgh Accounts, 1534-1624, ed. G.S. Pryde (SHS, 1937).

'Bagimond's roll: Statement of the tenths of the kingdom of Scotland', ed. A.I. Dunlop, *SHS Miscellany*, 6 (1939).

Bannatyne Miscellany, The (Bannatyne Club, 1827-55).

Beschlüsse des Rates Köln, 1320-1550, ed. M. Huiskes and M. Groeten (Düsseldorf, 1988-90).

Black Book of the Admiralty, The, ed. T. Twiss (Roll Series, 1873).

'Bouwstoffen voor de geschiedenis der laatmiddeleeuwse stadsdraperie in een klein Brabants produktiecentrum: Vilvoorde, 1357-1578', ed. J.P. Peeters, *Handelingen van de Koninklijke Commissie voor Geschiedenis*, 151 (1985).

Bronnen voor de Economische Geschiedenis van het Beneden-Maasgebied, J.F. Niermeijer (The Hague, 1968).

Bronnen tot de Geshiedenis van de Leidsche Textielnijverheid, 1333-1795, ed. N.W. Posthumus (The Hague, 1910-22).

Bronnen tot de Geshiedenis van den Handel met Engeland, Schotland en Ierland, 1150-1485, ed. H.J. Smit (The Hague, 1928).

Bronnen tot de Geshiedenis van den Handel met Engeland, Schotland en Ierland, 1485-1558, ed. H.J. Smit (The Hague, 1942).

Calendar of Close Rolls (London, 1862-).

Calendar of Documents relating to Ireland, 1171-1251 (London, 1875-86).

Calendar of Documents relating to Scotland, ed. J. Bain *et al.* (Edinburgh, 1881-1986).

Calendar of Early Chancery Proceedings Relating to West Country Shipping, 1388-1493, ed. D.M. Gardiner (Devon and Cornwall Record Soc., 1976).

Calendar of Entries in the Papal Registers relating to Great Britain and Ireland: Papal letters, ed. W.H. Bliss *et al.* (London, 1893-).

Calendar of Entries in the Papal Registers relating to Great Britain and Ireland: Petitions to the pope, ed. W.H. Bliss (London, 1896).

Calendar of Papal Letters to Scotland of Benedict XIII of Avignon, 1394-1414, ed. F. McGurk (SHS, 1976).

Calendar of Papal Letters to Scotland of Clement VII of Avignon, 1378-1394, ed. C. Burns (SHS, 1976).

Calendar of Patent Rolls (London, 1891-).

Calendar of Scottish Supplications to Rome, ed. E.R. Lindsay *et al.* (SHS, etc., 1956-).

Calendar of Signet Letters of Henry IV and Henry V, ed. J.L. Kirby (London, 1978).

Calendar of State Papers and Manuscripts, existing in the archives and collections of Milan, ed. A.B. Hinds (London, 1912).

Calendar of the Carew Manuscripts, preserved in the archepiscopal library at Lambeth, 1515-74 (London, 1867-73).

Calendar of the Justicary Rolls, or the proceedings in the court of the justiciar of Ireland, ed. J. Mills (Dublin, 1905-14).

Cartulaire de L'ancienne Estaple de Bruges, ed. L. Gilliodts van Severen (Bruges, 1904-6).

'Catalogue of accounts on the great pipe rolls of the pipe of the Irish exchequer for the reign of Edward III', *Reports of the Deputy Keeper of the Public Records in Ireland* (Dublin, 1869-), 43 (1912); 44 (1912); 47 (1915); 53 (1926).

C'est l'ordre qui a este tenu a la nouvelle et ioeuse entrée... (Paris, 1549), reprinted as appendix to I.D. McFarlane, *The Entry of Henri II into Paris, 16 June 1549* (Binghampton, 1982).

Charters and other Documents relating to the City of Edinburgh (Scottish Burgh Record Soc., 1871).

Charters and other Records of the City and Royal Burgh of Kirkwall, ed. J. Mooney (Spalding Club, 1952).

Charters of the Abbey of Coupar Angus, ed. D.E.R. Easson (SHS, 1947).

Charters of the Royal Burgh of Ayr (Ayr and Wigtown Archaeological Assoc., 1883).

Chartularies of St Mary's Abbey, Dublin, ed. J.T. Gilbert (Roll Series, 1884).

Chartulary of the Cistercian Priory of Coldstream, ed. C. Rodgers (Grampian Club, 1879).

Codex Diplomaticus Ordinis Sanctae Mariae Theutonicorum: Urkundenbuch zur Geschichte des Deutschen Ordens, ed. J.H. Hennes (Mainz, 1845-61).

'Contribution to the commercial history of medieval Wales, A', ed., E.A. Lewis, *Y Cymmrodor*, 24 (1913).

Collections des Keuren ou Status de tous les Métiers de Bruges, ed. O. Delepierre and M.F. Willems (Ghent, 1842).

Copiale Prioratus Sanctiandree, ed. J.H. Baxter (Oxford, 1930).

Correspondence, Inventories, Account Rolls and Law Proceedings of the Priory of Coldingham, The, ed. J. Raine (Surtees Soc., 1841).

Coucher Book of Furness Abbey, The. Volume II, ed. J. Brownhill (Chetham Soc., 1915-19)

Diplomatarium Danicum, 2. Raekke, xi, ed. C.A. Christensen (Copenhagen, 1950).

Diplomatarium Norvegicum (Kristiana, 1849-1919).

Dispatches with Related Documents of Milanese Ambassadors in France and Burgundy, 1450-1483, ed. P.M. Kendall and V. Illardi (Athens, Ohio, 1979-81).

'Documenten voor de geschiedenis van be beeldhowkunst te Antwerpen in de Xve eeuw', ed. G. Asaert, *Jaarboek van het Koninklijk Museum voor Schone Kunst, Antwerpen* (1972).

'Documents from the records of west Flanders relative to the carved stalls at Melrose Abbey', ed. M.O. Delepierre, *Archaeologia*, 31 (1846).

Documents illustrative of the History of Scotland, ed. J. Stevenson (Edinburgh, 1870).

Documents on the Later Crusades, 1274-1580, ed. N. Housley (Basingstoke, 1996).

Documents Origineaux de L'histoire de France (Archives Nationales, 1872).

Dublin Guild Merchant Roll, c.1190-1265, The, ed. P. Connolly and G. Martin (Dublin, 1992).

Exchequer Rolls of Scotland, The, ed. J. Stuart *et al.* (Edinburgh, 1878-1908).

Expeditions to Prussia and the Holy Land by Henry, Earl of Derby, ed. L.T. Smith (Camden Soc., 1894).

Extracts from the Records of the Burgh of Edinburgh (Scottish Burgh Record Soc., 1869-92).

Facsimiles of the National Manuscripts of Scotland (London, 1867-71).

Fasti Aberdonenses: Selections from the records of the university and King's College of Aberdeen, 1494-1854, ed. C. Innes (Spalding Club, 1854).

Foedera, Conventiones, Litterae at Cuiuscunque Generis Acta Publica, original ed., ed. T. Rymer (London, 1704-35).

Foedera, Conventiones, Litterae at Cuiuscunque Generis Acta Publica, Record Commission ed., ed. T. Rymer (London, 1816-69).

France Ecosse: Exposition organisée par les archives nationales (Archives Nationales, 1956).

France Gouvernée par Jean sans peur, La, ed. B.A. Pocquet du Haut-Jussé (Paris, 1959).

Frankfurts Reichskorrespondenz, 1376-1519, ed., J. Janssen, (Freiburg in Breisgau, 1863).

Foreign Correspondence with Marie de Lorraine, Queen of Scotland, 1537-1548, ed. M. Wood (SHS, 1923-25).

Gild Court Book of Dunfermline, The, 1433-1597, ed. E.P.D. Torrie (SRS, 1986).

Illustrations of the Topography and Antquities of the Shires of Aberdeen and Banff (Spalding Club, 1847-69).

Hamburger Burspraken, 1346 bis 1594, ed. J. Bolland (Hamburg, 1960).

Handelsrechnungen des Deutschen Ordens, ed. C. Sattler (Leipzig, 1887).

Hanseakten aus England, 1275-1412, ed. K. Kunze (Halle, 1891).

Hanserecesse. Zweite Abtheilung, 1431-76, ed. G. von der Ropp (Leipzig, 1876-92).

Hanserecesse, 1477-1530, ed. D. Schäffer (Leipzig, 1881-1913).

Hansisches Urkundenbuch, ed. K. Höhlbaum *et al.* (Halle, etc., 1886-1939).

'Holyrood Ordinale, The', ed. F.C. Eeles, *Book of the Old Edinurgh Club*, 7 (1914).

Inventaire Analytique des Ordonnances Enregistrées au Parliament de Paris, jusqu'à la mort de Louis XII, ed. H. Stein (Paris, 1908).

Inventaire des Archives de la Ville de Bruges, ed. L. Gilliodts van Severen (Bruges, 1883-85).

Inventaire Sommaires des Archives Départmental du Nord. Tome VIII: Archives Civiles, Série B, ed. J. Finot (Lille, 1895).

Inventaire Sommaires des Registres de la Jurade, 1520 à 1783, ed. D. le Vacher (Bordeaux, 1896-1947).

Issue Roll of Thomas de Brantingham, Lord High Treasurer of England, 1370, ed. F. Devon (London, 1835).

John of Gaunt's Register, ed. S. Armatage-Smith (Camden Soc., 1911).

Kämmereibuch der Stadt Reval, 1432-63, ed., R. Vogelsang (Cologne and Vienna, 1976).

Knights of St John of Jerusalem in Scotland, The, ed. I.B. Cowan, P.H.R. Mackay and A. Macquarrie (SHS, 1983).

Lay Subsidy Rolls for the County of Sussex, 1524-25, The , ed. J. Cornwall (Sussex Record Soc., 1956).

*Ledger of Andrew Halyburton, 1492-*1503, ed. C. Innes (Edinburgh, 1867).

Legislation by Three of the Thirteen Stanleys, Kings of Man, ed. W. Mackenzie (Manx Soc., 1860).

Letters and Papers, Foreign and Domestic, of the Reign of Henry VIII, ed. J. Gairdner *et al.* (London, 1900).

Letters of Abelard and Heloise, The, ed. B. Radice (Harmondsworth, 1974).

Letters of James the Fourth, The, ed. R.K. Hannay and R.L. Mackie (SHS, 1953).

Letters of James V, ed. R.K. Hannay and D. Hay (Edinburgh, 1954).

'Letters of a Scottish student at Paris and Oxford, c 1250', ed. N.R. Ker and W.A. Pantin in *Formularies which Bear on the History of Oxford, c.1204-1420*, ii, ed. H.E. Slater, W.A. Pantin and H.G. Richardson (Oxford Historical Soc., 1942).

Lettres de Charles VIII, Roi de France, ed. P. Pélicier (Paris, 1898-1905).

Liber Sancte Maire de Melros (Bannatyne Club, 1837).

Libri Commemoriali della Republica di Venezia: Regesti (Venice, 1883).

Livres des Priviléges (Bordeaux, 1878).

Local Port Book for Southampton, 1435-36, The, ed. D.B. Foster (Southampton, 1963).

'Lübeckischen Pfundzollbücher von 1492-96, Die', ed. F. Bruns, *HGb*, 13 (1907).

Making of King's Lynn, The: A documentary survey, ed. D.M. Owen (London, 1984).

Matrikel der Universität Köln, ed. H. Keussen (Cologne, 1928-31).

Memoranda de Parliamento, ed. F.W. Maitland (Roll Series, 1893).

Miteilungen aus dem Stadtarchiv Köln, 36-37 (1918), ed. J. Hansen.

Negocations Diplomatique de la France avec la Toscane, ed. A. Desjardin (Paris, 1875-76).

'Nieuw teksten over de Gentse draperie: wolaanvoier, productiewijze en controlepraktijken, c.1456-1468', ed. M. Boone, *Handelingen van de Koninklijke Commissie voor Geschiedenis*, 154 (1988).

Northern Petitions: Illustrative of life in Berwick, Cumbria and Durham in the fourteenth century, ed. C.M. Fraser, (Surtees Soc., 1981).

'Note et documents sur l'aparration de la 'nouvelle draperie' à Bruxelles, 1441-1443', ed. F. Favresse *Handelingen van de Koninklijke Commissie voor Geschiedenis*, 112 (1947).

Papers relating to the Scots in Poland, ed. A.F. Steuart (SHS, 1915).

Paston Letters, AD 1422-1509, The, ed. J. Gairdner (London, 1904).

Perth Guildry Book, 1452-1601, The, ed. M.L. Stavert (SRS, 1993).

'Plea roll of Edward I's army in Scotland, 1296, A', ed. C. Neville, *SHS Miscellany*, 11 (1990).

Pommeriches Urkundenbuch, ed. O. Heinemann *et al.* (Stettin, 1868-).

Procès de condemnation de Jeanne d'Arc: Texte, traduction et notes, ed. P. Champion (Paris, 1921).

Protocol Book of Gavin Ros, 1512-32, ed. J. Anderson and F.J. Grant (SRS, 1908).

Protocol Book of John Foular, 1503-1513, ed. W. Macleod and M. Woods (SRS, 1940-41).

Protocol Book of John Foular, 1528-34, ed. J. Durkan (SRS, 1985).

Quellen zur Geschichte des Kölner Handels und Verkehrs, ed. B. Kuske (Bonn, 1817-34).

'Question about the succession, 1364, A', ed. A.A.M. Duncan, *SHS Miscellany*, 12 (1994).

Raadsverdragen van Maastricht, 1367-1428, ed. M.A. van der Eerden-Vonk, W.J. Alberts and T.J. van Rensch (The Hague, 1992).

Recesse und andere Akten der Hansetage von 1256-1430, ed. W. Junghans and K. Koppmann (Leipzig, 1870-97).

Recueil de Documents Relatifs à l'Histoire de l'Industrie Drapière en Flandre. Première partie: des origines à l'époque bourguignonne, ed. G. Espinas and H. Pirenne (Brussels, 1906-24).

Recueil de Documents Relatifs à l'Histoire de l'Industrie Drapière en Flandre. Deuxième Partie: Le sud-ouest de la Flandre depuis l'époque bourguignonne, ed. H.E. Sagher (Brussels, 1951-66).

Rechtsbronnen der Stad Gouda, ed. L.M. Rollin Conquerque and A. Meerkamp van Embden (The Hague, 1917).

Rechtsbronnen der Stad Haarlem, ed. J. Huizinga (The Hague, 1911).

Records of the Earldom of Orkney, 1299-1614, ed. J.S. Clouston (SHS, 1914).

Records of Some Sessions of the Peace in Lincolnshire, ed. R. Sillem (Lincoln Record Soc., 1936).

Regesta Regum Scottorum, ed. G.W.S. Barrow *et al.* (Edinburgh, 1960-).

Register and Records of Holm Cultram, ed. E.F. Grainger and W.G. Collingwood (Cumberland and Westmorland Antiquarian and Archaeological Soc., Record Ser., 1929).

Register of Brieves, ed. T.M. Cooper, ed., (Stair Soc., 1946).

Register of John de Halton, Bishop of Carlisle, 1292-1324, ed. W.N. Thomson and T.F. Tout (Canterbury and York Soc., 1913).

Register of the Privy Council of Scotland, The, ed. J.H. Burton *et al.* (Edinburgh, 1877-).

Registres du Trésor des Chartres, ed. J. Viard and A. Vallée (Paris, 1978-84).

Registrum Cartarum Ecclesie Sancti Egidii de Edinburgh (Bannatyne Club, 1859).

Registrum de Dunfermelyn (Bannatyne Club, 1842).

Registrum Episcopatus Aberdenensis (Spalding and Maitland Clubs, 1845).

Registrum Episcopatus Moraviensis (Bannatyne Club, 1837).

Registrum Episcopatus Glasguensis (Bannatyne and Maitland Clubs, 1843).

Registrum Honoris de Morton (Bannatyne Club, 1853).

Registrum Magni Sigilli Regum Scottorum, ed. J.M. Thomson *et al.* (Edinburgh, 1882-1914).

Registrum Monasterii de Passelet (Maitland Club, 1832).

Rentale Dunkeldense, ed. R. Hannay (SHS, 1915).

Reports of the Royal Commission on Historical Manuscripts, 11th Report (London, 1887).

Rotuli Scotiae in Turri Londinensi et in Domo Capitulari Westmonasteriensi Asservati, ed. D. Macpherson *et al.* (London, 1814-19).

Rotulorum Patentium et Clausorum Cancellariae Hiberniae Calendarium, ed. E. Tresham (Dublin, 1928).

St Andrews Formulare, 1514-1546, ed. G. Donaldson and C. Macrae (Stair Soc., 1942-44).

'Scottish nation at Orléans, 1336-1538, The', ed. J. Kirkpatrick, *SHS Miscellany,* 2 (1904).

Scotia Pontificia: Papal letters to Scotland before the pontificate of Innocent III, ed. R. Somerville (Oxford, 1982).

'*Scotia Pontificia*: additions and corrections', ed. P. Ferguson and R. Somerville, *SHR,* 66 (1987).

Select Cases in the Court of King's Bench under Richard II, Henry IV and Henry V, ed. G.O. Sayles (Selden Soc., 1971).

Select Cases on Defamation to 1600, ed. R.H. Helmholz (Selden Soc., 1985).

Stralsunder Liber Memoriales, Der, ed. H.D. Schroeder (Schwerin etc., 1964-82).

Statuta Capitolorum Generalium Ordinis Cisterciensis ab anno 1116 ad annum 1786, ed. J.-M. Canivez (Louvain, 1933-39).

Statuti dell'arte dei Rigattieri e Linaioli di Firenze, 1296-1340, ed. F. Sartini (Florence, 1940).

Tabeller over Skibsfart og Varetransport gennem Øresund, 1497-1660, ed. N.E. Bang (Copenhagen and Leipzig, 1906).

Tax Book of the Cistercian Order, ed. A.O. Johnsen and P. King (Oslo, 1979).

Tol van Iersekeroord, De: Documenten en rekeningen, 1321-1572, ed. W.S. Unger (The Hague, 1939).

Tudor Royal Proclamations, ed. P.L. Hughes and J.F. Larkin (New Haven, 1964).

Urkundenbuch der Stadt Lübeck. Codex Diplomaticus Lubecensis (Lübeck, 1843-1905).

Wigtownshire Charters, ed. R.C. Reid (SHS, 1960).

'Wills of Thomas Bassandyne and other printers, The', *Bannatyne Miscellany* 2, (Bannatyne Club, 1827-55).

'Wool customs accounts for Newcastle-upon-Tyne for the reign of Edward I, The', ed. J.C. Davies *Archaeolgia Aeliana*, 32 (1954).

York House Books, 1461-1490, The, ed. L.C. Attreed (York, 1991).

Artistic, Literary and Narrative Sources

Adam, Salimbene de, *Cronica*, ed. G. Scalia (Bari, 1966).

'Adversus Jovinianum', *Patrologia Latina*, xxiii, ed. J.P. Migne (Paris, 1845).

Angels, Nobles and Unicorns: Art and patronage in medieval Scotland, ed. E. Sharrott and D.H. Caldwell (Edinburgh, 1988).

'The 'Auchinleck Chronicle'', ed. C. McGladdery in idem, *James II* (Edinburgh, 1990).

Auton, Jean d', *Chroniques de Louis XII*, ed. R. de Maulde la Clavière (Paris, 1889-95).

Ayala, Pero Lopez de, *Crónica del Rey Don Pedro y del Rey Don Enrique*, ed. G. Orduna (Buonos Aries, 1994).

Baker de Swynebroke, G. le, *Chronicon*, ed. E.M. Thompson (Oxford, 1889).

Barbour, John, *The Bruce*, ed. A.A.M. Duncan (Edinburgh, 1997).

Basin, Thomas, *Histoire de Charles VII*, ed. C. Samarins (Paris, 1964-65).

[Berchen, Willem van], *De Gelderse Kroniek van Willem van Berchen*, ed. A.J. de Mooy (Arnhem, 1950).

Beyeren, Herault van, *Het Haagse Handscrift*, ed. J. Verbij-Schillings (Hilversum, 1999).

Book of The Knowledge of All The Kingdoms, ed. C. Markham (Hakluyt Soc., 1912).

Bonet, Honoré, *The Tree of Battles*, ed. G.W. Coopland (Liverpool, 1949).

Borde, Andrew, *The Fyrst Boke of the Introduction of Knowledge* (Early English Text Soc., 1870).

Bouvier, G. le, dit le Hérault Berry, *Les Chroniques du Roi Charles VII*, ed. H. Courteault and L. Celiet (Paris, 1979).

Bower, Walter, *Scotichronicon, in Latin and English*, ed. D.E.R. Watt *et al.* (Aberdeen and Edinburgh, 1987-98).

Buik of Alexander, The, or The Buik of the Most Noble and Valiant Conquerour Alexander the Grit, ed. R.L.G. Ritchie (STS, 1921-29).

Buik of King Alexander the Conquerour, The, J. Cartwright (STS, 1986-90).

Buke of the Chess, The, ed. C. van Buuren (STS, 1997).

Brut, The, or the Chronicles of England, ed. F.W.D. Brie (Early English Text Soc., 1906-8).

Cellini, Benevenuto, *Autobiography*, ed. G. Bull (Harmondsworth, 1956).

Chastellain, George, *Oeuvres*, ed. K. de Lettenhove (Brussels, 1863-64).

Chronicle of Melrose, ed. A.O. Anderson and M.O. Anderson (facsimile edn., London, 1936).

Chronicon de Lanercost (Maitland Club, 1839).

Chroniken der Deutschen Städten vom 14.bis 16. Jahrhundert (Göttingen, 1968).

Chronique des Quatres Premiers Valois, 1327-1393, ed. S. Luce (Paris, 1862).

Chronique de Saint-Pierre-le-Vif de Sens, ed R.H. Bautier and M. Gillies (Paris, 1979).

Chroniques Asturennes, ed. Y. Bonnaz (Paris, 1982).

Columbus, Christopher, *The Four Voyages*, ed. J.M. Cohen (London, 1969).

[Commynes, Philippe de], *Memoirs*, ed. S. Kinser (Columbia, SC, 1969-73).

Corpus Chroniconum Bonotensium, ed. A. Sorbelli (Bologna, 1906-38).

Dei, Benedetto, *La Cronica dall'anno 1400 all'anno 1500*, ed. R. Barducci (Florence, 1984).

Deidis of Armorie: A heraldic treatise and bestiary, The, ed. L.A.J.R. Houwen (STS, 1994).

'Dethe of the Kynge of Scotis, The: A new edition', ed. M. Connolly, *SHR*, 71 (1992).

Discovering Western Civilization through Maps and Views, ed. G.A. Danzer and D. Buisseret (New York, 1991).

[Dunbar, William], *The Poems of William Dunbar*, ed. J.L. Kinsley (Oxford, 1979).

[Durham, Reginald, monk of], *Libellus de Admirandis Beati Cuthberti Virtutibus* (Surtees Soc., 1835).

Early Travellers in Scotland, ed. P. Hume Brown (repr., Edinburgh, 1978).

Escouchy, M. d', *Chronique*, ed. G. du Fresne de Beaucourt (Paris, 1863-64).

Eulogium (Historiarum sive temporis): Chronicon ab orbe condition usque.., ed. F.S. Haydon (Roll Series, 1858-63).

'Facsimiles of the Scottish coats of arms emblazoned in the *Armorial de Gelre*', *PSAS*, 25 (1890-91).

Févre, Jean le, *Chroniques*, ed. F. Morand (Paris, 1862).

Fordun, John of, *Chronicle of the Scottish Nation*, ed. W.F. Skene (repr., Llanerch, 1993).

Fortescue, John, *The Governance of England*, ed. C. Plummer (Oxford, 1885).

Froissart, Jean, *Chronicles*, ed. G. Brereton (Harmondsworth, 1968).

Froissart, Jean, *Méliador*, ed. A. Longnon (Paris, 1895-99).

Froissart, Jean, *Oeuvres*, ed. K. de Lettenhove (Brussels, 1867-77).

Gray of Heton, Thomas, *Scalacronica* (Maitland Club, 1836).

Grimani Breviary, The, ed. M. Salimi and G.L. Mellini (London, 1972).

Guiccardini, Francesco, *Storia d'Italia*, ed. L. Felici (Rome, 1967-68).

Guiccardini, Ludovico, *Descrittione de Tutti i Paesi Bassi* (Antwerp, 1567).

[Guisborough, Walter of], *The Chronicle of Walter of Guisborough*, ed. H. Rothwell (Camden Soc., 1957).

Hastings Hours, The, ed. D.H. Turner (London, 1983).

Haye, Gilbert of the, *Prose Manuscript, AD 1456*, ed. J.H. Stevenson (STS, 1901-14).

Higden, Ranulph, *Polychronicon*, ed. C. Babington and J.R. Lumby (Roll Series, 1865-66)

Hoccleve's Works I: The minor poems, ed. F.J. Furnivall (Early English Text Society, 1892).

'Idrisi's account of the British Isles', ed. A.F.L. Beetson, *Bulletin of the School of Oriental Studies*, 13 (1945-50).

Jerusalem Pilgrimage, ed. J. Wilkinson, J. Hill and W.F. Ryan (Hakluyt Soc., 1988).

Joinville, Jean de and Villhardouin, G., *Chronicles of the Crusades*, ed. M.R.B. Shaw (Harmondsworth, 1963).

Knighton's Chronicle, ed. G.H. Martin (Oxford, 1995).

Knox, John, *History of the Reformation in Scotland*, ed. W.C. Dickinson (Edinburgh, 1949).

Laing, H., *Descriptive Catalogue of Impressions from Ancient Scottish Seals* (Edinburgh, 1850).

Lancelot of the Laik, ed. M.M. Gray (STS, 1912).

[Lannoy, Ghillebert de], *Oeuvre de Ghillebert de Lannoy, Voyageur, Diplomate et Moraliste*, ed. C. Potvin (Louvain, 1878).

Laxdaela Saga, ed. M. Magnusson and H. Pálsson (Harmondsworth, 1969).

Libelle of Englysche Polycye, The: A poem on the use of sea-power, 1436, ed. G. Warner (Oxford, 1926).

Liber Pluscardensis, ed. F.J.H. Skene (Edinburgh, 1877-80).

Lindesay of Pitscottie, Robert, *The Historie and Cronicles of Scotland* (STS, 1899-1911).

Lindsay, Alexander, *A Rutter of the Scottish Seas*, ed. A.B. Taylor, I.H. Adams and G. Fortune (National Maritime Museum, 1980).

Lindsay, David, *Ane Satyre of the Thrie Estaitis*, ed. R.J. Lyall (Edinburgh, 1989).

Livres des Coutumes, ed. H. Barkhausen (Bordeaux, 1890).

Lopes, Fernão, *Cronicá de D. João I*, ed. M. Lopes de Almeida and A. de Magalhães (Porto, 1945).

Major, John, *A History of Greater Britain*, ed. A. Constable (SHS, 1892).

Malmesbury, William of, *Gesta Regum Anglorum*, ed. R.A.B. Maynors *et al.* (Oxford, 1988-99).

Mapping of the World: Early printed maps, 1472-1700, ed. R.W. Shirley (London, 1983).

Martorell, Joanot and Galba, Marti Joan de, *Tirant lo Blanc*, ed. D.H. Rosenthal (London, 1984).

Master of Mary of Burgundy, The, *A book of hours for Engelbert of Nassau*, ed. J.G. Alexander (London, 1970).

Mercanti Scrittori: Ricordi nella Firenze tra medioevo e rinascimento, ed. V. Branca (Milan, 1986).

[Monstrelet, Enguerran de], *La Chronique d'Enguerran de Monstrelet*, ed. L. Douet d'Arcq (Paris, 1857-62).

Murimuth, Adam, *Continuatio Chronicarum*, ed. E.M. Thompson (Roll Series, 1889).

[Nangis, Guillaume de], *Chronique de Guiiaume de Nangis de 1113 à 1300 et des continuateurs de 1300 à 1368*, ed. H. Geraud (Paris, 1843).

[Nogent, Guibert of], *A Monk's Confession: The memoirs of Guibert of Nogent* (University Park, Penn., 1996).

Pagine scelte in due codici appartenuti alla badia di S. Maria di Coupar-Angus in Scozia, ed. H.M. Bannister, (Rome, 1910).

Paris, Matthew, *Chronica Majora*, ed. H.R. Luard (Roll Series, 1872-83).

Parisian Journal, A, 1405-1409, ed. J. Shirley (Oxford, 1968).

Pegolotti, Francesco Balducci, *La Pratica della Mercatura*, ed. A. Evans (Cambridge, Mass., 1936).

Pii II, *Commentarii Rerum Memorabilium Que Temporibus Svis Contogerunt*, ed. A. van Heck (Vatican City, 1984).

Pilgrim's Guide to Santiago de Compostella, The, ed. W. Melczer (New York, 1993).

Pisan, Christine de, *The Epistle of Othea translated from the French text by Stephen Scrope*, ed. C.F. Bühler (Early English Text Soc., 1970).

[Pitti, Buonacorso, and Dati, Gregorio], *Two Memoirs of Renaissance Florence: The diaries of Buonaccorso Pitti and Gregorio Dati*, ed. G. Brucker (New York, 1976).

Playfair Hours, The: A late fifteenth-century illuminated manuscript from Rouen, ed. R. Watson, (London, 1984).

Political Songs of England from King John to King Edward II (Camden Soc., 1839).

[Reading, John of], *Chronica Johannis de Reading et Anonymi Cantuariensis, 1346-1367*, ed. J. Tait (Manchester, 1914).

Santiago de Compostella: 1000 ans de pèlerinage Européen (Ghent, 1985).

Scottish Annals from English Chroniclers A.D.500 to 1286, ed. A.O. Anderson (London, 1908).

Scottish Verse from the Book of the Dean of Lismore, ed. W.J. Watson (Edinburgh, 1937).

Scriptores Rerum Prussicarum, ed. T. Hirsch, M. Toeppen and E. Strehlke (Leipzig, 1861-74).

Stuart, Bérault, *Traité sur l'art de la guerre*, ed. E. de Comminges, (The Hague, 1976).

[Usk, Adam of], *The Chronicle of Adam of Usk, 1377-1421*, ed. C. Given-Wilson (Oxford, 1997).

[Usk, Adam of], *The Chronicle of Adam of Usk, A.D. 1377-1421*, ed. E.M. Thompson (repr., Llanerch, 1990).

Ursins, Jean Juvénal des, *Écrits Politique*, ed. P.S. Lewis (Paris, 1978-85).

Villani, Giovanni, *Cronica* (Florence, 1823).

Voraigne, James de, *The Golden Legend*, ed. G. Ryan and H. Ripperger (Salem, 1987).

Wales, Gerald of, *The History and Topography of Ireland*, ed. J.J. O'Meara (Portlaoise, 1982).

Waurin, Jehan de, *Chroniques et Anchiennes Istoires de la Grant Bretagne* (Roll Series, 1864-91).

Westminster Chronicle, The, ed. L.C. Hector and B.F. Harvey (Oxford, 1982).

Wyntoun, Andrew of, *The Original Chronicle* (STS, 1903-14).

Wyntoun, Androw of, *The Orygnale Cronykil of Scotland*, ed. D. Laing (Edinburgh, 1872-79).

SECONDARY SOURCES

Books and articles

Åberg, A., 'Scottish soldiers in the Swedish armies in the sixteenth and seventeenth centuries' in Simpson, *Scottish Soldier*

Adams, D., 'The harbour: its early history' in G. Jackson and S.G.E. Lythe, eds., *The Port of Montrose* (Tayport, 1993).

Aitken, W.G., 'Excavations of bloomeries in Rannoch', *PSAS*, 102 (1969-70).

Alexandre, P., *Le Climat en Europe au Moyen Âge: Contribution à l'histoire des variations climatiques de 1000 à 1425* (Paris, 1987).

Allmand, C.T., *The Hundred Years War* (Cambridge, 1988).

Andrews, M.C., 'Scotland in the portolan charts', *The Scottish Geographical Magazine*, 42 (1926).

Andrews, M.C., 'The boundary between Scotland and England in the portolan charts', *PSAS*, 60 (1925-26)

Antony-Schmitt, M.M., *La culte de Saint-Sebastien en Alsace* (Strasbourg, 1977).

Apted, M.R., and Hannabuss, S., *Painters in Scotland, 1301-1700: A biographical dictionary* (Edinburgh, 1978).

Aston, T.H., 'Oxford's medieval alumni', *PP*, 74 (1977)

Aston, T.H., Duncan, G.D., and Evans, T.A.R., 'The medieval alumni of the university of Cambridge', *PP*, 86 (1980).

Ash, M., 'David Bernham, bishop of St Andrews, 1239-1253' in D. McRoberts, ed., *The Medieval Church of St Andrews* (Glasgow, 1976).

Ayton, A., *Knights and Warhorses: Military service and the English aristocracy under Edward III* (Woodbridge, 1994).

Bald, M.A., 'Vernacular books imported into Scotland, 1500-1625', *SHR*, 23 (1925-6).

Balfour-Melville, E.W.M., *James I, King of Scots, 1406-1437* (London, 1936).

Balfour-Melville, E.W.M., 'Two John Crabbs', *SHR*, 39 (1960).

Balić, C., 'The life and works of John Duns Scotus' in J.K. Ryan and B.M. Bonansea, eds., *John Duns Scotus, 1265-1965* (Washington D.C., 1965).

Bannerman, J., 'The *clàrsach* and the *dàrsair*', *Scottish Studies*, 30 (1991).

Barbé, L.A., *Margaret of Scotland and the Dauphin Louis: An historical study* (London, 1917).

Barbé, L.A., 'The story of the 'long-tail' myth' in idem, *In Byways of Scottish History* (London, 1924).

Barber, R. and Barker, J., *Tournaments, Chivalry and Pageant in the Middle Ages* (Woodbridge, 1989).

Barker, J.R.V., *The Tournament in England, 1100-1400* (Woodbridge, 1986).

Barnhill, J.W., and Dukes, P., 'North-east Scots in Muscovy in the seventeenth century', *NS*, 1 (1972).

Barrell, A.D.M., 'The background to *Cum Universi*: Scoto-papal relations, 1159-1192', *IR*, 46 (1995).

Barrell, A.D.M., 'The papacy and the regular clergy in Scotland in the fourteenth century', *RSCHS*, 24 (1992).

Barrell, A.D.M., *The Papacy, Scotland and Northern England, 1342-1378* (Cambridge, 1995).

Barrow, G., and A. Royan, 'James, fifth Stewart of Scotland, 1260(?)-1309' in K.J. Stringer, ed., *Essays on the Nobility of Medieval Scotland* (Edinburgh, 1985).

Barrow, G.W.S., 'French after the style of Petithachengon' in B.E. Crawford, ed., *Church, Chronicle and Learning in Medieval and Early Renaissance Scotland* (Edinburgh, 1999).

Barrow, G.W.S., *Robert Bruce and the Community of the Realm of Scotland* (3rd ed., Edinburgh, 1988).

Barrow, G.W.S., *The Anglo-Norman Era in Scottish History* (Oxford, 1996).

Bartlett, R., *The Making of Europe: Conquest, colonization and cultural change, 950-1350* (London, 1993).

Bartlett, R., *Trial by Fire and Water: The medieval judicial ordeal* (Oxford, 1986).

Baumgartner, F.J., *Louis XII* (Woodbridge, 1994).

Bawcutt, P., 'An early Scottish debate-poem on women', *Scottish Literary Journal*, 23 (1996).

Bawcutt, P., 'Images of women in the poems of Dunbar', *Études Écossaises*, 1 (1991).

Baxter, J.H. 'Four new medieval Scottish authors', *SHR*, 25 (1928).

Beal, G., *Playing-cards and their Story* (Newton Abbot, 1975).

Beckett, W.N.M., 'The Perth Charterhouse before 1500', *Analecta Cartusiana*, 128 (1988).

Behault de Doron, A. de, 'La noblesse hennuyère au tournoi de Compiègne de 1238 [sic]', *Annales du cercle archéolgique de Mons*, 22 (1890).

Belhoste, J-F., 'La maison, la fabrique et la ville: l'industrie du drap fin en France, XVe-XVIIIe siècles', *Histoire, Economie et Société*, 13 (1994).

Bennett, J.A.W., *Poetry of the Passion: Studies in twelve centuries of English verse* (Oxford, 1982).

Bennett, M., *The Battle of Bosworth* (Stroud, 1985).

Bentley-Cranch, D., 'An early sixteenth-century architectural source for the palace of Falkland', *Review of Scottish Culture*, 2 (1986).

Bergier, J.F., 'Peages du XVe siècle au pays de Vaud', *Beiträge zur Witschafts- und Stadtgeschichte* (Wiesbaden, 1965).

Beveridge, J., 'Two Scottish thirteenth-century songs, with the original melodies, recently discovered in Sweden', *PSAS*, 73 (1938-39).

Bieganska, A., 'A note on the Scots in Poland' in Smout, *Scotland and Europe*.

Bing, C., *The Lairds of Arbuthnott* (Edzell and London, 1993).

Blake, J.B., 'The medieval coal trade of north-east England: some fourteenth-century evidence', *NH*, 2 (1967).

Blanchard, I., 'Lothian and beyond: the economy of the 'English empire' of David I' in R. Britnell and J. Hatcher, eds., *Progress and Problems in Medieval England: Essays in honour of Edward Miller* (Cambridge, 1996).

Blanchard, I., 'Northern wools and Netherlandish markets at the close of the middle ages' in Simpson, *Scotland and the Low Countries*.

Blanchard, I., *The Middle Ages: A concept too many?* (Avonbridge, 1996).

Blanchard, J., *Commynes L'Européen: L'invention du politique* (Geneva, 1966).

Blockmans, W., 'Manuscript acquisition by the Burgundian court and the market for books in the fifteenth-century Netherlands', in M. North and D. Ormrod, eds., *Art Markets in Europe, 1400-1800* (Aldershot, 1998).

Blockmans, W., 'The social and economic context of investment in art in Flanders around 1400' in M. Smeyers and B. Cardon, eds., *Flanders in a European Perspective: Manuscript illumination around 1400 in Flanders and abroad* (Leuven, 1997).

Bonney, M., *Lordship and Urban Community: Durham and its overlords, 1250-1540* (Cambridge, 1990).

Bowler, D., and Cachart, R., 'Tay Street, Perth: the excavation of an early harbour site', *PSAS*, 124 (1994)

Birch, D.J., *Pilgrimage to Rome in the Middle Ages* (Woodbridge, 1998).

Bliss, A., and Long, J., 'Literature in Norman French and English to 1534' in A. Cosgrove, ed., *A New History of Ireland. Volume II: Medieval Ireland, 1169-1534* (Oxford, 1987).

Boardman, S., *The Early Stewart Kings: Robert II and Robert III, 1371-1406* (East Linton, 1996).

Bois, G., *The Crisis of Feudalism: Economy and society in eastern Normandy, c.1300-1550* (Cambridge, 1984).

Bossy, J., *Christianity in the West, 1400-1700* (Oxford, 1985).

Brandmüller, W., *Das Konzil von Pavia-Siena, 1423-1424* (Münster, 1968).

Brill, E.V.K., 'A sixteenth-century complaint against the Scots', *SHR* 27 (1948).

Britnell, R.H., 'The English economy and the government, 1450-1550' in J.L. Watts, ed., *The End of the Middle Ages?* (Stroud, 1998).

Broadie, A., *The Shadow of Scotus: Philosophy and faith in pre-Reformation Scotland* (Edinburgh, 1995).

Brotherstone, T., and Ditchburn, D., eds., *Freedom and Authority: Scotland, c.1050-1650* (East Linton, 2000).

Brown, A.L., 'The Cistercian abbey of Saddell, Kintyre', *IR*, 20 (1969)

Brown, A.L., 'The priory of Coldingham in the late fourteenth century', *IR*, 23 (1972).

Brown, M., 'Regional lordship in the north-east. The Badenoch Stewarts, II: Alexander Stewart, earl of Mar', *NS*, 16 (1996).

Brown, M., *The Black Douglases: War and lordship in later medieval Scotland* (East Linton, 1998).

Brucker, G.A., *Renaissance Florence* (New York, 1969).

Brundage, J.A., *Law, Sex and Christian Society in Medieval Europe* (Chicago, 1987).

Brundage, J.A., *Medieval Canon Law* (Harlow, 1995).

Bryan, D., *The Great Earl of Kildare* (Dublin & Cork, 1933).

Bryce, W.M., 'St Roque's Chapel and the Lands of Canaan', *Book of the Old Edinburgh Club*, 10 (1918)

Bryce, W.M., *The Scottish Greyfriars* (Edinburgh, 1909).

Buchanan, P.H., *Margaret Tudor, Queen of Scots* (Edinburgh, 1985).

Bueno de Mesquita, M., 'Ludovico Sforza and his vassals' in E.F. Jacob, *Italian Renaissance Studies: A tribute to the late Cecilia M. Ady* (London, 1960).

Burns, C., 'Scottish bishops at the general councils of the middle ages', *IR*, 16 (1965).

Burton, J., *Monastic and Religious Orders in Britain, 1000-1300* (Cambridge, 1994).

Burns, J.H., 'The Scotland of John Major', *IR*, 2 (1951).

Burns, J.H., *Scottish Churchmen and the Council of Basle* (Glasgow, 1962).

Buuren, C. van, 'John Asloan and his manuscript: an Edinburgh notary and scribe in the days of James III, James IV and James V, c.1470-c.1530' in J.H. Williams, ed., *Stewart Style, 1513-1542: Essays on the court of James V* (East Linton, 1996).

Bynum, C., *Holy Feast and Holy Fast: The religious significance of food to medieval women* (Berkeley, 1987).

Bynum, C.W., 'The sprituality of regular canons in the twelfth century' in idem, *Jesus as Mother: Studies in spirituality of the high middle ages* (London, 1982).

Caillet, L., *Etudes sur les relations de la commune de Lyon avec Charles VII et Louis XI* (Paris and Lyon, 1909).

Cameron, A.I., *The Apostolic Camera and Scottish Benefices, 1418-1488* (Oxford, 1934).

Cameron, A.I., 'Scottish students at Paris, 1466-1492', *Juridical Review*, 48 (1936).

Cameron, N., 'The Romanesque sculpture of Dunfermline: Durham versus the vicinal' in Higgitt, *Art and Architecture of the Diocese of St Andrews.*

Cameron, S., 'Sir James Douglas, Spain and the Holy Land' in Brotherstone and Ditchburn, *Freedom and Authority.*

Camille, M., *Mirror in Parchment: The Luttrell psalter and the making of medieval England* (London, 1998).

Campbell, I., 'A Romanesque revival and the early renaissance in Scotland, c.1380-1513', *Journal of the Soc. of Architectural Historians*, 54 (1995).

Campbell, I., 'Bishop Elphinstone's tomb' in Geddes, *King's College Chapel* (Leeds, 2000).

Campbell, I., 'Linlithgow's 'princely palace' and its influence in Europe', *Architectural Heritage*, 5 (1994).

Campbell, L., 'The art market in the southern Netherlands in the fifteenth century', *Burlington Magazine*, 118 (1976).

Campbell, L., 'The authorship of the *Recueil d'Arras*', *Journal of the Warburg and Courtauld Institutes*, 40 (1977).

Campbell, L., 'Edward Bonkil: a Scottish patron of Hugo van der Goes', *Burlington Magazine*, 126 (1984).

Campbell, L., *The Early Flemish Pictures in the Collection of her Majesty the Queen* (Cambridge, 1985)

Campbell, L., *Renaissance Portraits: European portrait-painting in the 14th, 15th and 16th centuries* (New Haven, 1990).

Campbell, L., 'Scottish patrons and Netherlandish painters in the 15th and 16th centuries' in Simpson, *Scotland and the Low Countries.*

Campbell, L., and Dick, J., 'The portrait of Bishop Elphinstone' in Geddes, *King's College Chapel.*

Campbell, L., and Foister, S., 'Gerard, Lucas and Susanna Horenbout', *Burlington Magazine*, 128 (1986).

Campbell, T., 'Portelan charts from the late thirteenth century to 1500' in J.B. Hawley and D. Woodward, eds., *The History of Cartography. Volume I: Cartography in prehistoric, ancient and medieval Europe and the Mediterranean* (Chicago, 1987).

Cant, R.G., *The University of St Andrews: A short history* (3rd ed., St Andrews, 1992).

Carsten, E., *Geschichte der Hansestadt Elbing* (Elbing, 1937).

Cazel, F.A., 'Financing the crusades' in K.M. Setton, ed., *History of the Crusades* (Madison, 1969-89).

Cazelles, R., *Société, Politique, Noblesse et Couronne sous Jean le Bon et Charles V* (Geneva, 1982).

Challis, C.E., 'Debasement: the Scottish experience in the fifteenth and sixteenth centuries' in D.M. Metclaf, ed., *Coinage in Medieval Scotland, 1100-1600* (Oxford, 1977).

Cherry, A., *Princes, Poets and Patrons: The Stuarts and Scotland* (Edinburgh, 1987).

Chevalier, B., 'Les Ecossais dans les armées de Charles VII jusqu'à la bataille de Verneuil' in R. Pernoud, ed., *Jeanne d'Arc: Une epoque, une rayonnement* (Paris, 1982).

Chevalier, B., *Tours, ville royale, 1356-1520: Origine et développement d'une capitale à la fin du moyen age* (Leuven, 1975).

Childs, W.R., *Anglo-Castilian Trade in the Later Middle Ages* (Manchester, 1978)

Childs, W.R., and O'Neill, T., 'Overseas trade' in A. Cosgrove, ed., *A New History of Ireland. Volume II: Medieval Ireland, 1169-1534* (Oxford, 1987).

Chorley, P., 'The cloth exports of Flanders and northern France during the thirteenth century: a luxury trade', *Economic History Review*, 40 (1987).

Christiansen, E., *The Northern Crusades: The Baltic and the Catholic frontier, 1100-1525* (London, 1980).

Cipolla, C., 'Currency depreciation in medieval Europe' in S.L. Thrupp, ed., *Change in Medieval Society: Europe north of the Alps, 1050-1500* (New York, 1964).

Clark, J.M., *The Dance of Death in the Middle Ages and the Renaissance* (Glasgow, 1950).

Clouston, R.W.M., 'The bells of Perthshire: St John's kirk, Perth', *PSAS*, 124 (1994).

Cobban, A., *English University Life in the Middle Ages* (London, 1999)

Cockshaw, P., ed., *L'ordre de la Toison d'Or de Philippe le Bon à Philippe le Beau, 1430-1505: Idéal ou reflet d'une société?* (Brussels, 1996).

Cochet, M. L'abbé, 'Notice historique et archéologique sur l'eglise et l'abbaye de Saint-Saëns (Seine-inférieure)', *Bulletin de la Societé des Antiquaires de Normandie*, 20 (18??).

Colston, J., *The Town and Port of Leith* (Edinburgh, 1892).

Colvin, H., ed., *The History of the King's Works* (London, 1963-75).

Constable, G., 'The place of the crusader in medieval society', *Viator*, 29 (1988).

Contamine, P., 'Entre France et Ecosse: Bérault Stuart, seigneur d'Aubigny (vers 1452-1508), chef de guerre, diplomate, écrivain militaire' in J. Laidlaw, ed., *The Auld Alliance: France and Scotland over 700 years* (Edinburgh, 1999).

Contamine, P., 'Froissart and Scotland' in Simpson, *Scotland and the Low Countries*.

Contamine, P., 'La guerre de cent ans: le XV siècle du 'roi de Bourges' au 'très victorieux roi de France'' in idem, ed., *Histoire militaire de la France*, i, (Paris, 1992).

Contamine, P., 'La première modernité: des guerres d'Italie aux guerre de religion, un novel art militaire' in idem, ed., *Histoire militaire de la France*, i, (Paris, 1992).

Contamine, P., 'La première modernité: Louis XI, tensions et innovations' in idem, ed., *Histoire militaire de la France*, i (Paris, 1992).

Contamine, P., 'Scottish soldiers in France in the second half of the fifteenth century: mercenaries, immigrants or Frenchmen in the making?' in Simpson, *Scottish Soldier*.

Contamine, P., 'The war literature of the late middle ages: the treatises of Robert de Balsac and Béraud, lord of Aubigny' in C.T. Allmand, ed., *War, Literature and Politics* (Liverpool, 1976).

Contamine, P., *War in the Middle Ages* (Oxford, 1985).

Conway, A., *Henry VII's Relations with Scotland and Ireland, 1485-98* (Cambridge, 1932).

Coornaert, E., *Un Centre Industriel d'Autrefois: La draperies-sayetteries d'Hondschoote, XIVe-XVIIIe siècles* (Paris, 1930).

Cosgrove, A., 'Ireland beyond the Pale, 1399-1460', idem, ed., *A New History of Ireland. Volume II: Medieval Ireland, 1169-1534* (Oxford, 1987).

Courtenay, W.J., *Parisian Scholars in the Early Fourteenth Century: A social portrait* (Cambridge, 1999)

Cowan, I.B., 'Church and society', in J.M. Brown, ed., *Scottish Society in the Fifteenth Century* (London, 1977).

Cowan, I.B., 'Patronage, provision and reservation: pre-Reformation appointments to benefices' in idem, *The Medieval Church in Scotland*, ed. J. Kirk (Edinburgh, 1995).

Cowan, I.B., 'The church in the diocese of Aberdeen' in idem, *The Medieval Church in Scotland*, ed. J. Kirk (Edinburgh, 1995).

Cowan, I.B. and Easson, D.E., *Medieval Religious Houses: Scotland* (2nd ed., London, 1976).

Cowdry, H.E.J., 'The peace and truce of God in the eleventh century', *PP*, 46 (1970).

Craeybeckx, J., *Un Grand Commerce d'Importation: Les vins de France aux ancien Pays-Bas, XIIIe-XVIe siècle* (Paris, 1958).

Crawford, B.E., 'Foreign relations: Scandinavia' in J.M. Brown, ed., *Scottish Society in the Fifteenth Century* (London, 1977).

Crawford, B.E., 'Peter's pence in Scotland' in G.W.S. Barrow, ed., *The Scottish Tradition* (Edinburgh, 1970).

Crawford, B.E., ed., *St Magnus Cathedral and Orkney's Twelfth-century Renaissance* (Aberdeen, 1988).

Cruden, S., 'Glenluce abbey: finds discovered during excavations, part I', *TDGAS*, 29 (1952).

Cummins, J., *The Hound and the Hawk: The art of medieval hunting* (London, 1988).

Cunnigham, I., 'The Asloan manuscript' in A.A.MacDonald, M. Lynch and I.B. Cowan, eds., *The Renaissance in Scotland: Studies in literature, religion, history and culture* (Leiden, 1994).

Curry, A., 'The nationality of men-at-arms serving in English armies in Normandy and the *pays de conquête*, 1415-1450: a preliminary survey', *Reading Medieval Studies*, 18 (1992).

Cursiter, S., *Scottish Art* (London, 1949).

Cust, E., *Some Account of the Stuarts of Aubigny in France, 1422-1672* (London, 1891).

Danzig: Bild einer Hansestadt (Berlin, 1980)

Davidsohn, R., *Storia di Firenze* (Florence, 1956-68).

Day, J., 'The great bullion famine of the fifteenth century', *PP*, 79 (1978).

Deansley, M., 'Vernacular books in England in the fourteenth and fifteenth centuries', *Modern Language Review*, 15 (1920).

Degryse, R., 'De laatmiddeleeuwse herringvisserij', *Bijdragen voor de Geschiedenis der Nederlanden*, 21 (1966-67).

Degryse, R., 'De schepen in de haven van Sluis in het voorjaar 1464', *Mededelingen van de Marineakademie van Belgie*, 20 (1968).

Degryse, R., 'De Vlaamse haringvisserij in de XVe eeuw', *Annales de la Société d'Emulations de Bruges*, 88 (1951).

Delmarcel, G., *Flemish Tapestry* (London, 1999).

Dembowski, D., *Jean Froissart and his Méliador: Context, craft and sense* (Lexington, 1983).

Dennison, E.P.D., and Stones, J., *Historic Aberdeen: The archaeological implications of development* (Scottish Burgh Survey, 1997)

Derville, A., ed., *Histoire de Saint-Omer* (Lille, 1981).

Derville, A., 'Le marché du vin à Saint-Omer: ses fluctuations au XVe siècle', *Revue Belge de Philologie et d'Histoire*, 40 (1962)

Derville, A., 'Les draperies flamandes et artésiennes vers 1250-1350: quelches considerations critiques et problematiques', *Revue du Nord*, 54 (1972).

Dickson, C., 'Food, medicinal and other plants from the drain' in J. Malden, ed., *The Monastery and Abbey of Paisley* (Glasgow, 2000).

Dickson, G., 'The crowd at the feet of Pope Boniface VIII: pilgrimage, crusade and the first Roman Jubilee, 1300', *Journal of Medieval History*, 25 (1999).

Dilworth, M., 'Cluniac Paisley: its constitutional status and prestige' in J. Malden, ed., *The Monastery and Abbey of Paisley* (Glasgow, 2000).

Dilworth, M., 'Franco-Scottish efforts at monastic reform, 1500-1560', *RSCHS*, 25 (1994).

Dilworth, M., 'Letters from Paisley' in J. Malden, ed., *The Monastery and Abbey of Paisley* (Glasgow, 2000).

Dilworth, M., *Scottish Monasteries in the Late Middle Ages* (Edinburgh, 1995).

Dilworth, M., 'The first Scottish monks in Ratisbon', *IR*, 16 (1965).

Dilworth, M., 'The Schottenklöster at the Reformation' in D. McRoberts, ed., *Essays on the Scottish Reformation, 1515-1625* (Glasgow, 1962)

Dilworth, M., *The Scots in Franconia* (Edinburgh, 1974).

Dilworth, M., 'Two Scottish pilgrims in Germany', *IR*, 18 (1967).

Ditcham, B.G.H., 'Mutton guzzlers and wine bags: foreign soldiers and native reactions in fifteenth-century France' in C.T. Allmand, ed., *Power, Culture and Religion in France, c.1350-c.1550* (Woodbridge, 1989).

Ditchburn, D., 'A note on Scandinavian trade with Scotland in the later middle ages' in Simpson, *Scotland and Scandinavia*.

Ditchburn, D., 'Piracy and war at sea in late medieval Scotland' in T.C. Smout, *Scotland and the Sea* (Edinburgh, 1992).

Ditchburn, D., 'The pirate, the policeman and the pantomime star: Aberdeen's alternative economy in the early fifteenth century', *NS*, 12 (1992).

Ditchburn, D., 'The place of Guelders in Scottish foreign policy, c.1449-c.1542' in Simpson, *Scotland and the Low Countries*.

Ditchburn, D., and Hudson, B., 'Economy and trade' in S. Duffy, ed., *New History of the Isle of Man. Volume III: The medieval period, 1000-1405* (Liverpool, forthcoming).

Ditchburn, D., and Macdonald, A.J., 'Medieval Scotland' in R. Houston and W. Knox, eds., *The Penguin History of Scotland* (London, forthcoming).

Dollinger, P., *Die Hanse* (3rd ed., Stuttgart, 1981).

Donaldson, G., 'Foundations of Anglo-Scottish union', in idem, *Scottish Church History* (Edinburgh, 1985).

Donaldson, G., 'Justice across frontiers' in idem, *Scottish Church History* (Edinburgh, 1985).

Donaldson, G., 'The church courts' in idem, *Scottish Church History* (Edinburgh, 1985).

Donnelly, J., 'Thomas of Coldingham, merchant and burgess of Berwick-upon-Tweed (d.1316)', *SHR*, 59 (1980).

Dow, J., 'Scottish trade with Sweden, 1512-1580', *SHR*, 48 (1969).

Dow, J., *'Skotter* in sixteenth-century Scania', *SHR* 44 (1965).

Doyle, A.I., 'A Scottish Augustinian psalter', *IR*, 8 (1957).

Drummond, W., *The Genealogy of the Most Noble and Ancient House of Drummond* (Edinburgh, 1831).

Duffy, S., 'The Anglo Norman era in Scotland: convergence and diversity' in T.M. Devine and J.F. McMillan, eds., *Celebrating Columba: Irish-Scottish connections, 597-1997* (Edinburgh, 1999).

Dukes, P., 'Scottish soldiers in Muscovy' in *The Caledonian Phalanx: Scots in Russia* (National Library of Scotland, 1987).

Dunbar, J.G., *Scottish Royal Palaces: The architecture of the royal residences during the later medieval and early renaissance periods* (East Linton, 1999).

Dunbar, J.G., 'Some sixteenth-century parallels for the palace of Falkland', *Review of Scottish Culture*, 7 (1991)

Duncan, A.A.M., *Scotland: The making of the kingdom* (Edinburgh, 1975).

Duncan, A.A.M., *The Nation of Scots and the Declaration of Arbroath* (London, 1970).

Dunlop, A.I., *The Life and Times of James Kennedy, Bishop of St Andrews* (Edinburgh, 1950).

Dunlop, A.I., 'Remissions and indulgences in fifteenth-century Scotland', *RSCHS*, 15 (1966)

Dunlop, A.I., 'Scottish student life in the fifteenth century', *SHR*, 27 (1947).

Durkan, J., 'Further additions to 'Durkan and Ross': some newly discovered Scottish pre-Reformation provenances', *The Bibliotheck*, 10 (1980-81).

Durkan, J., 'Heresy in Scotland: the second phase, 1546-58', *RSCHS*, 24 (1992).

Durkan, J., 'The early Scottish notary' in I.B. Cowan and D. Shaw, eds., *The Renaissance and Reformation in Scotland* (Edinburgh, 1983).

Durkan, J., 'The French connection in the sixteenth and early seventeenth centuries' in T.C. Smout, ed., *Scotland and Europe, 1200-1850* (Edinburgh, 1986).

Durkan, J., 'The sanctuary and college of Tain', *IR*, 13 (1962).

Durkan, J., and Ross, A., 'Early Scottish libraries', *IR*, 9 (1958).

Durkan, J., and Russel, J., 'Further additions (including manuscripts) to John Durkan and Anthony Ross, *Early Scottish Libraries* at the National Library of Scotland', *The Bibliotheck*, 12 (1984-85).

Easson, D.E., 'The Lollards of Kyle', *Juridical Review*, 48 (1936).

Ebel, E., 'Das Bild der Fremden in den altwestnordlischen Quellen', *HGb*, 100 (1982).

Edwards, K.J., and Whittington, G., 'Palynological evidence for the growing of *cannabis sativa L.* (hemp) in medieval and historical Scotland', *Transactions of the Institute of British Geographers*, new series, 15 (1990).

Eeles, F.C., *King's College Chapel, Aberdeen* (Edinburgh, 1956).

Egli, E., 'Der Gotthard: Bedeutung und Auswirkung', *Geographica Helvetica* (1991).

Elliott, K., 'The Pailsey abbey fragments', *Musica Scoticana*, 1 (1996)

Esch, A., 'Importe in das Rom der Renaissance: Die Zollregister der Jahre 1470 bis 1480', *Quellen und Forschungen aus Italienischen Archiven und Bibliotheken*, 74 (1994).

Evans, G., 'The mace of St Salvator's College' in Higgitt, *Art and Architecture.*

Ewan, E., 'Mons Meg and Merchant Meg: women in later medieval Edinburgh' in Brotherstone and Ditchburn, *Freedom and Authority.*

Ewan, E., *Townlife in Fourteenth-century Scotland* (Edinburgh, 1990).

Fawcett, R., 'Late Gothic architecture in Scotland: considerations on the influence of the Low Countries', *PSAS*, 112 (1982).

Fawcett, R., ed., *Medieval Art and Architecture in the Diocese of Glasgow* (British Archaeological Association, 1998).

Fawcett, R., *Scottish Architecture from the Accession of the Stewarts to the Reformation, 1371-1560* (Edinburgh, 1994).

Fawcett, R., 'Scottish medieval window tracery' in D.J. Breeze, ed., *Studies in Scottish Antiquity presented to Stewart Cruden* (Edinburgh, 1984).

Fawcett, R., 'The medieval building' in Geddes, *King's College Chapel.*

Febvre, L., and Martin, H-J., *The Coming of the Book: The impact of printing, 1450-1800* (2nd ed., London, 1990).

Fedosov, D., *The Caledonian Connection: Scotland-Russia ties… A concise biographical list* (Aberdeen, 1996).

Ferguson, P.C., *Medieval Papal Representatives in Scotland: Legates, nuncios and judges-delegate, 1125-1286* (Stair Soc., 1997).

Fernández-Armesto, F., *Before Columbus: Exploration and colonisation from the Mediterranean to the Atlantic, 1229-1492* (Basingstoke, 1987).

Fernie, E., 'The Romanesque churches of Dunfermline Abbey' in Higgitt, *Art and Architecture.*

Fischer, T.A., *The Scots in Eastern and Western Prussia* (Edinburgh, 1903).

Fischer, T.A., *The Scots in Germany* (Edinburgh, 1902).

Flandrin, J.L., 'Internationalisme, nationalisme et régionalisme dans la cuisine des XIVe et XVe siècle: le témoinage des livres de cuisines' in D. Menjot, ed., *Manger et Boire au Moyen Age* (Nice, 1984).

Fliche, A., 'Le problème de Saint Roch', *Analecta Bollandia*, 68 (1950).

Foggie, J.P., 'Archivium Sacrae Paenitentiariae Apostolicae in the Vatican Archives as a source for Scottish historians', *IR*, 47 (1996).

Fontaine, L., *Histoire du Colportage en Europe, XVe-XIXe Siècle* (Paris, 1993).

Forte, A.D.M., 'Kenning be kenning and course be course': Alexander Lindsay's rutter and the problematics of navigation in fifteenth and sixteenth-century Scotland', *Review of Scottish Culture*, 11 (1998-99).

Forte, A.D.M., "Kenning be kenning and course be course': maritime jurimetrics in Scotland and northern Europe, 1400-1600', *The Edinburgh Law Review*, 2 (1998).

Forte, A.D.M., 'The identification of fifteenth-century ship types in Scottish legal records', *MM*, 84 (1998).

Fradenburg, L.O., *City, Marriage, Tournament: Arts of rule in late medieval Scotland* (Madison, Wis., 1991).

Fraser, W., *Memoirs of the Maxwells of Pollok* (Edinburgh, 1863).

French Connections: Scotland and the arts of France (Royal Scottish Museum, 1985).

Fraser, W., *The Douglas Book* (Edinburgh, 1885).

Friedland, K., 'Der hansische Shetlandhandel' in *Stadt und Land in der Geschichte der Ostseeraums* (Lübeck, 1973).

Friedland, K., 'Hanseatic merchants and their trade with Shetland' in D.J. Withrington, ed., *Shetland and the Outside World, 1469-1969* (Oxford, 1983).

Friedland, K., 'Kaufmannsgruppen in frühen hansisch-norwegischen Handel' in idem, ed., *Bergen als Handelszentrum des beginnenden Spätmittelalters* (Cologne and Vienna, 1971).

Friedland, K., *Mensch und Seefahrt zur Hansezeit* (Cologne, 1995).

Fritze, K., *Am Wendepunkt der Hanse: Untersuchungen zur Wirtschafts- und Sozialgeschichte wendischer Hansestädte in der ersten Hälfte des 15. Jahrhunderts* (Berlin, 1967).

Fudge, J.D., *Cargoes, Embargoes and Emissaries: The commercial and political interaction of England and the German Hanse, 1450-1510* (Toronto, 1995).

Gaier, C., 'The origin of Mons Meg', *Journal of the Arms and Armour Society*, 5 (1967).

Galbraith, D.L., 'Scottish seals from the continent', *SHR*, 27 (1948).

Ganshof, F., 'Pèlerinages flamands à Saint-Gilles pendant le XIV siècle', *Annales du Midi*, 78 (1966).

Gaucher, E., 'Les joutes de Saint-Inglevert: perception et écriture d'un événement historique pendant la guerre de cent ans', *Le Moyen Age*, 102 (1996).

Geary, J., *Furta Sacra: Thefts of relics in the central middle ages* (Princeton, 1978).

Geddes, J., ed., *King's College Chapel, Aberdeen, 1500-2000* (Leeds, 2000).

Geddes, J., 'The Bells' in idem, *King's College Chapel*.

Geer, I. de, 'Music and the twelfth-century Orkney earldom: a cultural crossroads in musicological perspective' in B.E. Crawford, ed., *St Magnus Cathedral and Orkney's Twelfth-century Renaissance* (Aberdeen, 1988).

Gemmill, E., and Mayhew, N., *Changing Values in Medieval Scotland: A study of prices, money, and weights and measures* (Cambridge, 1995).

Giesy, R.E., *The Royal Funeral Ceremony in Renaissance France* (Geneva, 1960).

Gilbert, J.M., *Hunting and Hunting Reserves in Medieval Scotland* (Edinburgh, 1979).

Gillet, E., *A History of Grimsby* (London, 1970).

Glenn, V., 'Court patronage in Scotland, 1240-1340' in Fawcett, *Art and Architecture*.

Goff, J. Le, 'Ordres mendiants et urbanisation dans la France médiévale', *Annales E.S.C.*, 25 (1970).

Goodman, A., 'A letter from an earl of Douglas to a king of Castile', *SHR*, 64 (1985).

Goodman, A., 'The Anglo-Scottish marches in the fifteenth century' in R.A. Mason, ed., *Scotland and England, 1286-1815* (Edinburgh, 1987).

Graham, A., 'Archaeological notes on some harbours in eastern Scotland', *PSAS*, 101 (1968-69).

Gransden, A., *Historical Writing in England II: c.1307 to the Early Sixteenth Century* (London, 1982).

Grant, A., *Independence and Nationhood: Scotland, 1306-1469* (London, 1984).

Graves, C.P., 'Medieval stained and painted window glass in the diocese of St Andrews' in Higgitt, *Art and Architecture*.

Griffiths, J., and Pearsal, D., eds., *Book Production and Publishing in Britain, 1375-1475* (Cambridge, 1989).

Griffiths, R.A., *The Reign of Henry VI* (London, 1981).

Grove, R., 'The animal bone', in G. Ewart, ed., 'Inchaffray Abbey, Perth & Kinross: excavations and research, 1987', *PSAS*, 126 (1996).

Guenée, B., *States and Rulers in Later Medieval Europe* (Oxford, 1985).

Guy, I., 'The Scottish export trade, 1460-1599' in Smout, *Scotland and Europe*.

Hamilton, B., *The Medieval Inquisition* (London, 1981).

Hammermeyer, L., 'Deutsche Schottenklöster, schottische Reformation, katolische Reform und Gegenreformation in West- und Mitteleuropa, 1560-80', *Zeitschrift für bayerische Landesgeschichte*, 26 (1963).

Hanham, A., 'A medieval Scots merchant's handbook', *SHR*, 50 (1971).

Harper, J., 'Music and ceremonial, c.1500-1560' in Geddes, *King's College Chapel*.

Harris, K., 'Patrons, buyers and owners: the evidence for ownership and the role of book owners in book production and the book trade' in Griffiths and Pearsall, *Book Production*

Harris, R., *Valois Guyenne: A study in politics, government and society in late medieval France* (Woodbridge, 1994).

Harvey, P.D.A., *Medieval Maps* (London, 1991).

Hay, D., *Europe in the Fourteenth and Fifteenth Centuries* (2nd ed., London, 1989).

Hay, G., 'A Scottish altarpiece in Copenhagen', *IR*, 7 (1956).

Hay, G., 'The late medieval development of the High Kirk of St Giles, Edinburgh', *PSAS*, 107 (1975-76).

Hay, G., and McRoberts, D., 'Rossdhu Church and its book of hours', *IR*, 16 (1965).

Hayes-McCoy, G.A., *Scots Mercenary Forces in Ireland, 1563-1603* (Dublin, 1937).

Heeringen, R.M. van, Koldeweij, A.M., and Gaalman, A.A.G., *Heiligen uit de Modder: In Zeeland gevonden pelgrimstekens* (Utrecht, 1988).

Heers, J., *Family Clans in the Middle Ages: A study of political and social structures in urban areas* (Amsterdam, 1977).

Henisch, B.A., *Fast and Feast: Food in medieval society* (London, 1976).

Henry, F., and Marsh-Michell, G.L., 'A century of Irish illumination, 1070-1170', *Proceedings of the Royal Irish Academy*, C62 (1961-63).

Heuvel, N.H.L. van de, *De Ambachtsgelden van s'Hertogenbosch voor 1629* (Utrecht, 1946).

Hieatt, C.B., 'Sorting through the titles of medieval dishes: what is, or is not, *blanc manger*?' in M.W. Adamson, ed., *Food in the Middle Ages: A book of essays* (New York, 1995).

Higgins, P., 'Parisian nobles, a Scottish princess and the woman's voice in medieval song', *Early Music History*, 10 (1991).

Higgitt, J., ed., *Medieval Art and Architecture in the Diocese of St Andrews* (British Archaeological Association, 1994).

Higgitt, J., 'Manuscripts and libraries in the diocese of Glasgow before the Reformation' in Fawcett, *Art and Architecture*.

Hill, M.C., *The King's Messengers, 1199-1377* (London, 1961).

Hill, P., *et al.*, *Whithorn and St Ninian: The excavation of a monastic town, 1984-91* (Stroud, 1997).

Hilton, R.H., 'Lords, burgesses and huxters', *PP*, 97 (1982).

Hodgson, G.W.I., and Jones, A., 'The animal bone' in J.C. Murray, ed., *Excavations in the Medieval Burgh of Aberdeen* (Edinburgh, 1982).

Holdsworth, P., ed., *Excavations in the Medieval Burgh of Perth, 1979-1981* (Edinburgh, 1987).

Holt, J., *Robin Hood* (London, 1982).

Hoshino, H., *L'arte della Lana in Firenze in Basso Medioevo* (Florence, 1980).

Housley, N., *The Later Crusades: From Lyons to Alcazar, 1274-1580* (Oxford, 1992).

Howard, D., *Scottish Architecture: Reformation to Restoration, 1560-1660* (Edinburgh, 1995).

Hudson, A., *The Premature Reformation: Wycliffite texts and Lollard heresy* (Oxford, 1988).

Hudson, B.T., 'Gaelic princes and Gregorian Reform' in idem and V. Ziegler, eds., *Crossed Paths: Methodological approaches to the Celtic aspect of the European middle ages* (Lanham, 1991).

Hughes, M.K., and Diaz, H.F., 'Was there a 'medieval warm period', and if so where and when?', *Climatic Change*, 26 (1994).

Hunt, E.S., and Murray, J.M., *A History of Business in Medieval Europe, 1200-1500* (Cambridge, 1999).

Hunt, N., *Cluny under Saint Hugh, 1049-1109* (London, 1967).

Hussey, S., 'Nationalism and language in England, c.1300-1500' in C. Bjørn, A. Grant and K.J. Stringer, eds., *Nations, Nationalism and Patriotism in the European Past* (Copenhagen, 1994).

Jacquart, J., 'Les Stuarts et les guerre d'Italie' in *Actes du Colloque: Des Chardon et des Lys* (Bourges, 1992).

Jones, J., *Balliol College Oxford: A history, 1263-1939* (Oxford, 1988).

Jope, E.M., ed., *Studies in Building History* (London, 1961).

Jordan, W.C., *The Great Famine: Northern Europe in the early fourteenth century* (Princeton, 1996).

Jorga, N., *Philippe de Mezieres, 1327-1405, et La Croisade au XIVe Siècle* (Paris, 1896; repr.,1976).

Kapelle, W.E., *The Norman Conquest of the North: The region and its transformation, 1000-1135* (London, 1979).

Kaptein, H., *De Hollandse Textielnijverheid, 1350-1600: Conjunctuur & continuïteit* (Hilversum, 1998).

Kemp, E.W., *Canonization and Authority in the Western Church* (London, 1948).

Kerling, N.J.M., 'Aliens in the county of Norfolk, 1436-85', *Norfolk Archaeology*, 33 (1965).

Kermode, J., 'The trade of late medieval Chester, 1500-1550' in R. Britnell and J. Hatcher, eds., *Progress and Problems in Medieval England: Essays in honour of Edward Miller* (Cambridge, 1996).

Krueger, H.C., 'The Genoese exportation of northern cloths to the Mediterranean ports, twelfth century', *Revue Belge de Philologie et d'Histoire*, 65 (1987).

Keussen, H., *Topographie der Stadt Köln im Mittelalter* (Bonn, 1910).

Keyser, E., 'Die Ermorderung des schottischen Grafen William Douglas in Danzig im Jahre 1391', *Mitteilungen des westpreussichen Geschichtsverein*, 27 (1924).

King, P., 'Scottish Abbeys and the Cistercian financial system in the fourteenth century', *IR*, 42 (1991).

Kirk, J., 'Iconoclasm and reform', *RSCHS*, 24 (1992).

Kirk, J., *Patterns of Reformation: Continuity and change in the Reformation kirk* (Edinburgh, 1989).

Klocke, F. von, *Alt Soester Bürgermeister aus sechs Jahrhunderten, ihre Familien und Ihre Standesverhältnisse* (Soest, 1927).

Knowles, D., and Hadcock, R.N., *Medevial Religious Houses: England and Wales* (3rd ed., London, 1971).

Köfler, M., and Caramelle, S., *Die Beiden Frauen des Erzherogs Sigmund von Oesterreich-Tirol* (Innsbruck, 1982).

Kratzmann, G., *Anglo-Scottish Literary Relations, 1430-1550* (Cambridge, 1980).

Labarge, M.W., *Medieval Travellers: The rich and the restless* (London, 1982).

Labaude-Mailfert, Y., *Charles VIII et son milieu, 1470-98: La jeunesse au pouvoir* (Paris, 1975).

Labaude-Mailfert, Y., *Charles VIII: Le vouloir et la destinée* (Paris, 1986).

Lachiver, M., *Vins, Vignes et Vignerons: Histoire du vignoble francais* (Paris, 1988).

Lauffer, V., 'Danzigs Schiffs- und Waarenverkehr am Ende des XV. Jahrhunderts', *Zeitschrift des Westpreussischen Geschichtsverein*, 33 (1894).

Laing, D., 'Notice of the death of Robert Blackader, archbishop of Glasgow, during a pilgrimage to the Holy Land, in the year 1508', *PSAS*, 2 (1859).

Lamb, H.H., *Climate, History and the Modern World* (London, 1982).

Lamb, H.H., *Climate: Present, past and future* (London, 1972-77).

Lawrence, C.H., *The Friars: The impact of the early mendicant movement on western society* (Harlow, 1994).

Lecler, J., *Vienne* (Paris, 1964).

Lequin, Y., *La Mosaïque France: Histoire des etrangers et de l'immigration* (Paris, 1988).

Lewis, B., *The Muslim Discovery of Europe* (London, 1982).

Lillehammer, A., 'The Scottish-Norwegian timber trade in the Stavanger area in the sixteenth and seventeenth centuries' in Smout, *Scotland and Europe*.

Lindenbaum, S., 'The Smithfield tournament of 1390', *Journal of Medieval and Renaissance Studies*, 20 (1990).

Loomis, L.R., 'Nationality at the council of Constance: an Anglo-French dispute', *American History Review*, 44 (1939).

Lopez, R.S., 'Hard times and investment in culture' in W.K. Ferguson *et al.*, *The Renaissance: Six essays* (New York, 1962).

Lourie, E., 'A society organised for war: medieval Spain', *PP*, 35 (1966).

Lowinsky, E.E., 'Music in the culture of the renaissance', *Journal of the History of Ideas*, 15 (1952).

Lyall, R.J., 'Materials: the paper revolution' in Griffiths and Pearsal, *Book Production*.

Lyall, R.J., 'Scottish students and masters at the universities of Cologne and Louvain in the fifteenth century', *IR*, 36 (1985).

Lyall, R.J., 'The lost literature of medieval Scotland' in J.D. McClure and M.R.G. Spiller, eds., *Bryght Lanternis: Essays on the language and literature of medieval Scotland* (Aberdeen, 1989).

Lydon, J.F., 'An Irish army in Scotland, 1296', *The Irish Sword*, 5 (1962).

Lydon, J.F., 'Edward I, Ireland and the war in Scotland, 1303-4 in idem, ed., *England and Ireland in the Later Middle Ages* (Blackrock, 1981).

Lydon, J.F., 'Irish levies in the Scottish wars, 1296-1301', *The Irish Sword*, 5 (1962).

Lydon, J.F., 'The hobelar: an Irish contribution to medieval warfare', *The Irish Sword*, 2 (1954-56).

Lydon, J.F., 'The Scottish soldier in medieval Ireland: the Bruce invasion and the galloglass' in Simpson, *Scottish Soldier*.

Lyons, M.C., 'Weather, famine, pestilence and plague in Ireland, 900-1500' in E. Crawford, ed., *Famine: The Irish Experience, 900-1900: Subsistence crises and famines in Ireland* (Edinburgh, 1989).

Lynch, M., *Edinburgh and the Reformation* (Edinburgh, 1981).

Lynch, M., *Scotland: A new history* (London, 1992).

Lynch, M., Spearman, M., and Stell, G., eds., *The Scottish Medieval Town* (Edinburgh, 1988).

Lynch, M., and Stevenson, A., 'Overseas trade: the middle ages to the sixteenth century' in P.G.B. McNeill and H.L. MacQueen, eds., *Atlas of Scottish History to 1707* (Edinburgh, 1996).

Lynch, M., and Stevenson, A., 'Restructing urban economies in the later middle ages' in P.G.B. McNeill and H.L. MacQueen, eds., *Atlas of Scottish History to 1707* (Edinburgh, 1996).

Lythe, S.G.E., 'Scottish trade with the Baltic, 1550-1650' in J.K. Eastham, ed., *Economic Essays in Commemoration of the Dundee School of Economics, 1931-1955* (Coupar Angus, 1955).

MacDonald, A.A., 'Anglo-Scottish literary relations: problems and possibilities', *Studies in Scottish Literature*, 26 (1991).

MacDonald, A.A., 'The Latin original of Robert Henryson's Annunciation lyric' in A.A. MacDonald, M. Lynch and I.B. Cowan, eds., *The Renaissance in Scotland: Studies in literature, religion, history and culture* (Leiden, 1994).

Macdonald, A.J., *Border Bloodshed: Scotland and England at War, 1369-1403* (East Linton, 2000)

Macdonald, A.J., 'Profit, politics and personality: war and the later medieval Scottish nobility' in Brotherstone and Ditchburn, *Freedom and Authority*.

Macdougall, N., *James III: A political study* (Edinburgh, 1982)

Macdougall, N., "The greattest scheip that ewer saillit in Ingland or France': James IV's 'Great Michael" in idem, ed., *Scotland and War, AD 79-1918* (Edinburgh, 1991).

Macfarlane, L.J., 'The book of hours of James IV and Margaret Tudor', *IR*, 11 (1960).

Macfarlane, L.J., 'The Divine Office and the Mass' in Geddes, *King's College, Aberdeen.*

Macfarlane, L.J., 'The elevation of the diocese of Glasgow into an archbishopric in 1492', *IR*, 43 (1992).

Macfarlane, L.J., 'The primacy of the Scottish church, 1472-1521', *IR*, 20 (1969).

Macfarlane, L.J., *William Elphinstone and the Kingdom of Scotland, 1431-1514* (Aberdeen 1985).

Macfarlane, L.J., 'William Elphinstone's library', *Aberdeen University Review*, 37 (1957-58).

Macfarlane, L.J., and McIntyre, J., eds., *Scotland and the Holy See: The story of Scotland's links with the papacy down the centuries* (Edinburgh, 1982).

McGavin, J.J., 'Robert III's 'Rough Music': charivari and diplomacy in a medieval Scottish court', *SHR*, 74 (1995).

McGladdery, C., *James II* (Edinburgh, 1990).

McIntosh, M.K., 'Local change and community control in England, 1465-1500', *Huntingdon Library Quarterly*, 49 (1986).

McKissack, M., *The Fourteenth Century, 1307-1399* (Oxford, 1959).

Macmillan, D., *Scottish Art, 1460-1990* (Edinburgh, 1990).

McNab, T.M.A., 'Bohemia and the Scottish Lollards', *RSCHS*, 5 (1935).

Macquarrie, A., 'Anselm Adornes of Bruges: traveller in the east and friend of James III', *IR*, 33 (1982).

Macquarrie, A., *Scotland and the Crusades, 1095-1560* (Edinburgh, 1985).

McRoberts, D., 'A St Andrews pilgrimage certificate of 1333' in idem, ed., *The Medieval Church of St Andrews* (Glasgow, 1976).

McRoberts, D., 'Bishop Kennedy's mace', in idem, ed., *The Medieval Church of St Andrews* (Glasgow, 1976).

McRoberts, D., 'Dean Brown's book of hours', *IR*, 19 (1968).

McRoberts, D., 'Notes on Scoto-Flemish artistic contacts, *IR*, 10 (1959).

McRoberts, D., 'St Edmund in Scotland', *IR*, 13 (1962).

McRoberts, D., 'The Fetternear banner [I]', *IR*, 7 (1956).

McRoberts, D., 'The Fetternear banner [II]', *IR*, 8 (1957).

McRoberts, D., 'The Greek bishop of Dromore', *IR*, 28 (1977).

McRoberts, D., *The Heraldic Ceiling of St Machar's Cathedral Aberdeen* (2nd ed., Aberdeen, 1976).

McRoberts, D., 'The medieval Scottish liturgy illustrated by surviving documents', *TSES*, 15 (1957).

McRoberts, D., 'The rosary in Scotland', *IR*, 23 (1972).

McRoberts, D., 'The Scottish church and nationalism in the fifteenth century', *IR*, 19 (1968).

McRoberts, D., 'The Scottish national churches in Rome', *IR*, 1 (1950).

Maczak, A., 'Wool production and the wool trade in east-central Europe from the fourteenth to the seventeenth centuries' in M. Spallanzani, ed., *La Lana come Materia Prima: I fenomeni della sua produzione e circolazione nei secoli XIII-XVII* (Florence, 1974).

Mallett, M.E., 'Anglo-Florentine commercial relations, 1465-1491', *Economic History Review*, second series, 15 (1962).

Marshall, R.K. *Mary of Guise* (London, 1977).

Martens, M.P.J., 'Some aspects of the origins of the art market in fifteenth-century Bruges' in M. North and D. Ormrod, eds., *Art Markets in Europe, 1400-1800* (Aldershot, 1998).

Marwick, H., *Merchant Lairds of Long Ago* (Kirkwall, 1939).

Matulka, B., *The Novels of Juan de Flores and their European Diffusion: A study in comparative literature* (New York, 1931).

Maxwell, A., *Old Dundee* (Dundee, 1891).

Mayhew, G., *Tudor Rye* (Falmer, 1987).

Mayhew, N., 'Alexander III – a silver age? An essay in Scottish medieval economic history' in N. Reid, ed., *Scotland in the Reign of Alexander III, 1249-1286* (Edinburgh, 1990).

Meek, D.E., 'The Scots-Gaelic scribes of late medieval Perthshire: an overview of the orthography and contents of the Book of the Dean of Lismore' in J.H. Williams, ed., *Stewart Style, 1513-1542: Essays on the court of James V* (East Linton, 1996).

Megaw, B.R.S., 'The barony of St Trinian's in the Isle of Man', *TDGAS*, 27 (1950).

Menzies, G., ed., *The Scottish Nation* (London, 1972).

Michel, F., *Les Ecossais en France, Les Français en Ecosse* (London and Edinburgh, 1862).

Mill, A.J., *Medieval Plays in Scotland* (Edinburgh, 1927).

Miller, G.J., *Tudor Mercenaries and Auxiliaries, 1485-1547* (Charlotesville, 1980).

Mirot, L., 'La colonie lucquois à Paris', *Bibliothèque de l'Ecole des Chartres*, 88 (1927).

Mitchell, R.J., 'Scottish law students in Italy in the later middle ages', *Juridical Review*, 49 (1937).

Mollat, G., *The Popes at Avignon, 1305-1378* (London, 1963)

Mollat, M., *Le commerce maritime normand à la fin du moyen age* (Paris, 1952).

Mollat, M. and Roncière, M. de la, *Sea Charts of the Early Explorers, 13th to 17th Centuries* (Fribourg, 1984).

Moonan, L., 'Pavel Kravar and some writings once attributed to him', *IR*, 27 (1976).

Moonan, L., 'The Inquisitor's arguments against Resby, in 1408', *IR*, 47 (1996).

Moore, M.F., *Lands of the Scottish Kings in England* (London, 1915).

Morrison, I., 'Climatic changes in human geography: Scotland in a North Atlantic context', *Northern Studies*, 27 (1990).

Morrison, I., 'Evidence of climatic change in Scotland before the age of agricultural improvement', *Scottish Archives*, 1 (1995).

Motta, E., 'Ladronecci ed assassini al Monte Ceneri nel quatrocento', *Bolletino Storico della Svizzera Italiana*, 16 (1894).

Munro, J.H., 'Economic depression and the arts in the fifteenth-century Low Countries', *Renaissance and Reformation*, 19 (1983).

Munro, J.H., 'Industrial protectionism in medieval Flanders: urban or national?' in H.A. Miskimin, D. Herlihy and A.L. Udovitch, *The Medieval City* (London, 1977).

Munro, J.H., 'The medieval scarlets and the economics of sartorial splendour' in N.B. Harte and K.G. Ponting, eds., *Cloth and Clothing in Medieval Europe* (London, 1983).

Munro, J.H., 'The origin of the English 'new draperies': the resurrection of an old Flemish industry, 1270-1570' in N.B. Harte, ed., *The New Draperies in the Low Countries and England, 1300-1800* (Oxford, 1997).

Munro, J.H., *Wool, Cloth and Gold: The struggle for bullion in Anglo-Burgundian trade, 1340-1478* (Brussels, 1972).

Munro, J.H., 'Wool-price schedules and the qualities of English wools in the later middle ages, c.1270-1499', *Textile History*, 9 (1978).

Murison, D., 'Linguistic relationships in medieval Scotland' in G.W.S. Barrow, ed., *The Scottish Tradition: Essays in honour of Ronald Gordon Cant* (Edinburgh, 1974).

Murray, A., 'The customs accounts of Kirkcudbright, Wigtown and Dumfries, 1434-1560', *TDGAS*, 40 (1961-62).

Murray, J., ed., *Excavations in the Medieval Burgh of Aberdeen, 1973-81* (Edinburgh, 1982).

Naville, C-E., *Enea Silvio Piccolomini: L'uomo l'umanista il Pontefice, 1405-1464* (Locarno, 1984).

Neilson, G., 'Caudatus Anglicus: A medieval slander', *Transactions of the Glasgow Archaeological Soc.*, new series, 2 (1896).

Neilson, G., *Trial by Combat* (Glasgow, 1890).

Newman, C.M., 'Order and community in the north: the liberty of Allertonshire in the later fifteenth century' in A.J. Pollard, ed., *The North of England in the Age of Richard III* (Stroud, 1996).

Nicholas, D., *Medieval Flanders* (Harlow, 1992).

Nicholson, R., 'A sequel to Robert Bruce's invasion of Ireland', *SHR*, 42 (1963).

Nicholson, R., *Edward III and the Scots* (Oxford, 1965)

Nicholson, R., *Scotland: The later middle ages* (Edinburgh, 1974).

Nicholson, R. 'The Franco-Scottish and Franco-Norwegian treaties of 1295', *SHR*, 38 (1959).

Nicholson, R., 'Scottish monetary problems in the fourteenth and fifteenth centuries' in D.M. Metclaf, ed., *Coinage in Medieval Scotland, 1100-1600* (Oxford, 1977).

Nijsten, G., *Het Hof van Gelre: Cultuur ten tijde van de hertogen uit het Gulikse en Egmondse huis, 1371-1473* (Kampen, 1992).

Norton, C., 'Medieval floor tiles in Scotland' in Higgitt, *Art and Architecture*

Ó Baoill, C., 'Some Irish harpers in Scotland', *Transactions of the Gaelic Society of Inverness*, 47 (1971-72).

Ó Mainnín, E.M.B., 'The same in origin and in blood: bardic windows on the relationship between Irish and Scottish Gaels, c.1200-1650', *Cambrian Medieval Celtic Studies*, 38 (1999).

Ó Siochrú, M., 'Foreign involvement in the revolt of Silken Thomas, 1534-5', *Proceedings of the Royal Irish Academy*, C96 (1996).

Ogilvie, A., and Farmer, G., 'Documenting the medieval climate' in M. Hulme and E. Barrow, eds., *Climates of the British Isles: Present, past and future* (London, 1997).

Ohler, N., *Reisen im Mittelalter* (Munich and Zürich, 1986).

Ollivant, S., *The Court of the Official in Pre-Reformation Scotland* (Stair Soc., 1982).

Oram, R.D., 'In obedience and reverence: Whithorn and York, c.1128-c.1250', *IR*, 42 (1991).

Origo, I., *The Merchant of Prato* (1963).

Otway-Ruthven, A.J., *A History of Medieval Ireland* (London, 1968).

Owen, D.D.R., *William the Lion: Kingship and culture, 1143-1214* (East Linton, 1997).

Palliser, D., 'Richard III and York' in R. Horrox, ed., *Richard III and the North* (Hull, 1986).

Pampaloni, G., 'Un nuovo studio sulla produzione e il commercio della lana a Firenze fra trecento e cinquecento', *Archivo Storico Italiano*, 140 (1982).

Parry, M.L., *Climatic Change, Agriculture and Settlement* (Folkestone, 1978).

Patourel, J. Le, 'L'occupation anglaise de Calais au XIVe siècle', *Revue du Nord*, 33 (1951).

Paul, J.B., 'Whitekirk church and its history', *TSES*, 6 (1920-21)

Paul, J.B., 'Royal pilgrimages in Scotland', *TSES*, 1 (1903-6)

Pearsal, D., 'Introduction' in Griffiths and Pearsall, *Book Production*.

Peddie, J.M.D., 'Note of a crucifix of bronze, enamelled, found in the churchyard of Ceres, Fife', *PSAS*, 17 (1882-83).

Penners-Ellwart, H., *Die Danziger Bürgerschaft nach Herkunft und Beruf, 1536-1709* (Marburg/Lahn, 1964).

Philips, C.R., 'The Spanish wool trade, 1500-1780', *Journal of Economic History*, 42 (1982).

Poerck, G. de, *La Draperie Médiévale en Flandre et en Artois: Technique et terminologie* (Bruges, 1951).

Pohl, H., 'Zur Geschichte von Wollhandel im Rheinland, in Westfalen und Hessen vom 12. bis 17. Jahrhundert' in M. Spallanzani, ed., *La Lana come Materia Prima: I fenomeni della sua produzione e circolazione nei secoli XIII-XVII* (Florence, 1974).

Power, R., 'Scotland in the Norse sagas' in Simpson, *Scotland and Scandinavia*.

Prestwich, M., *Edward I* (London, 1988).

Pryde, G.S., *The Burghs of Scotland: A critical list* (Oxford, 1965).

Purser, J., *Scotland's Music* (Edinburgh, 1992).

Queller, D.E., *The Office of Ambassador in the Middle Ages* (Princeton, 1967).

Randall, L.M.C., 'A medieval slander', *Art Bulletin*, 17 (1960).

Rankin, E.B., *Saint Mary's Whitekirk, 1356-1914* (Edinburgh, 1914).

Reid, W.S., 'Seapower in the foreign policy of James IV', *Medievalia et Humanistica*, 15 (1963).

Richardson, J.S., 'St William of Perth and his memorials in England', *TSES*, 2 (1906-9).

Riis, T., *Should Auld Acquaintance Be Forgot... Scottish-Danish relations, c.1450-1707* (Odense, 1988).

Riley-Smith, J., *What Were the Crusades?* (2nd ed., Basingstoke, 1992).

Robbins, M.E., 'Black Africans at the court of James IV', *Review of Scottish Culture*, 12 (1999-2000).

Roberts, A., 'The landscape as legal document: Jan de Hervy's 'View of the Zwin', *Burlington Magazine* (1991).

Rogers, C.J., 'The Scottish invasion of 1346', *NH*, 34 (1998).

Rooseboom, M.P., *The Scottish Staple in the Netherlands* (The Hague, 1910).

Roover, R. de, *Money, Banking and Credit in medieval Bruges* (Cambridge, Mass., 1948).

Roover, R. de, *The Rise and Decline of the Medici Bank, 1397-1494* (Cambridge, Mass., 1968).

Rose, R.K., 'Latin episcopal sees at the end of the thirteenth Century', in A. Mackay and D. Ditchburn, eds., *Atlas of Medieval Europe* (London, 1997).

Ross, A., 'Libraries of the Scottish Blackfriars, 1480-1560', *IR*, 20 (1969).

Ross, A., 'Men for all seasons? The Strathbogie earls of Atholl and the wars of independence, c.1290-c.1335', *NS*, 20 (2000).

Rouse, R.H., and Rouse, M.A., *Registrum Anglie de Libris Doctorum et Auctorum Veterum* (London, 1991).

Rubin, M., *Corpus Christi: The eucharist in late medieval culture* (Cambridge, 1991).

Sadourny, A., 'Le commerce du vin à Rouen dans la seconde moité du XIVe siècle', *Annales de Normandie*, 2 (1968).

Samsonowicz, H., Engländer und Schotten in Danzig im Spätmittelalter: Zwei Formen der Handelstätigkeit' in K. Friedland and F. Irsigler, eds., *Seehandel und Wirtschaftswege Nordeuropas im 17. und 18. Jahrhundert* (Ostfildern, 1981).

Samsonowicz, H., 'Handel zagraniczny Gdańska w drugiej połowie, XV wieku', *Przegald Historyczny*, 47 (1956).

Sanderson, M.H.B., *Ayrshire and the Reformation: People and change, 1490-1600* (East Linton, 1997).

Sanderson, M.H.B., *Scottish Rural Society in the Sixteenth Century* (Edinburgh, 1982).

Sawyer, B. & P., *Medieval Scandinavia: From conversion to Reformation, c.800-1500* (Minneapolis, 1993),

Schmitt, J.C., *The Holy Greyhound* (Cambridge, 1983).

Schmugge, L., 'Cleansing on consciences: some observations regarding the fifteenth-century registers of the papal penitentiary', *Viator*, 29 (1998).

Schwinges, R.C., 'Admission' in H. de Ridder-Symoens, ed., *A History of the University in Europe. Volume 1: Universities in the middle ages* (Cambridge, 1992).

Serre-Bachet, F., 'Middle ages temperature reconstructions in Europe', *Climatic Change*, 26 (1994).

Shaw, D., 'Thomas Livingston: a conciliarist', *RSCHS*, 12 (1958).

Sherborne, J.W., 'English barges and ballingers of the late fourteenth century', *MM*, 63 (1977).

Sherborne, J.W., 'Indentured retinues and English expeditions to France, 1369-1380', *English Historical Review*, 79 (1964).

Sherborne, J.W., 'John of Gaunt, Edward III's retinue and the French campaign of 1369' in R.A. Griffiths and J. Sherborne, eds., *Kings and Nobles in the Later Middle Ages* (Gloucester, 1986).

Sherborne, J.W., *The Port of Bristol in the Middle Ages* (Bristol, 1965).

Southern, R.W., *Western Society and the Church in the Middle Ages* (Harmondsworth, 1970).

Simpson, G.G., ed., *Scotland and the Low Countries, 1124-1994* (East Linton, 1996).

Simpson, G.G., ed., *Scotland and Scandinavia, 800-1800* (Edinburgh, 1990).

Simpson, G.G., *Scottish Handwriting: 1150-1650* (Aberdeen, 1973).

Simpson, G.G. 'The Declaration of Arbroath revitalised', *SHR*, 56 (1977).

Simpson, G.G., ed., *The Scottish Soldier Abroad, 1247-1967* (Edinburgh, 1992).

Simpson, G.G., and Stones, J., 'New light on the medieval ceiling' in J.H. Alexander *et al*, *The Restoration of St Machar's Cathedral* (Aberdeen, 1991).

Simpson, S., 'The choir stalls and rood screen' in Geddes, *King's College Chapel* (Leeds, 2000)

Simms, K., *From Kings to Warlords: The changing structure of Gaelic Ireland in the later middle ages* (Woodbridge, 1987).

Simms, K., 'Gaelic warfare in the middle ages' in T. Bartlett and K. Jeffrey, eds., *A Military History of Ireland* (Cambridge, 1996).

Simson, P., *Geschichte der Stadt Danzig bis 1926* (Danzig, 1913)

Slootmans, C.J.F., *Paas- en Koudenarkten te Bergen-op-Zoom, 1365-1565* (Tilberg, 1985).

Smith, C., 'Perth: the animal remains' in J.A. Stones, ed., *Three Scottish Carmelite Friaries: Excavations at Aberdeen, Linlithgow and Perth, 1980-86* (Edinburgh, 1989).

Smith, C., 'The animal bone' in A. Cox, ed., 'Backland activities in medieval Perth', *PSAS*, 126 (1996).

Smith, J.A., 'Notes on Melrose abbey, especially in reference to the inscriptions on the wall of the south transept', *PSAS*, 2 (1854-7).

Smout, T.C., ed., *Scotland and Europe, 1200-1850* (Edinburgh, 1986).

Smout, T.C., Landsman, N., Devine, T.M., 'Scottish emigration in the seventeenth and eighteenth centuries' in N. Canny, ed., *Europeans on the Move: Studies on European migration, 1500-1800* (Oxford, 1994).

Sneller, Z.W., 'Le commerce du blé des Hollandais dans la région de la Somme au XV siècle', *Bulletin de la Societé des Antiquaires de Picardie*, 42 (1947).

Snooks, G.D., *Economics without Time: A science blind to the forces of historical change* (Basingstoke, 1993).

Spearman, R.M., 'Workshops, materials and debris - evidence of early industries' in Lynch *et al*, *Medieval Town*.

Spencer, B.W., 'Medieval pilgrimage badges', *Rotterdam Papers: A contribution to medieval archaeology*, 1 (1968), 143.

Steer, K.A., and Bannerman, J.W.M., *Late Medieval Monumental Sculpture in the West Highlands* (Edinburgh, 1977).

Stell, G., 'The Balliol family and the Great Cause of 1291-2' in K.J. Stringer, ed., *Essays on the Nobility of Medieval Scotland* (Edinburgh, 1985).

Stevenson, A., 'Foreign traffic and bullion exports, 1331-1333' in P.G.B. McNeill and H.L. MacQueen, eds., *Atlas of Scottish History to 1707* (Edinburgh, 1996).

Stevenson, A., 'Medieval Scottish associations with Bruges,' in Brotherstone and Ditchburn, *Freedom and Authority*.

Stevenson, A., 'Notice of an early sixteenth-century Scottish colony at Bergen-op-Zoom and an altar once dedicated to St Ninian', *IR*, 26 (1975).

Stevenson, A., 'Trade with the south, 1070-1513' in Lynch *et al.*, *Medieval Town*.

Stevenson, W.B., 'The monastic presence: Berwick in the twelfth and thirteenth centuries' in Lynch *et al.*, *Medieval Town*.

Stevenson, W.B., 'The monastic presence in Scottish burghs in the twelfth and thirteenth centuries', *SHR*, 60 (1981).

Steuart, A.F., 'The Scottish 'nation' at the university of Padua', *SHR*, 3 (1905-6).

Stewart, A.M., 'The Austrian connection, c.1450-1483: Eleanora and the intertextuality of *Pontus und Sidonia*' in J.D. McClure and M.R.G. Spiller, eds., *Bryght Lantemis: Essays on the language and literature of medieval and renaissance Scotland* (Aberdeen, 1989)

Stewart, A.M., 'Do they mean us? The Nuremberg Chronicle (1493) and Scotland' in W. Ritchie, J.C. Stone and A.S. Mather, eds., *Essays for Professor R.E.H. Mellor* (Aberdeen, 1980).

Stewart, I.H., 'Some Scottish ceremonial coins', *PSAS*, 98 (1964-66).

Stalley, R., 'Ireland and Scotland in the middle ages' in Higgitt, *Art and Architecture*.

Stones, E.L.G., 'The mission of Thomas Wale and Thomas Delisle from Edward I to Pope Boniface VIII in 1301', *Nottingham Medieval Studies*, 26 (1982).

Storey, A., *Trinity House of Kingston-upon-Hull* (Grimsby, 1967).

Stringer, K.J., *Earl David of Huntingdon, 1152-1219* (Edinburgh, 1985).

Stringer, K.J., 'Periphery and core in thirteenth-century Scotland: Alan son of Roland, lord of Galloway and constable of Scotland' in A. Grant and K.J. Stringer, eds., *Medieval Scotland: Crown, lordship and community* (Edinburgh, 1993).

Strohm, R., *Music in Late Medieval Bruges* (rev.ed., Oxford, 1990).

Stuart, J., 'Notice of an original instrument recently discovered among the records of the dean and chapter of Canterbury...', *PSAS*, 10 (1875)

Summerson, H., 'Crime and society in medieval Cumberland', *Transactions of the Cumberland and Westmorland Antiquarian and Archaeological Soc.*, 82 (1982).

Sumption, J., *Pilgrimage: An image of mediaeval religion* (London, 1975).

Swanson, R., 'The university of St Andrews and the Great Schism, 1410-1419', *Journal of Ecclesiastical History*, 26 (1975)

Testa, J.A., 'An unpublished manuscript by Simon Bening', *Burlington Magazine*, 136 (1994).

Tolley, T., 'Hugo van der Goes's altarpiece for Trinity College Church in Edinburgh and Mary of Guelders, queen of Scotland' in Higgitt, *Art and Architecture*.

Thirsk, J., ed., *The Agrarian History of England and Wales* (Cambridge, 1967-).

Thompson, C., and Campbell, L., *Hugo van der Goes and the Trinity Panels in Edinburgh* (Edinburgh, 1974);

Thoms, G.H.M., 'The bells of St Giles, Edinburgh', *PSAS*, 18 (1883-84).

Thomson, J.A.F., 'Innocent VIII and the Scottish church', *IR*, 19 (1968).

Thomson, J.A.F., *Popes and Princes, 1417-1517: Politics and polity in the late medieval church* (London, 1980).

Thomson, J.A.F., 'Scots in England in the fifteenth century', *SHR*, 79 (2000).

Thomson, W.G., Thomson, F.P., and Thomson, E.S., *A History of Tapestry from the Earliest Times until the Present Day* (3rd ed., Wakefield, 1973).

Thorp, N. *The Glory of the Page: Medieval and renaissance illuminated manuscripts from Glasgow University Library* (London, 1987).

Thrupp, S.L., 'Aliens in and around London in the fifteenth century' in A.E.J. Hollaender and W. Kellaway, eds., *Studies in London History* (London, 1969).

Thrupp, S.L. 'A survey of the alien population of England in 1440', *Speculum*, 32 (1957).

Thurlby, M., 'Aspects of the architectural history of Kirkwall Cathedral', *PSAS*, 127 (1997).

Thurlby, M., 'Jedburgh Abbey church: the Romanesque fabric', *PSAS*, 125 (1995).

Thurlby, M., 'St Andrews Cathedral-Priory and the beginnings of Gothic architecture in northern Britain' in Higgitt, *Art and Architecture*.

Toorians, L., 'Twelfth-century Flemish settlement in Scotland' in Simpson, *Scotland and the Low Countries*.

Torrie, E.P.D., *Medieval Dundee: A town and its people* (Dundee, 1990).

Torrie, E.P.D., 'The early urban site of new Aberdeen: a reappraisal of the evidence', *NS*, 12 (1992).

Torrie, E.P.D., and Coleman, R., *Historic Kirkcaldy: The archaeological implications of development* (Scottish Burgh Survey, 1995).

Touchard, H., *Le Commerce Maritime Breton à la Fin du Moyen Age* (Paris, 1967).

Trautz, F., *Die Könige von England und das Reich, 1272-1377* (Heildelberg, 1961).

Tuck, A., 'A medieval tax-haven: Berwick-upon-Tweed and the English crown, 1333-1461' in R. Britnell and J. Hatcher, eds., *Progress and Problems in Medieval England: Essays in honour of Edward Miller* (Cambridge, 1996).

Turbet, R., 'Scotland's greatest composer: an introduction to Robert Carver, 1487-1566', in J.D. McClure and M.R.G. Spillar, eds., *Bryght Lanternis: Essays on the language and literature of renaissance Scotland* (Aberdeen, 1989).

Unger, R.W., 'The Netherlands herring industry in the later middle ages: the false legend of Willem Beukels of Biervlet', *Viator*, 9 (1978).

Unger, R.W., *The Ship in the Medieval Economy, 600-1600* (London, 1980).

Vale, J., *Edward III and Chivalry: Chivalric society and its context, 1270-1350* (Woodbridge, 1982).

Vanhaek, M., *Histoire de la Sayetteries à Lille* (Lille, 1910).

Vauchez, A., *La Sainteté en Occident aux Derniers Siècles du Moyen Ages* (Rome, 1981).

Vaughan, R., *John the Fearless: The growth of the Burgundian power* (London, 1966).

Vaughan, R., *Philip the Good: The apogee of Burgundy* (London, 1970).

Veitch, K., 'The conversion of native religious communities to the Augustinian rule in twelfth- and thirteenth-century *Alba*', *RSCHS*, 29 (1999).

Verger, J., 'Teachers' in H. de Ridder-Symoens, *A History of the University in Europe. Volume 1: Universities in the middle ages* (Cambridge, 1992).

Verhulst, A., 'La laine indigène dans les anciens Pays-Bas entre le XIIe et le XVIIe siècle', *Revue Historique*, 248 (1972).

Vermaut, J., 'Structural transformation in a textile centre: Bruges from the sixteenth to the nineteenth Century' in H. van der Wee, ed., *The Rise and Decline of Urban Industries in Italy and the Low Countries* (Leuven, 1988).

Vismara, G., Cavanna, A., & Vismara, P., *Ticino medievale: Storia di una terra lombarda* (Locarno, 1990).

Vrankrijker, A.C.J., 'De textielindustrie van Naarden, I: De laken industrie in de 15e en 16e eeuw', *Tijdschrift voor Geschiedenis*, 51 (1936).

Wade, J.F., 'The overseas trade of Newcastle-upon-Tyne in the late middle ages', *NH*, 30 (1994).

Wallace, P., 'North European pottery imported into Dublin, 1200-1500' in P. Davey and R. Hodges, eds., *Ceramics and Trade* (Sheffield, 1983).

Ward, R., 'A surviving charter-party of 1323', *MM*, 81 (1995).

Warner, M., *Alone of All Her Sex: The myth and the cult of the Virgin Mary* (2nd ed., London, 1990).

Watson, F., 'The expression of power in a medieval kingdom: thirteenth-century Scottish castles' in S. Foster, A. Macinnes and R. Macinnes, eds., *Scottish Power Centres from the Early Middle Ages to the Twentieth Century* (Glasgow, 1998)

Watson, F., *Under the Hammer: Edward I and Scotland, 1286-1307* (East Linton, 1998).

Watson, G.W. 'Wolfart van Borssele, earl of Buchan', *The Genealogist* (new series), 14 (1898).

Watson, G.W., 'Wolfart van Borssele, earl of Buchan', *The Genealogist* (new series), 16 (1900).

Watt, D.E.R., 'Abbot Walter Bower of Inchcolm and his Scotichronicon', *RSCHS*, 24 (1992).

Watt, D.E.R., *A Biographical Dictionary of Scottish University Graduates to AD 1410* (Oxford, 1977).

Watt, D.E.R. 'Scottish masters and students at Paris in the fourteenth century', *Aberdeen University Review*, 36 (1955-56).

Watt, D.E.R., 'Scottish student life abroad in the fourteenth century', *SHR*, 59 (1980).

Watt, D.E.R., 'Scottish university men of the thirteenth and fourteenth centuries' in Smout, *Scotland and Europe*.

Watt, D.E.R., 'University clerks and rolls of petition for benefices, *Speculum*, 34 (1959).

Watt, D.E.R., 'University graduates in Scottish benefices before 1410', *RSCHS*, 15 (1964).

Watt, J.A., 'Gaelic polity and cultural identity' in A. Cosgrove, ed., *A New History of Ireland. Volume II: Medieval Ireland, 1169-1534* (Oxford, 1987).

Wechmar, I. von, and Biederstedt, R., 'Die schottische Einwanderung in Vorpommern im 16. und frühen 17. Jahrhundert', *Greifswald-Stralsunder Jahrbuch*, 5 (1965).

Wee, H. van der, 'Industrial dynamics and the process of urbanization and deurbanization in the Low Countries from the later middle ages to the eighteenth century: a synthesis' in idem, ed., *The Rise and Decline of Urban Industries in Italy and the Low Countries* (Leuven, 1988).

Wee, H. van der, *The Growth of the Antwerp Market and the European Economy, Fourteenth to Sixteenth Centuries* (The Hague, 1963)

Wee, H. van der, 'Structural changes and specialization in the industry of the southern Netherlands, 1100-1600', *Economic History Review*, 2nd ser., 28 (1975).

Weiss, D., 'The earliest account of the murder of James I of Scotland', *English Historical Review*, 52 (1937).

Westergaard, W., 'Denmark, Russia and the Swedish revolution, 1480-1503', *Slavonic Review*, 16 (1937-38).

White, A., 'The impact of the Reformation on a burgh community: the case of Aberdeen' in M. Lynch, ed., *The Early Modern Town in Scotland* (London, 1987).

White, A., 'The Reformation in Aberdeen' in J. Smith, ed., *New Lights on Medieval Aberdeen* (Aberdeen, 1985).

Williams, N.J., *The Maritime Trade of the East Anglian Ports, 1550-1590* (Oxford, 1988).

Williamson, A.H., 'Scots, Indians and empire: the Scottish politics of civilisation, 1519-1609', *PP*, 150 (1966).

Wilson, S.C., 'Scottish Canterbury pilgrims', *SHR*, 24 (1926-27).

Wolff, P., *Commerce et Marchands de Toulouse* (Paris, 1954).

Woods, K., 'Some sixteenth-century Antwerp carved-wooden altar-pieces in England', *Burlington Magazine*, 141 (1999).

Wordsworth, J., *et al.*, 'Excavations at Inverkeithing, 1981', *PSAS*, 113 (1982).

Yates, N., *Faith and Fabric: A history of Rochester Cathedral, 604-1994* (Woodbridge, 1994).

Yeoman, P., *Medieval Scotland* (London, 1995).

Yeoman, P., *Pilgrimage in Medieval Scotland* (London, 1999).

Yeoman, P., *Secrets of Fife's Holy Island: The archaeology of the Isle of May* (Glenrothes, 1996).

Young, A., *Robert Bruce's Rivals: The Comyns, 1212-1314* (East Linton, 1997).

Unpublished Theses

Ditchburn, D., 'Merchants, Pedlars and Pirates: A history of Scotland's relations with northern Germany and the Baltic in the later middle ages' (University of Edinburgh, unpublished PhD thesis, 1988)

Finlayson, W.H., 'The Scottish nation of merchants in Bruges' (University of Glasgow, unpublished PhD thesis, 1951).

Grosjean, A.N.L., 'Scots and the Swedish State: Diplomacy, military service and ennoblement, 1611-1660' (University of Aberdeen, unpublished PhD thesis, 1998).

Stevenson, A.W.K., 'Trade between Scotland and the Low Countries in the later middle ages' (University of Aberdeen, unpublished Ph.D thesis, 1982).

Index

- Scots in English, 220-23, 230, 254
- Scots in French, 220, 225-30, 252, 254
- Scots in Irish, 219-20, 223-4, 226-7, 251, 253, 255
- Scots in Swedish, 231

Arms and artillery, 18, 191-2, 201; experts in, 201

Arran, earls of,
- Boyd, Thomas, 125
- Hamilton, James, 99

Arras (France), 116, 170
- cloth production in, 173-4
- tapestries of, 115
- university of, and students at, 235

Arrezzo (Italy) 25, 230

Art, 38, 52, 54, 113-20, 260

Artois (France), 170-1

Athilmer, John, scholar, 238

Atholl, earls of, 65, 67
- Patrick, 96
- Strathbogie, David, 198
- Thomas, 193

Auberive (France), abbey of, 24

Aubigny-sur-Nère (France), 150-1

Aubigny (France), lords of,
- Stuart, Bernard, 30, 68, 227-30, 249
- Stuart, Robert, 230

Audenarde (Belgium), 173

Augsburg (Germany), 20

Augustinians, religious order, 43-6, 57, 240

Austria, 69-70, 116, 124

Avignon (France), 25, 36, 62, 70, 81, 85, 234; university of, 235, 238

Averencia, Thomas of, musician 113

Ayala, Don Pedro, envoy, 30, 272-4

Ayala, Pero López de, poet, 276

Ayr (-shire), 3-4, 48, 53, 147, 152, 156, 158, 166, 168, 208 n.53

Bailleul (France), 170, 173, 175

Balantrodoch (Midlothian), 44

Balliol, Dervorguilla, 48

Balmerino (Fife), abbey of, 77, 166

Balyshannon (Ireland), 219

Bamberg (Germany), 214

Banff (-shire), 11

Bankers, 27-8, 204

Bannockburn, battle of (1314), 93, 96, 202, 266

Barbour, John, archdeacon of Aberdeen, 67, 92, 125

Barclay, David, of Brechin, knight, 69, 71

Barfleur (France), 220

Barratry, 80, 83, 194

Barton-on-Humber (England), 151

Basel (Switzerland), 22-3
- books published in, 129
- council of, 29, 36-7, 39, 80

Baugé (France), battle of, 278

Bavaria (Germany), 21, 125, 215

Beaufort, Joan, queen of Scotland, 6, 106-7

Beaugeau, sire de, 72

Beaton, James, archbishop of St Andrews, 55

Beatus of Liebana, scholar, 267

Beer, 152-3, 208; its use in communion services, 139

Beirut (Lebanon), 16

Bellinzona (Switzerland), 22

Bells
- from England, 130
- from Mechelen, 134

Benedict XIII, pope, 36

Benedictines, religious order, 43-6, 74-5

Benincasa, Grazioso, cartographer, 268

Benning, family of, artists, 118-9, 124

Bergen (Norway), 17, 20, 147-8, 155 n. 92, 207

Bergenfahrer, 18

Bergen-op-Zoom (Netherlands), 13, 15, 20, 22, 148, 206
- exports to Scotland, 154
- imports from Scotland, 169, 180
- Scottish altar in, 247
- Scottish emigrants in, 206-7, 211, 245-6

Bergue-Saint-Winoc (France), 174

Bern (Switzerland), 23

Bernham, David, bishop of St Andrews, 36

Bernham, William, student, 247

Berry (France), 244

Berwick-upon-Tweed (England), 4, 6-7, 13, 148, 203-4, 239, 254, 267, 273-4
- emigrants from, 243, 254, 259
- garrison of, 141, 202-3, 221
- gild of, 208
- merchants from, 162, 167
- religious houses in, 46
- shipbuilding in, 159
- trade of, 146, 156, 166, 168-9, 179 n.220, 203